The Social Context of Marriage

THIRD EDITION

The Social Context of Marriage

J. Richard Udry

University of North Carolina

J. B. Lippincott Company

Philadelphia   New York   Toronto

Printed in the United States of America

1 3 5 7 9 8 6 4 2

Library of Congress Cataloging in Publication Data

Udry, J. Richard.
   The social context of marriage.

   Includes bibliographical references.
   1. Marriage—United States. I. Title.
HQ535.U3 1974   301.42'0973   73-20059
ISBN 0-397-47305-2

Preface

This book was designed to provide a basic understanding of American marriage from a sociological perspective. It was written to be understood by the reader without a background in the social sciences, but with sufficient depth to be valuable to those with more extensive knowledge in sociology. The general approach is the organization of knowledge about the family around questions of interest to the layman in understanding himself and the world around him, rather than around the special interest of family scholars. Those familiar with earlier editions of this text will find that this edition is less doctrinaire in its sociological purity, and more informed by research in other disciplines. Because of the tempering of sociological research with findings from biology, medicine, psychology, and other fields, sociologists will not always find themselves either familiar or sympathetic with the conclusions reached.

The pace of change in family life in the 1970s makes a marriage text sound quaint after a very short time. The early seventies brought dramatic changes in birth rates, divorce rates, abortion laws and an accompanying crumbling of consensus on sex norms. Even the fundamental outline of the relationship between the sexes has become problematical. These are circumstances which lead an author to early revision to relieve himself and his students of the pain of reading things they know are no longer true.

The study of human heterosexual relationships contains many controversies. Toward most of these I have grown decreasingly impartial between editions. Issues considered "open" in early editions I now consider "closed." On the other hand, new controversies have arisen in the last decade, so that matters which were considered closed a decade ago have now become matters of controversy. In the field of marriage and the family, controversial issues cannot be saved for the advanced student, for they lie across the entry areas of the subject. I have therefore continued the emphasis on controversies as the keys to understanding the field. Consequently, instructors will continue to find with the new edition that the most common student complaint is that the text doesn't tell them what the answer is.

Susan K. Stiles played a special role in the preparation of this edition. Her editorial assistance resulted in the reorganization of some chapters. Her review of the literature and her eye for what was interesting and important account for many of the changes in the new edition. Her interpretation of a study sometimes helped me to see through some of my own biases. Her editorial judgment influenced many deletions from the old edition and additions to the new, and her help made it possible to present this edition in 1974 instead of some later year. Jenny Capparella and Winifred Shriver typed the manuscript. Cynthia McFadden developed the graphs for the new edition. Thanks are due to Judy Kovenock for her research assistance.

Thanks to Joseph E. Ribal for many of the case histories from his marriage counseling files. Thanks also to my students who have contributed so many valuable case histories to my files and to this text. I am indebted to several thousand former students in courses in the family and marriage who have given me confidence that material as complex as much of the text can be used successfully by students with little sophistication in the social and behavioral sciences. Appreciation is also due the many researchers and authors who have granted permission to quote from their works. Finally, my debt to others who have written texts in the area of the family, and from whose ideas I have drawn, will be clear to them.

J. RICHARD UDRY

Chapel Hill, North Carolina
February, 1974

Contents

Introduction

1

Of all the different kinds of human relationship, each society tends to emphasize one which has particular significance to its organization. Mother-daughter, father-son, same-sex friends, heterosexual peers — these are among the relationships which have been basic to the social structure of human life at various times, in various cultures. The twentieth-century United States has chosen to emphasize the significance of the heterosexual peer relationship. Not only does its popular literature focus on it, but American child-rearing is pointed toward it. The protracted period of adolescence in the United States now provides an entire decade for exclusive preoccupation with the sex-pair. Adult informal interaction is centered around it; the family system is built upon it. Americans expect the relationship to be their most important source of emotional satisfaction and support.

As a text on the sociology of marriage this book focuses on the heterosexual relationship. The book is not primarily concerned with the family *per se* or with childrearing, kinship structures, or other institutions of the society, except as they are related to heterosexual relationships. The justification for such a restricted focus is the growing importance in the United States of sex-pairs as the ultimate structural unit around which people organize their emotional lives.

The Importance of Marriage

Contemporary Americans, more than most groups of people, are fascinated with marriage, with the sex-pairs which are preliminary to marriage, and with the sex-pairs outside of marriage. American society has been said to be child-centered, and, as will be seen, most marriages eventually become child-centered, but it seems doubtful that many people plan it that way. Of hundreds of unmarried persons interviewed, very few have been motivated to marry primarily by the desire for children (at least as they see it). Seldom has an engaged couple broken an engagement on grounds of the incurable sterility of either partner. Of the whole gamut of kinship ties, none comes close in importance to the marital relationship. The parent-child relationship is conceded as temporary. The sibling relationship, although surprisingly strong, particularly between sisters, is weaker than that of marriage. In fact, it is probably fair to say that the marital relationship is the most highly valued role-set in American society. It appears that most middle-class Americans will choose a good marital relationship in any choice which pits it against any other role. They will enter what promises to be a good marriage even if it means no children. They will break up what seems to be a bad marriage, even though they think it is bad for the children. Women will forsake careers for which they have prepared and men will alter occupational aspirations, terminate educational programs, and change careers for the sake of their marriage. Religious values are no match for marital values. Even the ministers, priests, and rabbis recognize this when they recommend religion as a prop for maintaining a good marriage. "The family that prays together stays together" says something about the relative importance of praying and togetherness. Young people have been enjoined from marrying outside their churches, not because it is detrimental to their religion, but because it is detrimental to the marriage. The young couple whose marriage is threatened by religious differences rarely chooses to forsake the marriage and maintain the religion. Americans believe in marriage above all. They marry earlier, remain unmarried less often, and remarry after divorce more frequently and more rapidly than people of any other industrialized nation. They look to their marital relationship for their greatest satisfaction in life.

And what is a good marriage? Americans may disagree about the details of what marital behavior should be like, but the goals of marriage are clear: marriage should make the spouses happy, provide them with their basic source of emotional gratification and security, and give them love and companionship. This "cult of happiness," as Merrill (1959) terms it, is far more inclusive than the marriage values, but there can be little doubt that most Americans see their marriages as the primary potential source of happiness. When marriage fails to provide a "personal epic of pleasurable excitement" there is disappointment and disillusionment even for the sophisticated, who were skeptical from the beginning. The importance of the marital relationship in American culture, it appears, has led anthropologists and sociologists to posit unusual importance in the structure of society for the "nuclear family"—the husband-wife-offspring unit (Parsons and Bales, 1955). Not only do many other societies consider other kinship relations more important than the marital union (for sources of gratification, companionship, and life focus), but in several, the nuclear family unit itself seems unimportant in comparison to other kinship units in which it is imbedded. In fact, it is a justifiable generalization that where marriage is less important than other relationships, the nuclear family will not be an important functional unit in society—that is, it will not do many important things for the society or its individuals. A quick look at two non-Western societies will demonstrate the point.

In upper-class classical Chinese society, the most important kinship bond for social organization was the parent-child, and especially the father-son bond. Residence, authority, and family continuity were organized around this relationship. Apparently, the marriage was not expected to be a source of affection or personal gratification for the pair. Even childrearing was more the function of an extended kin unit rather than a nuclear unit, although members of what sociologists would call a nuclear unit were identifiable. Reciprocal obligations and involvement of husband and wife were minimal. However, indications are that in lower-class families the husband-wife relationship was basic to social organization.

Among the Nayar, a high-status Hindu caste along the Malabar coast of India, up until half a century ago there was no nuclear family as Americans know it, and marriage constituted only a formal ceremony entitling a girl to adult status, with practically no further interaction and obligation between "husband" and "wife." Residence was completely matrilocal, with no resident "husband" to complete any nuclear unit. (A family system is "matrilocal" if newly formed nuclear units reside with or near the wife's family and "patrilocal" if they reside with or near the husband's family.) "Married" women among the Nayar could then entertain the sexual favors of men of appropriate caste as they saw fit, with no reciprocal obligations developing between lovers. A woman's children simply became part of the matrilineage, and men provided authority and economic support for their mother's family rather than for their sexual partners and biological offspring.

The "matrifocal" organization of the Nayar kinship—organized around the mother—is approximated in numerous other places in the world, although apparently nowhere else in such clear-cut form. The importance of the marital bond frequently appears overshadowed by other kinship groupings. In ancient Greece, the importance of other kinship ties relative to the marriage is made clear in a story told by the historian Herodotus. Darius, King of Persia, had sentenced a man and his relatives to death for insurrection. Touched by the man's weeping wife, the king sent her the message that one of the prisoners might be chosen by her for reprieve. "If the king grants me the life of one only," she said, "I choose above all my brother" (Blood, 1962: 28).

The Interplay of Science and American Values

Americans believe in science. Science will provide us with the good life. Science will tell us what and how to eat to be healthy and wise; science will tell us how to build our dwellings to be warm and cozy. Science will tell us how to rear our children so they will be extroverted and adjusted. Increasingly, sophisticated Americans are looking to the social sciences to tell them how to live in order to best achieve their most important values. Perhaps this is an exaggeration; it would be more moderate to say that no one wants to be unscientific, and therefore everyone looks to science to offer support for what he already believes. Since social scientists are hardly ever unanimous in the support of any statement, individuals in a pluralistic society can pick according to individual taste from a pluralistic science those findings which will support their favorite values.

This is not to say that American behavior is not influenced by scientific conclusions. One might look at the interplay between science and values something like this: If strong scientific evidence helps to undermine a value of little strength, the value will collapse at once, and social change will ensue. If scientific evidence with poor credentials attacks a fundamental value, it is likely that the evidence will be either ignored or taken lightly. If scientific evidence supports a fundamental value, the scientific findings will be received enthusiastically with little regard to their credentials. If strong scientific findings undercut a fundamental belief, they may be suppressed, or a period of ideological conflict may ensue. Excellent evidence is available for each of these patterns. When strong science in the form of Darwinian theory opposed strong value in the form of religious beliefs of special creation, prolonged conflict ensued. When modest evidence was produced to the effect that smoking caused cancer, it was generally ignored. Now that the evidence is much stronger, however, the conflict is in evidence in the courtroom, legislature, classroom, and the individual psyche. When early studies in marital stability showed some tendency for those married within their faiths to have fewer divorces, this was taken by many churches as scientific evidence in favor of religious homogamy, even though the evidence, as well as the relationship shown, was rather weak. Fairly reputable evidence is now available to show that engaging in premarital intercourse will not ruin the subsequent marriage, yet weaker evidence to the contrary is widely disseminated and presented as the best and latest scientific evidence.

The discussion so far suggests that the science of human behavior is free of influence from the values of the culture it inhabits. Yet at numerous places in this book, the reader will note that the findings of scientists show unmistakable signs of influence by the value patterns of the period in which the research was done. Is it coincidence that during a period when educated American women were most career-minded and having fewest children, pediatric science recommended mechanical childrearing, while thirty years later, with women having won the right to careers, settling for domestic types of femininity, and surprisingly increasing their childbearing, scientific pediatrics recommended a warm, affectionate childrearing, overflowing with permissiveness and tender, loving care? A significant part of the influence of the culture on behavioral science is in the choice of ideas or problems to be researched. And, of course, this is no reflection on the motives or exactness of the researcher. Who should be surprised that the sociologist, as a member of his society, should be interested in, and therefore choose to study, the very things that interest everyone else? It is this tendency which insures the availability of data for this book on most of the subjects which rate high in student interest.

Some Caution on Scientific Methodology

Most of the readers of this text will not have had extensive training in research methods, and perhaps the majority will be unfamiliar with the techniques used by social scientists to arrive at conclusions. There is considerable consensus among social scientists on acceptable ways of testing statements for truth. Not many of the studies quoted in this book come very close to the ideal research designs necessary to provide answers to the questions asked. Furthermore, even those that do provide answers use words in special senses which do not always convey the same meaning to the student as they did to the researcher. Presenting a wide range of findings in a single text made it impossible to give the student enough detail on each particular study for him to know whether the research means what he thinks it means. Keep in mind the following problems in reading the chapters that follow:

1. Are the people studied representative of the people to whom one wants to apply the conclusions? The most accurate way of making sure the findings apply to everyone would be to study everyone. Because this is impossible, in most cases it is necessary to study a small group which is representative of the larger group. This is known as sampling. A good sample has the same characteristics (with known margins of error) as the group from which it was sampled. Not more than a handful of the studies to be quoted are drawn in such a way as to insure this. The best insurance is to draw the sample so that each person has an equal (or at least a known) chance of getting into the sample. If this is not done (and it rarely is), there is no real way of knowing whether the findings apply to anyone but those studied.

Subjects for the research studies are recruited in a number of ways. Instructors in colleges give questionnaires to their captive student audience. Sometimes the cooperation of all the members of a club is obtained. At other times, subjects are recruited by placing a notice on a college bulletin board offering an hourly wage to participants for research. At best they are selected at random from some particular student body, phone book, mailing list, or the residents of some particular city or county. Those studies based on samples which are representative of the entire American population are extremely few.

Even the best studies can only report behavior and conclusions for a particular time. Those done at different times may disagree because social behavior changed in the time between the studies. Many of the most valuable studies available are studies of the same kinds of groups or even the same groups over extended periods of time.

2. What are the meanings of the terms used? In scientific research, words mean what one says they mean and no more. However, the meaning is not always what is expected. Words like "understanding," "adjustment," "agreement," and "stability," when used in scientific studies must eventually be tied to something that the researcher can observe. What does it mean for a man to "understand" a woman? "Understanding" is a vague term with many nuances, meaning different things in different contexts. In studies of interpersonal relationships, it is frequently used to mean that the man can correctly guess which answers on a questionnaire the woman will choose. Perhaps this seems to be a trivial meaning, and the reader might like to propose a less trivial method for measuring the extent to which men understand women. From time to time the chapters which follow will describe how some of the concepts sociologists use are measured. If one does not know how the term was connected to people's actual behavior, he does not know what the word means.

3. Scientific observations do not speak for themselves. From any set of observations, innumerable interpretations can be drawn, some contradictory to others. The biases of the researcher can very well determine which of several equally acceptable interpretations he will make. In the chapters which follow, data will frequently be taken from a research study and conclusions drawn which are different and even opposite to those drawn by the original researcher. At many junctures, data will be presented in support of these conclusions. The sophisticated reader is at liberty to draw different conclusions from them than are given in this book.

4. Research cannot answer moral questions. It is possible to tell whether interfaith marriages are more or less stable than intrafaith marriages by doing a research study, but it is not possible to tell whether interfaith marriages are good in any ultimate sense. It is possible to determine whether homosexuality is innate or socially learned, but it is not possible to establish whether homosexuality should be a punishable offense. On the other hand, knowing the probable consequences of one's acts is necessary if the individual is going to have any control over his own destiny. It is with the consequences of acts that this book is concerned.

5. Not everything has been studied. Where no reliable information is available, it is probably best to remain silent. This book will not always show such restraint.

The Limits of Individual Autonomy

Most people would like to believe that they can make what they will of the marriage they undertake. If they will only try (and if they pick the right mate), they are convinced that they can control their matrimonial future. Since this is an article of faith, it is not especially amenable to modification. Yet, it is necessary that the intelligent person be acquainted with the limits, as well as the possibilities, of his control. The following restraints on autonomous control need to be considered.

1. Ignorance. For all the studies in behavior in the past fifty years, there are few questions asked by the layman that can be answered unequivocally.

2. Chance. Every day in every life brings unexpected contingencies over which one has little control, such as chance encounters; physical accidents; sickness; moodiness; being in the right place at the right time; accidentally finding out about a job or not finding out about a job; accidental pregnancies or unknown impediments to pregnancy. Autonomy consists largely of capitalizing on the fortuitous.

3. Social trends. In American society at this time, most people have certain ideas about marriage, and most marriages are of a certain sort because of larger forces transforming the society. The person who would have a pattern of heterosexual or family relationships which contradicts or ignores prevailing patterns will find that the social fabric is woven in such a way that it will entangle his plans while facilitating those of everyone else.

4. Personal characteristics. No one designs his own personality. By the time he is conscious of the forces producing him, they have already done their work. Personalities continue to change over a lifetime, but they do so primarily in response to changes in the relationships of the individual, and probably little in response to his own deliberate manipulation of himself. Autonomy can be achieved, however, by one's deliberate choice of his relationships.

5. One goal blocks another. By the nature of the interrelationships of behavior and events, the individual must choose to forego certain goals because they are inconsistent with certain others which seem nearly equally desirable. From no relationship do Americans demand as much as marriage. It is in the nature of the institution and the people whose interaction constitutes it that not all of these demands can be filled within one marriage for a lifetime. Autonomy consists, in part, of adjusting expectations to the possible, of substituting for happiness the intellectual satisfaction which comes from understanding what is happening and why when happiness is impossible.

The Family in a Changing Society

2

For generations, it has been popular for laymen and religious leaders to talk about the disintegration of the American family in modern society. The cause of this situation has sometimes been said to be lack of individual moral character; at other times it is said to be a product of civilization itself, to be remedied only by the return to some supposedly more simple state. These beliefs have been abetted by reputable philosophers, historians, and a few social scientists. "Cyclical theories" of history nearly always have pointed to a "disintegration of the family system" as one of the portents of deterioration for civilizations. Urban life in general, the decline of religious authority, industrialization—in fact, anything which is regarded to have been absent in the past—has been blamed for the disruption of family life. The disintegration is usually measured by the supposed disappearance of certain formerly existing patterns in families or by the initiation of new patterns supposedly not present until the decline. Divorce, desertion, adultery, premarital sexual relations, illegitimacy, women working outside the home, baby-sitters, decline in the birth rate, disobedient children—all have been taken as indicators of disintegration of the family system. Evils which are resulting from the alleged breakdown of family institutions range from juvenile delinquency, immorality in public office, and materialism to all of the items listed above which are supposed to be evidence of the breakdown.

Part of the confusion lies in the misconceptions widely held about the family of the immediate American past. Every society builds myths about its own past, and Americans share a myth concerning what family life was in the good old days. Family sociologist William Goode has aptly described the difference between the actual family and the prevailing cultural stereotype of the family of a century ago.

. . . I labeled this stereotype of the United States family of the past, when *praised,* "the classical family of Western nostalgia." It is a pretty picture of life down on grandma's farm. There are lots of happy children, and many kinfolk live together in a large rambling house. Everyone works hard. Most of the food to be eaten during the winter is grown, preserved and stored on the farm. The family members repair their own equipment, and in general the household is economically self-sufficient. The family has many functions; it is the source of economic stability and religious, educational and vocational training. Father is stern and reserved, and has the final decision in all important matters. Life is difficult, but harmonious because everyone knows his task and carries it out. All boys and girls marry, and marry young. Young people, especially the girls, are likely to be virginal at marriage and faithful afterward. Though the parents do not arrange their children's marriages, the elders do have the right to reject a suitor and have a strong hand in the final decision. After marriage, the couple lives harmoniously, either near the boy's parents or with them, for the couple is slated to inherit the farm. No one divorces.

Those who believe we are seeing progress rather than retrogression often accept these same stereotypes but describe the past in words of different emotional effect. We have progressed, they say, from the arbitrary power of elders toward personal freedom for the young, from cold marriages based on economic arrangements to unions based on the youngsters' right of choice, from rigidly maintained class barriers between children to an open class system, from the subjugation of the wife to equalitarianism and companionship in marriage, and from the repression of the children's emotions to permissiveness.

Like most stereotypes, that of the classical family of Western nostalgia leads us astray. When we penetrate the confusing mists of recent history, we find few examples of this "classical" family. Grandma's farm was not economically self-sufficient. Few families stayed together as large aggregations of kinfolk. Most houses were small, not large. We now *see* more large old houses than small ones; they survived longer because they were likely to have been better constructed. The one-room cabins rotted away. True enough, divorce was rare, but we have no evidence that families were generally happy. Indeed, we find, as in so many other pictures of the glowing past, that each past generation of people writes of a period *still* more remote, *their* grandparents' generation, when things really were much better.[1]

Compare your mental picture of family life in colonial America with this historically accurate picture based on John Demos' studies of Plymouth colony.

From the very beginning of settlement at Plymouth the family was nuclear in its basic composition and it has not changed in this respect ever since. One adult couple and their own children formed the core of each household—with

[1] William J. Goode, *World Revolution and Family Patterns* (New York: The Free Press of Glencoe, 1963), pp. 6–7. Reprinted by permission.

the addition in some cases of an aged grandparent or "servant." Only the latter term introduces a real element of difference from the pattern of our own day. Insofar as it designated children purposely "bound out" from some other family, it stands in some degree to confound us. Also (though less often) included among the servants were orphans and certain types of deviant or sick persons. But aside from this the typical domestic unit is easily recognized in our own terms. Moreover, the settlers' definition of kindred (beyond the immediate family) and the range of effective contacts between such people, seem equally similar.

Of course, families were considerably larger in the seventeenth century than they are today. And this difference is magnified by the further differences in typical house plans. Most Old Colony dwellings were extremely small by our own standards, and even so parts of them were not usable during the long winter months. There was little privacy for the residents, and little chance to differentiate between various portions of living space. Life in these households was much less segmented, in a formal sense, than it usually is for us; individuals were more constantly together and their activities meshed and overlapped at many points.

Still, despite this rather different set of physical arrangements, the usual alignment of roles and responsibilities within the family was basically similar to the modern American pattern. The husband was the head of the household, and, at least in theory, the final arbiter of its affairs. Yet the wife had her own sphere of competence and a corresponding measure of authority. In certain most important areas of family life—the sale of real property or the disposition of children—the couple would make decisions together.

Possibly the lines of authority between parent and child were much tighter and more formal than in our own society; but the evidence on this point is not conclusive. In any case, the experience of childhood and growth through time did follow a course most distinctively its own. Childhood as we know it did not last much beyond the age of six or seven years. After that participation in adult activities began in earnest. There was little schooling of the kind—the institutional kind—which in our own day helps to set apart a very broad age group. Instead children spent most of their time working (and relaxing) alongside older people, and were generally perceived as "little adults."

If six or seven marked the turning point of greater importance in the seventeenth than in the twentieth century, the opposite was true of adolescence. At Plymouth the "teens" formed a period of relative calm and steady progress toward full maturity. Courtships began at this stage; and, though officially restricted by requirements of parental approval, they seem in many respects to have followed the lines of personal inclination. Marriage came somewhat later than it does now, and needed at the outset substantial gifts of property from both sets of parents. But such gifts were never withheld, and were often framed so as to establish the complete autonomy of the recipients. The later years of life in Plymouth colony brought, in most cases, no new departures of any kind. The process of managing a family, and tending an estate, provided an essential continuity. Positions of power and prestige came chiefly to those over forty, and might indeed be retained to a very advanced age. Most men yielded reluctantly to "old age" proper, "retiring" only when forced to do so by real infirmity.[1]

A corrected picture of the American family of the past is very difficult to construct, since sociologists have little of the precise data necessary to reconstruct the typical family for any period before the twentieth century. The American family system grew from roots in a society which was preponderantly rural and nonindustrial in technology. The conjugal family system emphasizing husband-wife-children living units was established in northern Europe prior to the beginnings of the Industrial Revolution (Greenfield, 1961), and it is likely that a small-family system deemphasizing intergenerational and collateral kinship ties is as old as the language Americans speak. The English language has never had a kinship terminology beyond the bare minimum required to identify the closest relatives in gross categories like "cousin" and "aunt" which lump together several different kinds and degrees of kinship. No extended family tradition existed in America's history except among a very limited elite.

We do not know what the average age of marriage was in the early days of this country, but it certainly was no younger than today (Greenwood, 1956). Premarital sexual behavior in American historical times probably was different from what most people imagine (Smith, 1973). Parents probably never exercised anything like the control over potential suitors of their daughters that is imagined. Women bore many children and had more pregnancies, but infant mortality was extremely high by contemporary standards, so that the number of children who survived to adulthood was never large.

The average size of colonial households was near six. This is large compared to today's average household of near four, and large compared to English and European households of the 17th and 18th centuries, but not as different from today as our nostalgia sometimes imagines (Laslett, 1973).

How stern was father? To what extent did he make the important decisions? Some writers maintain that the frontier environment of the United States gave women an important voice in economic decisions of the family long before many women were employed outside their households. In an economy in which 90 percent of the employed persons were engaged in agriculture, it is not surprising that most sons continued in the occupations of their fathers. However, only a minority took over their fathers' farms, since most families had two or more sons. Families were certainly responsible for more educational functions than today, but the rapidity with

---

[1] John Demos, *A Little Commonwealth: Family Life in Plymouth Colony* (New York: Oxford University Press, 1970) pp. 181–182. Reprinted by permission.

which early communities set up primary schools for teaching the rudiments of reading and writing indicates a long-term recognition of public responsibility for educational functions in the early days of the nation. The family never was considered to have primary responsibility for religious education and practice. Both schools and churches were there to do the job, and the family played an auxiliary function in these areas. Studies of the content of American magazines in the late eighteenth century (Lantz et al., 1968), and of travelers' accounts of American family life in the early nineteenth century (Furstenberg, 1966), record some differences in emphasis in family concerns from then until now, but a remarkable similarity in family ideology and patterns of interaction over the entire two hundred years is the dominant impression.

The myth of the Western family of nostalgia probably represents an embodiment of the ideal of family life of a previous era more than it does a true description of the family life of our ancestors, just as the contemporary "companionship" family represents an embodiment of what Americans think family life *ought* to be like today, rather than a description of what it *is*. The ideal does serve a specific function, however, in that it affects our aspirations and is a standard against which we can measure experience.

American Values and American Marriage

Although contemporary society is very heterogeneous in many ways, there are certain belief systems which affect the shape of American family life in all classes and regions, even though the beliefs themselves are not shared by all Americans to the same extent. Four of these are worth examining individually: the Christian tradition, democratic equalitarianism, individualism, and secularism.

THE CHRISTIAN TRADITION

The doctrines of traditional Christianity still help shape American marital institutions and American thinking about the family even for those Americans who do not consider themselves Christians. Christians have, first of all, traditionally regarded the family as a religious institution. Although the Roman Catholic Church did not take over the rites of marriage as a sacramental function until the Middle Ages, the family today continues to have the status of a sacred institution in the minds of most Americans. Second, as a sacred union, marriage has been regarded by the Church as permanent. Various Christian scholars have pondered Matthew 19, containing Jesus' reply to the question, "Is it lawful to divorce one's wife for any cause?"

> He answered, "Have you not read that he who made them from the beginning made them male and female, and said, 'For this reason a man shall leave his

father and mother and be joined to his wife, and the two shall become one'? So they are no longer two but one. What therefore God has joined together, let no man put asunder." They said to him, "Why then did Moses command one to give a certificate of divorce, and put her away?" He said to them, "For your hardness of heart Moses allowed you to divorce your wives, but from the beginning it was not so. And I say to you: whoever divorces his wife, except for unchastity, and marries another, commits adultery" (Matthew 19:4–9, Revised Standard Version).

This passage contains ambiguities which are more clouded by comparable passages in other gospels. While scholars have proposed dozens of conflicting interpretations, on one thing it can be agreed: All Christian tradition recognizes marriage as a permanent bond, to be broken, if at all, only for grievous cause. Even those who do not profess Christian belief share this general attitude and are more or less shocked by the philosophy which does not take the permanence of marriage as an important value. Third, although the Old Testament patriarchs practiced polygamy, the bulk of the Judeo-Christian tradition requires monogamy, and the superior position and authority of men is taken for granted. This patriarchal position is emphasized in the Roman Catholic and Mormon faiths, but constitutes a fundamental substructure for other faiths as well. Fourth, Christianity holds that it is good to have children. Although the early Christians deemphasized the importance of marriage and childbearing because they felt the end of the world to be near (an antifertility bias which they shared with the pagans of their time), the later establishment of the Church as a major institution gradually led to a return to the Old Testament exhortation to be fruitful and multiply. Fifth, the Church has regarded sex outside of marriage as sinful and sexual pleasure as beneath the dignity of man. The Christian tradition poses sex as the enemy of religion (in contrast to some other religions which enlist sex in support of religious belief and ceremony). Founded by celibates, in a period of Roman history not noted for its sexual moderation, and anticipating the early arrival of Judgment Day, the Church, not surprisingly, fostered Chrisitan thinkers who chose celibacy as the highest spiritual state, later imposed it upon the clergy, and until modern times dealt with sex as a more or less necessary evil for the propagation of the race. Only in the past half century have some churches pronounced sexual pleasure as a legitimate end in itself. In the pleasure-affirming contemporary American culture, the pleasure-denying tradition of the Church has provided an emotional ambivalence to pleasurable activity of most kinds, and to sex in particular.

DEMOCRATIC EQUALITARIANISM

The doctrine of the equality of all men and the right of individuals to participate in the decisions affecting their fate began as a political creed but has selectively been diffused into other social relationships. A superficial equalitarianism has been remarked as characteristic of informal encounters among Americans, and privilege by ascription runs against the grain of at least our acknowledged social rules. Even superordinate-subordinate relationships such as military roles have been affected by this pervasive influence. Family relationships have been affected by the same forces, as have all relationships between men and women. Americans are now in the position of combining strong traditions which legitimize the authority of men over women and adults over children with a democratic-equalitarian attitude which undercuts this formerly legitimate authority and emphasizes the equality of the sexes and the rights of children to be spared from arbitrary authority. Under these circumstances, male-female relationships become a subtle blend of two contradictory orientations. Marriage becomes "a fifty-fifty proposition" in which most of the adaptability is required of women, in which an arbitrary domineering husband is unbearable, but in which the weak husband who does not provide leadership for his family is scorned. Democratic equalitarianism is early impressed on children, and by school age they will use it against their parents in pursuit of their demands. As their children grow older, parents can expect to have their commands honored less and less by simple virtue of their position and age.

INDIVIDUALISM

The philosophy of individualism asserts that the value of the individual is paramount over the value of social groups. The goals of the individual are given preference, and his well-being and happiness are the criteria for social and individual decisions. It is not the duty of the individual to sacrifice his happiness for the well-being of other people. The individual personality is honored, and the development of its potential is a worthy goal. The acceptance of this philosophy has given contemporary Americans wide tolerance of divorce and family disruption. It provides little support for family loyalty, and family goals emerge only as the goals of individual family members. Family traditions exert little hold on the imagination because the family is only the institutional vehicle through which individuals realize certain aspirations and gratify their needs.

SECULARISM

A *secular society* is one in which there is a generalized willingness to change social patterns and traditional beliefs, as contrasted to a *sacred society*, in which people are reluctant and resistant to social change of any kind. There is wide variation in people's willingness to change, depending on the institutions involved in the process. For example, Americans seem more willing to change a behavior which involves the use of a new piece of equipment than they are to change the nature of a family role. However, Americans are probably the most secularized major nation in the world. In most areas, they are not only willing to change patterns; they are enthusiastic for change to the point that, in some ways, the fact that a pattern is new is a recommendation for its adoption. Americans can hardly be said to have that degree of secularism in family relationships, but, even here, they have shown readiness to adopt new contraceptive devices, they practice new methods of childrearing from one child to the next in the same family, and they show considerable flexibility in dividing up the labor of the household.

Enthusiasm for change in areas other than family behavior encourages a rapidly changing society which, in turn, helps to transform family relationships in ways which are least intended. As the society becomes more secularized in its orientation to family behavior, the old patterns are no longer considered valuable in themselves. If they no longer make rational sense as vehicles for achieving their goals, Americans seem ready to transform them. In such an atmosphere, traditional religious values lose their effectiveness as social controls, with the result that religious institutions either rapidly change the emphasis of their teachings and in effect become "secularized" themselves, or else lose membership and influence in the society. Traditional Christian concepts of the good family have come to exert less and less influence as they have conflicted with more persuasive contemporary beliefs, and the emphasis of the church has been accordingly deflected. For example, most Protestant churches now emphasize the equality of the sexes rather than traditional male dominance, just as they rarely preach against usury. Divorced and remarried persons are now welcome in most churches. Where most churches condemned contraception fifty years ago, *all* have modified their positions toward greater acceptance today. A century ago most churches held that sex was for procreation only. Today many ministers are trained to counsel married couples in the manipulative techniques through which counselors believe greater sexual satisfaction is achieved. In a secular society, churches reflect rather than direct social change.

Functional Differentiation of the Family

Functional differentiation is one of the fundamental processes in the development of complex modern societies. In simple societies there are few social institutions, and each tends to be rather general in purpose. In simple societies, kinship groups, including the family, usually perform a wide range of functions, from local government and police protection through childrearing and occupational training. As societies increase in scale and complexity, the significance of larger coordinating institutions grows. Decision-making, which was formerly dispersed among families and villages, becomes centralized. The increasing complexity of the society makes it unfeasible for children to be educated and prepared for making their adult livelihood at home. These functions are located in specialized educational institutions. The removal of educational functions to specialized institutions tends to separate the youth into age-graded groups isolated from adults and to make children less dependent on their kinship group for emotional support. The economy shifts from agriculture carried out by household groups to specialized productive institutions. First husband and then wife engage in most of their productive activity outside the home. Today even such domestic activities as food preparation have increasingly devolved upon specialized outside agencies as the other services of the wife become more valuable. It has become more efficient to buy prepared foods than to have the wife prepare them.

By this process of functional differentiation, the kinship unit gradually comes to have fewer functions which it performs for individuals and for the society. At the same time it becomes more highly specialized. We need to distinguish nuclear families (husband-wife-children units) from larger kinship circles. Larger kinship circles have gradually ceased to perform any but friendship functions in contemporary society. It is true that jobs are sometimes secured through kin, and nonnuclear kin may be a source of status in the community. But these are peripheral functions of kinship circles. Nuclear family units, on the other hand, never performed some of the more general functions (such as local government or protection) which have been lost from the functions of larger kinship groups. Rather than saying that the "family" has gradually lost functions as the society becomes functionally differentiated, it should be said that the larger kinship group has lost functions and become relatively insignificant, leaving the nuclear family with some of its former functions (such as childrearing and companionship), while other functions (such as social security and occupational orientation), which now require larger social bases, have become the province of specialized agencies of the society not based on kinship. It is inaccurate to say that the nuclear family has become less functionally significant for the society and for the individual. In many ways, the nuclear family has become *more* important as a social unit, since it provides the major source of emotional security for adults and children during most of life. Marriage is the longest and most significant relationship in life. It is the major source of companionship for adults and provides the setting for the great preponderance of sexual activity in the society. The nuclear family is the basic consumption unit of the economy. It provides the only basis for initial status placement of individuals in the community. More than any other single institution, it determines what kind of life a child will grow into and what his chances will be to amount to something. It is hard to see why some social scientists have arrived at the conclusion that the family has few functions today. It simply has different functions, and it has become the only major focus of emotional life in the society. As other relationships become impersonal and take on the nature of formal transactions, the nuclear family becomes almost explosively emotional. The small child's emotional attachments are confined to the few people in his immediate family instead of being diffused over a wider group, with the consequence that parent-child relations are highly charged with feeling. The former preoccupation of family life with instrumental tasks may have tended to control emotional levels. With the basic needs of subsistence no longer problematical, husband and wife are more at liberty to consider the emotional adjustment of their children and the nuances of the marital relationship. (A wise man recently commented that Americans think sex is the most important thing in the world because they have never been really hungry.) Under contemporary circumstances, it is easy for families to become boiling cauldrons of emotionality. What is surprising is that a small group with such susceptibility to uncontrolled emotion should turn out to be so relatively stable.

The Family as a Basic Institution

The family has frequently been called the "basic" social institution. It has been said that the family is "fundamental" to the American way of life, that the survival of American civilization depends on the stability of the family. It is instructive to analyze what is meant by the family (or any other social institution) being a "basic" institution. Two alternate meanings come to mind. (1) The family is the primary determinant of the life chances of the individual born into it. (2) The family is the prime mover in a causal sequence determining either change or stability in the patterns of the society. The first meaning seems unquestionably true where children are reared in families. In this sense, the family is basic because, by giving the child his place in society and providing him with the resources which he needs to contribute to the society as an individual, the family perpetuates a class system in which differences in ability are accompanied by differences in opportunity to live the good life.

The second meaning is more complex, and the extent to which the family is basic in this sense is variable. Sociologists and historians, as well as economists, of the past fifty years have been inclined to see economic institutions as the seat of the "basic" forces which have transformed other institutions of the society. Thus, the family has been said to have changed from an extended family system to a conjugal system because of industrialization which took production out of the household. Because individuals had their sources of income outside the family unit and therefore were economically independent of the family enterprise, kinship organizations became weakened at the same time that the conjugal unit became emphasized. This is not an accurate description of the impact of industrialization on the family in northern Europe and America, since the extended family was never an important economic unit, even before industrialization. The credibility of the description for what has been taking place in non-Western societies has been seriously undermined by recent work in historical demography (Laslett, 1972). It had been argued that there is a compatibility in structure between an industrialized economy and the conjugal family system, so that the prior existence of this family form in northern Europe encouraged the rapid growth of an industrial economy, while the existence of strong comprehensive kinship organization elsewhere inhibited industrialization (Goode, 1963). It now appears that the preponderance of extended family structures in non-industrial societies was not nearly as great as we formerly thought, and that in fact hardly an example can be documented in which most people lived any substantial part of their lives in extended families (Laslett, 1972).

In Japan, the industrialization was carried out within the framework of a strong kinship system in the ruling class. While Japanese household size declined dramatically in the century before industrialization began (Laslett, 1973), the form of the industrial economy was profoundly affected by its having been grafted into the clan system of the elite. In this way the large industrial empires of Japan have taken on some of the social characteristics of kinship groups. For example, once a man is employed by a company, he usually becomes a permanent member of this economic "family," making his future within it, neither seeking advancement elsewhere nor being subject to the termination of his employment at the economic need of the employer (Wilkinson, 1962). In both of these examples, the family structure is the "basic" institution, causing, or at least facilitating, changes in economic forms.

Today it can hardly be argued that the family is basic in the second sense in American society. Rather, economic and political forces in the larger society alter the family forms. This may be done deliberately, as in the Soviet Union and China, or accidentally, as in the United States. The family may be simply "used" by the dominant institutions of society as a transmission agency, as some writers have suggested:

Agencies of socialization transmit culture: they do not necessarily create it. Primary groups may be the nursery of a human nature whose shapes and contours they do not determine. A sacred society will use its neighborhoods in one way, a secular society in another. The child must always be socialized within a small group, and the norms it is obliged to "interiorize" have another and a larger locus. The child is plastic, and he is molded to a large extent by his family, his play group, and his neighbors, but all these take their essential character from courses external to them. In modern society this is true with respect to the indispensable norms governing such phenomena as language, which certainly do not originate in any primary group, and it is equally true with respect to all major prescriptions and proscriptions.

. . . We may speak of the primary group as a transmission belt or a conveyor belt. Mechanized production requires the use of some such belt in a factory, regardless of what is being manufactured. The belt operates no less efficiently in conveying arms than in conveying automobiles, at a slow pace than at a high one, under capitalism than under socialism. The belt is *eo ipso* a neutral object, which must be adjusted to work norms and end products impersonally thrust upon it.

What this means in human terms can be seen if we pursue a point made by Cooley. He observes that in some countries we still find the neighborhood in all its ancient vitality, notably in Russia, "where the mir, or self-government village group, is the main theatre of life, along with the family, for perhaps fifty millions of peasants." Less than half a century later there is no mir. In Soviet Russia agriculture has been collectivized, the peasant way of life has been transformed, and self-government has been obliterated. But the primary group has survived all shocks and dislocations. It remains indestructible, flourishing now to serve purposes wholly inimical to its immemorial function. The institutional belt, which needed to be broken and refashioned, is now stronger than ever. What it transmits is something quite different.

Given such a highly symptomatic situation, one may legitimately inquire, "How primary is the primary group?"[1]

If there are Americans who believe that there is something about their family structure which is uniquely attuned to the American way of life and that it is somehow a bulwark of democracy or protectior against communism or some other sociopolitical system, it might be worth pondering the fact that changes in family structure in the Soviet Union closely parallel those in the United States. Not long a ago a Russian magazine published the results of a public opinion questionnaire on love and marriage. A typical response:

I cannot talk about family life, because mine was a marriage of convenience. . . . If it were possible to see even two months ahead into the future, many young girls would think twice before marrying for any other consideration except love. I say this on the basis of personal experience. Eleven years ago I married a man 20 years my senior because he had plenty of money and a highly paid job. Today I have everything—a TV set, a refrigerator, a radio, a vacuum cleaner, a washing machine, a Volga car—but not love; and all these material comforts about which so many other people dream merely weight me down, throttle me, don't let me breathe. My relationship with my husband is very bad. But we have a son who loves his father, and for his sake I must suffer in silence. I want to warn young people—a marriage of convenience is a terrible marriage (*Soviet Review,* 1962: 37).

[1] Bernard Rosenberg and Norman D. Humphrey, "The Secondary Nature of the Primary Group," in *Mass Society in Crisis,* Bernard Rosenberg, Israel Gerver, and F. William Howton, eds. (New York: Macmillan Company, 1964), pp. 76–77. Reprinted by permission.

When the Communist government took over China, the traditional family system constituted a detriment to rapid assimilation of new values and industrialization of the nation. In order to accelerate the process, the old family system was deliberately subverted and a new family system based on conjugal family units, marriage for love, self-selection of mates, feminine equality, and freedom from parental interference was encouraged to grow in its place. Because of the independence of each generation from the last, America's present family form facilitates rapid social change, urbanization, industrialization, and social and geographic mobility. It is, apparently, also peculiarly adapted to the facilitation of the social engineering practiced by powerful governments in mass societies.

Perhaps the form of the family has a determining influence on the outlook of individuals and the structure of society. Laslett (1972) suggests that "this determining influence may have been in fact of restricted significance. So little real variation in familial organization can actually be found in human history that examples of societies changing their character in accordance with changes in the family are very unlikely ever to be met with."

Equilibrium and Disequilibrium in the American Family System

Rapid change in any part of a society is likely to produce disruption and disequilibrium in other parts. In the latter part of the nineteenth century and the first part of the twentieth century, the United States was rapidly being transformed from a rural and small-town agricultural, nonindustrialized country to a highly industrialized, highly urbanized nation. It should not be surprising that the family would be somewhat transformed by the drastic change in the society, even if the existing family system were one which would facilitate the change. In the United States, it was necessary to invent new courtship forms, new bases for relationships between the sexes, and new relationships between family and community organization. Some dislocations occurred. Women moved into higher education and did not marry and have children to the extent that their less-educated mothers had. Courtship forms developed which were not sanctioned by tradition or the adult world. A period ensued when social norms had not developed fast enough to provide answers for the new situations people faced, even though the old answers would no longer work. When the society was built around a rural nonindustrial life, urban forms were found to be disruptive and look like disintegration.

By the 1950s, urbanization and industrialization had transformed the American way of life, and even rural areas shared most of the patterns of the new life. Americans became familiar with their new surroundings and took them for granted. They developed new forms of courtship, new patterns of marriage, new relationships among the unmarried, new parent-child roles. Social norms rapidly developed to support the new way of life. The birth rate returned to above population-replacement levels, especially among the educated. Marriage rates were at their highest in modern times. Courtship norms were stabilizing and developing wide social support. The divorce rate stabilized at a moderately high level. The American family system reached a state of equilibrium with the new society.

Not all scholars agreed with this picture, however. Jesuit sociologist Thomas was not willing to be optimistic, commenting that "it remains to be seen whether the emerging 'democratic' family is the final stage of a long evolutionary development or the first stage in the disintegration of a culture" (Thomas, 1955). However, even sociologists of an older generation, who thirty years ago were making historical analogies with the ancient world and predicting the decline of American civilization from what they saw as the state of decay of American families, became more optimistic. Zimmerman and Cervantes said:

> For some decades at the first of the century the family in this country, as well as some others, was losing ground, moving more and more away from its foundations. . . . In recent years there has been a reversal of this trend in the United States and in some other countries. . . . Our families have found out how to meet the new world with a workable system (Zimmerman and Cervantes, 1960: 200, 218).

By the early seventies disequilibrium was the picture. Birth rates plummeted to their lowest level in American history. Divorce rates doubled in less than a decade. The fundamental dimensions of sex-role differentiation were challenged. Social consensus on sexual morality was shattered. The sophisticated talked of alternatives to marriage. The unsophisticated wondered where it would all end. In the second edition of this text (1971), I wrote,

> . . . in nearly everything basic to the heterosexual relationships of American society, the present generation appears not to have changed as profoundly from its parents as both generations would like to believe.

The picture of glacial change in family structure that I painted sounds quaint today.

Social Forces and Individual Marriages

As unmarried persons read this book and discover "what happens" to married people, a frequent reaction will be: "That may happen to other people, but it will never happen to me. I will prevent it. This is something that only happens to others." Each person is different, and each marriage is different, but no marriage can escape the traditions of the society, the expectations of the community. No relationship is more personal and intimate than marriage. At the same time, no relationship is surrounded by so many cultural prescriptions, fables, myths, traditions, laws, and taboos. To be married is to be placed in a special relationship to another person—a relationship whose acceptable boundaries have already been established and whose general shape has already been determined. Even the terms used for spouses call forth social categories.

> In our society to speak of a woman as one's wife is to place this person in a category of which there can be only one current member, yet a category is nonetheless involved, and she is merely a member of it. Unique, historically entangled features are likely to tint the edges of our relation to this person; still at the center is a full array of socially standardized anticipations that we have regarding her conduct and nature as an instance of the category, "wife," for example, that she will look after the house, entertain our friends, and be able to bear our children. She will be a good or a bad wife, and be this relative to standard expectations, ones that other husbands in our group have about their wives too. . . . Thus whether we interact with strangers or intimates, we will find that the finger tips of society have reached bluntly into the contact, even here putting us in our place (Goffman, 1963: 53).

Most persons will be unaware most of the time of the social origins of their attitudes and expectations and of how very similar to other people's marriages their own are. Many young, sophisticated couples of intellectual bent will decide that the conventional patterns of marriage do not apply to them, that they will make their marriage what they will. These are the nonconformists. *They* will divide up the work the way they please. *They* will not be bound by the rules of jealous monogamy. *They* will rear their children as *they* see fit, not submitting to the pressures of the other parents in the neighborhood. *Their* children will not be permitted or encouraged to do things just because it is being done in their community. A nonconformist orientation to marriage and family life makes life interesting. It is also continuously frustrating and by definition subject to social punishments at every turn. Most couples cannot take this very long. Eventually they either isolate themselves from others, convert a small group of friends to their rules and limit themselves to this group, or find the new rules too difficult to maintain in the face of traditional patterns and gradually give them up. Everyone in a society is affected by the social changes and crises in the society in which he lives. These developments, more than the unique combination of personalities and experiences of particular family groups, will determine the destiny of the families caught up in them.

Sex Differences 3

Men and women behave differently from each other in American society. They do not just *happen* to behave differently from one another; the differences are systematic and expected. Men are expected to behave in certain ways because they are men and, for the same reason, not behave in certain other ways. Women are expected to do certain things and not others because they are women. In sociological terminology, these patterns of expected behavior for each sex are called sex roles. Investigations of societies other than ours indicate that every known society has sex-role differentiation; that is, each society expects men and women to behave with systematic differences.

Sex Differentiation in the United States in the Twentieth Century

DIFFERENCES IN PERSONALITY

Terman and Miles (1936) summarized the results of their landmark study of differences in the personalities of males and females as follows:

> From whatever angle we have examined them the males . . . evinced a distinct interest in exploit and adventure, in outdoor and physically strenuous occupations, in machinery and tools, in science, physical phenomena, and inventions. . . . The females of our groups have evinced a distinctive interest in domestic affairs and in aesthetic objects and occupations; they have distinctively preferred more sedentary and indoor occupations, and occupations more directly ministrative, particularly to the young, the helpless, the distressed. Supporting and supplementing these are the more subjective differences—those in emo-

Chart 3-1

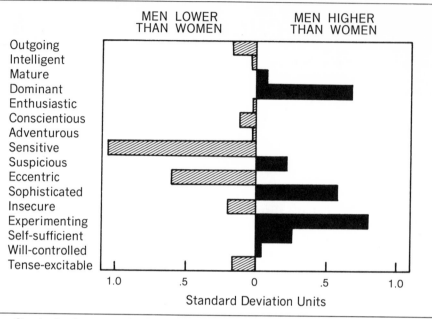

MALES AND FEMALES HAVE DIFFERENT PERSONALITY TEST SCORES
Index of difference, male and female scores on personality traits

MEN LOWER THAN WOMEN | MEN HIGHER THAN WOMEN

Outgoing
Intelligent
Mature
Dominant
Enthusiastic
Conscientious
Adventurous
Sensitive
Suspicious
Eccentric
Sophisticated
Insecure
Experimenting
Self-sufficient
Will-controlled
Tense-excitable

1.0   .5   0   .5   1.0

Standard Deviation Units

Source: Standardized norms on the Cattell 16 Personality Factor Test

tional disposition and direction. The males directly or indirectly manifest the greater self-assertion and aggressiveness; they express more hardihood and fearlessness, and more roughness of manners, language, and sentiments. The females express themselves as more compassionate and sympathetic, more timid, more fastidious and aesthetically sensitive, more emotional in general (or at least more expressive of the four emotions considered), severer moralists, yet admit in themselves more weaknesses in emotional control and (less noticeably) in physique (Terman and Miles, 1936: 447–448).

This description of differences will certainly not surprise many readers. In fact, its authors indicate that college students' descriptions of sex differences pretty much fit their findings. Every standardized personality test provides evidence that male and female personality scores are systematically different.

For example, Chart 3-1 indicates the differences between males and females for the 16 traits of the Cattell 16 Personality Factor Test. The differences described in this personality test are similar to those described by Terman and Miles.

It is interesting to note that the differences seem to be consistent with those described by the instrumental-expressive theory of feminine and masculine behavior. The theory was developed by sociologists observing small, same-sex decision-making groups. They noted that, in many of these groups, there seemed to be one person who led the group to "get things done," while another person was the "popular guy" who made people feel good. The person who got things done (known as the *instrumental* leader) performed one necessary function of the group—goal facilitation. The person who made people feel good (known as the emotional-*expressive* leader) performed the other necessary function for the group—maintenance of internal emotional equilibrium (sometimes called tension management). Talcott Parsons (1955) and many other researchers have associated women with expressive roles and men with instrumental roles. There is evidence that, in competitive situations, small groups of women work to keep each group member happy, while small groups of men are more concerned with winning. When men and women make up the same group, the men show exploitative behavior while the women are accommodative (Bond and Vinacke, 1961). Other group research suggests that women become as aggressive as men only when they cannot tell the effects of their actions on other members of the group (Lirtzman and Wahba, 1972).

Although females do tend to act in expressive ways while males tend to act in instrumental ways, this does not mean that men are always instrumental and women are always expressive. For example, Terman and Miles report that only 1 male in 100 scored higher on "femininity" than the mean of males did, but Kenkel (1963) shows that, in 1 out of every 5 married couples he studied, husbands acted in expressive ways more often than their wives.

An intriguing experiment by Matina Horner (1970) suggests that women are motivated to *avoid* achievement in competitive situations. Horner asked 88 men and 90 women to complete a story that began with the sentence she supplied. For the women the sentence read, "After first-term finals, Anne finds herself at the top of her medical-school class," and for the men it read, "After first-term finals, John finds himself at the top of his medical-school class." If a story contained imagery that showed negative concern about success, Horner scored it for fear of success. The stories written by 59 of the 90 women showed fear of success, while only 8 of the 88 stories by men indicated fear of success. Below are examples of the women's and men's stories.

FROM THE MEN	FROM THE WOMEN
"John is a conscientious young man who worked hard. He is pleased	"Anne is really happy she's on top, though Tom is higher than she—

with himself. John has always wanted to go into medicine and is very dedicated. His hard work has paid off. He is thinking that he must not let up now, but must work even harder than he did before. His good marks have encouraged him. (He may even consider going into research now.) While others with good first term marks sluff off, John continues working hard and eventually graduates at the top of his class."

"John is very pleased with himself and he realizes that all his efforts have been rewarded, he has finally made the top of his class. John has worked very hard, and his long hours of study have paid off. He spent hour after hour in preparation for finals . . ."

though that's as it should be . . . Anne doesn't mind Tom winning."

"Anne is a CODE name for a non-existent person created by a group of med students. They take turns taking exams and writing papers for Anne . . ."

"Anne is talking to her counselor. Counselor says she will make a fine NURSE. She will continue her med school courses. She will study very hard and find she can and will become a good nurse."

"It was luck that Anne came out on top of her med class because she didn't want to go to med school anyway."

METHODOLOGICAL NOTE

Horner's findings are so interesting that they have already found their way into many texts in marriage and the family. However, Levine and Crumrine (1973) repeated the study on a larger sample, with improved methodology, and found they could not substantiate the Horner results at all. Levine and Crumrine report that other unpublished replications of Horner have arrived at the same negative conclusions. At many other places in this text I have reported that influential studies whose results have become accepted fact, when repeated by other scholars, are contradicted by the results of the later study. In some cases the length of time between the studies allows us to imagine that "things have changed" between the studies. However, only three or four years elapsed between the Horner study and that of Levine and Crumrine. Different details of research methods frequently produce contradictory results. Small nonrandom samples from different college populations frequently produce different results. It pays to be cautious about placing confidence in the findings of a single study done on one small group, and never confirmed by subsequent studies.

While you may not agree that these stories show *fear* of success in women, they do indicate that women have more negative associations to success than men do.

DIFFERENCES IN ORIENTATION TOWARD THE WORLD

Males and females have different modes of orientation toward the everyday world. In a community study conducted by Seeley, Sim, and Loosley, sex differences emerged as the most fundamental division of the belief systems of the community.

> The deepest cleavage in the belief system of Crestwood Heights—more basic and deeper (we feel) than differences in age, ethnic group, or status—is created by the striking divergence in the belief systems of men and of women. The differences, the polarities, the selective, unlike, and emphatic emphases exist not merely at the level of detail, but, more important, at the very core of belief.
>
> This cleavage, which seems on the basis of our experience to appear in connection with virtually every important conviction, is obscured and covered over by another difference between men and women: as to whether, indeed, such important differences between them exist. Perhaps as a function of the conflict involved in the progressive emancipation of women in the last century or half-century, perhaps for other reasons, the ideology of the women tends to minimize the differences between the sexes. The "without regard to race, creed or color" pronouncement, the "people are people" view, the individualistic approach which tends to regard any categorization of people as wicked: these are used with perhaps even greater warmth and emphasis to play down or deny differences between men and women, other than those unblinkably given by anatomy. The women are thus—and here again they are in league with the experts—the promoters of an ideology of identity at the ideological level: men and women should, they feel, and would, except for irrational accidents of history, share a single value-system: the "maturity," individual-oriented values for which they themselves stand.
>
> The men, on the contrary, tend to exaggerate the cleavage, and even, ideologically, to regard it as an impassable gulf to be accepted with good humored tolerance. "Weaker sex," "inferior species" is now forbidden terminology, but the classification of "women and children" is more than a separation of convenience. Women are alleged to be unalterably sentimental, non-logical, and incapable of the heroic efforts needed for substantial accomplishment. This is supposed to be so much the case that the case cannot—in spite of all the evidence—be demonstrated to women. They must be "handled," like children, with careful concealment of the definition by which they are defined.
>
> . . . The men seem primarily concerned about the preservation of life against destruction, and they feel and believe accordingly. The women seem concerned about the creative and elaborative processes, and they believe and feel accordingly. The men attend to the *necessary* conditions for living; the women to the conditions that would make life *sufficing.* The men are oriented to the biological

and social substratum, to minima; the women to the social and psychological superstratum, to maxima. The men are concerned with the prevention of positive "evils"; the women with the procurement of positive "goods." The men live psychologically in an emotional climate of scarcity requiring the close and calculated adaptation of means to ends; the women, correspondingly, live in a climate of abundance requiring the wise selection and utilization of the riches available.

The disappearance of the patriarchal family from practice as impossible and from ideology as immoral has, seemingly, left untouched in the men the more general orientations which it bespoke, and to which under the then-existing conditions of life it was probably the best answer.[1]

EDUCATIONAL DIFFERENCES

There have been consistent educational differences between men and women for many years, but they are not as simple as is generally implied. For the last thirty years or more, the median years of school completed was higher for women than for men. This ended in equality in 1968. However, there have always been more men than women with college degrees. As can be seen in Chart 3-2, the ratio of men to women receiving college degrees in the 1960s reveals a shift away from a previous trend toward increasing male dominance in higher education, toward a somewhat larger proportion of higher degrees being awarded to women. Whether this shift is a harbinger of a trend toward greater participation of women in the professions, or whether it is a response to some other factor (such as the end of veterans' educational benefits), is too early to determine. However, the President's Council of Economic Advisers (1973) reports that the more education a woman has, the more likely she is to work, whether she is single, married, or separated (with children, if any, over six years old).

Sex differences in education are evident when major fields of study are examined. In 1970, women received 3.9 percent of the B.A. degrees and 9.3 percent of the M.A. degrees in business; they received 30 percent of the B.A. and M.A. degrees and 16 percent of the doctorates in biological sciences, but only 8.5 percent of the M.D. degrees. In 1971, 74 percent of the B.A. and 56 percent of the M.A. degrees in education were awarded to women (Economic Report of the President, 1973).

OCCUPATIONAL DIFFERENCES

A later chapter will deal in more detail with the relationship between women's employment and their family relationship. Here only the relation-

---

[1] John R. Seeley, R. Alexander Sim, and Elizabeth W. Loosley, "Differentiation of Values in a Modern Community," *Crestwood Heights* (New York: Basic Books, 1956). Reprinted by permission.

Chart 3-2

MORE MEN THAN WOMEN HAVE COLLEGE AND GRADUATE DEGREES
Ratio of men to women receiving college degrees, 1920 to 1970

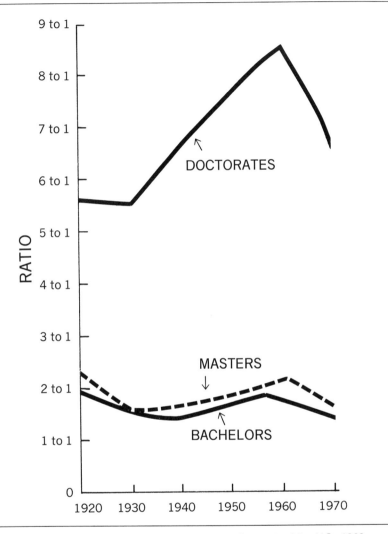

Source: Statistical Abstracts of the U.S., 1972, and Historical Abstracts of the U.S., 1960.

Chart 3-3

WOMEN LOSE GROUND IN THE PROFESSIONS, GAIN IN OTHER OCCUPATIONS
Percent of the workers who are female in major occupational groups, 1940-1970

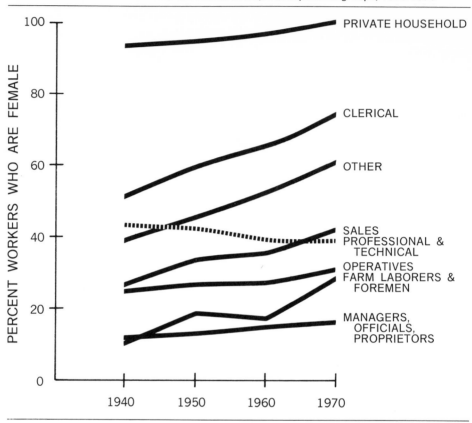

Source: Census data

ship of women's occupational patterns to those of men will be indicated. Chart 3-3 indicates the percentage of workers who were women in the various major occupational categories from 1940 to 1970. This chart clearly shows that while women constitute an increasing proportion of most major occupational categories, they continue to lose ground in the professional and technical occupations.

Women have come increasingly to dominate the clerical occupations, with more than 70 percent of clerical workers now women. In the professions, the proportion of women rose until 1920, but it has declined markedly since then, until the ratio of men to women in professions is now about down to the 1900 level. Table 3-1 indicates that even in the professions traditionally dominated by women (nursing, teaching, library science, religious work, and social work) and identified by Parsons (1955: 13-15) as essentially "expressive" occupations, the percentage of women is declining, while males continue to dominate most other professions at about the same level. These trends have continued undisturbed through the 1960s (Knudsen, 1969).

Table 3-1

MALES INCREASINGLY DOMINATE THE PROFESSIONS
Percent in Various Professions Who Are Male

	1940	1950	1960	1970
Architects	97.7	96.0	97.7	96.5
Authors	63.9	61.2	74.4	70.7
College presidents and faculty	73.5	76.8	78.1	71.6
Lawyers and judges	97.6	96.7	96.2	95.2
Physicians and surgeons	95.4	93.8	93.0	90.8
Social and welfare workers	35.7	30.8	37.2	37.3
Teachers	24.3	25.4	28.3	29.8
Nurses and student nurses	2.1	2.4	2.5	2.7
Librarians	10.5	10.9	14.3	18.1
Photographers	86.3	82.7	88.0	86.2
Religious workers	25.4	30.4	37.5	44.3

Source: Census data

The President's Council of Economic Advisers (1973) reported that in 1970 women made up 28 percent of college faculties, almost the same proportion as in 1930; 6.3 percent of managers of manufacturing firms, slightly fewer than 20 years ago; and 3.5 percent of dentists, only a little more than in 1910.

It is clear from all available sources that a greater percentage of women are working outside the home today, that a greater percentage of married women are working, and that a greater percentage of women with children of whatever ages are working than ever before. While in 1890 less than 20 percent of women were employed, according to the census, figures for 1970 indicate that more than 40 percent of women are working. In 1950 there were 190 women keeping house for every 100 women employed. By 1969, there were only 120 women keeping house for every 100 women employed. However, these figures can be somewhat misleading. Most working mothers do not really work a full schedule the year round. Three out of four working mothers with minor children work only part time or less than half the year in an average year. Among working wives with no children at home, only about half work full time the whole year (Smuts, 1959).

Of the people who work full time, black women earn less than white women, who earn less than men, black or white (Epstein, 1973). The percentage of black women who work is higher than that for white women, but the difference has been shrinking. From 1961 to 1971 the percentage of black women who worked rose from 48 to 49 percent, while the percentage of white women who worked rose from 37 to 42 percent (Waldman and Gover, 1972).

The percentage of women who have ever worked continues to increase (Blood and Wolfe, 1960), but the proportion going into full-time professional employment is declining. Parsons' appraisal of the trend seems to be correct: In occupational roles, "there can be no question of symmetry between the sexes in this respect, and . . . no serious tendency in this direction" (Parsons et al., 1955: 13–14).

Although it has been customary among sociologists to say that women work for the same reasons as men—to acquire money and prestige—this explanation no longer appears adequate. Studies of high school students looking forward to their occupational careers, at any rate, suggest that women expect the extrinsic rewards of work such as material wealth and prestige to follow from their *husbands'* job, not their own. Women look to their own careers to provide primarily intrinsic rewards—satisfactions that issue directly from doing the work itself. Furthermore, those women who value intrinsic rewards of work highly are those who are most likely to be planning careers. Most women who work are not working at careers but at jobs with few intrinsic rewards.

Changing Sex Roles

Although commentators on sex roles agree that sex roles have been changing, they disagree concerning *how* the roles are changing. In view of the widespread idea that males and females in American society are "becoming more alike," it is unfortunate that the social scientist does not have much data he can bring to bear on the subject. Before 1940, no one seemed to be very interested in collecting such information. There are only two pieces of information which may help one discover whether any changes are occurring in recent years in the difference between masculine and feminine personality. Terman and Miles (1936: 122–123), studying persons of different ages, discovered that males were most masculine in high school and females most masculine in college, after which both males and females gradually became

Chart 3-4

AMERICANS MAY BE BECOMING MORE MASCULINE
Masculinity of Americans, by age (as measured in the 1930s)

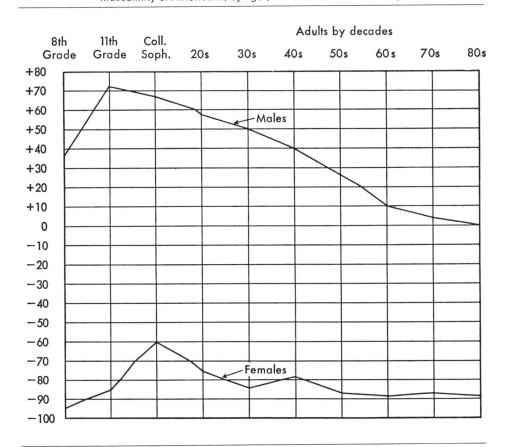

Source: Terman and Miles, 1936

more feminine, with the decline in masculinity by old age more than twice
for men what it is for women. In short, during the 1930s after the late teens,
the older the group studied, the less masculine it was. (See Chart 3-4.) This
was interpreted by Terman and Miles, quite understandably, to mean that
as persons get older, they become more feminine. The second piece of information, from Kelly's longitudinal study (1955), measured changes in personality over a twenty-year period and includes among his measures a masculinity-femininity scale adapted from Terman and Miles (with whom Kelly

worked). Kelly reported after the last follow-up of his sample that both males and females had become *more masculine* as they got older — exactly the opposite of the earlier finding. Assuming both samples to be comparable (and the test instrument was, in fact, identical), there is only one explanation which synthesizes these two findings: Masculinity does not change with age, but with the culture. Kelly's sample was studied for the first time in the early 1930s — exactly the same time as the Terman-Miles study was made. The persons studied were at an age when their masculinity should have been at its highest, yet as they grew older, they became more masculine. Kelly seems unsure of what his results mean, and suggests tentatively that perhaps anyone who had lived through the intervening twenty years (1933–1954) would have become more masculine. However, the two studies together point to the conclusion that American culture may have been gradually becoming more masculinized (as measured by the Terman-Miles tests) for a century, and the older people in the Terman-Miles study were less masculine because they had lived most of their lives in a culture which was less masculine than the culture in which the younger persons had grown up. This certainly contradicts popular and professional opinion alike, which has traditionally maintained that females were becoming more masculine and males were becoming less masculine.

MEASURING MASCULINITY AND FEMININITY: A METHODOLOGICAL NOTE

How does one go about measuring the attribute "masculinity" or "femininity"? The preceding discussion can be quite misleading unless the reader knows how the results were obtained. The pioneer work in this field done by Terman and Miles in the 1920s and the 1930s has been followed by nearly all subsequent researchers. In constructing their index of masculinity-femininity, Terman and Miles gave a very large number of different kinds of test and questionnaire items to men and women of different ages and occupations. The answers were then scrutinized to determine which items the two sexes responded to most differently. For example if a test item was normally answered "yes" by 10 percent of the women and by 90 percent of the men, then the item was considered "masculine" and included in the test. If 40 percent of the women and 42 percent of the men answered the item "yes," the item was defined as not measuring masculinity-femininity. The final masculinity-femininity test was constructed using only those items which males and females respond to with marked difference. The following items are representative of those included in the Terman-Miles test.

Instructions: In each case, draw a line under the word which goes best or most naturally with the one in capitals; the word it tends most to make you think of.

22. FLESH blood— color— meat+ soft—
30. EMBRACE arms— lover+ mother0 sin+
52. MARRIAGE children— divorce+ happy— license0
[Responses with + count a point for masculinity, with — count a point for femininity, and with 0 do not count either way.]

Instructions [abbreviated]: Underline the one word that tells what the drawing makes you think of most.

7.

dish —
ring 0
target +
tire 0

In each sentence draw a line under the word that makes the sentence true.

46. A buffet is used for   books0   clothes+   dishes—   food—
21. A boomerang is an   animal—   plant0   tool—   weapon+

Below is a list of things that sometimes cause anger. After each thing mentioned, indicate whether it angers you Very Much, Much, Little, or None.

16. Seeing someone try to discredit you with your employer   VM+ M0 L+ N—
17. Seeing someone laugh when a blind man runs into an obstacle VM— M+ L+ N+

Do you like or dislike these people?

2. Babies   like—   don't like+   neither+
4. People with loud voices   like+   don't like—   neither+ [1]

Several other types of items are included in the test. It is important to remember that the scores for masculinity and femininity are based on differences between male and female responses of persons taking the test in the 1920s and 1930s. It is probable that sex differences change from generation to generation and that the scoring of the items should be changed from time to time to take this into consideration. More recent researchers (Sannito et al., 1972) have challenged the Terman and Miles test because it is based on the assumption that masculinity and femininity are at either end of a continuum, so that femininity is the opposite of masculinity. They argue that in many instances the concepts of "most masculine person" and "most feminine person" are similar enough to insure that the same response to a test item could indicate both masculinity and femininity. These researchers

[1] Lewis M. Terman and Catherine Cox Miles, *Sex and Personality* (New York: McGraw-Hill Book Company, 1936), pp. 482–506. Reprinted by permission.

suggest that two separate scales, most masculine-least masculine and most feminine-least feminine, would be better measures of masculinity and femininity.

THE CHANGING FEMININE SEX ROLE

Margaret Mead believes that male and female roles are converging through the masculinization of the female role. She sees the roots of this change in the United States in the "frontier role" of the woman who was presumably required to be a self-sufficient companion in taming the wilderness (Mead, 1953: 14). At an earlier time, she saw the trend in more Freudian terms as a masculine protest of the feminist movement, which was motivated by envy of masculine superiority ("penis envy" in psychoanalytic terminology). Mead now interprets increasing convergence of sex roles as a product of heterosexual togetherness — the breakdown of sex segregated activities during elementary school and adolescence which used to develop and accentuate sex differences. In 1953, Mead wrote:

> In coeducational schools, girls and boys are educated alike, and taught to be individualistic, assertive, active, to want to make something of themselves. . . . The boy wants the girl to be independent, to have something to say for herself, to be able to make her own living. . . . To have a wife all to one's self, not to have to share her with a job . . . is still a pretty universal demand made by a man on his wife, but he does not want her all to himself because she cannot do anything else, but rather because, being able to do other things quite, but not superlatively, well, she chooses to stay home with him and have children. . . . Girls have become more like boys and their goals as human beings have steadily approached each other (Mead, 1953: 14–18).

Lundberg and Farnham, writing in 1947, and Deutsch, in 1945, saw a trend toward assertiveness and masculinization in women. They regarded the choice between acceptance of femininity and the neurotic striving after masculinity as a universal female dilemma. Modern women in the United States, they maintained, have been encouraged to make the neurotic choice by the feminist philosophy prevailing presumably in the 1930s and 1940s, a philosophy being promoted by sick women (Deutsch, 1945; Lundberg and Farnham, 1947).

Komarovsky, also working from data collected in the 1940s from American college women, discerned two contradictory roles with which modern women are said to be faced (a distinction since echoed by two decades of writers):

> One of these roles may be termed the "feminine" role . . . a set of personality traits often described with reference to the male sex role as "not as dominant or aggressive as men" or "more emotional, sympathetic." The other and more recent role is, in a sense, no *sex* role at all, because it partly obliterates the

differentiation in sex. It demands of the woman much the same virtues, patterns of behavior, and attitude that it does of the men of a corresponding age. We shall refer to this as the "modern" role (Komarovsky, 1963: 127).

Recently there has been a flood of new sex-role research accompanied by a more positive view of the convergence of sex roles. Masters and Johnson (1966, 1970) have made female and male sexuality of equal importance and interest. The negative effects of sex discrimination in such fields as medicine, the social sciences, and psychology has been the subject of many recent studies (Prather and Fidell, 1972; Ehrlich, 1971; Schneider and Hacker, 1972; Broverman et al., 1972; Chesler, 1971). The necessity, even the advisability, for mothers to provide all the care for their children is being questioned (Binstock, 1972). Women's, as well as men's, biases against women are being reported (Goldberg, 1968; Pheterson et al., 1971).

Sex Roles As Values

It is not at all inconceivable that a society could be built in which males and females were not sex-role differentiated beyond the differences in their contribution to the reproduction of offspring. As many anthropologists and sociologists have noted, this may not be an especially convenient or remarkably efficient arrangement, but it is clearly well within the range of human possibility. No social scientist could produce substantial evidence that this would be an untenable arrangement, likely to produce widespread social discontent or personal disorganization. Even with respect to socialization, it appears from limited data that the separation of love and discipline along sex-role lines of parents is not as effective as the situation where both parents are a source of both love and discipline.

This is not a recommendation for the abolition of sex-role differences, but the recognition of them for what they are—basic values around which a substantial part of American behavior is oriented. Every people has taken its sex-role differentiation as natural, and deviations from it as threatening. If sex roles are a basic axis of behavior differences in a society, then, when the sex roles change, many other types of behavior are disordered. In the United States in the past century, powerful changes in the organization of life have basically altered the relationship of men and women to one another, probably at first with no one recognizing the changes. When households were no longer agricultural production units, when individuals—male or female—were employed independent of family associations, when for substantial numbers of persons, sex and reproduction could be connected or disconnected from each other at will, when the influence of traditional religion had gradually declined under the philosophical impact of scientific rationalism, when the value of individual equality came gradually to be seen as applicable to more and more human relationships—then the foundation which supported the particular traditional sex-role differentiation in the United States had been effectively undermined. Sex roles began to change. It is easy to say that the change merely entailed the masculinization of the female sex role, but a look at the society fifty years ago suggests that nearly every exciting, intellectual, responsible task was within the male sex role, and the female sex role contained what men either could not do (bear children), or would not do. By today's perspective, it looks as though society locked women in the house and, when they tried to break out, castigated them for wanting to be men.

Whatever the changes are, they have made many people uncomfortable. Men are more likely to have been made uncomfortable because it was really their preserve which was invaded. Perhaps some males have found themselves impotent with women who did not fit their traditional concepts of femininity. When there is no consensus on roles, there is frustration for those who must interact in those roles. Behavior such as the male sex act, which is contingent on conditioned functions of muscle responses not under conscious control, will not respond to stimuli which are inconsistent with those to which it has been conditioned. The choices between alternate, and to some extent incompatible, sex roles have been experienced by many women with anxiety, the usual response to any role-conflict situation.

Concern over the Male Role

It should be expected that changes in the feminine role might be accompanied by changes in the masculine role. Although it is believed by many sociologists that men are today permitted to do many things formerly limited to women (e.g., changing diapers, child-care, housekeeping chores), there is no *systematic* evidence that men do this more than in the past. There is considerable evidence that no one considers such things as primarily the *responsibility* of the male even today, but rather as chores which the husband shares under certain practical circumstances as a helper to the wife. Hartley suggests that the husband's willingness to assume partial responsibility in domestic tasks corresponds to the wife's increasing willingness to work outside the home. In each case, "the activity is subordinate in importance both to the major responsibility of the sex involved and to the weight of the responsibility borne in the given area by the opposite sex" (Hartley, 1963).

In spite of the subordinate place the borrowed domestic tasks play in the lives of adult males and in the expectations of children, and the lack of empirical evidence demonstrating the actual occurrence of problems supposedly incurred by both spouses and children, a number of psychologists have expressed alarm concerning the "feminization of men."

But to talk about the "feminization of men" is deliberately to provoke anxiety. Furthermore, it subtly misses the real crux of the emerging changes

Chart 3-5

NORTH AMERICAN COLLEGE STUDENTS SUPPORT TRADITIONAL SEX ROLES
MORE THAN EUROPEANS

Percent "yes" responses to the question: "Do you support the idea that individuals and society function best if male and female roles in life remain essentially different though equal?" (Samples of college students)

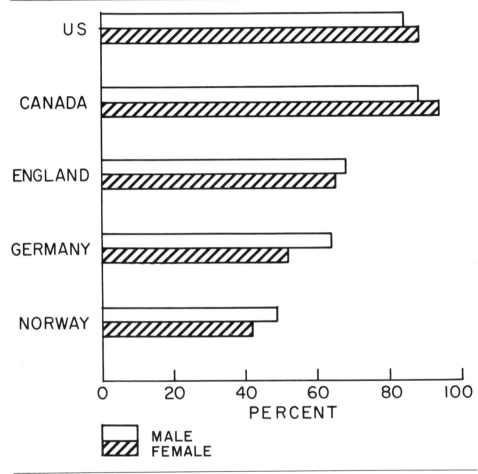

Source: Luckey and Nass, 1969

in male roles. An interesting investigation of the concepts which college students have of the ideal member of the opposite sex seems to have captured the essence of the changes coming about in males, at least among the well-educated. McKee and Sherifs asked college men to describe the ideal female of their age and women to describe what they thought men considered the ideal female. They also asked women to describe the ideal male of their age, and men to describe what they thought women considered the ideal male.

The results show that women believe men consider the ideal female to be restricted in her behavior to traditional feminine stereotyped behavior—and they are correct: men do believe this, but they are not as restrictive as women think. The male concepts in the test were especially revealing. The men believe that in the eyes of women, the ideal male is one who is not only everything society believes masculine, but also much that society alleges to be feminine. The researchers report, "We find a pressure by women to have men more oriented to interpersonal relations and more expressive of human (feminine in the stereotype) feelings." The data suggest that women put pressure on men not to be less masculine, but to add elements of femininity to the masculine stereotype. The researchers foresee the effect of this on the future:

> If college women now exert such pressure, and if they have communicated it to the men, then both men and women should, as they become parents during the next few years, teach these values in rearing the new generation of sons (and daughters) (McKee and Sherifs, 1960).

Yet in a survey done recently of college students in five countries, respondents were asked, "Do you support the idea that individuals and society function best if male and female roles in life remain essentially different though equal?" Chart 3-5 shows that American and Canadian students support traditional sex-role differences to a much greater degree than European students (Luckey and Nass, 1969).

A Hypothetical Society with Equality of the Sexes

What would life be like in a society in which there was no sex-role differentiation and the equality of the sexes was a fact? One must start with the assumption that the family system would be retained, that sexual behavior would continue to be basically heterosexual, and that a monogamous marriage arrangement would still prevail. As often as not, however, one would expect to find husbands tending children and doing housework while wives worked at careers. One would find entrance into occupations in which both sexes are equally capable to be irrespective of sex. Women locomotive engineers and male kindergarten teachers would be as common as their sex counterparts. Divorce would never provide for support of the wife. When married, couples would take the wife's name as often as the husband's, move for the convenience of her education or her job as often as for his. While middle-class women now consider it part of their role as wives to contribute to the husband's career development, one might expect husbands to be equally concerned with the development of their wives' full potential. Today it rarely occurs to a man that he has any such responsibility. Describing the contemporary scene, one sociologist remarks:

> Now wives in general have had much practice in playing the roles of friendly critic and stimulating audience. When their expectations sensitively run slightly ahead of their husband's performances, they account for many prodigies in male careers. But husbands are hardly prepared by cultural history to reciprocate as the most beneficent other in the development of wives for whom the performance of household duties no longer seems to challenge their capacities. . . . The commonest picture in American marriage is that in which the husband has no concept whatever of contributing by his manner of speaking and listening to the elaboration of his wife's career, particularly when she has no ostensible career (Foote, 1963: 20-21).

Sex equality would also mean the disappearance of nonreciprocal courtesies that men have traditionally extended to women. Practices of men holding doors for women, lighting their cigarets, giving their seats, standing when a women approaches the table, helping them on and off with wraps, and a thousand other niceties—all symbols of a women's helplessness and dependence—would be done away with.

Pay differentials for men and women at the same work have diminished, but they would disappear completely under conditions of sexual equality—as would laws providing special working conditions for women, such as shorter hours, mandatory rest periods, and the like.

Dating customs would be radically transformed. Girls would seek out boys as often as the reverse and initiate dating relationships as they pleased. There would be no particular reason why the males should pick up and deposit females at their homes, nor always provide the transportation. The practice of males paying the entertainment expenses would certainly disappear.

In fact, the longer one thinks about it, the more things occur that would be transformed under conditions of sexual equality. The strange picture presented by this hypothetical society is a measure of how far from a disappearance of sex-role differences contemporary American society is.

The Women's Liberation Movement

One of the most interesting social phenomena of the last decade has been the rebirth of the women's liberation movement, more or less dormant for almost half a century. The new movement is a loose association of formal and informal organizations, varying in their goals, but generally dedicated to the reduction or elimination of sex-role differences. In an age when the average American woman was confident that she was free, that she was not being put upon by men or society, the women's liberation movement has dramatically focused national attention on the continued existence of sex discrimination in jobs, wages, education, and general participation in the main stream of American society. It has directed the nation's attention to the fact that far from making strides toward equality of participation in higher education and the influential segments of the occupational world, women have been falling progressively farther behind men in these respects for four decades. It has exposed male-dominant attitudes in both men and women that most people take so much for granted that they do not even recognize them as sex-biased. More sociologically sophisticated than the earlier feminist movement, the new movement argues that the mechanism for perpetuation of the inequalities is the childhood socialization process, which prepares little girls to be dominated by men and to move into dependent adult roles. Most women therefore not only accept their restricted participation in the main business of the world, but do not experience this as an injustice, and in fact mostly find satisfaction within narrow confines. The movement therefore finds itself faced with the formidable task of educating millions of women to interpret their plight as one of exploitation, before it can tell them what they should do about it.

Sex differentiation is today the most fundamental dimension of personality difference in our society. Sex-role differentiation is so basic to the present organization of the social structure, that any group advocating its abolition can expect to be confronted with shocked disbelief, then ridicule. Proposals like nondiscrimination in employment, same work for same pay, and nursery schools for working mothers have found a wide and for the most part sympathetic hearing, and the movement can already claim achievements of importance in these areas. Proposals like rearing boys and girls alike, having men participate on an equal share basis in domestic chores and childrearing, and career equality of the sexes in marriage cut so deep into the basic structure of the present organization of life that they are greeted with anxiety and hostility by most men, and by many women.

REPRESENTATIVE LEGAL CHANGES TOWARD EQUALITY OF THE SEXES

While the women's liberation movement does not merit credit for all of the recent changes in legislation which have equalized the status of men and women, there is no question that its supporters have been influential in creating considerable change already. Among the most important changes of the past decade in the *legal* status of women in the United States, those of greatest import are changes in divorce laws of several states, and the Civil Rights Act of 1964.

Recent changes in divorce laws have generally been in the direction of imposing *equal* obligation on husband and wife for the support of the former spouse and the children, and allowing the court to decide to whom what obligation shall be assigned. These changes have in some ways removed women from the special privilege of being supported by an ex-husband after divorce, and have removed the husband from the special obligation of supporting his children after divorce. (Most states still retain the traditional laws in these respects.)

The Civil Rights Act of 1964 states that sex may not be a qualification for employment in a particular job, and that it is the obligation of the employer to prove that one sex or the other is disqualified on the basis of incompatibility with the nature of the work. It further states that persons of equal training, education, and experience must receive the same pay regardless of sex. Women are therefore protected by this law from job discrimination in the same way as other "minority groups."

The proposed Twenty-Seventh Amendment to the Constitution, the Equal Rights Amendment, now in the process of consideration by the states, reads: "Equality of rights under the law shall not be denied or abridged by the United States or by any State on account of sex." Its adoption is uncertain. At the time of this writing, 30 of the required 38 states have ratified the amendment, and 13 have turned it down. In 6 it was stopped before reaching a vote. Louisiana had not yet considered it.

IMPLICATIONS FOR BLACK AMERICANS

For American blacks legal and other changes in the definition of sex roles have somewhat different implications. Black women have always found it easier to get jobs than black men, and a far greater proportion of them have always worked than the proportion of workers among white women. When in the mid-1960s the federal government made a special push to hire more blacks, it was black women who mainly got the jobs. The black liberation movement and the women's liberation movement, although similar in pattern in many ways, find little sympathy in common because of the strong male-dominant theme in the black movement. In the past few decades there have been more professional black women than black men. Better job opportunities for white women in the job market may put them in direct competition with black men for jobs.

IMPLICATIONS FOR LOWER-CLASS WOMEN

The whole controversy over changing sex roles and new identities for women is strongly rooted in the problems of the middle-class educated woman, and has little relevance to lower-class problems as the lower-class people see them. In contrast to the middle-class educated group, the *ideology* of the lower-class American has always been more male-dominant than the *behavior.* On this level a high proportion of the women have always worked, not as a source of identity, but as a source of income. Work versus domesticity as a source of identity for women is not a salient issue among working-class wives (Komarovsky, 1964).

Origins of Sex Differences

Are sex differences in behavior determined biologically or culturally? Do men and women behave differently because of their genes or because of their upbringing? A century ago the answer would have been taken for granted. Biology was assumed to be the basis for the different behavior. The twentieth century saw the gradual rise to supremacy of the cultural explanation of the social scientist. We are even now in a period where most social scientists lean heavily to explanation of all sex differences in terms of differential socialization and different cultural expectations. In the last few years careful scholars have despaired of separating the effects of culture from the biological influences, and called the question meaningless. Recent studies of humans and other animals have allowed us to escape from this stalemate, and answer the question with increasing confidence.

The proponents of cultural determinants of sex differences argue that if sex-role differentiation were the same in every society—if masculine and feminine roles differed from one another in the same ways in every society—the biological explanation would be more acceptable. But sex roles are not differentiated everywhere in the same way, and even if they were, it would be difficult to prove that the differences were biologically caused. Table 3-2 shows that almost no activity is performed exclusively by women or exclusively by men in all societies. While the table does not dispute the possibility that it is more natural for one sex to do some kinds of work, it does suggest that any biological factor predisposing one sex to one kind of work is weak enough to be overridden by the culture.

There are obvious structural differences in males and females in primary sexual characteristics, in addition to other systematic secondary differences, which can only have a biological origin and cannot be considered culturally induced. A man's height is usually in his arms, legs, and chest (Leuba, 1961). His lungs and heart are larger and his chest and shoulders are broader than a woman's. A woman's height is predominantly in her abdomen to accommodate her uterus and her generally larger abdominal organs. She has broader hips; the muscles that support them are the only ones that are larger than the corresponding muscles in a man. A woman has a subcutaneous layer of fat and a metabolism more sensitive to temperature changes; because her metabolic rate decreases more rapidly in response to a rise in temperature, she perspires less than a man does. Men are usually the only victims of sex-linked defects such as color blindness and hemophilia. More miscarriages and stillbirths are males. A fetus develops into a male only if certain hormones prevent the development of female sex organs and induce the growth

Table 3-2

NO WORK IS EXCLUSIVE TO WOMEN OR TO MEN IN ALL SOCIETIES
Comparative data on the division of labor by sex

Activity	Number of Societies Where Work Is Done by				
	Men Always	Men Usually	Either	Women Usually	Women Always
Weapon making	78	1	0	0	0
Hunting	166	13	0	0	0
Boat building	91	4	4	0	1
Mining and quarrying	35	1	1	0	1
Trapping or catching of small animals	128	13	4	1	2
Lumbering	104	4	3	1	6
Fishing	98	34	19	3	4
Herding	38	8	4	0	5
House building	86	32	25	3	14
Body mutilations (such as tattooing)	16	14	44	22	20
Burden bearing	12	6	35	20	57
Manufacture of thread and cordage	23	2	11	10	73
Basket making	25	3	10	6	82
Mat making	16	2	6	4	61
Weaving	19	2	2	6	67
Gathering of fruits, berries, and nuts	12	3	15	13	63
Pottery making	13	2	6	8	77
Preservation of meat and fish	8	2	10	14	74
Manufacture and repair of clothing	12	3	8	9	95
Gathering of herbs, roots, and seeds	8	1	11	7	74
Cooking	5	1	9	28	158

Source: Stephens, 1963: 282–283

of male reproductive organs; if these hormones are not present, the fetus continues to develop as a female (Money and Ehrhardt, 1972).

Bone formation is more rapid in girls than boys, and girls reach puberty about 2 years earlier than boys. Diseases afflict and kill more men than women in any age group, and the life expectancy for men is 6 years below that for women (72 years for women, 66 years for men). For a comprehensive review of the research on biological sex differences, see Gadpaille (1972). The influence of the physical sex differences on behavioral predispositions of the sexes is at this time only a matter of conjecture.

The first edition of this text, based on information available in 1965, presented a thoroughly sociological explanation of the origin of sex differences in behavior. At that time I argued that sex differences were probably completely determined by socialization, and that any innate predisposition to different behavior by the two sexes was trivial by comparison with the effects of socialization. The second edition, on the basis of information I had in 1970, took a more moderate position. The information available today invalidates my previous explanations. Evidence on the role of sex hormones in differentiating the behavior of other animals had been accumulating for two decades. Primate behavior studies showed that monkeys had sex differences in behavior which closely paralleled those of humans. Harry Harlow's (1962) observations of rhesus monkeys led him to conclude that sex differences in behavior are largely genetically determined.

> The outstanding finding in both the playroom and playpen is that male and female infants show differences in sex behavior from the second month of life onward. The males show earlier and more frequent sex behavior than do females, and there are differences in the patterns displayed by the sexes. The males almost never assume the female sex-posture patterns, even in the earliest months. The females, on the other hand, sometimes display the male pattern of sex posturing, but this is infrequent after ten months of age. Predominantly, females show the female pattern and exceptional instances are to other females, not males . . . Thus, as soon as the sexual responses can be observed and measured, male and female sexual behaviors differ in form. Furthermore, there are many other behaviors which differ between males and females as soon as they can be observed and measured . . . males threaten other males and females but females are innately blessed with better manners; in particular, little girl monkeys do not threaten little boy monkeys . . . Contact play is far more frequent among the males than the females and is almost invariably initiated by the males. Playpen data show that real rough-and-tumble play is strictly for the boys . . . We believe that our data offer convincing evidence that sex-behaviors differ in large part because of genetic factors (Harlow, 1962: 3–6).

While it is perfectly true that the monkeys are learning their behavior in a social setting, the same sex differences emerge wherever monkeys get together. Surely we ought to consider it mildly curious that male and female monkeys differ from one another in their behavior in very much the same way as we have thought male and female humans did. But since they *were* in fact monkeys, and not humans, we could still protect ourselves with the conceit that the behavior parallels were a peculiar accident which meant nothing for us but amusement at the zoo.

Now the human data make it possible for us to begin sorting out sex differences into those which are underwritten by biology, however culturally embellished, and those which are genuine cultural options. The most important studies are those reviewed by Money and Ehrhardt (1972).

Money and Ehrhardt tested 25 genetic females who were born with ambiguous genitals but female reproductive organs because a male hormone (an androgen) had prevented normal development of the genitals. The hormone had been introduced in 15 cases because of a defect in the fetus' adrenal glands and in 10 cases because of hormone therapy the mother had received while pregnant. All 25 infants were raised as females from birth, and received estrogen treatments that counteracted the effects of the androgen after birth. At the time of the study the subjects ranged in age from 4 to 16 years. Money and Ehrhardt included a control group of 25 normal females matched with each patient for age, IQ, socioeconomic background, and race. Money and Ehrhardt hypothesized that any masculinization of the fetal brain by hormones could be pinpointed by discovering the differences between the patient and control groups. A trait that appeared often in the patients but seldom in the controls might be considered masculine, while behavior that occurred often in the control group but seldom in the patient group might be considered feminine. On the basis of interviews and sex-role tests of the 50 subjects, Money and Ehrhardt determined behaviors in which the patients differed significantly from their matched controls.

Twenty of the patients were regarded by themselves, their mothers, and their playmates as tomboys. Each expressed dissatisfaction at being a girl and either wanted to have been born a boy or could not decide whether she would rather have been born a boy or a girl. None wanted to change her sex, however. A statistically insignificant number of girls in the control group reported short periods of tomboyish behavior. The patients differed significantly from their matched controls on their high amounts of physical energy expenditure. They engaged in athletics and played rough games with boys more often than the control group did. Although the patients were more interested in rough games than the control group was, they did not differ from the control group on aggression. Mothers and patients agreed that the patients were not aggressive girls who picked fights. On the basis of this evidence, Money and Ehrhardt suggest that a measure of masculinity should be dominance assertion rather than aggressiveness. Dominance assertion in the patients was indicated by the finding that the majority of the patients wanted to subordinate marriage to a career or wanted both a career and marriage, while the majority of the control group felt that marriage superseded any career.

An interesting finding is that the 15 patients with adrenal malfunction differed significantly from their controls on their lack of enthusiasm for handling babies. One-third preferred not to have children, and all the patients were unenthusiastic about caring for infants, although they did not reject the idea of having children. The control group was extremely eager to have children. Perhaps lack of enthusiasm for handling small children could be considered a masculine trait. Such an idea might explain why the one task always assigned to women in every culture is the care of small children.

Money and Ehrhardt are careful to point out that the results of this one study do not indicate that hormones are responsible for sex differentiation, nor do they prove that androgens are responsible for the characteristics noted in the patients. They note again that the effect of a child's environment on his development is powerful and only vaguely defined. As an example of the effects of the culture on sex-role differentiation, Money and Ehrhardt cite the case of a normal male infant whose sex was changed at age 17 months because an accident during circumcision removed his penis. The parents treat the child and her normal twin brother in very different ways, and the children differ correspondingly. The girl enjoys neatness and dislikes being dirty, and she imitates her mother's behavior while the brother more often copies his father. It is interesting to note that, in spite of her femininity, the girl has many tomboyish traits, is extremely energetic and active, and is usually the dominant member in a group of girls.

Additional support for the intricate interaction between hormonal and cultural influences on sex differentiation is the fact that women with high levels of androgens in their bloodstreams tended to report an uncharacteristically large number of erotic dreams but that, although these women had erotic dreams as often as normal men did, the imagery in their dreams was appropriate to females, not to males (Money and Ehrhardt, 1972). Money and Ehrhardt conclude that ". . . human gender-identity differentiation . . . takes place . . . when a prenatally programmed disposition comes in contact with postnatal, socially programmed signals" (Money and Ehrhardt, 1972: 18).

We must now conclude that fundamental predispositions to sex-differentiated behavior are created in the early months of fetal development. In males, the fetal testes produce androgen. This androgen masculinizes the brain and the nervous system (as well as the anatomy) of the male fetus. If androgen is not present during this period, the nervous system is not masculinized, and the baby is born not only with female sex organs, but with predispositions to behave in characteristically feminine ways. If the androgen is present during this fetal period, the baby is born with a predisposition to behavior which is characteristically masculine. These differences continue to be evident regardless of socialization, and do not require continuous hormone support for their maintenance. The nervous system is preprogrammed by the fetal androgen or its absence, and the programming is evidently permanent. These androgen-programmed differences include at least the following:

1. Males have a predisposition to competition for dominance, while females do not.

2. Males have a greater predisposition than females for high energy expenditure.

3. Females have a greater predisposition to care for infants. This list is not meant to be exhaustive, nor does it exclude the possibility that other sex differences in behavior are supported by other biological factors which come into play at other times in life.

Sex roles may be seen as a social accommodation and elaboration on the basic differences in behavioral predisposition of males and females.

The achievement of "gender identity" (the identification of the self with being a male or female), and the learning of the appropriate ways of expressing that identity in a particular culture, is purely a socialization process.

An Interpretive Essay on Sex Differences

If differences in the behavior of men and women were solely determined by the social process, then presumably a society with consensus and determination could write its own scenario of the ideal society, specify any particular relationship between the sexes, and differences in the behavior of the sexes it chose, or no sex differences in behavior if that was preferred, and build a social structure to achieve it. The radical women's liberation philosophy is based on this assumption. It is an assumption which has the theoretical support of much of the social science community. Rear little boys and little girls in identical ways, the theory goes, and they will grow up different in plumbing only. Then half the Presidents of the United States will be women, and half the baby sitters will be men. Reverse the socialization processes we now have, rear girls as we now do boys, and boys as we now do girls, and we would get the world described in Thomas Berger's *The Regiment of Women:*

> It's the twenty-first century and all the roles are reversed; women dress in pin-striped suits, smoke cigars, strap down their bosoms, and hold all the positions of power; men dress [in panty hose] are secretaries, maids, and manicurists . . . Men hide behind tears, and women use force and profanity.[1]

We must now face very strong evidence which undercuts the theoretical support for such a position. It is no longer tenable to believe that males and females are born into the world with the same behavioral predispositions. Our theory of society and of the relationship between the sexes must accommodate itself to the fact that males and females are born with predispositions to behave differently. In the past, most societies have simply taken that for granted. Sex-role differences in most societies can be viewed as cultural elaborations and specifications which capitalize upon the innate proclivities of males and females to behave differently.

We must now be confident that if it were possible to rear boys and girls alike, they would still come out different. If we are thoroughgoing in our determination to eliminate sex-role differences, we must recognize that it will be necessary to work at cross-purposes with the natural propensity of the organisms. Specifically, we will have to reward dominance and punish submissiveness in women, while we reward submissiveness and punish dominance in men. No one can be sure what other problems such socialization might create, but we can be rather sure that it will not create Berger's twenty-first century.

[1] Review of *The Regiment of Women* by Thomas Berger, *New Republic,* June 30, 1973, vol. 168, no. 26, p. 32.

Development of
Sex Roles

4

In Chapter 3 we concluded that biological differences in males and females predispose them to behave in characteristically different ways along several dimensions. Every society elaborates a set of behavioral expectations appropriate for each sex. These behavioral expectations we call sex roles. Sex roles are usually consistent with the basic biological predispositions, and most societies capitalize on the differences laid down by biology. But all societies go far beyond the biology in laying down differences in sex roles. We cannot say that it is impossible for a society to develop sex roles which are inconsistent with, or even contradict, the biological predispositions. We can only say that no clear-cut cases of this can be documented.

This chapter develops *how* sex roles are learned by each new generation. Various explanations of the process are put forth by different scholars in different disciplines. Generally, the psychiatrist tends to stress the importance of experience in the earliest years of life and the overwhelming importance of parental relationships. Sociologists are less impressed with the importance of the first years in sex-role socialization, as well as in other developmental processes, and tend to see socialization as a continuous process extending into adulthood. Nearly all scholars are agreed on three points:

1. Sex roles are learned in primary groups, particularly the family and the peer group.

2. Deviations from a normal sex role should ordinarily be explained by deviant socialization processes rather than by departures from normal biology.

3. Sex roles in the United States (and probably elsewhere) are different in different parts of the society, so that, for example, lower-class sex roles will be in some ways different from middle-class sex roles.

The Concept of Socialization

The sociologist uses the term *socialization* in a very specific sense, and in a sense quite different from its use by the layman. Socialization is the process whereby persons learn how to behave in the ways which are expected in the groups in which they are members. Socialization may be seen as an extremely general process and one which begins whenever any person begins interacting in a new group. The family socializes new members into the family (and into society). Old members socialize new pledges into fraternities. Teachers and experienced students socialize new pupils into school systems. Inmates and guards socialize new prison inmates into appropriate prison behavior. New church members are socialized into appropriate church roles. A new kid on the block is being socialized into his play group when he learns who the tough guy is, finds out that you don't tell your mother what went on among your friends, and discovers that you get status by being able to spit twelve feet. Socialization is not something which occurs only in childhood and adolescence. A new resident in a home for the aged has a socialization process to undergo which is in many respects similar to that of a young child in his first week at camp or the new military recruit during his first week of basic training. In later sections of this book, several different socialization processes will be discussed. For example, the early period of marriage may be thought of as a process in which husband and wife reciprocally socialize one another to the marital role expectations of each.

Cross-Cultural View of Socialization for Sex Roles

Just as sex-role differentiation is found in every culture, so differences in the socialization of young boys and girls are a part of every society. Societies in which there are extended or large family groups involving high cooperative interaction tend to have the largest differences in socialization of boys and girls. Perhaps in large units the labor *can* be divided more strictly, and there is always another woman or man to substitute for a missing member. The relatively small differences in American sex socialization (and sex-role differentiation in adults, presumably) may be a product of our small-family system, where men and women may need to do a good deal of pinch-hitting in one another's roles (Barry, Bacon, and Child, 1957). *In most societies, girls experience heavy socialization pressures toward nurturance and responsibility, while boys are pushed to be self-reliant and achievement-oriented. Pressures on the other sex to acquire these traits are almost never found.* The sex traits emphasized in American socialization are basically similar to the pattern of emphasis elsewhere, but the difference in training of boys and girls is not as exaggerated as it is in most simpler societies.

Sex-Role Differentiation in Infancy

Initial sex-role assignment to the child is done at birth on the basis of the obvious genital configuration. Appropriate sex names are usually assigned by the parents at this time, and the fitting of the infant to a sex role is begun. Although the differentiation of bunting colors by sex (blue for males, pink for females) has begun to decline because of the availability of other attractive colors, it is still a part of the sex-role identification procedure of early infancy.

As the young child becomes aware of himself, he has a number of clues from which to decipher his sex role—his anatomy as compared to others, his parents' attitudes toward him, sex-role references to himself, and so on. During the early months of his life, the infant's parents may already be responding to him in sex-role terms, even though he will be unable to perceive them for perhaps two years. There is some difference among couples in this respect, but the general "neuter" gender of the infant in American culture is reflected in linguistic terms. The term "baby" is ungendered and may be replaced by the pronoun "it." Thus one hears: "Where is the baby?" "It's asleep." Some mothers and fathers use he-she gender pronouns from the beginning. Some families dress male and female infants alike for a long time, while others put on appropriate sex clothing in the early months. No systematic observations have been made on the topic, but one might suspect that sex-role socialization is begun earlier today in the United States than a century ago—perhaps earlier than a generation ago. Many people will find in their family albums a picture of a male ancestor at age four with long curls and a dress, and this seems to have been fairly common in the nineteeth century. On the other hand, it is inconceivable that this would occur in a contemporary family without quickly being identified as pathological. It is a common sight today to see one-year-old toddlers stuffed into frilly dresses, the costume completed with a ribbon in a wisp of hair, and a bulging waterproof diaper underneath. Blue-jeans with a zipper fly are available for boys who are not yet old enough to walk. Sex-stereotyped toys are made available during the second year, so that by age three most children make culturally appropriate choices of toys when presented with alternatives (Rabban, 1950), and can accurately classify adult items associated with one sex or the other (Vener and Snyder, 1966). If an early orientation to proper sex role may be taken as evidence of cultural pressures to adopt the sex role, apparently there is more pressure on boys than on girls to learn the behavior appropriate to their sex during the earliest period. The differences in the boy's problem of sex-role establishment, which is discussed below, will help make the reason for this clear. Any contemporary four-year-old boy who was allowed to wear female clothing would be a neighborhood curiosity, and it is likely that both he and his parents would be considered in need of psychiatric attention. On the other hand, American culture is not nearly so restrictive in eliminating masculine items from the behavioral repertoire of the young girl.

It might be interesting to speculate on the reasons for the apparent shift to very early sex-role emphasis, especially for boys. It might indicate that contemporary parents are not as confident of their boys growing up to become "masculine men" as previous generations were. Perhaps the general unclarity of sex roles in modern American society, abetted by frightening articles in popular magazines, leads anxious parents to work with especially great attention at getting boys to be boys.

The Social Psychological Interpretation of Sex-Role Learning

The process of sex-role learning is in some ways fundamentally different for boys than for girls. Exactly how one explains the difference depends upon whether the explainer is a social psychologist or a psychoanalytically oriented psychologist. Although essentially the same behavior is being observed and explained by the two points of view, the theoretical frameworks produce two very divergent explanations.

In the earliest period of parent-infant interaction, the infant has no awareness of sex-role differences. He learns his behavior from his mother in nearly every case. (It would be interesting to study the sex-role development of a sample of children reared by men—there must be a few.) This initial relationship leads the young child to develop behavior patterns which are similar to his mother's (a process sometimes referred to as "identification" with the mother). However, at the same time the mother reflects to the young child a set of behavioral expectations, or ways in which she expects the child to act with respect to her. This initial undifferentiated role of infant is one of dependence, obedience, and passivity. The mother reflects these requirements to the child, and they become a part of his initial orientation to social relationships. Insofar as the child is unaware of sex-role differences at this period, we may assume that even if the father is considerably involved with the young child, the differences in the roles of the mother and father are not perceived by the child. Both parents are sources of control and probably of affection; both expect dependence and obedience. Not only do both boys and girls initially "identify" with the mother (in the sense defined above), but both fall into what is essentially a "feminine" (passive-dependent) role with respect to *both* parents.

As the child's social perception becomes more sophisticated, he is able to discriminate between the behavior of his father and that of his mother and decipher from an abundance of cues that people are divided into two categories — male and female — and that he and one parent belong to one category, and the other parent belongs to the other. By age three, the boy will begin to perceive that some new requirements go with being male. Males are not supposed to be passive, compliant, and dependent, but on the contrary, are expected to be aggressive, independent, and self-assertive. The recognition of this by the boy is the point at which boys and girls encounter different sex-role problems.

At the point when the boy becomes aware of sex-role requirements, he is involved in a comfortable passive-dependent role with his mother and, to a much lesser extent, with his father. This is a fairly easy and satisfying relationship. Children and adults alike find it uncomfortable to reorient themselves to new role requirements. The easiest thing for the young boy to do is to remain in his "feminine" role. On the other hand, his parents control his reward structure to a great extent. They let him know they expect more assertive independence in *some* relationships (particularly with age-peers), although not with his parents, and especially more emotional control (not to cry when hurt). The reward structure of his life now begins to give the advantage to acting "masculine." If the mother and father both reflect the same requirements and reward the same new pattern (the parents form a "coalition" against the child, in the words of some writers), the boy responds to the expectations and altered reward structure and becomes more "masculine." As I indicated in Chapter 3, the boy's natural proclivities project him out of a passive, dependent role under ordinary circumstances. Therefore, the parental reinforcement pattern serves to support the usual natural inclination of the boy, and to play a primary formative role only when the boy's natural inclination is to stay in the dependency role.

However, the mother has some real emotional benefits in retaining the old relationship with the boy. As long as he is still "feminine" he is docile and easy to handle. He is also the dependent partner in a relationship which is very satisfying to mothers and, consequently, not easy to give up. If the mother yields to these temptations and encourages the boy to remain in his role of dependency, then the father becomes the main source of pressure for role disruption and independence. The mother and son are then in "coalition" to maintain his dependency against the demands of the father — "After all, he is still only a baby." Under these circumstances, it is not unlikely that the father will be perceived by the child as a source of uncomfortable demands and therefore the object of considerable hostility.

CASE

I can remember coming home with tear-filled eyes, bruise marks, rumpled clothes, disheveled hair, and whimpering to the tune of "so and so beat me up." The next day dad gave my brother and me a pair of boxing gloves. This, however, did not sit well with mother. She took the boxing gloves away from us. She tied us to her "apron strings" and throughout childhood my brother and I were dominated by our mother. Sitting on mother's lap may be part of the role of "loving, obedient little boy" assigned by her to myself, but as I continued going to school I learned that other boys took a dim view of lap sitting, and I began to resist my mother's continued overtures.

CASE

I was never very interested in sports except swimming so I would play with the girls at school, which distressed my father. He was always trying to get me interested in some physical activity. This had an opposite effect on me and even today I am more of a spectator than a participator when it comes to sports.

Normally, however, the mother finds it more rewarding to encourage masculine behavior on the part of the child, in large part because most boys will have a natural tendency to move toward less passive, more independent behavior. "Nonfeminine" is an appropriate term for the new role, because one of its major requirements is the elimination of previously acquired behaviors. Some writers say that the boy is required to "shift his identification" from his mother to his father (Lynn, 1961), which is another way of saying what has been said here. When the boy's natural inclination does not propel him toward a less feminine behavior pattern, and when the parents do not encourage the role shift in the boy, the rewards will sometimes remain with his essentially feminine role. Apparently this role shift must occur fairly early in life. Lynn writes:

> Those males who fail in forming same-sex identification are, for whatever reasons, unable to overcome the primacy of the early learned identification with the mother and remain "fixated" at that level. Perhaps the development of masculine identification typically progresses satisfactorily if it "once gets off the ground," that is, if the initial step is taken in early life. If the boy fails to make progress in this initial shift from mother to masculine identification, he may be unable to profit by the elaborate system of reinforcements provided males by the culture in developing masculine identification. If the boy is sufficiently fixated in his identification with his mother, these reinforcements for males may not even seem, to the boy, to apply to him at all. The mother-identified boy may consider these reinforcements to apply only to "those other children" falling in the male sex category to which he, phenomenologically, does not belong (Lynn, 1961: 374).

What circumstances in the boy's life encourage the development of masculine behavior? A substantial amount of research has been devoted to the topic. Sibling relationships apparently have a good deal of effect on the development of sex-role characteristics of boys. Brim (1958) has shown that for five- and six-year-old boys, at least in two-child families, boys with older sisters are distinctly less masculine and more feminine than boys who have

Table 4-1

BOYS WITH OLDER SISTERS ARE LESS "MASCULINE" THAN BOYS
WITH A BROTHER OR A YOUNGER SISTER
Frequency of masculine and feminine traits attributed to boys,
according to sex and age of sibling

	High Masculinity	Low Masculinity	High Femininity	Low Femininity
W/young brother	9	12	0	41
W/young sister	6	14	12	42
W/older brother	12	13	10	32
W/older sister	0	19	23	15

Source: Brim, 1958

a brother or a younger sister. The extent to which this would also be true at age twelve is unknown, but it might be hypothesized that the differences apparent at age five or six would be nearly obliterated by adolescence. Table 4-1 shows the frequency of masculine and feminine traits attributed to boys in Brim's sample, according to sex and relative age of sibling.[1]

Considerable research has been devoted to the effect of absence of a father on the development of masculine behavior in boys. Earlier studies rather consistently concluded that father-absent boys had more difficulty in identifying with the masculine role and establishing masculine behavior characteristics. Father-deprived boys showed more immature behavior, and less well-adjusted relationships with peers (Lynn and Sawrey, 1959; Sears, Pintler, and Sears, 1946). Later studies have thrown this conclusion into doubt. Hetherington (1966) discovered that in her sample, only those deprived of fathers before age five showed any difficulty. Other recent studies (Barclay, 1967; Thomes, 1968) have found no overt behavior differences related to presence or absence of father when other factors were controlled. It should also be pointed out that *none of the studies found father-absent boys to have less masculine behavior traits.* Various psychological hypotheses have been put forward to explain this negative finding.

The most popular explanation is that the father-absent boys have developed "compensatory" masculinity, especially through "reaction formation" (a defensive and violent reaction against characteristics which one rejects but fears in the self) (Miller, 1958). Barclay and Cusumano (1967) and others tell us that "on the surface" father-absent boys are just as masculine, but they have a deeply buried feminine identity which leads them to deal with the world in typically feminine ways. I prefer a peer-group explanation. This argument rests on the finding that father-absent boys are much more

[1] These results have since been confirmed by one study (Kammeyer, 1967) and not confirmed by another (Strodtbeck and Creelan, 1968).

dependent on their age-mates for guidance and status than father-present boys. It suggests that if a boy can't learn masculine behavior from a man at home, he learns it from his friends away from home.

METHODOLOGICAL NOTE: THE MEASUREMENT OF UNCONSCIOUS FEMININE IDENTITY

The ambiguities in the research on effect of father absence on boys' masculinity makes me hesitant to reach firm conclusions at this point. It might help the student to understand some of the hesitancy if we take a closer look at what the researcher did to arrive at his conclusions. Barclay and Cusumano (1967) measured overt masculinity on pencil and paper personality tests, and as noted above found no differences related to father absence. Deeply buried feminine identity was measured by having the boys try to hold a rod vertical inside a tilted frame. The father-absent boys deviated from vertical more than father-present boys. Since girls do more poorly on this test than boys, the father-absent boys were then judged to have an underlying feminine identity.

Other research shows that ease with which boys assume masculinity is facilitated by the pleasantness of childhood experience (Ferguson, 1941), by emotional involvement and high father-son interaction (Mussen and Distler, 1959), and by the father's role being a warm and affectionate one which is rewarding toward his son (Payne and Mussen, 1956; Sears, 1953).

In spite of the evidence pointing to the fact that *masculine identity in male children is facilitated through presence and involvement of the father with his son,* the *content* of the boy's masculine role does not seem specifically related to the way his father plays it. The young boy in American society appears to be presented with a cultural stereotype of the masculine role for his emulation. All boys receive essentially the same stereotype and conceive the masculine role in very similar ways, independent of the father's behavior. Exactly the opposite is the case for girls, whose feminine role identification is highly influenced by specific aspects of their mothers' role behavior (Lynn, 1961, 1962). Perhaps this is the product of a culture in which the way in which the feminine role is to be played is acted out in detail on a daily basis for every girl with a mother (or mother figure), while much masculine role behavior is in an absent and obscure occupational role, a few hours each evening, or after the children are asleep—at best available on a part-time basis to the boy, and in limited aspects. Thus even the boy's father can only present him, not with a specific role model, but with a stereotype of masculinity which is the same stereotype provided by the mother and by the society at large.

Because assumption of the demands of the masculine role requires the explicit rejection of prior feminine role components, *there is a strong element of antifemininity in early masculine role conceptions.* The concept of masculinity seems to filter through to the young boy as an upside-down concept of femininity. If his old "feminine" role calls for obedience, then masculinity consists of disobedience. If "nice little (feminine) boys" are clean, then big boys are dirty. It is easy for the boy to come to the conclusion that masculinity is "bad" and femininity is "good," but that he is required to be "bad." Children's conceptions of masculine and feminine differences tend to stereotype existing differences. A study with six- to eight-year-old children showed both boys and girls conceiving of males as being "stronger, larger, darker, more dirty, more angular, and more dangerous" than females (Dagan, 1961). Under conditions of lower-class culture, in fact, mothers consistently define men to their little boys as bad, giving social reinforcement to the tendency inherent in learning masculinity in American culture.

The repudiation of femininity for the emerging male comes to mean the repudiation of girls as playmates and scorn for their activities. One of the ways the masculine pattern of expectations is conveyed to the boy is the stricture against playing with girls. Boys may give up their girl playmates with some reluctance, especially when alternatives are limited, but it is the price of becoming masculine. The little acts of male aggression against girls, so familiar to teachers in the early elementary grades, can be seen as attempts of boys to reinforce their maleness. Throwing rocks at girls, breaking up their games, hurling epithets at them merely for being girls—in these ways the boy says to others and to himself, "How far away from those girlish things am I, and how little use I have for them now that I am a man." This rejection pattern is bewildering to girls who a year before played with boys as peers and now find themselves isolated from them and the object of jeers. The sex segregation which is begun by the withdrawal of boys into their own group during the first years of elementary school is the genesis of the enduring sex subcultures in American society which have such a profound influence on sex-role development.

Another reason for the difficulty of males in achieving proper sex identification and sex roles without anxiety is the teaching technique used in American society. While females are apparently taught femininity primarily by being *rewarded* for *appropriate* behavior, males are taught to be masculine primarily by what psychologists call "divergent feedback," or by being *punished* for *in*appropriate behavior. This helps to account for the preponderantly negative content of the youngster's conception of masculinity. Studies of learning processes have demonstrated rather conclusively that divergent feedback is an especially ineffective method of teaching, since to learn the same material takes much longer by punishing negative responses than by rewarding positive responses. Furthermore, divergent feedback causes more anxiety responses, and rather than causing the behavior to be "unlearned," merely suppresses it, causing dislike for the punishing person and dislike for the behavior punished. If this can be generalized to sex-role learning, it ought to be expected that American teaching techniques make *boys have more difficulty achieving sex-role identification than females, have more anxiety about their sex-role identification than females, and have greater hostility toward females and femininity than females have toward males.* All of these expectations have actually been confirmed (Lynn, 1964). The results of this method of teaching sex roles also help one to understand the origin of many differences between masculinity and femininity: the hostility component of masculine heterosexual behavior (largely missing in females), the tendency of men to emphasize and women to minimize the differences between the sexes, and the greater emotional ambivalence of men toward women in general.

FEMALE SEX-ROLE DEVELOPMENT

By implication, much of the early sex-role development of the girl has been spelled out in the description of the masculine process. In the earliest period of social interaction, the girl (as the boy) can only be in a dependency relationship to the parent, especially the mother. As awareness of sex-role differences develops and the girl deciphers from anatomical evidence and social expectations that she is a female who behaves differently from a male, she finds that the role requirements of femininity are those in which she is already socialized. Actually this statement makes it sound as if some sort of realization occurs, and this is probably not the case. Rather, when sex-role differentiation becomes obvious to the girl, she has already learned an appropriate behavior pattern, and so is quite removed, at least at that point, from the necessity of defining and learning her sex role. She already has it. *For a young girl, femininity is not something one* learns, *but something one* has. No special pressure from parents or peers is required, no hostility is aroused from giving up any comfort. Girls can apparently include in their behavior all kinds of masculine traits without interfering with a secure feminine identity, and later discard boyish behavior when it becomes inappropriate.

CASE

There weren't very many children living in the same neighborhood as me when I was five years old. Most of the children who were my age were boys, and as a result I started growing up under the boys' influence. For instance, there was a boy by the name of Jim, and he would always try to call me a sissy and this would make me so mad and I would do things that would prove to them that I wasn't a sissy. I remember one time when the boys teased me into climbing a very high eucalyptus tree. After I had climbed this tree, I sat up in one of the highest limbs making faces at them and laughing at them telling them that this was only a simple feat for me and I was really scared half out of my wits. When I reached the ground I was shaking from fright, and I used the excuse that it was really cold way up there. After that experience they seldom saw me up in a tree. I spent most of my childhood around boys, for when I was in grammar school, I would play all the games a boy would play instead of games girls would play. . . .

When I went into junior high I never thought about playing rough games with the boys. My whole attitude on boys changed.

The content of the feminine role is easily definable to the girl: mother plays it twelve to fourteen hours a day in more or less constant companionship with her. Consequently, concepts of femininity for each girl tend to be very specific to the way her mother plays the role (Lynn, 1961, 1962), in contrast to the stereotyped masculine pattern adopted by boys. As a result, there is considerably more variety in feminine sex-role preferences among girls than masculine preferences among boys (Brown, 1957). The direct patterning of feminine behavior from the mother may be the reason for the fairly rapid shifts in feminine behavior which have been accomplished in the recent history of American society. Masculinity appears to have changed much less and is probably stabilized by the existence of a culture-wide stereotype.

The understanding of the importance of mother and father in the development of adequate heterosexuality in both male and female children has probably been hampered by the Oedipus theory. The wealth of research on the development of sex roles has now led sociologists to an entirely new concept of how parents influence sex-role development of children. *The crucial step in establishment of adequate heterosexual adjustment in both boys and girls is breaking out of the mother-child relationship and establishing strong relationships with the father* (Johnson, 1963). It has been known for a long time that over-attachment to the mother inhibited the establishment of heterosexual relationships of boys, but it is now clear that the same is true for girls. An inadequate relationship with her father, combined with a great dependence on her mother, is the condition best designed to block the establishment of heterosexual relationships in the daughter. Conversely, those women who show the closest attachment to their fathers tend on the average to be the most advanced in heterosexual relationships (Winch, 1951).

CASE

During my childhood, between the ages of five and twelve, my family settled down. My father had to work late at night and sleep during the day. I remember not being very close to my father at this time. He was just another person whom I called by his first name. As a matter of fact, during this period I was always a little afraid of my father. I remember being afraid to ride in a car alone with him for fear he would run off with me. When we were alone I felt awkward in his presence and did not know what to say. My impression of him at this time is that of a very disciplinary man. . . .

I find that I have not had a satisfactory friendship relation with a person of the opposite sex. The boys I have gone out with have been mostly from school, but a few I have met through friends and relatives. I find that I have always found some reason to dislike or lose interest in a boy once he got too interested in me. The majority of the time I started comparing the boys with my father and found myself very dissatisfied with them. Another thing is that the moment a boy showed any sexual interest in me I began to distrust him. Until just recently I was afraid of having a boy like me because of sexual attraction, rather than for my personality. To be truthful, I still am a little afraid of this.

CASE

I do feel that because of the fact that my father was not around very much for the first fifteen years of my life that the showing of affection was embarrassing to me. I enjoy dating but I am afraid I am rather on the cold fish side.

CASE

I always felt I could tell my father when I was in trouble rather than my mother. I feel this has influenced me in feeling more at ease talking to persons of the opposite sex rather than ones of the same sex. Once when there was an accident and a group of us girls broke a window of a family's in town, I told my father immediately, knowing that he would hear the whole story before accusing me of being wrong. When my mother heard about it she was quite upset and furious, while on the other hand my father said "What is done is done."

The father who is nurturant and affectionate but demanding of his son, is encouraging his son's development of a secure masculinity; the father who is himself masculine in interests and attitudes but encourages his daughter to participate in sex-typed activities is encouraging the development of a confidently feminine daughter (Mussen and Rutherford, 1963). The father who remains aloof from the rearing of his children and who does not become emotionally involved with them in effect abandons them to the influence of their mother and ensures that they will have a difficult time establishing mature heterosexual adjustments.

The effect of the sex and relative age of siblings is different for sex-role assumption in girls than in boys. (See Table 4-2.) In families with one child of each sex, girls with a brother have many more masculine traits than girls with a sister, but more feminine traits as well (Brim, 1958). The presence of a brother, especially an older brother, does not in the least detract from a young girl's femininity, but simply expands her behavioral repertoire by the addition of masculine traits. A comparison of Table 4-1 for boys and Table 4-2 for girls is illuminating. These five- and six-year-old girls generally rate quite high on femininity, since feminine is what they have always been. Those who have had the opportunity to learn masculine patterns have acquired a number of masculine traits as well. The boys at the same age do not show nearly as many masculine traits as the girls do feminine traits, but generally they have high antifemininity scores. This is good evidence for the idea that the boy is repudiating femininity, but his concept of masculinity still lacks distinctly masculine items and still consists primarily of an anti-feminine orientation. The tables also reflect the permissiveness toward girls maintaining cross-sex traits in addition to feminine ones, but the necessity for boys to rid themselves of their cross-sex traits—characteristics which are inherent in the different way each sex learns his sex role.

This latter theme is evident in the sex-role differentiation of every age group in American society and helps to create the distinctive quality of each sex role. Girls can play baseball, but boys cannot have dolls. Girls can wear trousers, but boys must *never* wear girlish clothing. Women can work at otherwise masculine occupations, but men avoid distinctively feminine jobs and are practically *never* primarily responsible for the rearing of small children. Masculine women may not be extremely popular with men, but they are socially acceptable, while effeminacy in a man is a socially valid basis for scorn and ostracism in most groups.

Table 4-2

	High Masculinity	Low Masculinity	High Femininity	Low Femininity
SEX AND RELATIVE AGE OF SIBLINGS AFFECT BOTH MASCULINITY AND FEMININITY OF GIRLS *Frequency of masculine and feminine traits attributed to girls, according to age and sex of siblings*				
W/young sister	5	15	33	16
W/young brother	20	3	33	7
W/older sister	7	18	36	14
W/older brother	20	0	48	0

Source: Brim, 1958

The emphasis of the preceding paragraph, while still the dominant theme in American sex roles, needs to be tempered in the light of recent developments in certain segments of the generation now "under thirty." In some groups there has been a reaction against sex-stereotyped "role-casting" with emphasis on a less restrictive masculine role. This new masculine pattern encourages the personal adornment of men, appreciation for flowing locks, and a place in the male repertoire for the softer emotions and aesthetic appreciation. Many men welcome the freedom from being boxed in by the emotional restrictions of traditional "manliness."

A Psychoanalytic Interpretation of Sex-Role Learning

The psychoanalytic explanation of sex-role socialization is an attempt to explain the same behavior explained in the paragraphs above. Emerging from a different theoretical position, with a special focus on genital differences and eroticism, it casts an entirely different light on the process. The following selection is representative of the psychoanalytic point of view, reproduced in the words of a Freudian sociologist.

The Oedipus Complex. The male infant finds his first love-object in his mother. This incestuous desire is inhibited by the presence of the father. The male infant develops an antagonism for this rival who takes her away. The way in which the father reacts toward the infant's preoccupation with the mother, and of the mother with the infant, can exacerbate or neutralize or weaken this antagonism. In the male child's genital instinct lies the basis of his Oedipus complex—the desire to kill his father and marry his mother. So great is this male infantile desire for the mother and fear of his rival that he imagines the father would like to take away from him the organs associated with this desire; that is, he imagines that his father wants to castrate him. Thus is developed what is called castration-anxiety, a fantasied fear that his father will kill him since he identifies his genitalia with existence.

Castration-anxiety is heightened when the boy realizes that there are human beings without male genitalia, girls, whom he at first considers as being merely castrated males. Shunning castration, he inhibits overtly manifesting affection for the mother or overtly showing antagonism for the father. The amount of such anxiety he will accumulate during infantile sexuality and carry with him into maturity is dependent upon how much affection the father permits him to show to the mother and how much his mother permits him to show.

The young boy faces a tragedy inherent in infantile genitality; what he wants he cannot have even if it were permitted him, for he obviously is no coital match for the father nor could he maturely enjoy the coitus he desires with the mother. Here, indeed, is frustration denied to neither the rich nor the poor. But disappointment may be more than assuaged and the psychogenital energies may be constructively harnessed by identification with the father, the symbol of authority, by affection shown him by the father, and by affection permitted to be lavished upon him by the mother.

The female child in infantile sexuality is also originally attached to the mother. But as the female child becomes progressively conscious of the external world and of her own body she discovers her lack of male genitals and she feels castrated. Her castration-feelings are transformed into the desire to possess a penis, especially the father's. She feels that she has been thwarted and cheated by her mother, first in not having a penis and then in being denied her father's. She develops what is called penis-envy, which mixed with castration-fear develops into a castration complex.

Whereas the boy's feeling of castration leads him to seek identification with the father and thus resolve the Oedipus complex, the girl's penis-envy and castration-feelings set going her Oedipus complex. She longs for the forbidden object—her father or sometimes her brother. This forbidden object she finally possesses through coitus when she is sexually mature. The threshold of anxiety for this object is nailed down while she is working through the Oedipus complex. But "she accepts castration as an established fact, an operation already performed, whereas the boy dreads the possibility of its being performed. . . . The Oedipus complex in the girl is far simpler, less equivocal, than that of the little possessor of a penis; in my experience it seldom goes beyond the wish to take the mother's place, the feminine attitude towards the father. Acceptance of the loss of a penis is not endured without some attempt at compensation. The girl passes over—by way of a symbolic analogy, one may say—from the penis to a child; her Oedipus complex culminates in the desire, which is long cherished, to be given a child by her father as a present, to bear him a child. One has the impression that the Oedipus complex is later gradually abandoned because this wish is never fulfilled. The two desires, to possess a penis and to bear a child . . . help to prepare the woman's nature for its subsequent sex role."[1]

A comparison of the Freudian with the social-psychological interpretation of sex-role learning shows a number of similarities: initial identification of infants of both sexes with the mother, the simplicity of female sex-role development compared to the male, the young boy's hostility to the father. The attribution of the genital focus and adult sexual desires to the four-year-old appears to many sociologists as adult projection of adult motivations onto the young child. Sociologists generally maintain that there is no evidence to demonstrate that the child ever has the ideas and desires attributed to him. However, writers oriented toward the Freudian viewpoint point out that much of this goes on as an unconscious process and that the child *is* quite unaware of his desires. If the genitals are taken in the explanation as merely *symbolic* representations of masculinity and femininity, then the two explanations are not as far apart as they at first seem. While the Freudian interpretation is certainly the more colorful, the social-psychological explanation is simpler and stays closer to observable processes. For these reasons, it seems preferable to the majority of behavioral scientists.

Psychological Development and Sex Roles

One of the important theories of personality in contemporary psychology is the proposition that the basic outlines of personality are formed in the earliest years of life and that details of personality change later only within this basic framework. In a very important study of personality development

---

[1] George Simpson, *People in Families* (New York: Thomas Y. Crowell Company, 1960), pp. 36–37. Reprinted by permission.

of the same individuals over a period from preschool to early adulthood, the crucial importance of sex roles in providing this continuity of personality was discovered. In their conclusion, the researchers offer a statement which will contribute a great deal toward integrating the psychologist's emphasis on the importance of the early experiences and the sociologist's emphasis on the continuous effect of the social environment on behavior. These psychologists summarized their findings as follows:

> The most dramatic and consistent finding of this study was that many of the behaviors exhibited by the child during the period 6 to 10 years of age, and a few during the age period 3 to 6, were moderately good predictors of theoretically related behaviors during early adulthood. . . . These results offer strong support to the popular notion that aspects of adult personality begin to take form during early childhood.
>
> However, the degree of continuity of these response classes was intimately dependent upon its congruence with traditional standards for sex-role characteristics. The differential stability of passivity, dependency, aggression, and sexuality for males and females emphasizes the importance of cultural rules in determining both behavioral change and stability. . . .
>
> It appears that when a childhood behavior is congruent with traditional sex-role characteristics, it is likely to be predictive of pheno-typically similar behaviors in adulthood. When it conflicts with sex-role standards, the relevant motive is more likely to find expression in theoretically consistent substitute behaviors that are socially more acceptable than the original response. In sum—, the individual's desire to mold his overt behavior in concordance with the culture's definition of sex-appropriate responses is a major determinant of the pattern of continuity and discontinuity in his development. . . .
>
> . . . [W]hen a response displayed long-term stability, it was likely to be congruent with sex-typed behavior standards (Kagan and Moss, 1962: 266, 269).

This study suggests that sex-role *development,* as a major axis for orientation of personality growth, continues to play a basic part in the direction of growth long after the crucial period of the establishment of sex-role *identity.*

Differences in Sex-Role Acceptance

Since the young boy has to give up a comfortable dependent role and assume a more assertive one, one might assume that because of the possible difficulties in making the transition, there would be more men who did not achieve masculine identification than women who did not achieve feminine identification. It is the general impression of observers that males experience more anxiety than do females concerning the problem of achieving the proper sex-typed personality (Winch, 1963). Numerous studies, however, indicate that boys show much stronger preferences for the male role than girls for the female role (Brown, 1957), and that both men and women consider masculine traits superior to feminine traits (McKee and Sherriffs, 1959). Brown (1957) even shows that girls in elementary school are ten years old before they show a greater preference for the feminine than the masculine role. Numerous studies indicate that more women wish they were men than men wish they were women. There appear to be two reasons for these facts. First, ours (as are many others) is a masculine-oriented culture and the rewards and virtues are masculine. Remarks from early elementary school girls confirm that they already accept male superiority. This gives some impetus for boys to become masculine, and at the same time encourages masculine orientation of women as well. The second reason augments the effects of the first. Males must repudiate feminine traits as a part of becoming masculine and must therefore never admit feminine preferences even to themselves. On the other hand, girls, because of their less complicated acceptance of femininity, do not feel compelled to repudiate masculine items in the same way, and are not censured by cultural pressures when they respond to some of the cultural inducements to "superior" masculine behavior.

In spite of the preference for the male role indicated in the research cited above, when asked to indicate the sex preference they think their parents have, children do *not* attribute male preference to them. In four different culture groups studied, Hartley showed that "children perceive adults generally as having parallel (same) sex preference." In no group was the male child seen as preferred to the female, "even in culture groups which might be considered male-dominant, either in actual power structure or by tradition." When the children were asked to "have their parents agree" on the sex of an adoptive child, by and large the children thought the parents would select females. Their answers to "Why?" are instructive.

> They like girls best—they can cook and iron and all that stuff.
> They would like a girl because she could help clean up the house and all that.
> Mother would like a girl and my father would let my mother choose.
> A girl could help mother and help with other things.
> Girls—they like girls.
> Girls are nicer than boys. Their dresses make them nicer.
> Girls grow up and be clever.
> Daddy likes girls—we got a little girl and he plays with her.
> A girl don't get into mischief.
> A girl—when mother tells her to do something, she do it.
> A girl—What Mum wants, Dad wants.
> A girl—she works.

The composite picture is overwhelming. Not only is the girl prettier, less troublesome, someone Mum enjoys looking after (as by implication, she does not enjoy a boy) and Dad likes to play with, but she is a useful creature in the house, as boys are not in a sex-separated society. A picture of rootlessness for the eight-year-old boy emerges. By and large, he is not yet strong enough or clever enough to do the sorts of things Dad does, but custom separates him from the sorts of things Mum does, for which his abilities could suffice, as his sister's do (Hartley, 1969).

Although females generally do not experience anxiety over proper achievement of sex identity, this does not mean that women do not have anxieties over *management* of their sex roles. Greater confusion over the proper content of the sex role in adulthood, coupled with the uncertainty of the adolescent girl as to whether or not she will be "chosen" for marriage, serve to make the overall sex role of adolescent and adult women more anxiety-producing than the male role in many ways (Winch, 1963: 519).

Masculinity and femininity in these ways develop distinctive emotional tones for their possessors. From the beginning, and throughout life, masculinity for males is something to be achieved—the dragon to be slain, the other male to be vanquished, the occupational success to be secured, the muscles to be developed, and the woman to be won. In the adolescent male, this demonstration of masculine achievement approaches what might appropriately be considered compulsive masculinity, in which deviation from sex-typed behavior means cruel sanctions from the peer group (Winch, 1963: 515–516). It is the exceptionally secure man on the one hand, or the exceptionally effeminate man on the other, who does not feel the need constantly to demonstrate to others, his wife, himself, that he is manly. Femininity, in contrast, is something that each woman has had from the beginning, and few feel any compulsive need to demonstrate it to themselves and others. It is taken for granted. A girl becomes a woman by simply waiting for maturity. She will become a mother by simply being compliant. If she chooses, she can remain in a passive-dependent-compliant role from the beginning of her life to the end—first with her mother and father, then with her boy friends and teachers, and finally with her husband. The woman who recognizes the differences between herself and her boy friend, herself and her husband, will have come a long way toward understanding much otherwise baffling behavior on his part. Why does the husband become incensed and hurt when his wife laughs lightly at his clumsy efforts with saw and hammer? Why is the boy friend so sexually aggressive? Why is the middle-aged male so distressed with his declining sex interest? The woman can only understand these things in men, and the man in himself, when the meaning of masculinity as an achievement syndrome is understood. A look at the sex subcultures during preadolescence and adolescence will show how the initial differences in assumption of sex role are elaborated into adult differences in masculine and feminine behavior.

The Sex Subcultures in American Society

The repudiation of the company of his female peers by the young boy, and his retirement into interaction with boys alone marks the beginning of a pattern of sex segregation which has profound importance for subsequent sex-role development, and for adolescent and adult social behavior. The withdrawal of the boys into a same-sex group leaves the girls a same-sex group by default. For the following decade, peer interaction is organized by same-sex groups far more than, and at times to the virtual exclusion of, cross-sex peer interaction.

It is a basic postulate of sociological theory that consensus on attitudes, values, and roles is the product of social interaction within groups. A common outlook on life is generated by the continuous interplay in group life. When two groups of people have practically no interaction with one another and confine their interaction within their own group, these two groups will generate divergent and distinctive outlooks on life, especially if they face different kinds of problems. Thus, groups of people who formerly spoke the same language, but who have become completely separated for centuries, may not even be able to understand one another because their language will have drifted in different directions. In American society, as well as others, national and ethnic identity of groups is only maintained to the extent that interaction with the majority group is restricted. Racial, occupational, and class groups which, by virtue of their organization into separated interaction systems, developed distinctive attitudes and behavior—even distinctive language—are called subcultures. A subcultural group shares with the larger society its basic orientations but has developed characteristic differences from the larger society which make it recognizable as a distinctive way of life.

The separation of males and females at age five or six into same-sex groups lasts long enough, and appears at a period of life so important to later role and attitude development, that it gradually generates different outlooks on life between males and females. These differences are substantial enough to warrant the use of the term *sex subcultures* to describe them. The male subculture is that set of attitudes, values, and role concepts which is characteristic of males and not shared by females, and is best observed when males are interacting *as* males *with* males. The female subculture, likewise, is the set of behavior patterns, values, and world views which is found among the females in a society, and is unique to them. Separation of the sexes and the generation of sex subcultures occurs in most societies and should not be considered unique to ours. It is a natural product of sex-role differentiation (Stephens, 1963: 270–271). However, the strength of the two sex subcultures may not be equal in any society. For example, men may have a communal life with other men and develop a strong sex subculture, while women, as in classical Athens, are confined to their homes and are in no position to develop a distinctly feminine subculture. In such a case, the male subculture becomes almost identical to the main culture.

THE MALE SUBCULTURE IN THE UNITED STATES

Males enter the subculture at the beginning of formal schooling in the United States, and leave it when (and if) they begin to be involved with women for a major part of their informal interaction. With middle-class society today, this probably means leaving the male subculture at marriage, but it has not always been so. Even today in lower-class life, the masculine peer group remains the basic group for adult males, the major source of emotional support and informal companionship, broken only by temporary forays into the world of women and children (Miller, 1958). The male subculture is found in its most extreme form in situations where men are living together and isolated from women (barracks life of unmarried military personnel, frontier communities), and in less extreme form under circumstances where men are gathered together temporarily without women (camping expeditions, conventions and adolescent gang life). The young initiate into the masculine life learns appropriate masculine behavior in his peer group from the older members in much the same way he learned early masculine "identification." He is rewarded by approval and status for masculine behavior, and punished, humiliated, and ostracized for unmasculine behavior. He has norms to learn which are not part of his family norms and which, in fact, may contradict them; he has a vocabulary to learn which, before women's liberation, was the exclusive vocabulary of men.

The focal concerns of the masculine group, and hence the focal concerns of masculinity, are independence, emotional control, and conquest. At various ages and in various groups these concerns are manifested by different kinds of group interaction, but in most male groups in the United States, they are focused on sex, sports, and mechanics—especially automobiles. The focus on sex is the most important, most generalized, and longest lasting interest of the male subculture, and one which this book will explore in detail, since it has the most important implications for relationships between men and women.

SEX IN THE MALE SUBCULTURE

The elementary school boy entering the male life will not wait long before being introduced to the sexual interest of his peers. During the preadolescent years he will learn the forbidden male vocabulary, consisting of words for sexual and eliminatory acts and anatomy. Although subject to some regional variations, its core is fairly universal in all social classes and geographical regions. The vocabulary is identified from the beginning as forbidden except in the company of male peers, and it is a source of some masculine satisfaction to be able to use the words appropriately and, in some groups, lavishly.

They are written, singly or in various literary forms with accompanying illustrations, on school and other public restroom walls, as well as less frequently in public places. A four-letter, Anglo-Saxon word for coitus has been seen painted in block letters twenty feet high and legible from more than a mile away on a flood-wall in the Middle West, no doubt by males who felt it needed to be said again.

CASE

Until I was married I imagined and believed that when males got together they would talk using the same words common to girls.

Before, Jerry had lived in the dorms and then in an apartment with some friends. But when we were married he naturally didn't spend as much time with the boys as before. Now he wasn't able to use his vocabulary as much so as a result every now and then something would slip and I would hear a word I had never heard before. When I would ask for a definition, I would get no reply and only an apology. But if and when I was able to get the meaning behind some of these words or phrases I would be shocked.

Often some of his friends will come over and when I am in the kitchen making coffee or something for them I can overhear conversations that either shock me or are beyond comprehension for me due to the language used. But always when I return to the room or other girls are present the boy-type language is dropped and the conversation returns to "normal."

This case history dates from the mid-sixties. One of the most obvious changes accompanying the women's liberation developments flanking 1970 was the enormous increase in the use of sexual and excretory obscenities in the casual conversation of college women.

About half of the preadolescent boys are involved in sexual exhibition or other sex play with other boys at some time or other (Kinsey et al., 1948: 168). Nearly all boys hear about masturbation during preadolescence from other boys (Kinsey et al., 1948: 501), and by age thirteen (the end of elementary school), more than half the boys have masturbated (Kinsey et al., 1948: 500). Preadolescent boys are interested in *sex* more than in *girls*. Consequently, heterosexual sex play is less frequent in their experience than activities with other boys (Kinsey et al., 1948: 173). Kinsey remarks:

> The anatomy and functional capacities of male genitalia interest the younger boy to a degree that is not appreciated by older males who have become heterosexually conditioned and who are on the defensive against reactions which might be interpreted as homosexual. . . . [Among older pre-adolescents] there is social value in establishing one's ability [to effect orgasm], and many a boy exhibits his masturbatory techniques to lone companions or whole groups of boys (Kinsey et al., 1948: 168, 169).

By the time the conscientious middle-class mother gets around to deciding that her son is adolescent and may need some specific sexual information, he has very probably had a good deal of experience and information already in his activities with other boys. A majority of boys get their information on sexual activities from other boys (Lee, 1952; Terman, 1938: 240). Being sexually knowledgeable and sexually active is a source of status for the older preadolescent and early adolescent boy.

Among nearly all groups of adolescent boys, heterosexual interest and activity are a basis of status, while homosexual interests are strictly rejected. Masturbation becomes a status-losing activity, and although most males who will eventually go to college engage regularly in masturbation during adolescence, few will admit it to other boys.

Since status results from convincing other boys of one's heterosexual competence most early adolescent heterosexual activity is discussed in male groups. There is considerable fabrication and elaboration of experience, and boys learn to discount one another's tales of prowess. The emphasis in the descriptions is on anatomical and manipulatory detail and erotic responses. "They have a consuming interest in the proper methods and techniques for making sexual advances to a female" (Ehrmann, 1959: 340). Sex emerges as something which boys "do to" girls, which girls "let them have." Accounts of boys' early coital experience with girls show the boys to have been unconcerned with and largely unaware of the girl's own behavior (Kirkendall, 1961).

Through the experiences in the male subculture, a man's sexual activity becomes the crucial behavior on the basis of which he assesses his masculinity. Ehrmann says:

> Our culture, in innumerable ways, many of which are unrecognized, instills in the male the all-important idea that eroticism is essential to maleness, and that it is the mark of a man both to make sexual advances and to have some reasonable expectations of success . . . (Ehrmann, 1959: 361).

It is difficult for the average American woman to understand the *importance* of a man's sexual acts in his personality organization—the significance of his successes, the anxiety reactions to what he perceives as his sexual failures. When a man's self-respect is contingent on his conception of himself as strongly masculine, and masculinity means sexuality, every sexual act is fraught with meanings which cut to the core of the man's self-concept.

SPORTS

From elementary school through college, sports is a primary mode of masculine achievement. At some times, in some male groups, it exceeds sex as a focus of masculine interest and identity. In late elementary school, the boy who is successful at sports attains status among male peers and increasingly among adults—as evidenced by the intense parental interest in, and even radio coverage of, the results of Little League and similar baseball programs for elementary school boys. Boys who are not interested in sports are "sissies," and their parents, worrying about their masculinity, put pressure on them to exhibit sports interest. By secondary school, athletic prowess is the most important source of status for males among girls, and of masculine status among males themselves (Coleman, 1961).

CASE

When I was fifteen my parents moved away from the neighborhood. I didn't know until three or four years later that the reason we moved was to get me away from the crowd I ran around with in hopes of getting me to take a more serious approach toward school and life in general. I feel this is the best thing they could have done for me, but at the time I was unhappy. The new neighborhood was very different from the old one. All the boys my age were active in sports and as a result I started taking an interest in sports in order to be accepted by them. . . . At first I was the laugh of the neighborhood because I was so clumsy and such a poor player. It was because of this that I resolved to do my best and to excel in sports for two reasons: to prove within myself that I could do it, and in order to be accepted in the new environment. With a lot of help from my new friends and a lot of practice I played first-string football, basketball, and was all-state discus thrower.

The boy who is a failure at athletics is likely to perceive himself as thereby less masculine and look for substitute sources of masculine status. His alternate choices are limited.

Adult middle-class males do not look to sports achievement for masculine status, but an abiding interest in professional sports is characteristic of most males in the United States. Even those who are not interested must remain conversant with the activities of players and teams in professional sports; otherwise they find that they are unable to participate in a good deal of adult male conversation.

CAMARADERIE IN THE MALE GROUP

There is among young males a sense of camaraderie which is an important part of the feeling of masculinity, and which manifests itself in numerous subtle ways. This characteristic is nearly absent from female groups and might be thought of as activity peculiar to male solidarity. Loyalty to the male group is a distinctive part of maleness which really has no counterpart among females. Although young males compete with one another for women, for jobs, for status, and for athletic achievement, their sexual competition does not seem a divisive influence, as it is among females; rather it provides a set of common experiences which cement them as a male group, with girls as common objects of conquest. Because of the strong taboo against anything even vaguely suggesting homosexuality, there are no direct ways of expressing friendship and affection among males, but by a kind of upside-down logic, these emotions can be expressed indirectly through "horseplay" or "horsing around"—a kind of fake aggression in the form of bopping, tripping, wrestling, and other minor physical abuse. The verbal form for the same expression is insultive kidding, in which friendly males trade insults which would bring forth immediate violence from a nonfriend. In this way, males can measure the solidarity of their relationship with one another by the seriousness of the insults they can trade. In its purest form, this verbal exchange becomes the ritual of "doin' the dozens" among lower-class males—a rapid, witty exchange of insults of increasingly degrading nature, the object being not to lose emotional control and "blow up" or "flip" at what is being said about one's relatives, one's mother, one's sister.

Male camaraderie makes it important for the young male to "be one of the boys" and to be able to demonstrate to them that he is fairly independent of other influences, especially the influence of his parents. While among males, the boy usually feels called upon to speak of his parents as the outside enemy, although in other contexts he may not think of them in this way at all. To be under the control of one's mother, to have affectionate or tender thoughts about people, to be physically afraid or weak, is not to be "one of the boys."

The topics discussed above do not exhaust the content of the male subculture, nor does this description fit all male groups equally well. Influence and importance of the subculture seem far more important in lower-class life than in middle-class life, especially in adulthood when the husband-wife relationship has assumed major importance among middle-class men.

Serious heterosexual love relationships in adolescence, and increasingly early steady dating disrupt this pattern among middle-class males. After marriage it only recurs sporadically in stag affairs, the nostalgic "night out with the boys," the convention, or the hunting trip, where men can gather and reassert their independence from women and the too-civilized life that goes with family responsibility.

THE FEMALE SUBCULTURE

Girls enter the female subcultural life at the same time boys withdraw from them—at the beginning of elementary school. The focal concerns of the female subculture are sociability, popularity, and attractiveness. The interests around which these concerns are organized and around which most strictly female interaction centers (at least for unmarried women) are men, other women, and clothes, in approximately that order. For mothers, one can add their children close to the top of the list, since mother-identity becomes paramount for a number of years in most women with young children.

When females talk about sexual behavior, their concern is frequently with either the problems raised by the sexual aggression of the male in the dating situation, the threat of public exposure, personal regrets for sexual transgressions, or the justification of sexual activity as an expression of love . . . (Ehrmann, 1959: 340).

From casual observation, most observers believe that recent cohorts of girls are much more candid and explicit with other girls about sex, and sex is a more frequent and accepted part of casual conversation among girls than was the case a generation ago. This pattern brings the younger group of females closer to the typical male experience, and may be seen as another example of the reduction of socialization differences between the sexes.

The life of the elementary school girl is virtually free from sexual conversation. Although about half the girls in Kinsey's female sample reported some sort of preadolescent sex play, it usually consisted of genital exhibition only. Erotic arousal before adolescence was reported by 30 percent of the sample (Kinsey et al., 1953), but most of this was nonsocial (Kinsey, 1953: 197). Fewer than a third of the women reported as much as genital display in preadolescent experience with other girls (Kinsey, 1953: 105, 107).

Elementary school girls are likely to be already concerned with clothes, especially if they are from high-status families. Conversation is likely to center on who is whose best friend, whom people like and do not like, who is fat (and thin), who is giving a party or going to whose house to visit, who is the prettiest (or ugliest). Older elementary school girls are already talking about who is in love with which boy, whom they are going to marry, and who no longer likes whom. By this age, girls have already made a fine art of achieving status by bragging or complaining about their clothes and claiming ownership of some boy by displaying some token from him (Schwendinger and Schwendinger, 1963). Cutting or subtle derogatory remarks about other girls (present or not present) appear well developed at this age.

Girls talk about their own clothes, the clothes of other girls, and even men's clothes. By earliest adolescence, clothing has become such a focus of interest that shopping expeditions are already established as a form of recreation independent of purchase. It is difficult for an adolescent girl to have high status without being fashionably dressed, and this requires careful and constant attention to the clothes of other girls and to what the right magazines are showing. While the boys are looking at erotic pictures, the girls are studying the right styles from *Seventeen,* the fashion magazine for adolescent women. The older adolescent girl is painfully aware that her entire future probably hinges on being attractive to the kind of man who will provide the style of life she wants.

It is this important awareness which tends to focus the adolescent girl's concept of femininity *on personal attractiveness.* There appears to be wide consensus about feminine physical attractiveness in American society (Udry, 1965), both facial and anatomical. The entire advertising industry is organized to emphasize the ideal from which every girl must fall short. In this way, she comes to look to commercial products to make up for feminine deficiencies (Ellis, 1962). Girls fairly uniformly complain of body inadequacies, with most considering their weight, waist, and hips too large, and their busts too small (Jourard and Secord, 1955). Beauty is a feminine status item among nearly all female groups.

There is really no substitute for attractiveness as a prop for the female's self-concept. An older study shows that among college women, the prettier a girl was, the lower her grade point average was. Presumably it was enough to be pretty. The girls rated as plain and homely generally had the highest grades (Holmes and Hatch, 1938). No doubt it is this pattern which originated the idea that in women, beauty and brains do not go together. In fact, apparently beauty and brains do go together, but not beauty and grades. Lest anyone conclude that girls delude themselves on the importance of beauty in getting a man, social science research has shown that the beautiful women are the ones likely to get married first (Holmes and Hatch, 1938).

Not only are the beauties the first to marry, but they get the "highest quality" husbands. Elder (1969) showed that beauty was the main characteristic which identified working-class high school girls who would end up with educated, high-status husbands. Among American blacks, feminine attractiveness is still associated with having light skin (in spite of the recent trend toward increased racial pride among blacks), and it is the light-skinned girl from the lower-class who gets a high-status husband (Udry et al., 1971).

Clothing and other personal adornment, then, become identified as central to femininity through their association with personal attractiveness. A frequent line in advertising copy is that this or that brassiere, nightie, or blouse will make one "feel feminine." Whether the advertising created the feeling or the feeling the advertising, it apparently does cut through to the truth of the matter: A woman can enhance her feeling of femininity by putting on the right clothes. Furthermore, a woman's concept of herself as feminine or not very feminine can frequently be judged by the clothes she chooses. As women get older and can no longer support their self-concepts of femininity on physical attractiveness, clothes can play an independent role in maintaining feminine identity. And, of course, it is the construction of this identity on attractiveness which helps to make middle age a difficult period for American women, many of whom lack any alternate source of womanhood.

The one emphasis of the female subculture which dominates everything else is the orientation toward attracting males and, eventually, getting married. Almost universally, every other concern is secondary, and is placed as a secondary contingency against not getting married, or the possibility of needing to work after marriage or after divorce. All occupational considerations must be accommodated to marriage plans (Angrist, 1969).

For the married woman with children, motherhood and childrearing most often become the primary topics of female conversation, with husbands occupying a much less significant place. Perhaps this is because children absorb much more of a woman's time and energy than her husband. Most women come to derive a substantial part of their feminine identity from pregnancy, childbirth, and the rearing of children. It is, perhaps, unfortunate that the two most important bases for feminine identity should both be temporary and depart in middle age. The man, especially the middle-class man, is much better off in this respect. His masculine investment in active sexuality can be supported until old age (only 30 percent of Kinsey's older males were sexually impotent at age seventy) (Kinsey et al., 1948: 235), while his occupational role can support his masculine self-concept into his advanced years as well.

Implications of Subcultural Differences

The differences in men and women which are developed and elaborated in the sex subcultures serve to restrict the understanding which each sex has for the other. One can understand and therefore interact most smoothly with those who do not differ too greatly from him in their values. The sex subcultures, however, create fundamental value differences between men and women (Didato and Kennedy, 1956). The stronger the sex-role differentiation in a society, the stronger one would expect to find the sex subcultures which reinforce them, the more one would expect values and interests of the sexes to differ, and the less basis for mutual understanding, common purpose, and companionship between the sexes one would expect to find. However, when there are very strong sex subcultures, men and women do not find their companionship in one another, but with members of their own sex. Changes now evident in the organization of the sex subcultures in the United States are paralleling changes in sex-role differentiation and in the meaning of marriage and other heterosexual relationships.

The Decline of the Sex Subcultures

In the earlier traditions of American families, the sexual division of labor was far more significant in the functions of marriage, and companionship played a secondary and sometimes even insignificant role. Husband and wife did not expect to find intimacy of communication and companionship with one another. Companionship was found in the same-sex peer group at nearly all ages, and for both sexes. Dating was unknown as it appears today, and courtship was not the time-consuming operation it is at present. Sex-role differentiation was marked. It is a mistake to think of the solidarity of the traditional family in the United States as based on the shared activities of husband and wife. Husband and wife did not share tasks, but on the contrary divided them sharply into men's work and women's work. It was functional economic interdependence which constituted the structural support of the marriage. Consequently, men and women had in common only the joint enterprise. For conviviality they had nothing to talk to each other about except their work. Under these conditions the sex subcultures were strong, perhaps as strong as in most other societies (Stephens, 1963: 271). Recreation was primarily in same-sex groups. Movies portraying the old days like to show families all going to the church picnic together, but when they got there men, women, and children separated into one-sex groups for their fun until the time to return. In middle-class life until very recently, most formal organizations with the exception of the church have been one-sex organizations, and even church activities were likely to be segregated according to sex. In younger age groups, it was the same story, with little cross-sex interaction in adolescence and even less in preadolescence. Public school in the United States has always been coeducational, but college education for women flourished in the sex-segregated college in the late nineteenth and early twentieth centuries.

Today, segregation according to sex is largely disappearing. After World War II, enrollment in women's colleges declined during a period when other colleges were bulging, and one after another, all but the most famous women's colleges have become coeducational. One-sex schools came to be considered "unnatural" and "unhealthy," and even Catholic high schools, formerly almost uniformly sex segregated, are increasingly coeducational. Traditional men's clubs which usually excluded women from their premises except during special occasions, experienced radical declines in membership in the years after World War II. Today, those which maintain sex segregation are shadows of their former glory, while most others have opened their doors to wives and girl friends for dining and social activities.

Organizations especially for women have shown similar declines. Women's clubs in many cities have closed or contracted from lack of interest, while others have become "coed." Chapters of the American Association of University Women, an organization born in the struggle for recognition of women's rights and education for women, now have associated "couple's clubs" which in many places have come to dominate the other activities of the chapters.

With the prevalence of dating, the contemporary pattern of intensive courtship, and the increasing experience of repeated serious love involvements of adolescents before marriage, adolescence in the United States is being progressively occupied with heterosexual interaction. Couples dating steadily expect to spend most of their free time together. In a sample of steady daters in a southern California high school, it was found that most subjects were spending more of their free time with their steady date than with all of their same-sex friends combined.

Informal observers have noted that in the last decade, the practice of dating has been extending to earlier age levels. In earlier generations, dating was primarily limited to high school. In the fifties, dating had definitely moved well down to the junior high school, until today, heterosexual quasi-dating activities are increasingly found on the elementary school level among preadolescents. Thus, heterosexual interaction is invading the very periods when the sex subcultures are most important for attitude formation.

The entire pattern of interaction in elementary school is in transition. Studies done in the 1930s show little cross-sex interaction among grammar school children, and few cross-sex sociometric choices. This was taken as evidence of the "latency period" of Freudian theory, when the Oedipal conflict is resolved by the repression of heterosexuality. Today the pattern is changing.

Studies of late elementary school children during the 1960s reveal considerable cross-sex interaction at these ages. Chart 4-1 shows that there is wide variation from one type of community to another in the amount of involvement in heterosexual activity of eleven-year-olds, but that in each type of community, a sizable minority of children have "begun" involvement with the opposite sex (Rowe, 1966). Just to point up the ambiguity of the terms in Chart 4-1, we note that in some groups more children report having "gone steady" than report "dated."

The trend toward heterosexual companionship in the elementary school should not be construed as occurring in spite of school and parental discouragement. Many elementary schools offer instruction in dating etiquette and hold afternoon dances to which boys are encouraged to ask girls. Playground activity is organized in such a way as to make cross-sex interaction easy and "natural." Where thirty years ago many elementary schools maintained separate playgrounds for boys and girls, today this is rare. Although playground observations show most play groups are of one sex, it is not because this receives any particular encouragement from the authorities.

One might speculate that the return to heterosexual interaction by boys as young as ten years old is facilitated by the very early cultural demands for sex-role assumption and differentiation in young children. However, this cannot be the entire story, for the pattern is too general. All the changes fit into a single pattern: greater emphasis on husband-wife companionship, the near-equal age of couples at marriage, decline of same-sex clubs and other activities in adulthood, near universality of coeducation, extended courtship, intensive steady dating and dating at earlier ages, increasing prevalence of

Chart 4-1

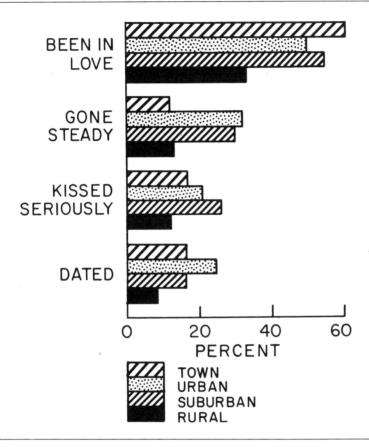

MANY ELEVEN-YEAR-OLDS ARE ALREADY ADOLESCENTS
*Percent of eleven-year-old girls who have ever had
certain experiences, by type of community*

Source: Rowe, 1966

cross-sex interaction in preadolescence, and a general blunting of the extremes of sex-role differentiation in the society. Americans are undergoing a fundamental shift in social interaction toward a preference for heterosexual relationships. The only period in life when this does not seem to be true is during the early elementary school period when boys are under greatest pressure to assume proper masculine behavior patterns. Since segregated interaction reinforces and elaborates differences in sex roles, one would expect the decay of same-sex patterns to reduce grosser sex differences and produce a more similar outlook on life for men and women. On the other hand, this process works both ways. One would expect that when men and women are not as sharply differentiated, they should be more comfortable with one another, and increased heterosexual companionship should be rewarding. These trends should enhance the probability that young couples of today will find in marriage the emotional companionship which every study indicates they value so highly (Blood and Wolfe, 1960: 150).

The middle-class pattern of sexual companionship is probably based on the rest of the structure of middle-class life. About the only job in middle-class life which cannot be done by both sexes is childbearing. Nearly all other tasks and occupations common to the class require symbolic but not muscular skills, and so much of the biological substratum support for traditional sex-role differentiation is undermined. Among middle-class people, human relationships are stable, economic opportunities are reliable, and husbands and wives run a joint enterprise for economic consumption rather than production. It would be inexplicable to find under these circumstances the same sex segregation that prevailed a century ago. In fact, much of what remains can be seen as traces of fading traditions. We can expect that the predominance of heterosexual relationships will grow rather than decline in the future.

In the lower class, the more traditional pattern of sex subcultures is still strong and because of the differences from middle-class life, should continue for a long time. Perhaps the enjoyment of heterosexual relationships generally, like the development of romantic love and the elaboration of erotic behavior, are the refinements of an educated, economically secure, cultivated class with enough leisure and sufficient symbolic sophistication to enjoy them. Or, from a less favorable point of view, perhaps they are evidence of the decadence which ensues when humans are freed from economic want and hard work, and may proceed to the unending search for individual pleasure.

The Origins and Development of Heterosexuality

5

In the previous chapter, the process of learning masculine and feminine roles was examined. This chapter will be concerned with a particular aspect of the sex roles—the sexual and, specifically, the heterosexual components, as they develop during adolescence. The topic is divided into two subsections:

1. The development of sexuality.
2. The development of social relationships with the opposite sex, especially the dating pattern.

The Biological Foundations of Sexual Behavior

Most human infants enjoy having their skin stroked. From infancy on, most humans find pleasure in genital stimulation. The degree to which individuals will seek out such stimulation is partly controlled by social learning experiences, but it is also underpinned by biological factors, which differ among individuals. The urge to seek out sexual stimulation we will call sex drive. Sex drive in males and females is at least in part determined by the male hormones called androgens (Salmon and Geist, 1943). In the male they are produced primarily by the testes. In the female they originate only in the adrenal glands. Preadolescents of both sexes have low levels of androgens, compared with adults. Although they are capable of most adult sexual behavior, and engage in most adult sexual acts in some cultures, preadolescents do not give much evidence of sex drive. Puberty brings a small increase in androgens to females, and a gradual increase over a several-year period in males to a level of androgens circulating in the blood which is about ten times that found in females. Studies of adolescent males show that the rise in sexual interest closely parallels the rise in androgen levels (Wieland et al., 1971). Similar studies have not been done in females. Deprivation of androgens dramatically depresses sex drive of either males or females, and in males reduces frequency of spontaneous erection. Restoration of androgens restores sex drive. Increase in androgens to females above normal levels causes marked increase in sex drive. It also sometimes causes permanent lowering of the voice and growth of beard in females. It is not clear whether the sex drive of a normal male can be increased by introducing additional androgens. But in the unusual case where a male has abnormally low levels of androgens, administration of androgens will increase sex drive. It is also not established whether androgen therapy increases the sex drive of aging males complaining of declining sex drive (Tamm, 1967).

The female hormones, the estrogens and progestogens, do not maintain sex drive in females, and there is some indication that progestogens decrease sex drive. Female hormones maintain the secondary sex characteristics of females, play an important role in pregnancy, and maintain the health of genital tissues. Complete deprivation of female hormones does not affect the sex drive in females (Money and Ehrhardt, 1972).

Whether there are any biological mechanisms which play a role in determining preference for the opposite or the same sex is still a matter of debate. While dogma in the homosexual world maintains that homosexuality is inborn, it is fashionable in the social sciences to scorn the possibility. In his controversial twin research, Kallman (1952) showed to the satisfaction of many researchers that there was substantial genetic determination of homosexuality. Other scholars are skeptical of his results. Several recent studies have shown biochemical differences between homosexual and heterosexual males (Margolese, 1970, Kolodny et al., 1971). Until we know more, it is premature to rule out biological factors.

Beyond the hormonal factors associated with sex drive, it is probable that all sexual behavior must be learned by humans, just as it must be by other primates. A group of chimpanzees of each sex was reared apart from sexually experienced chimps and from the opposite sex, until they had reached sexual maturity. At that point, the two sex groups were put together in common quarters. The chimps bounded about the cage together, wrestled, picked bugs off one another, and enjoyed themselves immensely. But they did not copulate. Finally, after a period of time in which an experienced group of chimps would have performed many copulations, sexually experienced chimpanzees of each sex were introduced into the group. Some very rapid learning took place. The naive group was clumsy, and there were many false starts and much bumbling. However, in a short while, all the formerly ignorant chimps were copulating in the normal manner of chimpanzees (Leuba, 1954). Apparently, chimpanzees do not copulate by instinct, but have to be taught. Since more instincts are not normally attributed to man than to less complex species, it seems unlikely that naive human subjects would have shown any more direct evidence of sexual competence.

It is part of American folk beliefs that sexually mature males develop stronger and stronger sex drives the longer they abstain from sexual behavior. Beach dismisses this notion once and for all:

> No genuine tissue or biological needs are generated by sexual abstinence. It used to be believed that prolonged sexual inactivity in adulthood resulted in progressive accumulation of secretions within the accessory sex glands, and that nerve impulses from these distended receptacles gave rise to sexual urges. Modern evidence negates this hypothesis. . . . What is commonly confused with a primary drive associated with sexual deprivation is in actuality sexual appetite, and this has little or no relation to biological or physiological needs (Beach, 1956: 4).

The Social Development of Sexual Behavior

It has been widely noted that mild local stimulation is innately pleasurable (Hardy, 1964), and that this is so from infancy. It may also be taken as axiomatic that the experience of genital orgasm is innately pleasurable. At precisely what average age individuals have orgasm capacity is not known, since most persons probably do not experience orgasm at as early an age as it is possible. Unquestionably, however, some preschool children are capable of genital climax. It is upon these two constitutional potentials that a sexual appetite is based and comes to develop. Several societies encourage children to engage in masturbation and coitus at early ages. This provides a wealth of experience with genital stimulation and the early development of an interest and desire for sexual activity on the part of children. Contemporary American parents observe the beginnings of sexual interest in their children in the form of self-stimulation of the genitals, but usually discourage the behavior. Furthermore, they discourage any other overt sexual behavior on the part of children, and prevent them, insofar as possible, from observing or learning about heterosexual behavior. As a consequence, *most* American children do not develop sex interest until their teens. This is conceived of as limiting the opportunity for the child to develop a sex drive, not "repressing" a drive that is there from the beginning. In the preceding chapter it was pointed out that the male subculture begins early to provide a set of sexual experiences and social encouragement for the development of sex drive in preadolescent males, but that it is a *sex* drive and not a "heterosex" drive which is developed. It was also noted that similar experiences are less frequent among females. This appears to adequately explain why males develop an earlier *sex* interest than females. From this discussion it may be concluded that *children will develop sexuality at the time and to the extent that they are encouraged or given the opportunity to learn the pleasures of sex.*

In American culture, adolescents are expected to develop heterosexual interest. In fact, adolescence might quite properly be *defined* as a social role which includes, for the first time, the expectation of social (and sexual) interest in the opposite sex. This sharply distinguishes adolescence (a social role) from puberty (a set of physiological changes). That they correspond to some extent in age at onset is probably due to the sex-drive enhancement associated with the gradual elevation of androgen levels in puberty. The organization of social life probably has limits in the extent to which it can delay the development of sex drive. Social pressures and expectations of parents and peers facilitate the development of a social and sexual interest on the part of girls in boys, and of boys in girls. Any individual who has learned an appropriate sex role will be strongly affected by these pressures toward heterosexual interest. Those (especially males) who have not established an appropriate role will not be affected in the same way. They may at this time develop socio-sexual interest in their own sex instead.

It is possible for the society to develop social interest in the opposite sex at one point in adolescence, but delay experiences which will develop specifically genital heterosexual drives until some other time. Observations in other cultures confirm that sex drive can be developed toward homosexual and heterosexual interest and activity at the same time, that a society need not even choose between the two. Different societies vary considerably in the overall level of sexuality developed, some making sex a major cultural theme and encouraging extremely high levels of sexual interest and activity, others minimizing its importance. There is particular variation in the extent to which feminine sexuality is culturally developed.

Sex should not be thought of as an organic "given," with which society must learn to deal. Societies play an important part in enhancing or minimizing the importance of sex. Social arrangements do not have to be accommodated to a biological constant in order to produce a "healthy" social order. Rather the mechanisms for the control of sex only need to be consistent with the socialization process by which the sex drives are shaped and developed in the society.

Dating

Not many persons reading this book will feel the need for a definition of dating. (One rarely tries to define those terms he uses commonly.) However, for the purposes of this book, dating will be defined as the recreational association of uncommitted heterosexual couples. Not many societies have made regular institutional arrangements for such relationships. The United States did not before the present century. In a few groups, preadolescent marriage eliminates the possibility. In others, the sexes are segregated until marriage, and marriage is arranged by parents. In the United States before the present century, although mates were not often selected by parents, there was little casual social interaction between adolescent boys and girls.

Some writers have implied that dating is an American invention. Although the particular dating institutions in the contemporary United States are certainly unique, it would be a mistake to suppose that casual noncommittal sex-pairing of adolescents was never common anywhere except in twentieth-century America. Young males in classical Athens and Rome were regularly involved with young women for purposes of fun (although not with women who were marriage-eligibles for them). A number of nonliterate tribes have been described by anthropologists in which adolescents regularly associate heterosexually with no marital obligations.

Western society has recently emerged from a period in which parents and children participated in mate selection, and in which noncommittal relationships among adolescents were not institutionalized. The twentieth century has brought profound changes in marriage values, emphasizing personality compatibility and emotional satisfactions. Under these circumstances, a plan had to evolve which would allow men and women to select their own mates on the basis of mutual personal attraction. The daily patterns which Americans approve and practice today serve that end.

This explanation, however, is a purely functional one and does not really explain the emergence of dating as a phenomenon of our time. In 1870, men were leaving school in early adolescence for some kind of employment and remaining unmarried until an average age of twenty-six, which would seem like perfect circumstances for some kind of dating system. Yet not until after World War I did dating become a widespread phenomenon in this country.

A causal explanation would interpret dating as a natural consequence of several factors. First, the initial quarter of the twentieth century was a period when Americans were becoming highly urbanized for the first time. Urban places and urban life provide circumstances where it is more difficult for parents to supervise the lives of their adolescent children. Second, geographic mobility and urbanization create circumstances where young people have no personal knowledge of a field of eligible mates without some sort of dating mechanism. Third, World War I and the years immediately succeeding it represent the peak of the feminine equality movement (which had been under way for a century or so). The new values made it more difficult to maintain the rigid standards of supervision for nubile but unengaged girls. These trends coincided with an increasingly liberal attitude toward premarital sex and the extension of coeducation into a greater part of adolescence. The situation was ideal for the development of an adolescent subculture within the society, separated from adult activities and dependent upon its own age group for emotional support, status, companionship, and normative standards (Coleman, 1961). From these circumstances, dating has been developed by adolescents themselves as a form of recreation, an end in itself. Each group of adolescents learns the norms from the preceding group and modifies them to fit new fashions, new circumstances, new values. The fact that dating eventually becomes mate selection is, in a way, quite irrelevant to its existence, as is the sociologist's observation that it provides status and experience in one's adult sex role. The fact is, dating provides experience in one's *adolescent* sex role, which is more or less unrelated to adult sex-role responsibilities. From another point of view, dating is a part of the general trend toward emphasis on heterosexual relationships in American society. It is the culturally patterned and approved form of heterosexual association from adolescence to marriage. Most people who have not given serious thought to the subject attribute the desire to engage in dating to the physical maturation of sexual drives at puberty. The preceding discussion of the social development of heterosexuality indicates the naïveté of this idea. Dating does not correspond in its inception to any particular physiological change in the individual. It has been observed that girls who mature physically earlier also begin to date earlier, but this is best attributed to the fact that if a girl *looks* old enough to date, people (especially males) will *respond* to her as though she were, and this will affect her self-concept and her social relationships in such a way as to propel her into the heterosexual world. This precocious heterosexual interest is a result of the social interpretation and the social expectation which is placed on her physical development.

DATING MOTIVATION

Motivation on the part of the individual adolescent to date is socially induced by the expectation of adults and older adolescents that he should "get interested" in the opposite sex and show this interest in the appropriate manner, that is, by dating. To date is to achieve valid adolescent status. To date is to show one has at least minimum heterosexual acceptability and to be more important in one's own eyes and the eyes of one's peers. Not to date is taken as a sign of immaturity, social unacceptability, or perhaps even homosexuality. The nondater in high school is not a part of things. His friends exert pressure on him to date and try to make dating arrangements for him; his parents encourage him and wonder if something is wrong with him. Under such conditions, even those who would really prefer not to, and who have no spontaneous interest in the company of the opposite sex, date. Eventually, not to date can frequently mean being the recipient of group ridicule.

As adolescents become familiar with dating and have dated frequently, the motivation for dating becomes more complex and, to some extent, different for males and females. Adolescent social life is increasingly oriented around heterosexual pairs. To participate in the social life requires a date.

All of this is quite independent of sexuality *per se*. For many, dating is motivated by a desire for sexual opportunities. For some, dating is an opportunity for the establishment of genuine affectionate relationships. For everyone, dating is a legitimate recreation—something that is just fun to do. The most common motivations for dating are summarized by Skipper and Nass (1966).

1. Dating may be a form of recreation. It provides entertainment for the individuals involved and is a source of immediate enjoyment.
2. Dating may be a form of socialization. It provides an opportunity for individuals of opposite sex to get to know each other, learn to adjust to each other, and to develop appropriate techniques of interaction.
3. Dating may be a means of status grading and status achievement. By dating and being seen with persons who are rated "highly desirable" by one's peer group, an individual may raise his status and prestige within his group.
4. Dating may be a form of courtship. It provides an opportunity for unmarried individuals to associate with each other for the purpose of selecting a mate whom they may eventually marry.

DATING AS A STATUS GAME

As an end in itself, dating can be taken as a game invented by adolescents for their amusement. It partakes of the nature of all games. Games are social encounters in which interaction between the participants is formally structured by a set of rules specifying the required and permissible behavior in the encounter, as the players attempt to achieve some arbitrarily defined goal. Goffman writes:

> Games can be fun to play, and fun alone is the approved reason for playing them. The individual, in contrast to his treatment of "serious" activity, claims a right to complain about a game that does not pay its way in immediate pleasure, and whether the game is pleasurable or not, to plead a slight excuse, such as indisposition of mood, for not participating (Goffman, 1961:17).

Games frequently have a quality of simulating real-life situations, that is, serious activities, except that the risks are lowered or removed and the rules become paramount. Thus cops and robbers, war games, even football and other team sports have structures which are similar to the structures in real-life situations. The rules and the goals, however, are arbitrary.

Dating is a courtship game. Just as the war game uses the language and gestures of war but the vanquishing of the enemy is only symbolic within the rules, so dating imitates the language and gestures of courtship (Thomas, 1959), but the players understand that it is only a game, and that the object is only to play the game well and to symbolically fall in love, with no further obligation, and no emotional commitment. The rules for the game have been developed by the adolescent peer groups and passed down from older to younger players with minor modifications for fifty years. Different groups of daters follow variants of the game with slightly different rules. Theoretically, any two unmarried persons of approximately the same age can play, provided they have not become involved in real courtship. In actuality, like so many games, only people of equal status usually play together, or if they are of different status, the rules change because the two cannot bring approximately the same skills and resources to the game.[1] As in most games, one usually enjoys it most with those of equal ability and status, because it is too easy to beat an inferior player.

An older generation of adolescents played the game like this. Only males could initiate a request for play, except for certain stylized turn-about occasions. Of course, girls could make it clear that they were available and skillful partners. The male picked up the female at her residence (since the game was usually arranged in advance). Partners were attentive to one another and were required by courtesy to show interest in one another. Players were not permitted to show erotic or affectionate interest in any other potential partner during a game. The male paid for expenses and performed other ritual chivalrous acts such as opening doors and holding coats. The object of the game was ego-enhancement. Formally it was a non-zero-sum game—that is, both could win, or both could lose. One did not expect to win at the expense of the partner's loss. Ego-enhancement came from two sources: the satisfaction derived from the interaction of the game itself, and the gain in status from being seen playing with a high-status partner.

When playing with a partner worth status points, players made it a point to be seen by those with whom they desired status. This helped them get higher-status partners in the future. The more signs of emotional involvement and affection one could elicit from the partner, the more ego-enhancement. The amount of display which was considered allowable within the game depended upon the dating group and the rules of its members. First dates in most circles did not normally require erotic behavior, nor did they prohibit it. Experienced players who were regular partners were expected in most circles to engage in more elaborate love-play. Love-play provided ego-enhancement to the male partner by reassuring his masculinity because he was sexually successful, while the primary ego-enhancement of the female came from the assurance that she was desirable, that she was popular. Normally, sexual intercourse signified a breakdown of the game framework in middle-class daters, because it indicated that the girl had taken the game seriously. Among lower-class and male cross-class daters, it indicated that the girl had lost, for in these groups, dating was played as a zero-sum game with sexual conquest as the male goal.

The game broke down, of course, and became real life when the daters became emotionally involved with one another, and at that point the game

[1] I am indebted to Goffman (1961) for the analysis of game structures.

became courtship. Commitments and obligations developed, and the interaction lost its formal structure and took on a much more personalistic orientation. It was no longer "fun" in the frivolous, nonserious sense. It broke down when one partner got involved and the other did not—the game was ended because the involved partner had lost. It broke down when partners broke the rules—they wouldn't engage in sex play when the rules made it obligatory, they did not limit their attention to the partner for that encounter, or they demanded more signs of affection or sex privileges than they had a right to demand under the rules. As with cheaters at most games, rule breakers in a dating group found it more difficult to get future partners. This was the way the rules were enforced.

These quaint customs of our recent male-chauvinist past are still perpetuated among conservative groups today. Meanwhile, new forms of association between the sexes are evolving which are too much in a state of flux to be set in the permanence of the printed text. Users of this book may profitably make their own comparisons between contemporary patterns and those I have described above.

WHO DATES WHOM: SOCIAL FUNCTIONS OF DATING

Although dating is not oriented primarily toward mate selection at any age, mate selection "happens" in the context of a dating relationship. Mate selection is made from a group which is no more inclusive than the dating group. Therefore, who dates whom is of great importance for the formation of families and for the social structure of the society. Men rarely date women who are older than they and frequently date women who are younger. It is difficult to imagine that age difference in marriage would produce as significant differences between individuals as the low range of age difference in dating might indicate, but the dating pattern is reproduced in the marriage pattern. In most other attributes, individuals are willing to date a broader spectrum than they are willing to consider marrying.

Men are frequently willing to date women of lower social status than themselves because normally they can get a more attractive partner in appearance by dating below their own social status. But most dating is between persons of similar social class (Hollingshead, 1949).

CASE

In our high school, which was all boys and Catholic, we had one of the strictest caste systems I've ever run across. A boy's social position was determined by the high school of the girl he went with. For instance we had three girls' Catholic high schools that catered to the needs of my school's students. One of the girls' schools was made up of mostly Mexican youth and girls from the west part of the city who were considered fairly loose moral-wise. The boys of the lower social class at my school went with these girls. Then we had the middle-class girls' high school for our middle-class students. This was the group I actually belonged in, but for some reason I dated the girls from the high-class school. This was the group whose fathers were in the top money brackets and the girls who held their proms at the Hilton and such places. Now needless to say this entailed putting out more money than I had, but my mother, who didn't really have it either, managed to put it up, so I would be able to travel in the proper circles.

On college campuses, where status distinctions have been developed into an art form, many observers have pointed out the fine status discriminations which are made in the dating system. Most colleges contain students who are fairly homogeneous in their social-class origins. Yet within this narrow band, students observe many status gradations, especially on campuses with well-developed fraternity-sorority systems. In one study done on a large state university campus, the researcher had each of the Greek-letter organizations on campus categorized by the students as high, medium, or low prestige. The "pinning" relationships between fraternity and sorority members were then traced. This revealed a strong relationship between the prestige of the sorority a girl belonged to and the prestige of the fraternity from which her boy friend came (Rogers and Havens, 1960). (See Chart 5-1.)

When a girl from a high-prestige sorority becomes involved with a man from a low-status group, she can expect to receive pressure from her sorority sisters to break off the relationship. Men are primarily status objects to women, and the sorority's major avenue to status is "ownership" of high-status males. Yet, at the same time, college daters emphasize personality characteristics as the basis for dating. If personality is actually an important factor in dating relationships, dating selection must be made with the same criteria which are used to select fraternity and sorority members.

It has been argued by some students of dating that the status aspects of dating have been overplayed by scholars. Perhaps this is true. Perhaps when college students approach actual mate selection they do not pay much attention to status characteristics. However, the status characteristics have already filtered out from the field of dates all who do not qualify on those grounds. In this way, dating serves as a social-status filter. Mate selection might then be performed from the remaining homogeneous status group on the basis of personality factors. But the influence of prestige ratings in college on mate selection can be seen from data on engagement relationships. Chart 5-2 shows clearly that the engagement relationships seen follow campus status lines even more closely than the pinning relationships. It is easy to see how the criteria used for admitting members to Greek-letter organizations on this campus become incorporated into the dating process and through dating eventually become factors on which mate selection is based.

Chart 5-1

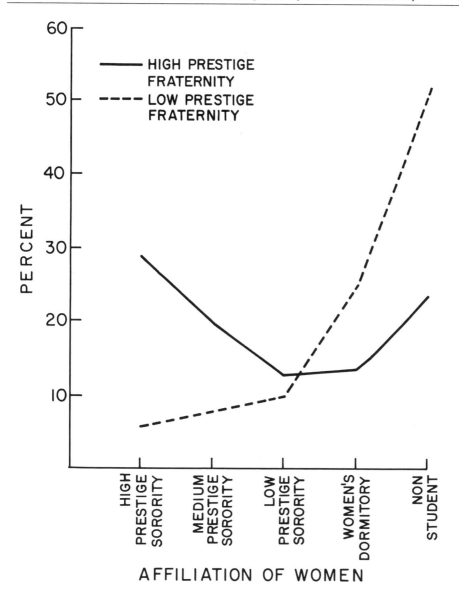

FRATERNITY PRESTIGE INFLUENCES WHO PINS WHOM
Affiliation of women pinned to fraternity men, by status of the fraternity

Source: Rogers and Havens, 1960

The Origins and Development of Heterosexuality 91

Sororities and fraternities in this way become strong structural supports for endogamous mate selection among high-status groups (Scott, 1965).

Unmarried students usually indicate a willingness to date outside of their religious groups more frequently than they are willing to marry outside them. Religious leaders opposed to intermarriage, however, have accurately recognized that it is not possible to predict in advance which dating relationships will lead to marriage. On these grounds, they have opposed interreligious dating. Given the goal of eliminating interreligious marriages, prohibition of interreligious dating is probably the only effective way to achieve it.

As high school education has become universal in the United States, dating relationships are more and more focused around the school. As colleges absorb a greater and greater number of high school graduates and as colleges become more and more differentiated according to status, it is easy to predict that the importance of dating as a filter on social characteristics for mate selection will become more important. Schools are organized in such a way as to maximize the effectiveness of peer-group pressures on dating partners. An additional effect of dating on campuses is that similarity in educational level of partners is encouraged.

When social background factors play a major part in the selection of dating partners, producing pairs of daters who are similar in most things, then the dating system guarantees that mate selection will be socially homogamous. The dating system, in this way, serves to perpetuate differences and cleavages in the social structure. Whether this is good or not depends on what kind of society and what kind of marriages are valued.

PHYSICAL ATTRACTIVENESS AND DATING

Physical attractiveness is so obviously important in the dating process that absence of research on the subject might be taken as simply an avoidance of studying the self-evident. On the other hand, it may indicate a reluctance on the part of family scholars to admit its importance. The invention of "computer dances" during the 1960s provided a made-to-order opportunity for its study. In one study (Walster et al., 1966), the researchers organized a dance for entering freshmen at a university. Those who signed up to come were rated on physical attractiveness, given personality measurements, and then assigned *randomly* to dates for the dance. The researchers had originally approached the problem with the following ideas: first, the physical attractiveness of the girls will be a much more important determinant of outcome than the physical attractiveness of the boys; second, individuals who are themselves very physically attractive will require that an appropriate partner be more attractive than will a less attractive individual. The latter hypothesis was based on the notion that individuals will try to match themselves with a partner who is neither much more attractive than they (for fear of rebuff or failure), nor much below (because they could do better). The results of the

Chart 5-2

PRESTIGE FRATERNITY MEN MARRY PRESTIGE SORORITY WOMEN
Affiliation of women to whom fraternity men were engaged, by status of the fraternity

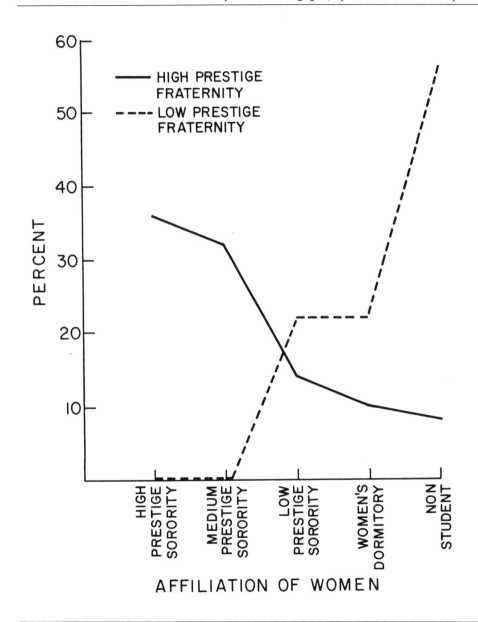

Source: Rogers and Havens, 1960

The Origins and Development of Heterosexuality 93

study were surprising on all counts. (Perhaps they will not surprise those who are presently involved in the dating game.)

> Regardless of the subject's own attractiveness, by far the largest determinant of how much his partner was liked, how much he wanted to date the partner again, and how often he actually asked the partner out was simply how attractive the partner was. Personality measures . . . and intellectual measures . . . did not predict couple compatibility. The only important determinant of the subject's liking for his date was the date's physical attractiveness (Walster et al., 1966).

This held *equally* for men and women.

> The more attractive a man is, the less physically and personally attractive he thinks his date is, the less he likes her, the less he would like to date her again, and the less often the date says he actually did ask her out again. Similarly, the more attractive a woman is, the less physically and personally attractive she thinks her date is, the less she likes her date, and the less she would like to date him again (Walster et al., 1966).

Both of the original ideas were found to be incorrect. There was not a significant tendency for subjects to try to date partners of approximately their own physical desirability. The most attractive girls were the most often asked out, regardless of the attractiveness of the man. Furthermore, the man's physical attractiveness was the only important determinant of how well he was liked.

This research should not be generalized too far. It should not be interpreted to mean that physical attractiveness is all that counts in the dating situation. What it does point up is that *in initial encounters,* physical attractiveness is the critical determinant of whether there will be *any more encounters* during which other factors such as personality might have a chance to have an influence.

DATING PARTNERS AND MARRIAGE PARTNERS

It is axiomatic that the same kinds of characteristics which make a good date do not also necessarily make a good mate. When college students are asked to list the qualities important in a good date and important in a marriage partner, there are some sharp discrepancies in the two. As an example, an interest in home life is obviously much less important as a dating characteristic.

Of course, the screening for dating and the process of falling in love are based on the characteristics of the dating partner. Where the dating and marriage criteria are different, the dating criteria are decisive because they are

Chart 5-3

EACH SEX HAS INACCURATE IDEAS ABOUT WHAT IS CRUCIAL
TO THE OPPOSITE SEX IN A DATING PARTNER
*Percent checking certain traits as "crucially important" to them in their selection
of dating partners, and thought to be crucially important to the opposite sex*

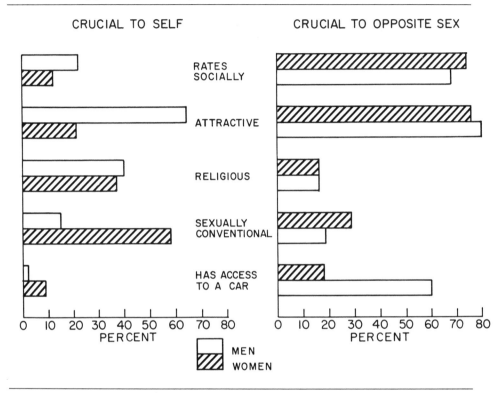

Source: Hewitt, 1958

the basis for prior screening of marriage partners. A particularly interesting feature (shown in Chart 5-3) is the difference between what people themselves consider crucial, and what they think the opposite sex considers crucial. For example, 1 woman in 5 said her date had to be attractive looking, but 4 men in 5 thought this was crucial to women. On the other hand, 3 women in 5 wanted sexually conventional dates, but only 1 man in 5 thought this was important to women. The misconceptions of the opposite sex revealed in this table are typical of the misunderstandings in heterosexual relationships. In the competitive situation of dating, it is certain that what a person *thinks* is important to the opposite sex will affect those qualities he emphasizes in his own behavior when he is with members of the opposite sex.

The Origins and Development of Heterosexuality   95

THE SIGNIFICANCE OF STEADY DATING

Scholars have noticed with interest, and laymen with alarm, that dating patterns have changed during the past thirty years from a pattern of "playing the field" with many different dating partners toward a pattern of longer-term relationships with one partner. Whereas exclusive dating was formerly associated only with courtship and immediately preceded marriage, it is now increasingly characteristic of early adolescent dating. The transition has been attributed by some to the growing insecurity of adolescents in an anxiety-ridden environment, and by others to a preoccupation with sex. A more reasonable conjecture might be that steady dating is becoming the norm in an increasing number of dating circles because, by trial and error, the adolescent group is evolving a more satisfying pattern. Initial encounters of dating partners, as most initial encounters, tend to be stereotyped role performances, with each person responding to the other in terms of stylized expectation patterns. Although this kind of date may satisfy the need to be seen publicly with an attentive, attractive member of the opposite sex, the interaction itself is not likely to be as satisfying as it would be if the partners were better acquainted. Heiss (1962) has shown that as a heterosexual relationship continues, the partners move away from stereotyped sex roles, do less "posing," and presumably develop a more intimate interpersonal relationship based on reacting to one another as individuals, rather than as representatives of the opposite sex. Repeated serious involvements with dating partners have become typical of the dating experience of the recent generation.

Hardly anyone has anything good to say about steady dating. It has been said to limit the number of partners of the opposite sex one knows, and therefore deprives daters of the experience necessary for proper mate selection. However, evidence indicates that those who have dated the largest number of partners have also had more steady relationships than those who have dated fewer partners. When steady dating becomes the norm in a group, it may be necessary to accept a steady arrangement (or simply find one's self in a steady pattern) or not date at all.

CASE

During my second year in high school, when sixteen, I became infatuated with a girl a year younger than myself. A bashful, reticent youth, I had had but little contact with the other sex. But the social life of a high-school boy renders companionship with girls essential. There are house parties, hikes, and dances; and it was at one of these affairs that I became acquainted with Ann. As she was presentable, unattached, and appeared acquiescent, I gradually grew into the habit of escorting her to and from these affairs. The all-observing eyes of school comrades noted this approaching liaison and furthered its progress in more or less overt ways. Boys would refrain from asking Ann to parties or other gatherings, assuming that I would take her, and other girls would avoid intimacy with me. Thus the group established our relationship (Burgess and Locke, 1953: 330).

Steady dating has been blamed for premature commitment to the "wrong partner." As the chapters on mate selection will explain, it is not clear what a wrong partner consists of, but there is no evidence to show that those who date steadily do a poorer job of mate selection than field players. At any rate, when steady dating is the established pattern, the individual may not have the option of choosing a field-playing approach unless he is an extremely attractive dating partner.

What appears to be the most serious charge leveled at steady dating is that it leads to early sexual intimacies between couples who cannot (or at least should not) get married to one another. It is true that girls experience their greatest sexual intimacies in steady relationships, but this is because feminine codes require emotional involvement as a prerequisite for sexual intimacy. However, the opposite is true for boys. Steady relationships apparently impose sexual controls and a greater sense of sexual responsibility on males than does random dating. If responsible sexuality for males is important, then steady dating is a boon. If minimizing the sexual involvement of females is more important, then steady dating is a detriment to this goal.

When the overall picture of exclusive dating is evaluated, it seems to contain more elements which are valued by Americans than alternative patterns. It is personalistic and nonexploitive. It minimizes superficiality. It fosters personal security and affection rather than status competition and anxiety. It encourages sexual responsibility for males. Though it may seem terribly monotonous and unexciting to an older generation reared in a more free-for-all system, it *is* monogamous, and in every other way it is more similar to marriage than the older system. Part of the objection of an older generation to steady dating is no doubt a misunderstanding of the meaning of the relationship. A generation ago, steady dating was implicitly a prelude to marriage. Today some steady dating is a prelude to marriage, but in the middle adolescent years and sometimes even later, steady dating is of a different type and meaning: it is non-marriage-oriented (Herman, 1955). Parents who themselves have grown up in a steady-dating period have come to take their children's similar behavior for granted.

THE TREND TOWARD EARLY DATING

Where dating used to begin for most persons in high school, it is now commonplace in early junior high school, and in many parts of the country ten- and eleven-year-olds are already dating. School systems and parents (some eagerly, some reluctantly) help to encourage this pattern by arranging social affairs and giving instructions in the heterosexual graces in elementary school. Dating dances in the afternoon are now standard practice for fifth graders in some localities. By the earlier definition in this book, the age of adolescence has been moved to somewhat before puberty. Whether or not this is a dangerous trend depends upon the value one places on the consequences of early dating.

It is interesting to learn who the early daters are. Are they the maladjusted, anxiety-ridden misfits looking for a heterosexual haven from the rigors of childhood? Are they the lower-class youngsters who are uninterested in school and who will drop out early to marry? Not at all. Rather, they are the distinctly American children from small families of high education and high socioeconomic status (Lowrie, 1961). More frequently than not, they have happily married parents (Landis, 1963). Apparently the children who have the best this society can offer are the most ready (or the most encouraged) to enter dating at an early age.

What are some of the probable consequences of early dating? Bayer (1968) has shown that within each socioeconomic stratum, those who begin dating earliest are most likely to marry early. A dating period now exists which spans a whole decade of life. Perhaps by the end of a decade of dating, even the most enthusiastic adolescent will have done everything twice, be bored with dating, and be ready for marriage.

Earlier dating means the imposition of heterosexual expectations at an earlier age. With the erotic practices which are a part of American dating culture, it might be predicted that this will lead to the early development of erotic desire on the part of girls, and to the intensification of the sexual interest of males because of their increasing involvement with heterosexual social relationships at early ages. A Roman Catholic spokesman expressed his belief that it would be impossible to put boys and girls into unmarried relationships with one another for so long a time and still maintain premarital chastity. He advises their elders:

> Either they abandon their concern for the observance of traditional Christian standards of premarital chastity, or they must change their approach to early teen-age dancing and dating. Why should American boys and girls be judged capable of engaging in long years of intimate cross-sex associations — when this has never been possible in any society known to man — without suffering psychological and moral harm? The majority of modern teen-agers are normal, although their elders apparently find this fact too shocking to think about (Thomas, 1963: 24).

The assumption that dating for a decade without sex will be harmful seems gratuitous, but it is realistic to predict that dating for a decade in a series of steady relationships will encourage more and more intimate sexual relationships among the unmarried.

Once dating patterns have become established in the early adolescent and late preadolescent years, it seems unlikely that concerted social action on the part of adults which will return things to the former pattern will materialize. The present generation of adults takes early dating more for granted than its parents did. Furthermore, the sharp age-grading of American society gives the behavior and norms of the adolescent group a certain autonomy from the adult system which adults can manipulate only with difficulty. Perhaps adults are no longer able to control the age at dating. Parents of younger children frequently maintain that when their children become late preadolescents, they (the parents) will certainly not allow *their* children to become involved in heterosexual relationships so early. However, parents overestimate the control they can exert over children in the face of countervening norms in the community. Probably the only recourse for the parent who expects to set dating norms for his children which contradict those established in the community (unless he is willing to generate an explosively hostile relationship with his offspring) is to withdraw the child from the community and find a community which shares his norms.

COMPUTER DATING

In an age when the electronic computer is being used to handle more and more complex problems, it is significant to note the development of computer applications to dating. Several commercial computer dating operations are now at work in various parts of the country providing clients with lists of dating prospects from a large pool of clients whose characteristics are stored on computer tapes. Several types of matching programs are used, but most match on age, height, and specified background and interest characteristics. These services grew up as a result of several experimental "computer dances" arranged by sociologists for the purpose of studying the dating process. In other places in this text we have noted that these experiments have shown that dates matched on interests and values are more successful than random matches, and more successful than matches designed to create complementarity of personality (Coombs, 1966; Strong and Wilson, 1969).

RECENT CHANGES IN DATING PATTERNS

We have no good national studies of dating, but studies at one eastern university done in 1958 and in 1968 show the following changes in a decade in college women's dating:

> "There had been no change in the ten year period as to the mean age at the first date for the two samples; in 1958 it was 13.3, and in 1968 it was 13.2. There was a significant difference in the number of different individuals ever dated by the coeds in the two time samples. In 1958, the mean number of different individuals dated was 53, while in 1968 it was only 25. In 1968 the coeds went out on dates just as often but went out more often with the same individuals in a dating relationship than did the coeds in 1958.
>
> "There was no significant difference in the two time samples as to whether coeds had ever gone steady. In 1958, 68 percent of the coeds had gone steady at least once, while in 1968 this had been the experience for 77 percent. Fur-

thermore there was no significant difference as to age at first going steady. In 1958 the mean age was 17 years and in 1968 it was 16.7 years" (Bell and Chaskes, 1970).

A GENERAL CONSIDERATION OF DATING TRENDS

In every society, there are some social relationships which are expected to provide more emotional satisfaction than others and some activities which are more valued than others. In some societies, adult same-sex friendships are regarded as the most satisfying and most important, while others emphasize the father-son or mother-daughter relationship. American society has increasingly focused its expectations of emotional gratification on the relationship between heterosexual peers in romantic-erotic intimacy. Not only has marriage been changed by this emphasis, but all of adolescence as well. Sexual relations have become a more important focus of expectation for gratification both in men and in women. Other relationships and other activities have, by comparison, suffered a relative decline in the "motivational economy of the personality." To some people this seems like sacrificing richness and challenge in life for a dull domestic security (Goodenough, 1957). Certainly it will not be experienced as a sacrifice by the present generation. Dating, early dating, steady dating—these are the ways in which the younger generation participates in what adult society values so highly. Perhaps the new values encourage early marriage by defining it as such a desirable relationship. There can be little question that the young people of today come to marriage with more extensive and intimate experience with the opposite sex than their parents did. It is hard to believe that the new patterns are a less realistic preparation for marriage than the dating patterns of a generation or two ago. In a way, the critics of contemporary dating are maintaining that dating has become *too good* a preparation for marriage.

Implications for Personal Autonomy

Most of the people into whose hands this book will fall have completed most or all of the dating experience. This chapter therefore mainly provides them with opportunities for hindsight, for understanding in more depth and complexity what has happened to them. As parents of the next generation, they may be alarmed and perhaps shocked at the dating system which will have evolved by that time, just as each generation in a fast-changing society alarms the previous one.

The most important implications in this chapter for decision making concern the origins and development of interest in the opposite sex. When heterosexual interest is looked upon as an instinctive or at least wholly organic "condition," the role of parents and society is only to bridle and guide the natural urges into acceptable outlets. Social responsibility is limited to a negative police function. When eroticism and heterosexuality are understood as shaped by the experience and social environment of each individual, parents and society become far more than repressive monitors of sex. Rather, they organize the experience and the environment of the next generation in such a way as to pattern the expression of heterosexual interest and sexual desire. To be sure, different individuals will respond differently to the experience, but the socialization process is basically predictable and controllable — that is to say, we know how to produce desired results. American society has never really been in this position before because it has not accurately understood the nature of the situation. If the desire is to produce adolescents and adults for whom heterosexual erotic pairing is the most consuming interest in life, the environment must be organized so that it is saturated with subtle and not-so-subtle messages that this is really all that counts. Early, continuous, and extensive experience in sexual arousal and gratification must be provided. It must be emphasized that human nature is fulfilled and optimum bliss achieved only in the heterosexual embrace. It should be expected that such a socialization process would also be accompanied by the collapse of restrictions on premarital sex.

On the other hand, if American society desires to produce adolescents and adults for whom cross-sex pairing is not very important and for whom sexuality plays a minor role in life, other relationships and other activities are emphasized. The concept of masculinity is focused on something other than sex — perhaps fatherhood, physical prowess, or outdoorsmanship. The extent to which the environment carries sexual messages is minimized. It is somehow made foolish or pathetic for a man to be interested in spending much time with a woman, and the opportunities for sexual stimulation are reduced. A systematic program of this sort should produce a new generation in which sex is far less important and in which cross-sex pairing takes a minor place in the lives of adults and adolescents. On the other hand, marriage would become quite different from what it is today.

The extent to which any single set of parents can take their own course is quite limited. In an environment which emphasizes sex and sex pairing, the child whose parents consistently shut him off from these influences will certainly be a social misfit. For many parents, social adjustment seems an unimportant sacrifice. On the other hand, parents can more easily play a positive role in such an environment, encouraging sexuality in their children, providing experiences and sexual opportunities, and emphasizing the importance and rewards of sex pairing. Some parents apparently do this unwittingly.

Premarital Sexual Behavior

6

Cross-cultural Perspective

No society is morally indifferent to sexual behavior. The focus of moral concern differs from one society to another, but every society is concerned with defining who has the right to do what with whom. The moral boundaries of sexual behavior involve consideration of kinship and marital status in every human group.

An examination of controls on premarital sexual behavior in societies other than our own led Murdock to report:

> . . . Non-incestuous premarital relations are fully permitted in 65 instances, and are conditionally approved in 43 and only mildly disapproved in 6, whereas they are forbidden in only 44. In other words, premarital licence prevails in 70 per cent of our cases. In the rest the taboo falls primarily upon females and appears to be largely a precaution against child-bearing out of wedlock rather than a moral requirement (Murdock, 1949: 245).

Premarital controls are more strict in complex than in simple societies. This generalization gives some support to the layman's conception of "primitive" groups as having a freer sex expression (Stephens, 1963: 256-259).

Why do some societies try to control premarital intercourse? The answer to this "why" needs to be given on two different levels. One answer reflects the reason a man will give when asked, "Why do you prohibit premarital intercourse?" In some groups, the answer is a religious requirement. In others (and Murdock thinks the majority), it is a "precaution against childbearing by the unmarried." Some writers do not agree with Murdock that the primary rationale is control of childbearing. In his sample,

Stephens finds the most common reason mentioned is the premium value of a virgin bride.

The second answer is phrased in terms of the consequences of the restrictions, or lack of them, for the society. Certainly viable societies can be maintained with or without the restriction. Numerous "latent functions" (consequences not necessarily intended) of premarital sex restrictions have been mentioned by sociologists and anthropologists. It is said, for example, to be a form of population control. However, Mead and others have remarked on the small number of pregnancies among the unmarried in permissive groups. Restriction is said to provide impetus for young people to marry, but marriage rates are usually lower and age at marriage older in restrictive than in permissive societies. It is said to be an attempt to be able to ascertain paternity of all children in patrilineal societies, but no one has shown that matrilineal societies are more permissive of premarital sex. No one has formulated any explanatory principle of the occurrence or nonoccurrence of premarital restrictions in societies. From the present vantage point, it appears to be largely a matter of historical and cultural accident that a society is permissive or restrictive. Where there is premarital license, sex for the young and unmarried appears to be viewed largely as "fun," not to be endowed with much symbolic significance.

Sexual Values in Western Tradition

Scholars agree that Western society owes its strict premarital sexual values to the ascetic tendencies in the Christian tradition. These values developed at a time when profligate sexuality seemed rampant to contemporary observers. It was easy for the early Christians to see uncontrolled sex as the cause rather than a symptom of the prevailing social disorganization. Sex became symbolic of the worldly and corrupt in early Christian thought, as it had been in early Hebrew tradition, and this symbolism has remained a part of our cultural heritage. A typical view of sex from the Christian heritage is given in the following selection from a medieval Christian writer:

> The world has fallen into such a state of decay that nowadays the beardless youth and the old man full of years alike love women madly. . . . To think of losing the glory of God for a fleeting moment of unrestrained appetite—vile, filthy, horrible. . . . You know of course that you cannot commit fornication with your own wife; that is, if you conduct yourself properly, and even if you do not, it is not deemed to be a mortal sin to yield to the gross appetites of lechery, but only a venial sin. . . . According to the doctors of medicine, lechery is the efficient and final cause of the weakening of the human body (Martinez de Toledo, 1959: 13, 19, 43, 48).

Thus, even in a nonscientific age, the practice of looking to the sciences for the support of moral values can be found. The cleric continues by telling us:

. . . how love is the cause of death, violence and war, how he who loves hates his father and mother, his kin and friends, how lovers lose the respect of others, how many go mad from loving, how love causes many to perjure themselves and commit crimes, how marriages are destroyed by love, how the learned lose their learning through love . . . Conclusion: how all evils proceed from love (Martinez de Toledo, 1959: v–viii).

It is not clear that this view of sex has ever prevailed among laymen at any time in Western history. Certainly the Renaissance alewife quoted by Taylor (1954: 141–142) does not share this view:

> *Ich am not cast away,*
> *That can my husband say:*
> *When we kisse and play,*
> *In lust and liking,*
> *He calls me his whiting,*
> *His mulling and his mittine,*
> *His nobes and his conny,*
> *His sweeting and honny,*
> *Thou are worth good and money;*
> *This make I my falyre Fanny,*
> *Till he be dreame and dronny:*
> *For, after all our sport,*
> *Then he will rout and snort;*
> *Then sweetly together we lye*
> *As two pigges in a stye . . .*

Contemporary works on the family frequently mention the effect of America's Puritan background on our generally negative view of sex. But Hunt's review of Puritan attitudes and behavior reveals a generally enthusiastic attitude toward sex. From one Puritan preacher we read that "marriage love" is a sweet compound of spiritual affection and carnal attraction, and this blend of the two is the "vital spirit and heart blood" of wedlock. Hunt finds seventeenth-century Puritanism "tight-lipped, severe, and pious, but simultaneously frank, strongly sexed, and somewhat romantic." In fact, he finds the origins of later American "puritanical" attitudes toward sex in the gentility of the nineteenth-century Victorians, not among the Puritans. Premarital intercourse was common in Puritan communities, although it was systematically but matter-of-factly censured by the authorities (Hunt, 1959).

Nineteenth-century Victorian thought generally viewed sex as beneath the dignity of man and beneath the nature of woman. Evolutionary theory was brought to the support of prevailing ideas. Man had really evolved above sex. To what extent these ideas permeated to the lower levels of the social structure is not known. It was into a society with these views that Freud probed, determining the source of all neurosis to be in sexual frustration and disorder. The Victorian act of love-making can be visualized as

—hasty, ashamed, and uncommunicative, the husband "taking his pleasure" while the wife either was, or tried to seem, inert and passive. It is only natural that the Victorian bedroom was so heavily muffled, shrouded and dark, for such surroundings must have somewhat reduced the embarrassment of performing so gross a function. This is not to say that Victorian marriages were loveless or unhappy, but that the quality of love in them was partly, and in a special way, desexualized (Hunt, 1959: 319).

It is against this Victorian background that trends in sexual behavior reported in the twentieth century and contemporary attitudes toward sex in the United States are seen in proper perspective. Each generation thinks it invented sex. A longer-term historical view reveals fluctuations in attitudes toward sex taking place in long cycles, with contradictory attitudes existing simultaneously at most periods. Even the attitudes of the Christian churches have changed with the times, during some periods being less antisex than during other periods. Twentieth-century sexual behavior seems permissive when viewed against a nineteenth-century background. The attitudes of contemporary church groups, although showing extremely wide variation, sound liberal when compared to those of a century ago, but do not sound remarkably different from those of seventeenth-century Puritanism.

Premarital Sex Codes Among Americans

In a society with so many different religious, national, and intellectual traditions, a society which is changing shape as rapidly as American society is, it would be surprising if Americans held to a single value framework for premarital sexual behavior (Reiss, 1960). Chart 6-1 gives the distribution of sexual philosophies prevalent among college students and adults in the 1960s in the United States.

The double standard has its roots in the oldest Old Testament traditions where a nonvirgin bride was to be stoned to death on her father's threshold but where no mention is made in regard to the male. This code, which is permissive for men but restrictive for women, is based on a male-dominant social system in which sex is for men only—behavior that women tolerate in exchange for something else. Double-standard values are predicated on the existence of two classes of women. "Good women" exchange sex for affection and security; "bad women" exchange sex for money or fun (Davis,

Chart 6-1

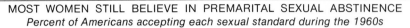

MOST WOMEN STILL BELIEVE IN PREMARITAL SEXUAL ABSTINENCE

Percent of Americans accepting each sexual standard during the 1960s

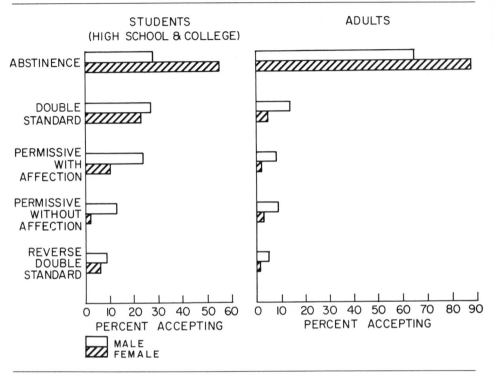

Source: Reiss, 1967

1960). Although most educated Americans have heard the concept of the double standard, it is not widely understood that the double standard is accepted by some women as well as men, as a source of self-definition and role prescription. Reiss reports that his male subjects who held the double standard said they felt disgusted with their female partners and themselves after the sex act was over. Double-standard values were apparently general in society in the nineteenth century, and it would not be surprising to find them latent and unrecognized in many contemporary persons who would repudiate them (Vincent, 1962: 78–79, 80).

American society is rapidly moving away from the double standard. A value orientation toward sex is replacing it which considers sex as a legitimate component of love relationships and as a physical expression of that love. This has led to the increasing acceptance of a premarital standard

Table 6-1

MALE AND FEMALE PREMARITAL SEXUAL PERMISSIVENESS SCALES

First decide whether you agree or disagree with the view expressed. Then circle the degree of your agreement or disagreement with the views expressed in each question. We are not interested in your tolerance of other people's beliefs. Please answer these questions on the basis of how YOU feel toward the views expressed. Your name will never be connected with these answers. Please be as honest as you can. Thank you.

We use the words below to mean just what they do to most people, but some may need definition:

Love means the emotional state which is more intense than strong affection and which you would define as love.
Strong affection means affection which is stronger than physical attraction, average fondness, or "liking"—but less strong than love.
Petting means sexually stimulating behavior more intimate than kissing and simple hugging but not including full sexual relations.

MALE STANDARDS (*BOTH* MEN AND WOMEN CHECK THIS SECTION)

1. I believe that kissing is acceptable for the male before marriage when he is engaged to be married.

	Strong		Strong
Agree	Medium	Disagree	Medium
	Slight		Slight

2. I believe that kissing is acceptable for the male before marriage when he is in love. (The same six-way agree-disagree choice follows every question.)
3. I believe that kissing is acceptable for the male before marriage when he feels strong affection for his partner.
4. I believe that kissing is acceptable for the male before marriage even if he does not feel particularly affectionate toward his partner.
5. I believe that petting is acceptable for the male before marriage when he is engaged to be married.
6. I believe that petting is acceptable for the male before marriage when he is in love.
7. I believe that petting is acceptable for the male before marriage when he feels strong affection for his partner.
8. I believe that petting is acceptable for the male before marriage even if he does not feel particularly affectionate toward his partner.
9. I believe that full sexual relations are acceptable for the male before marriage when he is engaged to be married.
10. I believe that full sexual relations are acceptable for the male before marriage when he is in love.
11. I believe that full sexual relations are acceptable for the male before marriage when he feels strong affection for his partner.
12. I believe that full sexual relations are acceptable for the male before marriage even if he does not feel particularly affectionate toward his partner.

FEMALE STANDARDS (*BOTH* MEN AND WOMEN CHECK THIS SECTION)

(The same series of questions used for Male Standards follows, substituting the word *female* for *male*.)

Reprinted by permission from Ira L. Reiss, *"The Scaling of Premarital Sexual Permissiveness,"* Journal of Marriage and the Family, *vol. 26 (1964).*

which Reiss (1967) characterizes as "permissiveness with affection." Affection becomes the prerequisite for full sexual relations. In his studies using a national representative sample of adults, and several groups of college and high school students, Reiss found that the permissiveness-with-affection orientation is particularly strong among younger generations of Americans. His most significant finding is that the more permissive the standards held by a group, the more that permissiveness is only justified by affection. Reiss measured values toward permissiveness and affection by the scale given in Table 6-1.

Items 4, 8, and 12 from this scale indicate acceptance of sexual permissiveness without affection and might be considered a measure of acceptance of sexual promiscuity. The most permissive groups, however, put items 4, 8, and 12 at the bottom of the scale. Thus they indicated more approval of full sexual relations before marriage in the presence of strong affection than of kissing not motivated by affection. Generally, adult groups were less swayed by the presence of affection in the relationship and more concerned with preventing the more intimate levels of sexual involvement, affection or no affection.

Table 6-2 gives the distribution among Americans of permissive attitudes toward premarital sex as indicated by recent Gallup surveys. This table shows that Americans are extremely divided in their attitudes about premarital sex. The young hold much more permissive attitudes than the old. Men are much more permissive than women, and the educated are far more permissive than the less educated. Sample studies of college students in recent years show them to be only half as likely to think premarital sex is wrong as the "under thirty" group as a whole. In 1972, 1 adult in 3, but 4 college students in 5, thought premarital sex was permissible. The dramatic changes in attitude shown between 1969 and 1972, when compared to attitudes just ten years or five years earlier (Chart 6-1) show that American attitudes toward premarital sex have been revolutionized in the decade.

Table 6-2

ATTITUDES TOWARD PREMARITAL SEX ARE CHANGING RAPIDLY
*Percentage of white men and women in the United States who believe
that premarital relations are not wrong, 1969 and 1972*

	1969		1972	
Age	Men	Women	Men	Women
Under 30	48	27	65	42
30–44	26	13	45	29
45 and over	12	10	21	12
Total	23	14	37	23

Source: Blake, 1973

Race Differences in Premarital Sexual Attitudes and Behavior

Comparison of the attitudes and behavior of white and black Americans with respect to premarital sex indicates that there are important differences between the races. *Blacks in every study show attitudes much more permissive of premarital sex.* Both in a sample of students and in a national probability sample, a far higher proportion of blacks than of whites gave highly permissive responses (Reiss, 1967). Furthermore, all comparisons of black and white premarital sexual behavior indicate that for both men and women, a higher percentage of blacks experienced premarital sex, experienced it at earlier ages than whites, and with more different partners. It has long been argued that these differences are primarily a reflection of the socioeconomic differences between whites and blacks in the United States. However, this is certainly not the case. A review of all studies cited in the book will demonstrate that in studies related to marriage and the family, controlling for socioeconomic differences between whites and blacks does not obliterate differences in their behavior. Reiss has shown that when his data are controlled for social-class differences by examining only responses of the lower-class part of his sample, race differences in sexual permissiveness are not even reduced (Reiss, 1968). Scholars have been recording and trying to explain these race differences for many years, and there is still no consensus. To say that the races simply have different cultures is to beg the explanation. Another common attempt at explanation is to say that the differences are remnants from slavery which systematically destroyed the family of blacks. Although this may be true, it is not a satisfactory explanation today. At this point we can only indicate that differences are observed between blacks and whites in the same socioeconomic setting, and that the differences between middle-class blacks and whites are generally as great as between lower-class blacks and whites.

The Scale of Sexual Intensity

Researchers have found what experienced adolescents have always known, that there is a rather inflexible scale of intensity in erotic behavior in American culture, beginning with simple lip kissing and hugging, continuing through deep kissing, breast manipulation over clothing, bare breast manipulation, breast kissing, manipulation of the genitals, to intercourse (Ehrmann, 1959). Among college students, it is an almost universal rule that no one experiences a more intense erotic stimulation without having experienced all the less intense levels. It should be pointed out that this sequence is not limited to premarital sexual behavior but is carried into marital sexuality in the preliminary petting which is the usual concomitant of marital sex in the middle class. It should also be pointed out that the preliminary petting behavior of the American middle class is almost exclusively devoted to the stimulation of females, with practically no attention to the male, whose stimulation is taken for granted.

Intimacy and Involvement

Although adults who have little contact with the peer culture of the young and unmarried frequently talk as though premarital petting is entirely promiscuous and done for "kicks," this is apparently much truer for males than for females. Christensen and Carpenter (1962) report that both men and women in three different culture groups saw increasing levels of erotic intimacy as related to the length of the relationship and its commitment level, although males asked for much less commitment. On the other hand, Ehrmann (1959) indicates that length of relationship and emotional involvement are only significant for the sexual intimacy of women, whereas most men are willing to initiate and accept intimacy on any level with any or no emotional involvement. This is a direct outgrowth of the difference of the place of sex in the sex role of males and females as developed in the adolescent sex subcultures. What this means is that in any erotic relationship, on almost any level in American society, it is assumed that the male will go into sexual intimacy as far as he is permitted by the woman. This leaves the control of sexual intimacy entirely in the hands of women, and for college women the level of intimacy permitted is more closely a function of the level of their emotional involvement than any other factor.

This requirement of affection for sexual access among women is fairly well known in the sophisticated reaches of the male subculture, where among the uncommitted and more predatory males there is a regular repertoire of techniques for simulation of emotional involvement to induce willingness to permit sexual intimacy. On the other hand, more than one male has "lost" this game by becoming emotionally involved when his initial intentions were strictly sexual.

Whether there is the same relationship between intimacy and commitment in the less-educated part of our population is not certain. Kirkendall (1961) reports uneducated girls pleading for some confession of affection from the boy, however cynical, as a requisite for permitting intercourse. This note, however, runs through reports of lower-class sexual behavior. The women hope to trade their sexual favors for a little affection. The male hopes to get his sex with as little emotional entanglement and commitment as possible (Rainwater, 1960). The effect of these differences in orientation to intimacy and involvement is the much greater promiscuity of males than females in the college population for every level of intimacy.

A number of studies show that males are far more likely than females to date below their class level and more likely to date outside the field of marital eligibles (Ehrmann, 1954, 1959; Hollingshead, 1949). A strong motivation for cross-class dating of high-status males is the widely held view in the male subculture that lower-class girls are not only more sexually available but are more passionate. Ehrmann found that:

> Male crossers of class lines in dating are usually sexually more active than non-crossers, and their extreme sexual experiences are more often with girls of a lower class and less often with girls of a higher social class (Ehrmann, 1959: 337).

In an earlier study of a smaller group, Ehrmann found that of the coital companions of the college females, every coital companion was a marital eligible, while half of the coital companions of the college males were not "acceptables" (Ehrmann, 1954).

Premarital Petting

For the purposes of this book, petting is defined as any deliberate erotic physical contact except intercourse. Although some people consider petting an invention of modern American youth, petting behavior is common among other mammals, practiced in all cultures, and has an ancient, rich, and honorable literature to attest to its long history in our own cultural past (Kinsey, 1953: 231–232). Even in the sexually restrained Victorian period, there was probably widespread occurrence of petting. Of the women in Kinsey's sample who were born before 1900 and therefore may be presumed to be at least partly "Victorian," some 80 percent reported premarital petting experiences of some sort, and about one-fourth reported at least one experience in premarital petting to orgasm (Kinsey et al., 1953: 243–244). Premarital petting has evidently become more widely practiced in later generations, and at somewhat earlier ages. Kinsey's data, which date to women born in 1930, indicate that each subsequent generation of women has shown a higher incidence of premarital petting and a higher incidence of petting to orgasm. Kinsey's data show that for women who did not have premarital coitus, the increase in incidence of various petting techniques occurred between those born before 1900 and those born in the next decade, while for women with coital experience, each subsequent generation had more experience and more intense experience in petting (Kinsey et al., 1953: 280–281). This is to say that petting which does not end in intercourse has not continued to increase in the later groups of women. The more elaborated petting techniques are mainly found among those women who also engage in intercourse. Comparable data is not available for males by age of birth, but the assumption can be made that there are fewer differences between earlier and later groups of men than there are for women.

Petting for most persons is an experience first encountered in the late teens, with an abrupt rise in incidence for both men and women between the ages of fifteen and eighteen, and is an almost universal experience of older adolescents. Though it is a feature of the premarital behavior of all social levels, elaborated petting is more common among upper-level persons and constitutes a larger part of the total sexual behavior of the educated than the uneducated.

In view of the general moral opposition of religious groups to petting, it is not surprising to find that religious training has something to do with the incidence of petting. For women, there is little difference in devout and inactive religious groups in the incidence of *some* petting, but petting to orgasm is far more frequent among the religiously inactive women than among the devout (Kinsey et al., 1953: 247–249). There are slight differences between the religious and the nonreligious male in petting behavior, but they are reduced to insignificance by the much larger differences between men of different educational levels (Kinsey et al., 1948: 477). *Whether or not a person engages in premarital petting does not have much to do with his religious training, but girls with devout religious orientation reject those kinds of intensive petting which are likely to lead to orgasm.*

Premarital Intercourse

It is widely believed among laymen that premarital intercourse is more common today than ever before in the United States. Little evidence is available which pertains to anything but the twentieth century. Several studies demonstrate that women born after 1900 are more likely to have had premarital intercourse than those born earlier (Burgess and Wallin, 1953: 331; Kinsey et al., 1953: 299; Locke, 1951: chapter 7). This applies to men as well as women in all the studies except those conducted by Kinsey, who finds no changes in the percentages of men who had had premarital intercourse. What is not widely known is that Kinsey's data show that the change began a long time ago and that all the groups of women born between 1910 and 1930 show the same new pattern (Kinsey et al., 1953: 299). In this sense, the increase in the number of persons who have premarital intercourse may be seen to begin with those who dated and married after World War I. These are the grandparents of the present generation of college students.

Recent changes in attitudes toward more permissiveness have made possible the conduct of surveys of sexual behavior among the unmarried

Chart 6-2

BLACK GIRLS ARE TWICE AS LIKELY AS WHITES TO HAVE INTERCOURSE
DURING ADOLESCENCE
*Percent of unmarried women aged 15–19 who have ever had intercourse
(U. S., 1971), by race.*

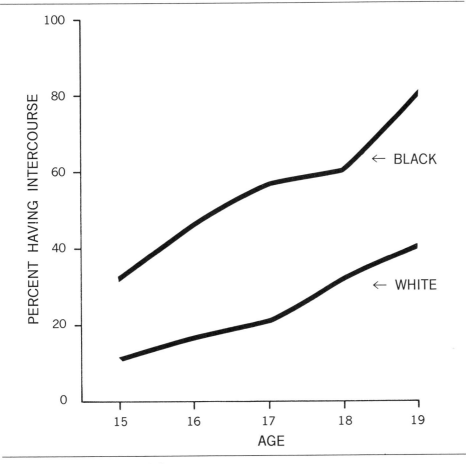

Source: Kantner and Zelnick, 1973

which would not have been possible even a decade ago. Two national surveys of the sexual behavior of adolescents were completed in the 1970s. The first, in 1971, was done by Zelnick and Kantner with a grant from the federal government. The second was done as a private venture by Sorensen in 1972. Zelnick and Kantner attempted to interview a representative sample of girls aged 15 to 19, and had a very low refusal rate (under 5 percent). Sorensen attempted to interview a representative national sample of males and females aged 13 to 19, but he was able to interview less than half of those who were supposed to be interviewed, largely because of refusals to be interviewed from the adolescents or their parents. Because of the large differences in the results of these two studies, and because of the probable serious bias in the Sorensen study caused by refusals, I will rely almost exclusively on Zelnick and Kantner's study.

Zelnick and Kantner (1973) found that in 1971, by age 15, 1 white girl in 10 and 1 black girl in 3 has had intercourse at least once. By age 19, 4 in 10 white girls and 8 in 10 black girls have had experience with coitus. (See Chart 6-2.) Differences in coital experience by socioeconomic status are not very important. Separate analyses show that girls from families of high income, education, or occupational status are as likely to be coitally active as those from less-privileged families. The only social variable that makes a difference is race. At every age, more than twice the proportion of blacks than whites is sexually experienced. Even when statistical controls are introduced to eliminate the effect of differences in socioeconomic status, the race difference is hardly diminished. This observation is consistent with those made in previous studies, and consistent with the more permissive attitudes of blacks which have been found in attitude studies (Reiss, 1967).

Contemporary studies indicate that something on the order of two-thirds of men who have been to college report that they have had premarital intercourse, while nearly all males with only grade-school education claim to have had intercourse. The *frequency* of premarital intercourse differs even more between the two educational levels of experienced males, with unmarried males of lesser education averaging two to ten times as frequent intercourse as the unmarried college-level males, and usually with many more different partners (Kinsey et al., 1948: 348). College-level males have traditionally found most of their premarital sexual experience in nonsocial outlets (masturbation and nocturnal emissions).

Recent Changes in Premarital Sexual Behavior

In the past five years a large number of studies have been published which all show similar significant changes in premarital sexual behavior in the past decade (Packard, 1968; Luckey and Nass, 1969; Bell and Chaskes, 1970; Bauman and Wilson, 1973). The proportion of college males who report having had coital experience remains unchanged from the Kinsey samples of thirty years ago. Studies in the early seventies report about two out of three college males coitally experienced. The main change in behavior for males is the virtual disappearance of experience with prostitutes (Packard, 1968). For female college students, the proportion who are coitally experienced continues to rise in every subsequent survey, with increases of from 50 to 100 percent during the decade of the sixties. One unpublished study from a southern state university, done in 1972, and using a careful random

Chart 6-3

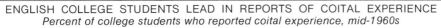

ENGLISH COLLEGE STUDENTS LEAD IN REPORTS OF COITAL EXPERIENCE
Percent of college students who reported coital experience, mid-1960s

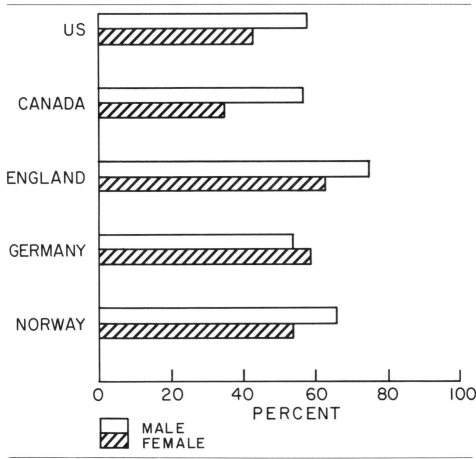

Source: Luckey and Nass, 1969

sample of students, showed for the first time that the proportion of coitally experienced males and females was the same (Bauman and Wilson, 1973). The trend toward greater involvement of women in premarital sexual intercourse, which began in the early part of the present century, is still continuing. This involvement is less and less limited to engagement, less limited to a single partner, and is more free from guilt than for earlier groups of women.

SEXUAL INVOLVEMENT OF COLLEGE STUDENTS: AN INTERNATIONAL COMPARISON

A five-nation study of the sexual attitudes and behavior of college students was completed in the mid-sixties, allowing us to compare the patterns in

Chart 6-4

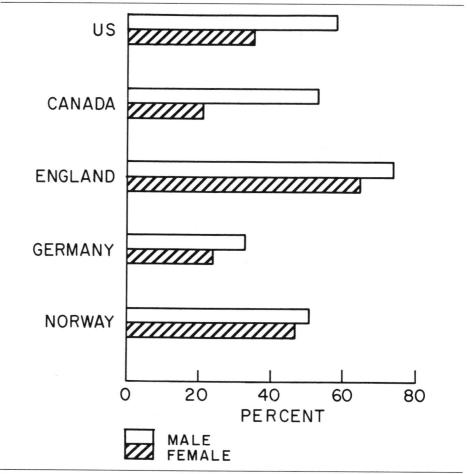

ENGLISH COLLEGE STUDENTS LEAD IN NUMBER OF SEXUAL PARTNERS
Percent of coitus-experienced college students who have had more than two partners

□ MALE
▨ FEMALE

Source: Luckey and Nass, 1969

the United States with those in other countries. Although considerable doubt remains as to whether this study accurately represents the total body of college students in each country, the data are certainly better than the guesses that pass for information in this area most of the time. Chart 6-3 shows the percentage of college men and women in each country reporting coital experience. Chart 6-4 compares the average number of coital partners for the experienced group in each country. The sample from England emerges clearly as the most promiscuous for both sexes.

Chart 6-5

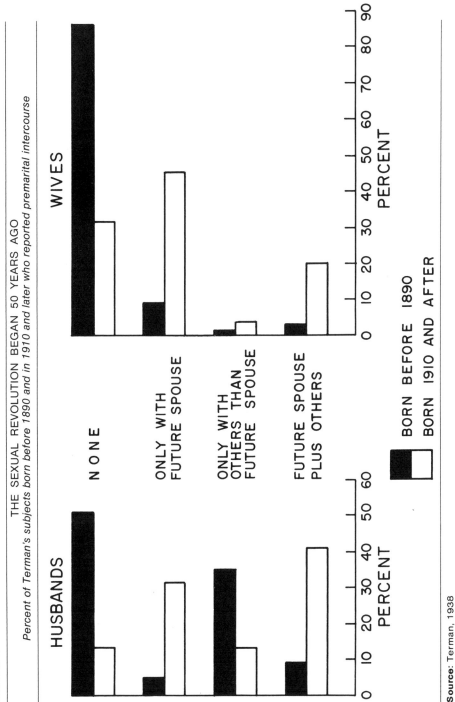

THE SEXUAL REVOLUTION BEGAN 50 YEARS AGO

Percent of Terman's subjects born before 1890 and in 1910 and later who reported premarital intercourse

WIVES

HUSBANDS

NONE

ONLY WITH
FUTURE SPOUSE

ONLY WITH
OTHERS THAN
FUTURE SPOUSE

FUTURE SPOUSE
PLUS OTHERS

PERCENT

PERCENT

BORN BEFORE 1890

BORN 1910 AND AFTER

Source: Terman, 1938

Premarital Sexual Behavior 117

Table 6-3

MOST SEXUAL LIAISONS OF COLLEGE MEN ARE NOT LOVE RELATIONSHIPS	
Premarital liaisons by level of involvement (200 college men)	

Level of Involvement	Percent of Liaisons at This Level
1. Prostitute	13.8
2. Pickup (strictly for sex, no involvement)	17.6
3. Casual date (begun for intercourse, no male affection)	33.2
4. Date who became sex partner before male became affectionally attached	17.4
5. Partner with whom male has considerable emotional involvement	14.2
6. Fiancée (strong emotional attachment)	3.8

Reprinted by permission from **Lester A. Kirkendall,** Premarital Intercourse and Interpersonal Relationships *(New York: Gramercy Publishing Co., 1968).*

Premarital Intercourse and the Nature of the Relationship

What is the social relationship between coital partners? Are most of the respondents promiscuous, or do they limit coital experiences to lovers or those to whom they are engaged to be married? A number of researchers have explored this topic, and their data are fairly consistent. The findings in Chart 6-5 are reported by Terman.

Similar figures are reported by Burgess, Locke, and Thomes (1963: 356). Most of the early increase in incidence of premarital intercourse among women after 1910 is accounted for by those who have intercourse with their future spouses only, although a substantial part is also accounted for by those who have had intercourse with their future spouses as well as other men. How many other men? In Kinsey's group, for women marrying at the usual ages, 60 percent of the experienced women report only one partner, and fewer than 10 percent report more than five different partners (Kinsey et al., 1953). The picture for men is somewhat different. The increase in premarital intercourse in younger generations of men is about equally divided between those who had intercourse with several women and those whose premarital experience was limited to those whom they subsequently married. Burgess and Wallin do report that there has been a decline in the number of men whose experience was limited to women whom they did *not* marry, which may be taken as evidence of a decline in the double standard. Put another way, more of the younger generations of men had intercourse with their future wives *as well as* other women.

Vincent, reporting on the relationship existing at the time of impregnation between unmarried mothers and their sexual partners (who are known to represent a fairly selected group of premarital sex pairs), shows that the

Chart 6-6

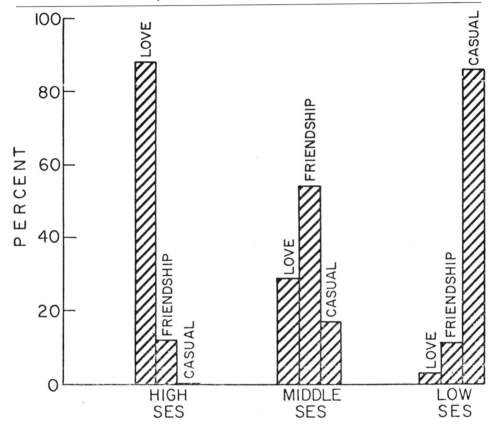

AMONG UNMARRIED MOTHERS, ONLY THOSE FROM HIGHER-STATUS
BACKGROUNDS WERE IN LOVE WITH THEIR SEX PARTNERS
*Relationship reported with their sex partners by unmarried mothers,
by socioeconomic status of the mother*

Source: Vincent, 1962

nature of the relationship between the sex partners is *very* strongly affected
by the socioeconomic status level of the woman. (See Chart 6-6.) These data
offer strong confirmation that the association between love and permissive
sexuality for women is found almost exclusively among higher-status women.
Few lower-status women report love relationships with their premarital sex
partners.

It is interesting to contrast this experience of unmarried mothers with
the premarital sexual liaisons of college men studied by Kirkendall. Of the
668 sexual liaisons reported by the 200 men, most could not be considered
as love relationships. Table 6-3 gives the percentage of liaisons reported
at each level of interpersonal involvement.

Table 6-4

GIRLS REPORT MORE SERIOUS INVOLVEMENT THAN
BOYS WITH FIRST SEX PARTNER

Relationship with first sex partner prior to intercourse

	Boys	Girls
My wife/husband after we were married	0%	2%
A girl/boy I was going steady with and planned to marry	7	36
A girl/boy I was going steady with but had no definite plans to marry	18	21
A girl/boy I knew well and liked a lot, even though we weren't going together	31	25
A girl/boy I knew slightly and was more or less friendly with	19	5
A girl/boy I had met only a little while before the time we had sex together	25	10
Someone who raped me	—	1
TOTAL	100%	100%

Source: Sorensen, 1973: 198

Kirkendall points out that the small number of liaisons reported at level 6 was probably a factor of the reticence of males to discuss sexual involvements with women to whom they were emotionally attached. However, he concludes that, much more frequently than boys, the girls involved became more attached to their sexual partner than the partner was to them (Kirkendall, 1961: 295). In a study of adolescent sexual behavior completed in 1972, boys and girls reported the nature of their relationship with their very first coital partner. Table 6-4 shows their responses. Almost 60 percent of the girls report they were at the very least going steady with their first sex partner, but only 25 percent of the boys report this kind of serious relationship existed. This is quite consistent with the differences in values of males and females, the differences in the meaning of sexual behavior to them, and the differences in their socialization with respect to love and sex. *In any premarital sexual relationship, there is a high probability that the girl will be more emotionally involved and interpret the interpersonal relationship as more serious than her male sex partner will.*

Religion shows a marked effect on premarital coital experience for both men and women. For all three major religious groups, about twice as many religiously inactive females have engaged in premarital intercourse as have religiously devout women (Kinsey et al., 1953: 305). Nonreligious males have a greater incidence of premarital coital experience than religiously devout males, but the differences between the religious groups are slight when compared to the differences between different educational levels. Put another way, the premarital (as well as all other) sexual experience of males appears to be profoundly affected by their class level, with religion playing a minor part. For women, religion is a much more powerful determinant, with (if the Kinsey data can be believed) class level playing a less significant part. But studies of the effect of religiosity on premarital coitus usually measure religiosity by frequency of church attendance. When a more complete measure of religiosity is used, the results are reversed; religiosity has more effect on premarital coital experience for males than for females (Clayton, 1972). On the other hand, religious participation and incidence of premarital pregnancy do not seem to be related. A small study conducted by Burchinal and Bock (1959) produced no evidence that religious participation deterred premarital pregnancies. In his more comprehensive study, Vincent reports:

> Some unwed mothers receive strict and extremely conservative religious teachings, from their parents and weekly church attendance. Some got moderate and liberal religious teachings from their parents, and attended church infrequently. Others received minimum religious teaching from their parents and were not affiliated with any church or religious group (Vincent, 1962: 179).

Do people who have engaged in premarital intercourse regret it? Most do not, according to their reports (Burgess and Wallin, 1953: 5, 30). On the other hand, in the devout religious groups where premarital experience was lowest, those women who were experienced reported regret three or four times as often as the nonreligious women. Regret is obviously a function of the strength of the moral code which has been violated. *Those people who are least likely to engage in premarital intercourse are those who are most likely to suffer from it if they do.*

Peer Group and Premarital Intercourse

People are strongly influenced by their friends' behavior, or by their perceptions of their friends' behavior. Teevan (1972) tested the influence of the peer group on the sexual behavior of 1,177 college students and found that students who saw their friends as sexually permissive were much more likely to have had coitus than students who felt that their friends were sexually conservative. The relationship held for males and females, although it was weaker for females.

Interpretation of Data on Premarital Intercourse

More men and women born since 1910 have had premarital intercourse than those born before the turn of the century. There is indication of a continuing increase in the experience of women born after 1930. The number of premarital coital companions each person has is very small for most women and rather limited for college-level men. This cannot be interpreted as a general trend toward promiscuous premarital sexual relations but as a trend, at least among the college-educated, to include intercourse as a part of serious emotional involvements. More than thirty years ago, Terman, after surveying his data, made the following prediction:

> *If the drop* [in virginity at marriage] *should continue at the average rate shown for those born since 1890* virginity at marriage will be close to the vanishing point for males born after 1930 and for females born after 1940. It is more likely that the rate of change will become somewhat retarded as the zero point is approached and that an occasional virgin will come to the marriage bed for a few decades beyond the dates indicated by the curves. It will be of no small interest to see how long the cultural ideal of the virgin marriage will survive as a moral code after its observance has passed into history (Terman, 1938).

Later research has shown Terman's time horizon to be too short. There has been little change in the proportion of premaritally experienced men since Terman's study. Meanwhile, women have been catching up. Most of the change since Terman's time has occurred since 1960. But the virgin bride is harder to eradicate than Terman imagined. Virginity at marriage is not about to disappear during the present generation.

Consequences of Premarital Intercourse

The objections and arguments put forth against premarital intercourse are legion. For many of these arguments, of course, there is no evidence which could be collected to support or refute them. Those based on religious grounds *alone* are by their nature irrefutable and equally unsupportable from observation. Certain alleged consequences will be treated in this section, because relevant data can be found.

PREMARITAL PREGNANCY

One of the most frequent arguments against premarital intercourse is that it will lead to premarital pregnancy with the concomitant social problems this entails. Lurid popular reports of the "fantastic" number of high school and college women who are pregnant, though unmarried, are mainly arguments against premarital sexual relationships. In Kinsey's sample, about 1 woman in 5 with premarital experience incurred a premarital pregnancy. Since about half of this sample was experienced, this means about 1 woman in 10 was pregnant before marriage (though not necessarily at the time of her marriage). Christensen's careful matching of marriage license records with birth records gives an index of the number of women who were pregnant

Table 6-5

UNMARRIED ADOLESCENTS ARE CASUAL CONTRACEPTORS
Percent of sexually experienced unmarried women aged 15–19,
according to contraceptive use status, United States, 1971.

Age	Percent who used contraceptives	
	Always	At last coitus
15	19	29
16	20	38
17	17	45
18	17	51
19	22	59
15–19	19	47

Source: Kantner and Zelnick, 1973

at the time of their marriage. The researcher conservatively estimates that in about 17 percent of the marriages the woman is pregnant at the time of marriage (Christensen, 1953, 1958). Estimates run as high as 80 percent for marriages in which the bride and groom are in high school. These figures only give a rough idea of the number of premarital pregnancies. Marriages with premarital pregnancies have been shown to be highly prone to divorce in the United States (Christensen and Rubinstein, 1956). Other studies suggest that their instability is related to the *acceptability* of premarital sex and premarital pregnancy in the culture group of the couple (Christensen, 1963). Previous study of a lower-class group showed stable marriages among second-generation Italian slum dwellers in spite of the fact that most marriages began with a pregnancy under way (Green, 1941).[1] In an important study comparing the extent and effect of premarital pregnancy in Denmark with two American groups, Christensen found premarital pregnancies much more common in Denmark, with its comparatively liberal sex code, than in the United States. The premaritally pregnant couples in Denmark, however, tended to take their time about getting married and were no more prone to divorce than those couples without premarital pregnancies. Sexual permissiveness was thus associated with higher incidences but lower negative effects of premarital pregnancies (Christensen, 1960).

PREMARITAL PREGNANCY AND AVAILABILITY OF ABORTION

During 1971 and 1972, the abortion law was transformed in the United States so as to make it legal to perform abortions in every state. In response to this, it might be imagined that illegitimacy rates would have dropped sharply, as the number of abortions rose. Tietze (1973) found evidence which indicated some slight effect of abortion on illegitimate births in New York.

---

[1] Perhaps this marital stability in an Italian slum is accounted for by the fact that most were Catholic marriages.

Unpublished data from my own research in other cities show that illegitimacy rates are declining where abortion rates are highest.

PREMARITAL INTERCOURSE AND CONTRACEPTION

Common sense might lead to the conclusion that contraception would be more common among the unmarried than the married, since few unmarried persons want to become pregnant. But interviews with a representative sample of unmarried girls aged 15–19 in the United States, completed in 1971, indicate that the young and unmarried are very casual contraceptors (Kantner and Zelnick, 1973). Table 6-5 shows that at last intercourse, fewer than half reported using any protection, while only 1 in 5 reported using contraception at every intercourse.

The contraceptives used most recently by the sexually experienced in this study are shown in Chart 6-7. This distribution of method use is probably affected by the reluctance of physicians to provide contraceptive methods to unmarried girls, which prevailed through 1970. By 1973, in most large cities in the United States, unmarried girls could obtain medically administered contraception without charge, no questions asked, at federally subsidized contraceptive clinics.

Older studies showed that the use of contraception by males was closely related to the degree of commitment to the sex partner, with nearly universal use in engaged pairs, and infrequent use in casual pairs. But the latest study shows no relationships of contraceptive use to marital intentions of the partners.

PREMARITAL INTERCOURSE AND ROMANTIC LOVE

Freud explained love as "aim-inhibited sex," by which he meant that the emotional experience of lovers was the result of the blocking of complete genital union by the couple. Most sociologists, Freudian and non-Freudian, have tended to accept this point of view. If it is true, then unmarried couples might contemplate whether consummation of the sexual relationship might not dissipate their love. The evidence for this proposition is ambiguous, however; reviews of the relationship between the existence of love and premarital sexual license in other societies have led researchers to different conclusions. Blood (1952) concludes from his comparisons that premarital sexual relationships and romantic attitudes are mutually incompatible. Stephens (1963: 206–207), on the other hand, compared ethnographic materials for several societies and found no clear relationship between love as a feature of courtship and restrictions on premarital sex. In a study by Burgess and Wallin, engaged couples who engaged in premarital coitus almost unanimously agreed that it strengthened rather than weakened their relationship (Burgess and Wallin, 1953: 372). Kirkendall, however, doubts whether

Chart 6-7

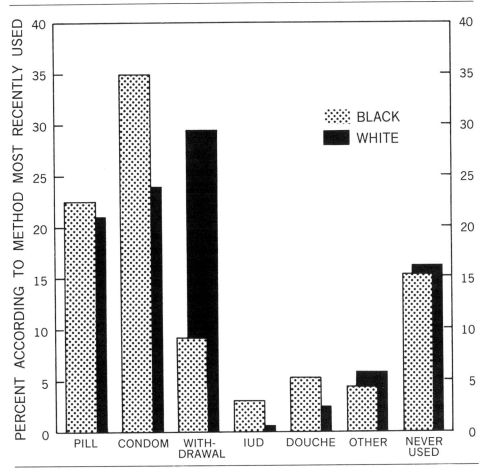

CONDOM AND WITHDRAWAL ARE STILL POPULAR AMONG SEXUALLY
ACTIVE ADOLESCENTS
*Percent of sexually experienced never-married women aged 15–19 who used
specified contraceptive methods' most recently, United States, 1971.*

Source: Kantner and Zelnick, 1973

they are in a position to assess its effect accurately, although he does not
conclude that it weakens any relationship which is strong before a sexual
relationship is begun (Kirkendall, 1961). Apparently there are exceptions
to this. The disenchantment process which couples experience with one
another after marriage (Pineo, 1961) has frequently been taken as evidence
that sexual consummation removes the emotional thrill from the couple's
interaction. Followed consistently, this argument might be used to dissuade

couples from marrying each other just as logically as to inhibit premarital intercourse. In view of the inconsistencies in sociological and psychological findings, *it cannot seriously be suggested to young couples that if they engage in premarital intercourse it will weaken their relationship to one another and destroy their feeling of love.*

EFFECT OF PREMARITAL INTERCOURSE ON MARITAL ADJUSTMENT

Premarital intercourse has been said to have an adverse effect on sexual adjustment in marriage and on general marital adjustment. This question has been carefully researched, though not in such a way as to establish cause-and-effect relationships. When people look at the results of this research, they usually look for scientific justification for a moral principle. Some research findings provide such justification. However, most of the recent research is in agreement on one point—*premarital sexual relations are not detrimental to marital sexual adjustment.* Terman and Kinsey both show a more satisfactory sexual adjustment among the premaritally experienced women and men. Although this does not necessarily demonstrate that premarital experience causes good sexual adjustment in marriage, this interpretation is not excluded by the findings. Most researchers are inclined to believe that women who have higher sex interest and responsiveness are most likely to engage in premarital intercourse and are *also* the most likely to have a good sexual adjustment in marriage (Hamblin and Blood, 1956). Burgess and Wallin's findings are intriguing but are inconsistent with other research. They report that husbands and wives whose only premarital coitus was with each other had lower sexual adjustment than those who had also had other partners as well as those who were virgin at marriage (Burgess and Wallin, 1953: 364).

In overall marital adjustment, all the marital adjustment studies agree: Those who enter marriage with no premarital coital experience are most likely to have high marital adjustment and are least likely to be divorced (Burgess and Wallin, 1953; Locke, 1951; Terman, 1938). Lest these results be misinterpreted, it should first be pointed out that the differences are in general very small and sometimes not statistically significant. Second, other findings from the same studies suggest caution in making any easy conclusion that premarital intercourse is bad for marital adjustment. For example, Terman found no difference to speak of in the marital adjustment of couples both of whom were virgin and both of whom had had relations only with each other. Furthermore, the marital adjustment of his most promiscuous group of women (17 women who had had relations with their husbands and more than 6 other men) was no lower than the adjustment of the virgin brides.

Most scholars today agree that one cannot interpret the results of the marital adjustment studies as demonstrating that if an individual avoids premarital intercourse he will have a happier marriage than if he had engaged in intercourse before marriage. Rather, it appears that those people who are most likely to engage in premarital intercourse have other characteristics which predispose them to report slightly less-well-adjusted marriages, while *those who do not engage in premarital intercourse have other characteristics which predispose them to report happier marriages.* Premarital intercourse, however, is still "unconventional" behavior. Conventionality of practically any sort has been found related to marital success as presently measured. Marriage is a very conventional institution, and those people whose values and behavior are most conventional fit into marriage best.

VENEREAL DISEASE

Another argument frequently given against premarital intercourse is the likelihood of acquiring a venereal disease. In spite of stories circulated in the male subculture to the contrary, venereal disease is practically never circulated by nongenital contact. Although 1 woman in 40 in Kinsey's sample who had premarital intercourse contracted a venereal disease (Kinsey et al., 1953: 345), we do not know the risk today.

Some Thoughts on the Past and the Pattern for the Future

What prompted the origins of the prohibitions against premarital intercourse in American tradition cannot be determined. It may have had to do with ancient patriarchal social organization in which women were the sexual property of men and premarital intercourse amounted to giving away the family property. In a society in which family membership, descent, and inheritance were traced through the father, and where pregnancy control was primitive, premarital prohibitions must have served to strengthen a patrilineal system. When pregnancy was the assumed possible result of any sexual intercourse and children were to be reared only in families, then prohibiting premarital sex served to eliminate difficulties.

It is suggested by some students of social structure that high valuations of virginity for women are characteristic only of strongly patrilineal societies. One scholar suggests that high valuation of virginity implies a grossly inferior status for women in society at large. When patrilineal organization declines in importance, especially if the society seeks to minimize the status difference between men and women as has been the case in our recent history, the toleration of a wide degree of sexual license for both sexes might be a natural concomitant (Leach, 1963). Perhaps one cannot have it both ways—

one of the unintended consequences of the achievement of equality of the sexes may necessarily be the undermining of controls over premarital sexuality.

Modern scientific technology has given to the married and the unmarried alike the ability to disassociate sex from reproduction at will. Under these circumstances, one might speculate on how many generations the prohibitions on premarital intercourse will continue. One might even wonder when the day arrives that venereal disease is not a problem (it is a problem now only because the society chooses not to wipe it out) and when everyone has at his disposal effective contraceptive devices, what stake society will have in the private sexual behavior of the unmarried.

In a recent paper, Winch gives his prediction on the effect of contraception on extramarital (including premarital) sex.

> To me . . . it seems that the prospect of an easy, efficient, readily available, inexpensive, and safe contraceptive—especially if used by the woman—is a development of critical significance for it truly provides a basis for distinguishing between procreational and recreational sex. Let us assume that such a procedure is developed in the next few years. What would follow?
>
> The rational basis for a society's prohibition of heterosexual intercourse outside marriage has to do with the consequences of such intercourse because many societies—probably most societies—do not have suitable provisions for raising children born outside of wedlock. As unwanted pregnancies would become rare to non-existent, the society would lose the basis of its interest in trying to control such behavior. Then—with some cultural lag—the strength of legal and moral sanctions against extramarital intercourse would weaken. Such a change in norms seems to be happening now . . . And we hear that the younger generation is critical of the cultural lag and speaks of the remaining moral sanctions as hypocrisy. The first consequence of the development of an efficient contraceptive and widespread access to it, then, would seem to be a disappearance of moral and legal sanctions against extramarital sex (Winch, 1970).

Today the double standard of sex morality is gradually being replaced with a single code for both sexes which legitimizes sex only within (and it is hoped as an expression of) love relationships. Older values held that sex had to do with marriage, and love had not much to do with it. Newer values in Western society hold that love and marriage go together, and that love and sex go together. Love, however, does not result in marriage as often as it does result in sex. One finds, at least in sophisticated and educated American groups, therefore, a gradual decline in exploitive sex among men and a gradual acceptance of sex as a "natural" expression of love among women. The consequence of this value shift is that sexual relations are found filtering into love relationships which have not (and some which will not be) formalized into marriage. The result is not promiscuity. The result is more premarital sexual relations, a greater percentage of which are within person-centered relationships. By placing an emphasis on sex as love, Americans have probably undermined the possibility of containing it within marriage. It seems improbable that American society will soon return to the rigorously observed standards of premarital chastity which are presumed to have prevailed during some previous centuries.

Implications for Individual Decision-Making

Some people would consider it immoral to suggest that there is any legitimate decision-making to be done concerning premarital sexuality. Generally, these are people who are not unmarried persons involved in heterosexual relationships. For the unmarried person, sexual dilemmas present themselves in contexts which demand decisions. The society no longer provides a clear-cut basis for making them. At least in previous American generations, there was social consensus that premarital sexual relations were immoral, and those who indulged knew this. Today that consensus is gone.

There are two basic patterns around which thoughtful individuals are now making their decisions concerning premarital sexuality. Fundamentally, neither involves ascertaining the empirical consequences of premarital coitus *per se.* These consequences are organized by the restrictive or permissive morality of the society and the individual actors involved and are largely controllable. The first pattern is simply to accept premarital chastity as an ultimate value, a good thing in life that does not have to be defended because it has more desirable consequences than some alternate choice, but because it is good in itself. Under this category are all decisions which are based on religious conviction, as well as those which can only assert that chastity is good and premarital intercourse is bad. All behavior decisions must finally be based on some irreducible values which can only be defended as ultimate, not on the evaluation of consequences. The second pattern establishes the meaning of sexual relations in the social context, and the meaning of sex determines its appropriateness in particular premarital settings. If sex is defined as a physical expression of love, then people in love who engage in sexual relations, whether they are married to one another, no one, or someone else, are behaving in a manner consistent with this definition. If sex is thought of as good clean "fun," then sexual congress with just about anyone is consistent with this meaning. If sex is symbolic of the exclusive commitment of married persons to one another, then only sex within the marriage relationship is consistent with this understanding. At this juncture in history, no one definition of the meaning of sex can be asserted as the only one having social support. One individual frequently holds several different contradictory meanings for different situations.

No one can look to social or medical or biological science to justify or condemn any sex code or meaning of sex. In the realm of science there is no warrant for premarital sexual freedom, restriction, or continence. Whether a nationwide consensus on a sex code will emerge from the present confusion, a few decades should tell. Meanwhile, those who live and love in the interim have the widest possible scope for autonomous decision-making.

Autonomous decision-making presupposes knowledge of the consequences of acts. For the unmarried American today, it is particularly difficult to predict the consequences of his sexual behavior (or nonbehavior) for himself or his partner. He probably has little understanding of the symbolic meaning of sex for himself or his partner and little appreciation of the interrelationships between his sexual behavior and other values he holds dear. (In this he is no different from married Americans, but at least for them the normative guidelines are more nearly universal.) There is a high probability that his partner has different sexual values than his own and, furthermore, that he does not know what his partner's values are. Under these conditions, it is not surprising that even the best-intentioned behavior has unintended outcomes. It is for this reason that cautious counselors advise adherence to traditional norms of premarital sexual chastity. On the other hand, the consequences in continent relationships are for the same reasons no less unpredictable.

Love

7

Contemporary Americans are so used to assuming that love is not only compatible with marriage, but a necessary condition for marriage, that it usually comes as a surprise to learn that earlier traditions in Western society held the contrary to be true.

> . . . Queen Eleanor of England had the following curious case brought before her court:—
>
> "A gentleman was deeply smitten with a lady who had given her affections to another. She, however, was so favourable to him, that she promised if ever a time should arrive when she should be deprived of her first lover, she would then give ear to his prayers and adopt him as the successor. A little time afterwards the lady and her first lover married. The gentleman immediately, pleading a decision of the Countess of Champagne's demanded the love of the newly-married lady, for in that decision it was solemnly laid down that real love cannot exist between married people. The lady, however, resisted his application, declaring that she had not lost the love for her lover by marrying him." After careful deliberation of the court, Queen Eleanor pronounced the decision as follows:—
>
> "We are not inclined to controvert the decision of the Countess of Champagne, to the effect that true love cannot exist between married people. This, a solemn and deliberate decree of the afore-mentioned court, ought to hold good. Accordingly we order that the lady grant to her imploring lover the favours which he so earnestly entreats, and which she so faithfully has promised. . . ." (Bernard et al., 1959: 149–150).

The Meaning of Love

Americans marry for love. The importance and generality in American culture of the value of marrying for love is not disputed by any scholar

Table 7-1

THE MEANING OF LOVE: DEFINITIONS OF COLLEGE STUDENTS	
Feeling or Attraction	
"Love represents a magnetic attraction between two persons."	
"Love is a feeling of high emotional affiliation . . . which sends a person's ego into dizzying heights."	
"Love is the emotional feeling two people receive when they both have sexual and Platonic love in the proper proportions."	40%
Companionship and Compatibility	
"Love is the physical and mental compatibility of two people."	
"Love is the end result of a mature union of two compatible personalities."	
"Love . . . is helping the other person whenever he needs it . . . being his companion. It's having common goals, dreams, and ambitions."	
"Love . . . is doing things together and liking it."	20%
Giving	
"Love is giving—time, understanding, yourself."	
"Love is to give of oneself to another."	
"Love is giving trust."	
"Love is a give and take relationship—and mostly 'give'."	
Security	
"Love is having security in being wanted and knowing you have someone to rely on."	
"When a person is in love the world is right and a person has security."	17%
Realistic or Practical	
"Love for the girl is cooking for him, washing his clothes and keeping the home in order. For the man it is providing security, safety, and helping his wife."	
"Love to me is faithfulness to my mate and caring for our children."	3%
Total	100%

known to this writer, nor would more than a small fraction of Americans reject the idea. Since the value is so widely accepted, it is for this very reason difficult to determine for what percentage of American marriages love is the major motivation. Other reasons such as economic gain, status achievement, rebellion against parents, escape from loneliness, "everyone else is doing it," and sexual gratification are either culturally unsupported or actually shameful. Perhaps under these circumstances it is necessary for most Americans to convince themselves they are marrying for love, whether or not this was the original motivation. Once they convince themselves, love can actually become the "real" reason for marriage.

When one asks the average American to define the kind of love for which he will marry, the usual answers are a pious potpourri of conventional Christianity, popular sociology, and parlor psychology. Table 7-1 gives a representative set of responses to the question "What is love?" from college students.

It is easy to determine where this confusion comes from. A sampling of definitions of love from marriage and family texts and the writings of psychologists, psychiatrists, philosophers, ministers of religion, poets, and other experts on love produces a similar conglomeration. Many persons when confronted with this terminological confusion try to maintain that actually the word has a different meaning for each person. While at first glance this might seem to be close to the truth, in fact it is a senseless conclusion. When Americans talk about being in love, whether they use the same definitions or not when pressed for definitions, they are talking about a common experience, more or less recognizable in the self and in other people. Although it seems unnecessary to set forth an explicit verbal definition, that of Goode is probably as widely acceptable as any: "A strong emotional attachment . . . between adolescents or adults of opposite sexes, with at least the components of sex desire and tenderness" (Goode, 1959).

Goode's definition intentionally avoids specifying the motivation for the emotional attachment, because here is where most of the disagreement about love arises among laymen and scholars alike. Here also is where the value judgments about love become inseparable from the definitions. Each "school" of love limits the "true" love to one based on motivations acceptable to its value system or its theoretical orientation. Erich Fromm, for example, maintains that the love must be self-less, not motivated by personal gratification to be received. This is quite consonant with traditional Christian theology and the idea of the unmotivated love of God, ultimately derived from the Greek concept of *agape,* or spiritual love. Love based on any other motivation is not "true" love. On the other hand, Winch maintains that love is essentially motivated by self-gratification. Any other explanation for its occurrence makes it "unmotivated," hence psychologically unexplainable (Winch, 1958).

Freud, as is now well known, explained love as "aim-inhibited sex." Though this definition is no longer widely held, it is still followed by a few scholars. Reik, an apostate psychoanalyst, takes his main issue with Freud on this point, maintaining that the roots of sex desire and love are quite distinct (Reik, 1945). These, however, are not disagreements over the emotional phenomenon itself, but over the explanation of its occurrences.

Rubin (1970, 1973) suggests that there are three components of romantic love: affiliative and dependent need for the loved one, a predisposition to help the lover, and absorption in the relationship to the exclusion of others. Items to measure these components comprise his scale of love (see Table 7-2). Answers to the items range from 1, "Not at all true; disagree completely," to 9, "Definitely true; agree completely." Rubin found that a high score is correlated with a couple saying they are in love and that the chances of their marrying are good; a low score correlates with a couple saying they are not in love and that they probably will not marry. Scores are not significantly related to the length of time a couple has been dating. The scale of liking in Table 7-2 was devised by Rubin to distinguish romantic love from friendship. Items in this scale define close same-sex friendships. As you can

Table 7-2

ROMANTIC LOVE AND FRIENDSHIP CAN BE MEASURED SEPARATELY
Correlations with total scale scores of love-scale and liking-scale items

Love-scale items	Women		Men	
	Correlation between love item and love-scale total minus that item	Correlation between love item and liking-scale total minus that item	Correlation between love item and love-scale total minus that item	Correlation between love item and liking-scale total minus that item
1. I feel that I can confide in ___ about virtually everything	.524	.274	.425	.408
2. I would do almost anything for ___.	.630	.341	.724	.530
3. If I could never be with ___, I would feel miserable.	.633	.276	.699	.422
4. If I were lonely, my first thought would be to seek ___ out.	.555	.204	.546	.328
5. One of my primary concerns is ___'s welfare.	.606	.218	.683	.290
6. I would forgive ___ for practically anything.	.551	.185	.394	.237
7. I feel responsible for ___'s well-being.	.582	.178	.548	.307
8. I would greatly enjoy being confided in by ___.	.498	.292	.513	.383
9. It would be hard for me to get along without ___.	.676	.254	.663	.464

see in Table 7-2, love and liking are separate phenomena; the 9 items that correlate significantly with love are not good measures of liking, and the 9 liking items are only insignificantly correlated with the love-scale items. (It is interesting that an additional item in an earlier version of the love scale, "I find it easy to ignore _____'s faults," had to be removed because it was more highly correlated with the liking than with the love scale; perhaps love is not blind after all.)

Driscoll, Davis, and Lipetz (1972) found that love changes over time, having fewer components of romantic love and more components of friendship as the relationship progresses. Like Rubin, they define romantic love as consisting of affiliative and dependent needs and feelings of exclusiveness and absorption but, unlike Rubin, they exclude the predisposition to help and include physical attraction and passion and idealization. They call the love that develops over time conjugal love, and define it to include such friendship components as trust, consideration, dependability, and uncritical acceptance. Forty-nine seriously dating couples and 91 couples who had been married for a mean of 4 years rated the amount of love, trust, and criticalness they felt for their partners. Couples performed this rating twice, the second time 6 to 10 months after the first. In this sample, love was more

Table 7-2 (Continued)

	Women		Men	
Liking-scale items	*Correlation between love item and liking-scale total minus that item*	*Correlation between liking item and liking-scale total minus that item*	*Correlation between love item and liking-scale total minus that item*	*Correlation between liking item and liking-scale total minus that item*
1. I think that ＿＿ is unusually well-adjusted.	.093	.452	.339	.610
2. I would highly recommend ＿＿ for a responsible job.	.199	.370	.281	.422
3. In my opinion, ＿＿ is an exceptionally mature person.	.190	.559	.372	.609
4. I have great confidence in ＿＿'s good judgment.	.310	.538	.381	.562
5. Most people would react very favorably to ＿＿ after a brief acquaintance.	.167	.366	.202	.287
6. I think that ＿＿ is one of those people who quickly wins respect.	.182	.588	.370	.669
7. ＿＿ is one of the most likable people I know.	.346	.402	.438	.514
8. ＿＿ is the sort of person whom I myself would like to be.	.253	.340	.417	.552
9. It seems to me that it is very easy for ＿＿ to gain admiration.	.176	.528	.345	.519

Source: Rubin, 1970, 1973, reprinted with permission

highly correlated with trust and uncritical acceptance for married than for unmarried couples, and for the unmarried couples, love became more highly correlated with the friendship components during the time between the first and second ratings.

Love: A Cross-Cultural Perspective

Judging from recent texts, one might easily come to the conclusion that Americans had invented love (at least "romantic love"), and more especially that the connection between love and marriage is a peculiarly American innovation. This view used to be popular among anthropologists, who as a group gave the impression that love as a social pattern exists only in the United States, or at least only in contemporary Western societies.

All societies recognize that there are occasional violent emotional attachments between persons of opposite sex, but our present American culture is practically the only one which has attempted to capitalize these and make them the basis for marriage. Most groups regard them as unfortunate and point out the victims of such attachments as horrible examples. Their rarity in most societies suggests that they are psychological abnormalities . . . (Linton, 1936: 175).

Yet, Stephens, reviewing ethnographic notes on 19 cultures, says that of these there are 7 in which romantic love is said to occur "sometimes," 5 in which it "seldom occurs," and 7 others in which it may be completely absent (Stephens, 1963: 204).

Goode, reviewing essentially the same studies as the previously quoted authors, suggests that love is a universal psychological potential. When the society allows unmarried heterosexual interaction, especially where there is a strongly developed adolescent peer group, a love pattern will develop. Societies vary, Goode says, mainly in the degree to which the structure of social interaction allows the conditions of love to flourish and in the extent to which they allow these love relationships to influence marital choice (Goode, 1959). There are many features of American society which encourage the freedom of love choices in directing mate selection. The emphasis on individualism in American culture justifies the choice of mate on the basis of the welfare of the individual rather than the family or some other collectivity. The emphasis on the pursuit of happiness as the worthy goal of life encourages selection of mates on the basis of love. Loyalty to kinship groups other than one's immediate family has little hold on Americans. Few Americans outside members of the most wealthy families need be concerned with preserving succession lines in the family enterprises, and for most people inheritance of land or wealth does not loom large enough to make mate selection a financial transaction. All of these factors combine to minimize the stake of the family and the community in the choice of mates. When these factors are combined with the ideology of marriage as an association for emotional gratification, the circumstances are ideal for love to dominate mate choice. American society sets up the conditions in which love flourishes and then allows it considerable freedom in influencing mate selection.

Love has a long historical tradition in Western culture. Far from having been invented in the twentieth century, as some discussions suggest, romantic love has been traced by Beigel back to the twelfth-century troubadours and the concept of "courtly love" (Beigel, 1951). Sussman maintains that by the eighteenth century the idea of romantic love as central to courtship was well established in Europe and was brought to America by the earliest settlers (Sussman, 1963).

Other writers find a love pattern in classical Greece and Rome (Hunt, 1959), and the following "Ode to Atthis," written twenty-five centuries ago by Sappho to her favorite girl friend, indicates that the symptoms were the same then as now:

> For should I but see thee a little moment,
>   Straight is my voice hushed;
> Yea, my tongue is broken, and through and through me
> 'Neath the flesh, impalpable fire runs tingling;

Nothing see mine eyes, and a voice of roaring
　　Waves in my ear sounds;
Sweat runs down in rivers, a tremor seizes
All my limbs, and paler than grass in autumn,
Caught by pains of menacing death, I falter,
　　Lost in the love-trance.[1]

The emotion of love has probably existed as a natural social phenomenon wherever young people were allowed to associate with the opposite sex. Wherever it has existed, it has had as much influence on mate selection as the society would let it have. American society seems to have conditions under which love flourishes, with maximum opportunity for love to influence marital selection.

Socialization for Love in American Society

In a society such as ours and a few others where love is institutionalized, that is, the focus of patterned, expected, and approved behavior, the children have more than their psychological impulses to depend upon for insuring that they will experience love. They have a training process as well. In American society this training process has certainly developed unplanned, but nevertheless appears as a pervasive program of socialization. The institutionalization of love is accomplished through what will be referred to as the romantic love myth. People can and do fall in love where the myth is absent, but the patterning of expectations provided by the myth insures that only those who are very obtuse, emotionally incapacitated, or perversely reared will be deprived of the experience of love.

Briefly stated, the romantic love myth is the idea that "for every girl there is a boy; when they know each other they will fall in love, experience bliss, and live together happily ever after."

CASE

It was one week to the day after my mother's death when I saw Georgia for the first time. I was flying back to my post from the funeral. A sailor, hitching a ride, shared my seat on the plane. I was reading a book when Georgia came aboard. The sailor whistled and I looked up. I saw Georgia in the aisle. Sunshine was tangled in her wonderful blond hair, and her lips and eyes were smiling. It was as though an inner voice spoke to me. Anyhow I heard my voice speak to the sailor. "Take it easy, bud," I said. "That's the girl I'm going to marry."

Compared to Georgia, who is intensely practical, I suppose I sound like a dreamy-eyed dope. But I still believe it was destiny that forced down our plane and gave me four days to court her. I know Georgia and I were meant to love each other and be happy (Popenoe and Disney, 1960: 169).

[1] Quoted by Morton M. Hunt, *The Natural History of Love* (New York: Alfred A. Knopf, 1959), p. 45.

Actually, few will admit that they believe the myth—but they know it by heart. They hope to experience it, and they organize their actions so as to maximize their opportunity to experience it. They are disappointed if it does not happen to them and are disillusioned after it goes away.

The telling of the myth is begun in the nursery with fairy tales: Cinderella, Sleeping Beauty, Snow White, Frog Prince, and half a hundred less famous stories. Hardly any child *believes* the tales, but they all have the same message: A handsome prince overcomes obstacles to marry the poor maid with whom he has fallen in love; they are married and live in bliss. Alternately, the handsome but poor peasant boy overcomes obstacles to marry the princess, with whom he has fallen in love; they are married and live in bliss. Always beauty, always obstacles, always love, always a class barrier (presumably changing from frog to human leaps an ethnic barrier), always married bliss. The unsaid last line of each story is "some day this may happen to you." Parents set the proper example for their children by relating to the child their own prince-and-beauty story. "Why did you marry Daddy?" "Because we fell in love."

The child of elementary school age today experiences a barrage of romantic symbols which is inescapable. He cannot help but notice the cult of the teenager, who becomes his behavioral model far into the preteens. What is the outstanding experience of adolescence? Romance. The popular song is part of the environment of the elementary school child, and one sociologist has estimated that 90 percent of popular songs are about romance (Horton, 1957). They tell how it feels to fall in love, what one does when one is in love, and with whom and under what circumstances one normally falls in love. They provide a vocabulary for love and a ready-made set of fantasies and symbols with which to experience and express love. By the second grade, every girl knows not to talk about a "boy friend" (as distinct from a "friend," which after kindergarten signifies only a friend of the same sex) unless she means someone she "loves" and "wants to marry." Middle-elementary-school children tease each other about love and boy friends and wanting to marry someone.

The adolescent milieu is so saturated with love symbols that it is difficult to see why some adolescents manage to take so long to fall in love. By mid-adolescence, whatever psychological proclivity for love there is in human beings has been powerfully reinforced and elaborated into a compelling set of expectations to use the emotional responses one has rehearsed and stored in readiness. The adolescent in American society should have developed an overpowering need to fall in love, and he usually does. Perhaps Linton is right that "in any ordinary population the percentage of individuals with a capacity for romantic love of the Hollywood type [is] about as large as that of persons able to throw genuine epileptic fits." Even Linton recognizes the powerful need created in American society, as he continues, "However, given a little social encouragement, either one can be adequately imitated without the performer even admitting to himself that the performance is not genuine" (Linton, 1936). As another writer put it, "by auto-suggestion and imitation she can usually convince herself of the unfathomable depth of her affection to anyone who speaks of love" (Beigel, 1951: 333).

This powerfully generated need for falling in love, coupled with the culturally provided cues for when and how it should happen, provides an important clue to the understanding of mate selection in American society. With his meticulous preparation, when the adolescent experiences the syndrome described so long ago by Sappho, he knows he is "in love."

CASE

I was first in love about two years ago. I couldn't see enough of my boyfriend. When he walked into a room I felt a kind of tingling sensation. He would walk me to every class and we would talk outside of the door until after the bell rang. I was always in a happy, ecstatic mood. I had a hard time sleeping at night because I was excited and I couldn't eat a thing. My parents really believed I was "living on love." I lost twenty pounds during this period, which is really great.

It used to be customary in texts on courtship and marriage to help the reader understand how he could tell when he is experiencing "true love" or when he was experiencing "mere infatuation." Various advisers offer different advice on this point. Infatuation was said to be a temporary phenomenon, while love was lasting. However, one must ask, how long is temporary? In order to distinguish feelings on this basis, one must, of course, wait until it is over; then he will know he was infatuated. Others maintained that infatuation was "mere" sexual attraction, while in love the sexual element is subdued or secondary. This gives the appearance, however, of moral judgment passing as science. To the person experiencing the emotion, the "cause" of the emotion is not susceptible to analysis. Further, experts, much less his parents and friends, are really not agreed enough to be able to tell him the "cause." In fact, it seems clear that infatuation is a word used only to describe a disapproved or devalued love relationship. Infatuated is what you were with him before you met me. Infatuated is what one's daughter is with that boy who rides the motorcycle. Infatuated is what the person with whom one is in love is with that little tramp. As an analytical term to assist in decision-making about the future of relationships, the word is worthless. Whatever the motivation or duration of the relationship, these are unknowables at the time. What is knowable at the time is the emotional experience, and that emotional experience is what Americans mean by being in love.

The reason for the debate over whether "it" is "true love" is America's close cultural association of love and marriage. If one says "It is love," he is in a way saying "and a proper basis for marriage." Perhaps the conceptualization could be refined to the place where one could say, "Love is one prerequisite for marriage; there are others; I have this one prerequisite: the feeling of love. If and when I get the other prerequisites (whatever they are), then I will marry." There seems to be something in the question of what is "true love," however, as one hears it discussed, which suggests that it is really only "true love" which is a prerequisite for marriage. This is what gives Americans the tendency to tie up with the emotional "bang" a number of unrelated social and psychological requirements and call the whole package "love." It is no wonder that there is confusion.

Love and Sex

The relationship between love and sex is of considerable importance to the person who wishes to understand his own behavior. Here, as in so many other areas of behavior where people would like definitive answers, different scientists give different answers. Discussion of the topic in this book needs to be divided into the answers to two distinct questions: first, what is the scientific explanation of the relationship between love and sex, and second, what do cultural values say should be the relationship between love and sex? The answers are interdependent.

What are the scientific explanations of the relationship between love and sex, and what is the evidence for each? Freud's famous aphorism, "Love is aim-inhibited sex," has already been quoted. Waller has given the statement more detail in his explanation: "Love is an idealized passion which develops from the frustration of sex" (Waller, 1938: 189). At all times in history, Freud maintains, "Wherever natural barriers in the way of satisfaction have not sufficed, mankind has erected conventional ones in order to be able to enjoy love" (Freud, 1922). The exhilaration of love, then, is explained as receiving much of its force from biological impulses blocked by cultural prohibitions.

A good deal of evidence can be advanced in favor of this explanation. If it is true that love comes from a blocked sex drive, one would logically have to maintain that with the unblocking of the sex drive, with the aim no longer inhibited, the love would perforce disappear. Likewise, where there is no cultural block to sexual release, love should not appear in the first place. Anthropologists have pointed to several cases which support this thesis. Mead observes its truth for the Samoans (Mead, 1928) and Malinowski for the Trobrianders (Malinowski, 1929). Pineo's twenty-year follow-up of the Burgess-Wallin couples indicates a *gradual* decline in love over the course of marriage which *might* be attributed to the disappearance of the sex blockage. On the other hand, he also notes a decline in sex interest as well (Pineo, 1961). Since Pineo's observations show a decline after twenty years that Burgess and Wallin did not notice after three years in the first follow-up, one might conclude (as Pineo does) that other factors are significant in the decline of love.

Blood reviewed the anthropological evidence available to him, including the studies by Mead and Malinowski, and concluded that romance and premarital intercourse are incompatibles—that both cannot exist in a society at the same time (Blood, 1952). Many writers of texts for functional family courses have maintained that these constitute important reasons for couples to save their sexual enjoyment of each other until marriage. One might argue just as logically, however, that if love is not to be damaged, one should follow the advice of the twelfth-century courts of love and avoid marriage with the loved one also (Beigel, 1951). A step further would be the continent marriage which was praised by some early Christian writers (Hunt, 1959: 93–100).

On the other hand, the anthropological and historical evidence for love as blocked sex is not nearly so compelling. Stephens, in his cross-cultural survey (Stephens, 1963: 207), provides the following run-down of societies: of 7 in which romantic love is said to be completely absent, 4 have extreme sexual liberty, 1 has moderate sexual liberty, and the other 2 are rather strict. Of 5 cases in which romantic love is said to occur "seldom," 2 have a good deal of sexual liberty, on 1 there is no information, and 2 have rather severe sexual restrictions. The evidence is certainly ambiguous. From literary and historical data, Hunt provides us with case history after case history where overt sexual relationships did not spell the end of love, and many cases where love in fact became a part of the relationship only after a sexual affair was well under way (Hunt, 1959). Kirkendall analyzed the interpersonal relationships of 200 college males to the 668 women with whom they were involved in premarital sexual liaisons. He could not come to the conclusion that when a love affair led to premarital intercourse, it had any particular detrimental effect on the love relationship (Kirkendall, 1961). Burgess and Wallin reported that couples who had premarital sexual intercourse did not hold different attitudes toward one another than those who did not have intercourse. Their affection and idealization of one another was apparently not affected by their sexual relationship (Burgess and Wallin, 1953: 239–242).

The most flagrant case of a love syndrome occurring in a society with widespread premarital sexual freedom is reported among the Gilyak, a Siberian hunting tribe. Blessed with a plentiful supply of game and the leisure to pursue the more aesthetic pleasures, the Gilyak's favorite recreation is premarital and extramarital sex. Groups of men make voyages to distant villages in search of sexual adventure. While at home, they divide their time between guarding the women in their families and seducing the wives and daughters of others. Yet, a very elaborate romantic love pattern exists. Most of the songs are love songs, the poetry is romantic, and the language of courtship is romantic. Young lovers who cannot marry often commit suicide in the best romantic traditions. This separation of romantic love from marriage is characteristic of the group, for marriage is not contracted on grounds of mutual attraction, but arranged by the parents on the basis of economic and family considerations (Chard, 1961).

Other Origins of Love

Not all scholars have accepted the sexual origin of love. The basic contribution of Theodor Reik to psychoanalytic thought was his development of a psychology of love as distinct from sex. In fact, Reik goes so far as to maintain that sex is really out of the realm of the psychologist and is the business of the biochemist and physiologist (Reik, 1945: 9). Love stems from purely psychic needs or, more specifically, from dissatisfaction with one's self — it rests in a discrepancy between the perceived self and the ego-ideal. One falls in love with that person to whom one attributes the characteristics of one's ego-ideal, and therefore, "two people who love each other are interchanging their ego-ideals" (Reik, 1945: 34). Put another way, Reik says that falling in love is a result of perceiving a deficiency in the self when compared to the ideal self, and finding another person to whom one can attribute the traits one lacks. By identifying with them, one makes up for this ego-deficiency. Falling in love is easiest with someone who makes the lover feel important and worthwhile. Martinson has shown that for both women (1955) and men (1959), those who marry first reveal greater signs of personal and social maladjustment than those who remain single for a longer period. Other marital adjustment studies have shown that self-sufficiency is negatively associated with marital adjustment. The self-sufficient, by definition, do not need enduring and intimate emotional involvement with anyone else. Cartoonist Jules Feiffer, in his book, *Harry, the Rat with Women,* presents a cruel satire in which love is seen as "a disease spread by the insecure to corrupt the self-possessed."

Ohmann defines love as a feeling of need for another personality to complete, supplement, or protect one's own (Ohmann, 1942: 28). Winch has developed this need-based theory of love into an elaborate theory of mate selection. His definition of love contains his explanation of the origins of love:

> Love is the positive emotion experienced by one person in an interpersonal relationship in which the second person either (1) meets certain important needs of the first, or (2) manifests or appears to manifest personal attributes highly prized by the first, or both (Winch, 1963: 579).

The explanations of love offered by Winch, Ohmann, and Reik (and many others) are fundamentally different from those theories which find the basis for love in the sex drive. Rather, love is seen as deriving from the fulfillment of certain kinds of personality needs of the lover—needs which may largely be socially generated (Winch, 1963: 574).

An Integrated Explanation of Love

The three theories of the origin of love that have been cited are not entirely mutually exclusive: certainly the blocking of sex fulfillment is culturally created. Feelings of inadequacy and other personality needs may certainly be seen as culturally generated. The culture—such as modern American culture—which has developed romantic love to its most important level certainly has a socialization process which predisposes people to fall in love.

The three theories of the origin of love might be integrated in the following way: *the emotion of love can be generated by the blocking of sex, by feelings of personal inadequacy and the meeting of personality needs in an interpersonal heterosexual relationship, and by conditioning everyone in a culture to expect to and need to experience the love syndrome.* The more of these processes a culture brings into play, the more important the love experience in that culture will be. Modern American society provides all three processes: sex blockage, heterosexual interaction with the opportunity for mutual meeting of needs, and a culturally induced expectation that everyone will fall in love. This should produce the maximum occurrence of love relationships. Furthermore, the loss of one, or even two, of the generating processes would not necessarily eliminate the experience, although it might substantially lower its frequency and intensity.

Examples of cultures can be found where love and sex bear little relationship to one another and others where they are joined or are expected to be joined. In American culture, middle-class values maintain that sex should be a way of expressing love. It is clear that Americans do not think that it always *is.* Exploitive sex relationships of men and prostitution in women are unacceptable because they do *not* embody a fusion of sex and love. Nearly everyone would agree that masturbation and nocturnal emissions are sex, but few would call them love. Sex and love are more closely fused for women than for men. On the other hand, the fusion of sex and love (or at least the *value* of the sex-love fusion) seems not to be a strong part of lower-class American life, especially for males (Green, 1941; Miller, 1958). Even on this class level, Kirkendall reports at least a vestigial trace of it among lower-class girls who ask for a profession of love, however trivial, as a preliminary to permitting coitus (Kirkendall, 1961).

In other societies, the extent to which love and sex are expected to be related varies widely. Gough reports that sex relations among the Nayar were devoid of lasting emotional attachment (Gough, 1952). Stephens' analysis indicates, as do most anthropological accounts, that there are some societies where love does not appear at all (Stephens, 1963), but there are no societies where sex does not occur (excluding certain religious communities, which could hardly be counted societies). In old Chinese fiction, men and women fell in love and had sexual relations (Winch, 1963: 611), but in real life love seldom occurred, and one was not expected to experience love with sex (Yang, 1945), although one was probably more affectionate with a concubine than with a wife. After all, a man picked his own concubine, but not his own wife.

Almost any pattern of relative occurrence of love and sex can be acculturated. In some places, there are no significant emotional heterosexual peer attachments which qualify as love under our original definition. In other places and other times, a sexual relationship develops with some people without love and with others with love, both by the same person. In still others, love is rarely experienced with sex partners, although it may be with other persons.

If love and sex can vary in their joint occurrence to such a great extent, it is unreasonable to maintain that the important root of love is frustration of sex. Americans are taught that they should feel the two together, and apparently to a considerable extent they actually do, though not as much as they think they should. For people who are not taught that sex and love must go together, however, they do not.

Falling in Love As an Interpersonal Process

When couples who have married or are in love are asked to describe falling in love, few say that it was a sudden occurrence. Nearly all describe a process of gradually falling in love. Different love relationships show different emotional trends. In a study of the emotional experiences in the broken love affairs of college students, Kirkpatrick and Caplow (1945) discovered almost a dozen different patterns.

Sociologists have attempted to describe the interpersonal processes involved in the development of a love relationship. Reiss (1960) has suggested the following model for love development. At the beginning of a relationship, a couple experiences a feeling of rapport with one another, a feeling of being at ease in one another's company, of a smooth flow of communication. If the feeling of rapport is not there, and they feel awkward, irritated, or ill-at-ease with one another, they are not likely to develop the relationship beyond initial interaction. The feeling of rapport is a form of mutual gratification, which then leads the couple to a process of gradual self-revelation, where previous experiences, private feelings, and future

Chart 7-1

LOVE AS A DEVELOPMENTAL PROCESS

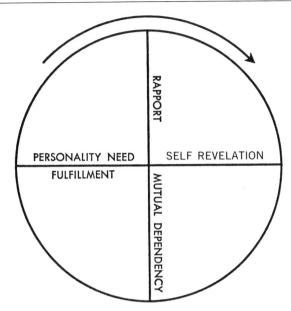

THE WHEEL THEORY OF THE DEVELOPMENT OF LOVE

aspirations are shared with one another. In the process of spending a large amount of time with each other, they gradually develop habits which are interdependent, so that the presence of the other is necessary to the performance of the habits developed. This mutual dependence in turn provides the setting for the fulfillment of the personality needs of each member of the couple, which should in turn enhance their feeling of rapport. Of course, it may be presumed that the initial feeling of rapport is based on fulfillment of felt personality needs. Because of the circular nature of this process, Reiss calls it a "wheel theory." (See Chart 7-1.)

Reiss points out that the wheel process can also unwind. Suppose that the process of mutual self-revelation produces incompatible views, offense, or argument. This should lead to a decline in the feeling of rapport and a decline in felt need fulfillment, with gradual disentanglement of interdependency as the response. In this way, the same model can be used to describe the deterioration of a love relationship as an interpersonal process.

Greenberg and Corwin (1962) give a psychological explanation of the process of falling in love. The need for a love satisfier, however developed, is seen as a learned drive which needs to be satisfied. As a single person gradually provides another sufficient pleasure over sufficient time, the drive is said to be "canalized" upon that individual, that is, that individual becomes more and more able to satisfy the drive, and other individuals therefore become relatively less satisfying in comparison to the loved one. This formulation is quite consistent with Reiss's above, emphasizing the cumulative nature of the love relationship.

Sex Differences in Romantic Experience

Traditionally most people have imagined that women were more given to romanticism than men: that they believed in romance, experienced romantic emotions more readily, and were more easily swept off their feet. But three decades of research have consistently contradicted this notion. Every study confirms that at least in questionnaire responses, women have more practical and realistic orientations toward love than men. In fact, relatively few college students of either sex agree with the typical statements on romanticism scales. Typical statements: "When you are really in love, you just aren't interested in anyone else; When love hits you know it; Love at first sight is often the deepest and most enduring type of love" (Knox, 1968: 25).

Either males or females can be considered the more romantic, depending on the criteria. Kanin, Davidson, and Scheck (1970) studied a group of college students' love experiences. They found that males tend to fall in love more quickly than females (and hence could be considered more romantic on that score), while the females, once in love, were more likely to experience the traditionally described euphoria of love (floating on a cloud, wanting to run, jump and scream, trouble concentrating, etc.) and to idealize the personalities of their mates.

Rubin (1970) found that love and liking were more highly correlated for men than for women (see Table 7-2), suggesting that women make sharper distinctions between love and liking than men do. Rubin also found that women liked their boyfriends more than their boyfriends liked them, although both scored high on love.

The Romeo and Juliet Effect

The literary tradition of Western society holds that romantic love thrives on obstacles. Parental opposition to the relationship is certainly one of the most celebrated obstacles. Driscoll, Davis, and Lipetz (1972) argue that this is consistent with theories in contemporary social psychology that "opposition to the group or restrictions of the group's activities and goals

. . . increases group solidarity." Working with a group of 49 dating couples and 91 married couples, these researchers showed that the more parental interference the couples reported, the higher their feelings of romantic love. The relationship was stronger for the unmarrieds than for the marrieds. Reinterviewing the couples 6 to 10 months later, they found that for the unmarrieds (but not for the marrieds), changes in the level of parental interference experienced were correlated with changes in the level of romantic love. They call this correlation "the Romeo and Juliet effect." It is satisfying to have statistical evidence to demonstrate what we intuitively know is true.

Multiple Loves

Apparently it is not only possible to fall in love many times, but also possible to be in love with more than one person at the same time. According to the romantic myth, of course, this is impossible. The person who claims to be in love with two at the same time simply does not understand the situation. This makes sense from the point of view of the mythology. If love and marriage go together, and monogamy is accepted as the norm, then by definition one cannot love two people at once. In this case, well-meaning friends and counselors may advise a person in such a quandary that they are either in love with one or the other, or are not "really" in love with either. This is, of course, mythology support, and should not be mistaken for objective evaluation. Ellis (1949), studying a sample of college women, found that 25 percent of the 500 women reported having had simultaneous love relationships. Today only about half of American adolescents buy the idea that you can't be in love with more than one person at a time (Sorensen, 1973: 403).

In a more recent study, Kephart (1969) found a sample of college students reluctant to classify their multiple involvements as "love." While about 1 in 20 men and women admitted to being in love with more than one person at the same time, 1 in 2 admitted having been "infatuated" with two at once. Kephart found multiple involvement as common for men as for women.

Since the romantic norms preclude two simultaneous loves, those who experience two at once might be supposed to be maladjusted in some way. In fact, Kephart found that men with simultaneous involvements were over-represented in the less-well-adjusted personality test scores. This was not true for women. One might ponder the reason for this sex difference. In American culture, with men as seekers and women as continuers of relation-ships, once a man is involved romantically with one woman, he is likely to discontinue relationships with others. Women, on the other hand, may continue to allow themselves to be pursued by two lovers at once and fall in love with both simultaneously. Simultaneous loves are "within the rules" for women but not for men.

Human beings may be presumed to vary in their ability to invest themselves in human relationships, but it could be supposed that some women might be capable of a higher investment in each of two love relationships at once than other women could muster for a single one.

In the past, family text writers' dim view of romance predisposed them to describe romantic experience as an indication of personality maladjustment, or at best a sign of immaturity. Recent studies throw light on this belief. In his sample of college students, Kephart (1969) found that romantic experiences were if anything more common among the best adjusted. Romantic experience is the "normal" experience of youth: it is almost a requirement for a complete life. Under these circumstances we would expect the "best adjusted" to fit most smoothly into the cultural pattern, and the "least adjusted" to fit least well. Knox (1970) studied romantic attitudes toward love of 100 high school seniors, 100 persons married less than five years, and 100 persons married more than twenty years. He found the young marrieds the least romantic in their attitudes, with those married more than twenty years registering attitudes as romanticized as those of high school students. Who is immature?

The Functionality of the Love Marriage

Is love a good basis for selecting spouses for American society? Does it produce the kinds of marriages Americans want, or is it interfering with the achievement of the marriage goals of individuals and of the society? For a subject on which there is little research data, writers on marriage have had a lot to say concerning the functionality of love for the basis of marriage. Discourse is confounded by the usual catchbasket definitions of love.

Some writers maintain that "mature love" is a good basis for marriage, but "immature love" is not (Lantz and Snyder, 1962). "Companionship love" is a more successful basis than "romantic love." No writer recommends mate selection on the basis of "infatuation," but everyone praises "conjugal love." When "love" is used to include in its meaning not only the positive emotional attraction but common interests, desire to have children and share an economic interdependence, consensus, and companionship, then most writers think it a good basis for marriage. When love is used to mean an emotional attraction, as it has been defined here, then most writers think it a poor basis for marriage, but would also qualify it as a pseudo-love of some sort. This appears to be an attempt of the scholar to keep within the framework of the American value system. One should marry for love, the writers seem to be saying, but let us redefine love so as to include all the factors which sociologists have found associated with marital stability and happiness; then we can say that love is a good basis for marriage.

Baum (1971) found that 65 engaged men and women defined love as companionship, understanding, sharing, and giving of mutual support and affection. They emphasized companionship and communication as the most important part of marriage. Baum suggests that marrying for love, as love is defined by her engaged subjects, is conducive to marital dissatisfaction in our society. People become dissatisfied with marriage because it does not provide the close companionship that they call love and that they marry to maintain.

Over the past twenty-five years, an interesting trend is becoming apparent in family sociology. The early treatments of the love-based marriage by an older generation of sociologists are uniformly pessimistic about the effect of the love-basis on the marital institution. Authors of more recent texts, however, are less cynical in this belief about the detrimental effect. In their second edition, Burgess and Locke maintain, "All our data . . . point to the conclusion that, on the average, marriages resulting from comradely affection turn out happier than those chiefly inspired by romantic attitudes" (Burgess and Locke, 1953: 436). The third edition deletes this message and only states that "the longer the period of intimate association before marriage, the greater the probability of marital adjustment. Such marriages are likely to be based on companionship" (Burgess, Locke, and Thomes, 1963: 323). Mowrer, Truxal and Merrill, and Groves all take what are essentially antilove positions. De Rougemont (1959) argues that basing marriage, which is lasting, on love, which is a passing fancy, has sabotaged the marital institution. Kolb (1948), on the other hand, sees benefical effects in the love-marriage tradition for the society, and Beigel sees it as a real benefit.

In his study of 218 married college couples, Spanier (1972) found no indication that romantic love, as opposed to conjugal love, was harmful to marital adjustment. He states that, "among married couples in a college community, romanticism is not generally excessive, and . . . in cases where there is unusually high romanticism, marital adjustment is not likely to be any lower. In fact, a slight positive correlation [between romanticism and marital adjustment] was found."

Hardly a discussion of the functionality of love-selection is based on anything which would be called scientific evidence. Any evidence on which the later conclusions are based was also available to earlier writers. It would be easy to see family sociologists as a very conservative group who have only grudgingly come to accept the point of view of the layman with respect to love and marriage and how they go together.

Consequences of the Love-Based Marriage for the Society

In considering the functions of a love-based marriage, a balanced approach requires examination of its consequences for the rest of the society. As family sociologist William Goode (1959) has made clear, love as an unrestrained emotional occurrence between two persons is potentially destructive to the structure of society.

> Kinfolk or immediate family can disregard the question of who marries whom only if a marriage is not seen as a link between kin lines, only if no property, power, lineage honor, totemic relationships, and the like are believed to flow from the kin lines through the spouses to their offspring. Universally, however, these are believed to follow kin lines. Mate choice thus has consequences for the social structure. But love may affect mate choice. Both mate choice and love, therefore, are too important to be left to children.
>
> Since considerable energy and resources may be required to push youngsters who are in love into proper role behavior, love must be controlled *before* it appears. Love relationships must either be kept to a small number or they must be so directed that they do not run counter to the approved kinship linkages.[1]

In American society, the pattern which has evolved restricts the possibilities of falling in love as much as possible to those who are considered to be socially eligible mates—those who might enter a marriage which would support the existing social structure. Just how this restriction of choice is accomplished will be dealt with in the chapter on social factors in mate selection. For a society which has placed as much emphasis on love as American society, the control of love becomes unusually crucial for the maintenance of social organization. Given this emphasis, the ideology which encourages lovers to marry might easily be seen as making a positive contribution to social stability. By virtue of the present structure of society, love is going to occur on a large scale whether or not it is beneficial to society. *By harnessing marriage to love, its potential disruptive force is channeled to propel socially appropriate couples into marriage.* Those who see the love-based marriage as disfunctional argue that the couples so propelled are not always appropriate (they are too young, too socially different, or have the wrong motives). The extent to which this is so will be examined in the chapter on social factors and marital success. The objection only points to the ineffectiveness of the social restraints on who falls in love with whom. The more fundamental question is, will love relationships be more destructive of the fabric of

[1] William J. Goode, "The Theoretical Importance of Love," *American Sociological Review,* XXIV (1959), pp. 38–47. Reprinted by permission.

society if they are socially restricted and channeled toward marriage or if they are not directed within the institutional family system, but left to their own development?

Summary

Love has been defined as a strong emotional attachment, with at least the components of sex desire and tenderness. This is what Americans consider a prerequisite for marriage. Any college freshman can tell you that no one really thinks that is all which is required for the selection of a spouse with whom one will be happy. There exists a tendency, therefore, in the layman and the scholar alike, to combine into the definition of love those *other* factors which have come to be widely accepted as *additional* prerequisites to successful marriage and to define those relationships which do not contain all the necessary prerequisites as pseudo-loves.

Love has been known in every culture, but most societies have restricted its influence in mate selection. American culture has built mate selection upon love, at least as a prerequisite. The structures of some societies encourage the development of love relationships—American society more than most. Some peoples have tried to fuse love relationships to sexual relationships; others have considered them to be quite separate, or at least separable. In middle-class American society the only "moral" sex is sex as an expression of love, or at least sex and love directed toward the same object.

Although some scholars still see love as a basis of marriage as flimsy, ill-advised, or immature, the present generation of sociologists have caught up with the public feeling and see an expanded version of love as a reasonable basis for marriage.

Social Factors in Mate Selection

8

A primary concern of sociologists has been the discovery of how social characteristics of human beings structure their interaction with others. The characteristics in which sociologists have traditionally shown the greatest interest are age, sex, religion, race, national or ethnic identification, education, occupation, income, and status (the last four often grouped and studied as "social-class" variables). The importance of any one of these variables in a society can be measured by the extent to which those persons who differ in a particular variable also differ from one another in many other ways. For example, religion is an important social variable in a society if, knowing how two groups of people differ in religion, one can also tell a great deal about how they will vary in many other ways—education, income, personality, persons with whom they interact and do not interact, status, and so on. Since marriage is a fundamental relationship in many societies, the social characteristics which are the most important variables in a society will also be important considerations in mate selection.

Cross-Cultural Perspective

The most simple human societies are spoken of as simple because social organization in them is not very differentiated. In the most simple society conceivable, all people would belong in the same social category, that is, there would be no social differentiation and even people of different ages and sexes would play socially similar roles. No society that simple is known. Even the most simple assign different roles to each sex and different roles to different ages. In the most simple groups, age and sex are relevant variables in mate selection. The importance of sex difference is, of course, obvious by definition (although a few societies have special arrangements whereby two men or two women may marry and even rear adoptive children).

Age differences are a consideration for mate selection in all known groups, but the socially appropriate age match is not always the same. In only one society are men regularly expected to marry women older than themselves (Hart and Pilling, 1966). Normally, spouses are expected to be the same age, or the husband older. How much older varies considerably—sometimes husbands are routinely as much as fifteen or twenty years older than their wives. This is related to three factors. First, in most societies superiority is related to age, and most societies are male-superior societies. Second, men of all ages have typically preferred young women as sexual partners. Third, the female reproductive period is limited to twenty or thirty years, with fertility rapidly declining in the latter part of the period. A man of marriageable age cannot have a wife too much older than himself if he expects to have children.

As societies become more complex, other factors divide the society into subgroups, and the most important factors become relevant for mate selection. When societies have a class structure, one of the measures of the importance of class divisions is the limitation it places on marriage partners. As the importance of class-related differences increases, interclass marriages may be treated with social reactions varying from raised eyebrows to prohibition. When there are differences in religion in a society, the importance of those differences for other behavior can usually be guessed from the extent to which religion divides the people into separate marriage pools. So with all of the other variables—the more significant to a society are the differences between two categories of people, the less they intermarry.

KINSHIP RESTRICTIONS IN MATE SELECTION

One restriction on the field of eligible mates which is so much taken for granted it goes unnoticed is the prohibition against marrying persons within certain degrees of kinship. One of the most nearly universal features of social structure in all societies is the prohibition against marrying within one's own nuclear family of orientation. The only well-known society in which parent-child and sibling marriages have been routinely condoned was Ptolemaic Egypt (Middleton, 1962). Exactly what degrees of kinship are prohibited from marrying varies widely among known societies. In the United States, first cousins and closer degrees are usually prohibited from marriage. In other societies, the prohibited groups to which the incest taboo applies may extend to all of those in one's clan, the entire village, or even larger groups. In classical China, one was prohibited from marrying anyone with the same surname, even though the common relative might have lived five centuries ago. This restriction might exclude several million persons as eligible mates.

Social scientists have been fascinated with the universality of rules against incest and rules requiring family exogamy. The scholarly literature is replete with competing explanations. Most of these explanations depend on a recognition of some favorable social consequence which flows from the restriction: reduction of sexual conflict in the nuclear family, strengthening of family alliances, simplifying inheritance, maintaining authority patterns, or preventing deleterious inbreeding. While these may in fact be consequences of incest taboos, they are not the kinds of explanations most people are seeking. Half a century ago, Westermarck (1921) argued that humans who are reared from birth together in the normal course of events simply did not develop sexual interest in one another. A social taboo or prohibition was only needed to deal with deviant developments. Forty years later, Talmon (1964) provided empirical support for this position.

Studies of the Israeli *kibbutzim,* where children live apart from their parents in peer groups from birth through adolescence, reveal that sexual attachments and marriages between members of the same peer group are almost nonexistent. Of the 125 marriages studied by Talmon (1964), not one marriage consisted of partners raised from birth in the same peer group. This aversion to inmarriage is not the result of cultural restrictions. According to Talmon, not only are there no sanctions against intra-peer-group marriages, but many parents prefer that the child marry a member of his peer group.

Social Factors and Marital Selection in the United States

The influence of social factors on mate selection is one of the best studied and best understood areas of family behavior. In this section, only who marries whom will be discussed; the influence of social factors on marital success will be explored later.

AGE AND MATE SELECTION

In 6 out of 7 American marriages, the groom is as old as, or older than, the bride. In 2 out of 3 marriages, the difference in age is less than 5 years. An indication of the increasing importance of companionship in American marriages is the tendency for the difference in age of bride and groom to narrow in recent years. Relatively few boys marry before age 18, but those who do pick girls a few months their senior. After that age, grooms are progressively older than their brides, so that males marrying at 20 are 1 year older than their wives. Those marrying at 25 are 3 years older than their brides, and those at 37 are 6 years older than their brides, with the differences growing even wider for those marrying in old age. The picture from the bride's point of view is strikingly different. Girls marrying at 15 choose husbands from a wide age range but averaging 5 years older than

Table 8-1

	AGE AT MARRIAGE HAS DECLINED OVER THE LAST CENTURY *Median Age at First Marriage, by Sex: 1890 to 1971*	
Year	Male	Female
1890	26.1	22.0
1900	25.9	21.9
1910	25.1	21.6
1920	24.6	21.2
1930	24.3	21.3
1940	24.3	21.5
1950	22.8	20.3
1960	22.8	20.3
1971	23.1	20.9

Source: U.S. Current Population Reports, 1971, p. 2

themselves. The difference between the bride's age and that of her husband gradually narrows, so that brides marrying at 20 are 2.5 years younger than their husbands, and those marrying at age 22 to 37 are on the average 2 years younger than their husbands (Jacobson, 1959).

The average age at first marriage of both men and women has apparently been declining for the past century in the United States. In 1870, the median age for grooms was 26 and for brides 22. In 1940, the median age for brides was still 21.5, but after World War II the average age dropped about 1 year, and then stabilized at nearly 20.5 for the past two decades. (See Table 8-1.) In recent years the trend has been slightly reversed.

On the other hand, more girls marry at age 19 than during any other single year of age (U. S. Department of Health, Education, and Welfare, 1971: 26). Yet, age at marriage is directly related to number of years of education, and the proportion of persons going to college has continued to increase. One effect of the interaction of these several trends is the increasing number of college students who are married.

Chilman (1966) compared the characteristics of married and unmarried samples of college students to determine factors which are different in those who marry early. She reports the following interesting findings:

1. Early physical maturation is related to early marriage for males, but not for females.

2. Early age at first going steady is related to early marriage for both males and females.

3. Early-marrying girls were more likely to engage in petting and premarital intercourse and to do this at earlier ages than late-marrying girls. However, early-marrying and late-marrying men did not differ in their premarital sex behavior.

Elder (1972) reported additional differences between women who marry early and women who marry late. In his long-term longitudinal study,

73 women were tested in high school in the 1930s and then participated in at least one of the three follow-up studies in 1953, 1958, and 1964. Elder found that:

1. Women who married early were more likely to report that their parents were detached or disinterested in them, while women who married late tended to report that their parents had considerable (often too much) control over their lives.

2. The women who married early had less self-esteem than the women who married late. Early marriers underrated, and late marriers overrated, their own popularity. In spite of the fact that all 73 women had very similar IQ scores, those who married early rated themselves lower in academic aptitude and got lower grades, while the late marriers highly rated their own academic aptitudes and did better in school.

PROPINQUITY AND MATE SELECTION

Since all human behavior takes place in space, and since time and energy are involved in covering space, any kind of social interaction is spatially patterned. Cities are found to be patterned with people who are alike on important social variables living together and those who are different from one another spatially separated. It should surprise no one, then, that sociologists have consistently demonstrated that the likelihood of any individual selecting any given other individual as a spouse, other things being equal, is inversely related to the distance between their homes. (A recent researcher found the likelihood of marriage inversely related to the square of the distance—almost an exact parallel to the attraction of gravity and magnetism!) Surveys in dozens of American cities have revealed the same pattern of residence (Kephart, 1961: 268). Clarke (1952) found that more than half of the persons who marry in Columbus, Ohio, live within sixteen blocks of one another at the time of their first date together. Summarizing these studies, Kephart says, "Cherished notions about romantic love notwithstanding, it appears that when all is said and done, the 'one and only' may have a better than 50-50 chance of living within walking distance!" (Kephart, 1961: 269). This study was done some time ago when fewer adolescents had automobiles than today. Today one might not find propinquity as important a factor in mate selection.

Why do people marry other people who live near them? First, with socially similar people sorted out into the same residential areas, even if there were no other reasons, persons living near one another would marry because they were socially similar. Beyond this, the probability of meeting another person is obviously contingent on being reasonably near him during some period. After having met, the farther two people live apart, the more trouble it is to continue the interaction regularly. Katz and Hill (1958) applied Stouffer's "intervening opportunity" idea to the situation to suggest that the farther two people live apart, the more intervening opportunities for mate selection there are, and the more likely one is to choose one of the other opportunities. Just as there are limits on the time and money a man will spend commuting to work when there is closer work, so there are limits on how much time and money a man will invest in commuting to a particular girl's house when there are closer girls.

Later work on residential propinquity indicates that sheer "time and energy costs of crossing the intervening distance to engage in interaction" are more important than the number of intervening opportunities to interact with other similar persons. It is not very romantic to have to say that *physical location is the most significant limiter of mate selection* (Catton and Smirch, 1964). Shrewd parents have known and used this principle for a long time to break up "unfortunate" love interests of their children by moving away or encouraging their son or daughter to attend a college remote from home, perhaps "to test the endurance of the relationship."

CASE

To eliminate this boy for good, she suggested I go to college in Michigan. Not being too bright and really not caring, I fell for the idea.

The first term of college I dated many different males and had many new and different experiences. In November I had rather settled upon one boy. At Christmas vacation I discussed him with my parents, and they did not seem too concerned. Now everyone is concerned—I've gone with him too long is the cry. We plan to be married next June, and I can faithfully predict many problems in store for us. One being: guess who is not returning to Michigan next fall to attend school?

Separation during courtship is one of the most frequent reasons given for breaking engagements (Burgess and Wallin, 1953: 287-288; Landis and Landis, 1963: 230). Specifically, the more time a couple spends together during courtship, the more likely they are to marry. The farther they are apart, the harder it is to spend much time together.

SOCIAL CLASS AND MATE SELECTION

To what extent do social-class differences affect one's choice of mate? A number of studies provide data on this point, every one indicating that *persons marry with greater than chance frequency within their own social class.* Using the father's occupation as his measure of class, Centers (1949) found that both men and women tended to marry close to the occupational status of their own families. Hollingshead, studying a New Haven sample, found the same pattern. His results indicate that when class lines are crossed, the man selects a woman from a lower class much more often than the woman selects a man from a class lower than her own (Hollingshead, 1950).

A recent study has failed to confirm this finding, and actually found that slightly more women marry "down" than marry "up." Rubin (1968) found that only in marriages linking the professional-managerial and white-collar classes do women marry "up" more frequently than "down." This study, based on a representative national sample, leads us to conclude that *any overall tendency for women to marry either "up" or "down" is negligible.*

Sociologists have always been interested in the rate of cross-class marriage in the society, because it is usually seen as one of the major mechanisms for maintaining an open-class society where one is not doomed to the class position of one's parents. Since Americans pride themselves on the opportunities presented in American society for individual qualities to surmount social distinctions, the matter is of more general interest to them. Studies conducted to find out whether the amount of social mobility in the United States is increasing or decreasing have been inconclusive, but they generally point to no great change in mobility rates in recent generations. A recent study designed to find out whether interclass marriage was increasing or decreasing reported that the trend is in neither direction (Rubin, 1968). Rather, there appears to be a decline in the proportion of marriages in which the class discrepancy of the mates is very large, as well as a decline in the percentage of marriages in which the mates are from identical status levels. People are paying less attention to small differences and more attention to larger differences (Dinitz, Banks, and Pasamanick, 1960). Yet during the same period, possibly because of the influence of popular sociology, college students since World War II have been far more critical of marrying outside one's social class than were college students in the 1920s and 1930s (Rettig and Pasamanick, 1959).

EDUCATION AND MATE SELECTION

Since education in the United States tends to be fairly closely related to occupation, income, and other social-class variables, it should be expected that mates will select one another from similar educational levels. On the other hand, since men marry women slightly their junior, one might expect some differences in education. Chart 8-1 shows the situation for couples married between 1950 and 1960. Generally speaking, the figures show a tendency toward homogamy in education. These statistics must be balanced against the available supply of spouses at one's own educational level. Recent male college graduates outnumbered recent female college graduates two to one at the time represented by this table, and men with very little education substantially outnumbered women with very little education. Furthermore, to this must be added the fact that, in spite of recent increases, from one-fourth to one-third of college-educated women were not marrying at this time (Glick, 1957). It is clear that the tendency for college graduate men to select women on their own educational level is really over-

Chart 8-1

AMERICANS PICK SPOUSES AT THEIR OWN EDUCATIONAL LEVELS
*Median educational level of husbands, by educational level of women
marrying between 1950 and 1960 for the first time*

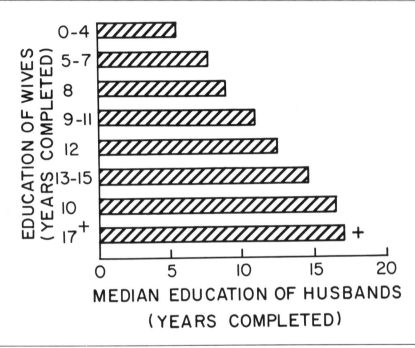

Source: U.S. Census of Population: 1960. Subject Reports. Marital Status. Final Report PC(2)-4E, p. 166

whelming, considering the relative supply of women available in the population. This fact has apparently not escaped notice by American women. The best way to get a potentially high-status husband is to go where he is—to college. On the other hand, this strongly suggests that college men are picking college women as wives because they are the most socially available and not because they prefer women with education similar to their own. For black women, however, college is not the marriage market it can be for white women. Black women who go to predominantly white colleges face a restricted social life, and even the women graduates of predominantly black colleges are more likely than white women to be single and to have no marriage plans (Epstein, 1973).

INTERRACIAL AND INTERETHNIC MARRIAGES

The proportion of marriages which occur across racial lines in the United States is small, underlining the fundamental cleavage in interaction between the races. Figures from Boston for a twenty-five-year period show that about one-tenth of 1. percent of whites married blacks (Wirth and Goldhamer, 1944), and national data for 1948 collected by Jacobson (1959) show a rate of 8 interracial marriages per 10,000 marriages, very close to the Boston figure. Interracial marriage rates must be taken with some caution because different states define what constitutes a different race in various ways. California is reported to have had an intermarriage rate of 1.4 percent of all marriages in 1959 (Barnett, 1963a), but of all white males marrying in that year, fewer than one-tenth of 1 percent took black brides, and of all white females marrying in that year, fewer than three-tenths of 1 percent took black husbands. Thus, at least for California, the great preponderance of "interracial" marriages are between whites and nonblacks, or between nonwhites. Many of these so-called "interracial" marriages are between persons that no biologist would consider of different races and are really between persons differing primarily in ethnic or national identification, rather than race in the usual biological sense. Heer (1966) believes that intermarriage is highest in areas where residential segregation is low, and where blacks and whites are similar in socioeconomic status.

Some writers and many laymen have accounted for the low rate of interracial marriage partly by the laws which, before the U.S. Supreme Court declared them to be unconstitutional, prohibited intermarriage in many states (Kephart, 1961). These laws have long existed in some northern states as well as the South. Recent U. S. Census data show that rates of black-white marriage are increasing. During the 1960s, about 1 black groom in 50 had a white bride, about double the rate in the previous two decades. During the 1960s about 1 white groom in 1,000 took a black bride. This is about the same rate as observed in the previous two decades.

There is no sign that black-white marriages are about to become commonplace. On the basis of his data Heer (1966) concludes that even with the highest projected intermarriage rates, racial intermarriage would have a negligible effect on the composition of the American population.

In a recent review of studies on international, interethnic, and interracial marriages, Barnett reports the following conditions associated with cross-nationality and cross-racial marriages:

1. Whites appear to be more willing to engage in interracial marriages with Orientals than with Negroes.
2. Protestants have the highest rate of mixed nationality marriages, and the Jews have the lowest, with Catholics standing between the two.
3. Apparently, among whites, it is the Protestant and Catholic male and the Jewish female who most frequently marry members of other races. In international marriages, it seems to be the Protestant and Catholic males who cross boundaries most frequently.

4. The religiously less-devout marry persons of different nationalities and races with a higher frequency than the religiously more-devout.
5. Persons who have experienced disorganized and stressful parental families are more likely to marry members of other nationalities and races than those who were raised in cohesive and stable families.
6. Persons living in urban areas cross nationality and racial lines to a greater extent than persons living in rural areas.
7. Persons crossing nationality lines to marry generally choose partners who are members of the same religion and of the same socioeconomic level. In interracial marriages, the spouses generally come from different religions and apparently from different socioeconomic levels; one study, however, reports that the majority of spouses in interracial marriages come from the same socioeconomic level.
8. Americans undertaking an international marriage are usually from lower-than-average socioeconomic homes. In interracial marriages, it appears that the non-white male has a higher-than-average socioeconomic status and the white male and female and the non-white female have a lower-than-average socioeconomic level; however, one study reports that the upper-class is highly overrepresented, the middle-class is greatly under-represented, and the lower-class is slightly overrepresented in interracial marriages.
9. In Negro-white marriages it is the Negro male who marries the white female in the majority of cases. In Oriental-white marriages, generally the Chinese male marries the white female and the white male marries the Japanese female.
10. Among those who undertake an interracial marriage, a greater-than-average number have been married previously.
11. Foreign-born white males more than native white males, and native white females more than foreign-born white females, undertake Negro-white marriages.
12. In Negro-white marriages, the family of the Negro spouse seems to be more willing to accept the couple than does the family of the white spouse.
13. American males and females marrying out of their nationality or racial group are generally older than the average at time of marriage.[1]

Low intermarriage rates are only partly explained by specific social pressures and obstructions against intermarriage. The whole structure of social relationships between whites and blacks in the United States has been organized in such a way as to prevent whites and blacks from meeting, especially under circumstances which would lead to identifying each other as eligible partners. Under these circumstances, the few interracial marriages which do occur are the ones which need explaining. Apparently, special facilitating conditions are required to produce interracial marriages (Golden, 1959). Much higher rates of racial intermarriage prevail in Hawaii, with its

[1] Larry D. Barnett, "Research on International and Interracial Marriages," *Marriage and Family Living,* XXV (1963), pp. 105–107. Reprinted by permission.

large Oriental population, than in the continental United States (Kimura, 1957; Cheng. and Yamamura, 1957). However, in Hawaii, the general structure of social relationships between Orientals and Caucasians is such as to encourage meeting and identifying one another as eligibles. For example, residential segregation of races in Hawaii does not resemble that of the continental United States, and there is not the large difference in class position between Orientals and Caucasians in Hawaii that there is between blacks and whites in the rest of the United States. Furthermore, even on the mainland, the racial difference between Orientals and Caucasians is not socially as large as the difference between whites and blacks (Burma, 1963). Nevertheless, although the interracial marriage rate in Hawaii is slowly increasing, white-collar men continue to be much less likely than blue-collar workers to contract interracial marriages (Schmitt, 1971).

The concern for the consequences of racial intermarriage which is evident among whites, especially in the states of the southeast, has been of interest to sociologists. Myrdal has shown, for example, that racial inter-marriage, in addition to being the form of equality that whites are least willing to grant, is also the form of equality in which blacks profess least interest (Myrdal, 1944).

RELIGION AND MARITAL SELECTION

The interest of Americans, laymen and sociologists alike, in religious inter-marriage has been phenomenal. More studies are available on the subject than on any other social variable. All studies have found that marriage within one's religion is far greater than chance occurrence. There is some disagreement only on the *degree* of the tendency toward religious homogamy. This chapter will deal with interfaith marriage only between major religious groups—Protestant, Catholic, and Jewish. This is an artificial distinction which implies that any Protestant marriage is religiously homogamous, when some Protestants differ in religion from other Protestants far more than they do from Catholics.

The rates for Catholic and Protestant intermarriage vary extremely widely from one part of the country to another. The percentage of Catholics who marry outside the Church has been reported as low as 6 percent in some areas (Hollingshead, 1950), and more than 70 percent in other areas (Thomas, 1951). National data are hard to come by, since the U. S. Census does not routinely ask questions about religion (unfortunately for the sociologist), and only two states (Iowa and Indiana) ask about religious affiliation in connection with marriage licenses. A national sample survey conducted in 1957, however, showed that 94 percent of the married couples consisted of husband and wife of the same major religious group. If people had married without regard to religion, only 56 percent would have had spouses who were the same in religious affiliation. In the 1957 sample, the rate of Protestant-Catholic marriage was only about one-fifth of what it would have been if marriage had occurred randomly with respect to religion. The intermarriage rate for Jews was by far the lowest, even though random mating would have given them the highest intermarriage rates (Glick, 1960).

A study done in Manhattan showed a far higher rate of intermarriage, which may be presumed to reflect greater interreligious contact in an urban area. The area was more than 50 percent Catholic, only 33 percent Protestant. In this representative sample, 1 in 4 of the respondents was intermarried. Catholics had an intermarriage rate of 21.4 percent and Jews a rate of 18.4 percent. The Protestant rate was much higher at 33.9 percent (Heiss, 1960).

Rates of intermarriage vary depending upon how they are calculated. If one spouse converts to the religion of the other near the time of their marriage, is it an interfaith marriage? A study done in the midwest found that 3 out of 4 marriages of partners raised in different faiths become homogamous through conversion of one of the spouses before or at marriage (Babchuck, 1967). Besanceney (1965) reports that in a sample of marriages in Detroit, 3 out of 5 marriages involving partners raised in different faiths become homogeneous marriages through the conversion of one or the other. When he calculated the number of marriages in which the spouses were still of different faiths, his figures coincided with those of Glick; that is, there were only about one-fifth as many as would occur by random mating. But when he calculated intermarriage rates based on *early* religious preference of each spouse, there were more than half as many as would be expected by chance. This demonstrates that Catholic-Protestant intermarriage is much more frequent than most people have suspected.

Likewise it has been shown that intermarriage rates are different for different parts of each religious group. Jewish intermarriage offers an excellent example. One study found that for three generations of Jews in Washington, D.C., the intermarriage rate was 1.4 percent for the first generation, 10.2 percent for the second generation, and 17.9 percent for the youngest generation, indicating a *current* intermarriage rate far higher than was formerly suspected. Furthermore, among highly educated Jews the intermarriage rate is much higher than among Jews generally, ranging from 20 percent to more than 50 percent (Sklare, 1964).

Several other nonreligious social factors account for the difference in Catholic-Protestant intermarriage rates in different parts of the nation. Three studies have demonstrated in a most conclusive manner that the lower the proportion of Catholics in a local area, the more Catholics marry non-Catholics (Locke, Sabagh, and Thomes, 1957; Burchinal and Chancellor, 1962a; Thomas, 1951). (See Chart 8-2.)

The greater the probability, therefore, *that the next person one meets will be a person of a different religion, the greater is the probability that one*

Chart 8-2

*Percent of interfaith marriages among all Catholic marriages and percent
of population which is Catholic, by geographic location*

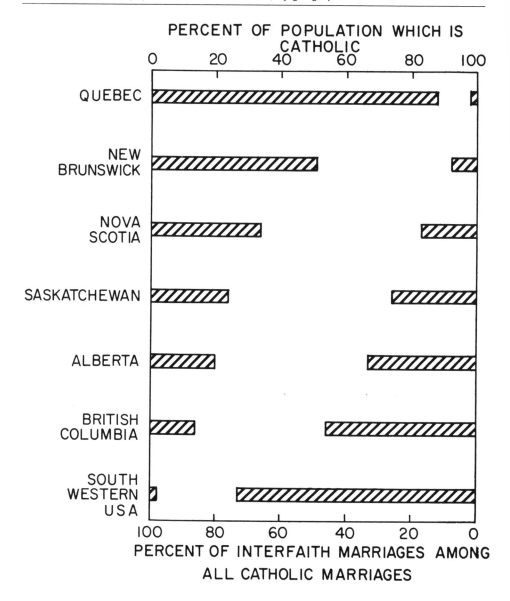

Source: Blood, 1962

will marry a person of a different religion. A second factor is ethnic differ-ences. When Catholics in an area are mostly of a single ethnic group, Catholic intermarriage rates are low, since intermarriage then involves crossing an ethnic as well as a religious line. A third factor is social-class differences. When class lines and religious lines in a community coincide, so that most Catholics tend to belong to a different social class than most Protestants, then Catholic intermarriage rates are lower, since intermarriage involves crossing a social-class barrier as well as a religious barrier (Thomas, 1951; Hollingshead, 1950).

Who marries outside his religion? Marriage outside one's religion, in the face of pressures from every church to marry within the faith, can be seen as the failure of social controls (Heiss, 1960). People who do marry outside their faith are different from those who marry homogamously. The very young, the rather old, and persons low in socioeconomic status are more prone to intermarry (Burchinal and Chancellor, 1962b). The very young might be presumed to be more romantic, on the one hand, and rebellious in other ways, as evidenced by the fact that they have married very young. The rather old have been shown to marry more exogamously than those marrying at the usual ages on other characteristics as well. Perhaps as one gets older, he is not in a position to be particular about religion. In addition, he is likely to be free from endogamous pressures originating with his parents. Lower-status persons generally have lower religious-participation rates and are therefore presumably not as subject to the pressures of church groups to select a mate of the same religion.

Rosenthal found that, among Jews, "Previous divorce leads to such a high level of subsequent intermarriage that it must be considered a leading factor in the formation of religious intermarriages" (Rosenthal, 1970: 435). In Indiana, marriages of previously divorced partners had an inter-marriage rate of 70.2 percent; the intermarriage rates of previously widowed and single spouses were 18.2 percent and 32.3 percent, respectively. Why should divorce be such a significant predictor of religious intermarriage? Rosenthal suggests that a person whose earlier, intrareligious marriage did not compensate for differences in social mobility or for personality con-flicts is motivated to remarry outside his religion to achieve what he wants. It is also possible that willingness to divorce—to indulge in relatively unconventional behavior—is in itself a factor in willingness to remarry outside one's religion.

A study of a representative sample of Manhattan couples showed that the religiously intermarried differed in other ways from the intramarried. The most significant differences were found for intermarried Catholics. Their parents were less religious, they had more unsatisfactory relationships with their parents, and were more emancipated from their parents at the time of their marriages. Thus they can be seen as removed from the social pressures which are organized to prevent intermarriage (Heiss, 1960).

Official church attitudes toward interfaith marriages. Nearly all major religious groups have issued statements discouraging interfaith marriages. The strongest and best organized opposition to intermarriage is from the Roman Catholic Church. Catholics have been encouraged to marry Catholics on grounds that it is both good for their marriages and a good influence on their religious devoutness. From 1918 until 1970, Roman Catholics were officially enjoined from marrying non-Catholics, and could do so with the Church's sanction only under certain conditions. In order for the marriage to be valid, a "prenuptial contract" had to be signed by both parties, promising that "all children of our marriage shall be baptized and brought up solely in the Roman Catholic Religion." It was also required that the marriage ceremony be conducted by a Catholic priest. The usual Catholic wedding ceremony was not permitted but instead a more limited ceremony was performed. During 1970, all of these restrictions were removed or modified. The non-Catholic partner no longer is required to promise to bring up all of his children as Roman Catholics, and "for serious reason" (presumably the objection of the non-Catholic partner would be serious) the marriage ceremony does not have to be performed by a priest in order to be valid in the eyes of the Church.

Protestant objections to intermarriage with Catholics appear to be mainly reactions to the concessions formerly demanded by the Roman Catholic Church as a precondition to intermarriage rather than being prompted by any serious concern about intermarriage *per se.* Older official statements of Protestant denominations therefore do not reflect response to the new Catholic position.

Jewish objections to intermarriage are based on different considerations. American rabbis have consistently taken the position that "mixed marriages are contrary to the tradition of the Jewish religion and should therefore be discouraged by the American rabbinate." This policy is evidently mainly based on prevention of assimilation and therefore disappearance of Jews as a culturally distinct group.

Are more people marrying outside their faith than in previous generations? Older studies indicate that there has been a long-time trend toward more interfaith marriage in the United States (Kennedy, 1944). Research based on a recent national survey indicates that for all three religious groups, interfaith marriage rates have doubled in the last generation (Bumpass, 1970). Decreasing differences in ethnic and socioeconomic status between religious groups is given major credit for the trend. Perhaps increasing religious intermarriage is a measure of the declining importance of religion in the United States.

SEX RATIOS AND MATE SELECTION

In a monogamous society which encourages marriage to age peers, one's chances for marriage are a statistical factor of the proportionate number of members of the opposite sex who are unmarried and the right age. Because of differential migration, some areas become heavily unbalanced in the direction of one sex, thus creating lower marriage chances for some persons.

Since marriage partners are selected from very close age groups, with men marrying women slightly younger, any abrupt change in the number of births causes a strain on the "marriage market" about twenty years later because of disproportionate sex ratios in the prime marriage ages. Akers (1967) explains it this way:

> Consider for example, girls born at the height of the post war baby boom. There were 1.9 million born between July, 1946, and June, 1947. In recent years, girls have married boys who were two years older than they on the average. Yet there were only 1.5 million boys born between July, 1944 and June, 1945. Thus 400,000 women (21% of all girls in the baby boom cohort) would find it difficult to find husbands. Since these women may delay marriage in hopes of finding someone of a suitable age, eventually, they must marry a man of less appropriate age, or not marry at all. The dilemma faced by girls now [1967] reaching the age of marriage has been referred to as "the marriage squeeze."

For the person who ranks high as a desirable mate, these sex-ratio differences have little importance, since he will have many chances to marry wherever he goes. For those with characteristics which put them farther down on the scale of mate desirability, a heavily unbalanced sex ratio can mean the difference between marrying and not marrying. Shrewd girls have taken this into consideration in choosing the college they attend. Highly attractive girls can afford to ignore it. A person in the marriage market who is in a racial, ethnic, religious, or socioeconomic category which is a small minority in a particular area and which has a badly unbalanced sex ratio among the unmarried may find that his "field of eligibles" is so restricted that he must marry exogamously, take a mate of low social desirability, or migrate if he wishes to marry at all.

Summary

Americans are marrying at somewhat younger ages than in the past, to someone nearer their own age. They are marrying someone who lives reasonably near them, whose family status is not too different from their own, and whose educational level is similar to theirs. They rarely marry outside their own race, but interracial marriage is more frequent than in the past. Most Americans marry within their own broad religious group, but there is considerable interfaith marriage, and its prevalence is increasing. Many of these factors must be seen as operating without the conscious knowledge of the persons selecting mates. In large part, they are the product of the overall organization of social life in the United States (and elsewhere) into subgroups of persons who interact more frequently because they are socially similar, and are similar because they interact more frequently. In almost every case, the probability of marrying someone in a given social category is proportional to the probability of meeting someone in that category. This is not the whole explanation, of course. Young Americans have distinct ideas about what categories of persons are "eligible" mates and what categories are not. The strength of these ideas automatically screens dating partners to a great degree and marriage partners even more carefully, to produce the overall effect: One is most likely to marry someone who is pretty much like himself in most of his social characteristics. This represents a considerable departure from the romantic myth and from American values of individualism and equalitarianism, but these are apparently values which are compromised when it comes to making individual decisions.

Implications for Individual Decision-Making

These, then, are the probabilities. What does this mean for the individual, unmarried person? It means that the individual's choice of mate is influenced by a whole series of social factors in the organization of his society of which he may be totally unaware. It would not go far beyond the facts to imply that picking a mate who is socially quite different from oneself usually takes a deliberate decision to do so. Interview evidence from intermarried couples sometimes indicates that this was the case—there was special motivation to marry across some conventionally observed barrier. Whether the motive be rebellion (Freeman, 1955), social reform, lure of the exotic, status-climbing, or other personal benefit (Blood, 1969), unusually heterogeneous marriages occur mainly to unusual people with unusual motivations, in unusual circumstances.

Interpersonal Factors in Mate Selection

9

Who selects whom as a mate for whom? Students know that different societies vary with respect to methods of mate selection, but the variation is often presented as almost a matter of whimsy on the part of a society, rather than being related to the structure of a way of life. Generally, there are three different answers to the question which opens this chapter:

1. The mates select for themselves, subject to no one's approval.
2. The mates select for themselves, subject to parental approval.
3. The parents select the mates, generally without the formal requirement of approval by the mates.

Each of these three variations is found somewhere. By all odds, the most common practice in the past was marriage arranged by the parents, but the pattern of mate selection by the young people involved is known in a number of cultures in addition to our own. A fairly good rule of thumb for determining what arrangement will prevail in a society is this: Who has a substantial stake in the selection? In almost all cases, this person will control the decision. When the young couple will be integrated into some existing residential unit, by moving in with the parents or by joining any larger kin-residence group, one can be fairly sure that the group which the couple joins will have an important voice in the selection. When marriage involves substantial exchanges of property or is fundamentally an economic arrangement, the mate selection will be controlled by the families. When the only substantial stake in the marital arrangement is that of the married couple then the selection will usually be done by the first parties (Stephens, 1963: 198–199).

Marital selection in the contemporary United States is dominated by the values of individuality and the "cult of personality" (Green, 1941). It is presumed that the couple will choose each other with complete freedom from interference. This idea is neither very old in American society, nor is it completely observed. The traditional European roots of American society are almost uniformly imbedded in arranged marriage systems. From earliest times into the nineteenth century, English custom called for matches arranged by the parents, with children having little to say about the matter. Mates frequently would not know each other before marriage; betrothals, and even marriages, were not uncommon in childhood. Frontier conditions of the United States modified the English traditions, so that arranged marriages were not as common here as during the same period in England. Still, "a young man was required by the laws of several colonies to secure consent of his prospective father-in-law before beginning the courtship, and this was not always easy to obtain" (Queen, Habenstein, and Adams, 1961: 255, 276, 277).

American traditions, therefore, contain nearly the entire spectrum of cross-cultural variation in mate selection arrangements, and all have been apparent in the last two or three hundred years. The change from colonial days to the present has involved the gradual attenuation of the residual parental approval, as it has become less possible, as well as less important, for parents effectively to exercise direct influence in the choice. However, parents today are not entirely uninfluenced by whom their child marries. "Good" marriages redound to the parents' higher status, while "poor" marriages are embarrassing and demeaning to the parents. Furthermore, one of the most frequent friendship interactions in the United States is that between relatives. Under these conditions, one should expect to (and does) see the attempt to influence mate choice still playing a part in American courtship.

From the discussion of social factors in mate selection in the preceding chapter, it is clear that Americans have always been influenced by social factors, although these may not have served as conscious criteria of selection. The most obvious force is that which determines the likelihood of two persons meeting under situations which allow them to define one another as eligibles. Intermarriage will seldom occur between social groups which have little in common and which seldom come in contact with one another. The decline in the barrier presented to mate selection by religion and social class suggests that these are not as fundamental axes of American social structure as they formerly were. In spite of such minor shifts in behavior, however, younger generations of Americans are still consciously and unconsciously using social criteria in screening mates. Individual selection on the basis of personal qualities obviously operates within a narrow framework imposed by the structure of society.

The Interpersonal Relationship

In the face of overwhelming consensus and empirical data, it will be assumed that Americans marry because they are in love. When love can be explained, mate selection can also be explained. The problem, then, resolves itself to this: What is the relationship between individual qualities of the two persons which "causes" them to fall in love? This is a more elaborate way of asking the familiar question, "What does she see in him?" Sociologist and layman alike have learned to pose the alternative possibilities as either "like marries like" or "opposites attract."

The question has not been asked by every society of itself, because in some, as has been noted, personal qualities of the mates are irrelevant to mate selection. In every society, however, some consideration is likely to be taken of how the two will get along with one another. This seems to indicate a rather widespread notion among human beings that there are some combinations of traits belonging to men and women that "go together" better than others.

The theory that opposites attract has had its proponents in Western culture for some time. Schopenhauer, writing in the first half of the nineteenth century, gave it one of its most colorful expressions:

> Accordingly, in the first place, every one will decidedly prefer and eagerly desire the most beautiful individuals, i.e., those in whom the character of the species is more purely impressed; but, secondly, each one will specially regard as beautiful in another individual those perfections which he himself lacks, nay, even those imperfections which are the opposite of his own. Hence, for example, little men love big women, fair persons like dark, etc., etc. The delusive ecstasy which seizes a man at the sight of a woman whose beauty is suited to him, and pictures to him a union with her as the highest good, is just the *sense of the species,* which, recognizing the distinctly expressed stamp of the same, desires to perpetuate it with this individual. . . . Thus what guides man here is really an instinct which is directed to doing the best for the species, while the man himself imagines that he only seeks the heightening of his own pleasure. . . . A man carefully chooses a woman with definite qualities which appeal to him individually, and strives so eagerly after her that in order to attain this end he often sacrifices his own happiness in life, contrary to all reason, by a foolish marriage, by love affairs which cost him wealth, honour, and life, even by crimes such as adultery and rape, all merely in order to serve the species in the most efficient way. . . .
>
> Since there do not exist two individuals exactly alike, there must be for each particular man a particular woman—always with reference to what is to be produced—who corresponds most perfectly. A really passionate love is as rare as the accident of these two meetings (Schopenhauer, 1928).

Here one sees the romantic myth of mate selection phrased in the language of philosophic biology: the only perfect mate, overpowering attraction at the recognition of "the one," the cutting through of social barriers—but without the promise of individual happiness.

Literally hundreds of studies have been done by sociologists on the comparison of social and personal traits of mates. Almost without exception, the studies concluded that in physical, social, and psychological characteristics, mates were more alike than they were different. These studies were criticized with respect to psychological characteristics because they were nearly all studies of married couples, and the possibility remained that the spouses had become alike psychologically during marriage. The Burgess and Wallin research, and several since, have reported that spouses were psychologically more alike than chance would allow even before marriage.

Still, it is clear that there is a preference for opposites in at least one characteristic—sex. Even here, however, the opposition is hardly a matter of choice. Further, it has even been shown that very masculine men do not prefer especially feminine women, nor do not-very-masculine men prefer not-very-feminine women. Those who deviate from the mean for their sex usually prefer those who deviate in the same direction as themselves (Lundy, 1958; Terman and Miles, 1936).

Since 1950, sociologists have devoted a great deal of attention to examining whether there are trends toward the selection of mates who differ from one another in some systematic way. A theoretical model for how and why they should differ was provided by Winch (1952). It has since been refined, and considerable research has been directed toward its verification. Winch's abbreviated statement of the theory is as follows:

> Love is an emotion based upon the lover's experience of having had his needs gratified by the love object, or on the expectation or hope or fantasy that the love object will gratify his needs. Motivation, or needs, may be conscious or unconscious. . . .
>
> Where love is regarded as a desirable precondition to marriage, it is theorized that mate-selection will take place on the basis of complementary needs. The central hypothesis of the theory of complementary needs states that within the field of eligibles, persons whose need patterns provide mutual gratification will tend to choose each other as marriage partners (Winch, 1963: 606–607).

The reader will recognize the theory in this form as a sophisticated way of saying that people fall in love with someone who satisfies them. The elaboration of the theory provides two types of complementarity, both based on the additional assumptions (not contained in the central hypothesis above) that the specific needs which gratify one another are different rather than similar, and the same need pair will be mutually gratifying. In the two types of complementarity which are provided, Type I specifies that if one spouse is higher in one need, the other spouse will be low. If one has a high need for achievement, for example, he will select someone with a low achievement need. Type II specifies that if one spouse is high in a particular trait, the other will be high (or low) in some other specific trait. For example, if one has high needs to dominate, it is predicted that he will be gratified by someone with a high need to be submissive (Winch, 1963: 585–586).

In order to test this theory, Winch and his associates worked intensively with a sample of twenty-five married college couples, using several different techniques of measuring complementarity as described above (Winch, 1955; Winch, Ktanes and Ktanes, 1954). The results, according to the authors, provide conclusive evidence of the complementarity of the couples as described in the theory (Winch, 1958). Two other studies since then have reported confirmation of systematic patterns of differences between couples which can be described as complementarity, although neither used the same categories of traits as the Winch group. Huntington (1958) reported finding a pattern of complementary differences in a sample of married couples, and Kerckhoff and Davis (1962) found a pattern of complementary differences among couples who subsequently reported courtship progress, in a sample of couples considering marriage.

As plausible, even compelling, as the theory sounds, other researchers have not been successful in finding a pattern of complementary differences (Bowerman and Day, 1956; Heiss and Gordon, 1964; Kernodle, 1959; Lundy, 1958; Murstein, 1961; Schellenberg and Bee, 1960; Udry, 1963; as well as every major marital-adjustment study). None of these used the intensive techniques of Winch, which included depth interviewing, but all are based on larger groups. Winch (1967) maintains that none of these studies is an adequate test of the theory. Murstein's latest study (1972a) used in-depth interviews (overcoming the criticism that paper-and-pencil tests used in other studies are too superficial), and couples who were engaged or seriously dating (overcoming the criticism that the patterns found were a result of living together over time). Although he looked hard trying to find complementary patterns, all he could find was greater-than-chance similarity between mates.

Many criticisms have been leveled at the idea of complementary needs. Several seem especially hard to answer. First, no study shows that the spouses themselves were aware of the complementary traits or that the existence of the traits had anything to do with the selection (Bolton, 1961). There is abundant evidence to indicate that there is considerable discrepancy between what people perceive as the traits of others and what the others are really like (Udry, 1963). People have sung for centuries of the blindness of love. Second, there is something implausible about the idea that when whichever sex has whichever trait, it will be equally satisfying to both spouses. For example, although it is intuitively plausible that a dominant male might choose a submissive female, it is not equally plausible that a dominant female would choose a submissive male. Rather, it is plausible that a dominant female might choose an even more dominant male so that the usual sex-role expectations would be maintained. Winch thinks that the female-dominant selection would still take place, but that it would later interfere with marital stability. He has subsequently suggested the following hypothesis on the relationship between complementarity of needs and marital stability:

> A pair of spouses who are attracted to each other on the bases of complementary needs will be a less stable pair if the complementariness is counter to the role-specifications than if it is consistent with the role specification (Winch, 1967).

CASE

I have found that I have a tendency to try to lead people. I think this need was developed when I was acquiring my high need for exhibition. I wanted to be a leader in school, and I certainly had to be able to lead a group. I don't think my need is too high. I still like men who dominate me. I would hate to be married to someone whom everyone considered to be henpecked.

In fact, however, research does not indicate a consistent pattern of this sort. The author's study of engaged couples shows *no* consistent pattern of personality trait matching, toward similarity or toward difference, or any other pattern beyond chance. Murstein (1961) discovers the same lack of pattern on the part of newlyweds.

Other provocative research is still being done on this problem. Another researcher has attacked the problem of combining complementary need theory with considerations of marital role orientation. Holz (1969) found in a group of recently married couples that if he divided the couples into those with traditional marriage role expectations and those with equalitarian role expectations, the couple with traditional role expectations showed Type I complementarity with respect to expressive needs, but similarity with respect to instrumental needs. The equalitarian couples, on the other hand, showed Type I complementarity on instrumental needs but similarity with respect to expressive needs.

Further research will be required to determine whether these results can be replicated, and therefore considered with confidence. The additional sophistication in the conceptualization of the idea of complementarity in mate selection will eventually lead us to a greater understanding of the mate selection process, as well as illuminate sources of marital satisfaction.

Can it be that people are not selecting each other on the basis of mutually gratifying need patterns? The couples certainly think they are. When they break their engagements, they mention "incompatibility of personality" as a frequent reason (Burgess and Wallin, 1953). The answer lies more likely in the discovery of *what people see in one another* than in what the objective outsider sees in each.

A Theory of Perceptual Complementarity in Mate Selection

Winch holds that love is based on the experience, expectation, hope, or fantasy of need gratification. That people choose someone to marry whom they *expect* to be gratifying to them seems so basic to the whole scheme of marriage in American culture as to be unassailable. The layman has noticed for a long time that people in love tend to see in one another things that outsiders do not see. Careful collection of data indicates that engaged persons (as well as married people) see things in one another that cannot be found by the test instruments available. Evidently, what they see in each other is what pleases them, whether another can find it or not. It has further been shown that what *he* sees in *her* is very closely related to what *he* is, but not to what *she* is.

With an open mind to the subject, then, one might say the relationship between what he is and what he sees in her could be defined as a complementary relationship. When one examines the relationships between what he is and what he sees in her, what she is and what she sees in him, one finds that a whole set of stable relationships is perceived by the couple. None of these relationships exist outside the minds of the couples, but it is these perceived relationships which determine how the people will react to one another. It should be pointed out that studies indicate that the perceived relationships do not fit the pattern of differences described by Winch but are much more complex. Dominant males do not pick females they perceive as submissive, and submissive males do not pick females they perceive as dominant. Evidently, this is not a complementary relationship as perceived by the couples, in spite of the fact that the pair of traits would logically *seem* to be complementary. Furthermore, the combinations of traits which males perceive as complementary are different from the combinations which females see as complementary. This is consistent with the general premise that men and women are not looking for the same sorts of gratification patterns in marriage, a fact that other studies have shown (Kernodle, 1959; Strauss, 1947). What prospective mates see in one another, they like, even though it apparently is not there.

Does this help one understand who selects whom to marry? A little. The lack of a consistent pattern in the personality relationships between spouses which is shown in the research suggests that, contrary to everyone's profound belief, mates are not selecting one another on any set of consistent personality trait relationships but are attributing to one another a set of relationships pleasing to the self, after having selected each other on some other basis. For example, Murstein (1972b) found that progress in courtship is much more likely when each member of the couple sees his mate as the mate sees *himself,* but that the improved relationship is much more highly correlated with the woman's ability to see her partner as he sees himself than with his ability to see her as she sees herself. This probably means that complementarity of mates will not help one understand mate selection very much. Much research is still under way in this area, and perhaps more definitive results in discerning personality relationships of mate selection will be forthcoming. *The studies to date, however, do not allow one to conclude that personality match is an important basis of mate selection.*

Then what are the important factors? Aside from social factors determining the probability of two people meeting and social factors defining mate eligibility, it really is not known what factors are important. One might speculate that a series of accidental contingencies such as perceived availability, considerations of relative dating status, the need to love someone, being in the right romantic circumstances at the right time, sitting at the same library table—little things like this may determine who gets whom. Nor need one take the pessimistic view of one college man who sees the selection process as one of accidental contingency.

CASE

Going the way I am now with the girls, I feel that I will probably never find her. I'm so lonely now that the first girl that comes my way I will probably marry her. We will have different personality needs and we will get along fine for the first few months, but later on we will get into patches of trouble and our marriage will end in a divorce.

Winch suggests that his kind of complementary mating would only work in circumstances where a person had a reasonable number of dating partners (say 25) from whom to choose (Winch, 1958). Something is known about the number of dating partners of the average college coed. Evidently, hardly anyone ever has 100, and the average number is around 25. Of these, suppose that the girl knows 5 of them intimately enough to form a complete picture of her "personality fit" to them to know that she could or does love them and would marry them. She will probably get only 2 proposals, or less formal opportunities to select 1 partner and commit herself. These 2 she is not very likely to get at the same time. With the steady dating pattern which has become prevalent in the United States, she really only has 1 prospect at a time, and she is not in a position to evaluate her personality fit to the next (unknown) prospect. Under these circumstances, it does not seem likely that profound and stable relationships will be found between the personalities of persons who have chosen one another for mates, beyond whatever similarity may be created by socially similar backgrounds.

Mate Selection on Physical Characteristics

An incredible amount of research has been done relating the physical characteristics of spouses. Spuhler (1968) lists over 300 studies, including 105 different physical characteristics. As one might expect, numerous studies show similarity of spouses on age, weight, and stature, but selection of similars is also documented on many other physical characteristics, including forearm length, hair color, general health, basal metabolism, and even pulse rate before exercise.

There is evidence that similarity in physical attractiveness is a factor in mate selection. Murstein (1972c) asked each member of 99 engaged or steadily dating couples to rate his own and his partner's physical attractiveness on a five-point scale ranging from "extremely good looking" to "considerably below average in looks." Photographs of the couples were rated on the same scale of physical attractiveness by a panel of 8 young professors and graduate students, 4 of them women and 4 men. Murstein then created a control group by creating artificial "couples": he randomly paired the ratings of self and partner given by one member of the couples with those given by another member of the couples. When he compared the actual and artificial couples' attractiveness ratings, Murstein found that self-concepts of attractiveness were much more similar among the actual couples than among artificial pairs, although each partner in an actual couple saw his partner as slightly more attractive than himself. In addition, Murstein's panel rated the photographs of actual partners as much more alike in physical attractiveness than the photographs of randomly paired men and women.

Consensus and Selection

Do people who agree with one another select one another as spouses more often than those who do not agree? A number of studies indicate that this is so. In fact, this tendency seems to be based on a process which is much more general than mate selection and may involve interpersonal selection and liking in all kinds of human relationships. Newcomb (1961, 1956) indicates that in same-sex friendship pairs, the more two people perceive one another agreeing on matters important to each, the more probable that they will continue interaction and the more they will like one another. Numerous other studies indicate that in almost any group of subjects, those who are friends will agree with one another on salient subjects more than if the people in the sample are randomly matched. Kirkpatrick and Hobart (1954) compared couples of different levels of commitment for their consensus on marital expectations and found that couples who were simply favorite dates shared more consensus than random couplings but that couples in each more serious commitment stage shared more agreement.

Kerckhoff and Davis (1962) tested a group of college couples who had marriage plans for consensus on marriage values then asked them nine months later whether they felt they were making progress toward a permanent relationship. Those couples with high consensus reported progress toward permanence significantly more often than those with lower consensus. However, doubt is cast on the generality of these findings by a later study reported by Levinger, Senn, and Jorgensen (1970). Using identical techniques on two separate samples of couples presumably similar to those studied by Davis and Kerckhoff, they were unable to find any evidence to support the idea that couples with high consensus will report courtship progress more than those low on consensus.

On the very generalized values (theoretical, aesthetic, social, religious, political, and economic) of the Alport-Vernon-Lindsey Study of Values it has been found that married couples are in far more agreement with one another than randomly matched persons from the same sample (Udry, Nelson, and Nelson, 1961). It can hardly be argued that all these couples show high agreement only because they come from more similar backgrounds, so that the real influence would then be similarity of social background rather than consensus. In each of the studies discussed, the entire sample was very homogeneous, consisting in every case of couples from a single college population, with similar educational and social background characteristics.

These studies clearly reveal the importance of a fairly broad consensus in the mate selection process. Evidently our perception that other persons agree with us on things that matter is an important source of our attraction to them. This should not be interpreted as meaning that any particular couple comes to agree with one another more and more as time passes or that consensus during engagement is necessarily predictive of marital success. These matters will be discussed later in the chapter on marital interaction processes.

The Ideal Mate Image

In a society such as America, where marriage looms so important, one would expect that before selecting a mate, the average person would devote considerable thought to what kind of a husband or wife he would like to have—his "ideal" mate. The image of the ideal mate is clearly formulated in the minds of some young people, while in others it is vague and not put into concrete terms until someone asks for it.

CASE

I am very particular about who I am going to marry. I will go out with guys but only to have a good time. If they don't meet my standards, I don't give them a thought. The person I choose will have to have a good sense of humor and a lot of understanding. I will need someone who will be able to dominate me and not cater to my every want. I don't want anyone who will need my support, because I will be unable to give it to him. He will have to be very aggressive because I don't like passive men. I have high ambitions, and my husband will have to be a professional man. I want someone who will share some of my interests in the out-of-doors, water sports, and spectator sports. If he doesn't share my interests, I don't think I would ever consider such a person. If he is an introvert, I could never find happiness with a person who doesn't like people.

Although there is almost no empirical research to indicate the origins of the ideal mate image, two major sources seem intuitively apparent: cultural values and personal needs.

CULTURAL INFLUENCES AND IDEAL MATE IMAGES

Every culture imposes some sort of ideal mate image on its members in terms of what is important in that culture and what functions marriage fulfills in that society. Whether the culture provides physical, social, or personality characteristics for the image again depends on what marriage means in that society. In an old movie on Scottish islanders, where marriage is primarily a division of labor and a matter of childrearing, a description of the ideal wife included strong stout legs and shoulders (for climbing mountains and hewing wood) and broad hips (for bearing children). Most cultures, apparently, include broad hips and breast development in the ideal qualities desirable in the wife. Ideal physical characteristics in men and women change rather rapidly in American culture to keep pace with changes in sex-role differentiation. In the late nineteenth century, with prevailing values still calling for sharply segregated sex roles, the ideal woman image emphasized the physical differences between men and women by accenting bulging breasts and generous hips. After World War I, in keeping with the trend toward feminine equality, the ideal woman image deemphasized the differences between men and women, producing the illusion of flat chest and general lack of contour. After World War II, and following the trend toward increased sex-role differentiation, the emphasis on physical differences again became evident in the ideal female mate image. With the deemphasis on sex-role differentiation of the 1970s, has there been another shift in the physical characteristics of the ideal wife in our cultural image?

Styles in physical fashion of ideal husbands seem more stable over the years, although there are modest changes from rugged to more polished ideals. It is not clear to what extent mass media initiate the changes in physical mate ideals and to what extent these changes emerge from changing emphasis in the culture independent of the mass media. It seems closer to the truth to say that the mass media help to conceptualize and spread to everyone the developing ideals of the culture.

Cultural prescriptions also provide the details of the society's descriptions of masculinity and femininity in personal characteristics, which in turn influence ideal mate images. Whether an ideal wife is supposed to be sweet and delicate, uncomplaining and stolid, or extroverted and sexually provocative is largely a matter of cultural definition. As American society changes its prevailing definition of sex differences in personalities, American cultural definitions of ideal mates change along with them.

The cultural definition of the ideal mate influences mate selection in two ways. First, since it represents consensus in the culture about what is desirable in a mate, it establishes the relative desirability of each person and makes the acquisition of those who most closely approach the ideal a matter of general status. This is the most plausible explanation of the status orientation to beauty (Beigel, 1953) and courtship (Waller, 1937). The person who gets the mate who most nearly fulfills the ideal mate image of the culture acquires admiration and esteem. What this means is that those persons with culturally desirable characteristics, if they recognize their desirability, will bargain in mate selection for a mate who is equally desirable. Those who depart more from the ideal will generally be excluded from top-level competition and will select mates on their own competitive level. Stroebe, Insko, Thompson, and Layton (1971) found that in comparison to college students who saw themselves as physically attractive, students who saw themselves as physically unattractive were more likely to say they would date an unattractive member of the opposite sex and less likely to say they would date an attractive opposite-sex person. Marital adjustment studies show similar dating histories or similar levels of adolescent popularity between mates. To underestimate one's own relationship to the cultural ideals is to settle for a mate with less status than might have been had.

The second way the cultural definition of the ideal mate is said to influence mate selection is by providing a set of desirable characteristics to be attributed to the person with whom one has fallen in love, independent of whether or not he in fact has them. This is the so-called process of "idealization of the mate." However, empirical studies give only limited support to this idea. There is little physical resemblance reported by subjects between their ideal mates and their actual mates (Strauss, 1947). With respect to psychological characteristics, ideal mates are apparently conceived with culturally defined desirable traits, but this tendency is much less marked in the perceptions that engaged persons have of their fiancés, although it is not entirely absent (Udry, 1963).

Table 9-1

MALE AND FEMALE IDEAL MATE IMAGES ARE SIMILAR
*Rank and personal characteristics in mate selection
based on mean value, by year and sex*

	Male			Female		
	1939	*1956*	*1967*	*1939*	*1956*	*1967*
1. Dependable character	1	1	1	2	1	2
2. Emotional stability	2	2	3	1	2	1
3. Pleasing disposition	3	4	4	4	5	4
4. Mutual attraction	4	3	2	5	6	3
5. Good health	5	6	9	6	9	10
6. Desire for home-children	6	5	5	7	3	5
7. Refinement	7	8	7	8	7	8
8. Good cook-housekeeper	8	7	6	16	16	16
9. Ambition-industriousness	9	9	8	3	4	6
10. Chastity	10	13	15	10	15	15
11. Education-intelligence	11	11	10	9	14	7
12. Sociability	12	12	12	11	11	13
13. Similar religious background	13	10	14	14	10	11
14. Good looks	14	15	11	17	18	17
15. Similar educational background	15	14	13	12	8	9
16. Favorable social status	16	16	16	15	13	14
17. Good financial prospect	17	17	18	13	12	12
18. Similar political background	18	18	17	18	17	18

Source: Hudson and Henze, 1969

THE CULTURAL CONTENT OF THE IDEAL MATE IMAGE

Several studies over the years have probed the ideal or desirable characteristics which young people sought in spouses. Table 9-1 presents data from studies over a period of nearly thirty years. An examination of the table will show a surprising overall stability, although there are some changes worthy of note. (For example, the importance of chastity declined in both males and females from tenth to fifteenth place.)

Sharp sex differences in ideal mates were found in a study of courtship values at the University of Colorado in 1950 (Smith and Greenberg-Monane, 1953). In this study, "open-ended" questionnaires were used which gave students the opportunity to build their own concepts within which to describe the qualities they desired, rather than making it necessary for them to respond in the conceptual framework of the researcher. The authors found that male concepts of mate desirability were heavily focused around desirable social graces. Contrast these results with those cited in Table 9-1. Unless these are very different student populations (which seems improbable), it appears that if males are left to present their own images, "good looks" appears very high on their list, but if they are given a list including many other "nice" traits, then "good looks" is rated very low. This is corroborated by results of another checklist study done at an Indiana state college in 1956.

Males and females to a large extent agreed on what was crucial in mates in using the checklist, and physical appearance did not appear on either the male or female list (Hewitt, 1958). There are indications from other studies that physical attractiveness is an important trait for girls in having dates and in progress toward commitment relationships in courtship. This does not seem as important for males (Winch, 1949).

In the following three cases, it is interesting to compare the two male descriptions with the female description following them.

CASE

My wife is very cute and shapely, two characteristics which our culture deems desirable, and I'm no exception when it comes to appreciating them. At least, these were responsible for first noticing her.

CASE

My greatest concern prior to making a date is the personal appearance of the girl, including a certain amount of sex appeal. An attractive feature in the opposite sex will often overshadow evident shortcomings. Tall women do not interest me and neither do short women. It pleases me to be seen with a woman of average height. I do not like to take out extremely thin women, and I do not like to take out extremely fat women. Here again I like a woman of average weight for her height, with curves in the right places. Like most men I look for a pleasing complexion in the opposite sex. I do not like the skin pigment too light or too dark but a shade between the two. The color of the girl's hair is not important to me. However, I do prefer shoulder length and am not in accord with the "bobs" which have recently come into style. Perhaps I am slow in adjusting my taste to the new style. I do not believe so. I have always preferred girls' hair to be shoulder length. The color of her eyes has never been a criterion as to whether I would date her. With a desirable combination of the above factors I am interested in taking a girl out. Some of the points I look for in a girl are not considered by other men. But for the most part I believe I have conventional standards as to their appearance. In particular cases I respect the opinions of my masculine friends regarding the physical appearance of a girl.

The appearance of a girl on a date is very important to me. I like attractive girls who dress smartly. It does my ego a lot of good to be with a girl that gets glances of notice and approval as she walks by. Neatness and dressing chic are my criteria for a date rather than beauty. A large part of a girl's appearance is made up by her manners. I want a girl who knows how to conduct herself naturally wherever you go. Stage mannerisms or just the lack of correct social manners bother me. Any crudeness, vulgarity, or cheapness cannot go along with an attractive girl in my estimation.

The first and most important qualification for a date is that she must be presentable. What could be worse than having a date I could not introduce to my friends? By presentable I mean a girl who has at least an average figure and who is clean looking. She should be neat and dressed with some taste. Also under presentable I include having a pleasant smile and not appearing to be hard and cold.

CASE

A date does not have to be an Adonis; in fact, they rather repel me since they generally think so much of themselves. I want a date to be a nice looking American Boy type, able to meet people easily and talk well. I don't like show-offs. They are uncomfortable to be with and generally don't have anything to show off about.

I like a date who has lots of friends and seems to be very well liked by both boys and girls. Perhaps that is because, although I stand up for individuality, I am still sensitive to other people's opinions and therefore like to go out with boys who are liked by my friends. Along that same trait, I like a boy who is at ease when he comes to call for me at my house and who will talk with the girls while there.

I like a date who has "been around" in the nice sense of the phrase, one who knows the proper things to do regarding manners, correct attire, etc. I like a man who is thoughtful about little things like opening the car door for you, helping you with your coat, introducing you to people you don't know, quick to strike a match for your cigarette. When I am with a certain boy, I like to feel that he is being reasonably attentive, not always in conversation with everyone else at the party or continually table-hopping.

Social ease and grace are necessary. Someone you can be proud to introduce to anyone and know he will make a good impression and be polite—this qualification is a "must." I like a date who knows what to do in the most elite places and at the same time can have fun doing it. There is nothing more uncomfortable than a self-conscious, uneasy boy who obviously has a miserable time trying to do the right thing. I also like a boy who is adjustable and can be just as happy in a dive as in a swanky night club. I enjoy being with a boy who has a versatile personality; that is, a date who can carry on a conversation with older people as well as with his friends.[1]

Other studies have documented the direct relationship between a woman's good looks and the probability of her getting married (Holmes and Hatch, 1938), and even pleasing appearance as influencing marital adjustment (Kirkpatrick and Cotton, 1951). From the evidence at hand, it appears that the low status awarded good looks in mate selection must be taken with a grain of salt. Good looks are obviously one of the characteristics which make a girl desirable and give her companion status. By itself, good looks serves mainly as a screening device for males with high status themselves. However, if one is screened out on the first screening, it does not make much difference what else she has.[2] Elder has shown that beauty is a working-class girl's best aid to upward mobility through marriage. In his study, the better looking a working-class girl was, the more likely she was to get a middle-class husband (Elder, 1969).

[1] Three cases from Ernest W. Burgess and Paul Wallin, *Engagement and Marriage* (Philadelphia: J. B. Lippincott Company, 1953), pp. 73–75. Reprinted by permission.
[2] For evidence that feminine beauty (not masculine) is an important part of the ideal mate image in more traditional societies than ours, see Noel P. Gist, 1954.

Among American blacks, an additional cultural criterion affects mate selection: skin color. Traditionally, light-skinned blacks of both sexes have been at an advantage in obtaining high-status mates. A recent study demonstrated that this was true for those married before 1960. But since 1960, with the growth of racial pride as a consequence of the black liberation and civil rights movements, a change has occurred in recent marriage cohorts, at least in the urban sample studied. Since 1960, the *darkest* Negro males have experienced a status advantage in getting high-status wives. For women the situation remains little changed, with the lightest women still at an advantage in getting high-status husbands. Evidently the criteria of desirability for women are more resistant to change (Udry, Bauman, and Chase, 1971).

PERSONAL NEEDS AND IDEAL MATE IMAGES

If one conceives of the marriage relationship as one from which the individual expects to derive much emotional gratification, then it would follow that ideal mate images should be strongly affected by the personality make-up of the individual holding the image, independent of cultural prescriptions or in addition to cultural prescriptions. This has been demonstrated to be true for psychological aspects of the ideal mate. When single subjects were asked to describe their own personalities and those of their ideal mates, their ideal mate descriptions were shown to be heavily influenced by their own personalities. For males, the ideal mate images were most affected by their self-sufficiency and suspiciousness, while for females, the ideal mate images were most influenced by their suspiciousness and conscientiousness (Udry, 1963). This gives strong support to the idea that mates are conceived as important sources of need gratification (Strauss, 1947, 1946; Winch, 1958, 1963). On the other hand, there is little evidence that the physical aspects of the ideal mate are influenced by the personality of the image-holder, suggesting that the physical aspects are culturally determined.

IDEAL MATE IMAGES AND MATE SELECTION

To what extent does the ideal mate image influence the actual selection of a mate? Clinical evidence and theory suggest that the image of the ideal mate guides the individual in the selection of a mate and causes one to fall in love with the person having the qualities of the ideal, or at least perceived to have them. Psychoanalytic writers have emphasized that falling in love involved the "exchange of ego ideals." The ideal mate is conceived as embodying the traits which the individual wishes he has but recognizes that he has not. When two people fall in love, each is said to attribute his own ego ideal to the other (Benedek, 1946; Reik, 1944: 40). No one, of course, would maintain that the loved one always has the characteristics attributed to him, since love is reputed to be blind. Nevertheless, some people report to researchers that they were consciously influenced in their mate choice by their ideal mate conceptions (Strauss, 1947: 188), and Strauss' subjects, who were already married or at least engaged, reported considerable similarity between their ideal mates and their actual mates. Did they select their mates to correspond with their ideal mate images? It is doubtful. Comparison of the ideal mate images with the characteristics of the image-holder reveals an entirely different pattern of relationships for engaged persons from those of single persons. From this one should conclude that ideal mate images change over time as one becomes involved with various persons of the opposite sex and is more a product of one's previous and current experiences than a determiner of mate selection (Udry, 1965).

CASE

I am not sure just what kind of person I expected before I was married. I expected to marry a younger girl, but my wife is five years older than I am. I expected to marry an American girl, but my wife is Danish. I expected to get married when I was twenty-five, but I was married when I was twenty. I guess I don't really know what I expected, but I am satisfied with what I got.

There is no good evidence that ideal mate images influence mate selection. This seems further to emphasize the validity of the conclusions stated earlier that mate selection is not determined by personality factors to any great extent.

PARENT IMAGE AND MATE SELECTION

The nostalgic barbershop song, "I want a girl just like the girl that married dear old dad," embodies an idea of mate selection which is shared by popular psychology and Freudian psychoanalysis. The idea in its Freudian guise is simple: one's first love is for the opposite-sex parent. This love is given up or repressed during the resolution of the Oedipus conflict. In adolescence, the person is again free to fall in love, but this time he selects a love object with the qualities of the opposite-sex parent. In a test of this theory, Strauss (1946) elicited descriptions of parents and of mates from engaged and married persons. He found a greater-than-chance relationship between an individual's conception of his opposite-sex parent and his mate, thus presumably demonstrating mate selection on the basis of parent image. On the other hand, he found that if a person reported not having a satisfactory relationship with the parent, then he did not report a similarity between the spouse and the parent. It might be questioned whether this is valid evidence of the influence of parent image on mate selection. Strauss' subjects, it should be remembered, were newly married or engaged. If they remembered the parent relationship as unsatisfactory, then they did not describe the mates as similar to the parents. However, it would be necessary to have discovered the parent image *before* mate selection to know whether mate selection was affected by a preexisting parent image. One's present relationships always color his memories of previous relationships. Another study done with men (Strauss worked with women) shows that men tend to describe their mothers and other women with the same personality concepts. The "other women" here were unknown women, not mates (Secord and Jourard, 1956). This suggests two possibilities: either in adulthood the mother of a man is perceived as a member of the class "women," all of whom are seen similarly, or a man's concept of women in general is based on his experience with his mother. It certainly raises strong doubts as to whether any similarity in the way spouses and parents are perceived can be taken to mean that the spouse was picked because of some resemblance to the parent. *Parent images do not seem to be an important influence on mate selection.*

In another partially related study, Luckey (1961) shows that satisfied wives saw their husbands and fathers as similar, while unsatisfied wives saw their husbands and fathers as dissimilar. (The relationship did not appear for men's conceptions of mothers and wives.) It might be easy to interpret this to mean that a woman will be more happily married if she picks a husband that reminds her of her father. But, of course, the extent to which the resemblance perceived between father and husband may be a *result* of the marital experience is not known, and one could just as easily (perhaps with more justification) conclude that if women are happily married, they come to see their fathers and husbands as similar.

Parental Involvement in Mate Selection

CASE

I am willing to have the help of my parents on the selection of my future husband. They are more experienced than I am. They have better judgment than I have. They can investigate into the family background of young men. They are in a better position than I am to judge whether or not our families would get along well together. It seems to me that American girls are at a great disadvantage having to find their own husbands. They cannot consider all the important aspects of the marriage, such as how the families will get along, whether he is dependable. My parents love me. They know and understand me. I trust them to find someone whom I can learn to love. They would not force me to marry a man I could not learn to love. That I would not care for any more than an American girl would. But it is pleasant to know that there is someone interested in you who will find men from among whom you can make a selection (Bernard, Buchanan, and Smith, 1959: 151–152).

Most Americans find this statement by a Japanese student emotionally incomprehensible. Yet, while the values of American society seem to imply that young American people select their mates without any participation by parents, voluminous case-history material in the files of counselors everywhere indicates that parents participate in numerous and subtle ways. Parents select their residential neighborhood, schools for their children, social-club memberships, and numerous other family relationships with the conscious purpose in mind of controlling the social companions of their children and in this way controlling mate selection. A study by Bates indicates that at least a generation ago, most children experienced some direct parental influence in mate selection. Sons reported that parental influence was brought to bear on their courtships by fathers in 49 percent of the cases and by mothers in 79 percent of the cases. One in five subjects reported extreme pressure from parents. Daughters reported much more frequent experience of pressures from parents, with fathers exerting influence in two-thirds of the cases and mothers in almost every case (Bates, 1942). To what extent this is true today is not known.

Burgess and Wallin report that all four parents approved of three-fourths of the engagements they studied (Burgess and Wallin, 1953: 288). Furthermore, it appeared that parental approval was predictive of continuance of the relationship. More than twice as many relationships ended in broken engagements or early divorce when both of the girl's parents disapproved (32 percent) as when both parents approved (13 percent). The approval or disapproval of the man's parents does not seem to be nearly as important (Burgess and Wallin, 1953). Driscoll, Davis, and Lipetz (1972) believe that in spite of the "Romeo and Juliet" effect they found, persistent parental interference undermines the courtship process and prevents marriages. In reviewing the most significant premarital items in predicting marital adjustment, Burgess, Locke, and Thomes (1953: 561) report that approval of parents has been found predictive of success in marriage in at least six different studies.

Many parents would like to interpret these results as a validation of the superior wisdom of parents when it comes to selecting mates for their children. Children (until they become parents) might as well counter with the equally plausible explanation that it is the parental disapproval (and probably subsequent interference) which disrupts the relationship, thus fulfilling the parents' own prophecies. Either argument can be made with equal justification, and there is really no basis available for choosing between them.

Whatever values American culture has with respect to parental participation in the mate selection process, what apparently happens is this: parents (particularly higher-status parents) exercise considerable indirect control over the associations of their offspring. In this way, *parents help to determine an appropriate field of eligibles from which their child will select a mate.* From this field of eligibles, the young person selects a potential mate in ways which are not entirely clear to him or to researchers. Parents are then in a position to express their approval or disapproval of the potential spouse and in this way can exercise a kind of residual veto. Girls are much more likely to experience parental pressures than boys. Although folklore has it that parental pressure is likely to force the couple into reaction against the parents and elopement (and Burgess and Wallin confirm that most elopements in their sample were from couples with strong parental disapproval), parental disapproval may be effective in breaking up a substantial number of unwanted engagements.

A study by Coombs (1962) reveals that the more parents are in contact with their children during courtship, the more homogamous with respect to church affiliation and socioeconomic status are their children's mate choices — presumptive evidence of the parents' direct or indirect influence on the mate selection process.

An Interpretive View of Mate Selection

In adolescence, American youth are expected to begin dating and gradually establish a series of more or less erotic relationships with members of the opposite sex. These partners are almost always selected from among an immediate peer group in the same community. The actual choice of dates is restricted by matters of size, age, and the equal match of desirable (status) qualities, so that the practical choice is quite limited. Typically, these dating relationships now take the form of quasipermanent arrangements in middle and late adolescence, with increasing emotional and sexual involvement. Particular relationships are likely to be broken if they are uncongenial. Primarily, this means that if the couple finds too many disagreements and conflicts involved in their recreational relationship, the relationship will be terminated. Any particular relationship is likely to be discouraged by friends and relatives if the courtship bargain is not fairly equal, and this discouragement is effective in terminating courtships. If the conditions are at all appropriate and nothing disrupts the relationship, the couple will fall in love. If they are at an age when marriage is impractical in terms of their plans, the relationship is simply continued as a love relationship until it wears off. During love relationships, many important personality needs are met by the courtship, but the basic needs are not met by virtue of the peculiar combination of qualities of the partner. Most of the needs met in courtship can be met equally well by any member of the opposite sex of appropriate status qualities; esteem in someone else's eyes confirms the worth of the self in its own eyes. Success with the opposite sex confirms one's value in his sex role. The need to fall in love and be fallen in love with does not require a particular other person. When these basic needs are met, the details of "personality meshing" of the pair are filled in imaginatively by the partners. The relationship between the two personalities is not the basis for initial selection of

dates, nor is it the basis for determining whether the love relationship termi-
nates in marriage or separation. Rather, the personality match probably
determines the shape of the relationship established by the couple.

If the lovers are at a stage in their careers where marriage is practical,
or if one or both have particularly pressing needs to marry, the love relationship, instead of completing its course and dying a natural death, is carried
over into a marriage, and one says that the couple selected one another as
mates. In a sense, they did select one another. In an equally accurate sense,
they "happened" to one another.

Summary

Persons who select one another for marriage have been shown to be similar
in social, psychological, and physical characteristics. The conclusions with
respect to similarity or complementarity of personality characteristics in
mate selection must be considered an open question at this time. Scholars
are not agreed, and their studies do not agree. The plausibility of an idea is
not sufficient grounds for its acceptance in the absence of consistent evidence. Certainly any blanket notion such as "opposites attract" is so naïve
as to be useless in describing mate selection. At any rate, there is only a slight
relationship between what a person thinks is the personality of the mate
he has selected and the actual personality of the mate. This phenomenon
may aptly be called the "idealization of the mate."

American culture supplies standard patterns by which Americans form
their images of ideal mates. These culturally shared images are organized
around sex-role stereotypes of masculinity and femininity to a considerable
extent. The male's cultural image of the ideal mate focuses much more on
physical attributes of the female, and the female's cultural image of the ideal
mate focuses much more on behavioral traits. These ideal images probably
play their part in mate selection by sorting mates according to their approxi-
mation of the cultural ideals. Individuals apparently hold ideal mate images
which are reflections of felt personality needs, but the importance of this
ideal mate image in influencing mate selection has never been demonstrated.
Contingency factors, many beyond the control of the individual, affect mate
selection to such a great extent that personality characteristics play a relatively insignificant role in the actual selection. This is an unpalatable finding
to many Americans because it so directly contradicts their cultural values
and intuitive feelings. Until evidence is produced to the contrary, however,
it will have to stand as the conclusion which most adequately summarizes
what is known at this time. The only consistent finding with respect to what
could be called a "psychological" characteristic is that people who share a
considerable area of agreement with one another on matters of importance
to them are most likely to choose one another as mates.

Engagement 10

Heterosexual relationships move along a continuum—sometimes rapidly, sometimes slowly—between casual, noninvolved, noncommital associations and intense, emotionally encompassing, permanent commitment relationships. It might be instructive to separate the emotional involvement and the permanent commitment factors for examination. Young couples with regular, frequent association with one another can rapidly become highly emotionally involved with no permanent commitment to the relationship. So-called "summer romances" are frequently of this sort. Continuous association builds up a high pitch of emotionality, but the partners know that "when the summer ends," they will go their ways separately, and the emotional exhilaration will disappear. On the other hand, couples not infrequently drift gradually into understandings of future commitment to one another without ever experiencing a high pitch of emotional involvement. The normal course of love relationships during adolescence includes periods of intense emotional interdependence, but with only short-term future obligation.

Changes in Courtship

In the contemporary courtship scene, most individuals will go through a series of such involvements. One or more for many persons ends in marriage. Farber contrasts this with the courtship pattern of forty years ago which was characterized by a "continuous narrowing of the field of prospective spouses" (Farber, 1964: 161). This new pattern contains within it at least the implicit recognition that hardly anyone believes anymore in the concept of the "one true love," and that love relationships are by their very nature temporary. Farber suggests that the new courtship pattern is conducive to a set of norms involving "permanent availability" as a mate rather than permanent commitment as a mate (Farber, 1964: 163). Blood (1962) takes another point of view, believing that a series of serious emotional involvements is better preparation for marriage than a series of dalliance relationships while narrowing the field. Perhaps these should not be seen as opposed points of view. The series of emotional affairs resembles a series of short marriages, at least in its emotional aspects. It is better preparation for marriage if marriage is viewed primarily as an emotional love affair, to be terminated and replaced if it proves unsatisfying. However, the concept of permanent commitment to the relationship is absent in both the premarital and marital affairs. Perhaps the addition of steps to the commitment continuum in the United States can be seen as cautiousness in admitting that one has incurred permanent obligations. In addition to the casual date, Americans have initiated going steady, dating steadily, pinning, engagement to be engaged, and engagement, all stages at which the relationship can be terminated with no breach of faith. "Breach of promise" suits have virtually disappeared from the American scene today, and a younger generation may not even have heard of their existence, because Americans are increasingly unwilling to view any human association as permanently binding. The prevalence of this point of view has fundamentally changed the nature of engagement.

A century ago, engagement was a public announcement of intent and promise to marry. To break an engagement was more or less disgraceful, implying the probable discovery of some impediment to the marriage or some shameful occurrence. To end an engagement was also likely to result in legal complications. How much America has changed since those days is indicated by the fact that in the Burgess and Wallin study of engaged couples in the 1940s, a third of the subjects had one or more previously broken engagements, and one in five broke the engagement they had at the time of their testing. Burgess and Wallin and many other writers in the field encourage couples to break engagements rather than enter marriages which will be unhappy. They feel that perhaps more marriages would be successful if more people broke their engagements when in doubt. This was particularly emphasized by the Burgess-Wallin finding that couples who have a great deal of trouble during engagement are highly likely to have a great deal of trouble in marriage (Burgess and Wallin, 1953). As a consequence of the prevalence of these ideas, few people hesitate to break an engagement if they think they can do better elsewhere, and few people hesitate to marry a person who has been engaged several times before. Engagement has become the last of several tentative steps toward greater involvement in the lives of two people and toward marriage.

The courtship patterns which resulted in marriage for three generations of American women give some insight into changes in engagement behavior in the period covered. The first generation consisted of married, college-

Table 10-1

THERE IS A TREND TOWARD SHORTER BUT MORE INTENSIVE COURTSHIP
Changes in courtship behavior of three generations of women

	Generation		
	3	2	1
Modal age	78	48	23
Dates per week during engagement	1	2	3
Discussed problem areas before marriage	4.5%		49%
Length of engagement in months	8.99	8.45	7.18
Knew mate one year or less before marriage	19%	22%	29%
Knew mate 7 years or more before marriage	23.5%	11.5%	12%
Median age difference of mates in years	4.45	3.78	2.74

Source: Koller, 1951

trained women, and the second and third generations were the mothers and grandmothers of the first generation. (The first generation would be the age of the mothers of present-day college women.) Table 10-1 compares the courtship experiences of these women with the men they eventually married for the first time. Generally, the latest generation had three times as many dates per week during engagement, indicating a more intense level of courtship interaction. Where the oldest generation rarely discussed problem areas before marriage with their fiancés, half of the youngest group did so. While the older generation knew their mates longer before marriage and had slightly longer engagements, the much more intensive level of interaction and the discussion of problems during courtship experienced by the younger group suggests that they almost certainly had much more complete knowledge of their mates before marriage than their grandmothers did (Koller, 1951).

Today among middle-class couples, engagement usually consists of two stages: first, the couple reaches a private understanding that they plan to marry; later (sometimes a year or two), if they are still sufficiently involved, the next step is taken in the form of a public announcement. (Sometimes intimate friends have known of the plans for a long time, of course.) The public significance of such an announcement is evidently far more important for the woman than for the man. College sorority and dormitory houses for women regularly have touching ceremonies to celebrate the engagement of members, and the announcement, in addition to the display of the ring, constitutes a signal for congratulations to the successful girl. However, little activity of this sort takes place on the part of males. *Her* picture appears in the newspaper, not his. At least the formal behavior of Americans still suggests that the girl is being congratulated for having won a commitment in a contest with a reluctant partner. Or perhaps these formal acts should be seen as an announcement of the removal of the girl from the marriage market.

Engagement As a Shift in Roles

Engagement introduces nonrecreational, nonfun aspects into the relationship for the first time. When a man and woman have agreed on plans for marriage, they can now overtly and publicly begin to see one another as prospective spouses. Under contemporary courtship situations, the transition to engagement frequently occurs by imperceptible stages and without a "proposal of marriage," so that couples just gradually come to realize that they are planning to marry. Once they have reached that stage, things begin to matter that were of no consequence in recreational courtship. For the first time, the partner's family may have to be reckoned with.

CASE

The only problem we have encountered which has not been or cannot be solved is the attitude of my parents toward us. My parents feel I am still their baby and are trying desperately to keep me that way without letting me do anything on my own, but also, I feel there is a fear on my mother's part of growing old, feeling if I stay young, so will she, and my engagement to Helen has burst this bubble of youth, and as a result, she (my mother) has turned hostile not only towards Helen but towards me also which bothers Helen more than it does me.

Can the mate have children? Does he want to have children? Does he know anything about contraception? Does he snore? What will he do for a living? How would I like my children to look like him? These and a thousand other questions engaged persons first ask themselves. Courtships successfully culminate in engagement primarily on the basis of recreational compatibility and emotional rapport; engagements flounder on more mundane obstacles. Couples who never had an argument during preengagement will frequently find their first grounds for disagreement in exploring the possibilities of an impending marriage with one another.

CASE

I was going to college when I started going with Marian. I was very much in love with her. She was still in high school, and we were going to get married after she graduated. We went together for nine months before we became engaged, and we were engaged five months before I broke up. When we started going together, we were both very happy. It wasn't until we became engaged when our differences conflicted and we continuously argued. It seemed that we both wanted our own way all of the time. I expected too much from Marian. It seemed that I wanted a perfect person rather than a human being, and I wanted to change her and found that to be impossible. This led to conflict. Neither of us were happy with each other, or away from each other. So I thought it best that we break up.

The solemnness of conversation between engaged persons indicates that couples take seriously the idea that it is important for them to talk over all the aspects of marriage to see if they agree. What they do not always understand is that marriage expectations and role conceptions are constantly changing and that they change rather markedly from before to after marriage. The discovery of agreement during engagement cannot be taken as a guarantee that in two years the very subject will not be one of disagreement. And, of course, disagreement on a subject during engagement may disappear with actual marital experience. Couples sometimes feel called upon to resolve differences of opinion during courtship that could well wait until later. For example, deciding during engagement how many children the couple is going to have or whether or not they are going to be strict or permissive disciplinarians approaches fantasy. These decisions emerge from later experience and not from engagement decisions. Couples nevertheless feel constrained to solve these "problems" in advance, and are so advised by their counselors, because they are convinced that the success of their marriage hinges on making a good initial choice of mate; they want to be sure they have chosen wisely.

Engagement As a Period for Screening Out Unsatisfactory Pairs

Most discussions of engagement emphasize its importance as a period for eliminating those couples from marriage who would not be successful as married pairs. As support for the idea that engagement performs this screening, many studies have shown that an engagement period of reasonable length is a predictor of marital adjustment (three months to a year or so being the usual recommendation). The fact that many engagements break up is also taken as evidence that unviable marriage pairs are the ones that break. Couples in one study (Burgess and Wallin, 1953) gave the following reasons for breaking engagements (in order of frequency):
1. Slight emotional attachment.
2. Separation.
3. Parental opposition.
4. Cultural divergences.
5. Personality problems.

The first factor, "slight emotional attachment," should be presented in more detail, but couples cannot be expected to give causal explanations of why their interest in one another has sagged. Separation is an understandable factor. However, one might surmise that some separations cause loss of interest, while some losses of interest cause separations. It is suspected that the advice frequently given to the effect that if a couple's love is "strong" or "true," it will survive separation is a cynical manipulation by those who disapprove of the relationship. If "absence makes the heart grow fonder," it is for someone who is not absent. Nothing more clearly demonstrates the destructive effect of long separation on even long-established marriages than the divorce rate after World War II. Parents whose children are about to contract undesirable engagements have long known and used this fact: it is intimate association which generates and maintains emotional relationships. Correspondence is a partial but pale substitute for physical presence. Probably the single best method of breaking an engagement is for the couple to be separated for several months, often by going, or being sent, to different colleges.

Broken couples frequently mention personality conflict or incompatibility as a reason for their breakup. However, two careful studies have been unable to distinguish the personality differences between those engaged couples who break up and those who marry (Burgess, 1953; Udry, 1967). Either personality match has little to do with the outcome of engagements, or the measuring instruments of the researchers are too blunt to ferret out the subtle factors involved.

There is some evidence, then, to support the notion that engagement is an effective period of testing the relationship on greater levels of involvement, since problems during engagement predict problem marriages, since those engagements which break differ from those which do not in some of the same ways that unadjusted marriages differ from adjusted marriages, and since an engagement of some duration is predictive of marital success. On the other hand, although they are statistically reliable, none of these relationships is particularly strong. Most couples who are engaged are convinced that their marriages will be successful; yet, from this group come bad marriages and broken marriages. No one can promise those with blissful engagements that they will live happily ever after. The absence of instrumental requirements in the relationship, the ability of strong erotic needs to help the couple "solve" engagement problems, and the general recreational nature of engagement activities keeps strains and disagreements at a minimum for most people and does not really "test" the relationship. Yet, the wide scope of eroticism and recreation as tension-reduction mechanisms for troubles during engagement has been disparaged by too many writers, who look at them as unrealistic escape mechanisms shielding the couple from a cold appraisal of problems. A more tolerant view would suggest that eroticism is for married couples also a basis for reducing interpersonal tensions, surmounting disagreements, and reasserting the solidarity and viability of the relationship in spite of disagreement and conflict. The marriage in which sex does not perform this function is missing one of its fundamental supports. It does not seem sensible, then, to recommend to the engaged couple that they avoid using their erotic attraction in this way. Likewise, recreation for married couples is time for the establishment of that psychological intimacy and the temporary freedom from concern over instrumental problems which provides carefree interludes in the marriage. Engaged couples who surmount their problems through eroticism and recreation are experiencing during engagement the same thing that will cement their emotional union if they continue through to marriage. Those writers who suggest a cold appraisal during engagement hope to see broken all those engagements which would lead to marriages with disagreement and conflict. This is a futile hope. Marriage, childbearing, and family life generate disagreement and conflict which cannot be ascertained from the vantage point of engagement. Nor can these problems always be resolved; frequently one only learns to live with them and, perhaps, outlast them. It seems more realistic to encourage couples during engagement to discover and exploit ways of drawing together, in spite of their problems, rather than to encourage ways of thought which make breaking relationships the alternative to harmonious bliss.

Sex and Engagement

In Chapter 6 the importance of the relationship between emotional commitment and sexual intimacy for women was emphasized. The high level of emotional involvement and the expectation of permanence of the relationship gives strong support to additional sexual intimacy during engagement. Actually, in European peasant groups, the social mores have permitted sexual intercourse to engaged couples for centuries, frequently under the fairly direct surveillance of parents, so this can hardly be considered a modern innovation.

It has become a part of the courtship ideology of certain groups of American youth that a relationship can only be completely meaningful if it includes sexual realization as well as other intimacies. Burgess and Wallin (Burgess and Wallin, 1953) asked engaged couples in their sample who reported premarital intercourse with one another whether they thought the experience had strengthened or weakened their relationship. Not surprisingly, 92.6 percent of the men and 90.6 percent of the women said that they thought it had strengthened the relationship, and practically none thought it had weakened it. This finding needs to be evaluated against the fact that engaged couples experiencing intercourse had lower engagement success scores in the study. The latter fact, on the other hand, should probably be interpreted to mean that those who establish their sexual relationship before marriage are less conventional in other ways and have other characteristics which lower engagement success, rather than that the intercourse itself was responsible for lower scores. It is not very meaningful to ask couples what effect intercourse has had on their relationship; they can hardly be expected to act as unbiased observers of their own behavior. Some relationships are probably damaged by sexual intimacy, and some are not. After extended interviews with college males, Kirkendall comes to what is probably the soundest conclusion on the subject:

> Some deeply affectionate couples have, through the investment of time and mutual devotion, built a relationship which is significant to them, and in which they have developed a mutual respect. Some of these couples are relatively free from the customary inhibitions about sexual participation. Some couples with this kind of relationship and background can, and do, experience intercourse without damage to their total relationship. The expression "without damage" is used in preference to "strengthening," for it seems that in practically all instances "non-damaging" intercourse occurred in relationships which were already so strong in their own right that intercourse did not have much to offer toward strengthening them (Kirkendall, 1961: 199-200).

Since complete sexual relations have become more common between engaged couples, one should expect those who engage in them to become the more ordinary rather than the more peculiar couples, with the probable consequence of a disappearance in subsequent studies of differences in success between continent and cohabiting engaged couples. Should coitus in engagement become the rule rather than the exception and should it become supported by conventional morality, one might predict that those who avoided intercourse would be the poor marriage risks. The couple who refrains from intercourse when everyone believes that intercourse is necessary to cement "meaningful relationships" may find that they do not have a meaningful relationship.

Engagement As a Preparation Period

For most couples, engagement is a decision to marry, not a decision to think about marriage and test the relationship. From their subjective point of view, engagement emerges as a period of planning and preparation. The "testing and screening" is really a "latent" function of engagement perceived by scholars who study courtship, and plays little part in the couple's thinking. It does not seem like reasonable advice to say to a couple which has decided to marry, "Now that you have decided to marry, you can use this period before marriage as a time for objective scrutiny of yourself and your prospective mate to decide whether this is really going to work out or not." If the engagement is broken, it will probably not be a result of the couple's decision that their marriage would be unsuccessful, but rather a result of their dissatisfaction with the courtship-engagement relationship *at that time.*

The Intrusion of Society

The approach of marriage for the engaged couple is accompanied by a series of rituals and other activities which serve to emphasize the broader commitments they are about to acquire, while deemphasizing the intimate, erotic-pair relationship which has until this time been so all-important. Philip Slater, in an article from which the following paragraphs are selected, suggests that it is the intrusion of other social groups on the sex-pair relationship which keeps everyone from withdrawing into sex pairs and thus atomizing society into pairs of lovers.

As the marriage approaches there is a rapid acceleration of the involvement of the families of the couple in their relationship. Increasing stress is placed upon an awareness of the ritual, legal, and economic significance of the relationship, and the responsibilities which must be assumed. In addition to the traditional evaluations made at this juncture of the bread-winning and home-making capabilities of the two individuals, there may even be, as Whyte has suggested, a concern about the social appropriateness of the wife for the organizational setting in which the husband must move.

But societal invasion on the free and exclusive intimacy of the couple (assuming this to have been the nature of the relationship prior to this time) is not limited to such overt influence. The entire ceremony constitutes a rehearsal for the kind of societal relationship which is expected of them later. First of all, the ceremony is usually a sufficiently involved affair to require a number of practical social decisions from the couple in preparation for the occasion. Much of their interaction during this period will thus concern issues external to their own relationship, and there will be a great deal of preoccupation with loyalties and obligations outside of the dyad itself. Guests must be invited, attendants chosen, and gifts for the attendants selected. The ceremony has the effect of concentrating the attention of both individuals on every *other* affectional tie either one has ever contracted.

Similarly, the ceremony serves to emphasize the *dependence* of the dyadic partners on other collectivities. In addition to the gifts given to the couple, it is made clear to them that much of the responsibility for their wedding rests with their families, who bear a far greater burden in this regard than they themselves. They are, in essence, "given" a wedding.

Their feelings of harassment and anxiety over the coming event, coupled with the realization that their role is at the moment a relatively minor one, and will throughout be a passive one, inculcates a feeling that the dyadic relationship is not their "personal affair." They become more aware that after marriage, too, life will involve instrumental responsibilities, extra-dyadic personal obligations, and societal dependence. It is usually during this period that the impulse toward dyadic withdrawal reasserts itself, and one or the other will half-seriously suggest elopement. By now there is a feeling that they have set in motion a vast machine over which they no longer have any control. But it is usually felt that things have "gone too far"—parents and friends would be disappointed and hurt, eyebrows would be raised—there is no turning back. The impulse is overwhelmed by the feelings of loyalty and obligation which the impending ceremony has aggravated, and the crucial moment passes.

. . . As the time for the wedding draws near, the forces drawing the couple apart become more intense. It is often believed to be "bad luck" for the groom to see the bride in her wedding dress before the ceremony, and, in general, contact between the couple on the day of the wedding is considered bad form. When they enter the church it is from opposite ends, as leaders of separate hosts of followers. Prior to the wedding day there are showers or a bridal supper for the bride and a "bachelor's dinner" for the groom, in which peer group ties are very strongly underlined. This tends to create the impression that in some way the couple *owe* their relationship to these groups, who are preparing them ceremonially for their marriage. Often this is made explicit, with family and friends vying with one another in claiming responsibility for having "brought them together" in the first place. This impression of societal initiative is augmented by the fact that the bride's father "gives the bride away." The retention of this ancient custom in modern times serves explicitly to deny the possibility that the couple might unite quite on their own. In other words, the marriage ritual is designed to make it appear as if somehow the idea of the dyadic union sprang from the community, and not from the dyad itself. In this respect, marriage in our society resembles the ritual of the parent who discovers a child eating candy, and says, "I didn't hear you ask for that," whereupon the child says, "May I?" and the parent says, "Yes, you may." The families and friends may actually have had nothing to do with the match, or even have opposed it. The members of the wedding party often come from far away, and some of them may be strangers to one another. The ceremony itself, however, its corollary rituals, and the roles which pertain to it, all tends to create an image of two individuals, propelled toward each other by a united phalanx of partisans.[1]

The number of decisions which have to be made in the months before marriage can be staggering if there is to be an elaborate wedding. For many college couples, educational and occupational decisions which have long-term implications for their future are probably being made at practically the same time. Housing has to be arranged (in some places still a major problem for the young couple); housekeeping equipment purchased; premarital physical examinations arranged; counseling sessions planned with a minister for church-oriented couples; arrangements made for the printing and mailing of invitations (and decisions as to who should be invited) to the wedding; decisions reached on the details and scope of the wedding itself, reception, or other formal festivities; clothing purchases, honeymoon plans, if any; purchasing the ring; and a thousand other little problems must be attended to at the very time when the couple's demands for privacy and intimacy are at a peak. It is small wonder that a few couples decide that formal plans are far too much trouble and cut them all short with a private marriage.

[1] Philip Slater, "Social Limitations on Libidinal Withdrawal," *American Journal of Sociology,* LXVII (November, 1961), pp. 296–311. Reprinted by permission.

Marital Interaction Processes

11

Americans do not know what happens after marriage. This situation seems strange in view of the fact that nearly everyone lives with a married couple during his childhood and should, therefore, have some reasonably accurate impressions of marriage. Yet, most married Americans do not know what has happened to their marriages; how can the unmarried be expected to be more knowledgeable? The ignorance of marital processes for the unmarried is sociologically quite understandable: As a child, one interacts with parents within a parent-child relationship. There is little in this interaction which gives a child much insight into the husband-wife relationship from which he is excluded. Furthermore, he can only observe his parents from the vantage point of his role as a child and their joint role as parents to him. Much of the most important husband-wife interaction is deliberately excluded from children's observation (sexual interaction, many arguments, and much of the intimate tête-à-tête which forms a significant part of marital interaction).

In this state of pluralistic ignorance, two myths describe the popular image of marriage: one is cynical, the other, idealistic. Both are held simultaneously by many people. The first myth says, "and they lived happily ever after." This is the myth which holds marriage to be a continuous courtship. The second myth is the picture of the domestic grind: the husband sits behind the paper, the wife moves about in morning disarray; the husband leaves for work, the wife spends the day among dishes, diapers, and dirty little children. Although, as with most myths, no one *really* believes either one of them, they continue to affect the behavior of most people. Perhaps most people faintly hope to live happily ever after, but rather fear dreary domesticity will be their lot.

Family sociologists, too, have their models of marital reality. Since they are scientific abstractions based on averages of thousands of diverse individual cases, the sociological models might be called statistical myths. At a time in which courses in marriage are part of the college curriculum, there

200

is a curious similarity between the sociological myths and the popular myths, each popular myth having its sociological counterpart.

The Period of Adjustment

The sociological model with the longest tradition lays out a scenario for the American marriage of today. Couples marry at the height of their romantic love for one another. The honeymoon period is one of continued courtship— a kind of extra holiday from the mundane responsibilities of conjugal life. After the honeymoon (about which sociologists are rather ambivalent, some endorsing it with qualifications, others seeing it as a barbaric custom best dispensed with), the couples enter the "period of adjustment." Gradually, or sometimes suddenly, they are presented with the realities of marital life. Their idealized pictures of one another from courtship crumble under the impact of sharing the same bathroom and listening to one another snore. Their "true selves" are revealed to one another in the harsh glare of marital reality. They discover that they have many problems which they either avoided or had no occasion to face during courtship. Their sexual life is troublesome because of their lack of experience and their clumsiness. Many problems arise for the first time. The first year or two is rough. However, they are in love, and love helps them solve some of their problems. There is give and take in decision-making in the good marriages, and petulance and obstinacy in those not so good. These problems are usually said to be things which could have been discovered and thrashed out during courtship, had not eroticism dominated their relationship then. Those people who did not select their mates properly are not able to solve the problems of the adjustment period, and the marriage eventually breaks up. Of course, the maladjustment may go on for a few years before the couple gives up, but generally, most marriages which are going to break up do so during this period of initial adjustment.

In the traditional pattern, the good marriages, where sensible mate selection prevailed and where the partners are "mature," come through the adjustment period, changed, however, from what they were. Romantic love has been transmuted into "mature" conjugal love which continues to be the basis of permanent marriages. The period-of-adjustment myth, then, is really seen to be a sociological sequel to the romantic courtship ideas of American society: A kind of romanticized domesticity is achieved by couples who have selected mates sensibly and survived the shattering of romance, while those who do not select sensible mates, or who are demoralized by the loss of romance, get divorced.

Divorce statistics based on the duration of the marriage give some insight into the period of adjustment. Jacobson provides the following interesting figures. He maintains that at the turn of the century, the divorce rate was at a maximum for those married about 4 years. By the 1920s, it was about 3 years. For those married after 1943, the peak rate is 1 or 2 years. It is not yet completely clear how much World War II was responsible for this shift, since the post-1943 figures Jacobson presents are greatly expanded by marriages contracted during the war years. Figures for marriages contracted in 1910, 1920, and 1930, however, show divorce rates remaining about the same for persons married 5 to 9 years as those married 0 to 4 years, and the divorce rate for persons married 10 to 14 years nearly as high. The changes since then are heavily distorted by the very high divorce rates immediately after the war (Jacobson, 1959: 94–95).

A more searching look at Jacobson's data shows that for those people married in 1928, the divorce rate for couples married 15 to 19 years was nearly as high as that of the first 4 years; those divorcing after 15 to 19 years of marriage were divorcing in 1943–1947. For those married during 1931–1934, the rates for divorce after 10 to 14 years of married life were *higher* than for marriages of shorter duration. Those divorcing after 10 to 14 years were divorcing in 1941–1947. Circumstances of the war years caused the high divorce rates for couples of *all* durations of marriage up to 20 years.

These data seem to indicate that the *early years of marriage are not as unusually precarious compared to the rest as one might suppose; rather, circumstances which try the marriage are likely to break it up at almost any period.* This probably even holds true for marriages of over 20 years' duration. The decline in divorce rates after 20 years of marriage may only be due to the fact that an increasing number of marriages during this period are broken by death.

No known important study shows an adjustment pattern of brief initial adjustment, conflict and lack of adjustment in the early year or years, followed by a continuous period of even-keel adjustment. In the cross-sectional studies (those which study a group of persons at one point in their lives only), the results are inconsistent. Starting with work in the early 1930s (Lang, 1932), and extending to the 1960s (Luckey, 1966), a dozen studies can be summarized as follows: *there appears to be a consistent decline in marital satisfaction during the first decade of marriage.* After that, most studies show inconsistent patterns with "ups and downs."

All of these studies were done by studying *once* a group of couples differing among themselves in the number of years married. Each is open to alternate interpretations. It may be that an older generation of couples simply did not contract as happy marriages as the younger ones, so that the couples married most recently score highest on happiness. The resolution for this problem of interpretation lies in studying the same couples over the years of marriage. Only two well-known studies have interviewed couples more than once in their marriages. The best known of these is the Burgess-Wallin study (Burgess and Wallin, 1953). These couples were first studied during engagement, next during the early years of marriage (3 to 5 years), and a

Chart 11-1

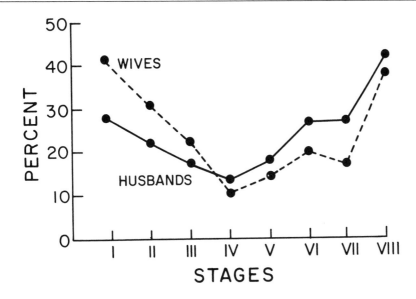

MARRIAGES GO LESS SMOOTHLY IN THE MIDDLE YEARS
*Percent of individuals at each stage of the family life cycle reporting
their marriages were going well all the time*

Source: Rollins and Feldman, 1970

third time after 18 to 20 years of marriage. They showed a consistent decline
in marital adjustment from the early to the later years of marriage. The
greatest decline was noted in the following areas: companionship, demonstration of affection, common interests, consensus, belief in the permanence
of the union, and marital-adjustment scores. On the other hand, there was
no change, according to Burgess and Locke (based on Burgess' analysis of
the data), in reported marital happiness, sex adjustment, rating of mate's
personality traits, and idealization of the mate's personality, among other
items. Burgess and Locke interpret these data to mean that the spouses
gradually grow apart over the years (what Pineo, 1961 calls "disengagement") but have not essentially changed their reactions and attitudes toward
the marriage or their mates (Burgess et al., 1963: 502-503). Pineo (1961:
10-11) interprets the same data to mean that "a process of gradually reducing marital satisfaction or euphoria typically characterizes the marriages
studied," but that this loss of marital satisfaction is not accompanied by an
equal loss of personal adjustment.

Another interesting finding from the middle years follow-up of the
Burgess-Wallin couples is that those couples who divorced between the first
and the second testings did not have very different mean engagement-

Chart 11-2

FAMILY LIFE IS LEAST SATISFYING AT THE LAUNCHING STAGE
*Percent of individuals in each stage of the family life cycle reporting
that their present stage of the family life cycle is very satisfying*

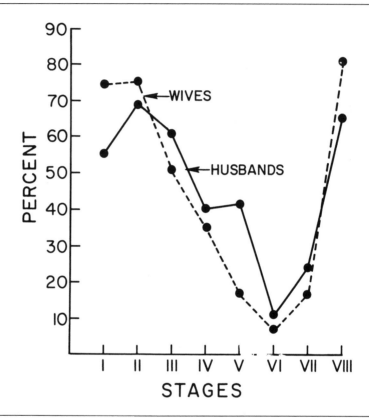

Source: Rollins and Feldman, 1970

adjustment scores from the couples who remained married. In fact, the divorcing men actually had *higher* engagement-adjustment scores than the remainder of the sample; they looked like "good" engagements, but they were divorced after 5 years (Pineo, 1961). There will be occasion to refer to this later in connection with mate selection and marital adjustment, but it might be suggested now that this points to the fact that the problem of adjustment is not necessarily an initial one, but something which arises in the processes of the marital relationship. Pineo puts it this way: "We feel that it is unforeseen *changes* in the situation, personality, or behavior which contribute most to the disenchantment occurring after five years of marriage." (Pineo, 1961: 7, emphasis added.)

Chart 11-3

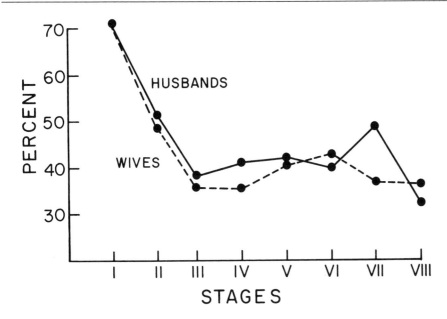

COMPANIONSHIP WITH THE MATE IS MOST
CHARACTERISTIC OF EARLY MARRIAGE
*Percent of individuals in each stage of family life cycle reporting positive
companionship experiences with their spouses at least once a day or more often*

Source: Rollins and Feldman, 1970

The most recent study available examined the pattern of satisfactions with marriage using a life-cycle approach. The subjects were couples living in middle-class white neighborhoods in a city in a northeastern state. Couples were classified on the basis of length of time married, age of the oldest child, and residence of the children, into the following stages of the family cycle:

    I. Beginning marriage (before children)
    II. Oldest child an infant
    III. Oldest child a preschooler
    IV. Oldest child an elementary school child
    V. Oldest child a teenager
    VI. Oldest child living away from home, other children at home
    VII. All children living away from home
    VIII. Husband retired.

Charts 11-1, 11-2, and 11-3 show the patterns of satisfactions at different family life-cycle stages. Chart 11-1 shows that the proportion of couples reporting that their marriages were "going well all the time" declined consistently from early marriage until reaching a low point in the group whose oldest child was in elementary school, after which it rose more or less regularly, reaching the highest point in the retirement stage. Chart 11-2 shows the proportion of couples reporting that their present stage in the life cycle is very satisfying. Here the pattern is a fairly consistent decline from stages I and II to a low point when the children are being launched into the world, after which it rapidly recovers and reaches a high point with retirement. Chart 11-3 shows that the proportion of couples reporting positive companionship experiences with their spouses at least once a day or more often rapidly declines from early marriage to a low point in the group with preschoolers, and never really recovers. Smoothness of the marital relationship and general satisfaction with family life evidently hit a low point during the rearing of children and then recover, but satisfying companionship with the mate is primarily an experience of the early years of marriage only (Rollins and Feldman, 1970). Roughly parallel results were obtained by Burr (1970) in a similar study published simultaneously.

Most of the studies quoted here lead to a formulation of the second sociological model of the marital process: "Loss of satisfaction is . . . generally an inescapable consequence of the passage of time in a marriage" (Pineo, 1961). This model has a remarkable similarity to the popular myth of the domestic grind.

Characteristics of Marriage Which Improve

Students are quick to point out that not every couple quietly watches its marriage deteriorate. Pineo's data suggest that as many as one couple in four actually improved its relationship between the early and middle years. Most students want to know the special characteristics of those which improve as contrasted to those which deteriorate most. An analysis of the final Burgess-Wallin couple data by Dizard (Dizard, 1968) contains some surprise answers. The couples who increased in happiness with their marriage were those in which the husband had experienced a decrease in income in the previous fifteen years or so, especially if he had also decreased his level of participation in other community organizations. The couples who were most likely to report decreases in happiness during this period were those in which the husband had experienced a great increase in income and had risen to the top of his profession in the past fifteen years or so, especially if this was accompanied by his increasing involvement with other community organizations, while the wife was decreasing her community involvement. Dizard interprets these data to mean that men who devote themselves to their wives and families at the expense of occupational success and community involvement will end up with happy marriages, while those who devote all their energies to occupational success and community activities to the neglect of their wives will end up with unhappy marriages. Other interpretations of the data are equally plausible, and the reader may wish to try his hand at a more satisfying explanation.

A second longitudinal study of changes in the marital relationship provided some especially valuable insights into the differences in good marriages and poor marriages. Three hundred couples were studied at engagement. Of these, about one-third were contacted again after eighteen years of marriage. Uhr compared the changes in the personalities of the most happily married with the changes in the least happy. The findings are intriguing. Happy couples were characterized by consistency of the husbands' personality and great change in the wives', while unhappy couples were characterized by great change for the husband and little for the wives. Of the four groups, unhappy women were the most consistent in personality over the twenty years, while the happy wives were the least consistent. Uhr concluded *that in happy marriages, the wives change to adapt to the marriage, while unhappy wives remain essentially the same in personality as they were during the engagement* (Uhr, 1957). One is tempted to account for the happiness by the change pattern, but it would be equally possible to explain the change pattern by the happiness.

Several other studies indicate that wives more than husbands determine marital adjustment. Kieren and Tallman (1972) found that the wife's flexibility, empathy, and motivation to solve marital problems was positively associated with the husband's marital happiness, but this was not true when the sexes were reversed.

Pineo's (1969) further analysis of the Burgess-Wallin couples weakens the argument for the influence of wives on marital adjustment. He found no indication that women made more adjustments in marriage than men, although the couples in the study *felt* that the wives made more adjustments. What he did find was the most dissatisfied couples made the most changes in their attitudes and behavior, although these changes did not increase marital satisfaction.

Adjustment-Happiness-Success

The marital-adjustment studies reported in this chapter have been criticized by a number of sociologists on many grounds. The most consistent criticism is leveled against the criteria for the dependent variable — success of the marriage. In most studies, the success of the marriage is measured by a composite instrument which taps such areas as amount of conflict, degree of agreement, shared activities, self-ratings on happiness, satisfaction or criticism toward the spouse, perceived permanence of the marriage, and other areas which are analytically quite distinct from one another. Every scholar who had conducted these studies would admit that marital adjustment has never been shown by anyone to be a single general factor—that is, that all of these separate areas of the composite are, in fact, systematically related on one dimension. Locke analyzed his marital-adjustment data and discovered several fairly independent factors but no *general* factor which could be called adjustment (Locke and Williamson, 1958). Another factor analysis of family problem areas produced five major factors but no general factor (Brim et al., 1961). Its authors conclude that family problems are specific to roles and areas of activity. They interpret their findings as contradicting the common assumption that economic problems are related to interpersonal ones and that interpersonal problems in the marital and parental roles are closely related. Other factor analyses lead to the same conclusion: when sociologists talk about marital adjustment, they are talking about a number of independent variables (Farber, 1962). It is important to keep this in mind in reading subsequent sections of this book and other books reporting on the marital-adjustment studies. This is unfortunate because it is confusing for the student. Since the major studies have been reported in terms of combined criteria of marital adjustment, their results are conceptually clouded.

Theoretically, at least, one can easily see that a couple might share fewer activities, yet rate themselves happier with the marriage than when they were sharing more activities; on the other hand, they might see the marriage as quite permanent, yet have a high level of conflict, be very critical of one another, share many activities, and be quite unhappy. It was stressed earlier in the book that the purpose of marriage in contemporary middle-class America, as perceived by the spouses, is personal happiness. It appears from Pineo's data that although the marital adjustment of most couples declined, their own personal satisfactions from life did not decline. Uhr's analysis indicates that the couples who rated themselves as least happy in their marriages actually had become better adjusted personally than they were when they were married, so that after twenty years there were no differences in personal adjustment between them and the couples who were happily married (Uhr, 1957). In a way, the object of the marriage was fulfilled even if the marriage was not perceived as the source of satisfaction. Looked at from another point of view, and perhaps a more defensible one, it appears that the longer couples are married, the less their satisfaction and personal adjustment depends on their marital relationship. Even though couples may be getting less from their marriages, they really do not think any less well of their spouses after twenty years than after three (Pineo, 1961).

Chart 11-4

MARITAL SATISFACTIONS AND TENSIONS MEASURE MARITAL ADJUSTMENT
Satisfaction and tension items on the Marital Adjustment Balance Scale

Satisfactions

I'm going to read you some things that married couples often do together. Tell me which ones you and your (husband/wife) have done together in the *past few weeks:*

Had a good laugh together or shared a joke
Been affectionate toward each other
Spent an evening just chatting with each other
Did something the other particularly appreciated
Visited friends together
Entertained friends in your home
Taken a drive or walk for pleasure
Gone out together—movie, bowling, sporting, or other entertainment
Ate out in a restaurant together

Tensions

Now I'm going to read you some things about which husbands and wives sometimes agree and sometimes disagree; would you tell me which ones caused differences of opinions or were problems in your marriage *during the past few weeks?*

Being tired
Irritating personal habits
Household expenses
Being away from home
How to spend leisure
Time spent with friends
Your (husband's) job
In-laws
Not showing love

Source: Orden and Bradburn, 1968

Table 11-1

MARITAL-ADJUSTMENT TEST IS RELATED TO REPORTED MARRIAGE HAPPINESS
Relation of three marriage-adjustment indexes to marriage-happiness ratings

Marriage-Adjustment Index			Marriage-Happiness Rating (Percent)		
Companion-ship[1]	Sociability[1]	Tensions	Very Happy	Pretty Happy	Not Too Happy
High	High	Low	77	23	0
High	Low	Low	73	27	0
Low	High	Low	70	29	1
High	High	High	62	38	0
Low	Low	Low	57	40	3
High	Low	High	57	40	4
Low	High	High	42	52	7
Low	Low	High	29	55	16
Total.			60	36	3

[1] Satisfactions index is made up of Companionship and Sociability indices.
Source: Orden and Bradburn, 1968

MEASURING MARITAL ADJUSTMENT:
A METHODOLOGICAL NOTE

Marital adjustment has been measured in so many ways and there are so many concepts related to adjustment (happiness, satisfaction, success) that if the reader is confused, he may take some consolation in the fact that scholars are confused by their own complex and sometimes redundant terminology. Burgess, Locke, and Thomes (1963) consider eight different criteria in their multiple index of marital success: permanence, happiness, consensus, companionship, satisfaction, integration, adjustment, and sex adjustment. Each of these criteria introduces a different meaning into the term "success."

The Marital Adjustment Balance Scale (MABS), developed by Orden and Bradburn (1968), is a simpler and perhaps more accurate measure of marital adjustment. A spouse's score on a scale of marital tensions is subtracted from his score on a scale of marital satisfactions. The two scales are shown in Chart 11-4. Since marital tensions are negatively correlated, and marital satisfactions are positively correlated, with marital adjustment, a high final score indicates high marital adjustment. The scale scores were positively correlated with the spouse's reported marriage happiness, and successfully differentiated degrees of marriage happiness, as you can see in Table 11-1. An interesting point not shown in the table is that the relationship between reported marital happiness and the MABS is much stronger for women than for men.

The concept of marital adjustment as it appears in the research will be clearer if the reader studies an actual instrument used to measure adjustment. The following test represents the shortest and perhaps the most carefully constructed of the tests. Each of the factors, it should be remembered, shows considerable independence of the others. Generally, the first choices for each question contribute to a high marital-adjustment score, and the last choices contribute to a low score. This is a good example of a test which is useful in *research* to separate married couples into groups of roughly the same "success" level, but which (as with all the other marital-adjustment tests) can hardly be recommended for use in individual decision-making.

Instructions: The test may be filled out by either the husband, the wife, or both. Frank and honest replies are of the highest importance. There are no "right" or "wrong" answers. The following points are to be observed in taking the test: (1) Be sure to answer all questions. Do not leave any blanks to signify "no" reply. (2) Do not confer with your mate in answering the questions or show your answers to him or her. (3) For each question circle the number given after the most appropriate answer.

I. *Companionship Factor*
1. When disagreements arise they generally result in:
   a. Husband giving in. 50
   b. Wife giving in. 31
   c. Neither giving in. 22
   d. Agreement by mutual give-and-take. 53
2. Do you and your mate agree on right, good, and proper behavior?
   a. Always agree. 61
   b. Almost always agree. 51
   c. Occasionally disagree. 40
   d. Frequently disagree. 40
   e. Almost always disagree. 13
   f. Always disagree. 22
3. Do husband and wife engage in outside activities together?
   a. All of them. 34
   b. Some of them. 24
   c. Few of them. 13
   d. None of them. 40
4. In leisure time, which do you and your mate prefer?
   a. Both husband and wife to stay at home. 44
   b. Both to be on the go. 51
   c. One to be on the go and the other to stay home. 31

II. *Consensus or Agreement*
1. Do you and your mate agree on aims, goals, and things believed
   important in life?
   a. Always agree. 26
   b. Almost always agree. 15
   c. Occasionally disagree. 40
   d. Frequently disagree. 22
   e. Almost always disagree. 31
   f. Always disagree. 13
2. Do you and your mate agree on friends?
   a. Always agree. 25
   b. Almost always agree. 70
   c. Occasionally disagree. 40
   d. Frequently disagree. 13
   e. Almost always disagree. 31
   f. Always disagree. 40
3. Do you and your mate agree on ways of dealing with in-laws?
   a. Always agree. 43
   b. Almost always agree. 52
   c. Occasionally disagree. 23
   d. Frequently disagree. 23
   e. Almost always disagree. 32
   f. Always disagree. 50

4. Do you and your mate agree on handling family finances?
   a. Always agree. 25
   b. Almost always agree. 16
   c. Occasionally disagree. 22
   d. Frequently disagree. 22
   e. Almost always disagree. 13
   f. Always disagree. 40
5. Do you and your mate agree on amount of time spent together?
   a. Always agree. 16
   b. Almost always agree. 60
   c. Occasionally disagree. 41
   d. Frequently disagree. 40
   e. Almost always disagree. 31
   f. Always disagree. 13

III. *Affectional Intimacy*
   1. How often do you kiss your mate?
      a. Every day. 25
      b. Now and then. 23
      c. Almost never. 50
   2. How frequently do you and your mate get on each other's nerves
      around the house?
      a. Never. 52
      b. Almost never. 60
      c. Occasionally. 50
      d. Frequently. 23
      e. Almost always. 32
      f. Always. 41
   3. Do you and your mate agree on demonstration of affection?
      a. Always agree. 16
      b. Almost always agree. 33
      c. Occasionally disagree. 41
      d. Frequently disagree. 14
      e. Almost always disagree. 23
      f. Always disagree. 32
   4. Check any of the following items which you think have caused serious
      difficulties in your marriage:
      Difficulties over money   ____
      Lack of mutual friends   ____
      Constant bickering   ____
      Interference of in-laws   ____
      Lack of mutual affection (no longer in love)   ____
      Unsatisfying sex relations   ____
      Selfishness and lack of cooperation   ____
      Adultery   ____
      Mate paid attention to (became familiar with) another person   ____
      Drunkenness or alcoholism   ____

Other reasons   ——
Nothing   ——
    a. Nothing checked. 44
    b. One checked. 80
    c. Two checked. 61
    d. Three checked. 24
    e. Four or five checked. 23
    f. Six or more checked. 22

IV. *Satisfaction with the Marriage and the Mate*
  1. Have you ever wished you had not married?
    a. Frequently. 31
    b. Occasionally. 22
    c. Rarely. 34
    d. Never. 26
  2. Do you and your mate generally talk things over together?
    a. Never. 31
    b. Now and then. 40
    c. Almost always. 33
    d. Always. 16
  3. How happy would you rate your marriage?
    a. Very happy. 17
    b. Happy. 43
    c. Average. 40
    d. Unhappy. 22
    e. Very unhappy. 13
  4. If you had your life to live again would you:
    a. Marry the same person?. 27
    b. Marry a different person?. 12
    c. Not marry at all?. 21
  5. What is the total number of times you left mate or mate left you
    because of conflict?
    a. No times. 54
    b. One time. 13
    c. Two or more times. 22

V. *Sexual Behavior*
  1. What are your feelings on sex relations with your mate?
    a. Very enjoyable. 43
    b. Enjoyable. 52
    c. Tolerable. 13
    d. A little enjoyable. 22
    e. Not at all enjoyable. 31
  2. Do you and your mate agree on sex relations?
    a. Always agree. 43
    b. Almost always agree. 33
    c. Occasionally disagree. 23
    d. Frequently disagree. 50

e. Almost always disagree. 41
f. Always disagree. 14
3. During sexual intercourse are your physical reactions satisfactory?
   a. Very. 34
   b. Somewhat. 25
   c. A little. 23
   d. Not at all. 14
4. Is sexual intercourse between you and your mate an expression of love and affection?
   a. Always. 52
   b. Almost always. 34
   c. Sometimes. 42
   d. Almost never. 22
   e. Never. 13

Based on Harvey J. Locke and Robert C. Williamson, "Marital Adjustment: A Factor Analysis Study," in *American Sociological Review,* XXIII (1958), 562-569.

Computing Scores

The first step in computing the marital-adjustment score is to add the digits of the number circled. For example, assuming a person circled 22 for the first question, his score for this question would be 2 + 2. A score for each question is obtained in this way and all are added together. Then 44 is subtracted from this score. This is because we added 2 points to the weight of each answer of the 22 questions in order to secure more combinations of digits.[1]

Burgess, Locke, and Thomes give the following advice on interpreting scores from the marital-adjustment test reproduced above:

The maximum score is 120 and the minimum is 49. Thus there is a spread of 71 points between the highest and the lowest possible score.

Anyone taking the marital-adjustment test generally wants to compare his score with some standard. A standard can be constructed by dividing the possible range of scores into approximate quarters. Scores from 103 through 120 represent the upper 25 percent of possible scores and can be considered an index of "good" marital adjustment. Scores from 85 through 102 represent the second 25 percent and indicate "above average." Scores of 67 through 84 are in the third quarter and indicate that the adjustment is "questionable." Scores of 49 through 66 are in the lowest quarter and indicate "poor" marital adjustment.

A poor or questionable rating does not always mean that a marriage is failing. And if the score is above average or good, the marriage may still be less adjusted than indicated by the test. . . . For a group the test will give an approximate measure of marital adjustment. For any given individual, however, it may be an incorrect measure of his marital success.

[1] Ernest W. Burgess, Harvey J. Locke and Mary Margaret Thomes, *The Family* (New York: American Book Company, 1963), pp. 301-306. Reprinted by permission.

Understanding and Marital Interaction

It is widely believed among family sociologists and laymen alike that husbands and wives come to understand one another better as they live with one another longer and that the better they understand one another, the better adjusted the marriage. Merrill maintains that:

> Even the most obtuse husband who lives for a quarter of a century with a woman gains some understanding of her motives. In a patriarchal society, formal power rested with the husband. The wife was forced to gain her ends by understanding the motives of her husband and getting around him as best she could. In an increasingly equalitarian family, however, authority roles are more nearly equal and the husband can no longer assert his dominance. Hence he must develop empathic ability to equal that of his wife (Merrill, 1959: 208).

Blood and Wolfe see understanding as practically the only growing part of the marriage over the years:

> Companionship may wane and love may wither, but the typical American wife can count on more lasting understanding from her husband. The passing years sap the energy which joint activities require and calm the fires of passionate love—but sheer living together provides the basic condition for understanding another person (Blood and Wolfe, 1960: 218).

Understanding in marriage is said by Locke to proceed to the place, "where a slight gesture, a facial expression, a word, or a phrase may have acquired great meaning" to the other spouse (Burgess et al., 1963; Locke et al., 1956). Such intuitive observations by sociologists, however, cannot be corroborated by empirical data to any great extent. Kirkpatrick and Hobart (1954) showed that in comparing sex pairs in varying stages of commitment, the more committed couples understood one another better (that is, could predict one another's responses more accurately). There was no indication, however, that the greater understanding of committed couples (engaged and married, as compared to casual date and going steady) was a product of their interaction with one another. Instead, it seemed to be the result of the weeding-out from among the more committed couples those of lesser degrees of commitment who had lower understanding scores. Other researchers have also failed to find a relationship between length of acquaintance or marriage and understanding (Budd, 1959; Udry et al., 1961). Wallin (1957) found that some slight portion of the understanding that couples had for one another could be attributed to actual direct acquaintance of the couple. The remainder was a result of spouses who were similarly assuming that the partner would respond in the same way as themselves.

Perhaps, however, the happy couples do come to understand one another better, and the less happy come to understand one another less well, leading to the negative results above. Put another way, maybe the couples who understand one another are happier than the couples who understand one another less well. Unfortunately, two decades of research have not been able to resolve this issue. For every study which shows that understanding is related to marital adjustment (Dymond, 1954; Hobart and Klausner, 1959; Karlsson, 1963), another of equal quality shows that it is not (Clements, 1967; Corsini, 1956; Locke et al., 1956). To complicate the matter, Luckey (1961) found that the self-concepts held by satisfied husbands agreed with their wives' perceptions of them more closely than was true of the less satisfied husbands, but that this was not true for satisfied and unsatisfied wives. Nothing provided by the social scientists justifies any easy assumption that mutual understanding of the spouses makes for good marriages.[1]

It is obvious that there is no simple correlation between accurate understanding of mates and their satisfaction with the marriage. In some cases, happy relationships are built on persistent misunderstandings. Stuckert (1963) shows that the husband whose view of marriage is quite different from his wife's, and who accurately perceives this, is an unhappy husband. On the other hand, the husband whose view of marriage is quite different from his wife's, but who does not perceive her expectations accurately, is generally satisfied if he thinks most other people have marriages pretty much like his. Both Stuckert and Luckey (1960) have arrived at an identical conclusion in two separate studies concerning the wife: *it is important for marital satisfaction that the wife accurately perceive her husband, but not important in itself that the husband understand his wife.* There is some reason to this, however unpalatable. Studies of marital adjustment consistently show that if marriages are successful, it is because the woman makes the greater adjustments; if they are not, it is because she has not changed. If wives must be the ones to make adjustments for the sake of successful marriages, it is obviously of some benefit if the wife knows what she is adjusting to (Luckey, 1960: 156–157).

The finding most devastating to the theory that understanding makes the marriage happy actually reverses that idea. One group of researchers, comparing the personality perceptions of happily married and unhappily married couples, found that the happily married persons showed more evidence of lack of realism in personality appraisals of their partners than unhappily married persons. The explanation apparently is that the situation of the unhappy marriage creates circumstances which encourage more accurate appraisal of the mate. Perhaps people on opposite sides of a con-

[1] A study by Stryker (1957: 286–296) shows that parents who do *not* understand their children will get along better with them than parents who are more perceptive of their children.

flict situation have more opportunities to take note of their opponent as different, rather than similar to themselves, whereas persons with strong feelings of love tend to see their partners as similar, rather than dissimilar to themselves, even though the similarity is actually slight (Preston et al., 1952).

THE MEASUREMENT OF UNDERSTANDING: A METHODOLOGICAL NOTE

The reader with little background in social research may wonder how researchers measure such a complicated thing as the amount of understanding one person has for another. "Understanding" is a word with many nuances of meaning, some of them suggesting a metaphysical awareness of the state of mind of another person. The behavioral scientists who have explored the phenomenon of interpersonal understanding have generally defined it as the ability of one person to predict the response of another to particular stimuli. This is clearly an aspect of the meaning of the term as used by laymen in such phrases as "I know just how you feel," or "I knew you'd say that." A number of different techniques are used. The wife may be asked to rank ten personality needs in the order of importance to her in her marriage:

1. Importance of love in marriage.
2. Being able to confide in one's spouse.
3. Showing affection.
4. Respecting ideals.
5. Appreciating the achievements of the other.
6. Understanding the other's moods.
7. Helping in making important decisions.
8. Stimulating the other's ambition.
9. Showing respect for the other.
10. Giving self-confidence in relations with other people.

When she has done this, the husband is asked to rank the same list in the order of importance *as he thinks his wife sees them* (Stuckert, 1963). Those persons who list their spouse's order most accurately can then be said, in one sense, to "understand" their spouse.

Another method is to give the husband a list of statements to respond to (agree, disagree, undecided), and then ask the wife to respond to the statements as she thinks her husband would. The following test sample is from the Kirkpatrick-Hobart Marital Expectations Scale used for the measurement of understanding. The wife whose predictions of her husband's responses are most accurate is said to "understand him best."

Instructions: Answer as follows:

> A—strongly agree; B—agree; C—undecided; D—disagree;
> E—strongly disagree.

1. I want the kind of marriage in which the family group has first claim on the husband's time, even if it interferes with his getting ahead in the world.
2. In my marriage I want to make whatever family sacrifices are necessary in order to have three or more children.
3. In my marriage I want the husband to provide the wife with an adequate personal allowance to spend as she wants.
4. In my marriage I want our babies to be given satisfaction with regard to feeding and training, rather than making them live on a strict schedule.
5. I want the kind of marriage in which the wife shows wifely devotion to her husband's convenience and comfort in the home.

Source: Unpublished test used in Kirkpatrick and Hobart, 1954

Communication in Marriage

Communication is a favorite nostrum for ailing human relationships. Business executives are sure their enterprises would be more successful if only there were better communication. More communication is said to be a solution to many of the problems which exist between nations. Young couples about to be married are convinced that their marriages will never break up "because we can talk to each other, because we can discuss our problems together." The assumption in back of these beliefs is that many, if not most, problems exist because people do not communicate and therefore do not understand one another. The complexity of the evidence for the effect of understanding on human relationships has already been commented on. It should, therefore, already be clear that it is not sheer volume or accuracy of communication which is crucial. Some researchers have shown evidence for there being a relationship between amount of communication and marital adjustment (Hobart and Klausner, 1959; Navran, 1967), but others fail to show any important relationship (Karlson, 1963; Locke et al., 1951). One study shows that the more husband-wife communication, the more likely the couple is to report that they solve most of their marriage problems (Petersen, 1969). On the basis of supervision of a family case-work program, Pollak reports,

> Actually, our experience suggests that . . . improved communication may (sometimes) lead to stagnation in the treatment process rather than to improvement in cooperation (Pollak, 1964: 219).

It has been widely observed that in disturbed marriages there is frequently a decline in communication and communicative efforts between husband and wife. Yet, it is almost certainly a mistake to assume that it is the lack of

Chart 11-5

COMMUNICATION CAN BE GOOD OR BAD FOR MARRIAGE
Items discriminating good and bad marital communication, by discriminatory power

1. Does your spouse have a tendency to say things which would be better left unsaid?
2. Do you find your spouse's tone of voice irritating?
3. Does your spouse complain that you don't understand him (her)?
4. Does your spouse insult you when he (she) gets angry with you?
5. Do you fail to express disagreement with him (her) because you're afraid he'll (she'll) get angry?
6. Does it upset you a great deal when your spouse gets angry at you?
7. Do you hesitate to discuss certain things with your spouse because you're afraid he (she) might hurt your feelings?
8. Do you find it difficult to express your true feelings to him (her)?
9. Is it easier to confide in a friend rather than your spouse?
10. Does he (she) seem to understand your feelings?
11. Do you help your spouse to understand you by telling him (her) how you think, feel, and believe?
12. Does your spouse nag you?
13. Do you feel he (she) says one thing but really means another?
14. Do you pretend you're listening to your spouse when actually you are not really listening?
15. Does he (she) try to lift your spirits when you're depressed or discouraged?
16. Does your spouse accuse you of not listening to what he (she) says?
17. Do you and your spouse engage in outside interests and activities together?
18. Are you and your spouse able to disagree with one another without losing your tempers?
19. Do you and your spouse ever sit down just to talk things over?

Source: Bienvenu, 1970

communication which has disturbed the marriage. Rather, it is the other way around: Disturbances in the relationship are caused by adverse reaction to the content of husband-wife communication and inhibit further communication as a defense against further damage. Some marriages which would have been dashed to pieces by a freer flow of communication between the spouses have been maintained on a tolerable level for years by this mechanism. On the other hand, couples who have found their communication with one another satisfying are encouraged to keep it on a high level.

Much of the literature directed toward helping couples with their marriages puts a great deal of faith in open sharing of feelings. But whatever positive consequences are said to flow from this unselective communication, we know that most of the nonadjustive responses couples make toward one another are a direct result of this open sharing of negative feelings about violations of the mates' expectations (Cutler and Dyer, 1965).

In devising a test of marital communication, Bienvenu (1970) formulated 19 items that significantly distinguished between couples with poor communication and couples with good communication. The items are listed in Chart 11-5, in decreasing order of their ability to distinguish poor and good communication. There are four possible responses to each item: "usually," "sometimes," "seldom," and "never." Optimum responses would be "usually" to items 11, 15, 17, 18, and 19, and "never" to the remaining items. Destructive communication leads all items in ability to discriminate good and bad communication.

In an even sharper departure from the traditional wisdom, in a laboratory study of newlywed couples (marriages of three or four months' duration), Goodrich and Ryder discovered to their surpise that their couples used lying as one of the most important methods of solving disagreements. These couples maintained marital harmony by falsely and deliberately creating an illusion of agreement. Both men and women were equally likely to resort to feigning agreement to stop an argument (Goodrich et al., 1968).

The process is no doubt more complicated than this. Probably *selective* communication is the key to the successful marriage. Some thoughts and desires and attitudes are destructive when communicated. A wife who continues to communicate to her husband her disappointment that he is not more affectionate when she has seen he is incapable of changing, a husband who continues to communicate to his wife his desire that she get more pleasure out of her motherhood when he knows this is not her nature — these are communicative acts which are not going to do anything but hurt the relationship. The development of a problem will usually lead a couple to considerable conversation in the problem area. The abandonment of discussion of this area when the problem is discovered to be insoluble and diversion of communication into other, more satisfying channels is probably a step toward solidarity of the marriage. These comments are speculative at this time and are only meant to emphasize that it is the fruitful control and direction of the communication process which distinguishes satisfying marriages, not the volume of the material communicated or the amount of time spent communicating it.

Nonverbal communication is an important part of communication; what a spouse is saying may be contradicted by his tone of voice or his posture, and nonverbal messages are just as subject to misreading as verbal ones. There is some evidence that couples who are satisfied with their marriages have more accurate nonverbal communication than dissatisfied couples. Dissatisfied couples are especially likely to misinterpret each other's nonverbal messages, and to put negative connotations on each other's attempts to communicate (Kahn, 1970).

Consensus and Marital Interaction

Sociological theory states that communication and other forms of interaction among human beings create the consensus that is the basis of social organization and that makes interaction harmonious and purposeful. Numerous studies with other than marital groups confirm the function of interaction in generating consensus. It is natural, then, that sociologists have assumed that marital interaction also generated the consensus which was the basis of family harmony and purpose. Thus, writers on marriage and the family regularly assert that, "The pattern of married life creates a value system by which it is justified" (Waller and Hill, 1951). However, not a single piece of research shows that this is true, and a number of studies show that husband and wife do not generate consensus, do not agree with one another more, or see life more similarly as they are married longer. This finding seems so contradictory to common sense that it would be hard to believe in the absence of compelling evidence. Americans seem so willing to believe that husband and wife do build a common outlook that it is still regularly asserted to be true in the face of the contradictory evidence.

Such evidence is offered by Kelly. Comparing attitudes toward marriage of couples at engagement and after twenty years of marriage, Kelly was unable to report a statistically significant trend toward similarity:

> There was a slight but not statistically significant tendency toward greater husband-wife similarity in these specific attitudes after twenty years of marriage, far less than one might expect on the basis of two decades of close interaction and shared experiences (Kelly, 1961).

It should be noted that this refers particularly to attitudes about *marriage itself.* When the full range of attitudes on which the couples were tested is taken into consideration, the couples had actually become *less* similar over the years (Kelly, 1955).

Pineo, reporting on the twenty-year follow-up of the Burgess-Wallin couples, finds a substantial *loss* of consensus over twenty years, including loss of consensus on finances, recreation, religious matters, demonstration of affection, friends, table manners, conventionality, philosophy of life, ways of dealing with in-laws, and intimate relations (Pineo, 1961). The results of the studies by Pineo and Kelly are especially persuasive because each includes data on the same couples at two different times. However, numerous cross-sectional studies (which, with one testing, compare couples with relationships of different duration) add support to the longitudinal studies (Kirkpatrick and Hobart, 1954; Udry et al., 1961). In each case, the studies show that couples with longer-term relationships have more consensus than random couples, but in each case the difference must be accounted for by the fact that mates *select* each other in the first place on some basis which provides for consensus but do not achieve more consensus over time. Until the time when a study conclusive enough to outweigh all this negative evidence is available, it must be concluded that married couples do not agree more, nor do they create a shared way of looking at life, in spite of their abundance of interaction; if anything, *couples have less consensus after many years of marriage than they did in the beginning.*

Is it possible that the consensus of a couple is not even related to their satisfaction with the marriage? No. Research results confirm common sense on this point. Terman (1938: 67) shows that the degree of agreement between the spouses is substantially related to the husband's happiness and even more closely related to the wife's happiness. Terman does not think that it is the agreement or disagreement which causes the happiness or unhappiness, however, and the method of his study makes it possible that the disagreement the couples indicated is only an expression of their unhappiness, rather than a cause of it (Terman, 1938: 71). Burgess and Wallin also report a relationship between consensus and marital satisfaction, but not one as important as Terman's. Later research has determined that the more happily married couples *perceive* more agreement between them than the unhappily married, but that *actual* agreement is only important for marital satisfaction when the agreement is in an area which is directly and instrumentally related to marriage goals. That is to say, agreement on international politics or the effectiveness of high school administrators would not be expected to be related to adjustment, but agreement on childrearing practices or divison of labor in the marriage might well be (Kimmel and Havens, 1966). Whether consensus during courtship is predictive of later adjustment cannot be shown.

Pineo's results (Pineo, 1961) justify the conclusion that the "most disenchanted" couples lost more consensus over the years than the "least disenchanted." *Common attitudes and consensus on matters of common concern contribute to marital happiness and the loss of this consensus is associated with dissatisfaction in marriage.* Part of the general loss of satisfaction with the marriage noted earlier is attributable to the fact that consensus is lost.

The results of these studies would certainly be clearer if the concept of adjustment were clearer. It may be of some interest to know whether, in the face of declining consensus, there is increasing conflict in marriage. Neither of the longitudinal studies answers this question. Sociologists would hypothesize that there would not be. It appears that over the years husband and wife become less involved with one another, both emotionally and in their shared activities. One might expect that there would be less conflict under these circumstances and, *in this sense only,* the couple might be said to have become adjusted. They have not settled their differences, but lack of conflict has been achieved through less involvement. Perhaps this is the best explanation of the decline in consensus noted in both studies. Consensus is not something that, once achieved, persists. Attitudes are more volatile than most people think, and those which have to do with marital and domestic matters are the most changeable of all (Kelly, 1955). If the basic sociological principle is accepted that it is interaction and involvement that maintain consensus in couples, then consensus might be expected to decline with time as interaction and involvement decline. Over the years, the behavior of individuals changes, but the behavior of spouses does not change in the same ways. The process is perceptively described by Pineo:

> If mating were by random pairing, as many gains in the "fit" between husband and wife would occur as losses. But marriage by personal choice implies that a marrying group, at the time of marriage, has a self-contrived high degree of fit between the individuals involved. Individuals do not marry unless, to some extent, they feel they have more basis for union than would have occurred if their mating were determined by chance. The fit between the two is maximized before marriage will occur, as is the satisfaction such "fit" brings about. Subsequently a regression effect occurs. The deviant characteristics which provided the grounds upon which the marriage was contracted begin to be lost, as later changes tend toward the population mean and the couples become more and more like ones who married at random rather than by choice (Pineo, 1961: 7).

It should now be clear why the author is not nearly as impressed as most laymen and many other sociologists with the importance of proper initial selection of mates as a make-or-break factor in marital success.

Effects of Personality on Marriage

The arguments on the importance of selection of the right mate in producing marital success are predicated on two assumptions: first, that personal characteristics are largely determined by the time of marriage and remain stable during adulthood; and second, that it is the relationship between the personal characteristics of the mates at the time of selection which is most closely related to their satisfaction in marriage. The data available must be dealt with separately to evaluate each of these propositions.

STABILITY OF PERSONALITY CHARACTERISTICS

Most early studies in the stability of adult personality indicate rather substantial stability. In fact, much of modern psychology, under the strong impact of psychoanalytic thought, is based on what is considered to be the overwhelming importance of experience during early childhood socialization.

If it is true that the earliest experiences set personality, then there should be little change during the adult years, regardless of adult experiences. The personal characteristics of an individual at the time of engagement should be an excellent indication of the characteristics to be maintained during the marriage. Later studies do not support these conclusions. Two of the more important longitudinal studies which indicate the continuous change which occurs in adult personalities will be cited here. Burgess and Wallin gave 390 of their couples the Thurstone personality items at engagement and again after three or four years of marriage. Interpreting the statistical rules somewhat loosely, it can be stated that the premarital personality scores accounted for less than 16 percent of the variation in marital scores three or four years later on more than half of the personality items, and for less than 25 percent of the variation in the later scores on every item but one. How much more the personalities had changed after twenty years is not indicated in Pineo's follow-up, but one may presume that the change would have been considerably greater (Burgess and Wallin, 1953: 532–533).

Kelly's study of the consistency of adult personalities covers a much longer period and is specifically pointed at measuring the changes in personality over time. Some of the personal characteristics were relatively stable over twenty years. On generalized values (as measured on the Allport-Vernon Study of Values), the engagement scores accounted for 48 percent of the variation in scores twenty years later. Personality items during engagement accounted for about 30 percent of the later personality variation. However, on the attitude scales (from Remmer's generalized attitude scales), there was little practical relationship between the engagement scores and the scores twenty years later. These scales especially cover attitudes toward marriage, church, childrearing, housekeeping, entertaining, and gardening—that is, primarily attitudes toward activities, most of which are presumably important in marriage and family life and in which husbands and wives are usually involved together. The engagement scores on these attitudes accounted for only about 8 percent of the variation in scores twenty years later (Kelly, 1955: 676). This, of course, says that most people changed a very great deal during the interval, but it does not eliminate the possibility that husbands and wives changed in similar ways. Their later "match," therefore, might still be based on their earlier "match." Kelly, however, says that most of the correlations between husband change and wife change were *negative,* indicating that what little relationship there was between the husband's change and the wife's change was in the direction of becoming less alike. There was no significant difference in the happily married and unhappily married in this respect (Uhr, 1957: 48).

PERSONALITY MATCHING AND MARITAL ADJUSTMENT

Even though there is no consistent pattern of personality matching achieved during courtship, this does not mean that certain types of personality matches might produce good marriages and other types of matches produce poor marriages. Even though spouses do not select one another on the basis of Winch's Type I and Type II complementarity,[1] the satisfaction of their marriage may be enhanced by the existence of these patterns. Winch, in

[1] See Chapter 9.

setting forth the theory (Winch, 1958), originally suggested that the relationship might be complex, with moderate levels of complementarity (as he defined it) conducive to marital happiness, but with very high complementarity probably associated with no reciprocal meeting of needs in the marriage, and consequent low happiness. The little information available on the subject at this time indicates that the types of complementarity discussed by Winch are probably associated with marital *dis*satisfaction rather than with happiness (Blazer, 1963). It is not known, of course, what the pattern of relationships between the personalities of these mates was at the time of their selection.

Although every marital adjustment study to date has concerned itself with the relationship between personality traits and the success of the marriage as measured by several criteria, the only relationships found consistently related to marital success are those of individuals, regardless of whom they marry. In addition to the individual traits which are predictive of marital success or failure, several studies have compiled lists of trait combinations which are said to be favorable or unfavorable. Terman (1938) presents such a list of personality relationships measured after marriage at the same time that the adjustment was measured. There is no way of knowing what *pre*marital trait combinations would have been favorable from the Terman analysis. Even here, Terman considered the relationships between spouses in personality to be such a poor correlate of marital happiness that the data for the main sample are not even presented. In general, no two studies have found the same trait combinations favorable or unfavorable.

The Burgess-Wallin study reports no reliable differences in the personality relationships at engagement of satisfied and unsatisfied spouses, nor does the study by Kelly (1955: 103). There are good reasons for all of these negative results in the face of such strong cultural beliefs. The best reason is the fact that personalities continue to change throughout life, so that the match that existed at engagement is not the same that exists five, ten, and twenty-five years later.

Still, work continues on this problem. Comparisons of stable and unstable married couples on one personality test show that in stable marriages the wife tends to be more introvert and the husband more extrovert, while in unstable marriages it is the other way around (Cattell and Nesselrode, 1967). Since this dimension of personality is relatively stable over time, it is likely that these were the personality matches at the time of marriage. This is a plausible and promising finding which may break the mystery of the "satisfying combination" in marriage.

In spite of this one glimmer of hopeful results, at this time we must reach an uncomfortable conclusion: *there is no convincing evidence that personality matching in courtship is important for marital success.*

INDIVIDUAL TRAITS AND MARITAL SUCCESS

To what extent will personal characteristics during engagement predict marital adjustment? This question has already partially been answered in two ways. First, if personality characteristics are not stable, one would not expect engagement characteristics to predict adjustment many years later. Second, marital adjustment cannot be considered by any stretch of the imagination to be a stable characteristic of the marriage; it evidently declines with considerable fluctuations, over the years. Therefore, one would not expect personality characteristics at one time to be a very good predictor of another variable which fluctuates over time.

Most of the cross-sectional studies show considerable relationship between personality characteristics and adjustment at the time of the test (Terman, 1938; Locke, 1951; Barton, Kawash, and Cattell, 1972; Barton and Cattell, 1972). However, in view of the demonstrations of variations over time in both personality and adjustment, this is not very convincing evidence of the relationship of engagement personality to later marital adjustment. Burgess and Wallin reported after their first follow-up that the correlation between engagement personality and their multiple marital success scores was .25 for men and .18 for women, indicating that engagement personality accounted for up to 4 percent of the variation in marital success scores three to five years after marriage (Burgess and Wallin, 1953: 536). Following up the same couples twenty years after engagement, Pineo (1961) reports: "Quite highly associated with marital adjustment and other indices of marital satisfaction within any time period, the [personality] indices demonstrate an unanticipated independence in the change analysis." In other words, changes in adjustment showed very little relationship to changes in personality. This points to the conclusion (although not stated by Pineo) that the *engagement personalities were certainly almost completely unrelated to the marital adjustment after twenty years.*

Family Constellation and Marital Success

Toman (1961) has argued that the particular constellation of brothers and sisters in which a person grows up has an important effect on his relationships with others as an adult. From his clinical cases he concludes that

> . . . marital partners of similar birth order will conflict over the rights which both had received in their early family constellation, and which by implication only one can now possess. Thus two eldest-sib spouses married to each other would be prone to get into conflicts over seniority rights. This would not occur for a senior-junior alliance (Levinger and Sonnheim, 1965).

He also maintains that if a person grows up in a group of siblings in which all are of his own sex, he is likely to have greater difficulty with an opposite-sex partner than if he grew up with siblings of the opposite sex. However, other researchers have not been able to duplicate Toman's findings (Levinger and Sonnheim, 1965). Until we have further consistent evidence, Toman's argument will have to be considered just an interesting idea, awaiting convincing demonstration.

Roles and Role Conflict

In a complex society such as America, where conceptions of marriage are in a process of transformation and where different marriage forms prevail in different social groups, some couples contemplating marriage find that they have conflicting expectations of husband-wife roles. Those who carefully consider their differences sometimes decide they are serious enough to dissolve the relationship before marriage. Others find ways of reconciling their differences or depend on their love for each other to transcend the differences. Still others remain unaware of how divergent their conceptions of marriage are until after they are married. Under these circumstances, one might expect differences in role expectations to constitute a source of conflict during marriage for many couples, and some studies confirm that this is true. One researcher interviewed college couples in their mid-twenties and found that the more areas in which the interview revealed role conflict between husband and wife, the lower was the marital happiness of the couple (Ort, 1950). Another researcher interviewed older middle-class couples and found that the greater the discrepancy in the importance assigned to certain roles by the two spouses, the lower were their marital-adjustment scores. This is certainly what one would expect intuitively. People who have different ideas about how husbands and wives should act will not get along well as husband and wife (Hurvitz, 1960). Jacobson (1952) found that divorced couples exhibit a greater disparity in their attitudes toward the role of husband and wife in marriage than do married couples. However, another study contradicts these results. Also studying middle-class, educated couples, Hobart and Klausner (1959) compared the marital-role disagreements (as registered on a marital-expectations test) of husbands and wives with their marital-adjustment scores, and found that no relationship at all existed between their differences in role conceptions and their marital adjustment. The results are difficult to reconcile with the other studies, but in view of the contradiction it must be said that *the function of role consensus in marital adjustment is in doubt.* It should be pointed out that none of these studies shows the significance or lack of significance of role disagreements *before* marriage to later marital adjustment.

THE ORIGINS OF MARITAL-ROLE EXPECTATIONS

Marital-role expectations are derived from two major sources, and each source tends to give different conceptions to husband and wife. The child's first concepts of husband-wife roles are derived from his parents, although it appears that the girl gets hers from the mother far more than the boy does from the father (Lynn, 1961). A new couple brings to marriage expectations derived from different parental homes which are not necessarily very similar. The second source of role expectations is mass media and the culture generally. As filtered through the sex subcultures, males come to marriage with somewhat different interpretations of marriage than females. In studies of high school students (Dunn, 1960) and college students (Lovejoy, 1961), males consistently show more conceptions of male dominance and more traditional views of the wife role than females. Yet, in the courtship process, those couples whose role conceptions coincide most closely are the ones who marry (Kirkpatrick and Hobart, 1954), so that husbands and wives *usually* define marital roles in fairly similar ways (Motz, 1950).

A third source of marital-role expectations which may account for some of the similar conceptions of husbands and wives is the interaction between husband and wife. This process is not yet explored by research. It is well known that while initial interaction between two people is governed by cultural role expectations, subsequent interaction between two people changes their expectations of each other. As two people become emotionally involved, each tends to respond to the other in terms of how he thinks the other sees him. This process usually goes on without conscious recognition by the persons involved. In this way, a husband may see that his wife expects him to be more forceful and dominant in the family decision-making and respond to this expectation by first behaving in a more dominant manner, and finally by incorporating a conception of his husband role into a self-concept which is closer to his wife's conception of his role. A wife may see that her husband expects her to be more active and aggressive in their sexual relationship, and respond to this perception by behaving more in accordance with it. She then redefines her self-conception in terms of how her husband sees her. The couple may actually never have been aware of the discrepancy in their original conceptions, and the conflict in role expectations is not "resolved" by "give and take" or any rational adjustment considerations of the couple; rather it is done by a process of responding to one another's role expectations. Conceptions of marital roles should not be conceived as determined by some certain early experience but as originating in early experiences and, from there, developing and changing through interaction (Ingersoll, 1948). This reemphasizes the thesis that *it is not some preexisting relationship between two people which determines the course of their marriage, but the responses of each to their interaction with each other.* The resolution of role conflict through accurate response to expectations of the mate is observed more frequently in well-adjusted than in unadjusted couples (Hawkins and Johnsen, 1969; Ort, 1950).

THE ASYMMETRY OF NEEDS IN MARRIAGE PAIRS

The differences in sex roles and personalities of males and females make the emotional needs and satisfactions sought from marriage different for each sex. Today Americans have come to accept the legitimacy of the norm of reciprocity in marital relationships: each spouse is entitled to as much from the relationship as the other. However, reciprocity of need satisfaction in marriage does not mean that husband and wife will satisfy the *same* needs to the *same* extent through the marital relationship. What is most important to one spouse in the marriage may be unimportant to the other, but the bargain is redressed with respect to some other aspect of the marriage in a kind of double-entry bookkeeping. In most marriages, parenthood will be far more important for the wife than for the husband. Sexual gratification *per se* may be more significant for the husband than for the wife. The adult companionship of marriage is usually more vital to wife than to husband. Even specific patterns of personality need satisfaction will usually be asymmetrical. In a satisfying marriage, a husband need not enjoy dominating a wife who enjoys being dominated; he may enjoy displaying her to his friends even though she receives no special pleasure from being displayed. *In a successful marriage, there is something for each spouse, but that something will likely be different for husband and wife.* This makes marriage a complex relationship and opens up possibilities of bargaining and strategy in marriage. The trump cards of each spouse are the ways in which he satisfies the other's needs. Not caring much about the companionship aspect of his marriage, the husband may bargain (sometimes even without being aware of using a stratagem) companionship for good cooking, more exciting sex, or whatever he values highly, providing only that companionship is more important to the wife. Marriage counselors rarely approve such bargaining, but it is a constant feature of marital interaction.

Young couples entering or contemplating marriage often appear to themselves to share such a unanimity of purpose that it is easy for them to imagine that all their marital interaction will be cooperative and that apparent differences can be dissolved through accurate and sympathetic communication. The complex reality of marriage is, of course, that spouses share some goals at some times, but also have goals which conflict with or are difficult to reconcile with those of the partner. In most marriages, goal conflict will engender a bargaining process between husband and wife which is in many respects similar to bargaining situations in other relationships. Although accurate communication is essential to the bargaining process, communication does not dissolve the problem.

Patterns of Interaction in Stable Marriages

Stable marriages are not necessarily stable because they are deeply satisfying. "A 'stable' married pair may on the one hand be deeply fulfilled people, living vibrantly, or at the other extreme entrapped, embittered, resentful people, living lives of duplicity in an atmosphere of hatred and despair" (Cuber and Harroff, 1963). Yet, in the most general sense, all such marriages may be said to be "adjusted" in the sense of having achieved some type of equilibrium which keeps the relationship on even keel. In a study of the heterosexual relationships of adult, upper-middle-class men and women between the ages of thirty-five and fifty-five, Cuber and Harroff (1963) described the types of interaction patterns developed in the marriages of this group. Based only on the study of marriages of persons married for at least ten years who had never considered separation or divorce and, "so far as they knew, no one, including members of the family, thought of them as other than normal American families," the following typology of relationships emerged.

> *Conflict-Habituated Relationships.* In this husband-wife configuration there is much tension and conflict—although largely "controlled." At worst there is some private quarreling, nagging, and "throwing up the past" of which members of the immediate family, and more rarely even close friends and relatives, have some awareness. At best, the couple is discreet and polite, "genteel about it" when in the company of others, but rarely succeeds completely in concealing it from the children—although the illusion is common among them that they do. The essence, however, is that there is awareness by both husband and wife that incompatibility is pervasive, conflict is ever-potential, and an atmosphere of equilibrated tension permeates their lives together. These relationships are sometimes said to be "dead" or "gone" but there is a more subtle valence here—a very active one. So central is the necessity for channeling conflict and bridling hostility that these imperatives structure the togetherness. Some psychiatrists have gone so far as to suggest that it is precisely the conflict and the habituated need to do psychological battle with one another which insures continuity of the marriage. Possibly so, but from a less psychiatric point of view, the overt and manifest fact of habituated attention to handling tension, keeping it chained, and concealing it, becomes the overriding life force. And it can, and does for some, last for a lifetime.

> *"Devitalized" Relationships.* Here the relationship is essentially devoid of zest. There is typically no serious tension or conflict and there may be aspects of marriage which are actively satisfying, such as mutual interest in children, property, or family tradition. But the interplay between the pair is apathetic, lifeless. There is no serious threat to the marriage. It will likely continue indefinitely, despite its numbness. It continues, and conflict does not occur in part because of the inertia of "the habit cage." Continuity is further insured by

the absence of any engaging alternatives, "all things considered." Perpetuation is also reinforced, sometimes rather decisively, by legal and ecclesiastical requirements and expectations. These people quickly explain that "there are other things in life," which are worthy of sustained human effort. But the relationship *between the pair* is essentially devoid of vital meaning, essentially empty, by comparison to what it was when the mating began and what was then considered to be its *raison d'être*.

This kind of relationship is exceedingly common. Many persons in this circumstance do not accurately appraise their position because they frequently make comparisons with other pairs, many of whom are similar to themselves. This fosters the illusion that "marriage is like this—except for a few odd balls or pretenders who claim otherwise."

While these relationships lack vitality, there is "something there." There are occasional periods of sharing at least of something, if only memory. Formalities can have meanings. Anniversaries can be celebrated, even if a little grimly, for what they once commemorated. As one said, "Tomorrow we are celebrating the anniversary of our anniversary." Even clearly substandard sexual expression is said by some to be better than nothing, or better than a clandestine substitute. A "good man" or "good mother for the kids" may "with a little affection and occasional companionship now and then, get you by."

Passive-Congenial Relationships. This configuration seems roughly about as prevalent as the preceding one. There is little suggestion of disillusionment or compulsion to make believe to anyone. Existing modes of association are comfortably adequate—no stronger words fit the facts. There is little conflict. They tip-toe rather gingerly over and around a residue of subtle resentments and frustrations. In their better moods they remind us that "there are many common interests" which they both enjoy. When they get specific about these common interests it typically comes out that the interests are neither very vital things nor do they involve participation and sharings which could not almost as well be carried out in one-sex associations or with comparative strangers. "We both like classical music"; "We agree completely on religious and political matters"; "We both love the country and our quaint exurban neighbors"; "We are both lawyers."

We get the strong feeling when talking with these people that they would have said the same things when they were first married—or even before. When discussing their decisions to marry, some of them gave the same rationales for that decision that they do now for their present relationship, some twenty or thirty years later. This is why we have said that they seem to be passively content, not disillusioned even though, as compared to the next type, they show so little vitality and so little evidence that the spouse is important—much less indispensable—to the satisfactions which they say they enjoy.

Vital Relationships. It is hard to escape the word, vitality, here—vibrant and exciting sharing of some important life experience. Sex immediately comes to mind, but the vitality need not surround the sexual focus or any aspect of it. It may emanate from work, association in some creative enterprise, childrearing, or even hobby participation. The clue that the *relationship is vital* and significant derives from the *feelings of importance about it* and *that that importance is shared*. Other things are readily sacrificed to it. It is apparent, even sometimes to the superficial observer, that these people are living for something which is exciting; it consumes their interest and effort, and the particular man or woman who shares it is the indispensable ingredient in the meaning which it has.

"Total" Relationships. The total relationship is like the vital relationship with the important addition that it is *multi-faceted.* This kind of man-woman relationship is rare in marriage or out, but it does exist and undoubtedly could exist more often than it does were men and women free of various impediments. One will occasionally find relationships in which *all* important aspects of life are mutually shared, enthusiastically participated in. It is as if neither partner had a truly private existence. Cynics and the disillusioned scoff at this, calling it "romance" and usually offering an anecdote or two concerning some such "idyllic" relationship which later lost its totality, if not its vitality too. This should not be taken to mean, however, even if accurately interpreted and reported, that the relationship had not been total at the prior time. Or it may simply be evidence of the failure of the observer to be more discriminating in the first place.

Relationships are not *made* vital, much less total, by asserting them to be so, by striving to make them so, or by deceiving the neighbors that they are so. This is not to deny, however, that the total relationship is particularly precarious; precisely because it is multi-faceted, it is multi-vulnerable as circumstances change.[1]

It should be kept in mind that this typology is developed from upper-middle-class marriages of middle-aged persons in the middle years of marriage, and that lower-status groups or marriages in the early years might show other types of adjustment. The patterns which are described are particularly enlightening for two reasons. First, the marriages which provided this typology were high-status couples who are generally more happily married than lower-status couples. Second, such high-status couples are generally *least* willing to put up with unsatisfactory marriages rather than divorce.

Predicting Marital Adjustment

Marital adjustment cannot be predicted on the basis of personality characteristics of the individuals before marriage, in part because personality is

[1] John F. Cuber and Peggy B. Harroff, "The More Total View: Relationships Among Men and Women of the Upper Middle Class," *Marriage and Family Living* XXV (1963), pp. 140–145. Reprinted by permission.

Table 11-2

PREMARITAL FACTORS PREDICTING LATER MARITAL ADJUSTMENT
AND NUMBER OF STUDIES REPORTING THE FACTORS

Premarital-Predictive Items	Number of Studies Reporting
1. Acquaintance: well, or over 6 months	6
2. Adaptability: good general adjustment	4
3. Age at marriage: 20 or older for women, 22 or older for men	7
4. Age differential: man older or the same age as woman	6
5. Attachment to father: close	4
6. Attachment to mother: close	4
7. Church attendance: 2 to 4 times a month	4
8. Church membership	4
9. Conflict with father: none or very little	5
10. Conflict with mother: none or very little	5
11. Discipline: not harsh	4
12. Educational level: some college or college graduate	6
13. Engagement: 9 months or longer	4
14. Friends before marriage: few or several women friends	4
15. Happiness of childhood: happy or very happy	4
16. Happiness of parents' marriage: happy or very happy	7
17. Married by: clergyman	4
18. Mental ability: equal	4
19. Occupation: professional	4
20. Organizations: member of some	4
21. Parents' attitude toward mate: approval	6
22. Savings: some	4
23. Sex instruction: adequate	4
24. Sex, source of information: parents	4
25. Sex relations, premarital: none or only with future spouse	8
26. Sunday-school attendance: some and beyond childhood	5

Source: Burgess, Locke, and Thomes, 1963

not a stable entity, and in part because marital adjustment and marital happiness fluctuate over the years. The farther one is from engagement, the less well he can predict subsequent adjustment from engagement personality. However, most research in marital adjustment has not tried to predict marital adjustment from personality alone, but from a combination of every available piece of information in the premarital history of the individual which could be shown to be related to marital adjustment. The list of predictive characteristics is impressive, but we will not attempt to list them all here. Burgess, Locke, and Thomes (1963: 318–319) list the twenty-six premarital predictive items found valid in four or more studies. (See Table 11-2.) The most interesting thing about this list is that only *two* of the items require reference to a relationship between two persons; all the other items could be answered without reference to a particular mate. The two relationship items are 1. mates of equal mental ability and 2. parents approve mate choice. Almost all the other items fall in the category of social background characteristics of the individual. The most predictive items on marital-prediction tests, then, are characteristics of the individual, independent of his mate choice. This would suggest that the marital adjustment of an individual is seen to be predictable without reference to whom he marries but mainly with reference to who he is, socially speaking. The high correlations reported by most studies between husband and wife adjustment might then be seen only as the result of social homogamy in mate selection leading people to select mates whose individual marital-adjustment potential is similar to their own.

PROFESSIONAL CRITICISM OF MARITAL-ADJUSTMENT TESTS

In addition to the shortcomings of a composite concept of marital adjustment on the one hand, and the attempt to predict this constantly changing potpourri of variables from the vantage point of before marriage, and in addition to the fact that the most predictive factors are personal ones and have nothing to do with the relationship between mates, a number of other criticisms have been made of marital-adjustment tests by other writers.

First, the items on the marital-prediction test which discriminate best are items which require conventional, "good," middle-class answers, such as having a happy childhood and having nice parents whom one liked. The concept of adjustment also is measured with a battery of items many of which are very traditional. If one goes to church, agrees with his spouse, kisses her regularly, settles agreements by give and take, and does not complain about his marriage, then he gets a good marital-adjustment score. Those people who give conservative, conventional responses on their engagement test are likely to give conservative, conventional responses on their marital-adjustment test, and this will get them a high grade. Does this mean that coming from a nice, conventional background insures a good marital adjustment? It does if the marital-adjustment test is made up from nice, conventional items. One writer says that a marital-adjustment score may merely be a measurement of deviation from middle-class norms (Kirkpatrick, 1963: 381).

Second, people who will admit things wrong with their background may also admit things wrong with their marriage. People who will cover up things wrong with their background may not admit things wrong with their marriage. This means that their marital-adjustment responses could be predicted with no difficulty from their background items, but that the prediction would not be worth much (Ellis, 1948).

Kieren and Tallman (1972) note that couples who admit to problems in their relationship score lower on adjustment than couples who say they have no problems. But marriages without problems are rare. Effective problem solving is indicative of good marital adjustment, and to solve problems efficiently a couple must be able and willing to recognize and admit to problems. Orden and Bradburn (1968) and O'Brien (1972) have found that degree of marital satisfaction cannot be measured by amount of marital conflict, or vice versa.

A more recent study by Edmonds, Withers and Dibattista (n.d.) shows that almost the entire relationship between conservatism and marital adjustment is due to the tendency of conservative persons to give conventionalized responses to test questions. They conclude that there is no real relationship between conservatism and marital adjustment; that is, that conservatives are not really more happily married than less conservative people, but that this appears to be so because conservatives more readily respond to test questions about their marriages with sweet-sounding, conventionalized responses.

PREDICTIVE ABILITY OF PREMARITAL TESTS

In spite of all of the qualifications presented above, the scores on marital-prediction tests are more useful than the discussion has so far indicated. By combining many different indexes, each of which by itself has low predictive ability, a modest level of accuracy is achieved by the marital-prediction tests. In general, they probably do as well as, for example, an IQ score does in predicting school achievement. Burgess and Wallin (1953: 551) report that when all the prediction factors for men were combined into a single index and correlated with all the multiple criteria of marital success, about 25 percent of the variation in marital success was accounted for by the engagement information. Similar predictability is claimed by other marital-adjustment studies, but none of the others got their predictive information before marriage. This may not sound like a very substantial prediction accuracy, but it is as good as most of the predictive devices in social science. Furthermore, the practical use to which marital-prediction tests are likely to be put — the screening out of the couples with lowest probability of success — makes the test more useful than if the entire range of scores were to be used for prediction. The test, like most others, is most accurate at its extremes. In the lowest 25 percent of the Burgess-Wallin scores, for example, the prediction accuracy for weeding out poor risks would have been three times as good as chance. Though this may not represent overwhelming accuracy, it is better than any other way of deciding. A couple with scores in the lowest quartile might well consider that the odds against them were high enough to be worth considering seriously in evaluating a decision to marry.

Summary

The first decade of marriage is characterized by a consistent decline in marital satisfaction, accompanied by a decline in intimate husband-wife communication, a decline in consensus, and a disengagement from joint activities. Most couples experience a general disenchantment with the marriage as a consequence of these trends. This process does not produce a generally less satisfying life, but fewer of life's satisfactions come from the marriage itself. Studies done among the upper-middle-class, where marriages are most stable and to outward appearance the most adjusted, conclude that few of these people find their marriages deeply satisfying.

Happy marriages are characterized generally by the wife's ability to adapt. It is important to marital satisfaction for the wife to understand her husband, but evidently less important that the husband understand his wife. Communication *per se* is not related to marital success. Rather it is the fruitful control and direction of the communication process which is characteristic of satisfying marriages. Consensus on matters of common concern contributes to marital satisfaction, and the loss of consensus over the years is reflected in a decline in satisfaction.

The social scientist has practically no useful advice on selection of mates on the basis of personalities and their relationships. This is because over the years of marriage, personalities of the mates bear little relationship to the personalities during engagement. These changed personality relationships interact with the unanticipated contingencies of married life to produce the shape of marriages.

Sociologists have designed a number of tests to measure and predict marital adjustment, but most of these tests have been criticized on the basis of their confused conceptualization. The best of these tests predicts marital success about as well as IQ tests predict school achievement: not very well, but worth considering as a warning when the score is quite low.

Implications for Individual Decision-Making

The layman and the sociologist are not nearly as far apart as it sometimes seems in their views of marital adjustment. For the layman's picture of "they lived happily ever after," the sociologist has substituted the "period of adjustment" where, after a difficult post-honeymoon period, couples either break up their marriages or "live happily ever after" in conjugal rather than romantic bliss, more and more becoming soul mates. For the layman's picture of the domestic grind, the sociologist has offered the picture of the marriage which gradually loses its emotional vitality and which provides declining satisfaction over the years. Of the two sociological pictures, the latter has the most convincing evidence, but it is a mistake to conclude that all marriages must inevitably deteriorate, as some writers have been prone to do. On the other hand, just what a couple might do to prevent this process is anyone's opinion, and there is little evidence to support any position. The young person contemplating marriage might be advised that the *usual* experience is gradual devitalization, although none will accept this as representing his own future.

To the young and to the idealistic, this description of the course of married life may sound grim. The value of any particular marriage for a person is measured against 1. his expectations of it, 2. his alternatives to it, and 3. comparison between his marriage and those of others similarly placed in life. These criteria will be studied separately.

EVALUATION OF MARRIAGE AGAINST EXPECTATIONS

Only the totally unrealistic expect the euphoria of the "in love" stage to be the permanent emotional tone of marriage. It might even be questioned whether the human organism is capable of sustaining such a profound emotional pitch for long periods. Yet all evidence indicates that Americans enter marriage expecting it to provide far more emotional satisfaction than is likely for far longer a period than is possible. If the discussion in this chapter does nothing more than establish a realistic base line for expectations, the discrepancy between experience and expectation will have been reduced, and the evaluation of the relationship on this criterion will have been improved.

EVALUATION BY COMPARISON WITH ALTERNATIVES

For most people, there *are* no serious alternatives to marriage. Some scholars have suggested that many persons are by temperament and character unsuited to marriage and that marriage "advocates" should consider the benefits of the single state as a "competing product." No studies have been done comparing the life satisfactions of those who marry with those who remain single, and the self-selection process involved in producing the two groups would probably make the comparison invalid. However, the organization of adult life around married pairs and family systems, with no institutionalized patterns for single persons outside the monastic life, would appear to minimize the possibilities of single "blessedness." Serial remarriage does not really solve the problem; rather, it simply repeats it.

Besides serial remarriage and singleness, a few couples today are trying out other alternatives. Of these, living together without legal entanglement or commitment is enjoying its greatest popularity since the urban bohemians rediscovered it in the United States in the 1920s. (It has always been popular among the poor.) More complex heterosexual associations involving several adults also have their advocates. For all but a miniscule minority, these patterns are associated with a short time in the life cycle. Such relationships are characterized by a short life span (under two years), but their instability cannot be described as a shortcoming, since some are deliberately temporary and noncommitting in concept. Although such relationships may be fairly common in certain age brackets in a few communities, fewer than one in a hundred Americans (excluding the single) is living in an arrangement which could be called an "alternative to marriage".

EVALUATION BY COMPARISON WITH OTHER MARRIAGES

For those married persons experiencing disenchantment and disengagement in their marriages, it should offer some support to know that most other married couples have the same experience, that it is nothing peculiar to them brought on through their inadequacy, poor marital choice, or the callousness of their spouses.

On a more fundamental level, Americans ask more of marriage than continuous emotional bliss. Marriages are instrumental towards the attainment of other goals: the convenience of a predictable daily routine, the rewards of parenthood, respectability and status as a responsible member of the community, security in sickness and age, the efficiency of a division of labor between the sexes — these are only a few of the many possibilities. What other human relationships provide as many benefits?

Most literature on mate selection stresses careful compatibility testing during engagement and assurance of a good fitting together of personalities because the marital choice is said to be crucial to future marital success and personal happiness. A review of the research, however, leads to the conclusion that personality and personality matching are of little consequence in the mate selection process because they are so little related to future marital success. Furthermore, there is good indication that marital success and personal adjustment in life are not very closely related, contrary to common sense. Personality, marital adjustment, and personal adjustment appear to be changing products of changing interpersonal situations, of changing roles, of unexpected contingencies. One perceptive sociologist draws a comparison between the nature of marriage and the nature of other friendship which sheds insight into the *process of continuous development* of marital relationships:

> Most friendships run for a term, subside, and expire. . . . The origin of friendships in connection with the development of new interests and their expiration with the arrest or decline of previous common interests, suggests than an ample supply of successive and concurrent common interests must be forthcoming to maintain the friendships of long duration. . . . Pairs of persons who never grow tired of each other are few and far between. There is no *a priori* basis for assuming that male-female pairs who do enjoy each other indefinitely are the people who always get married to each other. . . . Successful marriage may thus come to be defined . . . in terms of its potential for continued development [rather] than in terms of momentary assessments of adjustment (Foote, 1963: 17–19).

The most consistent premarital items predictive of marital success are the social background characteristics of the individual, independent of his marital choice. There are certain conventional middle-class backgrounds which predispose persons to be successfully married in the American marriage system. If one comes from the right background, he has a fairly good chance of being happily married. If one does not, his chances of successful marriage are fewer. A good marital prediction test is able to tell a young couple if they have the combination of characteristics which makes their chances of success low. If they have this misfortune, they might well be advised that the odds against them are strong enough to make a difference. On the other hand, simply changing the mate choice is not likely to put them into the best-risk category, since so many of the predictive items are not related to marital choice. Young couples should also be told this (though, apparently, they rarely are).

Most people will marry for love and whatever else they think is necessary and take their chances. Behavioral scientists do not have enough evidence, enough confident rules of good relationships between prospective mate characteristics, to suggest a better way of doing it. The best rules of relationship between couples which have been developed by the scholars of marriage will be discussed in Chapter 12.

Social Factors in Marital Success

12

Americans marry more within their own social categories than one would expect by chance. With some social characteristics, such as race, there is little intermarriage, while with others, such as social class, there is a larger number of intermarriages. Furthermore, it can be observed that the greater the difference on a particular characteristic, the fewer intermarriages there will be. The same thing can be stated in the form of a general principle of social homogamy: the more socially different two persons are, the less likely they are to marry. This is an important general principle of social behavior and helps the individual understand what social forces are shaping his life. However, it offers little assistance in individual decision-making where people are involved in what look to them like socially heterogeneous relationships.

What happens if one marries someone socially very different from himself? Does it make any difference? Are the marital outcomes affected by the difference? Are homogamous marriages happier, more stable? What other desired or undesired consequences follow from heterogamous marriages? For many social variables, the questions can be answered with some confidence. For others, the results are conflicting and appear to be affected by the values of the reporter more than by the regularities in human behavior.

Marital Stability and Marital Satisfaction: Different Criteria of Marital Success

Two indicators of marital success are recognized by most social scientists: stability and satisfaction. Marital stability (and instability) is measured by the incidence of divorce and separation, while marital satisfaction or adjustment is determined by questionnaires concerning marital happiness.

Throughout the literature on marriage success runs a tacit assumption that the same factors which lead to marital unhappiness are those which also lead to instability and divorce. To some degree, Locke's marital adjustment study (Locke, 1951) confirms this by finding the same factors associated with divorce as had been found associated with marital maladjustment. On the other hand some people tolerate what to others would be unbearable marriages, while some resort to divorce at much lower levels of frustration. Just because the survival rates of certain types of marriages are higher one cannot automatically assume that they are happier. The tendency of some groups to divorce when unhappy and of others to remain married when unhappy distorts the external picture of the relative success of these marriages (Landis, 1963).

As you read this chapter note that, if differences in unhappiness tolerance were removed, the difference in survival rates between religious and nonreligious marriages would shrink, the difference in divorce rates between the early married and the later married would shrink, and the differences between the divorce rates of the uneducated and the well-educated would *increase*.

The use of divorce rates only instead of divorce and separation rates can also distort information on marital stability. Marriages usually break up long before divorce occurs; a recent British study (Chester, 1971) indicates that the median interval between separation and divorce is almost three years. A cross-sectional study which does not measure both separation and divorce is likely to overrate marital stability. It is useful to remember that in many sources, instability does not include separation.

Relative Age of the Mates and Marital Outcome

Is the success of a marriage affected by the difference in age of the spouses? We know that the actual pattern of selection tends toward mates of the same age or pairs in which the husband is older, with men who marry at older ages picking women who are progressively younger than themselves. The studies on marital success and age differences have been inconsistent. Burgess and Wallin (1953) saw no pattern of age differences and marital success. Terman and Oden (1947) found it unfavorable in their sample of gifted persons for the husband to be younger than the wife, but Burgess and Cottrell (1939) found the same combination favorable to adjustment. King (1952), using a southern nonwhite population, Blood and Wolfe (1960) in Detroit, and Locke (1951), using a random sample of a rural Indiana county, all found it favorable for the spouses to be of the same age. A recent study by Bumpass and Sweet (1972) presents more reliable results because it was based on a large national sample and because other factors correlated with marital instability were measured and controlled. Bumpass and Sweet found that, when age level at marriage and religious differences were controlled, age differences had no significant effect on marital stability. People evidently have preferences in the relative age of spouse, and these preferences do not materially affect marital success. One might predict that the marriages would take on different interaction patterns in accordance with the age differences, and some research has found this to be true. Blood and Wolfe (1960: 38) carefully studied the decision-making structure of their couples and found that the balance of power usually lay with the older spouse. A smaller study of husband-wife influence in discussion undertaken by the author found no relationships to age differences of the spouse (Udry et al., 1961). It might be expected that if couples were closer to the same age their marriages would involve more companionship, while differences in age would entail less companionship with some other base supporting the marriage; but again, there is no evidence one way or the other. *Whatever other unstudied differences might be created by husband-wife age differentials, the effect on the success of the marriage is negligible.*

Age Level at Marriage and Marital Outcome

From the beginning of modern research on marital adjustment and marital stability, every study has shown that marital adjustment is lower in couples where the men were under twenty and the women were under eighteen at marriage, and that the divorce rate is higher for couples married younger, and lower for couples married older. However, because of the limitations of sample size, representativeness, or inability to introduce satisfactory statistical controls, older studies left important questions unresolved. We know that early marriage is associated with many other characteristics which are also known to be associated with marital instability: low educational level, low occupational status, premarital pregnancy, and the previous marital history of the marital partner.

The latest work, based on interviews with a representative national sample of women of childbearing age, conducted in 1970, remedies the problems of previous studies, and allows us to resolve the issues definitively. Bumpass and Sweet (1972) were able to look at differences in marital instability (defined as the proportion of first marriages ending in either separation or divorce), after controlling for the contaminating effect of wife's education, pregnancy status, wife's religion, stability of wife's parents' marriage, farm-nonfarm and regional differences, and first husband's marital history. The differences in marital stability by wife's age at marriage, when controlling for the influence of these factors, are shown in Chart 12-1. Statistical analysis shows that the contaminating variables only slightly

Chart 12-1

YOUTHFUL MARRIAGES ARE UNSTABLE
Rates of marital instability by age at marriage and race, U. S. 1970

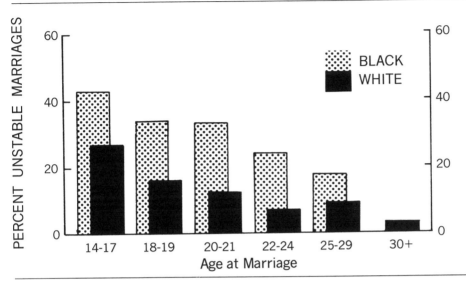

Source: Sweet and Bumpass, 1973

inflated the instability of marriages in which the wife was under eighteen but understated the stability of late marriages.

The Bumpass and Sweet analysis has allowed us to determine that the instability formerly thought to be associated with pregnancy at marriage is actually accounted for by the fact that such marriages occur at very early ages, and not the premarital pregnancy *per se.* Illegitimate births, however, are independently related to marital instability.

The apparent inadvisability of early marriage is exaggerated by the fact that men who marry at twenty-one or younger and women who marry at nineteen or younger are much more likely to end an unhappy marriage through divorce than are people who married at later ages (Landis, 1963). Perhaps their willingness to undertake divorce reflects their confidence that at an early age they still have a good chance to do better. Those who contract marriages quite late are likely to remain married even though unhappy.

A DISSENTING VIEW: EARLY MARRIAGE IN A FICTITIOUS SOCIETY

In the following section, psychologist B. F. Skinner presents in fictional form the argument that early marriages fail because society is structured to insure their failure, and that in a properly organized society (such as the imaginative Walden Two described) young marriage makes quite good sense.

"Certainly most girls are ready for childbearing at fifteen or sixteen. We like to ridicule 'puppy love.' We say it won't last, and judge its depth accordingly. Well, of course it doesn't last! A thousand forces conspire against it. And they are not the forces of nature, either, but of a badly organized society. The boy and girl are ready for love. They will never have the same capacity for love again. And they are ready for marriage and childbearing. It's all part of the same thing. But society never lets them prove it."

"Instead, society makes it into a sex problem," I said.

"Of course!" said Frazier. "Sex is no problem in itself. Here the adolescent finds an immediate and satisfactory expression of his natural impulses. It's a solution which is productive, honorable, and viewed by the community with admiration and pride. How very different from the secrecy and shame which most of us recall in connection with sex at some time or other! Adolescence is seldom pleasant to remember; it's full of unnecessary problems, unnecessary delays. It should be brief and painless, and we make it so in Walden Two.

"All your schemes to keep the adolescent out of trouble—your 'wholesome' substitutes for sex!" Frazier continued. "What is unwholesome about sex? Why must there be a substitute? What's wrong with love, or marriage, or parenthood? You don't solve anything by delay—you make things worse. The more or less pathological aberrations which follow are easily recognized, but there is a great deal more. A normal sexual adjustment is often prevented. And the sportive element in sex is played up—every person of the opposite sex becomes a challenge to seduction. That's a bothersome cultural trait that we're glad to avoid. Promiscuous aggression is no more natural than quarrelsomeness, or an inclination to tease, or jovial backslapping. But if you insist on making sex into a game or hunt before you let it become serious, how can you expect a sane attitude later on?"

"But isn't there one trouble?" said Barbara. "Do young people really know what kind of person they want to live with for the rest of their lives?"

"They seem to think so," said Frazier.

"But young people grow apart."

"Is that really true?"

"The figures," said Barbara, with obvious pride in talking in Frazier's terms, "show that early marriages tend to be unhappy."

"Because husband and wife grow apart, or because our economic system penalizes early marriage?"

"I don't know."

"Economic hardships could make people grow apart," said Frazier.

"All I know is, the boys I fell for when I was younger wouldn't interest me now," said Barbara, giving up the figures with relief. "I can't imagine what I saw in them."

"I wonder if that wouldn't be true at any age. We grow apart when we live apart."[1]

---

[1] B. F. Skinner, *Walden Two* (New York: Macmillan Company, 1948), pp. 108–109, 110. Reprinted by permission.

In a contemporary commune dedicated to carrying out the model of Walden Two, the founders, doing their commune building in the milieu of the late 1960s rather than the 1940s when Skinner wrote *Walden Two,* abandoned marriage altogether rather than institute an early marriage pattern (Kinkade, 1973).

Propinquity and Marital Success

Are marriages contracted between people whose premarital residences were close together more successful than those whose residences were farther apart? Only one author has thought to test this idea on the hypothesis that "people who live near one another are more likely to have similar background than those who live farther apart, and that similarity of cultural background facilitates the process of marital adjustment." A comparison of marriage rates with divorce rates in two samples leads to the conclusion that there is no relationship between distance separating premarital residences and divorce rate, suggesting that social homogamy is based on more than residential propinquity (Kephart, 1961).

Social-Class Differences and Marital Outcome

Do people married within their own social class have more satisfactory marriages than those married outside their class or those married to someone whose family is quite different in socioeconomic status? Few studies are pointed directly to the answer of this question. A number of studies report that "similarity of family background" is important in marital success, but not many of the items in the family background indices are direct indicators of social class. Thus, Burgess and Cottrell (1939) state that the more similar the spouses are in family background, the better the marital adjustment. Similarity of family background can be taken as a very indirect measure of similarity of socioeconomic status. A study by Roth and Peck (1951) specifically seeks the answer to the relationship between social-class similarity and marital adjustment, working with the data from the Burgess-Cottrell sample. Table 12-1 presents their results.

Table 12-1 shows that substantially more couples who are married within their own social class are well adjusted than those married outside their class. It also indicates that the more difference there is in the class level of the spouses, the more likely it is that there will be poor adjustment in the marriage. If this were not true, sociologists would be very surprised, since social class is believed to be one of the major axes of differentiation of behavior in American society.

Table 12-1

MARITAL ADJUSTMENT AND SOCIAL-CLASS DIFFERENCES OF SPOUSES
*Distribution of Total Cases According to Adjustment Index and
Similarity or Difference of the Social Class of the Spouses*

Social Class at Marriage	Adjustment Score of Each Subject, Percentage			
	Good	Fair	Poor	Total
Spouses of same class at time of marriage	53.5	26.0	20.5	100.0
Spouses one class apart at time of marriage	35.0	31.2	33.8	100.0
Spouses more than one class apart at time of marriage	14.3	38.1	47.6	100.0

Source: Roth and Peck, 1951:479

The Roth and Peck study of the Burgess-Cottrell couples is practically the only systematic study of the relationship between social-class homogamy and marital success. It has consequently been widely quoted but rarely studied carefully. First, it should be pointed out that of the 845 subjects classified by the researchers, more than 80 percent were classified as upper-middle- and lower-middle-class. As indicated in Table 12-1, their data do show that cross-class marriages have lower adjustment scores. However, this applies only to husbands and wives who were rated as different in social class *at the time of their marriage.* Most writers have failed to tell the rest of the story. For the smaller sample of 633 who gave sufficient information about their parents to permit class ratings to be made on them, there was *no relationship* between social-class level of the parents and the marital adjustment of their children, and *no relationship* between marital adjustment of the couple and *differences* in the social status of their parents, even for the 61 couples whose parents were more than one class apart. Thus, the conclusion from this study *should be* (as its authors state) that *difference in class* background *of the spouses has* no effect *on marital adjustment.* The fact that this has been consistently overlooked by other writers may be taken as evidence of an unconscious willingness to support class-endogamous marriages.

THE SOCIALLY MOBILE PERSON

The explanation of the findings of the Roth and Peck study can better be understood when it is realized that the sample of persons with which they worked included many persons who had changed their social-class position from that of their parents, that is, were upwardly mobile. Although less than 20 percent were themselves classified as lower class, twice that proportion of their parents were. Although the parental social class was irrelevant to marital satisfaction, the social class of the subject was important for marital satisfaction. Thus, the upwardly mobile person from a lower-class family can expect to have a well-adjusted marriage with a middle-class person but probably a poor adjustment with a lower-class spouse, since he himself is no longer lower class. *This is what counts.* It is not what one's parents were; it is what a person himself is that makes his marriage.

Why should social-class differences lead to marital instability and maladjustment in marriage? Several possible explanations are available. First, a number of other variables are closely associated with social class which are also predictive of marital trouble. Most of the adjustment studies have been done with samples which are predominantly college-educated. This was true with the Burgess-Cottrell sample from which Table 12-1 was developed.

Studies with broad status samples show that the higher the socioeconomic status of a marriage, the more stable and better adjusted it is. This means (as the authors indicate in most studies) that in a predominantly middle-class sample, couples are *all* fairly high on adjustment. It also means that any marriage which is very heterogeneous with respect to class has a high probability of containing one spouse from a low-status background. These cross-class marriages may be lower in adjustment than the average for the high-adjustment college sample, yet they may, at the same time, be better adjusted marriages than the average marriage where both partners are low status. Especially in the case of women marrying men of a status higher than their own, it is possible that the husband has a lower adjustment marriage than he might have had by marrying within his class but the woman has a *higher* adjustment marriage than had she chosen a man from her own low status. In fact, a careful analysis of the Roth and Peck data indicates that this is probably true.

Roth and Peck do not indicate what percentage of cross-class marriages in their study involved spouses from what particular class combinations. However, the marital adjustment record of spouses one class apart at the time of marriage is better than the adjustment record of upper-lower-class husbands in the whole sample and *substantially better* than the adjustment record of all upper-lower-class wives. It certainly cannot be concluded from this that anyone below middle-class status will be any worse off in his marriage for marrying a middle-class person.

HIGH-STATUS HUSBAND VS. HIGH-STATUS WIFE MARRIAGES

It is frequently suggested that marriages in which the wife is from a lower class status than her husband will work out well, whereas when the husband is from a lower status than the wife, the marriage is ill-fated (Blood, 1962: 87–88; Roth and Peck, 1951). It is unfortunate that so little knowledge of the effect of relative status of husband and wife is available. Roth and Peck believe that marriages in which the wife is of higher status are less successful, but their data are inconclusive. In an interesting comparison of a sample of dissolved marriages with a sample of intact marriages, Scanzoni (1968)

Chart 12-2

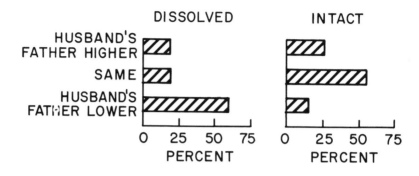

MARRIAGES IN WHICH HUSBAND IS BELOW WIFE'S STATUS LEVEL ARE UNSTABLE

Percent of couples at each relative occupational status of husbands' and wives' fathers in dissolved and intact marriages

Percent of couples at each relative educational level of husbands and wives in dissolved and intact marriages

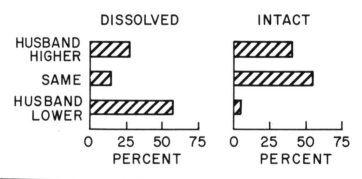

Source: Scanzoni, 1968

comes to the conclusion that marriages with differences in class background are more likely to be dissolved, as are marriages in which there is a discrepancy in educational level of the spouses. A reinterpretation of the data, presented in Chart 12-2, shows this to be incorrect. An examination of Chart 12-2 will show that on both class background and education of mates, there is actually a higher proportion of husband-high marriages in the intact group than in the dissolved group. The critical difference is in the proportion in the husband-low group. The intact marriages contain very few unions in which the husband comes from a lower status background than his wife, while the dissolved marriages are *more than half* made up of unions in which the husband has the lower status background or the lower educational attainment.

There are good theoretical reasons for *expecting* such marriages to be less successful than marriages in which the husband is of higher status. Students of social class point out that in the American stratification system, all members of a nuclear family occupy the same status position which is assigned primarily by the occupational status of the father-husband. Likewise, the family's style of life is primarily determined by the husband's status. Therefore, if a middle-class woman marries a lower-class man, the family can expect to be lower class and surrounded by a cultural environment which generates marital instability. On the other hand, if a lower-class woman marries a middle-class man, she can expect to have a family which is middle class and which is surrounded with a cultural environment supporting marital stability.

Additional difficulties for the cross-class marriage in which the wife is of higher status might be theorized on the basis of the patriarchal traditions of the society which, at least to some extent, equate masculinity with superiority. When a wife has status characteristics superior to her husband it might be assumed that this would be disturbing to both husband and wife because of its contradiction to symbolic masculinity-femininity differences. Thus, the wife with superior status characteristics might be presumed to make her husband feel less masculine and make him resent her. At the same time, it might be presumed that the wife would resent the husband's inferiority interfering with her prestige in the community. Marriages in which the wife is of higher status might theoretically be considered prone to fall into wife-dominant influence patterns, which have been found to be associated with marital unhappiness in several studies. Most of this is reasoning based on sociological theory for which there is little in the way of empirical evidence.

According to the interpretations of research and theory, a modification must be made of the usual idea that the greater the class difference, the poorer the marriage, to make it accurate and more useful for the individual. Such a modification might be: women should marry the highest-status males they can find; men should marry someone on their own status level, whatever it is. This, of course, follows from the fact mentioned in a previous section, that the status of the couple derives from the husband's position in society. A woman marrying down loses, but a man marrying down does not. In general, it can be said that high-status people have the characteristics which lead to high adjustment. If one is of high status or has a spouse who is, he can look for better than average marital stability and marital satisfaction.

The explanation is, of course, more complicated than the above argument implies. Persons who differ from one another in social class differ in many other characteristics which are relevant to the marriage. Middle- and lower-class persons rear their children differently (although not as differently as at one time). Middle- and lower-class persons have different concepts of masculinity. They have different ways of spending their leisure time. Their aesthetic tastes are different. The lower-class preference for action conflicts with the middle-class preference for manipulating symbols. Middle- and lower-class food preferences are different. Manners are different. Vocabulary is different. Ideas about what constitutes a good marriage differ along social-class lines. The sexual behavior of the classes is remarkably different. For example, elaborate erotic play before intercourse between spouses is to a large extent a middle-class expectation, considered unnecessary or even perverse by lower-class persons. Nudity in sexual activity is predominantly middle class and not common among lower-class couples. Ideas about spending money or saving it differ by class. Many of these differences are summed up by what the sociologists call the middle-class "deferred gratification pattern," in which middle-class persons plan for future gratification by denying it to themselves immediately. Lower-class life is not nearly so planned.

Education and Marital Success

The relationship between educational level and marital success is well-documented, and results are consistent: the more education one has, the lower the probability of his divorce, and the higher his probability of good marital adjustment. However, newer studies cast these old findings in a different light. The more education a person gets, the later his age at marriage. When Bumpass and Sweet (1972) controlled for wife's age at marriage, and other variables in their model, her educational level was not significantly related to marital stability, but her husband's education *was*. They conclude that differences in marital stability by wife's education are attributable to differences in age at marriage by education.

But husband's education is an important determiner of how much money he makes. According to Cutright's (1971) analysis, it is the husband's income which makes the contribution to marital stability. When he controlled for the husband's income, education had no additional effect. In fact, well-educated men with low incomes had more unstable marriages than men with little schooling but high incomes.

The studies of marital satisfaction have not employed the sophisticated statistical controls of the stability studies above. But their findings are unanimous that for each sex, better education is associated with marital satisfaction. Better educated women are more satisfied with the love and affection in their marriages (Blood and Wolfe, 1960: 229) and are more responsive sexually (Kinsey et al., 1953; Terman, 1938). Every serious study refutes the idea that education makes women unhappy with marriage. Since less-educated men and women tend to remain unhappily married, while college-educated persons tend to divorce if their marriages are unhappy (Landis, 1963), the tendency of the uneducated to tolerate marital unhappiness serves to minimize the already large difference in divorce rates between the educated and uneducated.

RELATIVE EDUCATIONAL LEVEL OF SPOUSES AND MARITAL SUCCESS

Is it better for the couple to be of the same educational level or better to have one or the other with more education? Results are not entirely consistent. Blood and Wolfe (1960: 256) report that representative Detroit wives used in their study were most satisfied when both busband and wife had equal education; the more the marriage departed from equality of education, the less the wives liked it, whether it was the wife or husband who had more education. Studies using narrower ranges of educational level do not show any significant relationship between differences in education and marital adjustment (Terman, 1938; Burgess and Wallin, 1953). It has generally been found that the more similar the husband and wife in educational level, the better they both like marriage (Burgess et al., 1963). Chart 12-2 indicates that in Scanzoni's study, mentioned above, marriages in which the husband has less education than his wife are more frequently ended in divorce than marriages in which the husband has as much or more education than his wife.

Bumpass and Sweet (1972) conclude that differences in education have no significant overall effect on marital instability, but support Scanzoni's finding that the incidence of separation and divorce was highest when the wife had a college education and her husband did not. We may reasonably conclude that similarity of educational level of husband and wife is of modest importance in marital *satisfaction,* while differences in education are associated with marital *instability* only when the wife is college-educated and the husband is not.

Religious Differences and Marital Outcome

The effect of religious differences on marital stability has been studied for fifty years. Early studies present results which are conflicting, and data analysis which does not control for other factors. Two recent studies, both linking divorce records to marriage records (Burchinal and Chancellor, 1963; Christensen and Barber, 1967), each found support for the following findings:

1. Catholic-Protestant marriages are less stable than pure marriages of either religion.

2. Among pure religious marriages, Jews have the most stability, Protestants the least, the Catholics intermediate.

Chart 12-3

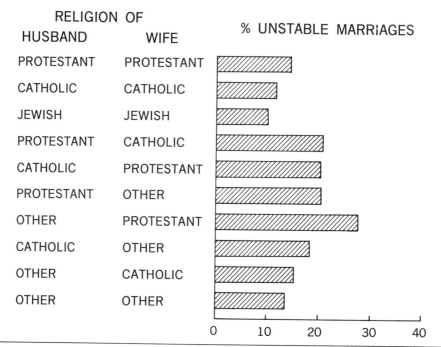

INTERFAITH MARRIAGES ARE LESS STABLE
Percent of marriages unstable, by religion of husband and wife, U. S. 1970

| RELIGION OF | | % UNSTABLE MARRIAGES |
HUSBAND	WIFE	
PROTESTANT	PROTESTANT	
CATHOLIC	CATHOLIC	
JEWISH	JEWISH	
PROTESTANT	CATHOLIC	
CATHOLIC	PROTESTANT	
PROTESTANT	OTHER	
OTHER	PROTESTANT	
CATHOLIC	OTHER	
OTHER	CATHOLIC	
OTHER	OTHER	

Source: Bumpass and Sweet, 1972

The most authoritative recent research is that of Bumpass and Sweet (1972), who analysed data from the 1970 National Fertility Study. The study was unique because it included data on the religion and age of both spouses at marriage and because it measured the incidence of separations as well as divorces. Many other variables besides religion and age at marriage were measured, including educational level and fertility. Controlling all variables except religious differences, Bumpass and Sweet found a significant negative correlation between religious heterogamy and marital stability. Interfaith marriages involving any combination of the three major faiths had higher levels of instability than intrafaith marriages. Protestant-Catholic marriages had higher instability rates than homogamous Protestant, Catholic, or Jewish unions. See Chart 12-3. Among intrafaith marriages, Jews had the lowest levels of instability, Protestants the highest, and Catholics were intermediate. Bumpass and Sweet found no evidence that Protestant inter-denominational marriages (as opposed to interfaith marriages) had higher instability rates than intradenominational marriages.

When tolerance for unhappy marriage is taken into consideration, the low survival rates of the marriages of nonreligious people take on new significance. Landis (1963) found that people who are indifferent to religion tend to end unhappy marriages in divorce, while more of those who are devout continue in unhappy marriages.

Another smaller study was designed to control the effect of premarital differences in couples' socioeconomic status, family background characteristics, parents' religiousness, and other factors which might influence marital outcome, to see what effect religious differences alone had on marital adjustment. In his exclusively urban sample, Heiss found that the differences between homogamous and interfaith marriages in marital adjustment were quite small, but concluded that there was a perceptible effect for Catholics and Jews. This is to say that *intermarriage lowered Catholic and Jewish marital adjustment slightly but did not have a perceptible effect on Protestants* (Heiss, 1961).

Numerous other studies have shown negligible effects of interfaith marriage on stability and adjustment. Locke (1951) found that differences in religion were just as frequent in his happily married group as in his divorced group and that marital adjustment was no different for the interfaith and intrafaith marriages. Neither Terman nor Burgess and Cottrell found differences in religion an important source of conflict in American marriages, and Landis found that of six major areas, more couples began marriage adjusted in their religious activities than in any other area with the exception of mutual friends. Mulhearn (1969) has recently shown that, contrary to earlier beliefs, those Catholics who marry non-Catholics but retain their Catholic affiliation score as high on Catholic devotional practices as those who marry Catholics. Intermarriage for this group evidently does not weaken the religious practice.

The secularization of the society in which this debate takes place is no better exemplified than in the arguments of religious leaders and religious persons against interfaith marriage. Ministers of religion have learned to speak to their congregations in terms which the layman can understand. In an essentially religious environment, one might warn against intermarriage on the grounds that it would lead one away from religion (a case for which a strong argument can now be made on the basis of the evidence). In American society, however, the young couple is warned not to marry outside the church because it is bad for their *marriage* (which is assumed to be a good deal more important to them). The billboard slogan, "The family that prays together stays together" is arguing for prayer because it is good for marriage.

Ultimately, this must be the explanation as to why interfaith marriages are increasingly prevalent (Thomas, 1951; Bumpass and Sweet, 1972), and why their survival rates are so high. Evidently, people for whom religion is a fundamental axis of their lives do not marry those of radically different religious belief very often. As religion becomes less central to the lives of Americans, more interfaith marriages can be expected, along with a gradually disappearing difference in their happiness and stability. One should not be surprised under these circumstances that *all* marriages are then less stable than before. The reason will not be that there are more interfaith marriages. Organized religion provides the strongest spokesmen against divorce, and religious convictions discourage divorce. If American divorce rates are higher in the future, it may be in part because Americans have lost their religious convictions against divorce.

Racial Intermarriage and Marital Outcome

Since racial intermarriages constitute only 8 out of every 10,000 American marriages (Jacobson, 1959), it is much more difficult to assess their outcome. No national figures are available and most of the data which are available do not indicate the exact racial composition of the marriage. No major marital adjustment study has included interracial marriages. Most sociologists believe interracial marriages are hazardous, but very little statistical evidence supports or refutes this belief. Case history material abounds, testifying to the difficulty the couple encounters. Black-white couples are said to be ostracized by the white community and the black community as well. One study of a sample of interracial marriages involved fifty black-white families in Philadelphia interviewed in 1949 and 1950 when interracial relations were somewhat different than they are today. Most of the couples reported that they had experienced severe pressure from their families to discontinue the relationship. The courtships were often concealed and the wedding was often secret. While the white families often refused to have anything to do with the black spouse, black families were at least willing to meet the white spouse, the researcher reports. Nevertheless, the author concluded that the chances of survival of the marriages were good because, under the circumstances, the couples had given a good deal more forethought to their marriages than most couples do (Golden, 1954). In a more recent study of black-white marriages, the author believes that the pressures and obstacles that such couples face actually enhance the marriage by bringing forth protective reactions (Smith, 1966).

Although much loose talk has been heard about the problems that are encountered by the children of interracial marriages (usually referring to white-black marriages), sociologists no longer consider this a special problem. The nearly universal experience is that the children are simply considered to be blacks, both by the white and the black communities. They are not more or less acceptable to either racial community than other black children with two black parents (Pavela, 1964). The problems usually spoken of in connection with children of interracial marriages must therefore come from the parents, who perhaps hope for a different response from the white community.

Two studies done in Hawaii throw interesting light on interracial marriage in a different interracial situation. Cheng and Yamamura (1957) note that although the interracial marriage rate is far higher in Hawaii than in the rest of the United States (mostly involving Orientals and Caucasians), the divorce rate is similar to the rest of the country. They report that most women who cross the race line marry into a higher socioeconomic status and have better chances for success than the few who marry into a lower status. Kimura (1957), also working in Hawaii, compared a group of Japanese war brides who had married Japanese husbands with a group who married non-Japanese. The comparison was based on difficulties with in-laws. Kimura reported that those with non-Japanese husbands got along more congenially with their in-laws than those who had married Japanese husbands.

A fascinating study on the stability of interracial marriages has recently been reported by Monahan (1970), using linked marriage and divorce records from Iowa for recent years. Monahan reported that black-black marriages were twice as likely to end in divorce as white-white marriages. But black-white marriages were *more stable* than black-black marriages. Furthermore, marriages in which the husband was black and the wife white had the lowest divorce rates of all—lower than white-white marriages. This report is for only one state, which may be atypical, but it is based on better data than any other studies of marital stability in racially mixed marriages done in the continental United States. Unless other studies are done which contradict this one, no one is justified in talking loosely about the instability of black-white marriages.

Recent studies of intermarriage in Hawaii, where rates of racial intermarriage are several times what they are on the mainland, reveal a more complicated but similar picture. Although the intermarriages as a whole show a somewhat higher rate of divorce than racially homogamous unions, several intermarriage categories had *lower* dissolution rates than within-race marriages as a whole (Lind, 1964; Monahan, 1966). And Schmitt (1969) found some evidence that age differences more than race differences accounted for the high divorce rates in racially mixed marriages in Hawaii.

It seems a reasonable conjecture that the difficulties to be experienced by a couple in an interracial marriage are proportional to the degree of cultural separation of the races involved. In the United States, the racial factor segregates people into groups more systematically than any other social variable. Under these circumstances, interracial marriage will continue to be rare, and those who marry across the race barriers can expect to receive powerful negative sanctions from their racial groups. *No evidence indicates that interracial marriages are less stable than marriages in which both partners are of the same race.*

Summary

AGE

Age at marriage is one of the most important determinants of marital stability. Women marrying before age eighteen and men before age twenty have distinctly elevated probabilities of divorce, while those marrying for the first time past age thirty have distinctly reduced probabilities of divorce. Early marriage is also related to lower marital adjustment. The instability of young marriages is not attributable to other social characteristics of those marrying early, but is a genuine function of age alone.

SOCIAL CLASS

Sociological studies indicate that the lower the social class, the less stable the marriage. This is almost certainly because the social and economic organization of lower-class life does not support marital stability. Lower-class marriages nearly always show lower marital adjustment as well, although this may be because testing measures are organized around middle-class ideals of a good marriage. Indicative of this is the finding that lower-class couples are less likely to use divorce as an escape from a bad marriage than are middle-class couples (Landis, 1963). Cross-class marriage is not an important source of increased marital stability or maladjustment. Rather, *stability and adjustment of the marriage are directly related to the income of the husband.* The lower the husband's income, the more unstable and maladjusted is the marriage (Cutright, 1971). Wives of middle status who marry men of low income can expect more unstable marriages than if they had married a man of higher income, *not* because they married out of their class, but because they married low-income men.

RACE

Similar comments are appropriate concerning interracial marriage. All persons, including sociologists, are convinced that the interracial couple will be exposed to a great deal of pressure from relatives not to marry, but hardly any interracial couple will need a sociologist to tell them that. The couple will also already know that they must expect problems in their marriage. However, no one can produce evidence which demonstrates that interracial marriages are less stable or less happy. In fact, black-white are probably *more* stable than black-black marriages. In this case, it is probably appropriate for the social scientist (and the counselor) not to express his own values. Is the fact that the community disapproves of interracial marriage sufficient grounds for professionals to discourage it? It is very easy to fall into the trap of saying "what is, is good, because people oppose anything else, and opposition means trouble." The recounting of a few case histories of troubled interracial marriage seems like flimsy evidence on which to decide issues which are of fundamental social significance.

EDUCATION

Educated persons are more likely than the uneducated to have well-adjusted marriages, are less likely than the uneducated to get a divorce, and yet are apparently more likely to get a divorce if they have an unhappy marriage. Educational similarity of the spouses seems to have a modest relationship to marital adjustment. Women who marry men with less education than their own have a higher risk of divorce than women who marry men with as much or more education than they have.

RELIGION

Catholics have lower divorce rates than Protestants, but this is almost certainly related to greater scruples against divorce among Catholics than to the unusual happiness of Catholic marriages. Catholic-Protestant marriages are less stable than Catholic-Catholic marriages, and less stable than Protestant-Protestant marriages. On the other hand, those couples in which neither spouse has religious affiliation are the least stable of all. This suggests that the increased instability of interfaith marriage over homogamous Catholic marriage is largely a factor of decreased willingness to tolerate marital frustration without resorting to divorce in the interfaith marriages, and not especially a factor of increased problems and frustrations of interfaith marriages.

The General Principle of Social Heterogeneity and Marital Success

Three different kinds of factors tend to produce marriages which are homogamous with respect to social characteristics. The first factor is the organization of society into groups which are similar on certain social characteristics, so that those who are socially similar are the most likely to meet and interact with one another frequently, and those who are socially dissimilar are unlikely to meet and interact with one another frequently (a prerequisite to marriage in American society). The second factor is social values which encourage persons to marry those in similar social categories to themselves and discourage those who are socially different from marrying. These social values help mate selectors to identify social similars as "eligible" mates and automatically to prevent dissimilars from identifying one another as "eligibles." The groups holding these values then bring interpersonal pressures upon individuals to encourage homogamous selection and to discontinue heterogeneous relationships which threaten to terminate in marriage. The third factor is the differences in personal behavior of socially different persons—differences in attitudes, mannerisms, and vocabulary which tend to facilitate easy interaction between social similars and to make interaction between social dissimilars more difficult and less satisfying.

Persons who are socially similar are, therefore, likely to find one another more attractive and gratifying than those who are socially different from themselves, other factors being equal. The greater the difference between two people on any particular social characteristic, and the more social characteristics on which two people differ, the more powerful each of these three factors is in discouraging marital selection. Therefore, the larger the social difference, the more social differences, and the greater the significance of the social differences, the fewer marriages will be contracted embodying these differences. One can imagine the small number of marriages there are between persons in which the wife is an upper-class, white, Protestant, forty-year-old, college-educated woman and the husband is a lower-class, black, Catholic, twenty-year-old, grade-school-educated man.

On the other hand, the larger the social differences between two people, the more social differences, and the more significant the social differences, the more likely their marriage is to be a source of conflict between them and other social groups (relatives, neighbors, friends, and social institutions). In addition, the more likely it is to be unsatisfactory to them, not only because of their conflict with groups outside the marriage, but because of the greater probability of conflict between them. Such marriages, therefore, lack the stability that comes from the support of other interlocking relationships in the society and are likely to lack the internal stability which is generated by a highly gratifying interpersonal relationship between the mates themselves. *Those who are least likely to marry are, therefore, most likely to have trouble if they do.*

For the individual contemplating a socially heterogeneous marriage, these principles can be of real assistance in decision-making. Differences between mates in certain social categories are not as important as in others. A small difference in a single social trait of minor significance will not lower the probability of success of the marriage enough to require attention. As the marriage involves more, larger, and more significant differences, the probabilities of lowered success and stability become cumulative to the point where any prudent person will want to take them into consideration *if* his major values in marriage focus around mutual gratification and personal happiness. The romantic will choose to ignore these probabilities because his romantic values are more important. The social reformer will choose to ignore them because his special social values are more important to him. Those with conventional social values are not likely to have become involved in such a relationship in the first place.

Implications for Individual Decision-Making

Few Americans are ever called upon to make a personal decision as to whether or not they should marry a person whose social background characteristics are different from their own. The structure of association patterns and the social values with which they are surrounded almost guarantee that they will not define as eligible mates persons who are socially very different from themselves. In fact, for most people with typical marriage motivations, the assumption can almost be made that if two people are willing to marry one another, the social differences between them are not as important as they might at first appear.

For those few persons who do become emotionally involved with and wish to marry a partner socially far removed from themselves, the application of sociological or laymen's labels to one another on the basis of some obvious social characteristics is not likely to clarify the situation for anyone. To label the man Jew and the woman gentile, or the woman middle-class and the man lower-class, and then respond in terms of the labels, is to distort the realities of the complicated interpersonal relationship which may exist between two people. A Jew who is alienated from the Jewish community who marries a gentile, or a man from a lower-class family who goes to college and marries a girl from a professional family are not necessarily creating heterogamous marriages in any sense which is important to the couple.

On the other hand, the young couple considering a marriage which is labeled as a mixed marriage by their families and associates might beware of the danger of the self-fulfilling prophecy: When people believe something to be true, they often behave in ways which confirm their beliefs. Thus, when a Catholic girl and a Protestant boy wish to marry and both sets of parents and clergy warn them that interfaith marriages are very unhappy and unstable, the young couple might remember that the parents and religious advisers are in a good position to see to it that their prediction comes true over the coming years. Even if there is nothing in the couple's relationship to one another which causes problems for them, they can expect well-meaning, devout friends and relatives to be a potential source of trouble for them and their marriage, especially after there are children.

CASE

A new problem has recently developed in our family with the engagement of my sister to a young man of the Catholic faith.

Our family has been baptized and raised Protestant. Religion has never been a prominent aspect of our family and yet my parents have not been able to accept this new hurdle of a change in religion for their grandchildren.

Although my sister has not decided to convert to Catholicism herself, she has agreed to raise her children Catholic. This is the part that my parents cannot accept. I can see already how our family is pulling apart and how hard it will be for George and Shirley to stay together if they do marry. On the other side of the to-be family, the engagement has been accepted completely with the family's complete approval. From the looks of things as they stand now, only time will tell the outcome of the mixed marriage.

The same process is apparent in interracial marriages and other marriages across socially defined lines of endogamy.

In spite of the pressures toward social endogamy, once a couple has become emotionally committed to one another, few are likely to sever the relationship on the basis of social differences unless they are perceived as current sources of trouble or conflict in their relations with one another. In the light of this fact, recent advice from officials in the hierarchy of the Roman Catholic Church that young people avoid social relationships with non-Catholics shows a perception of social reality. If one is *on principle* opposed to intermarriage of two groups, the only effective way to implement this is to restrict the kinds of initial contacts which are likely to eventuate in marriage. Attendance only at parochial schools, racial and ethnic segregation of schools, clubs, and neighborhoods—all are effective in preventing exogamous dating, friendships, and eventually love affairs and marriages. It is for this reason that conservative marriage texts advise young people that they avoid initial heterosexual involvements with those socially different from themselves. The ultimate effect of such advice, if it were followed, would be toward a crystallization and strengthening of present divisions in the social structure more than toward an increase in the proportion of happy marriages, although this consequence may be of little importance to the individual in the process of selecting a mate. Whether or not this result is good or bad for the society depends on one's beliefs about the shape of good society. The shape of the society is ultimately a product of the individual decisions of millions of people.

A broader view of the problems of exogamous marriages might show that those who contract exogamous marriages may have less stable and satisfactory marriages, not especially because of their exogamy, but because they are unconventional people in many other ways. Monogamous marriage, even in the United States in the twentieth century, is a very conservative and conventional institution and probably best designed to fit conservative and conventional people. Exogamy is only one form of nonconformity. Those who enter mixed marriages are in a way announcing to the world their disdain for its mundane rules. In many ways, marital adjustment is a measure of one's ability to make one's peace with the restrictions and conventions of proper society. To some extent, a low divorce rate in a group may indicate more happy marriages, but to a considerable degree it also indicates an unwillingness to upset apple carts, a willingness to compromise individual desires for the sake of upholding social obligations. It might be suspected that those who are willing to disdain the pressures for endogamy are not as willing to make these other compromises.

Sex-Role Differentiation in Marriage

13

This chapter is interested not in the general division of sex roles in the society, but in the division of roles between husband and wife. Of course, the two are intimately interconnected, and the actual role differentiation in any marriage is far more contingent on the conditions of the couple's involvement in the society than on any ideology they may hold. Put less fatalistically, the decisions made by the couple in many other parts of their lives also help unwittingly to shape the division of labor and influence in the marriage.

The Complexity of Sex-Role Specialization in Marriage

Before falling into the easy pattern of describing marital patterns in polar terms—traditional vs. equalitarian, togetherness vs. separateness, division of labor vs. no division of labor, instrumental vs. expressive—it might be worth a moment's thought to consider the complexity and diversity of possible arrangements of sex roles in a marriage. First, the roles of husband and wife may be thought of as including several sets of acts: those *vis-à-vis* one another, those *vis-à-vis* the children, those *vis-à-vis* the impersonal household tasks, and those which are involved in systems external to the nuclear family (e.g., outside employment; relationships with strangers, kinfolk, and with community institutions). Husband and wife may have quite differentiated responsibilities with respect to some external relationships but little or none in other areas. For example, only the husband may be employed as a breadwinner, yet the couple may assume equal and similar relationships to the church or to the children's schools. The pattern of external commitments must, in some ways, affect the internal arrangements of the family. If a husband is employed and a wife is not, it is very likely that their responsibilities in child-care will be quite differentiated. Yet, even here there is considerable room for variation. One employed husband may be quite involved with the children, while another never sees his except while they are asleep or excludes himself from their care. Consider the possible variations in the assumption of an emotionally supportive role. It appears from some recent research on parental roles that middle-class parents tend to be instrumentally oriented toward their same-sex children, but more emotionally supportive toward their cross-sex children. Consider again the varieties of job allocation within the household. Any particular task may fall totally to the husband, totally to the wife, or to one more than the other; they may always do it together, sometimes one will do it, sometimes the other; they may delegate it to a child, hire someone to do it, simply leave it undone, or combine any of these methods.

Instrumental and Expressive Roles Within the Family

Overall sex-role definitions in American society conventionally assign more expressive behavior to women and more instrumental behavior to men.[1] The extent to which this distinction is useful in describing family interaction is not at all clear. Studies of the role expectations and role perceptions of married and unmarried persons are somewhat at variance with actual observations of family behavior. When asked to define their marital-role expectations, adolescents show strong leanings toward similarity of sex roles and equalitarian norms, with great expectations of mutually sharing decision-making and expressive roles (Dunn, 1960; Lovejoy, 1961). Adolescent girls expect only slight sex differentiation in the conventional direction (Motz, 1950). Generally speaking, men expect more conventional differentiation than women, lower-class persons expect more conventional patterns than middle-class persons, and married persons are more conventional in their expectations than courtship couples.

The actual patterns of interaction in marriage are much more confusing than the expectations would lead one to anticipate. Perhaps they can be clarified by first setting forth some general sociological observations about roles. A social role is defined as a set of norms for the behavior of persons occupying certain positions in a society. They may be seen as generalized expectations held by people (with wide variation) that anyone in a certain position should behave in certain ways. These roles tend to be more stereotyped than the actual behavior of people occupying the position. For example, there are certain expectations as to how fathers should behave toward their children. In actual fact, there is far more variation in the behavior of fathers

[1] See Chapter 3 for discussion of instrumental-expressive roles.

than there is in people's expectations of fathers. When someone is a father, his behavior is in part controlled by the fact that he knows the general role of father. However, his actual behavior is modified by his personality, the personalities of his wife and children, his other role commitments (Does his occupation require him to travel? Is his wife an invalid?), and by pressures of daily family life.

Initial interaction between men and women who do not know one another is quite traditionally oriented in terms of male-instrumental, female-expressive roles. However, as males and females come to know one another better, they become less and less bound by the conventional definitions, and the differences in their behavior become less marked (Heiss, 1962). This is mainly due to a decrease in posing among women who are opposed to male dominance. That is, in early male-female interaction there is a tendency for all women to defer to men, but as they get to know one another better, those women who all along have been opposed to male dominance gradually become more assertive. The roles are modified by the personalities of the actors.

Within marriage there are a number of pressures which lead the couple away from conventionally expected role differences. Two factors seem fairly universal: The first is the fact that husband and wife know one another well, which minimizes posing; the second is the fact that in family interaction the mother usually has responsibility for supervision of the children, which includes (as every mother knows) far more than emotional-expressive functions. The result of the action of these forces is that family interaction is not as sharply differentiated along an instrumental-expressive axis as one might expect. Couples *think* that they will be more traditional in their role differentiation than they actually are (Kenkel, 1963; Strodtbeck, 1951).

An ingenious study by Leik (1963) demonstrated the effect of family situation on sex-role differentiation by observing the behavior of the same group of men and women with their own spouses and with spouses of strangers in otherwise similar situations. In these circumstances, the male-female differences on instrumentality and expressiveness were clear in the situation with the stranger but by comparison virtually disappeared when the subjects were in the same circumstances with their own mates. In spite of this, most observations of husband-wife interaction confirm that even within the family there is still a clear and traditional instrumental-expressive role division between husband and wife (Kenkel, 1963; Strodtbeck, 1951). This simple statement obscures more than it illuminates, however. In most American families, the husband is the main income provider (instrumental connection between outside world and family). In most families, the wife provides the primary care of the children (instrumental within the family). In most tasks with the family, there is task specialization between husband and wife, but both perform internal instrumental functions, albeit different ones. With respect to emotional-expressive behavior within the family, there is little evidence that this is more the domain of the wife than of the husband. With respect to one another, each appears equally important in providing emotional gratification and support to the other (Levinger, 1964). Because we cover up all of these complexities when we say that husbands generally play instrumental roles and wives play expressive roles, it is probably better to abandon that principle entirely in the face of our more detailed knowledge of the subject.

It is interesting to note in passing that lower-class persons consistently report more traditional attitudes toward sex-role differentiation (Dunn, 1960; Motz, 1950). Yet, actual lower-class patterns in the family appear to be less differentiated than in the middle-class family. This is no doubt associated with the peculiar occupational structure of lower-class life where the husband's occupational instability and wife's necessity of employment, coupled with the general instability of the marital relationship, place the lower-class wife in a far more instrumental position than the middle-class wife.

There is little basis for maintaining that instrumental-expressive role differentiation is associated with adjustment or maladjustment in the family. Some sociologists maintain on theoretical grounds that role differentiation in the traditional direction is necessary for successful family functioning (Parsons and Bales, 1955). No evidence is available to support this position. (One study does give evidence that well-adjusted wives *perceive* themselves as higher in expressive-role qualities than their husbands, while unadjusted wives do not [Kotlar, 1962].) Slater argues that in the American middle-class family, sharp differentiation of parental roles along instrumental-expressive lines would be detrimental to effective childrearing. At least in the early years, a child in the typical American family is far more influenced by his family alone than is the case in societies with more extended family structures. Under these circumstances, it is hard for him to adopt the values of a parent who is strictly a disciplinarian or strictly a source of emotional gratification (Slater, 1961). Another writer puts it this way:

> . . . Such differentiation reduces the influence of parents over children. The discipline of the father becomes coercive and the mother's love seductive. Only when discipline comes from a loving parent can it be accepted and internalized by the child. Only when a parent's love is concerned with the child's progress toward maturity does it avoid infantilizing him (Blood, 1962: 440).

It seems reasonable to conclude that in a family with children at home, *the human relationships and the emotional and instrumental requirements of living together are too complex for a simple division of roles along instrumental-expressive lines. Rather, each spouse is required to be sometimes instrumental, sometimes expressive in his behavior.* Husbands who are not emotionally supportive of their wives and affectionate to their children are probably disruptive to American families. Wives who cannot effectively direct the affairs of the daily household routine are probably disruptive to the emotional equilibrium of everyone in the family. (For a contrasting view, with some empirical evidence, see Epstein and Westley [1960].)

Decision-Making in Family Affairs

The prevailing value in middle-class families in the United States is that husband and wife decide most things together. "Marriage is a fifty-fifty proposition" is a favorite slogan. This value is held by the married and those who plan to marry, although perhaps with greater strength by the latter group. On the other hand, the value is more strongly held in some areas of decision than in others. Specifically, equalitarian norms seem to apply most strongly in childrearing, social participation, and recreation, and to a lesser extent in financial management and household tasks (Dunn, 1960; Dyer and Urban, 1958). Apparently, American families *are* quite generally equalitarian in their decision-making processes. Of the numerous investigations of family decision-making, equalitarian-democratic decisions are prevalent in most segments of the population (Blood and Wolfe, 1960; Middleton and Putney, 1960). It might be supposed that Roman Catholic families would be more husband-dominated than other groups in the population because of the Church's support of a patriarchal family. However, this proves not to be the case. Catholic families are, on the whole, not significantly more male-dominated than non-Catholic families (Blood and Wolfe, 1960).

The Bases of Family Power

Within the overall democratic orientation toward family life, there is considerable variation from couple to couple in the relative influence of the mates. The following factors are important in determining the relative power of the spouses:

1. Personalities of the spouses.
2. Relative age of the spouses.
3. Relative education of the spouses.
4. The employment status of the wife.
5. The occupational status of the husband.
6. The presence and number of children in the family.
7. The stage in the family cycle.

A METHODOLOGICAL NOTE: CONTRIVED SITUATIONS AND RETROSPECTIVE QUESTIONNAIRES

In evaluating the personal usefulness of the results of studies in family decision-making, it is important that the student consider how the data were obtained. The two common techniques relied upon by nearly every study quoted here are 1. retrospective questionnaires and 2. contrived situations, usually using the "revealed difference" technique. Students are no doubt familiar with retrospective questionnaires. In this technique, the research subjects are asked to report how decisions have been made on various issues in the past. There are a number of problems in this technique. Couples forget just what happened and report inaccurately. Then too, the two people involved each perceive the situation differently at the time, and frequently give conflicting reports. One study using this technique found that husbands and wives gave mutually inconsistent responses to almost half the items (Wilkening and Morrison, 1963). In addition, one's perception of past events is colored by the events intervening. Respondents underestimate their own power and overestimate their spouse's. Couples' responses to questionnaires indicate that husbands are dominant, but their actual decision-making was observed to be egalitarian.

In contrived decision-making situations, spouses are individually administered a questionnaire of some sort, and their answers are compared to "reveal differences." When the spouses disagree on any item, they are asked to discuss it and agree on an answer. The person whose original answers most resemble the joint answers is said to have the most power or influence. This technique has the advantage of not requiring recall of past events because the researcher can record the results as they occur. In addition, the researcher has the opportunity to observe the decision-making situation, which influences his interpretation of the results. The problems of this technique are as serious as with questionnaires. First, it is difficult to know whether the subjects really cared about the item to be decided in the first place. Do the differences make a difference? Second, because the situation is contrived and the subjects know that they are behaving for an audience (whether or not the observer can be seen), it is difficult to assess the effect of this extraneous factor. Kenkel (1961) has shown that even the sex of the observer has an influence over the process of interaction of married couples being interviewed. Third, the couple knows that the results of their deliberations are not actually going to affect anything. In one of Kenkel's studies, the couples were given a hypothetical $300 to spend and told to decide what they would buy. No one knows what the relationship is between the use of a hypothetical $300 and a real windfall of $300. However, the study would have cost $7,500 more to conduct with real money.

Olson and Rabunsky (1972) asked 15 married couples who were expecting their first child to predict who would have the final say on 27 items and to state who had the right to make the final decision. (To ensure that the items were relevant and important to the subjects, Olson and Rabunsky chose the items by asking couples with new babies about decisions they had made soon after the baby was born.) The couples then discussed the items on which they disagreed. About seven months later, after the births of their children, the couples were asked to recall who had made the final decision and what that decision was. Olson and Rabunsky found that the person predicted to have the final say is likely to be the one whose view prevails in the joint discussion, but that neither of these variables had any relationship to who later actually makes the decision. The person who is given the right to make the final decision is likely to be later recalled as the one who made the decision, but who actually made the decision is unrelated to these variables. Olson and Rabunsky conclude that a person can more accurately report what decision was made than he can report who made it, and that spouses' reports of who makes decisions therefore may not indicate who actually makes decisions in a family.

These comments are in no way meant to belittle the value of the research described, but the reader needs to realize its limitations. Certainly, it is better than intuition or casual observation of one's friends or parents. Something important will be said on this subject (and on most subjects talked about in this text) when observations of ongoing family behavior have been repeated at several different times (Walters, 1963). Meanwhile, the student will have to consider the available results for the little help they may be.

PERSONALITY OF THE SPOUSES

The student who is oriented toward thinking of human behavior in terms of individual personality traits might expect that the extent to which a person dominates the decision-making process in the marriage is largely determined by the personality traits of the individuals involved. Certainly, the whole theory of complementary needs in mate selection would lead one to this conclusion. Presumably, for example, dominant persons would choose spouses they expected to be able to dominate, and much of their gratification from the marriage would come from the practice of this dominance. Irrespective of the merits of this mate selection theory, there is a relationship between personality characteristics and the decision-making in a family. Kenkel's studies of the effect of personality, however, contain some surprises for the novice. Using a contrived decision-making situation, he compared personality traits of husband and wife to their influence. The *dominant* males, as expected, were more likely to get their own way, but the dominant women were less likely than the nondominant to have great influence on the decision outcome. *Persistent* males were less likely to influence decisions than less persistent males, and self-confident women seemed to have more influence than those with less self-confidence (Kenkel, 1961). In examining the way in which mates play roles, Kenkel concludes that the degree of influence in a family decision-making session is related to performance of traditional spousal roles. Wives with high or even medium influence generally played the more traditional wifely role, praising and rewarding their husbands, condescending to them, and only occasionally letting their own ideas be known. Husbands with high or medium influence generally played a quite different role. They "spoke up loud and long" and let their ideas and suggestions be known (Kenkel, 1957). *Personality can be seen to play a significant part in decision-making, but only as it is mediated by the strong cultural influence of sex roles.*

RELATIVE AGES OF THE SPOUSES

Although age is not considered as important a basis for power in the United States as it is in more traditional societies, it is still a basis for deference, and in the first half of life, large age differences are likely to influence nearly any social relationship. A century ago, age differences of five years or more (with the husband older) were the rule in this country. The age differences between spouses has now declined to under two years on the average. When there are large differences in age, the older spouse (nearly always the husband) is more influential, but when the differences are small they are irrelevant. Blood and Wolfe (1960) found in their study of a diverse sample that when the husband was more than ten years older than his wife, he was more influential than when the age difference was reduced. Other researchers, using subjects with less variation in relative age, have found the age differential an irrelevant factor (Udry et al., 1961). *For the vast majority of couples, age differences have no effect on the power structure of the marriage.*

RELATIVE EDUCATION OF THE SPOUSES

Taking a general view of influence structure, it might be predicted that persons with high-status characteristics would be more influential—that is, that influence is related to status. In American society, education is a status characteristic, and it is not surprising that in marriages *the mate with the highest educational level has more influence than he otherwise would have* (Blood and Wolfe, 1960). The influence edge is especially noticeable when one mate is college-educated and the other is not (Blood, 1962).

EMPLOYMENT STATUS OF THE WIFE

Many evils have been blamed on the wife's employment outside the home, and it is clear that many men have looked upon it as a threat to male dominance. These men may have been misogynists, but their perception of the situation is accurate. Wives who are employed full time have more influence in family decision-making than those employed part time, and the latter, in turn, have more influence than the unemployed housewives. Furthermore, the less the husband is employed (under full time) the less influence he has (Blood and Wolfe, 1960). Perhaps this finding can be explained by the fact that women who do not accept male dominance are more likely to go to work, as one report seems to indicate (Hoffman, 1960). More than likely it is the other way around. One team of sociologists asked a group of employed wives and a group of housewives how their attitudes toward authority in the marriage had changed since the time they were "going with" their husbands. Working wives more often reported changing toward equalitarian authority expectations, while housewives more often reported changing toward traditional (male-dominant) authority expectations (Blood and Hamblin, 1958). Even when couples in which the wife works and couples in which the wife does not work are equated for husband-wife differences in general personality dominance, working wives have more control over the decision-making process than their housewife counterparts. This is true for both middle-class and working-class couples (Heer, 1958). Evidently, the simple fact of the wife's outside employment is enough to either make her more assertive in family affairs or make her husband more willing to defer to her desires, or both.

A contradictory finding to the conclusions in the preceding paragraph casts some doubt over their universal applicability. The conclusions reported above were all based on retrospective questionnaires. However, a study of couples using the "revealed difference" technique to compare decision-making in couples in which the wife worked or did not work found that the housewives actually exerted *more* influence than their working counter-parts (Middleton and Putney, 1960). A breakdown of the areas in which decisions were made indicated that the working wives were significantly less dominant than housewives in childrearing, recreation, and role attitudes, while in the area of decisions about purchases and living standards—where the working wife might be expected to be more dominant because of her economic contribution—there were no differences between the two groups of wives. This finding is consistent with Motz's (1950) report that working wives (surprisingly) had a more conventional definition of marital roles than other wives.

When studies which are competently done turn up contradictions to one another, the results can usually be accounted for by differences in the people who were the subjects or differences in the methods used. In the above case, it was probably the difference in the method which produced the contradiction. Which result is closest to "real" marital decision-making no one knows. In addition, other factors influence the effect of the wife's working. For example, Kandel and Lesser (1972) found that whether the wife had a job was not so important as whether she worked inside or outside the home. In their study of Danish and American wives, they discovered that women employed full time *in the home* had less influence than women who worked part time or full time *outside the home*. And Safilios-Rothschild (1970) found that working women with high commitment to their jobs saw themselves as dominant in decision-making and giving in in arguments less often than their husbands. Working wives with low job commitment, unlike the wives with high commitment, reported that decision-making was egalitarian. The preponderance of evidence is in favor of the conclusion that *the wife who works has more influence in family decisions than the wife who does not.*

OCCUPATIONAL STATUS OF THE HUSBAND

In spite of the patriarchal values espoused by many working-class persons, and in spite of the so-called emancipation of the educated, middle-class woman, research into the decision-making structure of American families raises some question as to who is emancipated. A half-dozen studies have independently come to the same conclusion: *The higher the social status of a family, the more the decision-making process is dominated by the husband* (Blood and Wolfe, 1960), in spite of the fact that the wives in the high-status families constitute most of the well-educated women of America. Just why this is true is not easy to say. The more money a man makes, the less likely his wife is to be employed. Proportionally six times as many wives work whose husbands earn under $3,000 per year as do wives whose husbands earn $10,000 per year or more (Blood and Wolfe, 1960: 98). It is easy to interpret this as meaning that a high-income husband is so successful that his wife does not *have* to work and can afford to devote her full time to performing domestic services for her family and public services for the community. However, this is a clear acceptance of the husband's greater value and the wife's dependence on him. She owes her high status in the community not to anything she herself does, but by association with her husband. Since the husband provides her with so much in status and material possessions, she apparently shows proper deference to him. On the other hand, the low-income, low-status husband by comparison provides little status for his wife. Because of his probable low level of education and skills, her income-producing potential is often not much inferior to his. Furthermore, she is put into the position of feeling that she must use this potential — she *must* work because of the husband's inadequacy. Even if she does not work, she has less reason to show deference to her husband's wishes. Because he has so little to offer, his bargaining position is not great. It is interesting to note that the relationship between husband's power and his occupational status is exactly opposite in Greece and Yugoslavia. There the husbands with the lowest-status occupations have the most authority in family decision-making. For an explanation of this curious reversal, see Rodman (1967).

THE PRESENCE AND NUMBER OF CHILDREN

Childless couples are much more equalitarian in their power balance than couples with children (Blood and Wolfe, 1960), and there is some evidence that the more children there are in the family the more influence the husband has (Heer, 1958). These observations are consistent with Bossard's conclusion that the larger a family is, the more complex the problems of coordinating family activity and the more authoritarian becomes the power structure (Bossard, 1956). Heer (1963) offers another explanation for the power of husbands increasing with the presence and number of children. (His theory is also relevant to the other bases of family power.) Each mate, he maintains, implicitly compares the value derived from the present spouse with the alternative value of his own resources outside the marriage. The woman who is burdened with children is in a much less enviable position without her husband than is the woman who has no children, and the more children she has, the lower is her probable bargaining position for another husband and for jobs. According to this explanation, she recognizes that she has a good deal within the marriage and defers to her husband's wishes to the degree that this marriage arrangement exceeds any alternative in desirability.

THE STAGE IN THE FAMILY CYCLE

As other aspects of the marital relationship change over time, so the decision-making balance changes over time. Early in the marriage, before the arrival of children, when marriage is perhaps still a form of courtship, couples are at their most equalitarian stage. When the wife has preschool children at home and is most tied up in domestic chores—when her work hours are longest and her life hardest—then she has less say in family affairs than at any point in her marital career. Wolfe (1959) found that, as the children grow up, the balance in decision-making is gradually restored, so that middle-aged married life is nearly as equalitarian as preparental marriage. Very few wives over fifty are dominated by their husbands. On the other hand, Lewis (1972), in a study of 147 white families in varying stages of the family life cycle, found that husbands and wives with teenage children felt that the wife's decision-making power was at its peak, while couples whose children were grown felt that her power was at its lowest point. Lewis also found that the wife's satisfaction with the decision-making process was significantly related to the stage in the family life cycle, while the husband's was not.

Racial Differences in Family Decision-Making Patterns

According to Hyman and Reed (1969), "The American Negro family has been characterized as a *matriarchy* so often that the assertion is widely accepted as a truth rather than a proposition still in need of empirical evidence and critical analysis." This conception usually contains two different components: first, "father-absent families are relatively more frequent among blacks." (This is well-documented from census data, but its meaning is controversial.) Second, "even when the father is present, the mother is the dominant member of the intact black family." All kinds of sociological explanations have been offered for these two statements, but most revolve around the idea that the husband has less influence because of his disadvantage in providing economic support for his family on account of his inferior education and discrimination in the job market. Many studies have published data on the relative influence of husbands and wives in black and white families. One study comes to the following conclusion:

> The comparison of Negro and white blue-collar marriages shows significant differences in many variables in the direction of greater deprivation for Negro wives. In decision-making they get less cooperation from their husbands so they must make more family decisions unaided. In the division of labor at home, their husbands less often come to their aid in difficult circumstances. In the leisure time aspects of marriage, less interaction takes place between Negro husbands and wives. Negro men less often share their day's experiences with their wives and wives less often share their troubles in return. These objective deficiencies in marital interaction patterns are reflected in greater dissatisfaction of Negro wives with their mates (Blood, 1969).

TenHouton (1970) found that there is little black-white difference in the balance of decision-making in marriage. Jackson (1972) stated that wives do not dominate the marriages of elderly black couples. Other studies support this view. Yancey (1972) found that when he controlled for socioeconomic status, marital status, and sex, race differences were not significantly correlated with matrifocal attitudes. Among males, blacks were more matrifocal, but among females, whites were more matrifocal. In certain areas of family decision-making, however, black women do seem more powerful than white women. For example, Kandel (1971) found that black mothers are much more likely than white mothers to make decisions concerning their daughters without consulting their husbands. There are differences in the approach of the studies which will allow those who have decided what the conclusion ought to be to discount the study which contradicts their biases. However, we must again reluctantly conclude that *a conclusion is premature on the question of whether intact marriages of blacks are more wife-dominated than intact marriages of whites.*

Marital Decision-Making and Marital Adjustment

The kind of decision-making structure a marriage develops is closely related to the satisfaction the couple finds in the marriage. Good marital adjustment and satisfaction with the marriage are found most often in couples with democratic-equalitarian patterns of behavior, and least frequently when one spouse dominates the scene (Lu, 1952). More particularly, a wife-dominant authority relationship is associated with the lowest satisfaction of all (Blood and Wolfe, 1960: 45). This does *not* mean that marriages in which the woman has a more dominant *personality* than her husband are more unhappy. In fact, Terman (1938: 24) found that husband-wife differences in personality dominance were unrelated to marital happiness. *It is only when the marital relationship leaves the decision-making in the hands of the woman that the marriage is unhappy.* Why should this be? There are alternate possible explanations. A wife-dominant relationship contradicts the traditional sex-role differentiation expected in American society. Henpecked husbands have been objects of ridicule for centuries. This means that neither spouse can be proud of the husband under these circumstances.

CASE

I was more of an executive type than Jim so it was just natural for me to take the lead in making our decisions. I must have been too obvious about it because the fellows in our group of married couples began to make jokes about his being "henpecked" and about my "wearing the pants." Jim's reaction was terrific. He insisted on doing all the deciding. He took to ordering me about in the group. The worst thing about it was that his judgment was not as good as mine. Our family finances have suffered as a consequence. Worst of all, our happy relationship has become unhappy (Burgess and Wallin, 1953: 633).

Most scholars who have studied family decision structures are prone to believe that the wife-dominance is not what creates the unhappiness. Rather, it appears that the dominant wife "exercises power regretfully by default of her 'no good' or incapacitated husband" (Blood and Wolfe, 1960: 45). This suggests that the *unhappiness precedes wife-dominance and gives rise to it.* It is not so much that the wife succeeds in taking over the power and then does not like what she has brought about, but rather that the husband withdraws from the decision-making process, and the wife unhappily takes over the empty driver's seat. There is some indication that the attitudes of divorced couples are affected by this process. Divorced females have very high female-equalitarian attitudes toward marital roles, while divorced males have very high male-dominant attitudes (Jacobson, 1952). It is possible to read the female attitudes as a response to the upset power balances in their former marriages and the husband's attitudes as a response to the assumption of authority by their ex-wives. In any crisis, whoever is responsible for making decisions tends to decrease in power and be replaced. Bahr and Collins (1971) found that in marital crises the dominant family member was more often replaced than in noncrisis situations. In addition, the more equalitarian the conjugal power structure was in a noncrisis situation, the more likely it was that a change in the structure would occur in a crisis. Families dominated by one member were less likely to replace him during a crisis.

The Separate Allocation of Authority

Beside the long-range trend for wives to gain in influence as the couple is married longer, another long-range trend is apparent—*a trend toward the development of separate fields of authority.* The young couple tends to form decisions by discussion and resolution. This is consistent with the intimacy of the interaction of young marrieds. As couples are married longer, the intimacy is no longer so compelling, and as each develops separate areas of competence, it becomes efficient for each to have separate areas in which he has authority to make decisions without consulting the other. Most couples do not seem especially happy with this arrangement, that is, the happiest couples have this pattern less frequently. Nevertheless, it is found with increasing frequency as couples approach middle age (Blood and Wolfe, 1960).

A Neglected Factor: The Influence of Children in Decision-Making

The discussion so far has implied that all influence in decision-making is divided between husband and wife. Any parent with children over three years of age knows what a simplification this is. The presence of very little children has a profound effect on the decisions which parents will make, but the children can hardly be said to have influenced the decision themselves. As soon as children are verbal, they begin to make their wishes known. Although their power can hardly be said to be based on their alternatives outside the family (Blood, 1963), they have ways of influencing the family decisions through their ability to manipulate the reward structure within the home. A child who has lost a decision can fill the house with misery for an hour. Children have their techniques of punishing parents for not taking their wishes into account. Older children are able to appeal to the parents' sense of justice and democratic values to make parents seem unfair or autocratic for failing to make them part of the decision process, especially in middle-class households. The feelings of children on the subject may influence decisions as significant as whether or not to move to a new home, what type of family vacation will be taken, furniture purchases, and particularly, recreational decisions. In a formal decision situation using the "revealed difference" technique to study trios composed of husband, wife, and adolescent son, Strodtbeck showed by his method of scoring that the son's influence was nearly as great as that of the mother (Strodtbeck, 1954). It might be expected that the older the child, the greater is his share of influence on family decisions.

The Family Division of Labor

The division of labor in the family is related to, but not necessarily similar to, the division of power. One might easily conceive of a family where a highly authoritarian father made all the decisions of the family unilaterally but never contributed to the work; or of a family where all decisions were made jointly and with equal influence, while the work was done by one spouse and the children. The latter case might occur when one of the mates was physically incapacitated, or when the husband's work required his absence from home for long periods.

In American families generally, where the husband is nearly always employed outside the household and the wife is rarely employed full time outside the home for many years, most work seems to be divided in a way which is consistent with this work rhythm. Ideological concerns about what is "women's work" and what is "men's work" in the traditional division of labor seem of little importance to contemporary couples (Blood and Wolfe, 1960: 56). The actual division of labor appears to be pragmatically based. In families where the husband works outside and the wife does not, the traditional pattern is expedient and efficient. Under these circumstances, men do the heavy work, most of the outside work, and, particularly, jobs which come up only every once in a while (such as taking down the storm windows and mowing the lawn). Women typically do the tasks which recur daily and are not heavy work (such as ironing and preparing meals). In families where the outside employment pattern is not traditional, the pattern of household duties is adjusted, usually by additions to the husband's home responsibilities. When the wife has outside employment, the husband's share of the housework increases (Blood and Hamblin, 1958), but not by much.

CASE

Mom teaches school at the local high school. This means that she must be away from the house from about 7:30 in the morning until about 4:00 in the afternoon, Monday through Friday. This severely limits the time she has for getting the housework done. So Dad often pitches in, along with my brothers and sister, to help when they can. The problem here is that both Mom and Dad feel that studies should come first, and so the children are unavailable to help, for the most part, until Saturday mornings. Dad, therefore, helps with dishes, takes out the garbage, runs errands, and, on Saturdays, takes the sheets to the laundry and sometimes does some of the vacuuming. In these ways he helps take some of the work load off Mom, while she still prepares meals and does the washing, ironing, and mending.

SOCIAL CLASS AND THE DIVISION OF LABOR

The emphasis on the emotional rewards of family life which is characteristic of middle-class Americans and which has led couples to emphasize common activities is a consequence of a series of changes in contemporary society. Today's family has little instrumental function, is relatively isolated from other emotional supports in the form of relatives and permanent friendships by its mobility, and is an affluent family in an affluent society in which the problems of adequate food and shelter have been solved, and in which the lack of economic pressure allows the luxury of concentrating on the rewards of human intimacy and emotional response. Recent descriptions of the culture of poverty have dispelled any romantic notions Americans might have had about the emotionally satisfying life of the really poor. An emphasis on the nuances of human relationships is probably a luxury only to be achieved by the well educated and economically secure.

A sharp division of the sexes in task allocation is atypical in middle-class, educated families but more common in working-class and lower-class families, both in the United States and elsewhere (Blood and Wolfe, 1960; Bott, 1957). Middle-class families are much more interested in companionship, and especially those families with educated wives have less segregated husband-wife activities (Udry and Hall, 1965). Komarovsky (1963) argues that very high-income, high-status families have even more role specialization than the middle-class families, but the evidence is not very compelling. It is true that high-income husbands do less work around the house (Blood and Wolfe, 1960: 60). Perhaps this can be accounted for by the "value of the husband's time." High-status professionals and managers tend to become more absorbed in their work and work longer hours at it than men in lower-status occupations. Perhaps the inherent interest of the work they do leads them to prefer to work extra hours at their professions rather than do routine chores about the house. Wives are probably lenient in absorbing extra chores because the husband "has to work," and, of course, high-income families can always hire someone to do the work.

While the middle-class family emphasizes common recreation, joint involvement in tasks, and marital togetherness, *the lower-status family tradition in the United States (and elsewhere) is one of routine segregation of activities.* Certain tasks are done by one spouse, and other tasks by the other. Friendships are more likely to be separate, and each mate pursues his own recreational interests within his own circle. There is more traditional animosity between the sexes in the lower class, and by and large men and women do not have much in common beyond sexual interaction and the convenience of a division of labor. This is the tradition in the working-class

Table 13-1

HUSBAND AND WIFE REGIONS IN THE DIVISION OF LABOR AND AUTHORITY
Percentage Frequency of Interaction Patterns for a Typical Item in Each Region

Item	Region	Husband Decides			Both Decide			Wife Decides		
		H Does	Both Do	W Does	H Does	Both Do	W Does	H Does	Both Do	W Does
Ironing	Wife's household duties	—	—	—	—	1.3	18.7	—	—	80.0
Do the dishes	Common household duties	—	—	4.2	7.0	13.9	41.7	4.2	2.8	26.4
Table manners	Child control and care	—	1.3	—	6.3	46.3	38.8	—	1.3	6.3
Invite visitors	Social	—	—	—	1.3	74.4	12.8	—	5.1	6.4
Pay for holidays	Economic	4.3	7.2	7.2	13.0	44.9	18.8	—	—	4.3
Mow the lawn	Husband's household duties	64.3	7.1	8.9	5.4	5.4	7.1	1.8	—	—

Source: Herbst, 1960:344

family. However, things are changing. As economic well-being has increasingly spread to this class, and as geographic mobility has broken up the kinship-based networks typical of working-class neighborhoods, a new working-class group is emerging which is increasingly middle-class in its way of living. The new working-class family is characterized by less segregation in conjugal roles and more cooperative decision-making by husband and wife (Rainwater and Handel, 1963). But Komarovsky (1964) found working-class couples unable to find satisfaction in the new patterns. In a study of the problem-solving abilities of middle- and working-class families, Tallman and Miller have found that middle-class families solve their problems more efficiently when their decision-making process is egalitarian, but that among working-class families, problem solving is most efficient when the husband dominates the decision-making. Working-class egalitarian families are poor problem solvers.

THE REGIONS OF FAMILY TASKS

Herbst (1960) has shown that the actual division of labor in families groups the tasks into regions which may be arranged from highly sex-differentiated tasks (those which in nearly every family fall to the same sex and that sex only) to tasks which are as frequently associated with one sex as the other, or with both sexes interchangeably. Table 13-1 displays the arrangement. At the top are jobs which are strictly the work of the wife. Moving downward, subsequent regions each have additional male involvement. Responsibility for social activities is hardly sex-typed at all. The regions at the bottom of the table clearly become work of the husband. The tasks done by the members of individual families follow a very clear pattern with respect to these regions. If a husband is a heavy participant in the household, he will engage in tasks in all regions. If there is one region in which he is not involved, it will almost certainly be the wife's household duties. If there is another region in addition to this, it will be common household duties. The husband's "path of involvement" can be indicated like this:

Husband's Involvement in Total Family Tasks

Least Involved ⟵————————————————————⟶ Most Involved

| Economic duties | Social activities | Husband household duties | Child care | Common household duties | Wife household duties |

If a husband is involved in any area of activity, he will almost always be involved also in all areas to the left of that one. If he adds an activity, it will nearly always be the next one to the right. If he relinquishes a duty, it will be the last one to the right which he eliminates first. The wife's "path of involvement" is indicated like this:

Wife's Involvement in Total Family Tasks

Least Involved ⟵————————————————————⟶ Most Involved

| Wife household duties | Child care | Social activities | Common household duties | Economic duties | Husband household duties |

Of the couples Herbst studied, all wives were involved in the first three (boxed) areas on the left. If a wife is involved in only four activities (which is unusual), the fourth will be the common household duties. If she is missing one region, it will most likely be the husband's household duties rather than the economic area which she avoids. Herbst reports that by age eight, children have already taken on the "involvement paths" of the appropriate sex and are part of the family division of labor. From this study it can be seen that in spite of the pragmatic basis for the division of labor in families, the order of involvement in work around the household is really quite culturally patterned and institutionalized, however idiosyncratic it may seem to the families making the decisions.

DIVISION OF LABOR AND THE FAMILY CYCLE

The cozy picture which couples have during courtship of husband and wife doing the dishes together and marketing together is largely realized during the period immediately after marriage. Early marriage is in some ways an extension of courtship, a period of intimacy and mutual exploration of personality for most young couples. Two forces move the couple away from this idyllic pattern—boredom and desire for efficiency. As infants enter the family scene, the parents usually suddenly find that there is so much more to be done in the way of work, and that the child so restricts alternative actions, that a division of tasks is necessary to have any time left over at all. The particular tasks which are assigned to each spouse may be somewhat unorthodox at times, but the work is divided between husband and wife. Perhaps a more important reason for relinquishing the pattern of working together is that the couple becomes bored with being incessantly intimate. No person in the world can continue to be fascinating all the time for twenty years. Out of indifference, the mates gradually develop their separate spheres of activity. More often than not, their division corresponds a great deal to the division of other couples in their social situation in life. One indication that it is not primarily the force of necessity brought on by parenthood which drives the couple to their separate pursuits is the pattern observed in childless couples. Couples without children practice role specialization in just about the same way as those with children (Blood and Wolfe, 1960: 70; Silverman and Hill, 1967).

Are couples happier if they continue to work together rather than separately? Probably not. Blood and Wolfe (1960: 259) show that those wives whose husbands share some of the household tasks with them are happier than those whose husbands do not. Couples married several years frequently look back with some nostalgia on the early period when they walked arm in arm through the marketing. However, I suspect that the togetherness pattern is voluntarily relinquished by couples because they no longer find it satisfying, and not that they are unsatisfied because they have lost the closeness they once had. Lower satisfaction with marriage comes at the same gradual pace and at about the same periods in the family cycle as role specialization.

THE DEGREE OF PARTICIPATION

What determines how many regions of participation each family member has? Probably this is affected somewhat by the individual abilities and personalities of the members of the family. Some husbands like to do repair work around the house and some do not. Some like to care for children, and some even like to clean house. Some wives are good at figures and can keep the financial records of the family, while others are incompetent at this job. However, this is only half the story. Individual differences in family members may create a little leeway in the division of labor, but other commitments of the family members in addition to cultural expectations place limits on the extent to which work can be allocated according to the proclivities of personality. When the wife stays at home and husband goes to work, the culture says it is right that the woman should not expect as much of her husband's time in household duties as when she also goes out to work. The husband whose work takes him away from home for long periods will simply not do as much in the family division of labor as the husband who is home more regularly, and most wives will accept this as legitimate. If they do not, their husbands can validate their lack of participation by reference to its acceptability in the society. Other people will uphold him. For the same reasons, high-income husbands do less and over-employed husbands do less. Likewise, it is regularly found that when wives are employed full time, husbands do more housework, care for the children more, and cook and serve meals more (Blood and Wolfe, 1960). If they do not, the wives consider it unfair and find social support for their position.

When one spouse is sick, the other spouse rapidly picks up the slack in most cases. It is interesting to watch the differences in family behavior depending on which mate is sick. When a husband is sick, everything around the house can go on as usual except for his disrupting demands, because most of his jobs can be postponed or hired out. (Of course, for longer illness the loss of his income causes drastic alterations in the family pattern.) However, when the wife becomes sick, family life usually undergoes a shocking rearrangement. The proverb states, "many a fallen woman has been forgiven, but never for falling ill." Husbands frequently discover this for the first time at the birth of the first child, but the strain is even greater when there are already young children. Suddenly the husband has to do everything. Child-care has to be provided first. Meals have to be prepared. Groceries have to be bought, dishes done, beds made, pets fed, bills paid, and all this must be added to the husband's employment schedule. Many families will have a hard time avoiding the feeling that "it was a dirty trick for mother to get sick and leave us all in the lurch."

One of the beneficial consequences of having a "resident grandmother" in the house is a shift in the division of labor. Unless she is incapacitated by illness or age, she nearly always earns her keep through housework and child-care, thus relieving someone (usually the wife) of part of her burden. The difficulty encountered here, of course, is that there are no clear-cut cultural norms against which to validate the division of responsibility between the women. When the allocation of spheres of work has to be resolved through the interplay of personalities, there is a breeding ground for conflict.

Summary

Role differentiation in contemporary American marriages is too complex to be subsumed under any simple formula of instrumental-vs.-expressive roles. Each spouse is required to be both emotional and instrumental in different relationships. Power in family decision-making tends to fall more to the spouse with the most education when this differs between mates in low-status occupations. Employed wives are more influential than housewives, and husbands in high-status occupations are more influential than those in low-status occupations. Age differences do not seem to be very influential, but personality factors play an important role in the distribution of marital power. The more children there are in the family, the more power the husband has. When the wife wields the decision-making power by her husband's default, marriages tend to be unhappy.

Over the course of marriage, separate fields of authority develop, and division of labor is the characteristic pattern after the early years of marriage. This pattern is observed more quickly and more sharply in lower-class than in middle-class marriages. Most couples are not particularly pleased by the passing of joint decision-making and shared tasks, but it appears to be a natural evolution of the marital relationship.

Implications for Decision-Making

Not many couples during courtship anticipate having trouble in their marriage about who will decide what and who will do which jobs. The slogan that "marriage is a fifty-fifty proposition" seems to give them confidence that everything will be worked out without difficulty. Probably in the first year or so when sex-role differences in the marriage are minimized, their confidence is warranted. However, as the relationship becomes more complicated, decision processes and task allocation become increasingly troublesome. In one group of couples seeking help for problems in their marriage, household management and the sharing of household tasks were much more frequently stated as sources of trouble than in-laws, religious matters, child-rearing, and other areas where couples have traditionally been warned to expect trouble. In fact, only three areas—finance, personality, and sexual adjustment—were cited more frequently as trouble spots. The same trouble areas were also high on the list of a comparison group of couples who volunteered themselves as examples of well-functioning marriages (Mitchell et al., 1962).

No one can tell a couple what their decision structure should be or how they should divide labor in their home. However, some guidelines can be set forth on what to expect. The more the pattern departs from the usual pattern prevailing in a couple's social milieu, the more likely it is to give them trouble. When each spouse is doing what is "generally accepted" as his responsibility, there is social support from friends, neighbors, and relatives for the arrangement which can help to validate and stabilize it. On the other hand, the life which is worked out on the couple's own design is sometimes a good deal more interesting and exciting, though it is likely to be much more unstable and apt to generate problems which have to be resolved without reference to social norms to validate whatever solution is worked out. (This is no doubt why tradition and conformity have been shown to be consistently related to lack of conflict in marriages.)

Wife-dominated decision structures are regularly associated with unsatisfactory marriages. Couples who are deceived by the oversimplified theory of complementarity have sometimes come to believe that a husband who "wants to be dominated" will be quite pleased to be married to a woman who dominates him. However pleased he may be on some deep, unconscious level, it is unlikely that his wife will be happy with the situation.

There are many things that are not understood about family decision-making and division of labor. It is known that couples who consult with one another on decisions are more satisfied than those who do not, but it is not certain whether the lack of consultation is the cause or the result of the dissatisfaction. It is known that couples who share tasks and do things together are generally happier than those who do not, but it has not been determined whether the happiness is the result of the togetherness or the togetherness a result of the happiness. Perhaps each relationship works both ways.

If those contemplating marriage or just married know what to expect from the married years ahead, they may not be any happier with what they eventually get, but perhaps they will not become bitter. They will at least understand that their situation is typical of other couples their age. Most couples will develop increasing division of labor and increasingly separate decision areas as their relationship matures. Sociologists cannot tell them whether a concerted effort to prevent this will be effective, and, if it is effective, whether they will like the results better than what they would have experienced by drifting with social forces. Intuitively, one would guess that a more satisfactory plan is to continually revise one's expectations of the relationship. Nothing is more deadly than doggedly setting out to maintain a pattern which has outlived its ability to function and is no longer satisfying but is preserved out of nostalgia. Decision structures and job allocations are affected by other relationships in which the couple is implicated, by changes in other facets of their lives together. The changes brought about by the wife's employment or the coming of children are usually changes made in response to the pressures of the new situation which precipitated them—changes introduced because they prove to be efficient and satisfying.

Those couples with expectations which are not too rigid, those who are able to rise to crises, will be able to work out a satisfying procedure of consultation with each other and an equitable division of labor in most of the situations they meet in their life together. Some will not be happy with the changes they have to make.

External Roles and   14
Marital Interaction

I have sometimes discussed the dynamics of relationships among members of nuclear families as though families were self-contained social systems whose course was entirely determined by the relationships of the members of the family to one another. If any such families exist, living in self-imposed exile from the rest of society, they must be rather different from families embedded in a matrix of relationships. Families are not independent social units.

This chapter will be concerned with the effect on the marital and family roles of the relationships which husband and wife maintain outside the nuclear family. These relationships will be called *external roles*. Special interest centers on occupational roles, kinship roles, and friendship roles and their effect on husband-wife and parent-child relationships.

Marital Relationship and Kinship Ties

CROSS-CULTURAL PERSPECTIVE

In middle-class American groups, the most important human relationship is the marital relationship, and all other roles are subordinated to it (with the temporary exception of the mother-child role). Most Americans take seriously the Biblical injunction to leave their mothers and fathers at marriage and cleave unto their spouses. Thus, nuclear family ties completely eclipse all other kinship obligations and diminish their significance.

The marital relationship does not have such preeminence over other kin relationships in all societies. Rather, societies may be conceived as distributed on a continuum. At one end of the continuum, larger kin networks claim complete loyalty, and spousal obligations and involvement are reduced to a minimum. The traditional kinship system of the Nayar approximated this polar position. Kathleen Gough describes the Nayar system as follows:

At a convenient time every few years, a lineage held a grand ceremony at which all of its girls who had not attained puberty, aged about seven to twelve, were on the one day ritually married by men drawn from their linked lineages. The ritual bridegrooms were selected in advance on the advice of the village astrologer at a meeting of the neighborhood assembly. On the day fixed they came in procession to the oldest ancestral house of the host lineage. There, after various ceremonies, each tied a gold ornament *(tali)* round the neck of his ritual bride. The girls had for three days previously been secluded in an inner room of the house and caused to observe taboos as if they had menstruated. After the *tali*-tying each couple was secluded in privacy for three days. . . . Ritual husbands left the house after the four days of ceremonies and had no further obligations to their brides. A bride in turn had only one further obligation to her ritual husband: at his death, she and all her children, by whatever physiological father, must observe death-pollution for him . . . [A]fter the *tali*-rite and as soon as she became old enough (i.e., shortly before or after puberty), a girl received as visiting husbands a number of men of her subcaste from outside her lineage. . . . There is some uncertainty as to the number of visiting husbands a woman might have at one time. . . . It seems . . . that a woman customarily had a small but not a fixed number of husbands from within her neighborhood, that relationships with these men might be of long standing, but that the woman was also free to receive casual visitors of appropriate subcaste who passed through her neighborhood in the course of military operations.

A husband visited his wife after supper at night and left before breakfast next morning. . . . Either party to a union might terminate it at any time without formality. . . .

Although he made regular gifts to her at festivals, in no sense of the term did a man maintain his wife. Her food and regular clothing she obtained from her matrilineal group. The gifts of a woman's husbands were personal luxuries which pertained to her role as a sexual partner—extra clothing, articles of toilet, betel and areca nut—the giving of which is associated with courtship, and the expense of the actual delivery—not, be it noted, of the maintenance of either mother or child. The gifts continued to be made at festivals only while the relationship lasted. No man had obligations to a wife of the past.

In these circumstances, the exact physiological fatherhood of a child was often uncertain, although, of course, paternity was presumed to lie with the man or men who had paid the delivery expenses. But even when physiological paternity was known with reasonable certainty, the genitor had no economic, social, legal or ritual rights in, nor obligations to, his children after he had once paid the fees of their births. Their guardianship, care and discipline were entirely the concern of their matrilineal kinsfolk. . . .[1]

Near the other polar position is the socially and geographically mobile upper-middle-class family such as one finds in the United States, where

---

[1] E. Kathleen Gough, "Is the Family Universal?—The Nayar Case," Norman W. Bell and Ezra F. Vogel, eds., *The Family* (New York: Free Press of Glencoe, 1960), pp. 79–83. Reprinted by permission.

relationships with nonnuclear kin may be reduced to occasional letters and infrequent holiday reunions. It is easy to see that the kind of relationship which exists between married persons and their parents and parents-in-law is heavily influenced by the relative importance of the marital relationship and other kinship ties. In middle-class American society, a coalition of either spouse with his parent against the other spouse would be considered a breach of the solidarity of the marital tie. However, in classical upper-class Chinese families, where the patrilineal group was the basic kin unit and a husband's most important obligations were to his parents, a husband who did *not* side with his mother in her dispute with his wife would have been remiss in his responsibility to his mother.

Societies of many different kinds have recognized the troublesome nature of the relationship between mother-in-law and daughter-in-law, and almost as many find the relationship between mother-in-law and son-in-law a source of difficulty. Especially when the daughter-in-law moves into the home of her husband's parents at marriage, there is likely to be friction (Sweetser, 1966). Anthropologists have noted the existence in many places of elaborate rituals of "mother-in-law avoidance" as a way of dealing with potential problems. A man and his mother-in-law may be prohibited from touching each other, looking at each other, eating together, talking together, and even from being in the same room with one another (Stephens, 1963: 87).

RELATIONSHIPS WITH NONNUCLEAR KIN IN THE UNITED STATES

By comparison with the many societies studied by anthropologists, the American nuclear family is so much more important than any other wider kin organization that at first glance it appears to have no wider kinship circle. This has led certain sociologists to speak of the American nuclear family as being "isolated." The term *isolated nuclear family* as applied to the United States has been widely misunderstood, however, as implying that there are no significant social relationships between nuclear family members and other relatives. This is true only in comparison with unilineal kinship societies such as the Nayar or classical Chinese. Studies of social relationships among relatives in this country in the past decade and more have shown that most Americans maintain viable relationships with their parents and siblings after they themselves are married, and for large parts of American society, relations with relatives constitute a family's most important social contact (Sussman, 1959).

In their study of 120 young married couples, 120 of their parent families, and 120 of their grandparent families, Hill et al., (1970) found positive attitudes towards kin contact which were strongest among the youngest generation (see Table 14-1).

Table 14-1

THE YOUNGEST GENERATION VALUES KINSHIP INTERACTION MOST
Percent approving kinship interaction, by generation

		Percent endorsement by generations		
		Grandparent %	Parent %	Children %
A young couple and	Agree	60	42	36
their parents-in-law	Disagree	29	46	42
should go their	Undecided	11	12	22
separate ways and				
see each other only				
occasionally				
Children who move up	Agree	22	20	9
in the world tend to	Disagree	64	69	74
neglect their parents	Undecided	14	11	17
A young man has a	Agree	65	65	74
real responsibility for	Disagree	13	21	14
keeping in touch	Undecided	22	14	12
with parents-in-law				

Source: Hill et al., 1970: 60

A number of studies of migration patterns in the United States have shown that the most important factor in determining the specific city of destination of the migrant is the prior location of his relatives there (Blumberg and Bell, 1959). For rural migrants to urban areas, moving into a kinship group provides a kind of buffer for the new arrival before he establishes his own contacts with urban institutions. Recent immigrants to the United States are more likely to maintain closely knit kin groups than their countrymen who do not emigrate (Kassees, 1972). In times of crisis, married couples turn much more often to relatives than to professionals. For example, 293 victims of a heart attack reported contacting relatives and neighbors far more often during their convalescence than they contacted any social-service agency (Croog, Lipson, and Levine, 1972). Zimmerman and Cervantes (1960) found in a study of intact urban families that nearly half of the respondents indicated their most important friendships were with relatives. Sussman and Slater (1963) studied a random sample of Cleveland families and found that most were in regular contact with relatives by telephone, visiting, letters, and the exchange of help. These contacts are more likely to be maintained between parent and child than between siblings (Adams, 1965; Bellin, 1961).

The degree to which married children continue involvement with their relatives is not uniform in all levels of society. In both Britain (Wilmott and Young, 1960) and the United States (Sussman, 1960), kin ties are most important in lower- and working-class groups and least important in middle-

Table 14-2

	INTERGENERATIONAL VISITING ACCORDING TO SEX[1]					
	Parents-Grandparents		Child-Parents		Child-Grandparents	
	Male %	Female %	Male %	Female %	Male %	Female %
Daily	6	15	32	21	6	6
Weekly	30	39	42	48	26	35
Monthly	52	39	23	25	16	15
Quarterly-yearly	9	6	—	6	36	33
Yearly	3	—	3	—	16	10
Cases	33	46	31	48	31	48

[1] The percentage totals do not always add to 100 because of rounding.
Source: Hill et al., 1970: 62

class and professional families. In fact, most working-class families' social activities are likely to be restricted to members of the kinship group with non-kin friendships playing a relatively unimportant part. Straus (1969) found that farm wives reported more interaction with relatives than did urban wives, and high-income farm wives visited less often with relatives than did low-income farm wives. High-income urban wives had the least contact with kin. *In middle-class families, friendships outside the circle of relatives play the role that contacts with relatives play among the working class, and kinship ties themselves are far less important* (Adams, 1967; Dotson, 1951).

Hayes and Mindel (1972) found that black families may have more extended kinship networks than white families, even when socioeconomic status is controlled. In their comparison of twenty-five black and twenty-five white families matched for socioeconomic status, they found that black families saw more relatives more often than did white families, and that more relatives helped with child care more often in black than in white families.

Every investigation of kinship ties in the Unites States has shown that mother-daughter associations constitute the core around which most contacts with relatives are organized. This confirms the adage, "A son's a son till he takes a wife; a daughter's a daughter for all her life" (Bott, 1957; Young and Geertz, 1961). Mother-daughter relations are more important in working-class than in middle-class families, but even in the middle class they are likely to be the basis for whatever kinship ties are maintained (Adams, 1965; Wilmott and Young, 1960; Young and Geertz, 1961).

Hill et al., (1970), in their study of three generations of 120 married couples, found that married daughters do contact their parents and grandparents more often than married sons do (see Table 14-2), but that working-class men have more contact with parents and grandparents than do middle-class men.

Studies in England have suggested that if children move to different social-status levels after leaving the parental home, contact and affectional ties between parent and child are attenuated, but that mother-daughter ties withstand the status discrepancy better than ties with grown sons (Wilmott and Young, 1960). A recent study in a middle-sized city in a Southern state suggests that a different pattern exists in the United States. Adams (1965) showed that upward mobility of the children did not in any substantial way interfere with their parental ties for sons or daughters. Sons who moved to lower-status levels than their parents apparently continued the same types of contacts with parents as sons who had not lost status. It was the daughters who married beneath the status level of their parents who were cut off from contact and affectional ties with parents. In other words, the only way in which status mobility affected parent-child relationships was to weaken the relationship with her parents of the daughter who married beneath her parental status level. On the other hand, Hill et al., (1970: 62) note that both upward and downward mobility of the young married couple tend to weaken kin contacts.

KIN RELATIONS AND MARITAL INTERACTION

Any human being has a strictly limited amount of time which he can devote to social interaction and a limited capacity for investing himself emotionally with other people. The time and emotional commitment invested in one human relationship is not available for other relationships. This is one reason why, in human societies, the importance of other kin relationships is inversely related to the importance of the marital relationship—if parent-child relationships retain solidarity after the marriage of the children, the marital relationship will be less important. Where the marital relationship demands complete commitment, other kin relationships wither. Under such circumstances, there is an *inherent* conflict of emotions and interest between parents and the spouses of their children. In the American working class, marriage is not typically nearly as engrossing an emotional relationship as it is in the middle class, and ties to parents and siblings really compete for loyalty, especially among women. In the middle-class strata of this country, on the other hand, the marriage is the most important relationship, and strong loyalty to parents on the part of a husband or wife is likely to be interpreted as subversive to the marriage.

In most families, maintaining kinship ties is women's work. Consequently, *most in-law problems are women's problems.* Duvall (1954) found women involved in in-law problems six times as often as men. For example, wives dislike their mothers-in-law far more often than husbands dislike theirs. Perhaps this is because of the strength of the emotional attachment which mothers have to their sons (Winch, 1951). After marriage, women are more dependent on their parents than are men (Stryker, 1955; Wallin, 1954), but Stryker has shown that only the wife's attachment to her *mother* disturbs the marriage and the husband's relationship to his in-laws. The more dependent a woman is on her mother, the more trouble the husband has with his mother-in-law. On the other hand, "husbands are likely to be well-adjusted to their fathers-in-law when their wives report dependence on their fathers" (Stryker, 1955). Husbands are likely to be far less dependent on their parents and, as a consequence, difficulty is less often encountered here. However, when the husband *is* unusually dependent, particularly on his mother, this can be expected to be a real problem in the marriage as well as in relations between the wife and her mother-in-law (Komarovsky, 1950).

Young couples get along best with their parents and parents-in-law under the following conditions: parental approval of the marriage; meeting the prospective partner's family before marriage under friendly circumstances; maintenance of a separate household on the part of the young couple; happiness in the marriage of the parents; no religious differences with parents; traditional courtship and marriage; and similarity of cultural backgrounds between the mates (Marcus, 1951; Sussman, 1954).

A crucial determinant of interaction between parents and children is the geographic distance between them. It is hard to maintain intimate emotional ties where great distance separates parents and their married children. (It might also be suspected that how far a child is willing to move from his parents is some indication of how much emotional attachment remains.) Continuity between generations is obviously easier to maintain when the distance is small, *providing* harmonious relations already exist. However, when parental and in-law ties are already tense and difficult, the relationship can probably best be preserved if parents and their married children live at a distance which precludes regular visiting (Sussman, 1954). It is surprising how well couples maintain contact with their parents over long distances through letters, telephoning, and infrequent visiting. In fact, the amount of financial help a young couple receives from the parents does not seem to be in any way related to their geographic separation (Adams, 1964; Sussman and Slater, 1963).

In working-class and lower-class families, continued involvement of each spouse with his own kinfolk constitutes a continued threat to the stability of marriage. In case of marital conflict, each partner tends to retreat into his kinship group for support, and the mates tend to become polarized. The conflict then remains unresolved and the marriage weakened. It can be seen that it is not involvement with kin *per se* which weakens or competes with marriage. It is the circumstance under which the husband and wife continue to move each in his *own* kinship circle (Scanzoni, 1965).

LIVING WITH IN-LAWS

Very few American couples today share a household with their married children. The 1950 census reported more than 6 percent of married couples without their own households, but this was reduced to about 1.4 percent in the 1970 census. Most of this 1 percent is made up of parents living with children or children with parents. Yet, from 10 to 20 percent of young couples begin married life living with parents, usually the wife's parents (Schorr, 1962). Married children living in their parents' household is, therefore, seen to be a phenomenon of the early years of marriage, the only time when in-law problems are likely to be serious (Blood and Wolfe, 1960: 247). As the parents become old, the situation is reversed, so that about one aged couple in four is living with their children, while almost 40 percent of aged women who do not have husbands are living in their children's households (Schorr, 1962). Most living together, then, consists of newlyweds moving in with parents and of aged parents moving in with their married children. Arrangements for living together in the United States are much more common among low-income groups where financial assistance is more difficult to come by, and the arrangements are dictated by economic necessity.

Sociologists and laymen alike are nearly unanimous in saying that combined households are unsatisfactory living arrangements for Americans. A quarter-century ago, Parsons noted that "it is impossible to say that with us it is 'natural' for any other group than husband and wife and their dependent children to maintain a common household. . . . It is of course common for other relatives to share a household with the conjugal family but this scarcely ever occurs without some important elements of strain" (Parsons, 1962).

Most contemporary Americans agree with the experts. People's attitudes towards keeping an elderly parent in the home become much more negative as the likelihood of having to do so increases. High school and college students were more willing to have their aged parents with them when they were married than the parents were to have *their* parents move in with them (Wake and Sporakowski, 1972). And attitudes towards living with an elderly parent differ from actual behavior. Daughters who said they should move their ailing mothers into their own homes also said that in reality they probably *would* place their mothers in institutions (Wake and Sporakowski, 1972). People who share households report problems of privacy, space, and conflict over rearing children (Schorr, 1962). However, there really is no definitive evidence that shared living arrangements are more productive of stress than separate arrangements. Evidently, American values in support of separate households are so strong that even social scientists have not thought it worthwhile to demonstrate the benefits. A number of studies now available indicate that there are a number of benefits accruing to those who live together (Burgess, 1952). Grandparents play a major role in caring for the children of working mothers (Lajewski, 1959), and older parents living with the younger couple considerably lighten the domestic chores of the young wife. Schorr writes ". . . disaster studies which have been carried on since the Second World War find uniformly that families which include grandparents are more flexible and resilient in the face of the father's induction into the Armed Forces, and of flood, fire, or other disaster than are parent-child families" (Schorr, 1962: 424). Studies in England indicate that generations may choose to live together there for the benefits to be derived by both generations (Bott, 1957).

The fact that there are tensions which result from parents living with married children is not a valid basis for concluding that it is an "unnatural" living arrangement. Tensions are inherent in *any* living arrangement. The legitimate question which has not been answered is "are there significantly more tensions present in living-together arrangements over separate households?" Are there potential benefits which balance the tensions? Under what circumstances, if any, does living together produce more benefits than tensions? If social scientists concentrated their attentions on the strains inherent in marrying or childrearing, would they decide that these relationships were undesirable? Schorr suggests the following analogy:

> One may suppose that a visitor from Israel in the year 2000, third or fourth generation of a line of children raised communally in a kibbutz, would inquire whether Americans find it a strain to raise children *in the family home.* Do they not interfere with their parents' privacy; are they not insensitive and demanding; they must be an enormous physical and financial drain? Does not rearing children provoke unresolved conflict about dependency, and so forth? What can one answer to these questions but "yes," adding if we will that we find compensating satisfactions or that we do not like the alternative of raising our children communally. Moreover, a healthy family organizes itself so that these strains do not mount up as much as, to the uninitiate, it might seem. The useful questions about raising children, as about living together, are not categorical (that is, is there strain? or are there failures?) but discriminatory: when is strain greater and lesser? how are strains handled by those who handle them? what are the situations in which they cannot normally be handled? (Schorr, 1962: 426).

This is not a polemic in favor of parents and their married children living together. What needs to be clear is that most of the argument assembled by lay and scientific literature against living together is organized to support an existing value system in the society and is not based on substantial demonstration of the disadvantages of these living arrangements. When the value is firmly entrenched that living together is detrimental, one can look to the operation of the self-fulfilling prophecy for an explanation of why many people who do live together find it unsatisfying—they are so sure that it will be a source of serious difficulty that they organize their lives in such a way as to insure that they will experience the anticipated dissatisfaction. Those families who can approach combined households with open minds will occasionally find this a very satisfying way to live.

FINANCIAL EXCHANGE BETWEEN PARENTS AND MARRIED CHILDREN

In middle-class families, mutual aid between generations is more likely to be in the form of material or financial contribution and less in the form of living together than among working-class families. This is presumably because money is easier to obtain, and it is not necessary to resort to the most economical living arrangement. Although young people are likely to think of financial assistance as given from parent to child, it is important to keep in mind that the contributions go both ways.

In all cultures, every new generation of human beings is subsidized by the society for a number of years until the young are old enough to carry their own economic weight. Then it becomes their turn to subsidize the next generation. How many years this subsidy lasts depends on the complexity of the society and how many years it takes to train the new generation to do what is necessary to keep the society functioning.

In traditional American values, the mark of adult manhood was self-support. When a man had proven that he could support himself and a family independent of his father's assistance, he was ready to assume the additional responsibilities of adulthood, that is, marriage and parenthood. No records are available from previous generations of how much help married children received from parents, but in colonial days it was substantial (Demos, 1970: 182). Today the economic foundations of new families do not loom as important as the emotional foundations, either in the minds of the young couples or of their parents. When marriage is viewed as primarily a relationship to provide emotional satisfaction and security to adults, it is not surprising to find the criterion for marriageability shift from economic maturity to emotional maturity.

Although there is little comparative evidence to support the contention, it is the general feeling of family scholars that American middle-class parents are more willing to subsidize the marriages of their children today than previous generations of Americans have been. Furthermore, their children are more willing to accept the subsidy. It is taken for granted that emotional independence is the prerequisite of adult status. Marriage, rather than self-support, some sociologists think, now marks the assumption of adult roles which are not jeopardized by temporary and partial economic dependence of the married couple on their parents. For most couples from middle-class backgrounds, parental subsidy will prevent a drop in standard of living at marriage while the husband's earning power is mostly potential.

Even though most middle-class parents do help their married children (Sussman, 1953), the form that the help usually takes reveals that at least the feeling of economic independence is necessary for the couple's self-concept of adulthood (Adams, 1964). Rarely do the parents provide a regular money contribution. Rather, the assistance takes the form of help in making large purchases such as a home, gifts of furniture or appliances, presents to the grandchildren, or vacation trips. Although these forms of help may substantially boost the standard of living of the young couple, they evidently are not felt as "financial support." Financial help, like other forms of interaction between parents and their married children, flows from the parents to married daughters more often than to sons.

Financial assistance from parent to married children is likely to be most prevalent in the immediate postlaunching stage of the family cycle when parental incomes are at their highest and financial obligations have relaxed, and when the young couple's income is at its lowest and their expenditures are highest in relation to resources. As the parents become old and the children reach middle age, the financial flow is likely to reverse. Most of the help which married children provide their aged parents is in the form of living together rather than money. Not more than 10 percent of aged persons in the United States receive cash contributions from their children. Again, the help is more likely to come from daughters than sons. Personal relationships are probably easier when mothers get help from married daughters rather than married sons (Schorr, 1962). Once more the backbone of kinship ties is the mother-daughter relationship.

IMPLICATIONS FOR PERSONAL DECISION-MAKING

In the absence of any clear-cut mandate from research on the relative satisfactions of differing kin-relationship patterns, one can only suggest what are generally thought to be the conditions conducive to satisfaction, recognizing that these judgments are probably highly colored by personal values. Parents and their married children can probably live together in harmony under conditions which meet these criteria:

1. The arrangement must be voluntary on both sides—that is, it must appear to all parties that there are more benefits than disadvantages to the arrangement (Burgess, 1952).

2. Ordinarily, if there are two generations of married women in the household, there should be a clear division of authority and responsibility which is satisfactory to both generations (Sweetser, 1966). This would usually stipulate that authority for childrearing would be vested in the child's parents and not his grandparents. Other division of labor would probably depend on at what stage in the family cycle the families were. Each generation should probably be allocated *some* sphere of authority and *some* area of responsibility.

3. There should be physical arrangements for privacy for each nuclear family.

The problems of living together probably stem largely from the fact that the culture provides no norms which govern the allocation of responsibility and authority in a three-generation household; each family must work the problem out for itself with little support from the larger society. To most Americans the problems seem to be greater than the benefits to be derived. Therefore, it seems likely that few families try it except under pressure of economic necessity—conditions under which it seems least likely to be satisfying. Herein lies the explanation for the frequency with which three-generation living produces trouble.

Whatever pattern of relationship is developed between a young couple and their relatives, it is important for each generation to understand that this pattern is as much a product of the social structure of society and the family's place in it as a unique product of the personalities involved, of efforts to "keep the peace," and of what may look like particular circumstances in a particular family.

Occupational Roles of Men and Their Impact on Marital Roles

From the time a boy realizes that he will someday be a man, he knows that he will work at some regular job. Whether he comes to think of work as crucial to his identity as a male and a major source of his sense of self-worth, or whether he comes to think of work as an unfortunate but necessary way to provide the wherewithal for other satisfactions, he knows his adult life will be organized around work. That he will work is more certain (and perhaps more basic) than that he will marry and have a family. As a consequence, the family roles of men are organized in recognition of the important claims of work roles.

In more simple societies, work roles and family roles are not sharply delineated from one another. In America's complex social life, the actual performance of the work role may be quite distinct from the family role, but the functional importance of the work role for shaping family roles is great. The *income* from work is of the most obvious importance for the husband's family role as provider. The amount and stability of that income largely determine the standard of living of the family. More than that, low-level, unstable incomes mean unstable marriages. If a man is only sporadically employed in return for low pay (the two usually going together), he can only sporadically provide support for a family. His inability to provide stable support lowers his authority in the family, gives his wife less stake in keeping him around, and gives him little reason to remain in one place with one

Chart 14-1

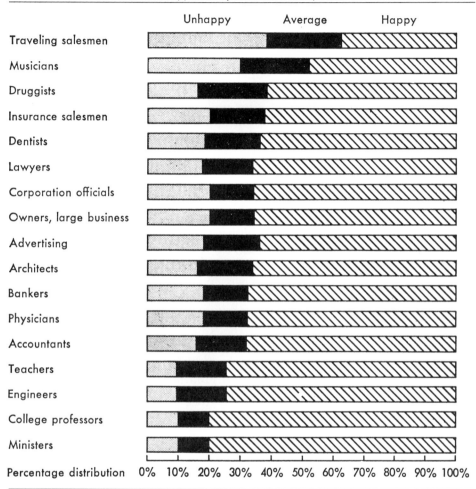

HUSBAND'S OCCUPATION INFLUENCES MARITAL HAPPINESS
Marital happiness by husband's occupation

	Unhappy	Average	Happy
Traveling salesmen			
Musicians			
Druggists			
Insurance salesmen			
Dentists			
Lawyers			
Corporation officials			
Owners, large business			
Advertising			
Architects			
Bankers			
Physicians			
Accountants			
Teachers			
Engineers			
College professors			
Ministers			

Percentage distribution 0% 10% 20% 30% 40% 50% 60% 70% 80% 90% 100%

Adapted from Blood, 1962:287
Source: Lang, 1932

woman. Where groups of men are found with sporadic work lives, as in the American lower class, the development of an unstable marital relationship with high desertion rates, high divorce rates, and high illegitimacy rates can be seen. Husbands are more valuable and reliable when they hold stable, high-income jobs. Under these circumstances, as in the American middle class, marriages are far more stable, divorce and desertion rates are very much reduced, and illegitimacy rates are low. The husband's authority in the family is greater. His material and emotional investment in his marriage and his family are higher providing strong motivation for him to remain with one family.

However, a man's occupation provides more than income. His position in the occupational structure is the most important single determinant of the family's status (prestige) in the community. How high the members of a family hold their heads in a community is a significant function of the occupation of the husband-father. His occupation is, in general, the most important determiner of the life style of his family—with whom they will associate, what their aspirations for their children will be, what they will do for recreation, where they will live, and a thousand other items which sociologists have found related to the social class of the family.

Although the husband's full-time employment *per se* may therefore be taken as necessary and compatible with his marital and family roles (which is not true in the same way for women), it is clear that some occupational roles are more compatible with typical family roles than others. Two different roles of an individual are spoken of as compatible if the expectations they impose on him do not conflict with one another, or, more positively, if the requirements of one role facilitate the performance of the other. The varying compatibility of occupations on roughly similar status levels is indicated by the happier marriages in certain white-collar occupations shown in Chart 14-1.

One might paint an idealized picture of the husband role from the point of view of impact of the occupation in the American middle class as follows: Husbands leave for work in the morning and come home from work at supper. They are home with their families in the evening and on weekends. They do routine maintenance jobs on the family home, have time to spend with their children, and are companions to their wives. The extent to which any occupation distorts this pattern is probably a good measure of incompatibility with the marital role, and hence an index of strain between the roles.

CASE

I am tired of running second. With Martin the church always comes first. When my father suffered a fatal stroke I went back to Ohio on the bus by myself. Martin sits up with the dying and comforts the bereaved; my mother and I dried our own tears. Anthony was born in my girlhood home town, and my parents saw me through the difficult birth. Martin was attending his eastern seminary and did not get there until I was out of danger, and our son was two weeks old. Throughout our marriage whenever I've felt weak and depressed and in need of masculine strength, somebody else has had first call on Martin's strength. As I cried out my heart last night, it seemed to me that if I lived to be as old as Methuselah I would never have a warm, satisfying marriage. It seemed to me my sons were half orphans and that they deserved a concerned, affectionate father. . . .

Just two weeks ago I dressed the boys and myself for church. A block before we reached there, I recalled Martin's text and wondered how I could sit and listen quietly to a sermon about love and charity delivered by a man who has love and charity for everybody—except his own flesh and blood. I became so ill I had to ask the boys to walk on by themselves; I turned around, went back home, pulled down the shades, and collapsed (Popenoe and Disney, 1960: 240).

On the other hand, the status and income-producing features of certain occupational roles are frequently tied in with the extent to which the man is willing to distort his family role by investing more time and energy in his work, by being willing to be absent from home for periods of time, or by being willing to take a job which has high status and pay but requires traveling.

CASE

When John and Stephanie were first married, he was still in dental school, and they had very little money. They lived in student housing near the campus. Stephanie hated the city and she hated the apartment. Their big dream was of the day he would be out of school and they could settle down somewhere with a practice of their own. They thought that then all their problems would be over, and they could spend more time and more money together.

By the time John graduated, they already had two children, and they were pretty much in debt. When they moved to San Bernardino, and John opened his practice, they discovered that things weren't going to be as easy as they thought. San Bernardino already has quite a few professional people, and John found it rather hard to break in.

John went right to work, trying to start a successful practice. He spent hours socializing with other doctors and dentists. Often he had dinner with his friends, and he took up golf on Saturdays. Stephanie wasn't able to be with him as much as she would have liked, because of the children.

To top it all, John took a job in a clinic in Los Angeles, for two days a week, so now he's away more than ever. He's really trying to get ahead, and be successful, but Stephanie resents a lot of it. She says she didn't spend all that time in a home she hated just so her husband could practically abandon her as soon as he graduated. John is getting ahead though.

Dizard (1968), in a study of 400 couples who had been married for fourteen to twenty years, found that husband's upward occupational mobility resulted in fewer marriage conflicts because it was less likely than downward mobility or stability to result in both husband and wife increasing in dominance. But upwardly mobile husbands and their wives report declining marriage happiness and consensus, although they were less likely to have considered separation or divorce. Dizard's findings should be interpreted cautiously. As Dizard points out, occupational mobility in either direction was slight because all 400 husbands started their careers as well-educated, white-collar workers. If Dizard's sample had included husbands whose income had changed drastically, his results might have been very different.

Chart 14-1 shows that the happiness ratings of the marriages of musicians and traveling salesmen are lowest; these are the two jobs on the chart which, because of irregular hours, periods away from home, and other factors, are most likely to impinge on the idealized picture of the husband role. To have a happy, stable marriage, a woman is well advised to marry a man at a high-status occupation with a stable location and regular working hours.

Differences in the importance of career and family to each marriage partner probably influence marital happiness. Bailyn (1970) divided a sample of 233 husbands into those who said their family relationship satisfied them most and those who said their careers were more important sources of satisfaction. Bailyn separated their 233 wives into those who favored combining a career and a family and those whose satisfactions came from their families alone. She then asked each couple to rate their marital happiness and found that the marriages of career-oriented men to women who combined a career and a family were most likely to be described as not very happy. Marriages of a family-oriented man to a family-oriented wife became more unhappy as the man became more satisfied with his career, but marriages of a family-oriented man to a wife who combined career and family became happier as the husband's satisfaction with his job increased.

Husbands' occupations, then, can frequently conflict with family responsibilities and be a source of difficulty between husband and wife. When a couple recognizes this source of conflict, the decisions necessary for its resolution are likely to be particularly difficult. It is not easy to decide which is more important, marriage or career. For lower-status persons, neither occupation nor marriage is crucial. For higher-status persons both are crucial. The problem situations are easy to pose but difficult to answer. Take the following situation: A husband's career in a company requires him at one point to take a traveling appointment as field representative if he is to move on to the next higher career level. Up to that point, the family's way of life and the husband-wife relationship have been built around marital companionship. His marriage now becomes seriously strained. Wherein lies his first obligation? If he resigns or refuses the assignment, he stymies his career development and limits the status and income he can provide his family. However, just as significantly, he may seriously fail to achieve his own capacities, suffer a loss of identification with his work, and an equal loss of sense of self-worth. If he continues in the assignment, he may break up his marriage or at least alienate himself from his wife. Important careers in politics, the arts, science, and business frequently pose similar dilemmas.

The most common value system in American society today makes the moral choice simple: one's first obligation is to his wife and family. When the career seriously endangers a man's family stability, it is a bad job and he should leave it for his family's sake. One reads nothing but scorn for the husband who discards his wife, whom he acquired early in his career, because she has become an impediment to his occupational advancement or career accomplishment. The choice may be practical as well as moral, because there is some evidence that a stable marriage enhances a man's career. In a study of 6,000 American men, Tropman (1971) found that marital stability was associated with upward occupational mobility. There are many possible explanations for this relationship besides one that attributes success to a happy marriage. The relationship may be a reflection of employer preferences for married men, or it may be that a man capable of participating in a stable marriage also possesses whatever it takes to rise in his profession.

Whether this same value choice ought to be forced upon every man—whether as a society America would benefit from everyone making a choice in favor of traditional family responsibility—cannot be answered so unequivocally. Perhaps there are some persons whose most important contribution to their fellowman will not consist of being a good husband to some woman and a good father to their children. Perhaps there are even temperamental incompatibilities between husbandliness and the qualities of success in some careers.

Those who believe that the fate of marriages is determined by mate selection will no doubt suggest that if couples only talked out their career plans and conceptions of marital roles before marriage, they could discover that the wife's expectations of a husband conflicted with the husband's expectations of his life work. Women who had traditional expectations could then choose husbands with compatible plans, and husbands with career plans which were not easily fitted into a traditional marital network could select wives with more unusual views of husbandhood. It would be ideal if life were so simple and behavior so predictable. However, people do not stop growing because of marriage. They affect one another's plans. Contingencies in lives cannot all be predicted at the time of marriage. Opportunities unfold and capabilities are discovered. Each new experience changes the response to subsequent experience. Those who expect to bind their marriage to a future agreed upon during courtship plan to live without learning from life.

Numerous allusions have been made to the relationship between the employment status of the husband and his influence in the marital relationship. At this point, a closer look is necessary. By now it is well documented that the higher the occupational status of the husband, the more dominant his influence in marital decision-making. It is also well established that the less the husband is employed, the lower his status in family influence. On the other hand, class ideologies directly contradict the actual observations of influence. Among lower-status persons, marriage ideologies are far more patriarchal than among higher-status persons who generally support a more equalitarian set of marriage values. What this means is that lower-status couples *believe* in husband-dominant marriages but because of the husband's inferior occupational position are *actually* not very husband-dominant; higher status couples *believe* in equalitarian marriages but are *actually* rather husband-dominated. The structural position of the husband in the occupational world is more important than the couple's private beliefs in determining the influence structure of their marriage. Under these circumstances, it might be expected that the effect of the belief system would only be to introduce a sense of frustration in high-status females and in low-status males. An indication that this is, in fact, the case can be inferred from the fact that the greatest marital satisfaction is reported by high-status couples with equalitarian relationships, while lowest satisfaction is reported by low-status couples with wife-dominant relationships.

RETIREMENT

Family sociologists have studied courtship and early marriage almost to the exclusion of interest in the later years of the relationship. Research, particularly by Burgess (1952), has shed much light on the processes of the later years which is at the same time helpful in understanding the rest of marriage. It has become clear that the role of the husband is organized more fundamentally around a work role than sociologists had understood. Much of the husband's status in his wife's eyes, as well as his sense of identity and self-worth, is organized around his work. At the same time, the rhythm of marital interaction is dictated by the husband's work hours. Sudden retirement of the husband requires a radical reorganization of married life. First, a man is likely to experience an "identity crisis" because of the removal of a basic axis of his self-concept. Few men of retirement age have alternate axes of equal importance to their identity which may be substituted for the work role. Second, and at the same time, the husband is made dependent on his wife as a companion after what in most cases has been thirty years of minimized companionship. His wife, however, is not suddenly made more dependent on him. She has had several decades in which to organize her daytime life without him. Without any additional focus of common interest added at the time of retirement, the wife may experience her husband's additional demands on her time as an intrusion. When recreation is all that is left to them, few couples can have fun playing together for the last decades of their life when they have not played together in the middle years. Furthermore, there is no basis in American culture for deriving from play a sense of personal importance. For many couples, the problem is exacerbated by the ill health of one spouse, further altering the dependency pattern.

From a statistical point of view, the problem of married couples in retirement concerns a relatively small minority. Only about half the persons

Chart 14-2

EACH NEW GENERATION HAS MORE WORKING WIVES
Percentage of wives in the labor force by number of years married, for three generations

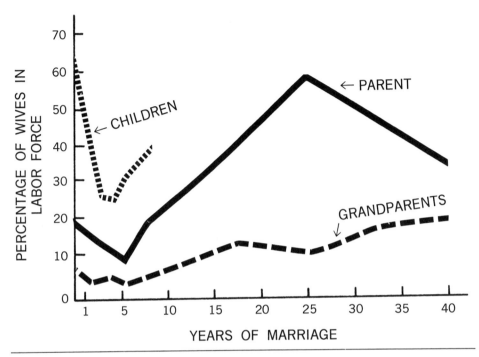

Source: Hill et al., 1970: 79

over sixty-five years of age are married. A clearer picture is obtained by separating the sexes. Seven out of ten men, but only one out of three women, over sixty-five are married (Winch, 1963). However, only 35 percent of the men and 18 percent of the women over sixty-five constitute married couples living in their own homes apart from their children and other relatives (Burgess, 1952).

Occupational Roles of Married Women

The traditional picture of the American woman's role is almost purely domestic: She marries early and spends the remainder of her life caring for her children and husband. This picture has so little relevance to contemporary American life that it is necessary to define the actual pattern in several stages to get an adequate picture of the married woman of today. In the

United States, the average girl marries very shortly after leaving school. More girls marry at age eighteen than at any other single year of age, while half are married before twenty-one. Very few remain unmarried. The median age of women at birth of the last child today is about twenty-six. This means that by age thirty-two, the average American woman has her youngest child in school. By the time she is forty-five, her children have all left home. In 1960, the woman who had survived to forty-five years of age could expect to live to be seventy-seven, leaving her thirty-two years after the end of responsibilities for children.

In their study of three generations of married couples, Hill et al., (1970) note that wives' participation in the labor force has changed greatly since the grandparent generation married. Chart 14-2 shows that less than 10 percent of the wives in the grandparent generation worked at the time of their marriage, and that the figure rose to 20 percent only after the children were raised. Over 60 percent of women in the married-child generation are working at the time of their marriage, and almost 40 percent are again employed eight years later. Census data from 1960 indicate that 10 percent of women whose youngest child was under one, and 17 and 19 percent of women with children aged one and two held jobs (Sweet, 1971). More black mothers than nonblack mothers were employed, and a higher proportion of black women than nonblack women returned to and remained at work after the births of their children. Because more than half of all the women who had worked returned to work after childbearing, Sweet feels that it "may be as accurate to say that young married women workers tend to have their work experience periodically interrupted by childbearing, as to think of them as sporadic workers with only a marginal commitment to the work force" (Sweet, 1971: 24).

The traditional role of wife calls for a woman to stay home, keep house, and rear children. In a previous age, "keeping house" meant more than housecleaning and meal preparation. It meant active participation in part of the productive labor of an economic enterprise. In contemporary urban society (and this includes most "rural" people today), the family is not engaged in economic production, and the few productive activities left to the housewife (outside of childbearing) are being gradually encroached upon by automation and pre-processing. Early and universal public education minimize the years devoted to full-time childrearing. In spite of the gradual reduction in the kinds of demands upon the wife which constituted most of her responsibility a century ago, the traditional role has not changed much in its external aspects. "Keeping house" has a different meaning than it had a century ago, and "rearing children" is perhaps conceived as an emotional rather than an instrumental responsibility today. The withdrawal from the household of much of the instrumental responsibility which was formerly woman's work has in a very peculiar way exaggerated the division of labor between husband

and wife. The trend toward woman's employment outside the household may be seen in perspective as a natural consequence of the movement of *all* production out of the household setting, including men's work as well as women's. When all a woman's functions could be fulfilled in essentially the same physical place, the integration of emotional and instrumental elements was not something anyone thought about. During a more simple age, it was taken for granted that women were productively employed and that this employment was a positive contribution to the well-being of her children and her relationship with her husband. It is only when the employment is outside the home that the question arises: Does it interfere with what was formerly taken for granted as a primary responsibility—the emotional health of her children and the level of satisfaction of her marital relationship? In the past there was really no question of priority of responsibility in the middle-class mores. A woman must put her "family" responsibilities first, while a husband may expect his family to orient their lives around his performance of occupational responsibility. Perhaps we are now to experience a generation of women who do not take this for granted.

The very fact that married women work intermittently or part time may be taken as *prima facie* evidence of strain between full-time employment and family responsibilities. A generation ago, sociologists and psychologists were more or less taking for granted that full-time employment of mothers was detrimental to performance as wife and mother. Employment of mothers was widely believed to be injurious to the emotional stability of their children, the happiness of their husbands, and the life satisfactions of the women themselves. Research by behavioral scientists in the past twenty years has made it clear that these blanket generalizations are far too sweeping where they are not clearly incorrect.

WIFE'S EMPLOYMENT AND MARITAL INTERACTION

The effect of the wife's employment on the structure of marital interaction seems quite clear. Blood writes:

> The wife decreases her housekeeping activities while the husband increases his by performing masculine tasks more unilaterally and by helping with feminine tasks. In an appreciable number of families the pressure for revising the division of labor results in conflict between husband and wife over marriage roles. The power structure shifts in the direction of a greater voice for the wife in major economic decisions and a lesser voice in routine household decisions (Blood, 1963: 303).

Later studies have confirmed this pattern for white families, but failed to find it in black families. In black families it appears that the employment of the wife results in less involvement of the husband in household tasks, and greater dominance of the household by the wife, even in the routine household decisions (Aldous, 1969). There is more general acceptance of the wife's working among blacks than among whites of both sexes. In a study of 67 black males and 565 white males in a random sample of households in a southern state, Axelson (1970) found that black men were more likely than white men to feel that their wives should work if they wanted to, and white males more than black males felt that the wife's working would have a detrimental effect on their children. In addition, black males in the sample were much more likely than the white men to agree that a working wife is less of a companion to her husband. White males more often than black males agreed that a successful man needed a wife who stayed at home. Epstein (1973), in a study of black women professionals, reports that, although the absolute numbers of black professionals (lawyers, doctors, dentists, professors, and journalists) of both sexes are very small, 7 percent of employed black women are professionals as opposed to 3 percent of all employed black men. College-educated black women have more positive attitudes towards working than their white counterparts, greater confidence in their ability to work in male-dominated occupations such as medicine, and are less inclined than white women to put marriage before a career (Epstein, 1973).

A closer look at the power balance is necessary. Some studies have shown that the husband-wife power balance in decision-making shifted toward the wife's favor as she went into employment (Blood and Wolfe, 1960; Heer, 1963). Studies of Danish working women (Noordhoek and Smith, 1972) show that a working wife participates more than the nonworking wife in making decisions about the family economy; the higher her income is in relation to the family's total income, the more she is likely to share in the economic decision-making. More detailed analysis using groups of working and nonworking wives who were matched on marital ideologies, husband's occupation, and age and number of children, suggests that the direction of causality should be reversed—that, in fact, women who were more likely to be influential in the marriage were the ones who on that account were also the most likely to accept employment (Hoffman, 1960).

Much recent work has concerned the dual-profession marriage, in which both husband and wife pursue professional careers such as medicine, law, and college teaching. Garland (1970) found that husbands of career-oriented wives did not seem dominated or emasculated, but he noted that no wife in his sample wanted to be more successful than her husband. The one factor that negatively affected these professional marriages was the wife's making more money than the husband, and in most cases the wife deliberately kept her own salary below that of her husband. Poloma and Garland (1971, 1972) found that while husbands' attitudes towards their professional wives' careers varied from active support to active discouragement, their wives consistently reported that the husbands were favorable to their working. Interviews with 53 dual-profession couples revealed that the wives did most of the household chores in addition to their professional work, and that almost every wife did not expect her husband to share the housework. While both partners agreed on who actually performed certain household tasks, the wives tended to overrate their husbands' contributions while husbands were more realistic about the paucity of help they gave (Poloma and Garland, 1972). In all but 6 of the 53 professional couples they studied, Poloma and Garland found that "the wife was *responsible* for the traditional feminine tasks (although usually the husband did 'help' in varying degrees) while her husband was *responsible* for providing the family with status and income" (Poloma and Garland, 1971: 534).

It is interesting that a recent poll showed that 31 percent of American wives feel that "a woman's ultimate fulfillment in life is the realization of her own personal goals," while 67 percent feel that "a woman's ultimate fulfillment in life is marriage and motherhood." In addition, most wives reject the idea of complete equality with their husbands; 60 percent of the women who wanted more from life than a husband and children did not want complete equality with their spouses (Overholser, 1973).

On the surface, one might expect that the employment of the wife would decrease the amount of interaction she had with her family, but this appears to be untrue. Blood reports that "dual income couples expect more interaction and joint activity in their leisure time," although some of the more time-consuming uses of leisure together are curtailed (Blood, 1963: 303). Women who are not employed at all have been shown to play a *less* companionate role with their husbands than those employed full time (Weil, 1961). Whether the mother works part time or stays at home may not make much difference to the time she spends with her family. Rossi concludes that "women devote to household chores four times as many hours as they do to interaction with their husbands and three times as many hours as they do to interaction with their children" (Rossi, 1972: 1059). Family recreational roles are apparently not affected to any degree by the wife's assumption of the role of provider (Nye and Hoffman, 1963: 371).

What about marital happiness? The first careful studies of the effect of wife's employment concluded that there was no difference in the marital adjustment of working and nonworking wives but that what really mattered was the husband's attitude toward his wife's employment (Gianopulos and Mitchell, 1957; Locke, 1951). A later study was not able to confirm the importance of the husband's attitude as the crucial variable (Nye, 1962). Orden and Bradburn (1969) found that both partners experience more tensions and less companionship in their marriage when the wife works by necessity rather than by choice. When the wife works only because she wants to, both husbands and wives are lower in tensions and higher in companionship than if the wife chooses to stay at home, but the partners are just as likely to *report* that they are happy when the wife chooses to stay at home as when she chooses to work. Orden and Bradburn also found that marriages tend to be happier when the wife chooses part-time work over both full-time employment and staying at home. They note that the stage in the family life cycle influences the effect of women's employment on marriage happiness. "Among those who are free to choose between [the home] market and the labor market, there are some differences at varying stages of the life cycle. When there are preschool children in the home, husbands and wives are both happier in marriage if the wife chooses the home market than if she chooses the labor market. Seven out of ten comparisons favor the home market choice. When there are grade school children in the family, all of the comparisons favor the labor market choice. When the youngest child in the family is of high school age or older, there is little or no difference in marriage adjustment between the labor market and the home market choice" (Orden and Bradburn, 1969: 407). Although the wife's working has little effect on her husband's reports of consensus in the marriage, the nonworking wife is much more likely than the working wife to report decreasing consensus in her marriage over time (Dizard, 1968).

Nearly all recent studies show a relationship between wife's full-time employment and marital conflict, but the relationship is not clear and not simple. Blood and Wolfe (1960), using Detroit Area Study couples, found employed wives as a whole did not differ significantly from the nonemployed wives in their evaluation of their marriages. However, they observed a slight trend toward highest marital satisfaction among employed wives of low-income husbands and nonemployed wives of high-income husbands. Nye considers present data to be sufficient to support the contention that employment of mothers increases conflict in the marital relationship (Nye, 1958, 1959; Nye and Hoffman, 1963: 272, 324). One ingenious study controlled the effect of education and income on marital adjustment and found that if education and *family* income of working and nonworking wives were controlled, then the working mothers "would report more marital unhappiness than their housewife counterparts" (Feld, 1963: 345). Put another way, the fact that the wife works is evidently a source of marital *conflict*, but the income she brings home puts the family in a higher socioeconomic bracket which has a *positive* effect on marital adjustment. The two effects balance each other out, so that *the net effect of the wife's employment on marital adjustment is negligible.*

WIFE'S EMPLOYMENT AND CHILDREARING

A great deal of work has been devoted to exploring the relationship between employment of mothers and the emotional well-being of their children, and it would not be possible to review all of the studies here. Early studies, inspired by the Freudian concept of maternal deprivation, firmly established in the layman's mind that the full-time employment of mothers deprived the children (especially very young children) of the maternal attention they needed and fostered the development of emotionally distorted and delinquency-prone children. This idea has now been badly undermined. Most studies find no significant differences in the emotional adjustment of the children of employed mothers, either when the children are young (Hand, 1957; Nye et al., 1963; Siegel et al., 1959), or during adolescence (Burchinal, 1963; Nye, 1963; Peterson, 1961).

On the other hand, a few studies cast a shadow of doubt over this clean bill of health for the children of working mothers. Hoffman (1961) probed the personality adjustment of the children of working mothers to see if there were differences that corresponded to whether or not the mother liked working. She reported disturbance patterns in *both* groups of children. The difference in the two was the *nature* of the disturbance. Mothers who liked their work had children who were "non-assertive and ineffective," while mothers who disliked working had children who were "assertive and hostile." This finding is not congruent with the findings reported above.

A good bit of evidence now leads sociologists to suspect that *the effect of the mother's employment is different for boys than for girls. Generally speaking, the reported effects are positively valued for girls and negatively valued for boys.* Nye (1958) and Gold (1961) both report higher delinquency in the sons of working mothers than those of nonworking mothers from *middle-class* families, but find no association for *lower-class* families. Another scholar has found that the effects of maternal employment on sons is detrimental only when the motives for the mother's working tell something about the failure of the father as the head of the household (Douvan, 1963: 163). Other studies suggest (somewhat inconclusively) that sons of working mothers are more dependent and withdrawn (Nye and Hoffman, 1963: 202), and one study finds that adult sons whose mothers worked before the sons were sixteen are more receptive to innovation (Schooler, 1972).

No studies report unfortunate effects on girls, on the other hand. Douvan concludes that a mother's employment appears to be an important contributor to her daughter's personality integration:

> . . . the kind of woman who assumes an occupational role through a desire for self-realization exerts an influence on her daughter's development in which the girl identifies with and incorporates many of her mother's ego characteristics (Douvan, 1963, 163).

The girls of working mothers are found to admire their mothers more, have a concept of the feminine role which includes a wide range of possibilities, a more clearly formed self-concept, and generally a less "traditionally feminine" personality (Nye and Hoffman, 1963: 301).

Whatever the effect on the children, mothers who are employed have a better adjustment to their children than those who are not employed. Hoffman (1961) finds that employed mothers who like working are high on positive affect for their children and use mild discipline. In small families (three or fewer children), employed mothers get more pleasure from their children than nonemployed mothers (Nye and Hoffman, 1963: 324). This applies both to mothers of preschoolers and to mothers of school-age children (Nye, 1963). On the other hand, the employed mothers report more frequent doubts and feelings of inadequacy as parents than nonemployed mothers. However, black mothers who hold high-paying jobs have fewer guilt feelings about working when their children are young than white mothers do; in addition, they are more likely to have relatives available and willing to provide long-term or short-term care for the children (Epstein, 1973). Feld writes:

> For women with children at home, the employed mothers are unquestionably more generally satisfied with life and free from emotional disturbance. Employed mothers show more self-acceptance and fewer physical symptoms of distress. . . . are less likely than housewives to complain of pains and ailments in different parts of their body and of not feeling healthy enough to carry out the things they would like to do (Feld, 1963: 340, 344).

Mothers employed full time find more satisfaction in their work than their nonemployed counterparts find in housework. Their overall level of satisfaction from life is higher, especially among the college-educated working mothers. The nonemployed women include a very large group of women who are generally dissatisfied with their lives (Hoffman and Nye, 1963: 323–326).

Social Networks and Marital Roles

Every person enters marriage with a set of preexisting social relationships with friends and relatives. The nature of these existing relationships helps to determine the marriage relationship. When a man and woman marry who have lived all their lives in the same neighborhood, when all of their friends are mutual, and when they establish their married home in their old neighborhood, the highly articulated structure of their premarital ties remains intact.

In an intensive study of twenty couples in the London area, Bott (1957) pursued this line of argument. Under these conditions, she reasoned, the young spouses are not dependent on one another for companionship. Their friends, who have probably married one another also, are still their friends, and these friendships can be expected to continue to play an important part in the social and emotional life of each spouse. To a certain extent this implies a continuation of activity of each spouse in the life of the sex subcultures, to the deemphasis of the marital relationship. She found in her couples that those which were embedded in a closed friendship network had sharper role differentiation, a more complete division of labor, less time spent in companionship with the spouse, and more time spent in companionship with friends and relatives.

As compelling as the logic seems, studies using American couples have not been able to confirm Bott's findings in England (Aldous, 1965; Udry and Hall, 1965). For the time being, at least, this intuitively appealing idea will have to be put on the "interesting but unproved" shelf.

As the marriage relationship matures, as other roles become more demanding, and perhaps as the intimacy becomes boring, most marriages eventually become "embedded" in a gradually developing social network anyway. A study of middle-class, middle-aged couples indicates that by this time in their marital careers, most couples' relationships have taken on a character of their own. At this stage in the life cycle, companionship and division of labor in the marriage have become independent of the particular type of social network in which the couple circulates, but are more closely related to the educational level and employment role of the wife. At least there is a suggestion that in the middle years, couples with college-educated, employed wives are the ones with least segregated roles (Udry and Hall, 1965; Weil, 1961).

Friendship Groups as Alternatives to Companionate Marriage

Nelson (1966) has provided us with a new way of looking at the relationships between marriages and other groups outside the marriage. He studied a sample of working-class wives, and found that some had very companionate views of marriage, while others expected marriage to provide primarily economic security and a convenient division of labor. The latter group is characterized as having a traditional orientation toward marriage. He found that for those having a traditional view of marriage, involvement in close-knit cliques of friends and relatives served to replace the intimacy and companionship of the marital relationship. Women so involved reported themselves quite satisfied with their marriages. Women with companionate expectations from marriage who were involved in close-knit friendship circles appeared to be unhappy with their marriages. For the companionate-oriented women, the clique group was an unsatisfactory substitute for the intimacy of marriage. The traditionally oriented women never expected their marriages to provide companionship which they found quite satisfactorily in close-knit friendship groups.

Summary

The importance of marriage compared to kinship relations varies from one society to another. In some the marriage is almost invisible by comparison to the importance of kinship ties. In American society, kinship ties take a poor second place to the marriage tie. This is less true among lower-class couples, where competing kinship groups weaken the strength of marriages. In-law problems are female problems in the United States and largely confined to the early years of marriage. Living with in-laws is considered to be a source of trouble by Americans, but little evidence can be produced that it is on balance destructive, unless it is evidence of the lack of emancipation of one of the spouses from his parents.

Some occupational roles are more concordant with the responsibilities of fatherhood and husbandhood than others, and conflict of obligations between these roles can be a source of marital strife. Few couples ever consider the possibility that husbands could assume the domestic role. Occupational roles for women are more often a source of marital conflict because of the traditional dominance of the domestic role in women's married lives. The occupational world is organized to make it difficult to reconcile with the time demands of child-care and housekeeping without the assistance of husbands or hired assistance at domestic tasks. The employed mother is likely to experience somewhat more marital conflict than if she were not working. She is likely to produce daughters who are somewhat like herself — less traditional, more oriented toward self-expression. Whether her working will be a negative influence on her sons is less clear, but if she is working because of a failing husband, it is the husband's failure and not her employment which is detrimental to the son. In spite of the additional conflict with her husband, the employed woman will be happier in her marriage, have a more positive attitude toward her children, and be more satisfied with her life in general (especially if she is well educated), than a comparable housewife.

Sexual Interaction in Marriage

15

In previous chapters, the impact on the American family structure and marital relationship of the value complex associated with equality of the sexes was explained. The increasing emphasis in the United States on marriage as primarily a relationship for emotional gratification of the spouses has been commented on in several places. Three value systems related to equality of the sexes have combined with this development to produce the picture of the ideal American marriage. First of all, the marriage is a relationship of mutual gratification. When it does not perform this function for the spouses, it is not likely to continue. Second, the American values of the love-marriage specify that the gratification from marriage should come from mutual affection and "being in love" with the spouse. Third, the values of equality of the sexes indicate that women are entitled to the same things out of life as men. Translated into the marital relationship, equality of the sexes has come to mean that the relationship should be one of equals with similar goals in marriage and similar sources of gratification. The expectation is developing in the American marriage that husband and wife will find the same meanings in marital interaction and derive from it the same rewards. The togetherness complex implies that these gratifications will be achieved through interaction with one another and from one another.

The Equalitarian Ideal and Mutual Reciprocity

Of particular significance for the present topic is the effect which the value of equality of the sexes has on sexual interaction in marriage. The common ideology developing in the middle class around this value is that men and women are basically equal in most of their intellectual, emotional, and temperamental capacities, and specifically in their sexual behavior. Men and women, then, have equal rights to the enjoyment of marital sex and should derive equal enjoyment from it. The operation of this norm is shown in couples' reports of preferred frequency of intercourse. Where the husband's actual preference is higher, both husband and wife tend to underestimate the discrepancy in desires. Where (one couple in six in the Burgess-Wallin sample) the wife's actual preference is higher, both husband and wife tend to report equality of preferred frequency (Levinger, 1966; Wallin and Clark, 1958). Furthermore, this basic equality seems to imply that not only should the enjoyment be equal, but of the same kind, and that the sexual response patterns of both sexes should, therefore, be similar. Husbands and wives both expect that the woman should have the same desires as the man—that she should initiate sexual activity as often as he, that their passions during sexual activities should reach the same intensity, that each should climax with a similar explosive orgasm, and that this orgasm should be simultaneous in both. Failure at any point to achieve this sequence is presumed to have a similar frustrating effect on each sex. Inability to achieve this sequence is accounted for by inhibitions due to repressive training (usually of the woman), lack of knowledge of technique on the part of the husband, or both. Well-educated couples, failing achievement of the ideal sequence, are likely to seek outside assistance to determine how it may be achieved.

These inhibitions are said to be overcome by careful handling, re-education, the use of certain techniques by the husband on the wife who is not *too* neurotic, and, in severe cases, by professional therapy.

Variety in sexual techniques and behavior is emphasized as a positive value in the ideal pattern. Failure to appreciate a variety of positions for intercourse and elaboration of technique as ends in themselves is held to represent prudery or inhibition which had best be overcome.

It is difficult to trace the development of this ideal pattern in the layman. It seems clear from centuries of erotic literature that men have found desirable women who could approximate this pattern. It is less clear when and why they began to *expect* their *wives* to behave in this manner. General prevalence of this expectation among the educated male seems to be of fairly recent origin. The ideas are of even more recent prevalence among females. Even today they hardly constitute a universal pattern of ideal expectations and self-definitions among females. When 450 female undergraduates were asked the question, "From what you know of your present sexual feelings, after you have been married a year in what proportion of your sexual relations do you expect to have an orgasm?" 62 percent of the women answered "always" or "usually" (Clark, 1965).

The description presented above is a *belief system.* Some of these beliefs (for example, the belief that failure to appreciate variety can be explained by inhibition) are subject to empirical confirmation or refutation, but as *beliefs,* they form a basis for the evaluation of one's own experience, regardless of their objective truth value.

This belief system has also influenced the interpretation of research results by scholars, and the kind of research they design. Scholars generally share the prevailing cultural beliefs in the areas they study. For example, the Kinsey studies of the forties and fifties contain a mountain of data and important analysis of sexual behavior. From this source, many writers reach the conclusion that Kinsey has shown the basic sexual similarity between men and women. But in the "female" volume, Kinsey and his associates present a comprehensive comparison of the volumes on the two sexes, which points to profound differences in the nature of male and female sexuality. The work by Masters and Johnson in the 1960s is usually interpreted to demonstrate the basic similarity of sexual response in males and females, and the differences revealed in their work are now usually overlooked. The reader may wish to try to read between the lines in this text to see how this author's biases affect his interpretations of the data.

Sex in American Marriages: The Traditional Picture

Most of the available research on marital sex in the United States is based on the study of couples and individuals who are now over fifty if they are still alive. This research, involving the couples primarily during early marriage and the childbearing years, showed the following general pattern.

1. Sex was not of equal importance to husband and wife, but was of much greater importance to the husband. Women did without sex for extended periods while their husbands were absent, or during widowhood, and generally did not report this as sexually frustrating.

2. Sex had quite a different meaning for husbands than for wives. Men showed much greater appreciation than women of the visual aspects of sexual encounters. Men showed much greater interest in experimentation with different sexual techniques and positions than women. Women far more than men viewed sex as an expression of love. Men were more drawn to a variety of partners, while women reported this much less frequently.

3. Husbands generally preferred intercourse with greater frequency than their wives. Three times as many men as women reported higher preferred frequency of intercourse than their spouses reported.

4. The most common complaint about their sex lives made by husbands was that their wives were not interested enough in sex, and were not sexually responsive enough. The most common complaint by wives was that their husbands were oversexed.

5. Most of the attention in love-making was devoted to the sexual stimulation of the wife, with the husband's stimulation taken for granted.

6. Female orgasm was of problematic occurrence. Its absence or infrequency was one of the best predictors of marital maladjustment in every study which included data on this issue. The sex lives of many couples were organized around the problem of bringing the wife to orgasm.

7. Unless the wife was unusually interested sexually, she generally set the upper limit on sexual frequency, and the husband generally set the lower limit. Christensen and Gagnon (1965), in detailing the pattern prevailing for the sample interviewed for the Kinsey studies in the 1940s, described the typical sexual interaction pattern:

> The general pattern of interaction is one in which the husband makes a series of approaches and then receives either encouragement or a refusal for each approach as the female sets her coital limit (Christensen and Gagnon, 1965).

A Note on Sexual Terminology

Much confusion is introduced into discussions of sexual behavior because of the vagueness of reference of the terms we use. We have a tendency to equate the terms *drive, behavior, desire, capacity, response,* and *receptivity,* in various ways. Distinctions between these terms will clarify some of the dimensions of sexual behavior usually misunderstood. Sex *drive* is usefully limited to refer to behavior which actively seeks sexual activity. Sexual *behavior* (either orgasm, intercourse, or any other type of expression) is what the individual actually *does* sexually. He may *do* very little even though his drive is high if there is little opportunity or if he is regularly refused. Or he may *do* a lot with very little drive because he attracts partners with drive. *Desire* is a subjective awareness of a need for sexual expression, which may or may not lead to active behavior. *Capacity* refers to the physiological limits of behavior. It may be little related to drive or behavior under certain circumstances. Few people know what their sexual capacity is, because they have never had occasion to test it. A man may have the capacity to have thirty orgasms per day, but lack the desire for more than thirty per year. *Response* refers to the physical reactions to sexual behavior. A woman might have high drive (seeks out contacts), high capacity (can have coitus dozens of times per day), but little or no *response* (nothing happens when she does). *Receptivity* is willingness to have sexual contact when approached. There is no reason to expect a close relationship between receptivity, response, and drive. Try making these distinctions when thinking about or discussing sexual behavior, and see how it clarifies the process.

The Origins of Sex Differences in Sexuality

To what extent will these be the prevailing features of the married sex lives of persons reading this text today? We can get some reading on the answer to this question by considering three approaches to explaining the origin of the traditional pattern: a psychodynamic approach, a biological approach, and a cultural approach.

A PSYCHODYNAMIC EXPLANATION

The *psychodynamic explanation* of the differences in male and female sexuality interprets the lack of sexual responsiveness in females as mental pathology. Sexual responsiveness and enjoyment of heterosexual intercourse are assumed to flow from the natural development of the organism. Failure to experience orgasm and lack of natural responsiveness is attributed to repressive childhood training, to disturbances of the parent-child relationship in early childhood, or to traumatic sexual events such as rape, seduction by a relative, or observation of parents at intercourse. Lack of response is defined as frigidity and considered a neurosis. A typical psychodynamic explanation follows:

> It has been found in other cases of frigidity that the woman too closely identifies her husband with her father. Precisely because the woman has done such a good job of finding a substitute for her father she cannot have intercourse with him. Her aversion and disgust will prevent her from carrying out her unconsciously perceived incest with her husband-father. In other cases where the husband and father are unconsciously confused, sexual intercourse is possible, but not enjoyable. The long-sought alliance with the father is realized, but punishment for the "crime" is exacted through her inability to obtain any pleasure from it. Such a woman may seek passionless intercourse with her husband not, in this case, to disappoint him, but to disappoint and punish herself (Kenkel, 1960).

A BIOLOGICAL EXPLANATION

The *biological explanation* of differences in male and female sexuality interprets lack of sexual responsiveness or lack of sexual interest in females as flowing from biological differences in the nature of the sexes. At one point, it appears that Freud himself accepted this explanation. He confessed not to be able to understand female sexuality, but reached the conclusion that females simply did not have any biological sex drive.

Today many scholars believe that differences in exposure to the influence of male and female hormones create basic differences in sexual behavior. First, they believe that males are more sexually conditionable than females. What this means is that initially nonsexual stimuli come to have sexual stimulus value because in the experience of the individual they have been associated with sexual stimulation. For example, seeing or touching female undergarments may be sexually stimulating to men because it has become associated with sexual stimulation. In this way, it is argued, a male gradually comes to experience sexual stimulation from a wide variety of nonsexual stimuli. This apparently does not occur as easily in females. (Animal researchers have reported this same difference in many other mammalian species.) Through this process, it is argued, males are continually aroused by their environments in a way which does not occur for females.

Second, biologically-oriented scholars argue that there are hormone-related differences in the *reinforcement value* of sex for men and women. An experience has reinforcement value if it tends to cause the repetition of the behavior which makes the experience possible. We usually say that if an experience is pleasurable it will tend to be repeated. But here it is argued that however pleasurable sex may be for men or women, any particular sexual experience does not shape subsequent behavior of women toward repetition of it as much as it affects subsequent behavior of men. This is the kind of difference which Kephart was thinking of when he described the following possibility:

> A woman who has been sexually responsive during coitus may not have specific after-thoughts of sex or desire for sexual intercourse for a period of weeks, or months, or even longer. Extended periods without coitus may well have no adverse effects. In short, although she actively enjoys coitus *when it occurs,* her sexual needs remain low as compared with most men (Kephart, 1961).

Third, students of the effects of human sex hormones believe that testosterone, a male hormone, is the source of whatever internally induced desire for sex humans have, both males and females. But females, by comparison with males, produce very little testosterone. Furthermore, experimental studies with women have demonstrated that injections of testosterone cause most women to experience an increase in sex drive. (The idea that there are no true aphrodisiacs is no longer widely held among well-informed scholars in the area.) Following this line of reasoning, no one should be surprised if men experience more active sex desire than women, on the basis of their hormones alone.

A CULTURAL EXPLANATION

The *cultural explanation* of differences in male and female sex behavior maintains that the values of our society encourage the development of male sexuality, but discourage the development of sexuality in females. According to this theory, the social life of males is organized to provide them with easy access to sexual experiences, and strong encouragement to take advantage of the opportunities provided. Furthermore, males learn to think of sex as a critical element in their own concepts of masculinity. On the other hand, the social life of females is organized to shield them from access to sexual experience, and strongly discourages them from taking advantage of whatever opportunities arise. Finally, females do not have any training which would make sex a crucial part of their own concepts of femininity. This is not to say that sexuality is inhibited or repressed in females so much as to say that their experience is organized in such a way to minimize its development. Under these circumstances, it is argued, males learn to develop high sex interest, while females do not.

No one has to choose among the three different explanations offered above. Each explains certain types of differences and not others. Certainly some women suffer from repressive or traumatic sexual neuroses. (However, it should be pointed out that sexual perversions appear to be far more common among men—perhaps a piece of evidence of their greater conditionability compared to women.) Certainly the cultural emphasis on male sexuality in the past has emphasized the differences in sex interest of the sexes. The biological differences are today more controversial, and perhaps less well understood. The prevailing aversion among liberal social scientists from explaining any difference between two groups by biological factors has certainly played a part in downgrading the importance of biological sex differences. But perhaps more important than this is the lack of biological knowledge among most social scientists.

For the student, the wisest course is probably to accept all three of these explanations as significant in maintaining different orientations toward sex by men and women in the past. But given that these explain the traditional differences of the past, what are their implications for the future?

The Future of Sex Differences in Sexuality

The biological differences are not likely to disappear. They must be taken as a kind of starting point. The psychodynamically related sex differences are a consequence of the culturally prescribed differences in sexual behavior. Suppose, then, that our society in the future gave the development of sex interest equal emphasis in men and women. This would still leave us with the biological differences, predisposing men to become more sex-oriented. If Americans are really interested in "creating" sexual equality of men and women, our theories indicate that we will have to go beyond eliminating sexual repression of females. But these same theories make it quite reasonable to assume that differences in sexuality between males and females can be eliminated (or even reversed) by reorganization of the socialization process. If our theories are correct, any society that wishes to produce women who are *predominantly* highly and actively sexed will have to organize the experiences of women with this goal in mind. One family sociologist suggests the form this would take:

> Culture is not necessary to stimulate sexuality in men. Unless actively discouraged, male sexuality can be taken for granted. But a cult of sex is necessary to stimulate a high level of sexuality in women. A culture can attempt to equalize sexuality or at least minimize the differences by either downgrading sexuality in men or upgrading sexuality in women. Chivalry and the Victorian model dealt with the problem by downgrading sexuality in men and upgrading it only for some women. The Pacific Islanders, on the other hand, upgraded sexuality in women. In fact, sex was a way of life for everyone. It was a major cultural theme (Bernard, 1964).

If a cult of sex is necessary, its effectiveness would probably be enhanced by the encouragement of childhood sexuality. This is commonly done where sex is a major cultural theme. Hardy writes:

> Cross-cultural data show the extensive elaboration of sexual behavior (masturbation, mutual masturbation, sexual games, attempted coitus, coitus itself) in cultures which are permissive, encouraging, or demanding of sexual activity pre-pubertally. In such societies, virtually no secrecy is associated with sex, and little or nothing is done to inhibit the sexual activity of the youngsters. Ford and Beach report that in a few cultures, regular heterosexual intercourse occurs from ages 8–10 onward; e.g., among the Chewa it is believed that youth will not mature unless intercourse begins early in life; similarly, the Lepcha believe that girls will be infertile unless they participate in coitus pre-pubertally.
> The extent of sexual activity in childhood among the peoples mentioned above is a powerful demonstration of the hypothesis that sexual interest is not dependent upon the maturation of the sex gland (Hardy, 1964: 2).

The cult of feminine sexuality which would probably be necessary to produce an equality in the sexuality of males and females might well be organized around a female subculture based on the model of the existing male subculture. Active sexuality represented as the core of the concept of femininity and prestige accorded for sexual activity might provide the cultural encouragement and reinforcement which would facilitate a high level of learned desire in women. The fact that this reinforcement must work against the "disadvantage" of a lower conditionability indicates that it is probably not possible to overdo it.

In the cultural atmosphere produced by such a cult, it would probably not be difficult to make it as acceptable, or even fashionable, for women to take a sex-stimulating drug (Wheeler, 1955), as it is now taken for granted that a woman not provided by nature with attractive breasts will make up the deficiency cosmetically. It is hard to believe that many males would find the practice objectionable.

Given a thoroughgoing effort toward the creation of such a cult, *there can be little doubt that a society of women could be produced equal in sexuality to men.* On the other hand, the society would almost certainly lose any restraints which exist on premarital sexual relations (unless it would introduce child marriage). It is commonplace observation that almost all the control which is now exercised over premarital intercourse in American society is exercised by females. It should be expected that with the transformation of female sexuality, one would no longer expect women to be a restraining influence.

Some observers believe that Americans have already moved a considerable way toward the achievement of sexual equality. Certainly, there have already been changes in the socialization process of females. Early and prolonged dating careers and increasing sexual experience for females is the trend in adolescence. This should work in the direction of higher female sexuality. In more and more movies directed at the younger generation, the young heroines are portrayed as being overwhelmed with sex desires and are active in effecting their consummation. Merrill (1959) cites the following trends which indicate that Americans are closely approximating sex relationships in marriage which are reciprocal and more nearly equal:

1. The decline in prostitution (attributed to greater accessibility and response of respectable women).

2. Increase in premarital coitus by women (indicating a change from the double standard to the male standard).

3. The decline in the frequency of marital coitus because the husband is deferring to the wife's lower drive in order to achieve reciprocity (of course, this is not unequivocally in the direction of the ideology).

4. Increase in marital sexual foreplay.

5. Increase in female orgasm in marital coitus. These changes support the idea that sex differences are based on socialization differences; they predict that sex differences in sexual responsiveness and drive would weaken if the socialization of male and females was identical.

Other writers, who believe that a great increase in feminine sexuality will be achieved simply by relaxing repressive and inhibitory training, already profess to see problems for the immediate future (or even the present) in excess feminine sexuality. Bell attributes past differences in masculine and feminine sexuality to repression of the female. Accordingly, his predictions for the future of American marital sex life are startlingly different.

One implied assumption has been that, once the restrictions on marital sex are removed, the wife will catch up to the husband in sexual desire and they will then be sexual equals. What generally has not been recognized is that some women may pass their husbands in sexual interest. The social and psychological sexual liberation of the woman has led some wives to shed many restrictions and inhibitions and emerge with greater sexual interest than the husband. In the writer's study, when the wives were asked to assess the frequency of sexual relations in their marriages, 25 percent said that it was "too infrequent." One out of four wives were saying that, for a variety of reasons, there was not enough coitus in their marriage to satisfy them. This is a recent and generally unanticipated sexual response for wives to make. . . .

A number of married couples may find themselves in a situation where the sexual interests of the wife have increased to a point greater than those of the husband. But because of the biological limitations on the man, he, unlike the woman, cannot normally function as a sex partner without some interest. While this difference is probably not an important problem early in marriage, it may become one as the couple grows older, with the sexual interest of the woman often increasing and many of her early inhibitions removed. As he grows older, the male's sexual drive as well as, in some cases, his sexual interests are often decreasing. Thus, the older wife may desire more frequent coitus while her husband is neither physically nor psychologically capable of satisfying her need. This can be extremely important to the male who makes a close association between his sexual potency and his sense of masculinity.

In the future, the number of marital sexual problems involving a lack of satisfaction for the woman will possibly increase. While an ironical switch from the past, the situation is not the same because of the basic differences required of the male and female for sexual intercourse. The results may be far more serious for the inadequate or uninterested male than they were for the restricted female in the past.[1]

Bell is not alone in his apprehension that women are about to overwhelm men in sexual desire. Psychiatrist Karl Menninger is quoted as reporting that for every woman who complains of her husband's excessive virility, a dozen complain of their husband's apathy or impotence (Hunt, 1959: 382). Betty Friedan in her best-selling book conveys the same impression:

> I have heard from many doctors evidence of new sexual problems between man and wife—sexual hunger in wives so great that their husbands cannot satisfy it. "We have made of woman a sex creature," said a psychiatrist at the Margaret Sanger marriage counseling clinic. . . . She waits all day for her husband to come home at night to make her feel alive. And now it is the husband who is not interested. It is terrible for the woman, to lie there, night after night, waiting for her husband to make her feel alive (Friedan, 1963: 29).

Research is now beginning to discover that many of our old notions about the differences in type of sex interest between men and women cannot be demonstrated with contemporary studies. For example, it has generally been assumed that with its focus on sexual variety, genitals, and bizarre

---

[1] Robert R. Bell, *Marriage and Family Interaction* (Homewood, Illinois: Dorsey Press, 1963), pp. 312-314. Reprinted by permission.

sexual behavior, pornography is generally not stimulating to women, and in fact, few women in surveys report ever having been sexually aroused by it (Kinsey and Pomeroy, 1953). However, this may be only because the women have never been exposed to it. In a carefully done laboratory study, Jakobvits (1965) has turned our traditional belief upside down. His study is worth pondering.

Jakobvits prepared two groups of ten short stories each. One group of stories was written to meet the criteria of erotic realism: "The writer of erotic realism intends to depict the realities of life, such as they are, not excluding the sexual side which he considers to be an important aspect of human behavior." The other group of stories was written to meet the criteria of hard-core obscenity: "The main purpose of the writer of hard-core obsenity is to excite the reader sexually and to provide a psychological aphrodisiac, and this at the expense of credibility and the necessary limitations imposed by the requirements of the real world."

Jakobvits had male and female subjects read the stories, and report their evaluations of them. To his surprise, the women found the hard-core obscenity more sexually stimulating than the men did. Furthermore, the men found the erotic realism more interesting and stimulating than the hard-core obscenity, while the women found the hard-core obscenity more interesting and sexually stimulating than the erotic realism.

Other recent research contradicts this finding. A study done on West German college students, using photographs, found results which reinforce the traditional assumptions on sex differences (Sigusch et al., 1970). But the Jakobvits findings suggest that we need to be cautious in assuming that informal observations on previous generations are a valid basis for describing contemporary generations.

Sexual Adjustment and Marital Adjustment

The significance of sexual satisfaction for the general success of marriage has been argued by laymen and scholars, but it is surprising how little conclusive evidence is available on which to base an opinion. Kinsey estimated that sexual factors make at least some contribution to 75 percent of the divorces of upper-middle-class persons, but he did not study this aspect of sexual behavior. Other writers are convinced that sexual adjustment is not a cause of marital adjustment at all but merely a reflection of it. Sexual adjustment ranks among the top few problem areas both in successful and unsuccessful marriages, but it ranks farther down the list of problems among successfully functioning couples than among those having trouble (Mitchell et al., 1962). Every study of marital adjustment and marital happiness shows a strong relationship between marital adjustment and sexual adjustment, but the direction of causation simply cannot be disentangled.

SPECIFIC SEXUAL FACTORS

Two related sexual factors which have been demonstrated to bear close relationships to marital satisfaction are the relative level of sexual desire of the partners and the "orgasm adequacy" of the wife. On the first point, Burgess and Wallin summarize their findings as follows:

> The problem of sexual adjustment appears to spring most often from a divergence between husbands and wives in their attitudes toward sexual intercourse and the frequency of their desire for it. The findings of the research of Terman and of Burgess and Wallin show that women are more likely than men to have a negative orientation to sex relations and to desire them less frequently. There is some evidence, although it is not conclusive, that men tend to have greater sex drive and more positive attitude toward sexual activity than do women, before as well as after marriage.
>
> Despite this apparent difference wives are less disposed than their husbands to be critical of, or dissatisfied with their sexual relationship. The explanation for this may be that women do not expect as much as men from the sexual sphere of marriage. . . . These wives are apparently not greatly disturbed by being deprived of sexual satisfaction (Burgess and Wallin, 1953: 696-697).

Results of Locke's studies confirm that equality of sex interest is much more characteristic of happily married than divorced couples (Locke, 1951).

Every study of sexual adjustment in marriage has found that the wife's ability to respond with orgasm during sexual relations is related to the marital adjustment of both husband and wife. From Hamilton's study in the twenties, through Terman and Burgess and Wallin, to Thomason's study in the fifties, this factor has emerged as one of the two or three most significant factors for sexual adjustment and has shown strong relationships to marital adjustment. In three of these studies, it has emerged as the most significant sexual factor. Furthermore, these authors are inclined to interpret orgasm responsiveness as a genuine causative factor in adjustment. Terman says:

> Among the sex factors investigated are two that not only correlate markedly with happiness scores, but are in all probability genuine determiners of them: *viz.,* the wife's orgasm adequacy, and husband-wife difference in strength of sex drive (Terman, 1938: 374).

Thomason, studying a group of married couples a generation younger than Terman's couples, came to exactly the same conclusion:

. . . the quality of total marital and sexual adjustment of both husbands and wives was decidedly increased if the wife always had a climax in sexual intercourse. Wives who rarely or never had a sexual climax scored significantly lower on both total marital adjustment and sexual adjustment than wives who always had a sexual climax (Thomason, 1955: 163).

Because of the importance of the woman's orgasm for the quality of the marriage shown in every study, researchers from the 1930s to the present have tried to identify the determinants of "orgasm adequacy" in the woman's socialization, in the quality of the relationship she has with her mate, and even in her physical and biochemical characteristics, but with no success. Perhaps Fisher's (1973) monumental work will end this search. Fisher's study examined every possible determinant of orgasm pattern that any other researcher had ever suggested, and a number no one before had thought of. He found no important relationship between orgasm pattern and *anything* else of consequence. Masters and Johnson (1966, 1970) have written that any woman with a little instruction can learn to have orgasm rather easily using an inexpensive electric vibrator. Nevertheless, the differences in orgasm pattern seem to be randomly distributed in the population of women, evidently inborn, a stroke of luck in genetic roulette.

SOME THOUGHTS ON SEX AND MARITAL ADJUSTMENT

In understanding the relationship between sexual adjustment and marital adjustment, some reflection on the differences in the *context* of male and female sexuality which were discussed in previous chapters is required. First, sexuality has traditionally been more fundamental to masculine than to feminine personality organization. Second, love comes to men in a sexual context, while sex comes to women in a love context. This would lead one to expect that if a man is unsatisfied with his sexual relationship with his wife it should interfere with his love for her and cause him to have unsatisfactory marital adjustment (although a good sexual relationship in itself will not guarantee that he will have high marital satisfaction). On the other hand, a woman with otherwise high marital adjustment should not be made generally unsatisfied with her marriage on account of low sexual satisfaction. In fact, high marital satisfaction and love for her husband ought to cause better sexual adjustment. In addition, if her marriage is generally unsatisfactory and her love for her husband declines, this would be expected to interfere with her sexual satisfaction. In an important recent analysis of the Burgess-Wallin couples, Clark and Wallin (1965) have confirmed the general accuracy of this reasoning. After examining data derived from the early years of marriage and from eighteen to twenty years of marriage, they reach the following conclusions concerning the relationship between a woman's sexual responsiveness and the quality of her marriage over the years:

. . . the passage of time offers women no assurance of becoming more responsive. Whether having intercourse hundreds of times through the years will enhance their chances of experiencing orgasm appears to be related . . . to the quality of their marriage. . . . When women are classified by the quality of their marriage a consistent association between responsiveness and the length of the marriage is found for wives having a more positive marital relationship, *but not for those whose marriages are of relatively negative quality.* (Emphasis added)

. . . wives whose marriages are consistently positive in quality are increasingly likely to be sexually responsive *up to the time they have been married about five years.* (Emphasis in original) If by then they do not usually or always have orgasm in intercourse with their husbands, they will probably not do so in the years that follow. Similarly it appears that a shift from negative to positive in the quality of marriages from the early to the middle years is not accompanied by any increase in the responsiveness of the wives who are party to these marriages. On the other hand, the findings indicate that a deterioration in the quality of marriages after their early years often is accompanied by a decrease in responsiveness and that this may also occur in marriages which are consistently of negative quality. This decrease in responsiveness is almost certainly in most instances a consequence of the cultural norm which proscribes a woman "giving herself" in a relationship which has been designated as negative in quality. The negative quality of a marriage thus can inhibit women's responsiveness even when a pattern of responsiveness has already been established (Clark and Wallin, 1965).

For each sex, then, there is the same *correlation* between marital adjustment and sexual adjustment, but the main direction of causation is opposite for the two sexes. For a man, the level of sexual adjustment has a causal effect on his marital adjustment with little reciprocal effect of general marital adjustment on his sex life; for a woman, the level of general marital satisfaction has an effect on the sexual adjustment with little reciprocal effect of the sexual adjustment on her general satisfaction with the marriage.

Chart 15-1 probably accurately represents the relationship between sexual adjustment and marital adjustment for couples studied over the past thirty years. The arrows indicate the direction of causation, with heavy arrows representing the major causal direction, and light arrows minor causal influences. It is interesting to note that for women who are highly religious, lack of sexual gratification affects their general marital satisfaction less than for religiously uninvolved women. However, religion has no mitigating effect in the case of men. The marital satisfaction of the most and least religious men is equally affected by sexual dissatisfaction (Wallin and Clark, 1964).

Given the predicted changes in the nature of sexual interaction for future generations, we would surmise that Chart 15-1 will be out of date for them, and the arrows in opposite directions would have to be represented as more nearly equal in strength for each subsequent cohort.

Chart 15-1

HIS SEXUAL ADJUSTMENT AFFECTS HIS MARITAL ADJUSTMENT; HER
MARITAL ADJUSTMENT AFFECTS HER SEXUAL ADJUSTMENT
The relationship between marital satisfaction and sexual satisfaction

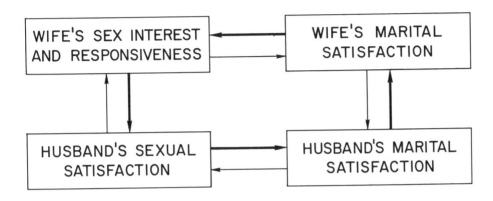

Sex As Play

With the widespread use of contraception in the United States, sex for millions of people has been dissociated at will from its reproductive consequences. Procreation has increasingly become a deliberate decision rather than an unintended consequence of sexual intercourse. As a pleasurable activity with no necessary consequences for the future, marital sex has now entered the group of activities engaged in simply because they are fun. The male subculture has long emphasized the fun aspects of sex. The female subculture on the other hand, and surprisingly nearly all scholarly writing on sex, has consistently failed to develop this aspect of sexuality.

Now that a new value with respect to sex is permeating American society, recognizing women as legitimate participants in the pleasure of sex and implicitly or explicitly recognizing men and women as equal participants in sexual activity, perhaps a discussion of sex as one of man's favorite recreational activities should be included. Yet, there is still a reluctance in serious discourse to admit the legitimacy of such a value as an end in itself. Nelson Foote has suggested a reason for this reluctance and the misconception on which it is founded.

> As our advertisers imply daily in a thousand ways, the attractions of sex make it the favorite form of play for millions of Americans. Why do not our thinkers go on from there to contemplate the kind of social life which might result from formal recognition of this fact, rather than implicitly or explicitly reverting to the prejudice that sex as play is bound to be sinful or at best amoral? Is it because to grant its status as play is felt to legitimize its pursuit without restraint? If so, the thinker does not understand the nature of play.

For play—any kind of play—generates its own morality and values. And the enforcement of the rules of play becomes the concern of every player, because without their observance, the play cannot continue; the spoilsport is sternly rejected. To be sure, the development of rules intrinsic to the game itself does not guarantee that they will be the same rules outsiders would like to impose, and when outsiders repress the play itself as illicit, the development of rules can hardly occur at all. But the social psychologists of play, from Spencer and Groos to the present, all seem to agree that no system of government whatever can approach play in making the enforcement of rules the felt interest of every participant.

With regard to sex, an example may clarify this point. A male student not long ago spent a year doing academic work in Sweden. He learned that in that enlightened country the double standard is almost extinct, and women both permit and are permitted the same liberties as men in premarital relations. This knowledge excited in him the hope of enjoying such an unrestrained orgy of self-gratification as other college males only dream of. After a series of frustrating and bewildering encounters with some Swedish young women, however, he was left a sadder and wiser person, for he found himself disgraced and outcast as an oaf and boor. He had not played the game correctly nor had he realized how strictly its rules are enforced in that highly moral and law-abiding country. It is not that he was mistaken about the greater sexual freedom of Scandinavia, but that coming from an American background, he did not rationally foresee the context through which order and responsibility are nonetheless maintained.[1]

Since Americans are just in the initial phases of defining sex as legitimate play, they are only beginning to specify the rules for enjoying the game. At the present, Americans are engaged in a national moral debate concerning who may legitimately play. Although an increasing minority maintains that the criterion for participation is being in love, the legitimacy of married partners as participants is everywhere acknowledged. Let us, therefore, take it from that point.

Sex is a game which husband and wife play together, with no one else, under the normal rules. (Wife-swapping clubs have received a good deal of notoriety because the rules of the game they play violate the normal rules of the game.) There are several requirements for successful games. First, they require a focus of attention without distraction of the players. The players must be interested in the game and "take it seriously." Just as it is no fun to play chess with a bored partner, it is no fun to play sex unless the playmate is absorbed in the play. Second, the players usually agree on how the game is to be played. Some things are not allowed, others are required. Partners who have played together for years develop their own set of house rules for sex based on their own preferences and abilities as players. Third, as in most forms of play, there are techniques and skills to be learned, and

[1] Nelson Foote, "Sex as Play," *Social Problems,* I (1954), pp. 159–163. Reprinted by permission.

some players are more skillful than others. In a good marriage, the more skillful partner can teach the less skillful if he is tactful and a good teacher as well.

Inventive couples create many variations on sexual games. The "seduction drama" is a perennial favorite. Some couples specialize in gymnastic variants. Others manipulate the psychological environment with changes in music, lighting, clothing, smells, and surroundings. A larger number only repeat the basic format without change for years. If this is the way they like to play, no scientific book on sex can tell them that is not the way to do it. However, the basic ingredient in sex, as in all games, is tension and excitement—physical tension, psychic tension, dramatic tension—generated for the fun of it and for the pleasure of its release. Husband-wife teams which provide this ingredient in good measure for themselves and each other are likely to continue to enjoy playing together.

Sex As Work: The Marriage Manual Approach

The "marriage manual" (which is really a sex manual) in American culture takes on a different meaning in the context of this discussion. Although most marriage manuals are written by psychiatrists and physicians and make a great point of presenting scientific information about correct sex practices, there is nothing "scientific" about most of them except the language. They are more useful (and less dangerous) when they are viewed as a handbook containing the authors' preferences and suggestions for maneuvers which they think make the game interesting. Taken in this light, they resemble books on how to enjoy golf or how to get more fun from bridge. When the unwary or inexperienced reader takes as scientific truth such advice as "failure of the woman to achieve sexual climax is a sign of unconscious hostility toward her husband," or "inability to achieve sexual satisfaction except through intercourse is a form of sexual perversion," he is likely to ruin his appreciation of the play aspects of sex, as well as invite new frustrations in his sexual relationship. No book can provide scientific information on the *correct* way to enjoy sex. As helpful hints for appreciation of the game, a good sex manual can provide even oldtimers with some interesting new techniques. As manuals of sexual orthodoxy, they can have a pernicious influence.

An insightful analysis of contemporary marriage manuals by Lewis and Brissett (1967) reveals marital sex, as depicted in the marriage manuals, to be "an activity permeated with the qualities of work." Readers are advised to prepare for sex in the same way that they would prepare themselves for a job. The "product" manufactured in this job is orgasm. This product is so important that the stability of the whole marriage industry depends on its regular production. There are certain techniques and job skills which must be learned, and even a certain range of equipment which must be mastered by the untutored sexual craftsman if the product is to be produced. Furthermore, according to these job specification manuals, female orgasms are much harder to manufacture. One writer presents a diagram of the woman's genitals, advising the husband to study it, and on the bridal night compare the diagram to his wife's genital region, presumably to identify all the working parts of the machinery which actually grinds out the product. The properly organized orgasm manufacturing process consists of several production phases, each of which must be mastered and taken in order. One manual states that "All three stages must be fitted into this time. None must be missed, and none prolonged to the exclusion of the other." A skillful and experienced couple will in these ways be able to produce orgasms of which they can be proud.

Brissett and Lewis (1970) report that the marriage manuals portray an unequal division of sexual labor between husband and wife. The manuals emphasize husband's responsibilities for exciting his wife, and describe complicated and difficult means to excite her. The wife's "job," on the other hand, is merely to be passive and accepting. The manuals urge both partners to control impulses and regulate their behavior in order to please each other. This practice has its drawbacks, as Brissett and Lewis observe. "It seems highly questionable that people continually should have to constrain, control, and suppress their emotions, impulses, and passions, in order to achieve a satisfactory sex life; at the very least, it seems unfortunate" (Brissett and Lewis, 1970: 47).

There may be a change in marriage manuals published later than those examined by Brissett and Lewis. Gordon and Shankweiler (1971: 462) report that more recent books "place more emphasis on spontaneity and the willingness to experiment," although initiative and responsibility are still attributed to the male.

Sex and Aging

It has been argued by some writers that males reach the height of their sexual capacity in their teens while women reach the height of theirs in the early thirties. This conclusion has been reached on the basis of the study of the Kinsey data on males and females which show highest "outlets" at those ages. A diagram similar to Chart 15-2 is frequently presented to defend such a view.

With the abandonment of the view of sexual behavior as produced solely by innate urges, Chart 15-2 takes on an entirely different meaning. The level of sexual activity of an individual is related to a number of different social factors. Monogamous marriage suddenly imposes an equal rate of sexual activity on a man and a woman with very different prior rates of sexual

Chart 15-2

MALE SEXUAL-ACTIVITY LEVELS REACH A PEAK AND BEGIN TO
DECLINE EARLIER THAN FEMALE SEXUAL-ACTIVITY LEVELS
Comparison of aging patterns of total outlet in human female and male

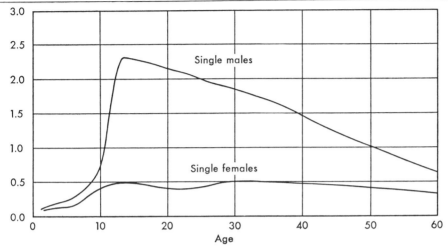

Source: Kinsey et al., 1953: 714

activity. Yet, no one supposes that any radical change in "sex drive" has suddenly occurred in the partners. The frequency of intercourse in the marriage will be determined almost entirely by the husband's desires. Kinsey has shown that the frequency of intercourse in marriage is highest in the early years and declines gradually thereafter until old age. This gradual decline has usually been attributed to the decline in the male's "sex drive" with increasing age. No doubt advanced years slow down the capacity for physical activity of all sorts, and sex is an intensely physical exertion, but the decline should not be laid to this fact alone.

Two other factors seem to be more cogent explanations: habituation and accommodation. The principle of habituation states that "the gratification which comes from an initial experience occurs with lessened intensity upon subsequent occasions" (Hardy, 1964: 3). Part of the thrill of any sexual experience is novelty, and marital sex with the same partner one hundred times a year for ten years is likely to lack novelty. Consequently, there is a declining interest in sexual relations with the same partner over the years. The fact that the decline is not due to the lessening of some specific innate drive can be demonstrated by introducing a new sex partner. To the extent that marriage partners are concerned with reciprocity in the sexual relationship, one would expect that the husband would come to desire sexual relations less frequently as he becomes aware of his wife's less pressing level of desire. If a considerable part of the pleasure from sex is now conceived to be derived from the pleasurable response of the mate, women should become gradually more interested from experiencing their husbands' pleasure, while men should become somewhat less interested. One would expect this process to reach a point of minimum difference after a few years of marriage, followed by a parallel decline on the part of both mates.

The sex life of a married couple is one of the most enduring parts of their relationship, continuing far into old age. By age seventy, most couples are still sexually active. The same factors that are significant in younger persons differentiate the sexual behavior of the aged: males are more active than females and lower-status persons are more active than higher-status persons. Those who describe their sexual urges in youth as very strong still report moderate sex desires in old age, while those who describe their youthful urges as moderate or weak report themselves without sexual feeling in old age (Newman and Nichols, 1960).

The husband continues to control the frequency of intercourse in old age. Pfeiffer, Verwoerdt, and Davis (1972) found that the elderly men and women in their sample who had stopped having intercourse said the responsibility for stopping had been the husband's.

The reasons for the decrease in sexual activity with age are different for each sex. Pfeiffer and Davis (1972) found that the older woman's sex drive and activity are affected by marital status, age, and her enjoyment of sex in youth; the aging male's sex drive and activity are affected by past sexual experience, age, social status, and his own and others' evaluations of his health.

Typical Patterns of Sexual Response

Students interested in a detailed description of the phases of the coital episode, with observations on the physiological responses of various parts of male and female anatomy at each phase, are referred to the groundbreaking work of Masters and Johnson (Masters and Johnson, 1966). This work reports detailed observations of a variety of sexual contacts as observed and measured with special equipment under laboratory conditions. Masters and Johnson have served a valuable function in exploding old ideas derived from inaccurate observation, and replacing them with accurate information.

Extramarital Sex

Except among the Gilyak of Siberia, where Sternberg reports that adultery is the favorite cultural sport (Chard, 1961) and a few other places, sexual involvement of a married person with someone other than his spouse is forbidden (with allowances for certain ceremonies and special circumstances). In every state in the United States and all Western European nations which permit divorce at all, adultery is grounds for divorce. American college students consider it a serious moral offense, although their attitudes today are not as severe as they were a generation ago (Rettig and Pasamanick, 1959). However, it is not clear that extramarital sexual relations are becoming more common. Kinsey's data show that women born after 1900 are more likely to have engaged in extramarital sex than those born before, but more recent generations of women show about the same incidence as those born between 1900 and 1910 (Kinsey et al., 1953: 423). Of those women in the Kinsey sample born after the turn of the century, about one in three had extramarital coitus by age forty. The data for men appear to be surprisingly similar in view of the widespread assumption of greater masculine preference for variety. About a third of Kinsey's men engaged in extramarital coitus, although Kinsey admits that the records on this point are quite inadequate and is sure that the actual incidence rate is much higher (Kinsey et al., 1948: 585). Because of the inadequacies of the available data, and because Kinsey is quite sure that there was considerable cover-up on the extramarital sex histories of the males studied, it is not known whether these proportions are representative of Americans generally. A cautious conclusion would be that it is not known how many men and women engage in extramarital coitus, though it is probably a substantial percentage. Neither is it known whether women or men are more likely to be involved. It *is* known that extramarital sex accounts for only an infinitesimal proportion of American sexual behavior. In the case histories where it occurs, it tends to be sporadic, episodic, and limited to one or a few partners. It is known that there is a considerable amount of extramarital sexual petting which does not lead to intercourse and that those women who engage in premarital sexual relations are about twice as likely to engage in extramarital sexual relations as girls entering marriage as virgins (Kinsey et al., 1953).

CAUSES, MOTIVES, AND REASONS

Kinsey gives numerous explanations offered by respondents for their extramarital involvements. Among them are desire for variety in partners, social status, accommodation of a friend, assertion of independence from the spouse, new sources of emotional satisfaction, poor sexual relationship with spouse, and encouragement of spouse (Kinsey et al., 1953: 431–436). Among laymen, the favorite explanations are in terms of an unsatisfactory sex life within the marriage. No one has ever shown that this is in fact the case, and one study suggests that it is entirely spurious. In a study of marital conflicts involving an affair by one of the partners, Cumming (Cumming, 1960) reported that only one-third of the men and one-sixth of the women in these affairs gave poor marital sexual adjustment as the most important reason for their extramarital activities. Rather, their reasons suggested a general dissatisfaction with the emotional aspects of their marriages. (It is interesting to note that one-third of the women reported that their affairs did not even include sexual intercourse.) A comparison of the personality scores of those involved in extramarital affairs with average test scores indicates that affairs are characteristic of people with unconventional personalities who are less sensitive than the average person to social restraints generally. As a matter of fact, those involved in extramarital affairs tended to be more satisfied with their marital sex than those who only had "fantasy" extramarital involvements. In short, it appears that extramarital sex is engaged in by those who do not respond to the usual social restraints, not by those who are unhappy with their marital sex lives (Neubeck and Schletzer, 1962).

Extramarital sexual involvement is one of the most frequently cited sources of trouble in divorcing couples, many couples reporting it as the cause of the divorce. In most cases where the spouse knows about it, an adulterous relationship is disruptive of the marriage. In some cases, no doubt, marital difficulty of a nonsexual nature has driven the couple apart and into extramarital liaisons, while in others, involvement in extramarital sex preceded any other serious difficulty, and its discovery actually precipitated the marital problem.

ORGANIZED EXTRAMARITAL SEX

One of the more interesting social developments on the sex scene is organized extramarital sex. In some parts of the country this is called "swinging," in others "mate swapping." (It was called "wife swapping" by a less equalitarian generation.) The key feature of this pattern is that husband and wife together and with each other's cooperation arrange to have sexual intercourse with other similar couples, sometimes friends, but frequently strangers. It is a no-emotional-involvement arrangement by design. It is strictly for recreation. It is now found in all parts of the United States, and has its own newspapers and magazines through which contacts with new couples are made by advertisements. Although it involves in some degree a wide social spectrum of individuals, most participants are under forty, most are upper-middle-class, and most are in all other aspects of their lives highly conventional individuals. "Swinging" is their only deviant behavior.

Most couples report that they originally entered the game of swinging at the urging of the husband, and with misgivings on the part of the wife. However, with time the wives often become the most enthusiastic participants, with the husbands' interest waning. Parties organized for the activity have their own rules and rituals. Male-male pairings are strictly taboo, but female-female pairings are usual (as, of course, are male-female). In fact, it is reported in some groups that their parties usually end up with the men

Chart 15-3

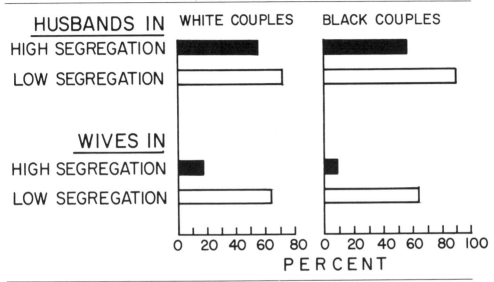

LOWER-CLASS COUPLES IN HIGHLY SEGREGATED RELATIONSHIPS
FIND LESS ENJOYMENT IN SEXUAL RELATIONS
*Percent of lower-class respondents expressing great interest
and enjoyment in sexual relations*

Source: Rainwater, 1966

sexually exhausted, somewhat resentfully watching the females pair up and continue the evening's activities into the night. (For four serious papers devoted to the study of this phenomenon, see the May, 1970, issue of the *Journal of Sex Research*.)

Because of the recentness of this pattern, we have little idea how extensive it is, only general outlines of the characteristics of the participants, and no idea about the consequences. Spanier and Cole (1972) found that 10, or 1.7 percent, of their sample of 579 married people in a midwestern community reported that they had participated in mate swapping at least once. Female swingers are usually in their late twenties, males in their early thirties. Certainly it is a clear indication of continued movement toward breakdown of the traditional confinement of sex within a single marital relationship.

Sex and the Social Context of the Marriage

The nature of the sexual relationship between husband and wife is heavily influenced by the total nature of the marital relationship and its place in the

Chart 15-4

LOWER-CLASS COUPLES IN SEGREGATED RELATIONSHIPS GET ONLY PHYSICAL PLEASURE FROM SEX
Percent of couples who get only physical pleasure and release from sex

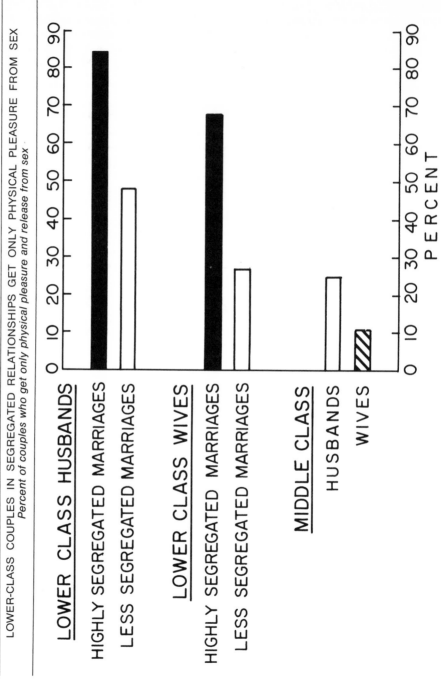

Source: Rainwater, 1966

general social matrix. Where conjugal roles are highly segregated and marital interaction is built around a division of labor, as is characteristic of some lower- and working-class groups, a close and mutually satisfying sexual relationship is not likely to develop because husband and wife do not customarily relate to one another in an intimate, personal way. Rainwater, after studying several such systems, suggests:

> . . . a close sexual relationship has no particular social function in such a system, since the role performances of husband and wife are organized on a separate basis, and no great contribution is made by a relationship in which they might sharpen their ability for cooperation and mutual regulation. It is possible that in such a system, a high degree of intimacy in the marital relationship would be antagonistic to the system since it might conflict with the demands of others in [the spouse's] social network (Rainwater, 1964: 463).

Chart 15-3 shows that for lower-class black and white couples alike, those in highly segregated relationships do not find sex of great interest, but the interest of women particularly is sensitive to the effect of marital role segregation.

The appreciation of the interpersonal and emotional satisfactions of sex as something of value beyond the physical pleasure and release is a product of the emotional involvement of spouses that is rarely developed in highly segregated marriages. Chart 15-4 indicates that lower-class persons generally fail to appreciate the more subtle social pleasures of sex, but that this kind of appreciation is almost completely absent from highly segregated lower-class marriages (Rainwater, 1966).

Summary

The traditional marital sexual relationship in the United States was one in which the husband was more interested in sex than his wife. Her desire for sex was less than his, and her sexual responsiveness was a critical factor in his marital satisfaction. Cultural definitions of appropriate sexual behavior for the two sexes no doubt were a major contributor to the production of this traditional pattern, by providing the two sexes with fundamentally different sexual socialization, in which sexuality of males was encouraged, while females were shielded from sexual stimuli and were provided with a nonsexualized image of themselves. The part played by biological factors in producing the observed differences in the sexes is more disputed, but it seems probable that biological differences in the sexes predispose men to generally greater sexuality, all other factors being equal.

The contemporary cultural emphasis on equal and similar sexuality of men and women is already changing the pattern of marital sexual relationships. Sexuality is receiving more emphasis and encouragement in the socialization of women. Equality of the sexes in sexuality can be produced in this way, but probably only by more encouragement of female sexuality than is now the case. We should expect this change in the socialization of women to cause further increases in premarital and extramarital sexual behavior.

Implications for Individual Autonomy

Individuals vary in their biological potential and in their acquired appetite for sex, not only in their levels of desire and responsiveness, but in the kinds of sexual activity they find satisfying. Today we know enough about the origins of these differences and their consequences to understand that any two people of opposite sexes who marry one another cannot automatically expect to find their mutual sex lives gratifying. With the increasing centrality of sex to marriage, this lack of satisfaction with sex is likely to be tolerated less well than in the past. This is especially true of women, who in the past did not expect much from sex, but who expect more today.

For those couples who want assurance of sexual compatibility in the early years of their marriage, extensive premarital sexual experience with one another is probably the best way to determine sexual compatibility. It is hard to imagine why we ever thought otherwise, yet texts of the past regularly asserted that this was not true, in the face of evidence to the contrary. Kanin and Howard summarize their exploration of sexual adjustment before and during the honeymoon period as follows:

> The present findings on the honeymoon period indicate the importance of premarital intimacy with the spouse not only in terms of immediate postmarital sexual satisfaction, but in terms of altered postmarital behavior (Kanin and Howard, 1958).

Hamblin's and Blood's reanalysis of the Kinsey data (1956) allows some refinement of this conclusion. They found that premarital experience *per se* was not related to the wife's sexual adjustment. Rather, those women who were unresponsive in intercourse before marriage also showed the lowest response levels within marriage. Those women who were more responsive in intercourse before marriage were also by far the most responsive within marriage. Those without premarital experience can be considered unknown quantities. But a woman with no premarital orgasm experience has a low probability of frequent orgasmic response after marriage (Kinsey et al.,

1953). In fact, whether a woman's responsiveness before marriage is in intercourse, petting, or other activities seems to make little difference. It still predicts marital response.

For those who have moral or psychological restraints from premarital sex, and for those who are more patient teachers and learners, it is probably never too late to learn new sexual behavior. The sexual responsiveness of inexperienced women increases during the early years of marriages which are otherwise satisfying. Couples who are flexible in their behavior, open minded in their preferences, and willing to try anything promising will have more chances of developing satisfying ways of relating sexually to one another than those who have already decided what sex is supposed to be like.

For those couples who work too hard at good sex, and for those couples who get tangled in one another's sex problems, it is good to know that effective behavior therapy can now untangle most sexual problems (Masters and Johnson, 1970).

Over the course of a marriage, companionship declines, children are born, grow up and leave home, youth and beauty decay, but sex endures. Sexual needs may change, and sexual preferences may alter, but couples who are still listening to one another can retain sensitivity and learn new sexual patterns as they get older. If sex dies in middle age for some couples, it dies of boredom. Those who are blessed with interesting and interested sex partners will be sexually active when they are old.

Perhaps as important as any of the above suggestions is the importance of remembering that in marriage, sexual behavior is above all symbolic behavior, and sexual interaction is symbolic interaction. Sensitivity to the *meaning* of the sexual relationship in the marital relationship as a whole gives sex a whole new dimension which for many couples will make the emphasis on a special pattern of physical reaction seem a concern for trivia by comparison. Failure to understand the symbolic functions of sex in the marital relationship is a failure to understand the human sexual relationship at all. The sexual relationship is a subtle form of communication between husband and wife of ideas that can be communicated as well in no other way. It may be a veiled and acceptable way to express minor hostilities; it nearly always becomes a symbolic affirmation of the exclusiveness, privacy, and psychological intimacy of the husband-wife relationship. (In contemporary marriage, the damage to the relationship done by adultery is its symbolic shattering of the value of exclusive commitment.) For most couples, their sexual relationship becomes (at least in part) a symbolic ritual through which social estrangements generated in other facets of their relationship can be transcended and the equilibrium of their psychic intimacy reestablished. It is a symbolic reaffirmation of the masculinity of the husband and the femininity of the wife, and the difference between them and their complementarity. Without its symbolic element, the marital sexual relationship becomes only a mechanical sort of tension release. For most human beings, the symbolic nature of sex is an integral part of every sexual relationship.

As sex becomes a more important focus of the emotional relationship in marriage, and as the society becomes less sexually repressive and puts more positive emphasis on the enjoyment of sex, the sexual problems of the past, rooted in negative and repressive orientation toward sex, should be reduced in importance. It is doubtful that this will produce a generation which is more satisfied with its marital sex life. Emphasis on the increased importance of sex raises everyone's level of expectation of the amount of sexual satisfaction he should experience, while it makes people less tolerant of sexual frustration. The widespread knowledge of, and view of, other people's sexual behavior can be expected to lead to the development of sexual performance norms, which may be the foundation of a new generation of sexual problems.

Fertility Control 16

Parenthood in American life has become a deliberate, planned role. Childbearing is not considered as a necessary consequence of sexual activity but as a consequence of deliberate decision on the part of the parents. The discrepancy between one's holding this value and the actual occurrence of childbirth should not obscure the existence of the value. What this means is that parents view children as something to be had *because they want them when* they want them. The voluntary quality of parenthood affects the entire atmosphere of childrearing among contemporary parents.

Why do people want children? People want them because they perceive children as sources of pleasure and satisfaction. Few people say they have children because of some social or moral obligation (although this would certainly be a socially acceptable response). In this sense, the bearing of children may be viewed as motivated by selfish and individualistic wishes, however selfless or even self-sacrificing it may appear to those who already have children. Whatever economic considerations may have motivated the production of large families a century or more ago, under contemporary American urban conditions, children cannot be considered anything economically but a loss. Each child represents an investment on the part of a middle-income parent of something on the order of $30,000 before he becomes self-supporting. From this the parent will get no economic return, nor can he even expect to be supported in his old age. Every generation makes this investment in the next generation, which on the ledgers of society represents a return of the investment made in it by the previous generation (though not many parents see it this way). For the individuals deciding on parenthood, the fact cannot be avoided that *every decision to have a child means a decision to accept a lower standard of living in return for the satisfactions of parenthood.*

Trends in Childbearing in the United States

A historical review of the last century in the United States with regard to childbearing will give some insight into the thousands of childbirths which represent individual decisions of couples. From 1860 to 1930, every single index of fertility declined steadily and gradually in the United States. Fertility measures are a complex and specialized subject in themselves, and discussions of family size or the number of children born per family rarely take into consideration the difficulties of specifying exactly what is meant by a change in family size and exactly how this is to be measured. While this is not the proper place for an elaborate discussion of the problems involved, discrepancies between the description here and other descriptions may sometimes be accounted for by differences in the particular measures of fertility used. Considerable understanding of the changes in fertility has come from what is called "cohort analysis." By this technique, the childbearing experience of a group of women who were born during a particular year is compared with the childbearing experience of other groups of women born in other years. Looking at the total number of children born per thousand women, it is discovered that women born each year up to 1910 had fewer children born to them by the end of their fertile period than women born in the previous years. On the other hand, women born between 1910 and 1940 have had *more* children than women born in 1910. This means that women who married after about 1930 have been having more children than the women older than they. It is impossible to tell how many children a woman will have until she is through the childbearing age (usually figured between fifteen and forty-five), so that the production record of any woman born after 1930 is still not definitely known.

Birth rates after World War II were higher than before, and the trend of the 1950s was upward, reaching a high point in 1957. Since 1957, birth rates have declined. (Chart 16-1 gives the trend in birth rates for recent years.) Demographers expected birth rates to "bottom out" in the late sixties, and to rise in the early seventies, because of the unusually large number of women entering the prime childbearing years during this period. As Chart 16-1 shows, after levelling out in the late sixties, birth rates dropped precipitately in the early seventies, reaching the lowest levels ever seen in the United States. It is only mildly embarrassing to have to admit that we have no better explanation for the decline in births during the seventies than we had for the decline in the sixties. Nevertheless it appears that women born after 1940 will have smaller completed family size than the generation of women immediately preceding them. With anticipated availability of a new generation of contraceptives, and increasing spread of legal abortion and sterilization in the next decade, together with the widespread availability of government-subsidized family planning services, the generation now in

Chart 16-1

BIRTH RATES HAVE DECLINED DRAMATICALLY IN RECENT YEARS
Births per 1000 women age 15–44, United States, 1940–1972

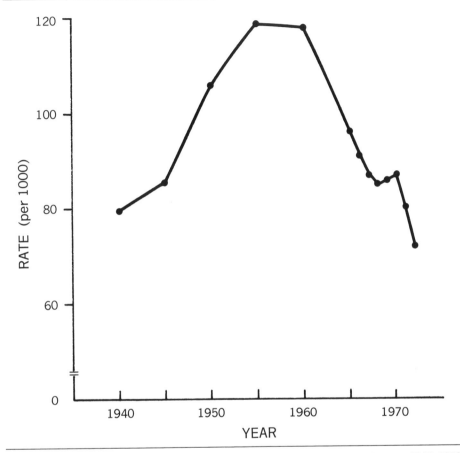

Source: Statistical Abstracts of the United States, 1972; Monthly Vital Statistics Reports, 1969–1972

its early childbearing years will be the first to have real control over its fertility.

For at least 150 years there has been an inverse relationship between socioeconomic status and fertility in the United States—the lower the status, the higher the fertility. While this is still true, the difference between the lowest and the highest status couples has narrowed sharply in the past thirty years.

The effect of economic trends in the United States on fertility patterns is well known. Parents are very aware of the economic commitment to the future which they make when they conceive a child. Since the early part of the century (there is no data before this time), with the downward fertility trend, short-run fluctuations of fertility have always followed the economic cycle with about a year's lag. When economic conditions are promising, people conceive children. When economic futures look uncertain, people who know how postpone conceptions. The effect of economic conditions on childbirth has a slight effect on first births, and an exaggerated effect on second births. This suggests that the symbolic significance of the first child to a couple makes economic considerations unimportant in timing its birth. The second child comes when circumstances are more propitious. As more and more people become educated and enter ways of life consistent with fertility planning, it can be expected that these short-run changes will be more and more abrupt and also more pronounced, with periods of heavy childbirth followed by periods in which few children are born.

Short-range changes in birth rates have all kinds of unexpected consequences for immediate and long-run use of resources in the United States. Consider: at the height of the baby boom in the fifties, there were half again as many births each year as there were in the early seventies. This meant overcrowded obstetric wards in the late fifties, while hospital building plans swung into action. Bulging elementary school enrollments followed behind the birth rates by six years. There was a brisk market for elementary school teachers. By 1972, hospitals were desperately searching for new ways to use their obstetric facilities. Elementary school enrollments were already falling. The supply of elementary school teachers built to handle the baby boom was far in excess of needs for the early seventies. This will become accentuated even more in the late seventies when the very low birth crops from 1971 and 1972 hit the first grade.

But the consequences do not stop here. In the seventies, the babies from the boom years of the fifties hit the job market, at the rate of more than four million a year. This kind of a labor supply depresses the economic life-chances of this entire cohort of births. In comparison they will receive lower incomes and slower promotions, have a harder time getting jobs, and take lower-status jobs than had their birth cohort been smaller. Consider, by comparison, the fate of the birth cohort of the early seventies. In the early 1990s, in a nation with a much larger population, this cohort will enter the job market with a million per year fewer job aspirants. They should really do well.

Cross-Cultural Perspective on Fertility Control

The world-wide population explosion since World War II is an entirely different phenomenon from the increase in fertility observed in the United States and Western Europe during the same period. The increase in the United States and Western Europe can be traced directly to the increase in births. In the rest of the world, there has been little increase in births, and the so-called population explosion can be traced largely to a decrease in deaths, especially infant mortality. This has been achieved through the application of Western medical technology and sanitation to societies little changed in other respects. In some countries, infant mortality has been cut in half in a few years. With no change in the high birth rates, populations previously stabilized by mortality can double in twenty years.

The recent changes only emphasize the fact that traditional societies, especially technologically simple societies, have almost always had high birth rates. Furthermore, their values have almost always emphasized the importance and desirability of high fertility. Generally, they have been more concerned with methods of assuring fertility than methods of checking it. High mortality rates have meant that only societies with high fertility rates could survive.

Yet, for one reason or another, most societies have wished to exercise some control over fertility under certain circumstances, and every society is organized in such a way that the existing fertility rates are far under those possible within the biological capacities of humans. Among the structural features which depress fertility (although no one may consciously consider them fertility control) are monogamy, premarital sexual prohibitions, proscriptions of incest and adultery, pregnancy and postpartum sex taboos, and late marriage, to mention only a few. Many societies have folk remedies which are supposed to prevent conception or induce abortion.

In the Western traditions, methods of preventing conception have been known since very early times. The Hellenistic period in Greece and the days of Imperial Rome are not famous for their sexual restraint, yet they achieved some of the lowest birth rates known. These were achieved, it is believed, by methods which today are not considered very effective, especially *coitus interruptus.*

Fertility control is predicated on a value structure and a philosophy of life which makes fertility control meaningful. Where the culture has the values which encourage striving for a higher standard of living and an attitude toward the future which acknowledges the possibility of rational planning and human control of destiny, then contraceptive technology can effectively control fertility. Therefore, most population control programs today are making a two-pronged attack on the problem. On the one hand they are attempting to provide family planning technology for the majority of women who are already having more children than they desire. On the other hand, they are attempting to change the cultural circumstances to those which are less favorable to high fertility. This includes, among other things, trying to reduce infant mortality rates and diseases of childhood so that parents can expect all of their children to grow up, and trying to stimulate economic growth, so that the future is worth planning for.

Religious Beliefs and Fertility Control

Major religious groups have distinctly different attitudes toward fertility control. In general, the differences may be summarized as follows: Jews and most Protestant groups have no explicit religious ideology concerning fertility control, and religious leaders have been either permissive or noncommittal in public statements; the Roman Catholic Church provides an explicit religious ideology which stipulates the permissible motives for fertility control and the permissible control techniques. Specifically, the Roman Catholic Church states that fertility control for spacing or limitation for reasons of health or economic difficulties are legitimate but restriction for "selfish" reasons, such as to achieve a higher standard of living or to avoid the inconvenience or emotional difficulty of childbearing and parenthood, is strictly enjoined (Ahearn, 1959). Two methods of conception control are now permitted under Catholic doctrine: sexual abstinence and the "rhythm method," or abstinence during the woman's fertile period.

In recent years a very serious internal conflict in the Roman Catholic Church has developed over the acceptability of other forms of birth control, particularly birth control pills. Many persons within the Church expected the Pope to make a formal change in church doctrine in 1968. But the papal encyclical, "Humanae Vitae" of 1968 maintained the Church's opposition to birth control unchanged. Interviews of Catholic women in the United States showed that the majority were against the policy of the encyclical. Among young Catholic women, more than three out of four opposed it (Westoff, 1969). Westoff and Bumpass (1973) predict that 90 percent of young Catholic women will use Church-disapproved methods before they finish their childbearing years.

Catholic-Protestant differences in fertility belief and behavior are usually cited as a major source of potential conflict in interfaith marriages between these groups. It is unfortunate that nothing but impressionistic observations are available on this point. There is some evidence that those Catholics who marry non-Catholics are atypical in their practices, and it is possible that the importance of conflict over contraception in mixed Catholic marriages has been overestimated.

Family-Size Preferences

Family-size preferences have been measured regularly in the United States for a number of decades. The number of children actually "desired" is always somewhat smaller than what is considered "ideal." Chart 16-2 shows desired number of children for American women in 1965. Blacks desire considerably fewer children than white non-Catholics, who in turn desire considerably fewer children than white Catholics.

Chart 16-2

MOST CATHOLICS WANT FOUR OR MORE CHILDREN, MOST NON-CATHOLICS WANT THREE OR FEWER CHILDREN
Desired family size, by race and religion, among women with incomplete fertility, 1965

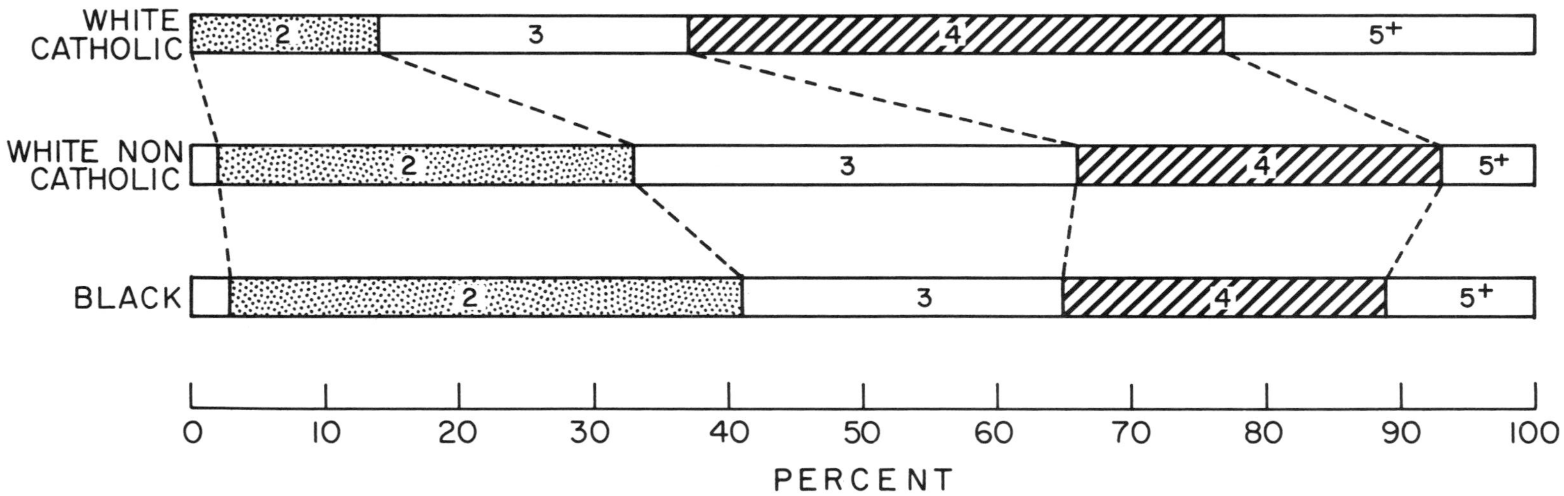

Source: Ryder and Westoff, 1969b

Table 16-1

THE FOUR-CHILD IDEAL IS FAST VANISHING
Percent of Americans saying four or more is the ideal number of children

	1967	1971
National	40	23
Men	34	19
Women	45	26
Age 21–29	34	15
Age 30–49	40	24
Age 50 and over	42	27
Protestants	37	22
Catholics	50	28

Source: Wattenberg, 1971

By the early 1970s, the distribution of desired family sizes in the United States had shrunk far below those shown in Chart 16-2. Values were changing so fast that valid predictions about the future of American population growth became futile. Table 16-1 shows that just between 1967 and 1971, the proportion saying four or more children was an ideal family size dropped almost 50 percent, or more percentage points than it had changed in the previous decades.

Today in the United States, desired family size does not differ much by educational and economic status.

Chart 16-3

BLACK WOMEN HAVE A HIGHER PROPORTION OF
UNWANTED BIRTHS THAN WHITE WOMEN
*Percent of women who said last birth was unwanted among those who
intend no more children, by years of education completed, 1965*

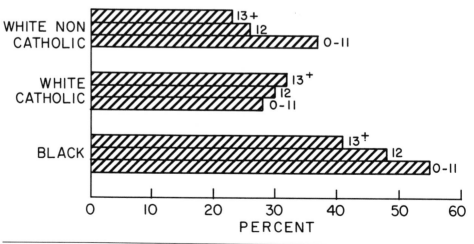

Source: Ryder and Westoff, 1969a

Chart 16-4

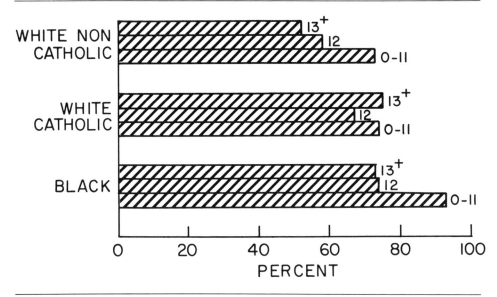

MOST WOMEN ARE UNSUCCESSFUL IN CONTROLLING
THE SPACING OF THEIR CHILDREN
*Percent of ever-pregnant women who have experienced a timing failure
in birth spacing, by education (years completed)*

Source: Ryder and Westoff, 1969a

Unwanted Fertility

Given the fact that almost all fertile couples in the United States today use some form of contraception after they have had all the children they want, it is surprising the number of couples who have unintended pregnancies. Surveys done in the mid-1960s (Ryder and Westoff, 1969a) indicate that about a fourth of American couples with wives under age forty-five who did not intend to have more children, already had more children than they wanted. Among blacks, about half had more children than they wanted. See Chart 16-3. Westoff estimated that about 40 percent of the population growth in this country in the early 1960s was contributed by births which the parents did not wish to have. Surveys of recently delivered mothers conducted in the early seventies by the author show that the proportion of births which are unwanted has declined dramatically in the past decade, with a substantial part of that decline coming since 1970.

When we look at pregnancy timing failures, the figures show that most couples who intend no more children have had at least one child sooner than they wanted it. Sixty-four percent of whites and 82 percent of blacks reported some births had come too soon. See Chart 16-4. These data indicate how far Americans are today from having only as many children as they desire, and when they desire them (Ryder and Westoff, 1969a). A closer look at Chart 16-3 reveals that for blacks and for white non-Catholics, fewer educated women have births they don't want than the less educated do. For white Catholics, the educated women are more likely to experience unwanted births than the less educated. This curious reversal is brought about by the fact that the more-educated women are closer in touch with the doctrines of the Catholic Church with respect to birth control, and attend church more often. This causes them to avoid effective means of birth control to a greater extent than less-educated Catholic women do. As a consequence, less-educated Catholics have better control over their own fertility than better-educated Catholics.

Chart 16-4 also makes quite clear that the least-educated whites have better control over the number of children they have than do the most-educated blacks. At this time we do not understand why this race difference is so marked.

The Current Use of Contraception in the United States

Although there remains a small group of Americans who report in surveys that they are opposed to the use of any method of preventing births (fewer than 10 percent in the latest surveys), it is safe to predict that of women now entering the childbearing years, nearly all who marry will at some time use a contraceptive method. The fewer couples who do not will almost all be couples with fertility impairments who have not been able to have as many children as they desired.

Since 1960, when the oral contraceptive was introduced in the United States, the use of contraception has been revolutionized. Chart 16-5 shows the shift in method usage which occurred in the five-year period between 1965 and 1970.

Hormonal Contraception

Hormonal contraception is best known to the layman today in the form of "the pill," although many other forms of hormone administration are now becoming available. All work through the administration of a drug related to female hormones in such a way as to inhibit fertility of the woman.

CONTRACEPTIVE PILLS FOR WOMEN

Three basic forms of contraceptive pills are available for women today, although dozens of different formulations of these basic pills are produced

Chart 16-5

CONTRACEPTIVE USE IS SHIFTING TOWARD PILL, IUD, AND STERILIZATION
*Percent of contracepting married couples currently using specified
methods, United States, 1965 and 1970.*

Source: Westoff, 1972

by different manufacturers. All are available through prescription only in this country and in Europe, although in many other countries they are available on the open market. The three forms are *combination* pills, *sequential* pills, and *minipills* (or *everyday* pills).

Combination pills contain a synthetic estrogen and a synthetic progesterone (the two basic types of female hormones). These pills are taken every day for three weeks, discontinued until menstruation occurs, and then resumed a week after they were stopped. Their method of operation is complex, but for most women they appear to inhibit ovulation. Hence there is no egg to be fertilized. On the smaller dosage combination pills now in use many women apparently ovulate, but they do not become pregnant. In actual field usage the pregnancy rate for women using the combination pills is extremely low (less than one pregnancy per 100 woman years).

Sequential pills consist of two different medications taken in sequence. Beginning on the fifth day of menstruation, a pill containing only estrogen is taken for two weeks. Then a pill containing estrogen and progesterone is taken for about a week, after which pills are discontinued for a week. Their method of operation is prevention of ovulation. Sequential pills have very low pregnancy rates, but not quite as low as combination pills. (Latest figures indicate a pregnancy rate with the sequential pills of about one pregnancy per 100 woman years).

Minipills are at the time of this writing still under investigation, using large samples of women. The minipill contains a small dosage of progesterone only, and is taken continuously, once a day, for as long as infertility is desired.

THE CONTROVERSY OVER HEALTH RISKS OF THE PILL

From the introduction of hormonal pills to the present day a considerable controversy has raged among physicians and researchers concerning the potential risks to health of long-term use of the pill. (We are not concerned here with minor side-effects such as nausea, weight gain, tender breasts, irregular bleeding, etc., which are annoying and may cause many women to give up the pill, but which are usually temporary, and have no important health implication beyond the symptom.) Many researchers and physicians have worried that hormone pills (especially those containing large amounts of estrogen) might cause cancer if used over long periods. There is no evidence that contraceptive pills cause cancer in human females. However, women taking pills are at an elevated risk for some disorders related to clotting of the blood, and to some disorders related to spasms of the arteries. Physicians can identify from patient histories those women who are likely to experience this increase in risk, and for these women hormonal pills are usually not prescribed. This is not the place for detailed medical discussion of the problems involved, and the reader is referred to his own physician for details. But it is worth taking a few lines to discuss the concept of increased health risk. It has been estimated that in the United States, about three deaths per hundred thousand women using the pill will occur each year from thrombo-embolisms which would not have occurred had women not used the pill. But what would have happened to these hundred thousand women had they not been using the pill? The competing risk must also be examined. More deaths would result from the accidental pregnancies likely to be experienced while using a less effective method of contraception than result from the use of the pill.

Since the pill has been in widespread use in the United States only about a decade, it is of course impossible to say that other effects will not be noticed which are detrimental to health after some women have taken pills for twenty years. On the other hand, it is difficult to imagine that physicians will continue to prescribe pills for the same women for twenty consecutive years. We will discuss this later in connection with sterilization.

The research now available on the pills tells us more about the pills than is known about any other medical preparation or procedure ever used. Perhaps if we knew as much about aspirin, mouth wash, or cosmetics applied to the skin as we know about contraceptive pills, we would be less exercised about the danger of pills, and more worried about many of the common products we use casually every day.

OTHER HORMONAL CONTRACEPTIVES FOR WOMEN

Several other methods of hormone administration are now being field tested in various parts of the world. (By field tested, we mean tried out on large groups of women for contraception, rather than laboratory tests on animals.) *Injections* of hormones in an oil base into body muscle to be absorbed over a period of one to three months have been under test for several years. *Implants* (under the skin) of hormone capsules which release a measured amount of hormone each day into the system for a period as long as five years without further medication are now being field tested in the United States and elsewhere. The daily amount of hormone is very slight, and side-effects are expected to be at a minimum. Once the capsule is in place the woman does not have to remember to do anything except to go back after a few years to have the capsule replaced if she desires continued infertility, or to have it removed if she desires to become pregnant. It is expected that pregnancy rates for this method will be somewhat higher than for present combination pills, but that for many women the convenience and absence of side-effects will be worth the slight increase in pregnancy risk.

A *vaginal ring* impregnated with progesterone is now being tested. The plastic ring is inserted into the back of the vagina, where it can stay in place indefinitely, and where it will not be felt during intercourse. The ring releases into the vaginal tissue a small amount of progesterone continuously. This is subsequently absorbed into the system in sufficient amount to prevent pregnancy. Its method of operation is therefore very similar to the minipill described above.

The *morning-after pill.* The "morning-after pill" is a very large dose of estrogen which is administered by a physician within a few days after intercourse in which a woman fears she might have become pregnant. Research is still under way to determine the exact method of operation of this technique. At this time it is believed to either prevent implantation of the fertilized egg, or to cause the destruction of an already implanted fertilized egg. This method has recently been approved for routine medical practice in the United States.

At the time of this writing it is impossible to predict when these methods will be available for widespread use. With the rapid development of new methods in this area, the only thing which can be said with confidence about the future is that the next generation will be using contraceptives which are as different from those of the present generation as those of the present generation are different from the traditional coitus-connected methods.

Intrauterine Devices

Intrauterine devices (IUDs) are manufactured of plastic, metal, or other inert material, and then inserted into the uterus through the cervix with a special inserter. Once in place, they offer high protection against pregnancy for as long as they are there. The way in which IUDs prevent pregnancy is still under study. Usually an attached string protrudes through the cervix into the vagina. The woman can check to see that the string is still there, and thus be assured that the device is still in place and she is protected from pregnancy. A small number of women expel IUDs spontaneously. For others there are unpleasant side-effects, such as unusually heavy menstrual flows, intermittent menstrual bleeding in the middle of the cycle, and occasionally some women experience cramps. The large majority of women can retain the device without side-effects. IUDs are now manufactured in a large variety of sizes, shapes and type of material. In the most recently developed IUDs, side-effects are at a minimum, spontaneous expulsions are rare, and the protection against pregnancy is nearly as effective as with hormonal pills.

When IUDs were first introduced there was considerable fear that "introducing a foreign body" inside the human body would have unfortunate health consequences. There was particular fear in some places that IUDs would cause cancer of the uterus or cervix. Thorough research on this problem has proved these fears to be completely unfounded. It therefore seems likely that a new generation of IUDs will soon take its place alongside hormonal contraception as one of the two methods of choice for pregnancy prevention among married women and other women regularly exposed to the risk of pregnancy, but who have not yet had all the children they desire.

Older Methods of Contraception

RHYTHM METHOD

The rhythm method of contraception dates to the 1930s, when it was definitely established that ovulation occurred at a fairly predictable part of the menstrual cycle. The ovum is known to have a fertile life span of probably not more than forty-eight hours, and probably much less. The life span of a sperm is not known as well, but most observers believe that it is probably not more than forty-eight hours or so. It is therefore clear that if the time of ovulation is definitely known, avoidance of intercourse at and around the time of ovulation will effectively prevent conception. Unfortunately, the problem is not as simple as it seems. Since the original presentation of this method, a great deal of research has been devoted to ways of determining the exact time of ovulation. At present, however, no simple method can reliably and closely predict the time of ovulation. It turns out that the amount of irregularity of the menstrual cycle in most women is a great deal higher than anyone thought thirty years ago. And of course methods of practicing rhythm require a good estimate of the length of the menstrual cycle. Furthermore, we now know that ovulation is not by any means as regular as was once thought. The latest research on the rhythm method indicates that if couples using the method will limit intercourse to the period beginning two days *after* there is an indication that ovulation has occurred (a rise in basal body temperature), then the effectiveness of the method is very high—probably almost as good as the IUD or the pill. By using this adaptation of the rhythm method, the "safe period" for most couples will be not more than ten days per month, followed by menstruation, during which most couples do not have intercourse, followed by about two weeks of abstinence from sex. At this point we do not know how many couples will be willing and able to limit intercourse to the latter ten days of each menstrual cycle. Any other pattern of using the rhythm method has been shown to result in so many unintended pregnancies that it cannot seriously be recommended as an effective method of contraception. In fact the only reason it continues to be discussed in texts and researched in the clinics is because of the official position of the Catholic Church which makes rhythm method the only approved method of contraception. The fact that about 80 percent of American Catholics have used other methods of contraception, and that clinics which offer instruction in the rhythm method have few takers, suggests that unless there is a real breakthrough in predicting the time of ovulation, the rhythm method will be relegated to historical interest only.

CONDOMS

The condom is a thin rubber sheath which is rolled over the erect penis prior to intercourse. Prior to introduction of the contraceptive pill, it was the most widely used method of contraception in the world, and is still a very important method in the United States today. Many couples still rely exclusively on the condom for contraception. Its use is also widespread among the unmarried, for whom its universal availability without professional medical advice, its emergency availability (as compared to the pill, for example, the use of which must be begun at a certain time in the menstrual cycle and continued regardless of immediate need), and the fact that it is the only contraceptive which also offers protection from venereal disease infection, make it an ideal method. Consistently used, the condom is a highly reliable method of contraception—probably nearly as good as the IUD. There are no side-effects. In many informal discussion groups with married men and married women of widely varying educational level, the author must report that although all knew of the condom, and most had used condoms at least at some time, few people had anything positive to say about the condom as far as satisfaction with its use during intercourse was concerned, except for the fact that it prevented pregnancy. On the other hand, those who were familiar with the lubricated condom (which most couples had not heard of) were quite positive toward it. High-quality lubricated condoms will be found widely acceptable as a method of contraception for those who only occasionally must concern themselves with pregnancy risks.

DIAPHRAGMS

A diaphragm is a thin rubber hemisphere with a stiff but flexible ring around the outside. It is customarily filled with contraceptive jelly and inserted into the vagina in a very precise fashion, before intercourse, so that it offers a barrier to sperm entering the cervix. Properly inserted and left in place for several hours after intercourse it is a highly effective method of contraception—about as effective as IUDs. A diaphragm must be fitted by a physician (diaphragms come in several sizes). Up until the introduction of the contraceptive pill, the diaphragm was practically the only method recommended by physicians and contraceptive clinics. It is still used among the generation of middle-class women who were married before the pill became available. Among other groups it has found a very low acceptance rate. It will probably continue to be a useful method in the repertoire of contraception for a small number of persons who cannot retain IUDs, have medical reasons for not using contraceptive pills, and do not wish to be sterilized for one reason or another.

FOAMS, JELLIES, CREAMS, SUPPOSITORIES, AND SIMILAR PREPARATIONS

There are a number of foams, jellies, creams and other chemical and mechanical barrier preparations available without prescription in the average American drug store. Many now come in aerosol cans, and most come with an applicator. A measured amount of the preparation is inserted into the vagina with the applicator before intercourse. The most effective of the aerosol foams have been shown to be very effective contraceptives—on the same order of effectiveness as the IUD. Some users consider them to be too messy or to produce too much lubrication during intercourse, or to be generally offensive on aesthetic grounds. On the other hand, millions of couples have used such preparations and are highly satisfied. Their method of operation is twofold. They form a mechanical barrier which prevents sperm from entering the cervix, and they usually contain a chemical which either kills or immobilizes sperm. They are frequently recommended for use temporarily by some physicians who do not prescribe pills or insert IUDs until several weeks after a woman has given birth. Until the woman can be begun on a recommended method, she is instructed in the use of contraceptive foam. Although clinical trials of foam have shown very high contraceptive effectiveness, the author's interviews of 30,000 newly delivered mothers in hospitals show a disproportionate number of foam failures compared to condoms and prescription methods.

The Use of Contraception Among the Unmarried

Ordinarily, one would imagine that a couple engaging in sexual relations, but unmarried, would have a greater stake in preventing pregnancy than married couples. And over the past few years, newspapers, magazines for men, and worried parents have talked about the common knowledge that so many unmarried girls are on contraceptive pills, just as a few years before we regularly read of the unmarried girls who carried a diaphragm in their purses for any emergency opportunity. Yet studies of contraception among the unmarried indicate that their attention to contraception is extremely casual. In a recent study of unmarried adolescents Kantner and Zelnick (1973) recorded that fewer than half reported using contraception at their last intercourse, and only one in five reported always using contraception. Even among college women, only three in four reported contracepting at last intercourse. Even among college students, who are presumably the best informed about contraception, the use of birth control in an effective manner is relatively unusual. A study by Bauman found that in one state university, in a representative sample of undergraduate girls, *none* of them had been on pills at the time of their first intercourse (Bauman 1970). The most common method used was the condom—oldest of all the effective methods—and just what their grandparents used when they were in college. Why do college women who are sexually active not protect themselves with better contraception? The most common reason given by college women is that contraception is so unromantic. Since romanticism is still the most common justification for sex among college women, it is easy to imagine why a girl does not begin on contraceptive pills on January 4th because she expects to get romantically carried away sometime late in February, at which time she will need to be protected. As long as romanticism is an important justification for sex among the unmarried college population, we can expect continued occurrence of pregnancy among unmarried college women.

Induced Abortion

Induced abortion is the deliberate termination of an early pregnancy, causing destruction and/or explusion of the fetus. In the world today it is probably the most widely used and effective method of birth prevention. In January, 1973, the Supreme Court of the United States transformed abortion law in the United States. At that time, state laws varied widely, with some extremely permissive, and some completely restrictive. This state of affairs led to a large interstate business in abortion in the permissive states during the early 1970s, especially in New York. The Supreme Court decision of 1973 essentially laid down the guidelines for a national abortion law.

> For the first three months of pregnancy the decision to have an abortion lies with the woman and her doctor, and the state's interest in her welfare is not "compelling enough to warrant any interference." For the next six months of pregnancy a state may "regulate the abortion procedure in ways that are reasonably related to maternal health" such as licensing and regulating the persons and facilities involved.
>
> For the last ten weeks of pregnancy, the period during which the fetus is judged to be capable of surviving if born, any state may prohibit abortions if it wishes, except where they may be necessary to preserve the life or health of the mother (*New York Times,* January 23, 1973: 1).

Most states are now in the process of rewriting their laws to conform to the Court's decision. It is now expected that for the next few years, at least, there will be more than a million legal abortions performed each year.

METHODS OF ABORTION

Dilation and Curettage. The traditional medical method of abortion is dilation of the cervix, and scraping the wall of the uterus with a spoon-like instrument, in the process removing the fetus from the uterine lining. It is a surgical procedure, requiring proper medical facilities, and necessitating careful antiseptic precautions to prevent infection and skill to prevent hemorrhage. When performed by a skilled physician under proper conditions no later than the third month of pregnancy, it is extremely safe. Reports from eastern Europe indicate that the risk to life from such an abortion performed by an experienced physician in a hospital on a healthy woman in the first three months of pregnancy is far smaller than the risk ordinarily associated with pregnancy and childbirth (Tietze and Lehfeld 1961).

Vacuum extraction. The vacuum extraction method of abortion is a recent addition to American obstetric practice. In this method, a small flexible vacuum pipe is inserted through the cervix into the uterus, and the products of conception are simply "sucked out" through the pipe. Those who are using it report considerably less chance of shock, hemorrhage, or infection from this method than from traditional D and C. This method is also limited to the first three months of pregnancy, and requires the same circumstances for its safe use that are required by D and C. Vacuum extraction will probably make do-it-yourself abortions safe and common in a few years.

Hypertonic injection. The hypertonic injection method of inducing abortion involves injecting a saline solution into the uterus by means of a large hypodermic needle inserted through the abdominal wall. This method is only used *after* the third month of pregnancy. It causes destruction of the fetus and spontaneous delivery within twelve to eighteen hours. Under hospital conditions performed by an experienced physician, the method usually empties the uterus cleanly, with very slight risk of complication.

Prostoglandin. The prostoglandin method of abortion is a recent development, and is under experimental study at the present time. Prostoglandin is a hormone-like protein substance which was originally discovered in semen, and at that time thought to be produced by the male prostate gland. Its use in abortion involves the intravenous administration of a prostoglandin solution to the pregnant woman at a slow but continuous rate for from twelve to eighteen hours, at which time labor occurs, and the fetus is expelled. It is the only "drug" method of abortion now in medical use (unless the morning-after pills work as an abortifacient).

Although abortion makes sense as a "backup" method for contraceptive failures, it is an inefficient substitute for contraception. The Japanese experience in this regard has been very frustrating. Of women having first abortions, half were back for a second by the time eighteen months had passed (Green, 1967). As an emergency population-control measure in countries sorely pressed by the pressure of numbers, it can be remarkably effective. Japanese sources compute that abortion cut the number of births by more than half in that country in 1955 (Muramatsu, 1960). When abortion is used instead of contraception, however, the necessity of its frequent repetition makes it a very expensive method.

In countries where abortion is legal, freely available, and limited to the first three months of pregnancy, deaths from abortions reach extremely low rates. In eastern Europe and in Japan, where legal abortion is easily available, there is less than one maternal death in 20,000 abortions (Tietze and Lewit, 1969). It seems likely that recent advances in abortion techniques will lower even these low rates.

THE EFFECT OF ABORTION ON THE BIRTH RATE

When liberalized abortion laws were enacted in Japan and certain European countries in the 1950s, dramatic declines occurred in the birth rates of these countries. Therefore, some have expected a similar decline in the United States. An examination of the experience of New York City in the two years preceding the Supreme Court decision is instructive. New York liberalized its abortion law in early 1970. The number of legal abortions jumped sharply. During 1971 and 1972 the birth rate dropped 25 per cent in New York City (Tietze, 1973). During this period there was one abortion on a resident woman for every two resident live births. Tietze concludes from his analysis that half the decline in births was due to abortions. Similar data which have been developed by the author for other cities lead to a different conclusion: cities with large numbers of resident abortions and cities with small numbers of resident abortions experienced similar birth declines in 1971 and 1972. There is no reason to assume that national availability of abortion will lower birth rates.

Sterilization

The average American woman today is completing the family size she desires by age twenty-six, and of women thirty years old, most have all the children they ever want. This leaves the average woman with something like fifteen to twenty years in which she is capable of becoming pregnant, but does not want to have any more children. Since the death rate of infants over one year of age in the United States is practically insignificant, American couples with as many children as they want have highly efficient contraceptives available to them. But statisticians have recently demonstrated that even with the available contraceptives, about half the couples who have reached their desired family size can expect to have an undesired pregnancy before their fertile years have ended. An increasing number of physicians are coming to the conclusion that it is simply not good medical practice to leave a woman on daily contraceptive medication for twenty years. Experts on fertility are beginning to recommend that when a young couple has completed their fertility, they should seriously consider sterilization. There are two basic sterilization operations presently being performed: tubal ligation for women, and vasectomy for men.

VASECTOMY (MALE STERILIZATION)

Vasectomy is a simple operation which ties off the tubes which transport sperm from the testicles into the male reproductive tract. Sperm continue to be manufactured, but they are reabsorbed into the testicles and destroyed. The operation produces no changes in the circulating levels of hormones in the male, and no biologically-induced changes in sexual behavior. The ejaculate is unchanged in quantity or quality, but simply contains no sperms.

Recent years have seen considerable research devoted to making vasectomy "reversible," so that should the man change his mind, he could have his ability to impregnate restored. Although considerable progress has been made, the results of reversal operations are so unreliable that the method should be considered permanent. At one time we expected that the "sperm bank" would protect men from being sorry later about a vasectomy. Recent experience with stored sperms has not been reassuring. The longer the sperm is stored in a sperm bank, the lower the likelihood of its producing a pregnancy. Sperm batches stored for several years have very low remaining fertility.

Surveys conducted by the author indicate that the majority of men have grave misgivings about vasectomy. Even though they are reassured that it will not affect their sexual desires or performance, the general reaction is they they do not want to take any chances. A carefully controlled longitudinal study gives some insight into the psychological reactions of some men to vasectomy. Rodgers *et al.,* (1965) interviewed and gave psychological tests to a group of couples in which the man was about to undergo vasectomy, and a control group of couples in which the wife was about to begin taking contraceptive pills. The couples were then reinterviewed and tested two years later, and again four years later. The men were almost unanimous in maintaining that they were happy with the operation, would have the operation if they had it to do over, and would recommend it to their friends. But in fact, few had recommended it to their friends, and most had kept secret the fact of the operation. Both husbands and wives reported increases in socially approved behavior associated with masculinity, when compared with the control group. But during the follow-up period, both husbands and wives in the vasectomy group showed increased personality disturbance on the psychological tests. From their studies, the authors conclude that vasectomy appears to be viewed by the males as a threat to their masculine self-image, which in turn leads to compensatory masculine behavior and a deterioration in personality adjustment. All of these changes are of course clearly psychologically induced responses to an unfortunate perception of the operation as demasculinizing.

In view of the simplicity of the operation, and its freedom from side-effects affecting health, we should not be surprised at its growing popularity. As the operation becomes more familiar to Americans, we should expect to see the psychological side-effects become minimized, and the perception of the operation as demasculinizing become a myth limited to the uninformed. Nevertheless, for the present, men who suffer from real doubts about masculine adequacy should probably be discouraged from undergoing the operation. For the psychologically confident male, it is the best method for terminating fertility when a couple has completed its desired family size.

TUBAL LIGATION (FEMALE STERILIZATION)

The most common form of female sterilization is tubal ligation, or the surgical severing of the fallopian tubes which transport the ovum from the ovaries into the uterus. Many other surgical procedures performed on women have the effect of sterilization, even though the ostensible purpose of the operation is not sterilization. Tubal ligation as now performed is a hospital surgical procedure, requires several days confinement, and costs several times as much as a male sterilization. However, new surgical techniques are now in the process of development which may make female sterilization a minor surgical procedure, less expensive, and perhaps even reversible. Tubal ligation has no biological effect on the woman's sexual desire or performance, but no adequate studies have been done measuring its psychological effects. For couples who have completed their desired family size, and who are for some reason afraid of vasectomy, tubal ligation appears to be the most sensible choice for terminating fertility, especially for those couples with many fertile years ahead.

Fertility Impairments

A substantial proportion of American couples want more children than they are able to have. This is attested to by the chronic excess of demand over supply of adoptable infants. Advances in knowledge about human reproduction have helped to reduce this number below previous levels so that relatively few marriages remain childless today. The appropriate steps to be taken to increase the probability of conception depend on which causes of infertility are operating for each couple. Among the more common causes for infertility are:

1. Failure of the woman's ovary to mature or release eggs.
2. Failure of the male testes to produce viable sperm, or production of defective, weak, or too small a number of spermatozoa.
3. Certain chemical conditions of the uterus.
4. Physical blockage of the cervix or fallopian tubes, sometimes by pathological formation or growth.
5. Viscosity of the vaginal and cervical secretions.

This is not meant to be an exhaustive list. Indeed, occasional cases turn up in clinical practice where the couple is infertile because they have not discovered penile-vaginal intercourse.

Another method of minimizing infertility which is just beginning to be used with any frequency is artificial insemination. If the husband is producing viable sperm but the sperm count is low, or if it is high but no conception has occurred under conditions of normal regular intercourse, a sample of the husband's semen may be mechanically placed in the reproductive tract of the wife by a physician in such a way as to maximize likelihood of conception. This is done at the time in the menstrual cycle when ovulation is most likely to occur. If the husband is sterile, it is possible to use fertile semen donated by an anonymous male in the same way. In this way couples are able to have children who otherwise could not.

Chart 16-6

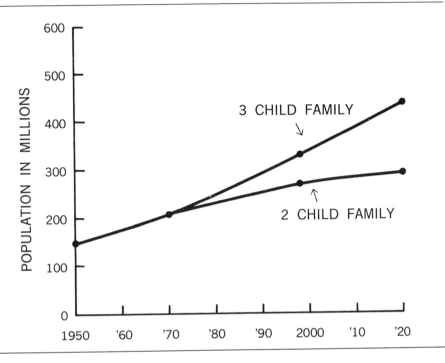

THREE-CHILD FAMILIES MEAN A CROWDED FUTURE
Population of the United States, 1950–1970, and projected to 2020

Future Population Growth in the United States

Birth rates at any one time are a relatively poor indicator of population growth trends in the United States. When we talk in terms of the completed family size of a group of women we can get a much more personally applicable interpretation of growth of population. Because of the extremely low death rates in the country today, if every couple beginning childbearing in 1970 had two children, and one couple in ten had three, the American population would level off and stop growing in about the year 2035, after increasing about 50 percent in size between now and then, leaving us with a population of about 300 million Americans (Frejka, 1968). Chart 16-6 compares the population growth for the next century in the United States given a two-child average family with the growth given a three-child average family. The differences are startling. Present desired family sizes indicate a United States future closer to the bottom line than the top line in Chart 16-6.

Policy of the United States Government

Up until 1965, the federal government officially spent no funds for birth-control programs in the United States, although in the early 1960s it adopted a policy of providing technical assistance to other nations who requested help with their problems of population growth. Beginning in the mid-1960s the federal government first began to allow funds from certain health programs for the poor to be spent to provide birth-control services, although the money so spent was not to be identified. (Southeastern state and county governments had been providing birth-control services to a few women for several decades.) In 1966, the first specific federally sponsored family-planning programs were begun by the Office of Economic Opportunity and family-planning services were added as a part of the Maternity and Infant Care programs funded by the Children's Bureau. Large-scale funding of family-planning programs by the federal government was not under way until 1969. The policy of these federal programs is to provide services for people who cannot afford or who otherwise do not have access to private physician services in family planning. The policy explicitly repudiates a population-control intent, and is designed only to help people realize their own childbearing plans. Although by 1973, three million women had received services from programs subsidized by the federal government, recently completed studies by the author reveal that the provision of subsidized services was in no way responsible for the birth dearth of the early seventies.

Summary

The last decade has seen revolutionary changes in the control of fertility. Today most couples have access to birth-control techniques which are nearly perfect in their ability to prevent conception without interfering with sexual enjoyment. Couples who are less educated still have more problems with controlling the number and timing of their children than more-educated couples, and blacks have more trouble than whites in this regard, even controlling for differences in education. Catholic couples are rapidly shifting away from the Church's unchanging position against mechanical and chemical contraception, so that only a few relatively well-educated Catholics use the rhythm method exclusively.

A new generation of contraceptives may soon supplant even the excellent methods available today. These new methods, plus the increased popularity of sterilization among couples who have completed the number of children they want, should go a long way toward reducing the number of couples who have more children than they want. Government subsidy of family-planning services is another step in this direction. Sweeping changes in laws governing abortion now give women real access to legal and safe abortion. Almost all the future population growth in this country will come from couples who want more children than it takes to replace themselves.

Implications for Individual Decision-Making

The contemporary generation of young couples is the first in history to be presented with the techniques to thoroughly and safely disassociate sexual pleasure from reproduction at will. For most of these couples, reproduction will become a deliberate decision and not simply an accidental by-product of their sex life. Although there is no firm knowledge of how this affects reaction of parents to their children, it is probable that the deliberateness of parenthood changes the quality and meaning of parenthood. When children just happen to people, parenthood is the gift of fate. No one need ever ponder the advantages or disadvantages of having another child; no one need be sure that he is enjoying the children he has in order to justify the decision to have them. When reproduction becomes subject to rational control, it enters the realm of the marital decision-making process and becomes part of the economics of marriage as a pleasure-giving relationship. This cannot help but complicate the parent-child relationship. Certainly, it must create a heightened "ego investment" of the parent in each child with more opportunities for the development of guilt, pride, possessiveness, and bitterness, as well as feelings of responsibility. As it introduces possibilities of more creative childrearing, it gives the parents opportunity for the expression of their own personalities through their children. The negative aspect of the process is the probable tendency to "use" children in the service of parental neurosis or as pawns in manipulating the dynamics of the marital relationship. The problems introduced into parenthood are probably not greater than those introduced into any facet of human life by man's achievement of control over the immediate consequences of his own behavior.

The widespread use of contraception, sterilization, and other methods for the control of fertility, combined with increasing knowledge of how to overcome natural impediments to fertility, has tended to bring about an increasing uniformity in family size among Americans. Widespread social values encouraging moderate-sized families combine with other unrecognized features of the social structure to make the family with two to four children the norm from which few couples depart. Thousands of young couples, acting autonomously but subject to the same social forces, make identical fertility decisions and produce similarly sized, similarly spaced broods. It is perhaps inevitable that in a mass society such as America, the possibility of universal fertility control should have reduced rather than increased the individual variation which biology and circumstance had previously produced.

17

Marriage and Parenthood

In our previous discussion of the basis for mate selection and marital inter-action, the fact that almost all marriages which persist for any length of time produce children was completely ignored. This omission has been intentional, since the focus of the book is on the interaction of the heterosexual pair. Certainly, in the mind of courtship couples, childbearing, or even the advent of children, is not uppermost in their minds and for most plays a very minor role in mate selection and marriage planning. It is true that most couples discuss before marriage how many children they will have (and perhaps the sex distribution), and many middle-class couples discuss contraception and child spacing. However, the desire for children is a minor motivation for marriage for both men and women in the United States. In a way, the fact that there will be children is simply taken for granted. Although some women give considerable thought before marriage to their future roles as mothers, hardly any young man has given his role as father more than the most casual thought. While most people grow up in families, few have any realistic notion of what little children are like until they have them, and many adults hardly know what to say to a young child. The average adult's unfamiliarity with children is reflected in the peculiar tone of voice and diction which he uses when he talks to little children.

Yet children are desired by most couples, most of whom are disappointed when they have no children from their marriage. American middle-class people increasingly have children "on purpose" by a deliberate decision to cease practicing contraception. This is to say that there are positive motives for having children for most people. It is not likely that many have them out of duty to society. Some are prompted by religious duty. Most people have children for reasons that they themselves do not at all understand. The motivations are complex and not well studied. Most people expect pleasure, gratification, or satisfaction from their children.

In this chapter, the functional relationship between the children and the marriage will be explored. The problem will be explored from both sides: First, what effect do children have on the marriage? Second, what effect does the marriage have on the children?

The Effect of Children on Interaction and Adjustment

Marriage is a twosome; three is a crowd. Studies of many kinds of groups have shown that of all human patterns of association, triads are the least stable. Unusually stable threesomes are the subject of fiction *(Three Musketeers, Drei Kameraden),* but even they eventually break up. Pair interaction appears to be by far the most prevalent pattern of association, at least among Americans (James, 1951), and is evidently the most satisfying form. Why this should be is not known. Addition of a third person to any pair radically changes the interaction between the pair, and a whole new pattern of behavior emerges quite different from that which existed before the addition.

It should not be surprising to learn, then, that the addition of a child to a family fundamentally alters the family structure. Where formerly there was one relationship, now there are four: baby and I, baby and spouse, spouse and I, and we three. Life has become complicated. How does the addition of a baby change a family? How are families with children different from those without? The culture provides answers for these questions. Children are said to bring husband and wife closer together, to give them interests in common; childless homes are said to be unhappy places, and having children is an immunization against divorce. Babies are said to be "bundles of joy," and appealing mother-and-child photographs and paintings assure everyone of the pleasure. Only the cynical sociologist would have thought it worthwhile to collect evidence to verify such undisputed truths.

THE EFFECT OF FAMILY SIZE ON INTERACTION AND ADJUSTMENT

Sociologists have for decades been interested in the effect of group size on interaction (Hare, 1952; James, 1951; Simmel, 1902). Every study shows that groups of different sizes have distinctly different social properties. It should, therefore, not be surprising that different-sized family groups have also been shown to have distinct properties. Those couples interested in planning the size of their families will find it useful to know how families of different sizes differ in family behavior. Bossard (1952, 1960), the sociologist who has devoted the most attention to large families, describes the following differences between small families and large families (families with five or more children):

1. Parent-child emotional relationships are less intense in large families than in small families.

2. Large families are better equipped to handle minor crises but are peculiarly vulnerable to major crises as compared to smaller families.

3. Large families tend to be group oriented rather than individualistic.

4. Large families are more authoritarian and put more stress on discipline, conformity, and cooperation.

5. Task specialization is likely to be much greater in large than in small families.

Parents of large families use more physical punishment of their children than parents in small families, even when the influence of social class is eliminated. In fact, the difference in physical punishment of different-sized families is greater than the difference in families of the same size but different social classes.

Value similarity between parent and child is greater in small families than in large families (Clausen, 1966).

Bossard reports that the children from large families report they think they are happier and better adjusted than children from smaller families (Bossard, 1956), and he sees "a certain balance and sanity in childrearing" in the large family which he believes is absent in the small family (1960). The mother of many children simply does not have the time to be over-solicitous, overanxious, or overprotective of each child. However, personality testing of children from large and small families does not confirm this viewpoint.

Careful studies of the personal adjustment of children from different-sized families show that children from larger families have significantly poorer relationships to their parents than children from smaller families but are not significantly different in other phases of personality adjustment (Hawkes, 1958; Nye, 1952).

Several studies have shown that the more children there are in a family, the lower their intelligence. This relationship is not due to the larger families of the culturally deprived, because it has been found to be true within each socioeconomic class examined separately. Children from large middle-class families have lower scores on IQ tests than children from small middle-class families. However, the impact of increased family size in reducing IQ of the children is more marked in the lower social class. The reason for this phenomenon is not completely understood; a large family size may reduce the amount of verbal communication between each child and adults, which might lower the child's vocabulary level and verbal facility, skills that are heavily weighted on intelligence tests (Clausen, 1966). Class differences differentially affect large and small families in other ways too. Adolescents in large middle-class families report that their parents exert more control over them than adolescents from small middle-class families do, but there are no differences in the reports of adolescents from lower-class families, large or small (Peterson and Kunz, n.d.).

THE ONLY CHILD

Americans have a bias against having only one child. About one out of seven completed families has only one child. A good proportion of these are in families where the parents desired more children but did not produce them. The reasons parents give for not having an only child almost always deal with the welfare of the child—parents think it is detrimental to the child's development for him not to have siblings. Less than 1 percent of American women consider one child an ideal number to have (Freedman et al., 1959: 222), and only 3 percent of college men and 4 percent of college women in a recent study preferred to have one child (Blake, 1972).

Studies of only children and their adjustment have produced inconsistent conclusions. Early studies described them as being "selfish, dependent, aggressive, domineering, or quarrelsome" (Bossard, 1956), "more inclined to be leaders, . . . self-confident and aggressive," "not unique," and "higher in intelligence, less subject to stealing, lying and truancy, more restless, overactive, with more school difficulties" (Bossard, 1960: 95). Later studies fail to find significant differences between only children and those with siblings when their adult personalities are compared (Cutts, 1954). An interesting exception to this is Veevers' (1973) finding that wives who were only children were over-represented in a sample of voluntarily childless wives. *The differences between only children and those with siblings have been grossly exaggerated.* Many of the differences cited above may have nothing to do with being an only child but are simply characteristics commonly found in the children of parents in the social strata most likely to produce only children. If their parents had had more children, there is no reason to believe that these only children would have been different. Furthermore, many children who are not classified as only children are really only children on most of the criteria thought to be of importance—for example, they have siblings either much older or much younger with whom they never interact as peers. The idea that only children are deprived of playmates seems to be a case of myopia on the part of people with several children. No researcher has ever demonstrated that not having siblings reduces the number of playmates. It will obviously reduce the number of sibling playmates, but my casual observations suggest the hypothesis that because of their "only-ness," only children are *more* likely to have playmates outside the home than those with siblings who can fall back on the companionship of their brothers and sisters rather than make outside friends. Even this is probably an unusual phenomenon. It used to be said that only children were prone to make up imaginary playmates to fill in their loneliness. The only study testing this notion found imaginary playmates just as common among those children with siblings as those without (Cutts, 1954: 95–96). It would probably be closer to the truth to say that the real reason people have only children as infrequently as they do is because they themselves want more children, especially children of each sex.

NUMBER OF CHILDREN AND MARITAL ADJUSTMENT

Many studies have explored the effect of differing numbers of children on marital adjustment. While the results of different studies are not entirely consistent, several studies have found that couples with a smaller number of children have better adjustment than those with a large number. In view of the many studies showing no relationship, there is no proof that having many children produces poor adjustment. In one study of couples in a student housing community, a strong inverse relationship was found between number of children and marital adjustment. However, the interview responses of the couples suggested that the poor marital adjustment was related to two factors: difficulties in being a parent and attending college at the same time and inability to control fertility in accordance with the couple's desires (Christensen, 1952). Although some studies have shown a relationship between having no more children than desired and marital adjustment, this could probably be accounted for by the negative reactions to additional children of those who have poor marital adjustment already.

Marital adjustment and family interaction are different *in large families. Parent-child relations appear to be more strained in larger families than in smaller families.* Whether particular parents will be happy with large families or small families is evidently not a factor of size *per se,* but of parental reaction to that size, which is not now predictable. A review of all the important studies of the question reveals that "more important to marital success than just how many children and how long between them is how successful the couples become in controlling the number and spacing according to their desires, or else in adjusting their desires to conform with reality, or some of both — but, in any event, reducing the discrepancy between desire and occurrence" (Christensen, 1968).

The number of children wanted before marriage is a poor estimate of the number actually born to a woman. Rather the number actually born is usually more closely related to the number later reported as the number desired. That is to say, those who are satisfied report that they desire the number they have, while the less satisfied are not happy with the number they have (Westoff et al., 1957). The number of studies which have found no relationship and the contradictory results of those with positive findings lead to the conclusion that *there is no reliable relationship between the presence or number of children and marital adjustment.* Regardless of their enthusiasm about large families, the children from large families do not go on to have large families themselves. Bossard says:

> As a system, the large family seems not to perpetuate itself. Rates of marriage and of reproduction are relatively low, as compared with the population as a

whole. Many reasons for this appeared in the course of the study. Economic pressures resulting from the mere fact of numbers; the crises, often major ones, that appeared in so many families; the problems that arose from incompetent and unwise parenthood; the stresses and strains of limited space—all of these and others often overshadowed the other compensations of the large family. In only 30 percent of the families were parents and informants agreed that it was wholly good. Most often, the over-all attitude of siblings could be expressed in the words of one informant: "It was nice, it was fun, but—" It is the *but* which is the key word in interpreting the failure of the large family system to perpetuate itself (Bossard, 1960).

If the major function of children for the parents is to provide emotional gratification for them, it is probable that two to four children provide *more* emotional gratification for the parents than larger numbers.

CHILDREN AS A DIVORCE PREVENTIVE

Many people believe that children can solidify weak marriages and are therefore preventives of divorce. Many marriage counselors hear women clients say that if only they would have a child, then everything would be better. Data on the childlessness of divorced couples produce clear evidence that among divorcing couples, childlessness is much higher than among those not divorcing. More than half of divorced couples have no children (Jacobson, 1959), and the average number of children for divorcing couples with children is only two. Furthermore, the more children there are, the lower the divorce rates. On the surface, this would seem to support the common-sense beliefs. In 1955, for couples without children, the divorce rate was 11.9 per thousand. Where one child was present, the estimated rate was 10.9, and for families with four or more children, it was only 4.1. One might note that the difference between one-child and no-child marriages is slight. Furthermore, there are certain factors which tend to inflate the difference. For example, fewer divorced spouses are from rural areas, which usually have higher fertility. Also, divorce is more common in the early years of marriage when more couples are childless. When these and other factors are taken into consideration, the difference in divorce rates of those with one child and those with no children is insignificant. It is probable that couples who are having serious trouble in their marriage or are contemplating divorce will not continue to have children deliberately, and many couples sever their sexual relationship long before the divorce is granted. When Chester (1972) matched married and divorced women on the time between marriage and the divorcees' divorces, he found that divorcees had lower fertility rates than the married women. But when he matched married and divorced women on the time between marriage and the divorcees' *separations,* divorcees showed higher fertility than the married women. These factors seem satisfactory to account for the low divorce rate among those with several children. Consequently, *few family scholars today consider the presence of children to be a real deterrent to divorce.* One authority on the subject has this to say:

> . . . the relative frequency of divorce is greater for families without children than for families with children. Yet the presence of children is not necessarily a deterrent to divorce. It is likely that in most cases both divorce and childlessness result from more fundamental factors in the marital relationship. Moreover, while children may hold some marriages together, in others pregnancy itself and the additional strains involved may disintegrate rather than cement the marriage. It is also probable that some unsuccessful marriages are not legally dissolved until the children are grown up. However, their number is undoubtedly less than is popularly believed in view of the small difference in the divorce rate between the two groups at the later years of marriage (Jacobson, 1959: 135).

PARENTHOOD AND CONVENTIONALITY

I have mentioned that marriage is a conventional institution into which conventional people fit with the least difficulty. Having children is one of the conventional expectations of married persons. Therefore, those couples who go on to have children are probably more conventional than those who do not—that is, their parenthood is an index of their conventionality. If it is true that couples with children are less likely to divorce than those without children (probably less true than formerly—see Chart 18-4), it is probably in part because having children signifies the conventionality—and hence the probable marital stability—of those who are parents. Thus, parenthood and stability are both the products of initial conventionality to some degree.

However, this relationship between conventionality, stability, and parenthood is probably also reciprocal. In ways which most young couples are ill-prepared to understand, parenthood itself exerts strong pressures toward conventional behavior on couples. "The child's welfare" may require a steady income from a dull job in preference to an exciting but unreliable occupation. It nearly always means the withdrawal of the mother from whatever employment she had into the most conventional of all occupations, housewifery. It tends to impose regular hours on the household. Living accommodations are selected on the basis of their being appropriate to children. Neighborhood selection takes into primary consideration the availability and social appropriateness of playmates for the little members of the family, rather than quaintness or convenience for parents. Being in the right school district is a consideration which only the childless take lightly. In turn, each of these steps toward conventionality imposes further encouragement to live the conventional life which is so conducive to marital stability. In this way, parenthood produces conventionality which leads to marital stability.

PRESSURES FOR PARENTHOOD AND THE VOLUNTARILY CHILDLESS

Most married couples have children because they do not see the alternative as a viable option. There are few role models for childless marriages; children obviously cannot look to their parents for such models, and the mass media are oriented towards parenthood. The proportion of childless marriages has been steadily decreasing since the 1940s, partly because of improved control of venereal disease and partly because of a decrease in voluntarily childless couples (Veevers, 1971). Voluntary childlessness is rare; Veevers (1973) estimates that 1 wife in 10 never has children, but only about half of these is voluntarily childless. In the 1965 National Fertility Study sample, of the married women aged 40 to 44, only 1 white woman in 20 had never had a child, but childlessness among comparable blacks was more than twice as common. Couples who do decide not to have children, and couples who postpone having children, face pressures for parenthood from relatives and friends. Societal pressures to have children are powerful and pervasive, as Schulz (1972) aptly describes.

> If you should decide to suggest openly that you do not want to have children when you marry, or if you are married and do not yet have children, you will know what subtle means can be utilized to bring pressure to bear upon your waywardness. Mothers who wish to become grandmothers, neighbors who lack the capacity for conversation about anything but children, friends who feel that something must be wrong with you—the general assumptions of all that a couple must have children in order to be normal—are but a part of the informal pro-natalist policy. Tax structures favoring children by providing exemptions are but a part of the formal policies (Schulz, 1972: 371).

Who advocates parenthood, and who are the voluntarily childless? Maxwell and Montgomery (1969) found that 55 percent of 96 married women, aged 21 to 84, felt that a married couple should begin having children within the first 2 years of married life, while 35 percent favored delayed parenthood. Women who encouraged early childbearing were older (married 15 years or more), were lower class rather than middle class, and had not completed high school. Lopata (n.d.) found that women with the least education tended to rank motherhood as a woman's most important role; the more educated the woman, the more likely she was to rank "wife" over "mother" as a woman's most important role. And Overholser (1973) reports that 5 out of 8 black wives in a national sample said their children took priority over their husbands; 50 percent of the white wives in the sample put husbands' needs before the children's. Gustavus and Henley (1971), who studied 72 childless couples applying for sterilization, described their sample as unlikely to have had a miscarriage or an abortion and likely to be living in a large metropolitan area, to be of high socioeconomic status, to have been married about 5 years, to be about 30 years old, and to say they have no religion.

Married couples who are parents pressure childless couples to have children, partly because the "presence of childless couples, and their flaunting of an alternative life style, threatens the parent's conviction that the children are 'worth it all' . . . If one is married and has children, a situation which apparently is permanent, then it is comforting to believe either that these states are inevitable, or that if one had a choice, one made the right choice to maximize one's happiness" (Veevers, 1972: 586, 587).

There are few studies of the voluntarily childless. An exploratory study by Veevers (1973), of 52 wives married at least 5 years who had deliberately avoided having children, suggests that women who decide not to have children have had past experiences that make them see childlessness as a viable option. For example, some of the women in Veevers' sample were oldest children in large families and had been responsible for the care of their younger siblings. Having experienced the constraints of child care in their own childhoods, these women may have been predisposed to think of the advantages of childless marriages. Other reasons for remaining childless, given by the 72 couples studied by Gustavus and Henley (1971), are concern over population growth, health problems, career interests, being too old to have children, and simply disliking children.

The Impact of the First Child

Whether or not children influence the marital adjustment of their parents, their impact on the marital relationship is profound. A large part of this effect can be traced to the fact that the birth of the first child tremendously complicates the wife's role, demanding far more time and emotional energy from her than from the husband, whose role, in comparison, remains relatively unchanged. Although the modern middle-class father participates in the rearing of his children far more than lower-class husbands, his fatherhood is essentially peripheral to his life organization. As they become mothers, women tend to become engulfed in the motherhood role because it is so demanding of the self. Even during pregnancy, women describe themselves as preoccupied with their new role. As the foetus matures, it comes physically between the parents, makes their love-making awkward, and reduces their interest in sexual relations with one another.

The changes which occur in the marital relationship at the birth of the first child are seriously disorganizing enough to be described by some parents as a real crisis in the lives of the young couple (Dyer, 1963; Le

Masters, 1957). In studying a sample of parents and their reactions to the birth of the first child, LeMasters summarizes the parents' responses:

> The mothers reported the following feelings or experiences in adjusting to the first child: loss of sleep (especially during the early months); chronic "tiredness" or exhaustion; extensive confinement to the home and resulting curtailment of their social contacts, giving up the satisfactions and the income of outside employment; additional washing and ironing; guilt at not being a "better" mother; the long hours and seven days (and nights) a week necessary in caring for an infant; decline in their housekeeping standards; and worry over their appearance (increased weight after pregnancy, et cetera). The fathers echoed most of the above adjustments but also added a few of their own: decline in sexual response of wife; economic pressure resulting from the wife's retirement plus additional expenditures necessary for child; interference with social life, worry about a second pregnancy in the near future; and general disenchantment with the parental role (LeMasters, 1957: 354).

With the birth of the first child, the amount of time the wife must spend in housework doubles, and the amount of time she spends in conversation with her husband is cut in half. Even when there is time, it is difficult for husband and wife to carry on an adult conversation when there are little children in the room. As the child becomes a social being, after about one year of age, he resents the attention which parents pay to each other which cuts him out. Toddlers are famous for screaming or upsetting milk when their parents are in conversation at the meal table and for pulling on one parent or trying to jam themselves between parents during a goodby kiss. The intimate give-and-take of communication which helps to maintain the special feelings spouses have for each other may have to be limited to the time after the children are in bed, and by that time the young mother may be folded up on the couch asleep. Having their love-making interrupted by an infant squawl is an experience few young couples greet with enthusiasm. Husband and wife may come to think of themselves as parents first and husband and wife to one another only secondarily. One woman (without children) cynically describes the relationship of wife to husband:

> She becomes so much the mother that she may one day find herself treating that tweedy, commuting chap who was once her husband and lover as just another one of the brood—another runny nose to wipe, another mouth to pop a vitamin pill into, another finicky appetite to cater to—an overgrown and petulant child. He even calls her "mom." She calls him "dad," and that sums up their relationship. "No, you may not have another Martini before dinner," she will say in exactly the same tone in which she would forbid the six-year-old another slice of chocolate cake (Greene, 1963: 10).

Feldman (1971) found that married couples with a small child reported a significantly lower level of marital satisfaction than childless couples, even when the length of the marriage was controlled. Couples who reported *increased* marital satisfaction after the birth of their first child tended to have less companionate marriages, talked to each other less frequently, and had a more rigid and conventional divison of labor before the birth than the couples who reported decreased marital satisfaction. The impact of the first child seems to be no greater than that of subsequent children. The birth of a child, whether it was the couple's first or fifth, caused "lowered satisfaction in marriage, perceived negative personality change in both partners, less satisfaction with home, more instrumental conversation, more child-centered concern and more warmth towards the child, and a lowering of sexual satisfaction after childbirth" (Feldman, 1971: 121).

Other researchers have studied the "crisis" of parenthood and failed to find many couples who define the birth of the first child as a serious crisis (Hobbs, 1968). In later studies, *parenthood emerges as a mildly stressful transition, weathered without serious difficulty by most new parents.* Perhaps later cohorts or parents are more prepared to cope with parenthood realistically than parents in previous decades. Or perhaps they are less willing to admit to the occurrence of a "crisis."

INTERRUPTION OF THE SEXUAL RELATIONSHIP

The effect of the new child on the sexual relationship of his parents is symbolic of the general effect of his presence on the marriage, since the sexual relationship is symbolic of the privacy and intimacy of the married couple. Before the birth of the child, sexual interest of the couple in one another wanes as the mother's distended abdomen makes her more and more awkward and intercourse more difficult. Although any detailed marriage manual contains explanations and diagrams of special positions for facilitating intercourse during late pregnancy, many couples find them distasteful or peculiar. Few men know ahead of time that contemporary medical practice recommends discontinuance of coitus from six to eight weeks before expected delivery. To this is added another six to eight weeks of abstinence after the birth until the tissues of the woman's genital area have returned to their usual shape and size, any delivery damage is healed, and there is no longer danger of postpartum infection. Altogether this constitutes about three months' discontinuance of the sexual relationship for husband and wife. This may well be the longest period of sexual abstinence for the husband since he became sexually active at or before adolescence, and some husbands experience considerable sexual frustration during this period. Women do not seem to be as frustrated by this period of sexual abstinence, and pregnant wives may find it difficult to understand their husbands' problem. Many couples, of course, find individual ways to continue sexual relations without intercourse during this period. Imagination and an open mind can usually deal with the problem.

After the birth of the child and after postpartum abstinence, many husbands report they are disappointed with the decline in their wives' sexual responsiveness. Disruption of old routines and the wife's assumption of new and sometimes exhausting duties is likely to distract the wife from the interest in sex she had before childbirth, even if the previous relationship was satisfactory. Wives who found sex uninteresting, boring, or distasteful before parenthood may be even less interested after motherhood.

The presence of small children in the home restricts the erotic play of spouses to times when the children are not around, which usually means to bedtime. A few couples report that this stifles the spontaneity of their lovemaking, but most couples come to limit their sexual activities to bedtime without the assistance of children. Most couples return to the sexual patterns they had established before the birth of the child within a few months and are none the less adjusted for the experience. However, during the transition period, the sexual relationship, or absence of it, may be trying for new parents.

THE JEALOUS HUSBAND

Since it is primarily the wife who has a new focal role with the advent of the child, and since this inevitably means less attention to and less involvement with her husband, many husbands react to the new situation with a feeling of being cut out of things—a feeling of being neglected by their wives. In fact, this is almost exactly what does happen and is not a distortion on the part of husbands. The needs of the new baby *do* come first, and husbands must often be left to their own devices, have their interesting stories interrupted, their meals delayed, and the wife's affection shared with what amounts to a new rival. Where the husband-wife relationship before parenthood was satisfying, the wife will probably be motivated to minimize the husband's feeling of abandonment. In couples with poor preparental adjustment, the wife can use the new motherhood role as a primary source of emotional gratification, thereby reducing her dependence on an unsatisfying relationship. In working-class couples, the husband's loss of intimacy with his wife at this period is likely to be more marked and may represent an end to the primacy of the marital relationship over the parental relationship.

CASE

I like to plan ahead. Dan likes to act impulsively. For thirteen years I followed his impulses. I wasn't working, and we had no children. I could devote all my thoughts to pleasing him. I wanted a baby from the first, but he wasn't interested in having a family. At last I talked him around.

From the day of Peter's birth, Dan showed he wasn't fond of our son. He was selfish, unreasonable. He took the position a baby could be introduced into a home without fuss, without bother, without change. I had much less time to spend with him, but he wanted more of my time. His sexual demands increased, although my interest in sex was diminished both by fatigue and by his indifference to our child.

During those days, his drinking became intolerable. He'd got drunk before, but in a less objectionable way. Busy as I was with Peter, I noticed he was throwing all control to the winds. I begged him to stop drinking. Several times he went on the wagon. Invariably he fell off. Once he made a public scene because I took Peter with us on a two-day automobile trip instead of leaving him with my aunt. Dan has always wanted to leave Peter behind, while I have wanted to take him along (Popenoe and Disney, 1960: 217–218).

THE EFFECT OF PROBLEMS IN CHILDREARING ON THE MARRIAGE

Disagreement over childrearing is a common problem of parents. There is no consensus in the United States on how children should be reared, and young couples contemplating marriage infrequently discuss childrearing. At that point in their relationship, the discovery of fundamental differences with respect to the philosophy of childrearing would probably not be a deterrent to marriage for most couples in love. It has been widely assumed that problems between spouses over childrearing have a detrimental effect on the husband-wife relationship. This rests on the general idea that all problems of family life become interrelated, and problems in one area stir up problems in other areas. Although clinical literature emphasizes the interrelatedness of problems, empirical studies attempting to show this interrelationship have been wanting. In a survey of 448 normal families from all parts of the United States, the relationships between twenty-five different family problems were studied. Five different and *independent* problem areas were determined, consisting of problems related to: childrearing, husband-wife relationships, style of life (socioeconomic status), community activity, and religion (Brimm et al., 1961). This contradicts the clinical assumption that interpersonal problems in marital and parental roles are closely related *in normal families,* although they may be in highly disturbed families. Most couples, it appears, are able to keep problems in different phases of family life distinct, so that *problems of childrearing remain unrelated to problems in husband-wife relationships.* Perhaps this is the best explanation of the inability of researchers to find a consistent relationship between the presence of children and the *marital* adjustment of the couple.

ROLE SPECIALIZATION

While the preparental period of marriage is likely to be one of shared roles and shared activities for the young couple, parenthood means a sharp increase in role differentiation and role specialization. At least for a few years, most wives give up outside employment and economic contribution to the family and move into the full-time role of housewife. This means the wife has become much more dependent on her husband than before, and her dependence on him is reflected in a fairly distinct shift in the power relationship from one of shared responsibility to husband dominance (Blood and Wolfe, 1960). This is only the usual pattern of the relationship between the wife's employment and her influence in the decision-making process.

Shared activities give way to role specialization. Where husband and wife did the dishes together before the birth of the child, now the wife may do the dishes while the husband watches the baby. *The reduction in shared activities is part of the long-term disengagement process which most marriages undergo but which is apparently accelerated by the birth of children.* It is likely to mean that where husband and wife went out together to do things, now the husband goes out but the wife stays home to tend the children. Although working-class wives thrive on this pattern, well-educated women may not find it satisfying. At any rate, separate spheres of activities become the rule. Requests for indulgences from the children are likely to be met by the father with "go ask your mother." Spouses increasingly make decisions in their special spheres without consulting one another. This is not a particularly cozy or companionable arrangement, but it is more efficient. The young couple without children can afford the luxury of little role specialization. However, the pressures of parenthood require of most people the elimination of inefficient methods, and the specialization of tasks is a more efficient way of running a family as a going concern. Most people react with disappointment to this loss of intimacy, but it is apparently one of the facts of married life with children, and couples learn to make their peace with it.

With the arrival of children, then, there is a fundamental shift in the focus of family behavior from a husband-wife relationship to a parental relationship. Yet, the engaged couple hardly gives a thought to this parental function which in a few years may come to dominate their interaction with one another. Many couples will philosophically accept the change; others will find it a major source of frustration and disillusionment. Parenthood is apparently romanticized far more than marriage itself. Those couples who accept the transformation of the relationship learn to substitute the pleasures of childrearing for the lost intimacy of the marriage. Those who find the transformation disturbing may wish to consider what can be done to minimize it. The romantic couple contemplating marriage can rarely contemplate such a future change with equanimity. For these people, it is appropriate that ways be discussed in which the impact of parenthood on the marital relationship can be minimized.

CONTROLLING THE IMPACT OF PARENTHOOD

A number of different suggestions have been made for young couples to follow if they wish to keep the intimacy of early marriage after parenthood. Unfortunately, for most of these suggestions, little evidence is available which indicates their effectiveness. Bearing in mind the nonempirical base of the discussion, what courses of action might the couple consider?

1. Wait for a few years before the first child? If parenthood represents a crisis, then many writers recommend that the young couple postpone parenthood until they have made the early marital adjustment and cemented their relationship. In an earlier chapter, the inaccuracy of considering only the first year or so of marriage as the adjustment period has already been commented upon. Of course, for one marriage in four this recommendation is beside the point, since their first pregnancy occurred before marriage. For the remainder, what are the advantages of waiting for the first child? The advantages lie outside the marital relationship itself and in the area of economic stability of the family. Most couples start marriage with limited financial resources. After a recent study of the relationship between child-spacing patterns and family economic position, Freedman and Coombs reach the following view:

> Those who have their children very quickly after marriage find themselves under great economic pressure, particularly if they marry at an early age. Opportunities for education or decisions involving present sacrifices for future gains, are difficult. They are less able than others to accumulate the goods and assets regarded as desirable by young couples in our society. They are more likely than others to become discouraged at an early point and to lose interest more quickly than others in the competition for economic success (Freedman and Coombs, 1966).

It is only indirectly that these economic consequences affect the marriage relationship through the higher marital satisfaction and marital stability associated with increasing income.

2. Avoid having children? Perhaps the couple might avoid having children altogether and thereby save the primacy of the marital relationship. The previously quoted studies on the presence of children and marital adjustment do not give any unqualified encouragement to this step. The Detroit study by Blood and Wolfe (1960) gives the best information differentiating the childless from those with children. This study included a large sample of couples with children but only about fifty without children and with marriage duration similar to those with children. The researchers reported that childless couples had a more democratic power structure than those with children but otherwise did not have consistently less role specialization. The childless wives were not more satisfied with their husbands'

love or understanding and did not share their troubles with their husbands more frequently than the mothers did. The overall marital satisfaction of the childless women was actually lower than for those with children. No information was obtained from husbands. (It would be interesting to know if they would show the same response.) At least half the childless couples are probably voluntarily childless. Not wanting to have children has been found in other studies to be associated with unhappiness, while involuntarily childless couples show high adjustment (Burgess and Cottrell, 1939). In the study by Blood and Wolfe, the childless couples regularly showed more companionship than those with children.

On the basis of the information available, it cannot be said that a couple will retain the intimacy of early marriage by avoiding parenthood. Parenthood apparently only accelerates and gives a demarcation line for a process which is inherent in the marital relationship whether or not there are children.

3. Emphasize importance of the father role? If fathers feel jealous of the wife-deprivation that parenthood entails, their increased participation in infant care and childrearing might offer some control over this feeling by substituting for it a more important father role. This would have the additional effect of minimizing role specialization. Apparently just this sort of process occurs in many middle-class families, at least with the birth of the first child. In the early months, many middle-class fathers change diapers, baby-sit, and generally take advantage of being a father. This participation is usually shortlived and is replaced by a minimum father role in the pre-school period. In lower-class families, child care is defined as unmasculine (as it is by some middle-class males who are insecure in their own masculinity), and here the participation of the father is largely absent from the beginning. However, as a device for minimizing the problems of transition to parenthood, the father's help may not only make him feel more a part of what is going on, but by relieving the pressure on his wife make her a more interesting and energetic companion in whatever time is left over for husband-wife intimacy. The couple's feeling of participation in a joint enterprise should prove to be beneficial for most marriages.

4. Create time for husband-wife interaction? Parenthood is so demanding, especially for the wife, that unless the couple takes special pains to prevent it, it can engulf the marriage. However, many couples have found that they can *create* time and opportunity to be husband and wife. Child care is a twenty-four-hour proposition. It is true that babies sleep more than adults. (Many couples who have heard they sleep twenty hours a day are in for some surprises.) However, even when they are asleep, someone must be there. As they become older they sleep less and less and cut more and more into the time left over for the spouses. The middle-class answer to the question of how to have time for the marriage is the modern institution of

the baby-sitter. Sitters cost money, which is something new parents often do not have in abundance. It is simply a matter of allocating financial resources to meet the most important needs. For most couples in modest circumstances, this means the necessity of diverting money from other things into baby-sitting. Most couples find they can buy an evening out together for a few dollars, a whole Saturday for ten dollars, and a weekend for twenty. On the other hand, this may mean foregoing a new car, television set, or wall-to-wall carpeting in the living room. Some couples prefer the furnishings; others find that an investment in shared leisure and time for intimacy is necessary for the survival of their marriages. Most middle-class couples discover that private times together away from the children add zest to their marriage and make them appreciate their children more.

Parents who have children of, say, five years of age and over can demand time to themselves on occasion. Some couples set aside a half-hour or so after the husband returns from work for relaxing and sharing the day's events together. Children are often very possessive and may resent not being allowed to intrude, but they can be taught to respect the parents' right to conversation, especially when there are also times for their participation. It is not unhealthy for a child to know that his parents' relationship to each other is important to them.

CASE

My parents have been married for twenty-two years and have managed to set aside a time when they can be alone each day and talk over the events that happened to each other and their mutual problems. For as long as I can remember, when my father came home from work, usually around 5:30 in the evening, he and my mother would sit in the kitchen while she was preparing dinner. My father would usually mix cocktails and they would sit around the kitchen table talking. My sisters and I were told to "get lost" for that hour or forty-five minutes before dinner. While younger, I think we resented not being included in the conversations and visiting with Daddy when he came home, but now I realize that my parents needed this intimacy together to strengthen their interpersonal relationship, and to sustain the sentiment of love that thrives on interaction.

5. Know what you are in for ahead of time? One of the best ways to minimize the shock of any experience is to have accurate foreknowledge of what it will involve. Americans have presumably romanticized parenthood with some notion that this encourages childbearing. There is no self-evident need, however, to encourage most couples toward parenthood. A realistic preparation for parenthood is not likely to constitute discouragement of parenthood. It is difficult for the instructor to demonstrate in the educational situation the impact of several little children on a twenty-four-hour schedule. The baby-sitting that most adolescent girls do is so sporadic and brief, and their responsibilities are so limited, that its impact in reproducing

reality is evidently minor. Perhaps it is an unavoidable time of crisis—part of the maturation process of the young. Marriage is a transition to new roles and responsibilities, but under modern American conditions, the adjustment to marriage is not as great as the adjustment to parenthood which, for most people, is the last big step toward adult responsibility.

The problems of parenthood have been dealt with at great length to the exclusion of its joys and subtle satisfactions. However, the emphasis of the culture adequately presents the bright side. Many a young couple has stood arm-in-arm beside the crib of their sleeping child and felt an emotional bond toward one another which the childless do not experience. Still, most of the rewards of parenthood are rewards to the individual parent and are not especially a contribution to their relationship to one another.

The Rewards of Parenthood

The individual rewards of parenthood are what lead people to have children and, having had one, to have another and another. To present a balanced picture, the satisfactions of parenthood should be examined. They are not always the same satisfactions as those which parents mention when asked.

PROJECTION

Just as children identify with their parents and in some way live the lives of their parents, parents identify with their children and have the opportunity to live vicariously through them. In this amplification of life, the parent can relive the satisfying experiences of childhood. The other side of this coin is that he will also relive the humiliations, defeats, and frustrations of childhood. The adult who has resolved the childhood problems of his own life will be content to encourage the development of the child's own direction, while the parent with unresolved childhood conflicts will be tempted to influence the life of his child for the gratification through projection of his own childhood desires. The man who was an unmanly little boy may push his own boy to anxiety in the achievement of masculinity; the woman who was an unpopular adolescent may distort her daughter's social life in a frantic effort to be popular through her identification with her daughter.

POWER AND CONTROL

Many otherwise submissive people find themselves dominant in a social relationship for the first time with their own children. At last, there is someone who imitates them and does what they say. Most people find this very satisfying, even if the relationship is with a two-year-old. To be important to someone else is to have an increased sense of self-importance. Parenthood gives most people a sense of self-worth. These rewards are available to even the permissive parent. The problem is that children are not without their own power, and they do not always respond submissively. Parents who depend on this reward are also those who are most upset by the obstinate, defiant behavior which is characteristic of children of certain ages. In addition, the control over one's children is shared with other children, teachers, and the community in such a way that the control of others often leads the child against the parent.

COMPLETION OF EXPECTED PATTERNS

A more subtle satisfaction from parenthood, but one which is frequently overlooked, is the fact that it fulfills a person's general expectations of life. Most adult Americans grew up in families, but even those who did not have a picture of adult life as taking place in a family situation. As a child one learns that people grow up and have children, the children, in turn, have children, and so on for generations. When one reaches adulthood, he also expects to have children, not especially for any particular gratification but just because "people do." A life cycle without parenthood is for most people an uncompleted life cycle. When adults do not have children it just does not "seem right," and it is assumed that they must be unhappy in their childlessness, even though this is often not the case. Adult women with children have something to talk about with other mothers their age. Those without children may feel left out of the conversation which focuses on the rearing of children probably more often than any other single subject.

How much is left in middle-class society of the traditional association of fatherhood with virility is not known. The distribution of symbols of masculinity (cigars) by the "proud" father at the birth of a child and the special satisfaction which some men find when that child is male suggest that a vestige of the association remains. How voluntary childlessness is interpreted with regard to the self-concept is unexplored, but middle-class culture defines it as evidence of selfishness. Friends and neighbors expect young couples to have children, and parents usually relish becoming grandparents. It is surprising how many people one can make happy simply by having children.

In general, people who have children find them rewarding, and if they had it to do over they would have them again. This is the ultimate endorsement of parenthood.

Summary: Effect of Children on the Marriage

Because the evidence is, in part, conflicting, one cannot conclude that the presence of children makes marriages either happier or less happy. Nor can the idea any longer be accepted that children hold marriages together which would otherwise end in divorce. The fact that these two propositions are still widely believed in American society indicates something of the extent to which children, childbirth, and childrearing are romanticized among Americans. Couples are so ill-informed on the nature of babies and children and so ill-prepared for their impact on the marriage relationship that they often experience a crisis with the arrival of the first child. The child transforms marital interaction, interferes with marital intimacy, and complicates life far beyond what misty-eyed parents-to-be expect. Most couples experience considerable disenchantment with parenthood during their early months of experience. It is unfair to say that the children cause the disengagement of their parents, for this process apparently occurs in childless couples as well. However, parenthood marks an acceleration of disengagement and may usurp the central place in the interpersonal relationships of the spouses that the marriage occupied before the birth of a child. Parents who wish to maintain the primacy of their marriage will usually have to deliberately organize their lives to achieve it.

Most middle-class Americans derive real pleasure from their children. They enjoy playing with them, going places with them, instructing them, and just being with them. To most people, their own children are intrinsically satisfying. The frustrations of childrearing and the impact of children on the marriage still leave most parents with a positive balance of gratification from parenthood. In an earlier chapter, it was concluded that although the satisfaction derived from the marital relationship over time declines, the general life satisfactions of married people do not. Other relationships and responsibilities become more important sources of gratification as the marital relationship provides less. Parenthood is one of these alternate sources.

Implications for Individual Decision-Making

A person from another culture might well find the discussion above somewhat incomprehensible, for it is predicated on the value that marriage is the most important relationship in life and that children ought not be allowed to interfere with it. The reader might reply that the marriage is the basis for family organization in the United States and that the reason for marrying is the cultivation of the husband-wife relationship which will, after all, probably be there long after the children have departed—especially in these days when early marriage and births completed by the mid-twenties are common for many couples. All this is quite true, of course. The fact remains that in many societies the parent-child relationship is far more important than the husband-wife bond, both for the emotional gratification of individuals and for the structural stability of the family. One should not lose sight of the fact that for many people in American society, childrearing and parenthood are more important than marriage as sources of gratification and a sense of self-worth. This is more often true for women and especially working-class women. If husbands grow dull and sex becomes tedious, the children continue to need a mother and will absorb as much of her time and emotional energy as she is willing to let them have.

Other couples will find parenthood essentially unsatisfying and, without neglecting their children, will minimize their emotional investment and identification with their parental role. This does not mean that they will not love their children or that their children will suffer from taking second place to their parents' marriage or even their jobs (see Chapter 14). Children do not come into the world with a conception of what family life is but acquire their expectations in the context of the family they have. Such families may produce a different kind of child, but there is no evidence that they produce less healthy or wise children.

Most couples will choose the middle road. They will have children and enjoy them. They will derive considerable sense of self-worth from their identification with the parental role. They will get satisfaction from being needed and being looked up to. However, they will sometimes be wistful about the relationship they enjoyed before having children and will find ways to maintain the emotional significance of the husband-wife relationship. It can be done, but the initiative will more likely than not have to come from the husband.

Effect of the Qualities of the Marriage on the Children

In many people's minds, the effect of the marital relationship on the adjustment of the children is a more important social issue than the effect of children on the marital relationship. Divorce and poor marital adjustment on the part of parents are widely believed to affect unfavorably the social adjustment of the children. A sizable amount of empirical data has been amassed on the subject showing the effect of marital adjustment of parents on the lives of their children to be far more complicated than most of the usual explanations indicate.

MARITAL ADJUSTMENT AND THE DESIRE FOR CHILDREN

Poor adjustment of a couple to their marriage usually reduces their wish to have children. This is shown in the large number of divorces of couples who have no children. In the Burgess-Cottrell study, couples with good adjustment and no children generally desired children. Other studies have found a similar relationship between good marital adjustment and desire for children (Locke, 1951). This finding is probably a product of the tendency of many respondents to give consistently conventional responses.

ADJUSTMENT OF THE PARENTS AND ADJUSTMENT OF THE CHILDREN

There has been a good deal of interest among students of child development in the effect of good marital adjustment of the parents on the adjustment of their children. It certainly seems plausible that the two should be related.

Three different studies on this subject are available, and their results are not entirely consistent. The first two studies assessed the child's adjustment and the marital adjustment of the parents independently. Stroup (1956) explored the relationship between the personality adjustment of preadolescent children and the marital adjustment of their *mothers*. He was able to find no relationship. The adjustment of the children of the mothers of the poorest marriages was no different from those of the mothers in the best marriages. Another group of researchers tested the marital adjustment of *fathers* and the personality adjustment of their fifth-grade children and again found no relationship (Burchinal et al., 1957). None of the researchers was entirely satisfied with his results. The third study did not measure the parents' adjustment directly but had the children rate their parents' marriages. Whether there is any relationship between the marital adjustment of parents and their children's perception of this adjustment is a matter which has not been thoroughly explored. This last study is not directly comparable to the other two on another count: While the first two used elementary-aged children, the last studied adolescent children. Considering for the time being only those from *unbroken* homes, those adolescents who rated their parents' marriages as happy showed far better general psychological adjustment than those who rated their parents' marriages as unhappy (Nye, 1957).

There are two ways of reconciling these studies. At this time, which of the two is the correct way is not known. First, marital adjustment of parents may only affect the personality adjustment of children after adolescence. Second, the personality adjustment of adolescents as well as younger children may be unaffected by their parents' marriage adjustment, but other factors which disturb children's personalities may cause them to *perceive* their parents' marriages as unhappy, even though there is really no relationship. In the first explanation, it might be conjectured that it is only after adolescence that the social perceptions of children are subtle enough to penetrate the relationship of their parents in such a way as to affect their own adjustment. In any case, *we cannot now be sure what the relationship is between the marital adjustment of parents and the personality adjustment of their children.* (See Chapter 18 for the effects of divorce on the personality adjustment of children.)

Two other findings of the Nye study are of interest. First, the results showed that parents' marital adjustment was not related to school performance. This should come as a surprise to many high school teachers and counselors who generally concede that the children in families where there is marital conflict are more likely to have trouble in their school work. This is probably evidence of the biasing effect of clinical observations. It might be expected that those students from unhappy homes who are having trouble with school work are most likely to turn up at the teacher's or counselor's desk with their problem, while those from unhappy homes who are doing well in school do not bring their home problem to the attention of school authorities. In this way, the impression is created that children whose parents are having trouble with one another do poorly in school (Nye, 1957). The second finding is that the students who rate their parents' marriages as unhappy report that they have engaged in more frequent or more serious acts of delinquency than those from happy homes (as measured by the Nye-Short Delinquency Scale), although they do not have more delinquent companions. In view of the fact that the students rated their own parents, it is too soon to conclude that children from more maladjusted marriages are more delinquent. It may only be that the psychologically maladjusted delinquent reports more negative relationships of the people around him because he perceives the world more negatively. There is evidence for this suggestion. Novak and van de Veen (1970) compared emotionally disturbed adolescents and their "normal" siblings and found that the disturbed adolescents' concepts of their real and ideal families were much farther apart then the real and ideal families described by their siblings.

MARITAL ADJUSTMENT OF PARENTS AND PARENT-CHILD RELATIONS

To what extent does the marital adjustment of the parents affect the relationship between them and their children? Although a previous study cited found no relationship between the occurrence of childrearing problems and marital problems in a family (Brim et al., 1961), the relations between children and parents have been shown to be more strained in the poorly adjusted marriages. Porter (1955) found that those couples with happy marriages accepted their children more than those with unhappy marriages. Wallin (again relying on children's reports of parental happiness in marriage) found that the more unhappy a person rated his parents' marriage, the greater conflict he reported between himself and each parent.

Dielman, Cattell, and Rhoades (1972) found that fathers who were dissatisfied with their home lives had children who were "thick skinned" and tough minded, and that fathers who combined dissatisfaction with life at home and strictness of discipline had extroverted, emotionally unstable, and apprehensive children. McIntire and Payne (1971) found the school achievement of third- and fourth-grade boys was significantly related to fathers' behavior and adjustment at home, and was not related to mothers' adjustment. In happy parental marriages, the children report high attachment to both parents, while in unhappy marriages, both male and female children report a greater attachment to the mother. This is an easily understandable finding. When the marriage is unhappy, the children, who generally are with their mothers far more than they are with their fathers, are led to "side" with the mother and become alienated from their fathers (Wallin, 1954). The Nye study cited above confirms the finding that parent-child relations are less amicable where children report unhappy parent marriages (Nye, 1957).

MARITAL ADJUSTMENT OF PARENTS AND THEIR CHILDREN'S MARRIAGES

If children come from unhappy marriages, does it sour them on marriage? Yes and no. Men are generally more favorably disposed toward marriage the more happy they perceive their parents' marriages to be. For women, the picture is more complicated. Those women who see their parents' marriages as very happy have highly favorable attitudes toward marriage. Those who see their parents as moderately happy have less favorable attitudes, but women whose parents are seen as unhappily married have attitudes as favorable as those whose parents were very happy. The researcher who reported these findings gives the tentative explanation that the women from unhappy parental marriages are more highly motivated to reject the image of marriage given to them by their parents and are determined to have a better marriage themselves (Wallin, 1954).

What about the actual marriage experience of the children? Is it affected by their parents' marital adjustment? Almost without exception, the marital-adjustment studies say "yes." It has become one of the most thoroughly accepted tenets of marital-prediction analysis that children of unhappy marriages are poor marital risks themselves. In the short marital-adjustment test included in Chapter 11, the item "degree of happiness of your parents' marriage" is given the highest weight of any item on the test. In spite of the unanimity of results, it is not at all clear just *why* it should be true. Do the children learn marital roles from their parents which are conducive to marriage failure? Remember that girls apparently learn their sex roles in detail from their mothers (at least before adolescence), but that the boys' sex roles are not clearly affected by specifics of their fathers' role. Furthermore, it might be expected that the way a person rears his children is likely to be similar to the way he was reared, because he participated with his parents in a parent-child role-set and presumably learned a parent role in order to know the appropriate ways to behave as a child; but he did not play a *spousal* role in his parental home, so there is no theoretical basis for assuming that he would carry the spousal roles of his parents into his own marriage.

It may be that the adjustment of the child's marriage is not affected by the parental marriage relationship directly at all but is affected through the acquisition of personality traits through his parents—traits which lead to poor marriages independent of the pattern of marital interaction of the parents. Fisher and Mendell have described patterns of the transmission of neuroses from one generation through the next and even the third generation in a family (Fisher and Mendell, 1956). Presumably other, nonneurotic traits prognostic of poor marriages would be similarly transmitted. Of course, all the relationships reported between parental marriages and the marriages of their children are dependent on the children's reports of their parents, which are of unknown validity. Nevertheless, for whatever reason, it must be presumed that *the child from an unhappy marriage has a poorer than average chance of a happy marriage himself.*

Summary: The Effects of the Quality of the Marriage on the Children

One of the first signs of the quality of the marriage is whether it produces children at all. Couples with marriages that are not working out do not want to have children or continue having them. It is not clear whether poorly adjusted marriages produce poorly adjusted children. The children of poor marriages appear to score higher in delinquency but do about as well in school as those from happier marriages. Children from happy marriages get along better with their parents, are more attached to both parents, and are more accepted by their parents. In unhappy marriages, the father is the parent most likely to be alienated from the children. The children from happy families generally take a more positive view of marriage, but women from unhappy parental marriages seem determined not to repeat the experience of the parents. In spite of this, those who see their parents' marriages as unhappy are almost universally conceded by family researchers to have the least chance for marital success.

Implications for Individual Decision-Making

Most married couples want children, and most will produce children. Although marriage is rarely undertaken with children as the major motivating force by young people in the United States, it is a responsibility which most take seriously enough when it comes. Children introduce into the marriage a responsibility to make the marriage work well which transcends the personal gratification of the parents, for with the arrival of children, many other people have a stake in the success of the marriage. "Good" marriages produce healthy children who are an asset rather than a detriment to the community and who go on to have "good" marriages and healthy children themselves. It is this widening circle of responsibility with parenthood which has led most sociologists and anthropologists to see the function of the social control of marriage as a license to bear and rear children rather than primarily a license to sexual relationship. The broadening social inplications of parenthood give the community the right to restrict marriage to those who look like good parental risks, although the restrictions are often based on the wrong criteria. Those couples who try to cement their crumbling marital relationship by having children are not only fooling themselves but are compromising their children. For what more exploitive reason could childrearing be undertaken? Evidently, most couples are aware of this on some level of consciousness. However, marital success is not a static quality determined at the beginning of marriage, and some marriages decay after the children are born. Marriages deteriorate in part because people let them deteriorate. To this extent, parents owe it to their children to repair their own marriages. It will be shown in Chapter 18 that if a marriage cannot be made satisfactory to the parents, however, it is better for the children for it to be broken than held uncomfortably intact "for their sake." Not enough is known about marriage to enable every failing marriage to be repaired. The children from these marriages will probably be the worse for this.

Perhaps American values put too high a premium on personal happiness. Perhaps the children from unhappy marriages are not all blessed with marital happiness themselves. The focus may be too narrow: Can it be determined that their lives are not just as productive, just as worthwhile, and just as satisfying in other ways?

18

Divorce and Remarriage

The divorce rate in the United States seems to be of considerable concern. For a generation, Americans have been told that their family system is disintegrating, as evidenced by the fact that so many marriages are breaking up. Since it is widely believed that the strength of American society is built upon the stability of individual marriages, it is not surprising that some people have become alarmed. Governors have held conferences on the problem, clergymen and lawmakers have recommended new legislation. Newspapers report that at certain times and places there were as many divorce filings as marriage license applications. Serial marriages and publicized divorces of celebrities help give the impression that the institution of marriage is crumbling. Serious writers are maintaining that the soaring divorce rate is evidence that the institution of marriage is no longer suited to modern society, and are leading the search for alternatives.

Very few young couples marry with the expectation that they will take recourse to divorce if their marriage does not work out. In one group of couples questioned while waiting in line for marriage licenses, the idea that divorce was a possible escape in the event of unhappiness had evidently not even occurred to four out of five. They seemed to have "a kind of infantile confidence in the ability of mere communication to guarantee a successful marriage" (Hillsdale, 1962). It is one of the happy features of courtship that it gives the couple confidence that all problems are soluble.

A Cross-Cultural Perspective on Divorce and Marital Stability

Practically all societies make some arrangement for divorce. In one study of a sample of forty different societies, Murdock (1950) found only the Incas had

Table 18-1

GROUNDS FOR DIVORCE VARY WIDELY AMONG SOCIETIES
Grounds for Divorce in Forty Societies

	Permitted			
	Definitely		Inferentially	
Reasons	To Man	To Wife	To Man	To Wife
Any grounds, even trivial	9	6	5	6
Incompatibility, without more specific grounds	17	17	10	10
Common adultery or infidelity	19	11	8	12
Repeated or exaggerated infidelity	27	23	8	10
Childlessness or sterility	12	4	15	18
Sexual impotence or unwillingness	9	12	24	21
Laziness, non-support, economic incapacity	23	22	11	9
Quarrelsome or nagging	20	7	7	12
Mistreatment or cruelty	7	25	19	9

Reprinted by permission from George P. Murdock, "Family Stability in Non-European Cultures," The Annals of the American Academy, 272 (1950), pp. 195–201.

no provision for dissolving marriages. In all the rest, he reported, not one required a couple to remain married where there were reasons that most Americans would consider really important for breaking up. In some societies, divorce is relatively rare, but in approximately half the groups he examined, Murdock reported that "permanent separations appear substantially to exceed the present (1949) rate in the United States throughout the lifetime of the individual." Occasional groups are described in which permanent union is unusual. Observers have reported that only about one Navaho in four lives with the same spouse throughout life, and it is common for a man to have half a dozen wives in succession. In one Eskimo tribe, women are sometimes married and divorced two or three times a year (Stephens, 1963: 234–235). According to Murdock,

> In one of the societies of the sample—the Crow Indians—public opinion, instead of exerting its usual stabilizing influence, actually tends to undermine the marital relationship. Divorce is exceedingly frequent, and a man subjects himself to ridicule if he lives too long with one woman. Rivalrous military societies make a sport of stealing wives from one another, and any husband feels ashamed to take back a wife thus abducted from him, however much against her will and his own (Murdock, 1950: 198).

Grounds for divorce vary widely, depending on the nature of the marital relationship in each society, from no reason or trivial whims to the most strict and serious reasons. Table 18-1 gives the acceptable grounds for divorce in the forty societies sampled by Murdock. In modern nations, divorce rates have varied widely over time and from one nation to another.

Chart 18-1

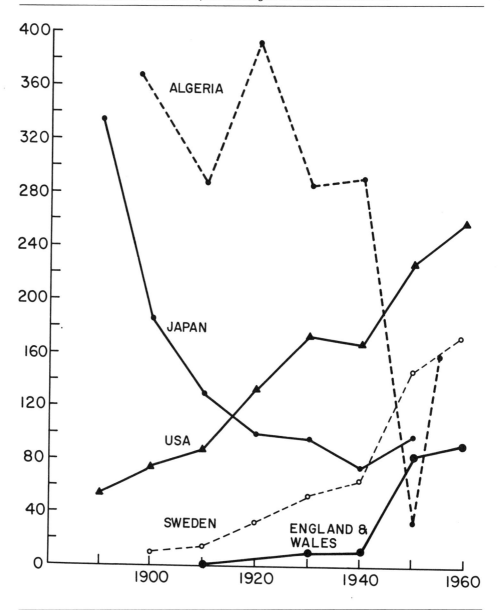

DIVORCE RATES VARY WIDELY BY NATION AND TIME PERIOD
Divorce Rates Per 1,000 Marriages for Selected Countries

ALGERIA

JAPAN

USA

SWEDEN

ENGLAND &
WALES

Source: Goode, 1963

Chart 18-2

DIVORCE RATES HAVE DOUBLED IN THE LAST DECADE
Divorce Rates Per 1,000 Married Women, United States, 1920–1973

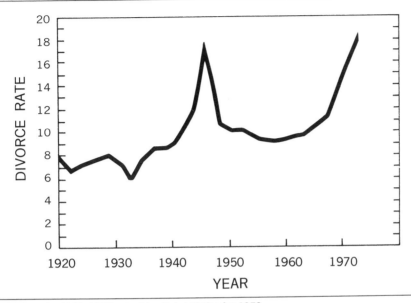

Source: Plateris, 1969, 1973, monthly vital statistics for 1973

Chart 18-1 gives rates for selected periods in a few countries for comparison. From Chart 18-1, it is clear that the United States has the highest divorce rate of the Western nations, though other modern nations at other times have had far higher rates.

Divorce Rates in the United States

American divorce rates look high because Americans have recently emerged from a period of *very low* incidence of divorce. Chart 18-2 shows the trend of divorces for the past fifty years in this country. After relative stability between 1954 and 1963, the rate increased sharply after 1963, doubling in a decade.

What percentage of people marrying will eventually get divorces? What percentage of marriages end in divorce? These are the kinds of questions that people want answered, but they cannot be answered in such form. It can be determined how many marriages were contracted for each divorce granted in any one year, but this figure changes rapidly in response to changes in economic circumstances, marriage rates, age distribution, and other factors. Alternatively, the number of divorces during a year for each 1,000 persons or for each 1,000 existing marriages can be given. In 1956, for example, there were 259 divorces granted for every 1,000 marriages performed. If that rate continued for a half-century, one might say that about 1 marriage in 4 was ending in divorce. The actual proportion of *first* marriages ending in divorce would be closer to 1 in 5. Of course, the rates do not stay constant. On the other hand, if one asks how many of all the people married in a certain year will get divorced, the question can be answered only for years far enough in the past that all who married in that year are now dead. In addition, one can find the percentage of marriages contracted in any particular year which have survived a given number of years. For instance, of all first marriages contracted in the state of Iowa during the years 1953 to 1959, 97 percent survived the first year, 92 percent survived the first 4 years, and about 88 percent survived the first 7 years, according to estimates prepared by Burchinal and Chancellor (1962). Glick and Norton (1973) predicted that "between 1 in 4 and 1 in 3 women around 30 years old today are likely to experience divorce during their lifetime." For women younger than 30, latest divorce rates make 1 in 3 look like the reasonable estimate.

One can learn a great deal about American marriage by examining who gets divorced and who does not. It has been observed that in countries where attitudes and laws concerning divorce are very restrictive, only the well-to-do have enough influence and money to divorce. Where laws and opinion are more liberal, the highest divorce rates are among the less privileged groups (Goode, 1963). This is because of the many difficulties posed by the lower-class environment for successful married life. In the United States, divorce rates are highest in the unskilled, low-income, poorly-educated classes, with progressively more stable marriages in the higher-status groups. Burchinal and Chancellor's Iowa data show divorce rates for low-status husbands which are five times those for high-status husbands. This may be taken as fairly typical. Recent experience in providing federally subsidized legal services for the poor suggests that divorces would be even more common among the poor if they could afford it. These experimental services were set up in 1966 to help protect the poor from exploitation by unscrupulous landlords and merchants. But in the early days of the program, 84 percent of the cases involved divorce actions. Many people who had wanted divorces for years, but who could not afford them, filed suits when the services were free. It is interesting to note that Britain had an almost identical experience with government-subsidized legal services in 1950 (New York *Times,* 1966).

Among religious groups, Roman Catholics have lower divorce rates than non-Catholics, but Monahan and Kephart (1954) were surprised at the sizable proportion of divorces among Catholics in Philadelphia. On the other

Chart 18-3

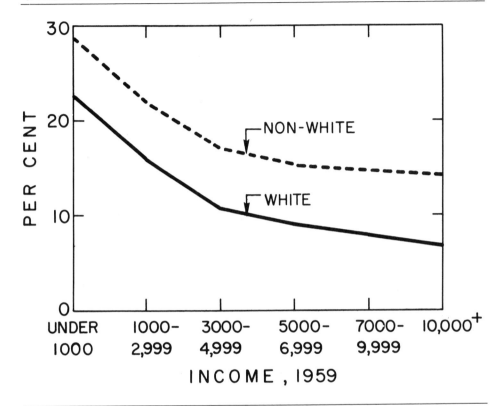

BLACKS HAVE HIGHER MARITAL INSTABILITY THAN
WHITES WITH THE SAME INCOME
*Percent of Ever-married Males 25–34 Years of Age Who Were Separated, Divorced,
or Had Been Married More than Once at the Time of the 1960 Census, by Income and Race*

Source: Udry, 1967

hand, they found that Catholics appear in desertion cases far out of proportion to their relative number in the population. Other studies cited elsewhere in the text show direct relationships between divorce rates and youthful marriage, absence of religious affiliation, marriages in which the bride is already pregnant, marriages in which the couple goes to another state to be married (Kephart and Strohm, 1952), and a host of other socially identifiable factors.

BLACK-WHITE DIFFERENCES IN MARITAL INSTABILITY

Black Americans experience much higher divorce and marital disruption rates than white Americans. The reasons for this difference are highly controversial and explanations of the difference proved to be politically explosive during the 1960s. It was formerly thought that the differences were attributable to the fact that most blacks were poor, and it was a well-established fact that poor people had higher divorce rates than the rest of the population. Data available from the 1960 census definitively eliminated this explanation. Chart 18-3 shows that at every income level, more blacks than whites have experienced marital disruption (divorce or separation). Although disruption rates decline for both races with increasing income, the racial difference is much greater among high-income than among low-income persons (Udry, 1967). Much the same pattern of differences holds between blacks and whites equated for education or occupation (Udry, 1966). A 1967 survey by the Bureau of the Census confirms the black-white difference. When blacks and whites who entered marriage twenty years or more ago are equated for age at first marriage, in every age-at-marriage category black divorce rates are at least twice those of whites (Glick and Norton, 1971). Interested readers may wish to sample the bibliography of this and other chapters in search of explanations.

Unhappiness and Divorce

Only the unmarried need to be told that whether or not a couple divorces has to do only in part with whether or not they are unhappy. The willingness of one or both partners to tolerate a given level of unhappiness is a function of many different factors, some of which are understood. Given the same level of unhappiness, low-income couples will stay married when high-income couples divorce — partly because divorce costs money and it is sometimes too expensive to terminate a marriage. However, there is perhaps a more important reason for the differential. In lower-class groups, marriage plays a smaller part in the satisfactions expected from it relative to other facets of life, whereas in middle-class groups, the marital relationship is viewed as a major source of life's satisfactions. If a high-status marriage is unsatisfactory, it leaves a bigger hole in the lives of those concerned than if a lower-status marriage is unsatisfying. Persons who marry young are less likely to tolerate an unhappy marriage than those who marry at later ages. Perhaps those who marry late do not expect much from marriage and for that reason are not in a hurry to get into it. When they are unhappy, it does not surprise them. Or, perhaps if those who marry late divorce, their chances for getting a good second marriage are less than for those who are younger. Those who are religiously devout are more likely to tolerate an unhappy marriage than those who have little religious interest (Landis, 1963). No doubt this is because religious beliefs usually make divorce a moral issue, and one's religious duty is to tolerate an unhappy marriage because the permanence of the marriage is a more important value than the happiness of the partners.

Chart 18-4

MOST DIVORCES INVOLVE CHILDREN

Percent of Divorces Involving Children, and Mean Number of Children per Divorce Decree, 1952–1969

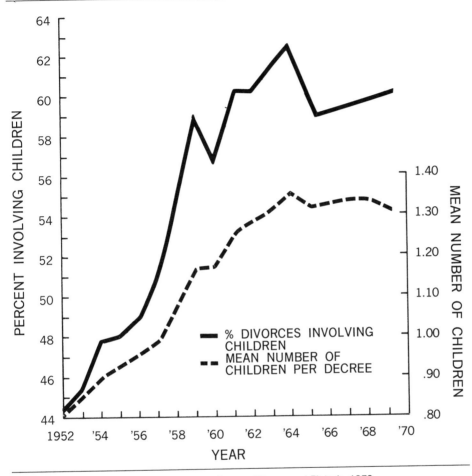

Source: Children of Divorced Couples: U. S. Selected Years; and Plateris, 1973

Looked at from a secular point of view, the decision whether or not to end an unhappy marriage will usually be resolved around the question, What are the alternatives to the marriage? If public opinion will not be too oppressive, if economic conditions look favorable, if single life by comparison seems attractive, or if the likelihood of a good replacement marriage seems high, and if divorce is not a moral issue, then marital frustration tolerance will be low, and people will dissolve marriages often (providing legal complications are not too great). The Soviet Union has demonstrated that the level of the divorce rate can be radically altered simply by manipulating legal requirements. It should be pointed out that none of these conditions has anything to do with making marriages more or less happy *per se,* but only affects the willingness of married persons to tolerate unsatisfactory marriages.

Divorce and Children

The strongest arguments made against divorce are usually in behalf of the children of divorced parents. It has been widely argued that children are damaged by divorce and that the children of divorced parents are more delinquent, more emotionally maladjusted, and generally less well off than children of intact marriages. This has led to the common remark that parents who are unhappily married ought to stay together "for the sake of the children." Chart 18-4 suggests that Americans with children are increasingly willing to divorce. A number of studies confirm that when children from broken homes are compared with children from unbroken homes, the ones from the unbroken homes score better in emotional adjustment and relationships with parents (Bowerman and Irish, 1962; Koch, 1961; Russell, 1957). However, these comparisons are quite misleading. To get a fair comparison, it would be necessary to make sure that the marriages did not differ in the two groups in other ways than in their being broken. When Burchinal (1964) investigated the effect of divorce on school relationships and adjustment characteristics of adolescents, controlling social-class differences in the two groups, he found no support for the detrimental effect of divorce on the children. The adolescents from divorced families were none the worse off when compared with their classmates from intact families.

The crucial comparison of a group of children from broken homes with those from unbroken *but unhappy* homes was made by Nye (1957). In this study, the children from broken homes fared better every time, whether the home was broken by divorce or not. The adolescents from broken homes showed *less* psychosomatic illness, *less* delinquent behavior, and *better* adjustment to parents than the adolescents from intact but unhappy homes. This and a later study (Perry and Pfuhl, 1963) showed no difference in the adjustment of children whether they were in one-parent homes or reconstituted homes with a stepparent. The effects of divorce and subsequent father absence on daughters seem to appear at adolescence. In a study of adolescent daughters of divorced, widowed, and married mothers, Hetherington (1972) found that both father-absent groups of daughters had difficulty relating to males; girls whose mothers were divorced were aggressively open and physically demonstrative with men while daughters of widowed mothers

Chart 18-5

DIVORCE RATES FOR COUPLES WITH AND WITHOUT MINOR CHILDREN

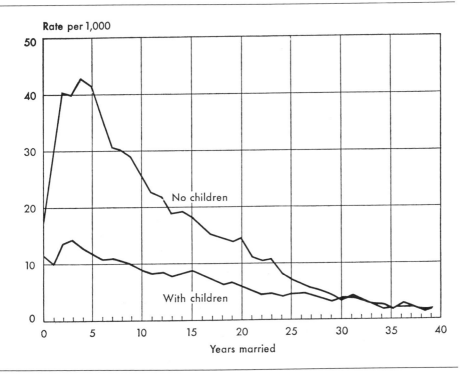

Source: Jacobson, 1959, p. 134, reprinted by permission.

tended to avoid contacts with men. Earlier studies had shown that the children of divorced parents were more likely themselves to be divorced (Locke, 1951) or at least less happy. The latest studies confirm the early findings for women, but contradict them for men. Bumpass and Sweet (1972) showed that women whose parents' marriage was broken by divorce were at a definitely increased risk of marital disruption themselves, but that this was not true for those whose parents' marriage was broken by a death.

A recent study based on a national representative sample of American *men* comes to a different conclusion for men. It showed that "the experience of growing up in an intact family does not increase the probability that a man will be found living with his wife in adulthood" (Duncan, 1969). However, this study did conclude that growing up in an intact family increases a man's chance of holding a high-status occupation. "Men raised in intact families not only have superior job qualifications, but also translate their educational attainment into occupational achievement more efficiently . . ." This finding should not be interpreted as implying a lack of concern about the educational achievement of their sons on the part of husbandless mothers. Evidence suggests that these mothers are even more concerned about their son's educational progress than mothers with husbands, but because of their predicament are unable to make their concern effective (Kriesburg, 1967).

We conclude that *children from happy marriages are better adjusted than children from divorced marriages, but those of divorced parents are better adjusted than those of parents whose marriages are intact but unhappy.* These studies ought to lay to rest the idea that divorce *per se* is bad for children in any way. Rather, they tend to show in general that parents who "stick it out," thinking they are doing their children a favor, are doing the worst thing for their children. If they cannot succeed in their marriage, apparently the best thing they can do is to break it up and try again.

In view of the widespread notion that parents ought to stay together when they have children, it is not surprising that sociologists have found that most divorces are given to couples without children. In fact, it is widely believed among laymen that the presence of children in a family acts to "hold families together." Chart 18-5 shows the rates of divorce for couples with and without minor children at various durations of marriage for 1948, the only year for which data are available. This graph confirms the common belief, at least for the early years of marriage. For the later years, when couples who have stayed together in spite of an unhappy marriage might be expected to be breaking up (therefore raising the "no children" line in Chart 18-5 for those marriages of twenty years' or more duration), the line continues to go down, suggesting that not many parents are simply waiting for their children to mature to dissolve the marriage. When corrections are made for other differences between the childless and those with children, the divorce rate for the childless is probably not more than one-and-a-half times as great as that for those with children. Even this difference should not be taken as evidence that children hold marriages together. Jacobson writes

> . . . the presence of children is not necessarily a deterrent to divorce. It is likely that both divorce and childlessness result from more fundamental factors in the marital relationship. Moreover, while children may hold some marriages together, in others pregnancy itself and the additional strains involved may disintegrate rather than cement the marriage (Jacobson, 1959: 135).

Couples whose marriages are falling apart are not likely to continue to have children. Most marriages which break up are in difficulty for some years before the actual divorce, and this period is likely to be one in which the couple will not deliberately conceive children. Because of these factors, not many sociologists today believe that children tend to prevent divorce, and no one would recommend them as a divorce preventive. It is hard to imagine a more cruel trick to play on a child than to conceive him as an attempt to prop up a failing marriage. It is not only a cruel trick; it does not work.

Remarriages

There is no question that with the increase in incidence of divorce has come an increased tolerance of divorce as a nonmoral issue. Further, divorced persons encounter little difficulty in finding another mate. In fact, divorced persons are more likely to remarry within any given period than either single or widowed persons of the same age. At age twenty-five, for example, divorcees have 99 chances in 100 of remarriage, while single women of the same age have only about 88 chances in 100 of marriage (Jacobson 1959: 82). This offers conclusive evidence that divorced persons are rarely soured on marriage as such but only on *that* marriage. Divorced men and women are generally eager to remarry. Men divorced in their twenties are usually married within less than two years, while women divorced in their twenties are remarried in three years or less (Jacobson, 1959: 87). Those women with children are almost as likely to remarry and do so as quickly as those who are childless at divorce.

HOW SUCCESSFUL ARE REMARRIAGES?

If one could tell those who are contemplating divorce that they would almost certainly not do better in a second marriage, this might be a convincing argument for staying in an unpleasant marriage for all except those who would find single life a welcome alternative. Most persons have already heard it said that second marriages are more likely to end in divorce than first marriages. A number of studies have been done on the subject, all with consistent conclusions: *first marriages are most stable, a marriage in which one partner is remarrying is less stable, while a marriage in which both have previous marriages is least stable and perhaps twice as likely to end in divorce as the average of all first marriages* (Monahan, 1952). (But Vallot [1970], in a more recent study of remarriages in Paris, found that divorce rate among remarriages was highest when one of the partners had previously been divorced but was low when both partners had previously been divorced.) However, these studies are prejudicial against remarriage because they do not offer the right comparison. People who are divorced are predominantly from lower-middle- and lower-class groups which have higher divorce rates generally. When the divorce rate of remarriages is compared to the divorce rate of first marriages in the same part of the class structure, the difference is not striking. Furthermore, those who are divorced differ from those married more in their willingness to divorce than in the unhappiness of the first marriage. That is, those who remarry after divorce constitute a group of people who have already demonstrated that they will end a marriage which is unsatisfactory. By this fact alone, it should be very surprising if more second than first marriages did not end in divorce.

When the marital satisfaction of those who are remarried is compared with that of those married once, findings are different for blacks and whites. Renne (1971) found that remarried black women under forty-five are more likely to be satisfied with their marriages than black women who have been married only once. Remarried white women under forty-five are more likely to be *dissatisfied* with their marriages than white women who married only once. The really important question, however, is how do remarried people compare their second marriages to their first? They could hardly maintain that their second marriages are better than first marriages in general. However, do they think their second marriages are an improvement over the first? Overwhelmingly. Bernard's (1956) study of remarried couples found that the majority were rated as successful marriages by friends and acquaintances. Goode (1956) asked the divorced women in his study to compare their second marriages to their first. Ninety-two percent said that their second marriages were better or much better than their first. It is not known to what extent men are this pleased with their second wives. There is some indication that divorced men are poorer marriage risks than divorced women (Locke, 1951; Locke and Klausner, 1948). Perhaps if they were interviewed concerning second marriages, they would be less enthusiastic.

There are many factors which contribute to the satisfaction which people find in second marriages after divorce. The divorced person has probably learned something about marriage from his first failure. If age contributes anything to maturity, he should be able to make a more mature choice the second time. The significance of sex is transformed, since it can be more taken for granted in the approach to second marriage. Second marriages have the advantage of being compared with a marriage which recently ended in bitterness and conflict. The second time around, the first-time loser has probably readjusted his expectations of marriage and is simply easier to please than those without previous marital experience.

The following case history is typical of the experience of many who fail at their first marriage through a combination of circumstance and interpersonal conflict, but who profit from the experience and make second marriages which are satisfying.

CASE

Both the husband and the wife of the first marriage were from about the same type of background. He was from a well-to-do family with two older brothers who were much more forceful and much brighter than he. He was good looking but weak looking. She was not pretty but stunning, extremely popular with men and much sought after. They married when he was about twenty-one or twenty-two and she about a year older. He had had two years at college and probably flunked out. She had had a year of finishing school. She was much brighter than he and much more forceful. He was considered a good catch because he came from a wealthy family. They had two children. The early years of their married life were just one constant financial struggle, because they were part of a social set whose plane of living was beyond what they could afford. In addition, there was serious illness which was expensive. They were constantly in debt. His family became disgusted with him.

She was the kind of person who . . . was always being called upon to help other people with their problems. Where her own were concerned, she fell down. There was always a good deal of bitter quarreling. She would flounce out of the house in disgust. . . . Yet he continued to seem enamored of her.

They finally moved in with her mother and father, which didn't help matters because both the mother and father had bad tempers and interfered with the children. But the financial strain was removed.

After almost twenty years of married life the war came along and her brother was called into the army. She took over his position in her father's business and made an enormous success—in fact, she made her father a rich man. . . . At about this time his father died and he received stock in their company which had always been successful and became more and more successful. But now she decided she wanted a divorce.

A peculiar circumstance now developed. She had always been a highly sexed woman. But over a period of years he had become as weak sexually as he had been in other ways. He never approached her sexually for months at a time. He proclaimed his love for her over and over again, but made no attempt to have any contact with her. In the meanwhile she was attractive to many men and he was jealous. . . .

He pleaded with her not to divorce him and sought out friends to plead with her. . . . His family said they did not blame her but asked her not to divorce him; he would go to pieces. But she persisted. . . . She obtained her divorce when she was about forty-two or forty-three. . . . He threatened suicide. . . . Because he was so unhappy . . . about the divorce, the family sent him to New York to take charge of the New York office. . . .

About a year after the divorce, . . . this man who had been about to commit suicide remarried. He married a woman entirely different from his first wife. She was a divorced woman with a married daughter, in fact a grandmother. She was strictly feminine, a clinging-vine type, the kind that curls up in his lap in public. She was the exact opposite of his first wife in almost every way. Where the first wife had been forceful, the second wife was yielding. She allowed him the initiative in everything. She built him up as a man. She did not show him up by her superiority. He was completely wrapped up in her.[1]

CHILDREN IN REMARRIAGES

Children offer a real complication in remarriages and in the courtship leading to them. Folklore has it that children never get along very well with their stepparents, and at least one sociological study has found the adjustment of

[1] Jessie Bernard, *Remarriage* (New York: Dryden Press, 1956), pp. 297-299. Reprinted by permission of Holt, Rinehart and Winston.

the stepchild to his parents to be more difficult and less harmonious than that of children in a "normal" home (Bowerman and Irish, 1962). Here again, the comparison must be made not to "normal" homes but to the previous marriage situation. Remarried mothers making this comparison almost always feel that their children are better off in the new family than in the old (Goode, 1956: 329), and personality and interview material from children in remarriages fails to reveal indications that the children are any worse off for the experience (Bernard, 1956: 318).

The "Causes" of Divorce

When the causes of divorce are discussed, the three different kinds of causes which are frequently involved in discussions of divorce should first be disentangled. When one asks what causes divorce, he may mean any one of the following:

1. What were the problems and motivations of particular couples who subsequently divorced, and how did these problems and motivations lead to the divorce?

2. What are the characteristics (social and personality factors) which are found in divorcing couples as compared to nondivorcing couples?

3. What are the factors in the society which produce a high divorce rate as compared to a low divorce rate?

The first two questions have been dealt with at a number of different places in the text. The third does not apply to individual couples but explains the nature of the "divorce problem" in the nation as a whole.

One of the most fundamental reasons for the high divorce rate of Americans is the fact that divorce is less socially stigmatized today than ever before. In the past hundred years, Americans have redefined the nature of marriage. An increasing proportion of the population defines marriage not as a religious institution ordained by supernatural sanction and therefore indissoluble, but as an arrangement of mutual gratification. Once this redefinition is made, it becomes impossible to marshall social pressure against divorce. Conditions are provided which allow couples to see divorce as a natural solution for marital difficulty. There are an indefinite number of ways to deal with the problem of an unhappy marriage: One can grin and bear it, or he can relegate the marriage to an insignificant corner of his life and find his satisfactions from life in other activities. He or she can take a mistress or lover and retain the marriage intact. A woman can bury herself in motherhood and domestic chores. A man can look for an occupational routine which will remove him from the scene of the marriage for as much time as possible. Husbands and wives can legally separate but not divorce. However, prevailing cultural expectations of marriage among Americans today encourage the couple in trouble to see divorce as a possible solution. When marriage is viewed as the most important source of personal satisfaction, and when this view is held by lawyers, judges, clergymen, and most married people, it is not going to make much difference what the "legal" grounds for divorce are. Those involved in the divorce process will find a way to facilitate it, and couples in trouble can be expected to seek divorce if their problems seem insoluble. The more people that are divorced, the more divorce becomes acceptable as a solution to marital unhappiness. Actually, the fact that as many marriages escape divorce as do is surprising in view of the high expectations of emotional gratification which Americans place on one long-term relationship.

Evaluation of the Magnitude of the "Divorce Problem"

Divorce is always a problem for the couple seeking it. When divorce is spoken of as a social problem, the suggestion is that it is in some way detrimental to the society as a whole. The divorce picture in America has caused many people to talk of the disintegration of the family. It is said that the stability of the family is basic to the American way of life and that family disintegration is the prelude to the collapse of American civilization. Divorce is said to cause juvenile delinquency, to raise taxes for the support of children and wives from broken homes, even to fill prisons and mental institutions with the children from these divorces. These are alarmist views which find little support from the social scientist.

Although divorce occurs frequently in American society, there is no serious reason to believe that Americans, on the whole, divorce frivolously. Divorce represents something of a crisis for most couples and is not undertaken lightly. High divorce rates do not indicate that marriage is no longer considered important by Americans. Rather, it indicates that marriage has become so important a source of emotional satisfaction that few people can endure a relationship which does not provide this. If only one out of three first marriages ends in divorce, Americans are either phenomenally successful at marriage or phenomenally tolerant of poor marriages. The latter conclusion seems the more likely. It has been noted that upper-class marriages are very stable and that upper-middle-class persons are more willing to resort to divorce than lower status persons, given an unhappy marriage. Yet, a study of upper middle-class marriages concluded that among middle-aged couples in this class, there are very few really deeply satisfying marriages (Cuber and Haroff, 1963). This certainly does not suggest that Americans, in general, resort to divorce casually.

Divorces are concentrated in the lower socioeconomic strata where rates are up to five times as high as in the upper strata, yet these lower strata persons resort to divorce less given an unhappy marriage than higher strata persons. The conditions of life in the lower strata of American population make stable, happy married life fairly rare. Yet the majority live with the same spouse until death. Of the first marriages ending in divorce, probably two-thirds of the partners go on to a second marriage which is their last. This leaves perhaps 10 percent of the population or less in the actual multiple-marriage category. This hardly augurs the collapse of the American marriage system; rather, it indicates its basic strength. The divorce safety valve for marriages under conflict almost certainly strengthens rather than weakens the family structure of the nation. Very few social scientists take the American divorce rate as an indication of pathology in the marital institution.

How high would the divorce rate have to go before one should worry about it? This is impossible to say flatly, because the decision would depend on remarriage rates and the general state of heterosexual relationships. Probably, divorce rates could be doubled or trebled within America's present social system without serious repercussions. It is not at all unreasonable to predict that a strong family system could be maintained in America's present general society even though *all* first marriages eventually ended in divorce, with remarriage the rule. Divorce does not "cause" juvenile delinquency; it does not disturb children as much as homes filled with conflict. It does not lead to general immorality or lack of respect for the marriage bond.

The matter of divorce, as all other issues in this text, has been approached from a functional, nonreligious point of view. From a religious point of view, all of the discussion is irrelevant. Most religious groups rest the purpose of marriage and the ground for its dissolution on a supernatural base. From this point of view, for example, Roman Catholics maintain that divorce is a sin because Roman Catholic doctrine defines indissoluble marriage as good in itself. Nothing which has been said above can contradict this. No social scientist can say that divorce is good or divorce is bad on moral or other grounds. He can say that divorce has this or that set of observable consequences. I do not believe it can be shown that the present divorce pattern has any destructive consequences for the society or for the family institution. It can be shown that it has generally happy consequences for those who find themselves in intolerable marriages.

What are the particular problems which lead couples to seek divorce? Chart 18-6 reports the marital complaints of 600 couples applying for divorce during the 1960s in Cleveland, Ohio. Husbands and wives evidently have very different complaints about their marriages. Levinger makes the following comparison of complaints from middle- and lower-class respondents:

Chart 18-6

DIVORCING HUSBANDS AND WIVES HAVE DIFFERENT COMPLAINTS
Marital Complaints of Couples Applying for Divorce

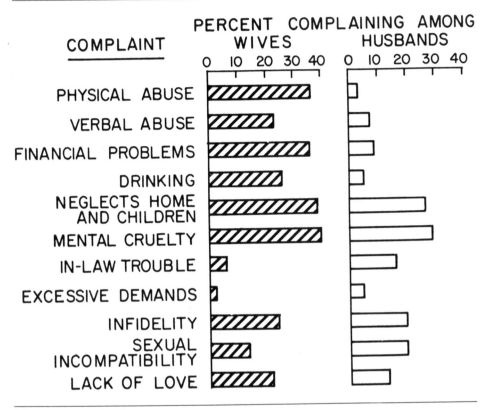

Source: Levinger, 1966

Middle-class wives were significantly more prone to complain about lack of love, infidelity, and excessive demands. Middle-class husbands paralleled the wives in their significantly greater concern with lack of love; on the other hand they were significantly less likely than lower-class husbands to complain of the wife's infidelity (Levinger, 1966).

Yet middle-class husbands complained more frequently than lower-class husbands about "sexual incompatibility."

These reasons are not listed as explanations of divorce. The problems of divorcing couples are not different from those of couples who do not divorce, they are only more intolerable to the persons concerned. It might be noted, however, that two difficulties which are common explanations for divorces—sexual incompatibility and religious conflict—have never been found to be frequent themes of major complaint in any study of divorced persons.

Divorce As an Unintended Outcome

In the ordinary course of a marriage, husbands and wives use many strategies in dealing with one another. Sometimes they are successful strategies in the sense of accomplishing their aims. In other marriages, the strategic play backfires with unintended consequences—consequences frequently not desired by either party. Divorce sometimes occurs to couples with otherwise sound relationships, who wake up one day and wonder how it happened. A strategic threat which does not succeed and must be carried out, a counter-move by the spouse, followed by a disruption of communication, and one mate or the other may find himself in a position where there seems to be no alternative to divorce (Bernard, 1964). It is for such situations involving marriages with no fundamental problem that courts of reconciliation, marriage counselors, "cooling-off periods," and interlocutory decrees may serve some function in salvaging the relationships.

Attitudes Toward Divorce

With one or two possible exceptions, no society has ever had a positive attitude toward divorce (Murdock, 1950). The extent of negative feeling has varied from attitudes verging on indifference to the strictest and most complete condemnation. In the United States, attitudes toward divorce have become more lenient on every front in the past century. Urbanites are more tolerant of divorce than rural residents, men are more tolerant than women, and those with more education are more tolerant than those with less (in contrast to the actual divorce record by education). The more religiously devout a person is and the more doctrinally strict his religious affiliation, the more he opposes divorce (Goode, 1963: 83).

American churches are quite diverse in their attitudes toward divorce. On the one hand, some churches seem indifferent to the issue, although none actually expresses favor with it. It is impossible to characterize the Protestant point of view because there are too many viewpoints, ranging from a liberal, psychological point of view to outright condemnation. The Roman Catholic position is quite clear:

> It is divorce itself, not the variety of divorce laws, which is the principal element in the rotting away process which is destroying the lines mooring

civilization to the family. A uniform divorce law for the nation will undoubtedly eliminate many of the legal entanglements resulting from the conflicting and varying laws of the different states, but a uniform divorce law will do nothing to save the disintegrating family unit. The knowledge that civil divorce may be obtained if the marriage should turn out unsatisfactorily, is one of the principal factors robbing the family of that security which God and Nature intended. . . . The only course which will save the "disintegrating family unit" is a return to the Christian concept of indissoluble marriage . . . (Ploscowe, 1955: 254-255).

Discussing the same matter of uniform divorce laws, a Rabbi presents his view:

A uniform divorce law for the entire nation is most desirable and a feasible solution of the problem. Such a law should be drafted with a sense of the realities of the situation with due regard to the frailties of human nature and the exigencies of modern society. Judaism, which has always maintained a realistic view with respect to divorce, would be in favor of a liberal divorce law, which would safeguard the security of the family, but would provide for the dissolution of an intolerable marriage . . . (Ploscowe, 1955: 255).

Protestant policies with respect to divorce have shown some tendency toward liberalization in the past three decades.

Protestant acceptance of the idea that divorce might be justifiable in particular cases did not mean a complacent attitude toward problems of the family. On the contrary, Protestant ministers during the 1940's and 1950's undertook much more seriously than ever before their responsibility to counsel couples before and after marriage. Believing that divorce was the result, rather than the cause, of wrecked marriage, they sought the aid of doctors, psychologists, and social workers in getting at the real sources of family friction. With much of this new emphasis the Roman Catholic Church could agree. Like their Protestant counterparts, Catholic priests became increasingly involved in organizing classes for young people planning to marry and in counseling with husbands and wives involved in family quarrels.[1]

Public opinion polls give some measure of popular attitude toward divorce. In the 1930s, Americans were asked, "Should divorce be easier to obtain in your state?" More than three out of four respondents thought not. In the 1940s, they were asked, "Do you think the divorce laws in this state are now too strict or not strict enough?" Only 9 percent said laws were too strict, while 35 percent said they were not strict enough, and 31 percent said the laws were about right (Goode, 1963: 84). Studies of the moral

[1] Nelson Manfred Blake, *The Road to Reno* (New York: Macmillan Company, 1962), pp. 229-232. Reprinted by permission.

attitudes of college students over four decades give a time perspective on the attitudes toward divorce of this select group. From the twenties to the late fifties, there was a gradual increase in the severity of judgment against divorce among college men and a more marked increase in severity among women. In spite of the increase in severity relative to other items of morality, the only "offenses" considered less serious by the latest generation of students were married persons using birth control devices, betting on horse races, girls' smoking, and killing in defense of one's own life. Nonvoting, living beyond one's means, and falsifying a child's age to secure a reduced fare were moral offenses of more import than divorce to these students (Rettig and Pasamanick, 1959).

In spite of the little actual censure of divorce today, divorce is embarrassing to the couple involved and to their friends. It indicates failure on someone's part, and no one wants to appear to have failed. Further, Americans do not really have any institutionalized ways of responding to divorce.

> Few of us know what to say to a friend or colleague who is obtaining a divorce or being divorced. The divorce situation is relatively unstructured; there are no standard ways of dealing with the occasion. This circumstance contrasts with the norms related to marriage or death. In the latter instances we are expected to congratulate the marital pair (although it is sometimes difficult to know how to act toward the parents in the reception line) or express our sympathy to the bereaved. But how should we act with our friend whose home and family are in the process of breaking up? Should we congratulate him or express sympathy? If we do either we may be hurting his feelings. Does the person in a divorce action feel both relief and sorrow? Do we really know what he is thinking and does he know his own feelings in the matter? What conception does he have of the attitude expected of him in this situation? (Nimkoff, 1963: 450).

The anomalous role of the divorcing person is one of the most important reasons for the prevalence of remarriage. Adult social life is built around husband-wife units. When a person leaves a husband-wife unit, he no longer fits into the prevailing pattern of adult life. It is the awkwardness of the situation rather than any disapproval of the status *per se* which causes friends and associates either to avoid former friends who have been divorced or to put subtle and not-so-subtle pressure on them to remarry.

The Legal Complexities of Divorce

Divorce laws are made by the individual states. They differ from state to state in an almost haphazard fashion. It has also come forcibly to the attention of some divorced couples in the past few years that divorces granted by some states and several foreign nations are not always considered valid in other states. This is true where the state granting the divorce is not conceded to have legal jurisdiction over the couple. This matter is so complex that it would require a chapter in itself to set forth an outline of the problem.

The most interesting feature of the legal divorce procedure is the direct contradiction between the actual divorce practice and the formal divorce codes. Nimkoff writes

> The existing legal codes respecting divorce hold, in brief, that an unhappy marriage may be terminated only if (1) the divorce is sought by one of the parties and opposed by the other; (2) the one who seeks the divorce is entirely without blame; and (3) the plaintiff has been offended by an act on the part of the defendant included in the limited list of allowable causes of divorce to be found in the statutes of the several states.
>
> The reality is very different. (1) In most cases, both members of the unhappy marriage contribute to the cause of their unhappiness. (2) The causes of marital unhappiness are not those which the law recognizes as allowable grounds for divorce. The actual causes are more numerous and more complex. . . .
>
> In actual practice those seeking a divorce usually adjust to the requirements of the divorce code as follows: (1) The couple agrees upon one of the allowable grounds on which to rest their case; if possible, one that will be least damaging to them psychologically and socially. . . . (2) The petition for divorce is presented by the wife, for practical and chivalrous reasons, and is not contested by the husband (Nimkoff, 1963: 457).

Over the years there has been a gradually greater proportion of divorces granted to wives. A century ago, 64 percent of divorces were granted to wives. Today it is over 70 percent (Jacobson, 1959: 121).

GROUNDS FOR DIVORCE

In almost all states, divorce is permitted on grounds of cruelty, desertion, adultery, and drunkenness, with about half the states granting divorce because of neglect to provide. The shift in the usual grounds for divorce over the past century is indicative of the change in legal interpretation and change in the marital relationship itself. Table 18-2 shows that in the 1860s, most divorces were granted for desertion and adultery, while by 1950 these had become minor grounds and more than half of all divorces were granted on the grounds of cruelty.

RECENT CHANGES IN DIVORCE LAWS

Many experts have pointed to the discrepancy between divorce law and actual divorce practice and to the differences in divorce laws among the states, suggesting that a uniform divorce law is needed for the United States which would take into consideration the actual reasons why people want to break up their marriages.

Table 18-2

CRUELTY AS A LEGAL GROUND FOR DIVORCE IS INCREASING
*Percent of Absolute Divorces and Annulments by Legal Ground,
United States, 1867–1950*

				Legal Ground			
Period	Cruelty	Desertion	Adultery	Drunken-ness	Neglect to Provide	Com-binations	All Others
1867–70	12.4	35.4	26.4	3.0	1.6	13.4	7.8
1935	44.4	26.1	6.9	1.9	3.3	6.6	10.8
1950	58.7	17.6	2.7	2.9	2.1	1.7	14.3

Source: Jacobson, 1959: 121

Most marriages are broken because husband and wife do not get along well together anymore. In most marriages, both are partly responsible for the failure of the marriage. It is particularly recommended that the "adversary" style of proceeding, in which there must be a guilty party and an innocent party to accuse him, be done away with. Instead, it is frequently suggested that divorce courts be run in conjunction with some kind of marital counseling service which would try to save the marriage, if at all possible, before the couple is permitted to divorce. Only if this failed would the divorce be granted, and strict "grounds" for divorce might then be dispensed with.

Increasing dissatisfaction with divorce laws in this country in recent years has resulted in a clear-cut trend away from the adversary procedure, and to the enactment of laws which are in keeping with contemporary sentiments about marriage and divorce. The most important changes are in the following directions:

1. Introduction of a period of separation without cohabitation as sufficient grounds for divorce in itself. More than twenty states now have such grounds, but in many of these the separation period is three to five years. North Carolina, Nevada, and the District of Columbia now require only one year of separation as sufficient grounds for divorce. In effect, such laws permit divorce by mutual agreement.

2. Introduction of general grounds for divorce, such as "irreconcilable differences," which in their effect abolish the necessity for specific grounds. California's new divorce law, effective in 1970, is a case in point. There are now only two grounds for divorce in California: (1) irreconcilable differences, which have caused the irremediable breakdown of the marriage, and (2) incurable insanity. If, from evidence at a hearing, the court finds that there are irreconcilable differences which have caused the irremediable breakdown of the marriage, it orders the dissolution of the marriage, or a legal separation, whichever the participants are seeking. During these proceedings, any testimony or evidence of specific acts of misconduct are improper and inadmissible, except of those cases where child custody must be determined

by the court, and evidence of serious misconduct on the part of a parent would be relevant (Civil Code of California, 1969).

No American state has yet reached the freedom to divorce by mutual consent, typified by new marriage and divorce laws in the Soviet Union, which became effective in 1968. Where there are children involved, the Soviet law reads very much like the California law: "A marriage is dissolved if the court ascertains that a couple's continued cohabitation and preservation of the family have become impossible." Where no children are involved it is simpler. "If spouses who have no minor children consent mutually to dissolution of the marriage, the marriage is dissolved by the agencies for registration of documents pertaining to civil status," and does not require any court action at all (*Soviet Press,* Oct. 16, 1968).

Another important characteristic of the new California divorce law (also appearing in the Soviet 1968 law and other recent American and European revisions) is that *either husband or wife* can be required to support the other, and either or both can be required to support their minor children, depending on the court's judgment. Support is no longer unilaterally required of the husband alone.

An Interpretive Review: What Holds Marriages Together

In order to get an overview of what causes marriages to break up, it is useful to ask, "what holds marriages together?" A valuable integration of research findings by Levinger (1965) and a similar integration by Nye, White and Frideres (1966) have conceptualized the problem in much the same way. Three components are distilled:

1. Positive rewards within the marriage.
2. Barriers to the disruption of the marriage.
3. Alternative sources of satisfaction in the case of disruption.

"Positive rewards within the marriage" is what we have generally meant when we talk about marital satisfaction. It comes from many sources: companionship, sexual satisfaction, mutual affection, childrearing, and other mutual need-meeting. But low marital adjustment does not necessarily mean divorce, nor high adjustment stability. It depends on the strength of the barriers against disruption. If everyone you know frowns on divorce as unforgivable, if legal restrictions are formidable, then many very unhappy couples will stay married. If legal restrictions are negligible, and if no one cares very much whether anyone else divorces, then disruption may be common, even in couples who are not terribly unhappy with their marriages, *if* there are attractive alternatives to the marriage. If a woman can easily support herself and her children without a husband, or if she is attractive enough to get another husband easily, and if other potential mates look more attractive and are available, or if society is organized so that unmarried life competes with married life as far as available satisfactions are concerned, then marital disruptions will be common, even when the present marriage is tolerable. Marital satisfaction can be seen as only one of three major determinants of marital stability. (The answer to "what holds marriages together" can be applied with equal cogency to any human relationship.)

Summary

Divorce rates in the United States have doubled in a decade. About three in ten first marriages end in divorce. Divorce rates are higher among non-Catholics than among Catholics, higher among blacks than whites, and higher among lower-class than middle-class people, even though middle-class couples are more prone to seek divorce from unhappy marriages. Children from divorced marriages are more poorly adjusted than children from intact happy marriages, but better adjusted than children from intact unhappy marriages. In spite of this, children of divorced parents do not have an elevated risk of divorce themselves. The presence of children is not a deterrent to divorce for contemporary American couples.

The trend in the divorce laws of the states is away from requiring specific grounds, away from determining guilt through adversary proceedings, and toward granting divorce to couples when their marriages have become intolerable. The newest divorce laws allow judges to assign obligations for support of children and ex-spouses to either husband or wife.

A high level of divorce is not a sign of decaying family structure in a society when most divorced persons remarry, but a sign of the emotional importance of marriage. Under these circumstances even much higher divorce rates are not necessarily a cause for grave concern.

Implications for Decision-Making

Of the persons exposed to this book, few will get divorces and fewer yet will be legally separated from their spouses. Those who are opposed to divorce on religious grounds will have no decisions to make about divorce in their marriages. For the others, a substantial number will have marriages which are to a greater or lesser degree, and for longer or shorter periods, unhappy. Divorce is one (perhaps, in some ways, the most difficult) solution to a problem marriage which they will consider. It is maintained by some divorce judges and counselors that nine out of ten marriages which apply for divorce can be saved. For the couple involved, the question will not usually be *can* the marriage be saved. *Any* marriage *can* be saved. Several alternatives to divorce have been listed in this chapter, most of which involve relegating the marriage to the background in one's life. For most couples, the question will be, is the marriage *worth* saving? The rational answer to this question lies in comparing the benefits and deficits derived from the marriage with the unpleasant experience of divorce and the available alternatives to the present marriage. Most divorced persons remarry, and educated, young divorced persons remarry most frequently of all. Furthermore, their remarriages are better than their first marriages in nearly every case. Their children will be better off if they divorce than if they try to endure a marriage which is full of conflict. With satisfactory custody arrangements, the children will probably be more satisfied with the new than the old arrangement. They will not become delinquents on account of their parents' divorce. The couple need not feel that they are contributing to the collapse of the American family system or to the demise of the American way of life. Evidence indicates people use divorce as a last resort, although they do not always know how many different alternatives they have. Couples who have tried everything else, including outside help, and who have been unsuccessful can consider divorce as a promising solution to their marital problems. How much they are willing to sacrifice to hold a marriage together depends on their hierarchy of values and what other things will be jeopardized by divorce. A presidential candidate may sacrifice his political future by divorcing at the wrong time. A professor of marriage education at a religious college may lose his position by disrupting his marriage. On the other hand, many a person has had to choose between breaking his marriage and jeopardizing his career. A hundred years ago, the society would have helped him make his choice: Marriage would have been defined as the obligation overriding all others. Today, the choice is likely to be made by the individual couple, and the society is not much help. For some people, careers are more important than marriages.

Given people's actual goals in life, marriages are not always reparable. Two people cannot always will themselves, or be manipulated by someone else, into a state of marital bliss or even of tolerance. How does one make an undemonstrative mate affectionate? How many who are bored by sex can be transformed into interesting sex partners? (It is easy to tell somone *else* that these things are not very important, after all.) Forever is a long time. A young couple at twenty has little way of foreseeing what life has in store for them. A bright, pretty, affectionate coed may make a wonderful wife for a college man, but ten years later they may have made one another's lives miserable and there may be nothing that can be done about it. Couples in the present generation will probably not be satisfied with the view that it is simply good to save marriages and bad to break them. They will more and more frequently ask, "What is worth saving about this marriage?"

19 *Marriage Counseling and Marriage Education*

Marriage Counseling

Marriage counseling, broadly defined, is any consultation of a person with anyone else about marriage. It is a very ancient activity found in every society. It will be fruitful to retain this broad definition of marriage counseling during the discussion in this chapter, differentiating between the persons who provide the consultation. Most marriage advice and consultation is provided by friends, relatives, and spouses. There is no precise information on the subject, but it seems reasonable to assume that almost everyone has talked to someone else about his marriage, either before or after the ceremony. Therefore, virtually all adults have experienced marriage counseling, and almost all have provided it. A survey of the mental health attitudes and practices of the nation found that only one person in eight had sought *professional* help for any kind of personal problem. Problems with the marriage or the mate were nearly three times as frequently the reason for seeking professional help as the next most frequent reason. If problems with children are included, family problems constituted the majority of all professional help-seeking (Gurin et al., 1960: 309). It is particularly interesting to note that the majority who do not seek professional counsel apparently do not experience less distress on the whole, nor do they avail themselves of informal social contacts for help any more frequently (Gurin et al., 1960: 380).

As the behavioral sciences have matured in the last quarter century, and as American society has become more psychiatrically oriented, the legitimacy of professional marriage advice has gradually been established. For centuries, the church has provided the basic source of professional help to married persons, perhaps more frequently to women than to men. Today the clergyman is still the major source of professional marital advice for

416

Chart 19-1

CLERGYMEN AND PHYSICIANS PROVIDE MOST OF THE MARITAL COUNSELING
Sources of Help Sought for Marital Problems

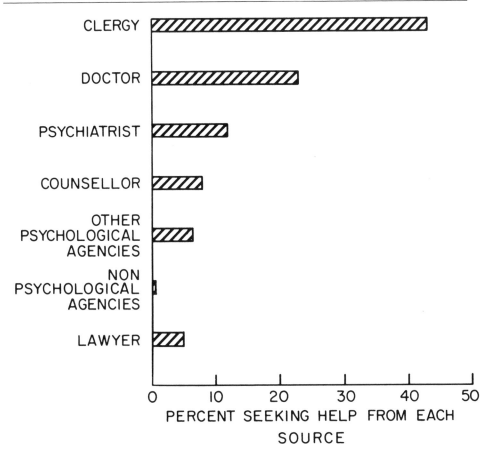

Source: Gurin, Veroff, and Feld, 1960

Americans. Chart 19-1 indicates the proportionate use of various types of professional assistance sought for marital problems (Gurin et al., 1960: 309).

Recent studies of the role which young clergymen perceive for themselves indicate that while the church of the past may have given primarily religious advice on marital problems, churches of today are increasingly likely to provide psychiatrically oriented counseling. In fact, the counseling role has begun to loom larger than the preaching role in the minds of a sizable proportion, perhaps the majority, of young clergy. The curricula of seminaries have come increasingly to emphasize pastoral counseling. Courses in marriage counseling, techniques of psychotherapy, Jungian analysis, and related subjects are commonplace. There is, of course, wide variation from one church group to another, but the counseling by most "progressive" churches is not likely to differ fundamentally in approach from that which would be received from a marriage counselor or clincal psychologist. Since the clergy is being called upon to provide the bulk of marital counseling, it is understandable that the churches have responded by providing the kind of secular professional training a secular society expects of its religious experts. Although it cannot be said that today most clergymen are psychologically trained marriage counselors, this development is probably not far in the future. The clergy is also becoming more involved in dispensing family planning information as part of marriage counseling. Where fewer than 20 percent of married seminary students report that the minister who married them gave helpful birth-control advice, 80 percent of these students plan to offer family planning information to couples they marry (Allen, 1969). How helpful the information they provide will be is uncertain; less than 40 percent of the seminarians felt that they were adequately trained in family planning counseling (Allen, 1969).

The second most common professional source of marriage counseling is from nonpsychiatric physicians. For years, physicians have provided the majority of marriage manuals on the market, and sexual advice has quite commonly been treated as a "medical aspect" of the marital relationship (Lantz and Snyder, 1962: 359–363). The role of the medical profession in fitting and prescribing contraceptives and dealing with problems of fertility and infertility has served to validate this claim. The physician's ability to alleviate his patients' sexual problems is impaired by his uncertain knowledge of human sexuality. Courses in human sexuality are now taught in many medical schools, but a study of one such program for second-year medical students showed that common misconceptions about sex were not changed by the course (Golden and Liston, 1972). Physicians have little formal training in the social and psychological aspects of marital relationships and therefore might be expected to emphasize the technical and anatomical aspects of marriage. However, this does not seem to interfere with their effectiveness as marriage counselors.

All other types of professionals taken together (psychiatrists, marriage counselors, lawyers, and other psychological and nonpsychological agencies) provide perhaps one-third of professional marriage-counseling services. These include *all* those professions specially trained to provide this kind of service. Put another way, only one or two adults in a hundred have ever consulted any professional other than a clergyman or physician concerning a marriage problem.

With the increasing specialization of the "helping professions," the past thirty years has witnessed the development of a professional group of specifically trained marriage counselors. The American Association of Marriage Counselors is their national organization. As with most professional groups, there is an attempt by this and related groups to set up special qualifications for performing the service, along with special programs in graduate schools to provide what is considered to be adequate professional training. Adequate professional training is credited as a doctoral degree and extensive supervised experience in counseling (Rutledge, 1957). Some graduate schools are already providing such training programs.

Who seeks professional help about marriage? Premarital counseling is likely to be sought primarily by "young, educated, open-minded and progressive persons who are highly motivated to make their marriage work and wish to do everything possible to that end" (Merrill, 1959: 374). This is also the same group which is most likely to seek help with problems that develop within the marriage. The less educated and the old are least likely to seek help, just as they are least likely to receive personal psychiatric attention when they become mental patients (Hollingshead and Redlich, 1958). Tyndall (1972) reports that, in England, white-collar workers are more likely than blue-collar workers to seek counseling after marriage. Wives twice as often as husbands first apply for counseling, and only 5 percent of all counseled couples apply together.

THE GOALS OF MARRIAGE COUNSELING

Marriage counseling differs from the process of medical treatment in that in medical treatment there is usually a clear understanding of how the organism should operate and a general social consensus that having it operate that way is desirable; in counseling (and psychotherapy) the proper organization of a personality or a marriage is not nearly so decided, and different parties to the counseling may have quite different value systems and goals. Whose goals are to be realized, whose values implemented in counseling? Most counselors would say "not the counselor's," but this is easier to say than to practice. Is the goal to be "saving" the marriage, that is, its permanence? Is it the happiness of both spouses or the happiness of the spouse who has sought counseling? Is the goal lack of conflict? Is the well-being of children paramount? Are there religious goals to be achieved? All of these are "healthy" objectives, but they may be mutually exclusive. The importance of the goals of the counselor can be seen beneath the surface of the following recommendation by a nationally known authority on marriage counseling:

> Divorce is not the best solution to most of the personality and relationship problems seen in marriage counseling. In most cases where the marriage will break up before the couple can rediscover meaningful potential together, the counselor should take an active stand that the marriage is worth saving. In some instances a couple should be kept together, in conflict, so as to involve them in individual therapy, even though the indications are that the marriage ultimately should be ended. In the occasional case where a careful marital

diagnosis conclusively indicates that a marriage should be ended, for a variety of reasons, the marriage counselor should support plans in this direction and, if needed, recommend and even urge divorce (Rutledge, 1963: 324).

Although the recommendation is couched in the language of a physician recommending an excision of an inflamed appendix, the personal values of the counselor guide the recommendations. A more orthodox position appears in a draft of a proposed code of ethics for the American Association of Marriage Counselors and gives the counselor a much more cautious and neutral role:

> While the Marriage Counselor will feel satisfaction in the strengthening of a marriage, he should not feel obliged to urge that the married partners continue to live together at all costs. There are situations in which all resources fail, and in which continued living together may be severely damaging to one or several persons. In such event it is the duty of the Counselor to assess the facts as he sees them. However, the actual decision concerning separation or divorce is a responsibility that must be assumed by the client and this should be made clear to him. If separation or divorce is decided upon, it is the continuing responsibility of the Counselor to give further support and counsel during a period of readjustment, if that appears to be wanted and needed, as it often is. (Quoted by Dorothy E. Barrier in her discussion of Rutledge, 1963: 325).

Judgments concerning healthy and pathological relationships all too often represent only personal judgments concerning the good life. It is inevitable and proper that these judgments should be made by counselors. Those who seek counseling should take care to recognize the differences in kind between the "diagnosis" of a severely damaging relationship and a diagnosis of tuberculosis.

THE EFFECTIVENESS OF COUNSELING

Complex values make it very difficult to talk about the success or effectiveness of marriage counseling or other forms of counseling and therapy. What will be the criterion for effectiveness? Is a marriage counselor, all of whose clients divorce and remarry happily, more or less successful than another counselor, all of whose clients decide to remain married and find their satisfactions in life from hobbies and children? Is it enough that those counseled are pleased with the results, or must one discount their enthusiasm in favor of giving more weight to some objective measure of "improvement"? Suppose a couple is just as unhappy after as before counseling but now has profound insight into the nature and insolubility of their problem. Have they been helped? To what extent is the counselor free to guide his clients into behavior which violates prevailing morality or to stand as the guardian of traditional values? Should he be judged unsuccessful if his clients have learned to feel neither guilty nor jealous about adultery, or successful if his clients foreswear an existing extramarital liaison to return to a

Chart 19-2

MARRIAGE PROBLEMS ARE HELPED BY PROFESSIONAL THERAPY
LESS OFTEN THAN ARE OTHER TYPES OF PROBLEMS
Percent Who Said Therapy Did Not Help Them, by Type of Problem

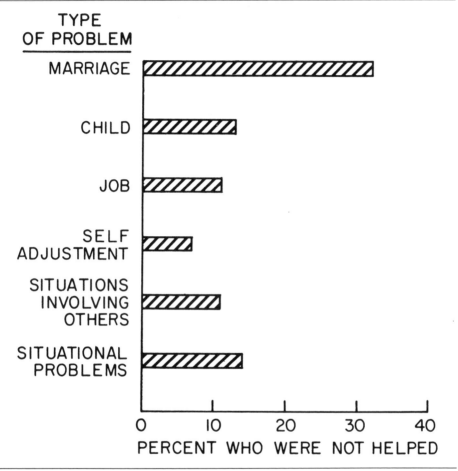

TYPE
OF PROBLEM

PERCENT WHO WERE NOT HELPED

Source: Gurin, Veroff, and Feld, 1960

deadening but acceptable marital union? Marriage counseling is too new and too limited for conclusive scientific information to be available now on its ability to achieve stated goals. In addition, the goals themselves are too unclear. The best information now is the opinions of the counselors, who are understandably enthusiastic, and the responses of selected clients. In the national mental health survey cited above, those who sought help for marital problems (the most frequent problems) felt that they were helped less than did those who sought help for any other kind of problem. (See Chart 19-2.)

Those who seek counseling because they see some defect in themselves are far more likely to feel that they were "helped a lot" than those who sought help because of a defect in someone else. Since marriage counselors are likely to have clients who see their problem as the relationship with, or a defect in, another person, it is not surprising that the researchers must observe (on the basis of far too few cases to be conclusive) that "of all sources of help, the marriage counselors are perceived as least effective" (Gurin et al., 1960: 319). The clergy and physicians have the most enthusiastic counselees, perhaps because the problems they deal with are more easily dispatched, perhaps because those who choose them are most willing to perceive improvement in the situation, or perhaps because they are the most effective in helping people.

No experimental studies have been done comparing the satisfaction, happiness, or adjustment of counseled couples with those who have not been counseled. Like personal problems—even those called neuroses—marital problems also come and go over the years. Some are not solved but are simply superseded by more pressing problems and hence decline in importance. Others arise in the course of some crisis in the world outside the marriage and decline with the disappearance of the crisis. Some are characteristic of one period in the family cycle. Others fester in a corner of the marriage for years during which everyone is too busy to notice, only to become a general inflammation in the relationship when everyone has time to concentrate on them. Counseling provides no panacea for marital or personal problems.

Nothing in the available evidence demonstrates that there are not certain *types* of marital problems from which relief can usually be obtained through outside counseling. Indeed, it seems probable that future research will discover that professional counseling regularly solves many categories of marital problems. Other factors besides the type of marital problem may affect the success of counseling. In one study of forty-one married couples with varying marital problems, Freeman, Leavens, and McCulloch (1969) found that counseling was most successful when the husband attended all the counseling sessions and when the counselor was an experienced psychiatrist rather than a psychiatric trainee. "Success" in this case was measured by the couple's and the counselor's reports of improvement in the marriage one to three years after the counseling. Many couples in trouble will want to try professional help on the chance that they will be helped. Many persons do report that their difficulties were cleared up by counseling.

Perhaps this represents too dim a view because it focuses too narrowly on the happy solution to marital problems as the criterion of successful counseling. If counseling provides the couple with a significant intellectual understanding of what is wrong, is this not a contribution to the individuals?

A marriage is at least more meaningful and profound a relationship if those who are involved in it understand why it is unhappy. Interpersonal understanding is independent of satisfying relationships. At times, the ability to understand makes something unbearable that was tolerable as long as it was misperceived. One should not be surprised to find that, in some cases, counseling, by clarifying issues and confronting problems, might well serve to disrupt a relationship which was surviving by not being looked at too carefully. In terms of adding drama and excitement to life, in terms of restoring honesty to relationships which have become mutual subterfuges, and in terms of adding dignity to life, counseling might be considered to have contributed significantly to worthwhile goals even when, at the same time, it puts the quietus on a relationship or makes two people unhappy.

Marriage Education

The growth of formal courses of instruction in marriage education is an excellent indication of the changing status of the marital institution in the society. In most societies, it has been taken for granted that family and peers would teach the neophyte what he needed to know to be married. In American history, marriage education in the form of outside instruction has long been a province of religious education programs. However, in a rapidly changing, secularized society, neither religious nor family-provided instruction is in keeping with the modern outlook on marriage. The emphasis on the intrinsic features of the marital relationship itself as a pleasure-giving arrangement, together with the development of a social science with some pretensions of being able to provide scientific information which might be useful for personal decision-making, has inaugurated specific programs in "family-life education." The general orientation of the programs is that an "expert" with specialized knowledge provides instruction in "successful" family living. The courses are extremely varied and are taught both in high school and college by teachers from many different disciplines who apply many different criteria to the concepts of knowledge and success. Home economists emphasize the domestic aspects of budgeting, decision-making, prenatal care, and infant care. Religious educators emphasize family morality arguments and may be tempted to use scientific studies to strengthen them. Clinically oriented psychologists teach courses in which personal insight and personality analysis are emphasized. Some courses are directed primarily at providing sexual information and technique. All operate under the same basic assumption that formal courses can help achieve certain goals in the marriages of those who take the courses.

THE GOALS OF MARRIAGE EDUCATION

What should be the goals of a marriage-education program? Who should decide what the goals are? The following statements represent some of the values which people hope to see realized through marriage education:

1. Marriages should be permanent. Divorces represent failure.

2. Marriages should be pleasure-producing. Nonpleasurable marriages represent failure.

3. People should marry. Not marrying represents failure.

4. Marriages should produce children. Not to reproduce represents failure.

5. Married people should enjoy childrearing.

6. Children should be reared in such a way that they become well-adjusted, emotionally healthy, independent adults, contributing to the community according to their potential. Emotionally disturbed, delinquent, or criminal offspring represent failure.

7. People ought to observe conventional standards of behavior: they should not have intercourse except with a spouse; at not too early an age, they should marry someone who is from a similar social environment, of their own race and religion, for reasons which are socially acceptable; they should rear their children in accordance with presently accepted fashion. Unconventionality is failure.

8. People should make marriage the central focus of their emotional lives. Emotionally peripheral marriages are a sign of failure.

9. People should marry for love and should continue to love each other for the rest of their lives.

Normally, the goals for a marriage-education program are *not* set by the students being educated. One might wonder in how many college classes complete unanimity of opinion could be found on any single one of these values. For practical reasons, the goals for any course are implicitly set by the instructor. Because of the value-laden content of the subject area, it is inherent in the classroom situation that by his very selection of subjects, the instructor establishes the goals of the educational program. Since some of his values will conflict with those of the students, it is difficult for the instructor to avoid the role of moralist, and many do not try.

THE EFFECTIVENESS OF MARRIAGE EDUCATION

Educators can rarely measure the effectiveness of their efforts because of the complexity of the measurement problem. One course is a small piece of experience. Thirty or forty hours of instruction would hardly be expected to alter the main direction of many lives. However, the first problem is to specify the goals of the educational program and then to detail the criteria for effectiveness in meeting those goals. Marriage education, like other facets of the educational program, has many goals, not all of which are articulate and some of which are contradictory to others. The goals of permanence in marriage and happiness in marriage are obviously in part mutually exclusive.

Another problem in measuring effectiveness is student selectivity. Those who go to college are more likely to have "successful marriages" by most criteria than those who do not. Those who take elective courses in marriage and family life are likely to have characteristics which make them distinctly better than average marriage risks on most counts.

A number of small-scale studies have been made in attempts to measure the effects of single courses in marriage, but none comes close to meeting the requirement that those who take the course be matched on the most relevant characteristics to a comparison group who have not taken the course. One study showed that when matched samples were used, a larger proportion of those who took the course got married, but the researcher was not able to attribute this fact to the course. Rather, he was led to the conclusion that the taking of such a course did not demonstrably affect subsequent behavior with respect to getting married, staying married, and having children (Finck, 1956). In another study which compared those who had completed a course in preparation for marriage with a control group who did not take the course but who were matched for year in school, college, and sex, a significantly greater number of the control group rated themselves "less than happy" in their marriages (Dyen, 1959). In a follow-up of 3,700 Stephens College alumnae some years ago, high grades in the marriage course were shown to be related to success in marriage (Ellzey, 1949)! Of course, in none of these studies can the differences in the groups be seriously attributed to taking the single course. Other attempts have been made to measure the effect of family life education. After evaluating attempts to measure the effectiveness of education for childrearing, Brim (1962) could only say: "The issue of how effective is parent education in changing parents or children therefore remains unresolved at present." A review of attempts to demonstrate the effectiveness of marriage courses in reaching any of the goals previously mentioned would have to come to the same conclusion. It is not known whether courses in marriage make people have happier, more permanent, more fertile, more conforming marriages. It is known that good college courses can give the student sophisticated knowledge, analytical tools, and a more heightened perception of the world around him. Good courses in marriage can do the same. I would expect exacting studies to be able to demonstrate that such courses provide the student with knowledge which he then uses for the achievement of his own goals and the realization of his own values. These will be different at different stages in his life. The insight used to select an appropriate spouse at twenty may be used to dispose of one at thirty-five.

To put it more broadly, marriage courses provide knowledge. Some people will be able to combine this knowledge with fortuitous circumstance and useful personal characteristics to achieve a measure of control over their destinies. They will be able to predict better the consequences of their own and other people's actions and to choose better from alternative courses of action. For most people, life contains many goals and conflicting values. The most important are not at all times those concerning family life. Nor does the ability to control the course of one's existence necessarily make one happy and contented. There is no one-to-one correlation between autonomy and happiness, just as there is no relationship between understanding and happiness. Marriage education can provide understanding and, through understanding, autonomy. It is the last sequence which represents the goal of this book.

Three impediments block the sequence from education, to understanding, to autonomy. The first, which prevents proper education, is the lack of knowledge on the subject. If half of the conclusions in this book could be considered so well established as not to be subject to dispute, sociologists would know many times as much as they do now. This drawback can eventually be remedied but not in time to be much help for the present generation. The second impediment, which stands between education and understanding, is unwillingness to learn. Especially in the areas of sex, courtship, marriage, and childrearing, most people hold ideas which give them such great emotional satisfaction and support that they are steadfastly reluctant to change them in the face of their inaccuracy. For this impediment there is no remedy. Perhaps some of these beliefs serve useful social functions. Perhaps the myth that marriage provides a lifetime of deeply satisfying interaction serves to guide into approved marital grooves many who with the destruction of the myth would not marry and who would, therefore, be difficult persons in the social structure of adult life. The third impediment, which will be called circumstance, stands between understanding and autonomy. By circumstance is meant all the uncontrollable factors which serve to reduce the scope of autonomous behavior: personality characteristics which one finds himself with as an adult; sickness, death, and accident; an ordered social system; the uncontrollable behavior of other autonomous persons seeking their own goals; and the complexity of life, which presents one with so many variables to think about and control that any particularly desired outcome becomes problematic. By its nature irremediable, the impediment of circumstance often makes it necessary for one to accept, as a substitute for autonomy where it is impossible, the pleasure of understanding as an end in itself.

Sex Education in Public Schools

During the 1960s one of the most significant curriculum developments in elementary and high schools across the United States has been the introduction of sex-education programs. For various reasons, from unwillingness to indicate that sex was being considered out of its moral context, to the desire to avoid public conflict, these programs have been given many different titles, perhaps most frequently, family-life education. It is the sexual-education content of these programs which represents a new and distinctive element, and it is the sex content which has generated the enormous amount of controversy and acrimony in communities across the country.

Sex-education programs have appeared in many forms, from single courses organized for a single year or semester or part of a semester in high school to integrated educational sequences beginning in the first grade and introducing new elements every year through high school graduation. The substantive content is sex and reproduction from a social, psychological, and biological perspective. The most thoroughgoing programs introduce into the high school and junior high school years a complete instructional program on the biology of sexual behavior and reproduction, consideration of dating, mate selection, premarital sex, sexual perversions, contraception, sexual techniques, psychology of sexual behavior, and an introduction to the sociology of sex.

The goals of sex-education programs depend on the nature of the community and differ widely. Generally, conservatively inclined communities see sex-education programs as a way of reducing premarital sexual involvement of adolescents. Liberals are inclined to view sex education as a means to achieving a fuller appreciation of the sexual nature of man in adulthood, emphasizing appreciation of sex as a social relationship to enhance marriage, and making a strong point of the concept of sexual responsibility. Controversy has been provoked in many communities over the introduction of sex education. Conservatives have argued that exposure to sexual material in the classroom at early adolescence will encourage sexual experimentation and provoke sexual interest prematurely. Liberals have generally argued that precocious sexuality is not developed through sex education. There is no evidence to support either assertion. Conservatives have argued that sex education must be presented in a firm context of moral and religious teaching. Liberals have argued that individuals must be encouraged to develop their own values around the concept of taking responsibility for one's own sexual behavior. Liberals tend to look at sex education as having mental health value, while conservatives are more concerned with maintaining social control of sexual behavior. It is too early in the development of widespread sex education to determine what effect if any it is having on the sexual behavior and attitudes of young Americans.

Since teachers evidently get little training for teaching sex-education courses, and since they have varying attitudes towards their own and others' sexuality, the effects of their teaching probably vary. A survey of teachers' colleges (Malfetti and Rubin, 1968) revealed that few schools offered special courses in teaching sex education and few students took the courses when they were offered. People who become sex educators may be motivated by certain moral views; one study found that women who were teaching sex-education courses were less permissive of premarital sexual relations for women than women who were not sex educators, and 75 percent of the 180 sex educators studied felt that adolescents behaved with more sexual abandon than was proper (Rubin and Adams, 1972).

A dispassionate observer might predict that sex education is not likely to be an effective mechanism for the reassertion of community control over individual sexual behavior. Nor is it likely to encourage the flowering of a sexual renaissance in America. If it emphasizes the teaching of contraception to adolescents, it may reduce illegitimacy and premarital pregnancies, but we cannot be sure that it will not at the same time increase the prevalence of premarital intercourse. Serious efforts are being made to determine the effect of sex-education programs through careful research.

Toward a More Temperate View of Marriage Counseling and Marriage Education

To present a proper perspective on the success of marriage counseling and the effectiveness of marriage education, it is necessary to point out that research validation is absent for the effectiveness of many other processes in American society, the effectiveness of which we take for granted—either assuming that their efficacy has been demonstrated or that the demonstration is unnecessary. In the field of education, new teaching techniques and new curricula replace the old without any research validating the necessity of the replacement. In medical practice, new drugs until *very* recently have entered the market and been used to treat illness with no scientifically satisfactory evidence of their therapeutic value. Preventive and therapeutic surgery of various sorts is performed with little besides haphazard clinical evidence to support its value. New laws are passed to encourage certain kinds of behavior and discourage others, and rarely is an attempt made to determine whether or not the laws are, in fact, successful in achieving their goals.

It is in no way suggested that it is not desirable for marriage counseling and marriage education to be subjected to rigorous tests to determine whether they are doing what one wants them to do. However, until more convincing evidence is available, it is necessary to continue in ignorance of their beneficial or detrimental effects. Nevertheless, the absence of validation of professional effectiveness in the areas of marriage counseling and marriage and sex education should make practitioners in these fields modest in their claims. It should make them cautious when they warn the layman to take his problem to the expert and not to his friends and relatives. The counsel of friends and relatives has not been shown less effective *in relieving the problem* than the most highly trained, professional assistance money can buy.

Summary

Marriage counseling is a recent addition to the helping professions, and marriage counselors are mainly available in metropolitan areas. In the past, more people have taken their marriage problems to physicians than to any other professional. Those who have used marriage counselors have not reported they were helped as often as those using other professionals, perhaps because those who go to marriage counselors have more intractable problems. Research is sorely needed to demonstrate what kinds of marriage counseling are successful in treating what kinds of problems, for we know nothing on this subject at present. It is more difficult to evaluate marriage counseling than many other services because it is so difficult to specify the goals which are sought.

The introduction into public school and college curricula of courses in marriage education and sex education has been a source of public controversy because of the lack of a community moral consensus on the purposes to be served by these programs. The solution to the controversy is to provide the student information and opportunity for thoughtful analysis, to which he can apply his own moral code, from wherever derived, in arriving at guidelines for his own behavior.

Bibliography

* Denotes citation or reference in the main text.

CHAPTER 1   INTRODUCTION

As, Berit, and Tiller, Per Olav, "Marriage—A Value of the Social Scientist," *Acta Sociologica,* vol. VIII, pp. 7–14, 1964.

Bendix, Reinhard, "Sociology and the Distrust of Reason," *American Sociological Review,* vol. XXXV, pp. 831–843, 1970.

Furstenberg, Frank F., Jr., "Industrialization and the American Family: A Look Backward," *American Sociological Review,* vol. XXXI, no. 3, pp. 326–337, June 1966.

* Hunt, Morton M., *The Natural History of Love.* Alfred A. Knopf, Inc., New York, 1959.

Kunstadter, Peter, "A Survey of the Consanguine, Matrifocal Family," *American Anthropologist,* vol. LXV, pp. 56–66, February 1963.

Lantz, Herman R.; Britton, Margaret; Schmitt, Raymond; and Snyder, Eloise C., "Pre-Industrial Patterns in the Colonial Family in America: A Content Analysis of Colonial Magazines," *American Sociological Review,* vol. XXXIII, no. 3, pp. 413–426, June 1968.

* Merrill, Francis E., *Courtship and Marriage,* revised edition. Henry Holt & Company, New York, 1959.

* Parsons, Talcott, and Bales, Robert F., *Family, Socialization, and Interaction Process.* Free Press of Glencoe, Inc., Glencoe, Illinois, 1955.

Reiss, Ira L., "The Universality of the Family: A Conceptual Analysis," *Journal of Marriage and the Family,* vol. XXVII, pp. 443–453, 1965.

Silverman, Irwin; Shulman, Arthur D.; and Wiesenthal, David L., "The Experimenter as a Source of Variance in Psychological Research: Modeling and Sex Effects," *Journal of Personality and Social Psychology,* vol. XXI, no. 2, pp. 219–227, February 1972.

Sklare, Marshall, "Intermarriage and the Jewish Future," *Commentary,* vol. XXXVII, pp. 46–52, 1964.

CHAPTER 2   THE FAMILY IN A CHANGING SOCIETY

Ball, Donald W., "The 'Family' as a Sociological Problem: Conceptualization of the Taken-for-Granted as Prologue to Social Problems Analysis," *Social Problems,* vol. XIX, pp. 295-307, 1972.

Bardis, Panos D., "Marriage and Family Customs in Ancient Egypt: An Interdisciplinary Study," *Social Science,* part 1, pp. 229-245, October 1966.

Belcher, John C., "The One-Person Household: A Consequence of the Isolated Nuclear Family?" *Journal of Marriage and the Family,* vol. XXIX, pp. 534-540, 1967.

Berardo, Felix M., "Kinship Interaction and Communications Among Space-Age Migrants," *Journal of Marriage and the Family,* vol. XXIX, pp. 541-554, 1967.

Berardo, Felix M., "Kinship Interaction and Migrant Adaptation in an Aerospace-Related Community," *Journal of Marriage and the Family,* vol. XXVIII, pp. 296-304, 1966.

Berger, Bennett; Hackett, Bruce; and Millar, R. Mervyn, "The Communal Family," *The Family Coordinator,* vol. XXI, pp. 419-427, 1972.

Blood, Robert O., Jr., "Impact of Urbanization on American Family Structure and Functioning," *Sociology and Social Research,* vol. XLIX, pp. 5-16, 1964.

Bock, Wilbur, and Iutaka, Sugiyama, "Urbanization, Social Mobility and the Maintenance of the Extended Family: Brazilian Data," presented at the annual meeting of the National Council on Family Relations, 1968.

Camilleri, Carmel, "Modernity and the Family in Tunisia," *Journal of Marriage and the Family,* vol. XXIX, pp. 590-595, 1967.

Cancian, Francesca M., "The Effect of Patrilocal Households on Nuclear Family Interaction in Zinacantan," *Estudios De Cultura Maya,* vol. V, pp. 299-315, 1965.

Chauhan, I. S., "Three Families in a Small Town: A Study in Social Change," *Journal of Social Research,* vol. VIII, pp. 83-90, 1965.

Cohen, Nathan E., and Connery, Maurice F., "Government Policy and the Family," *Journal of Marriage and the Family,* vol. XXIX, pp. 6-17, 1967.

* Demos, John, *A Little Commonwealth: Family Life in Plymouth Colony.* Oxford University Press, New York, 1970.

Dumont, Louis, "Marriage in India: The Present State of the Question," *Contributions to Indian Sociology,* vol. V, pp. 75-95, 1961.

Dumont, Louis, "Marriage in India: The Present State of the Question," *Contributions to Indian Sociology,* vol. VII, pp. 77-102, 1964.

Dumont, Louis, "Marriage in India: The Present State of the Question," *Contributions to Indian Sociology,* vol. IX, pp. 90-114, 1966.

Edwards, John N., "The Future of the Family Revisited," *Journal of Marriage and the Family,* vol. XXIX, pp. 505-511, 1967.

Firth, R., "Family and Kinship in Industrial Society," *The Sociological Review Monograph,* pp. 65-87, 1964.

* Furstenberg, Frank F., "Industrialization and the American Family: A Look Backward," *American Sociological Review,* vol. XXXI, pp. 326-337, 1966.

* Goffman, Erving, *Stigma: Notes on the Management of Spoiled Identity.* Prentice-Hall, Inc., Englewood Cliffs, New Jersey, 1963.

* Goode, William J., *World Revolution and Family Patterns.* Free Press of Glencoe, Inc., New York, 1963.

Gordon, Michael, and Bernstein, M. Charles, "Mate Choice and Domestic Life in the 19th-Century Marriage Manual," presented at the 1969 Meeting of the American Sociological Association.

Goshen-Gottstein, Esther R., "Courtship, Marriage and Pregnancy in 'Geula'," *Israel Annals of Psychiatry and Related Disciplines,* vol. IV, pp. 1-24, 1966.

* Greenfield, Sidney M., "Industrialization and the Family in Sociological Theory," *American Journal of Sociology,* vol. LXVII, no. 3, pp. 312-322, November 1961.

* Greenwood, David, *Essays in Human Relations.* Public Affairs Press, Washington, D. C., 1956.

Haavio-Mannila, Elina, "Sex Differentiation in Role Expectations and Performance," *Journal of Marriage and the Family,* vol. XXIX, pp. 568-578, 1967.

Harmsworth, Harry C., "Family Structure of the Fort Hall Indian Reservation," *Family Life Coordinator,* vol. XIV, pp. 7-9, 1965.

Heckscher, Bridget Tancock, "Household Structure and Achievement Orientation in Lower-Class Barbadian Families," *Journal of Marriage and the Family,* vol. XXIX, pp. 521-526, 1967.

Herrmann, Robert O., "Families in Bankruptcy—A Survey of Recent Studies," *Journal of Marriage and the Family,* vol. XXVIII, pp. 324-330, 1966.

Kaplan, Benjamin, "The Shtetl Family: A Socio-Psychological Survey," proceedings of the Southwestern Sociological Association, 1966.

Kharchev, A. G., "Motives of Marriages in the USSR," *Acta Sociologica,* vol. VIII, pp. 142-154, 1964.

Korson, J. Henry, "Dower and Social Class in an Urban Muslim Community," *Journal of Marriage and the Family,* vol. XXIX, pp. 527-533, 1967.

Kurokawa, Minako, "Lineal Orientation in Child Rearing Among Japanese," *Journal of Marriage and the Family,* vol. XXX, pp. 129-136, 1968.

* Lantz, Herman R.; Britton, Margaret; Schmitt, Raymond; and Snyder, Eloise C., "Pre-Industrial Patterns in the Colonial Family in America: A Content Analysis of Colonial Magazines," *American Sociological Review,* vol. XXXIII, pp. 413-426, 1968.

* Laslett, Peter, "The Comparative History of Household and Family," in Michael Gordon, editor, *The American Family in Socio-historical Perspective,* pp. 19-33. St. Martin's Press, New York, 1973.

* Laslett, Peter, and Wall, R., editors, *Household and Family in Past Time.* Cambridge University Press, New York, 1972.

Lee, S. C., and Brattrud, Audrey, "Love and Marriage," *Soviet Review,* vol. III, August 1962.

Lee, S. C., and Brattrud, Audrey, "Marriage Under a Monastic Mode of Life: A Preliminary Report on the Hutterite Family in South Dakota," *Journal of Marriage and the Family,* vol. XXIX, pp. 512-520, 1967.

Magrabi, Frances M., and Marshall, William H., "Family Developmental Tasks: A Research Model," *Journal of Marriage and the Family,* vol. XXVII, pp. 454-461, 1965.

Marris, Peter, "Individual Achievement and Family Ties: Some International Comparisons," *Journal of Marriage and the Family,* vol. XXIX, pp. 763-771, 1967.

Mayer, John E., "People's Imagery of Other Families," *Family Process,* vol. VI, pp. 27-36, 1967.

McGinn, Noel F.; Harburg, Ernest; and Ginsburg, Gerald P., "Dependency Relations with Parents and Affiliative Responses in Michigan and Guadalopia," *Sociometry,* vol. XXVIII, pp. 305-321, 1965.

Mencher, Samuel, "Social Authority and the Family," *Journal of Marriage and the Family,* vol. XXIX, pp. 164-192, 1967.

Morioka, Kiyomi, "Life Cycle Patterns in Japan, China, and the United States," *Journal of Marriage and the Family,* vol. XXIX, pp. 595-606, 1967.

Neubeck, Gerhard, "Notes on Russian Family Life Today," *Acta Sociologica,* vol. VIII, pp. 324-326, 1965.

Nye, Ivan I., "Values, Family, and a Changing Society," *Journal of Marriage and the Family,* vol. XXIX, no. 2, pp. 244-248, 1967.

Olson, David H., "Marriage of the Future: Revolutionary or Evolutionary Change?" *The Family Coordinator,* vol. XXI, pp. 383-393, 1972.

Osmond, Marie W., "Toward Monogamy: A Cross-Cultural Study of Correlates of Type of Marriage," *Social Forces,* vol. XLIV, pp. 8-15, 1965.

Parke, Robert, Jr., and Glick, Paul C., "Prospective Changes in Marriage and the Family," *Journal of Marriage and the Family,* vol. XXIX, pp. 249-256, 1967.

Pollak, Otto, "The Outlook for the American Family," *Journal of Marriage and the Family,* vol. XXIX, pp. 193-205, 1967.

Rapoport, Robert N., "The Male's Occupation in Relation to his Decision to Marry," *Acta Sociologica,* vol. VIII, pp. 68-82, 1964.

Rodman, Hyman, "Talcott Parsons' View of the Changing American Family," *Merrill-Palmer Quarterly,* vol. XI, pp. 209-227, 1965.

Rodman, Hyman; Nichols, F. R.; and Voydanoff, Patricia, "Lower-Class Attitudes Toward 'Deviant' Family Patterns: A Cross-Cultural Study," *Journal of Marriage and the Family,* vol. XXXI, pp. 315-321, 1969.

*Rosenberg, Bernard, and Mumphrey, Norman D., "The Secondary Nature of the Primary Group," in Bernard Rosenberg, Israel Gerver and F. William Howton, editors, *Mass Society in Crisis.* The Macmillan Company, New York, 1964.

Rosenthal, Joel T., "Marriage and the Blood Feud in 'Heroic' Europe," *British Journal of Sociology,* vol. XVII, pp. 133-144, 1966.

Schlesinger, Benjamin, "The Family in Communist China," *Social Science,* pp. 221-228, October 1966.

Schlesinger, Benjamin, "Family Patterns in the English-Speaking Caribbean," *Journal of Marriage and the Family,* vol. XXX, pp. 149-153, 1968.

Schlesinger, Benjamin, "Family Patterns in Jamaica: Review and Commentary," *Journal of Marriage and the Family,* vol. XXX, pp. 136-148, 1968.

Schlesinger, Benjamin, "Modern Family Life Around the World: Recent Literature in the Journals," *Family Life Coordinator,* vol. XIV, pp. 144-148, 1965.

Schottland, Charles I., "Government Economic Programs and Family Life," *Journal of Marriage and the Family,* vol. XXIX, pp. 71-123, 1967.

* Smith, Daniel Scott, "The Dating of the American Sexual Revolution: Evidence and Interpretation," in Michael Gordon, editor, *The American Family in Socio-historical Perspective.* St. Martin's Press, New York, pp. 321-335, 1973.

Steyn, Anna F., and Rip, Colin M., "The Changing Urban Bantu Family," *Journal of Marriage and the Family,* vol. XXX, pp. 499-517, 1968.

Straus, Murray A., "Westernization, Insecurity, and Sinhalese Social Structure," *International Journal of Social Psychiatry,* vol. XII, pp. 130-138, 1966.

Straus, Murray A., and Libby, Diane J., "Sibling Group Size and Adolescent Personality," *Population Review,* vol. IX, pp. 55-64, 1965.

Sussman, Marvin B., "Current State and Perspectives of Research on the Family," *Social Science Information,* vol. VII, pp. 35-50, 1968.

Sussman, Marvin B., and Cogswell, Betty E., "The Meaning of Variant and Experimental Marriage Styles and Family Forms in the 1970s," *The Family Coordinator,* vol. XXI, pp. 375-381, 1972.

* Thomas, John L., "Theory and Research in Family Sociology," *American Catholic Sociological Review,* vol. XXVI, June 1955.

Vincent, Clark E., "Familia Spongia: The Adaptive Function," *Journal of Marriage and the Family,* vol. XXVIII, pp. 29-36, 1966.

Wassink, M. W. Graeff, "Opinion Survey on Mixed Marriages in Morocco," *Journal of Marriage and the Family,* vol. XXIX, pp. 578-589, 1967.

Whitehurst, Robert N., "Some Comparisons of Conventional and Counterculture Families," *The Family Coordinator,* vol. XXI, pp. 395-401, 1972.

* Wilkinson, Thomas O., "Family Structure and Industrialization in Japan," *American Sociological Review,* vol. XXVII, pp. 678-682, October 1962.

Winch, Robert F.; Greer, Scott; and Blumberg, Rae Lesser, "Ethnicity and Extended Familism in an Upper-Middle-Class Suburb," *American Sociological Review,* vol. XXXII, pp. 265-272, 1967.

Yamane, Tsuneo, and Nonoyama, Hisaya, "Isolation of the Nuclear Family and Kinship Organization in Japan: A Hypothetical Approach to the Relationships Between the Family and Society," *Journal of Marriage and the Family,* vol. XXIX, pp. 783-796, 1967.

Young, Frank W., and Young, Ruth C., "The Differentiation of Family Structure in Rural Mexico," *Journal of Marriage and the Family,* vol. XXX, pp. 154-160, 1968.

Zimmerman, Carle C., "The Future of the American Family: I. The Revolution," *International Journal of Sociology of the Family,* vol. I, pp. 1-9, 1971.

Zimmerman, Carle C., "The Future of the Family in America," *Journal of Marriage and the Family,* vol. XXXIV, pp. 323-333, 1972.

* Zimmerman, Carle C., and Cervantes, Lucius F., *Successful American Families.* Pageant Press, Inc., New York, 1960.

CHAPTER 3   SEX DIFFERENCES

American Association of Marriage Counselors, *Marriage Counseling: A Casebook.* Association Press, New York, 1958.

* "A Stunning Approval for Abortion," *Time,* vol. CI, pp. 50-51, February 5, 1973.

Bieber, Irving, et al., *Homosexuality: A Psychoanalytic Study.* Basic Books, Inc., New York, 1962.

* Binstock, Jeanne, "Motherhood: An Occupation Facing Decline," *The Futurist,* vol. III, pp. 99-102, 1971.

Blood, Robert O., Jr., *Marriage.* Free Press of Glencoe, Inc., New York, 1962.

* Blood, Robert O., Jr., and Wolfe, Donald M., *Husbands and Wives: The Dynamics of Married Living.* Free Press of Glencoe, Inc., New York, 1960.

* Broverman, Inge K.; Vogel, Susan Raymond; Broverman, Donald M.; Clarkson, Frank E.; and Rosenkrantz, Paul S., "Sex-Role Stereotypes: A Current Appraisal," *Journal of Social Issues,* vol. XXVIII, pp. 59-78, 1972.

* Chesler, Phyllis, "Women as Psychiatric and Psychotherapeutic Patients," *Journal of Marriage and the Family,* vol. XXXIII, pp. 746-759, 1971.

* Deutch, Helene, *The Psychology of Women,* vols. I and II. Grune and Stratton, Inc., New York, 1944, 1945.

* *Economic Report of the President,* pp. 89-112, 155-159. U. S. Government Printing Office, Washington, D. C., 1973.

* Ehrlich, Carol, "The Male Sociologist's Burden: The Place of Women in Marriage and Family Texts," *Journal of Marriage and the Family,* vol. XXXIII, pp. 421-430, 1971.

* Epstein, Cynthia Fuchs, "Positive Effects of the Multiple Negative: Explaining the Success of Black Professional Women," *American Journal of Sociology,* vol. LXXVIII, pp. 912-935, 1973.

* Foote, Nelson N., "Matching of Husband and Wife in Phases of Development," in Marvin B. Sussman, editor, *Sourcebook in Marriage and the Family,* pp. 14-21. Houghton Mifflin Company, Boston, 1963.

* Friedan, Betty, *The Feminine Mystique.* W. W. Norton & Company, Inc., New York, 1963.

* Gadpaille, Warren J., "Research into the Physiology of Maleness and Femaleness," *Archives of General Psychiatry,* vol. XXVI, pp. 193-206, 1972.

* Gitter, A. George; Kozel, Nicholas J.; and Mostofsky, David I., "Perception of Emotion: The Role of Race, Sex, and Presentation Mode," *Journal of Social Psychology,* vol. LXXXVIII, pp. 213-222, 1972.

* Goldberg, Philip, "Are Women Prejudiced Against Women?" *Transaction,* vol. V, pp. 28-30, 1968.

* Harlow, Harry F., "The Heterosexual Affectional System in Monkeys," *American Psychologist,* vol. XVII, pp. 1-9, 1962.

* Hartley, Ruth E., "Some Implications of Current Changes in Sex-Role Patterns," in Marvin B. Sussman, editor, *Sourcebook in Marriage and the Family.* Houghton Mifflin Company, Boston, 1963.

* Horner, M. S., "Femininity and Successful Achievement: A Basic Inconsistency," in J. Bardwick et al., editors, *Feminine Personality and Conflict.* Brooks/Cole Publishing Company, Belmont, California, 1970.

Johnson, Miriam M., "Sex Role Learning in the Nuclear Family," *Child Development,* vol. XXXIV, pp. 319-334, 1963.

* Kangas, Jon, and Bradway, Katherine, "Intelligence at Middle Age: A Thirty-Eight-Year Follow-Up," *Developmental Psychology,* vol. V, pp. 333-337, 1971.

* Kelley, E. Lowell, "Consistency of Adult Personality," *American Psychologist,* vol. X, pp. 659-681, 1955.

* Kenkel, William F., "Observational Studies of Husband-Wife Interaction," in Marvin B. Sussman, editor, *Sourcebook in Marriage and the Family.* Houghton Mifflin Company, Boston, 1963.

* Knudsen, Dean D., "The Declining Status of Women; Popular Myths and the Failure of Functionalist Thought," *Social Forces,* vol. XLVIII, no. 2, pp. 183-193, 1969.

* Komarovsky, Mirra, *Blue Collar Marriages.* Random House, New York, 1964.

Komarovsky, Mirra, "Cultural Contradictions and Sex Roles," in Robert F. Winch, Robert McGinnis, and Herbert M. Barringer, editors, *Selected Studies in Marriage and the Family,* pp. 126-133. Holt, Rinehart & Winston, Inc., New York, 1962.

* Komarovsky, Mirra, "Functional Analysis of Sex Roles," in Marvin B. Sussman, editor, *Sourcebook in Marriage and the Family,* pp. 125-132. Houghton Mifflin Company, Boston, 1963.

* Leuba, Clarence J., *Man: A General Psychology.* Holt, Rinehart & Winston, Inc., New York, 1961.

Levine, Adeline, and Crumrine, Janice, "Women and the Fear of Success: A Problem in Replication," presented at the annual meetings of the American Sociological Association, New York City, August 1973. Mimeographed.

* Lirtzman, Sidney I., and Wahba, Mahmoud A., "Determinants of Coalitional Behavior of Men and Women: Sex Roles or Situational Requirements?" *Journal of Applied Psychology,* vol. LVI, pp. 406-411, 1972.

* Luckey, Eleanore B., and Nass, Gilbert D., "A Comparison of Sexual Attitudes and Behavior in an International Sample," *Journal of Marriage and the Family,* vol. XXXI, no. 2, pp. 364-379, May 1969.

* Lundberg, Ferdinand, and Farnham, Marynia F., *Modern Woman: The Lost Sex.* Harper & Brothers, New York, 1947.

* Maccoby, E. E., editor. *The Development of Sex Differences.* Stanford University Press, Stanford, California, 1966.

Martinez de Toledo, Alfonso, *Little Sermons on Sin.* University of California Press, Berkeley, California, 1959.

* Masters, William H., and Johnson, Virginia, *Human Sexual Inadequacy.* Little, Brown & Company, Boston, 1970.

* Masters, William H., and Johnson, Virginia, *Human Sexual Response.* Little, Brown & Company, Boston, 1966.

* McKee, John P., and Sherifs, Alex C., "Men's and Women's Beliefs, Ideals and Self-concepts," in Jerome M. Weidman, editor, *The Adolescent.* Holt, Rinehart & Winston, Inc., New York, 1960.

* Mead, Margaret, *Growing up in New Guinea.* William Morrow and Company, Inc., New York, 1930.

* Mead, Margaret, "Introduction," in A. M. Krich, editor, *Women: The Variety and Meaning of Their Sexual Experience,* pp. 9-24. Dell Publishing Company, New York, 1953.

* Mead, Margaret, *Male and Female.* William Morrow and Company, Inc., New York, 1949.

* Mead, Margaret, *Sex and Temperament.* William Morrow and Company, Inc., New York, 1935.

Mercer, Marilyn, "Is There Room at the Top?" *Saturday Evening Post,* pp. 18–22, July 27, 1968.

* Money, John, and Ehrhardt, Anke, *Man and Woman, Boy and Girl.* Johns Hopkins University Press, Baltimore, 1972.

Mussen, Paul, and Rutherford, Eldred, "Parent-Child Relations and Parental Personality in Relation to Young Children's Sex Role Preferences," *Child Development,* vol. XXXIV, pp. 589–608, 1963.

* Olesker, Wendy, and Balter, Lawrence, "Sex and Empathy," *Journal of Counseling Psychology,* vol. XIX, pp. 559–562, 1972.

* Parsons, T.; Bales, R. F.; and Shils, E. A., *Working Papers in the Theory of Action.* Free Press of Glencoe, Inc., Glencoe, Illinois, 1955.

* Pheterson, Gail I.; Kiesler, Sara B.; and Goldberg, Philip A., "Evaluation of the Performance of Women as a Function of Their Sex, Achievement, and Personal History," *Journal of Personality and Social Psychology,* vol. XIX, pp. 114–118, 1971.

* Prather, Jane, and Fidell, Linda, "Put Her Down and Drug Her Up!" presented at American Sociology Association, August 1972.

Reiss, Ira L., *Premarital Sexual Standards in America.* Free Press of Glencoe, Inc., New York, 1960.

* Sannito, Thomas; Walker, Ronald E.; Foley, Jeanne M.; and Posavac, Emil J., "A Test of Female Sex Identification: The Thorne Femininity Study," *Journal of Clinical Psychology,* vol. XXVIII, pp. 531–539, 1972.

Schiffman, Jacob, "Marital and Family Characteristics of Workers," *Monthly Labor Review,* LXXXV, pp. 9–16, 1962.

* Schneider, Joseph W., and Hacker, Sally L., "Sex Role Imagery and Use of the Generic 'Man' in Introductory Texts: A Case in the Sociology of Sociology," presented at the annual meetings of the American Sociological Association, 1972.

Seeley, John R.; Sim, R. Alexander; and Loosley, Elizabeth W., "Differentiation of Values in a Modern Community," in Norman W. Bell and Ezra F. Vogel, editors, *The Family.* Free Press of Glencoe, Inc., Glencoe, Illinois, 1960.

Seidman, Jerome M., editor. *The Adolescent.* Holt, Rinehart & Winston, Inc., New York, 1960.

* Smuts, Robert W., *Women and Work in America.* Columbia University Press, New York, 1959.

* Stephens, William N., *The Family in Cross-Cultural Perspective.* Holt, Rinehart & Winston, Inc., 1963.

* Terman, Lewis M., and Miles, Catharine Cox, *Sex and Personality.* McGraw-Hill Book Company, Inc., New York, 1936.

* U. S. Bureau of the Census, *Detailed Characteristics* (summary of U. S. Census of Population, 1960), PC (1) 1D U. S., p. 528. U. S. Government Printing Office, Washington, D. C., 1964.

U. S. Bureau of the Census, *Historical Statistics of the U. S., Colonial Times to 1957,* 1960.

* U. S. Bureau of the Census, "Labor Force," vol. III of *Population* (16th census of U. S., 1940), p. 75. U. S. Government Printing Office, Washington, D. C., 1943.

U. S. Bureau of Labor Statistics, "Marital and Family Characteristics of Workers, March, 1966," *Monthly Labor Review,* vol. XC, pp. 29–36, April 1967.

U. S. Department of Health, Education, and Welfare, *Converging Social Trends, Emerging Social Problems.* Washington, D. C., 1964.

U. S. Department of Labor, Bureau of Labor Statistics, *Employment and Earnings: Annual Supplement Issue, 1961.*

Waldman, Elizabeth, and Gover, Kathryn R., "Marital and Family Characteristics of the Labor Force," in U. S. Bureau of Labor Statistics, *Monthly Labor Review,* vol. XCV, pp. 4–8, 1972.

* Zelditch, Morris, Jr., "Role Differentiation in the Nuclear Family: A Comparative Study," in Talcott Parsons and Robert F. Bales, editors, *Family Socialization, and Interaction Process.* Free Press of Glencoe, Glencoe, Illinois, 1955.

CHAPTER 4   DEVELOPMENT OF SEX ROLES

* Angrist, Shirley S., "The Study of Sex Roles," *Journal of Social Issues,* vol. XXV, pp. 215–231, 1969.

Barclay, A., and Cusumano, D. R., "Father Absence, Cross-Sex Identity, and Field-Dependent Behavior in Male Adolescents," *Child Development,* vol. XXXVIII, pp. 243–250, 1967.

* Barclay, Allan G., and Cusumano, D. R., "Testing Masculinity in Boys Without Fathers," *Transaction,* vol. V, pp. 33–35, December 1967.

* Barry, Herbert; Bacon, Margaret K.; and Child, Irvin L., "A Cross Cultural Survey of Some Sex Differences in Socialization," *Journal of Abnormal and Social Psychology,* vol. LV, pp. 327–332, 1957.

* Beach, Frank, editor, *Sex and Behavior.* John Wiley & Sons, Inc., New York, 1965.

* Blood, Robert O., Jr., and Wolfe, Donald M., *Husbands and Wives.* Free Press of Glencoe, Inc., New York, 1960.

Brim, Orville G., Jr., "Adolescent Personality as Self-Other Systems," *Journal of Marriage and the Family,* vol. XXVII, pp. 156–162, 1965.

* Brim, Orville G., Jr., "Family Structure and Sex-role Learning by Children," *Sociometry,* vol. XXI, pp. 1–16, March 1958.

* Broderick, Carlfred B., and Fowler, Stanley E., "New Patterns of Relationships Between the Sexes Among Preadolescents," *Marriage and Family Living,* vol. XXIII, no. 1, pp. 27–30, 1961.

* Brown, Daniel G., "Masculinity-femininity Development in Children," *Journal of Consulting Psychology,* vol. XXI, pp. 197–202, 1957.

Brown, Daniel G., "Homosexuality and Family Dynamics," *Bulletin of the Menninger Clinic,* vol. XXVII, pp. 227–232, 1963.

Brown, Daniel G., and Lynn, David B., "Human Sexual Development: An Outline of Components and Concepts," *Journal of Marriage and the Family,* vol. XXVIII, pp. 155–162, 1966.

* Burton, Roger V., and Whiting, John W. M., "The Absent Father and Cross-sex Identity," *Merrill-Palmer Quarterly,* vol. VII, no. 2, pp. 85-96, April 1961.
* Coleman, James S., *The Adolescent Society.* Free Press of Glencoe, Inc., New York, 1961.
  Coombs, Robert H., "The Socialization of Male and Female: Sex Status and Role," in Clark E. Vincent, editor, *Human Sexuality in Medical Education and Practice.* Charles C. Thomas, Springfield, Illinois, 1968.
* Dagan, Jerome, "Child's Symbolic Conceptualization of Parents," *Child Development,* vol. XXXII, pp. 625-636, 1961.
* Diamond, Milton, "A Critical Evaluation of the Ontogeny of Human Sexual Behavior," *Quarterly Review of Biology,* vol. XL, pp. 147-175, 1965.
* Didato, S. V., and Kennedy, T. M., "Masculinity-femininity and Personal Values," *Psychological Reports,* vol. II, pp. 231-250, 1956.
* Ehrmann, Winston W., *Premarital Dating Behavior.* Henry Holt & Company, Inc., New York, 1959.
* Elder, Glen H., Jr., "Appearance and Education in Marriage Mobility," *American Sociological Review,* vol. XXXIV, pp. 519-533, 1969.
* Ellis, Albert, *The American Sexual Tragedy,* second edition. Lyle Stuart, Inc., New York, 1962.
  Fararo, T. J., and Sunshine, Morris H., *A Study of a Biased Friendship Net.* Youth Development Center, Syracuse University, Syracuse, New York, 1964.
* Ferguson, L. W., "The Cultural Genesis of Masculinity-femininity," *Psychological Bulletin,* vol. XXXVIII, pp. 584-585, 1941.
  Gagnon, John H., "Sexuality and Sexual Learning in the Child," *Psychiatry,* vol. XXVIII, pp. 212-228, 1965.
* Hartley, Ruth E., "Children's Perceptions of Sex Preference in Four Culture Groups," *Journal of Marriage and the Family,* vol. XXXI, pp. 380-387, 1969.
  Henry, Jules, and Henry, Zunia, "Doll Play of Pilaga Indian Children," in Clyde Kluckhohn and Murray Henry, editors, *Personality in Nature, Society and Culture.* Alfred A. Knopf, New York, 1948.
  Hetherington, E. M., "A Developmental Study of the Effects of Sex of the Dominant Parent on Sex-Role Preference, Identification, and Imitation in Children," *Journal of Personality and Social Psychology,* vol. II, pp. 188-194, 1965.
* Hetherington, E. M., "Effects of Paternal Abuse on Sex-Typed Behavior in Negro and White Preadolescent Males," *Journal of Personality and Social Psychology,* vol. IV, pp. 87-91, 1966.
* Holmes, S. J., and Hatch, C. E., "Personal Appearance as Related to Scholastic Records and Marriage Selection in College Women," *Human Biology,* vol. X, pp. 65-76, 1938.
* Houwink, R. M., and Jansen, L., "Masculiniteit en Femininiteit bij de Middelbare Schooljeugd in Zuid-Oost Nederland," *Ned. Tijdschr. Psychol.,* vol. VI, 1951, 439-445 (Abstract).
* Johnson, Miriam M., "Sex Role Learning in the Nuclear Family," *Child Development,* vol. XXXIV, pp. 319-334, June 1963.
  Jourard, Sidney M., and Secord, Paul F., "Body-Cathexis and the Ideal Female Figure," *Journal of Abnormal and Social Psychology,* vol. L, pp. 243-246, 1955.

* Kagan, Jerome, and Moss, Howard A., *Birth to Maturity: A Study in Psychological Development.* John Wiley & Sons, Inc., New York, 1962.

Kammeyer, Kenneth, "Birth Order and the Feminine Sex Role Among College Women," *American Sociological Review,* vol. XXXI, pp. 508-515, 1966.

Kammeyer, Kenneth, "The Feminine Role: An Analysis of Attitude Consistency," *Journal of Marriage and the Family,* vol. XXVI, pp. 295-305, 1964.

* Kammeyer, Kenneth, "Sibling Position and the Feminine Role," *Journal of Marriage and the Family,* vol. XXIX, pp. 494-499, 1967.

* Kephart, William M., *The Family, Society, and the Individual.* Houghton Mifflin Company, Boston, 1961.

* Kinsey, Alfred C.; Pomeroy, Wardell B.; and Martin, Clyde E., *Sexual Behavior in the Human Male.* W. B. Saunders Company, Philadelphia, 1948.

* Kinsey, Alfred C.; Pomeroy, Wardell B.; Martin, Clyde E.; and Gebhard, Paul H., *Sexual Behavior in the Human Female.* W. B. Saunders Company, Philadelphia, 1953.

* Kirkendall, Lester A., *Premarital Intercourse and Interpersonal Relationships.* Gramercy Publishing Co., New York, 1968.

* Kronhausen, Eberhard, and Kronhausen, Phyllis, *Pornography and the Law.* Ballantine Books, Inc., New York, 1959.

Landis, Judson T., and Landis, Mary G., *Building a Successful Marriage,* fourth edition. Prentice-Hall, Inc., Englewood Cliffs, New Jersey, 1963.

* Lee, Margie Robinson, "Background Factors Related to Sex Information and Attitudes," *Journal of Educational Psychology,* vol. XLIII, pp. 467-485, 1952.

Leuba, Clarence J., *Man: A General Psychology.* Holt, Rinehart and Winston, Inc., New York, 1961.

* Lynn, David B., "Divergent Feedback and Sex-Role Identification in Boys and Men," *Merrill-Palmer Quarterly,* vol. X, no. 1, pp. 17-23, 1964.

* Lynn, David B., "Sex Differences in Identification Development," *Sociometry,* vol. XXIV, no. 4, pp. 372-383, December 1961.

* Lynn, David B., "Sex-role and Parental Identification," *Child Development,* vol. XXXIII, pp. 555-564, 1962.

* Lynn, David B., and Sawrey, William L., "The Effects of Father-Absence on Norwegian Boys and Girls," *Journal of Abnormal and Social Psychology,* vol. LIX, pp. 258-262, 1959.

Maccoby, Eleanor E., editor, *The Development of Sex Differences.* Stanford University Press, Stanford, California, 1966.

* Mamiya, Takeshi, "Seisa Kenkyu: Seisa Kenkyu No Taikeika to Seisa Ishiki ni Kansuru Kendyu," *Japanese Journal of Educational Psychology,* vol. VI, pp. 205-216, 264, March 1959 (Abstract).

McCord, Joan; McCord, William; and Thurber, Emily, "Effects of Maternal Employment on Lower-Class Boys," *Journal of Abnormal and Social Psychology,* vol. LXVII, pp. 177-182, 1963.

* McKee, John P., and Sherifs, Alex C., "Men's and Women's Beliefs, Ideals and Self Concepts," *American Journal of Sociology,* vol. LXIV, pp. 356-363, 1959.

* Meyer, William, "Relationships Between Social Need Strivings and the Development of Heterosexual Affiliations," *Journal of Abnormal and Social Psychology,* vol. LXIX, no. 1, pp. 51-57, July 1959.

* Miller, Walter B., "Lower-class Culture as Generating Milieu of Gang Delinquency," *Journal of Social Issues,* vol. XIV, pp. 5-19, 1958.
* Money, John; Hampson, Joan G.; and Hampson, John L., "Imprinting and the Establishment of Gender Role," *American Medical Association Archives of Neurology and Psychiatry,* vol. LXXVII, pp. 333-336, March 1957.
  Moss, Howard A., Review of *The Widening World of Childhood* in *Merrill-Palmer Quarterly,* vol. XI, pp. 171-179, 1965.
  Moss, Howard A., "Sex, Age and State as Determinants of Mother-Infant Interaction." Manuscript presented at the 1966 Merrill-Palmer Conference.
  Moss, Howard A., and Kagan, Jerome, "Report on Personality Consistency and Change from the Fels Longitudinal Study," *Vita Humana,* vol. VII, pp. 127-138, 1964.
  Mueller, William J., "Need Structure and the Projection of Traits onto Parents," *Journal of Personality and Social Psychology,* vol. III, pp. 63-72, 1966.
  Mussen, Paul, and Distler, Luther, "Child-rearing Antecedents of Masculine Identification in Kindergarten Boys," *Child Development,* vol. XXXI, pp. 89-100, 1960.
* Mussen, Paul, and Distler, Luther, "Masculinity, Identification, and Father-Son Relationships," *Journal of Abnormal and Social Psychology,* vol. LIX, pp. 350-356, 1959.
  Mussen, Paul H., and Parker, Ann L., "Mother Nurturance and Girls' Incidental Imitative Learning," *Journal of Personality and Social Psychology,* vol. II, pp. 94-97, 1965.
* Mussen, Paul, and Rutherford, Eldred, "Parent-Child Relations and Parental Personality in Relation to Young Children's Sex-role Preferences," *Child Development,* vol. XXXIV, pp. 589-608, September 1963.
* Packard, Vance, *The Hidden Persuaders.* David McKay Company, Inc., New York, 1957.
  Parsons, Talcott, "Age and Sex in the Social Structure of the U. S.," in Robert F. Winch, Robert McGinnis, and Herbert R. Barringer, editors, *Selected Studies in Marriage and the Family,* revised edition. Holt, Rinehart & Winston, Inc., New York, 1962.
* Payne, Donald E., and Mussen, Paul H., "Parent-Child Relations and Father Identification Among Adolescent Boys," *Journal of Abnormal and Social Psychology,* vol. LII, pp. 358-362, 1956.
* Rabban, M., "Sex Role Identification in Young Children in Two Diverse Social Groups," *Genetic Psychology Monographs,* vol. XLII, pp. 81-158, 1950.
  Reese, Hayne W., "Attitudes Toward the Opposite Sex in Late Childhood," *Merrill-Palmer Quarterly,* vol. XII, pp. 157-163, 1966.
* Reiss, Albert J., Jr., "The Social Integration of Queers and Peers," *Social Problems,* vol. IX, no. 2, pp. 102-120, fall 1961.
  Rowe, George P., "Patterns of Heterosexual Development Among Preadolescents," presented at the 1966 annual meetings of the National Council on Family Relations.
  Safilios-Rothschild, Constantina, " 'Good' and 'Bad' Girls in Modern Greek Movies," *Journal of Marriage and the Family,* vol. XXX, pp. 527-531, 1968.

* Schwendinger, Julia, and Schwendinger, Herman, "Big-shots, Fatsos and Smarty-pants: Social Types Among Pre-teens," presented at the annual meetings of the Pacific Sociological Association, Portland, Oregon, April 26, 1963.

* Sears, Pauline Snedden, et al., "Child-Rearing Factors Related to Playing of Sex-Typed Roles," *American Psychologist,* vol. VIII, p. 431, 1953.

* Sears, R. R.; Pentler, M. H.; and Sears, P. S., "Effect of Father Separation on Preschool Children's Doll Play Aggression," *Child Development,* vol. XVII, pp. 219-243, 1946.

* Sears, R. R.; Whiting, Nowlis; and Sears, P. S., "Some Child Rearing Antecedents of Aggression and Dependency in Young Children," *Genetic Psychology Monographs,* vol. XLVII, no. 2, pp. 135-234, 1953.

Sigusch, Volkmar; Schmidt, Gunter; Reinfeld, Antje; and Wiedemann-Sutor, Ingeborg, "Psychosexual Stimulation: Sex Differences," *Journal of Sex Research,* vol. VI, pp. 10-24, 1970.

* Simpson, George, *People in Families.* Thomas Y. Crowell Company, New York, 1960.

Singer, Jerome E., "The Use of Manipulative Strategies: Machiavellianism and Attractiveness," *Sociometry,* vol. XXVII, pp. 128-150, 1964.

Smith, Thomas E., "Social Class and Attitudes Toward Fathers," *Sociology and Social Research, An International Journal,* vol. LIII, no. 2, pp. 227-241, January 1969.

* Stephens, William N., *The Family in Cross-cultural Perspective.* Holt, Rinehart & Winston, Inc., New York, 1963.

Stevenson, Harold W., and Allen, Sara, "Adult Performance as a Function of Sex of Experimenter and Sex of Subject," *Journal of Abnormal and Social Psychology,* vol. LXVIII, pp. 214-216, 1964.

* Strodtbeck, Fred L., and Creelan, Paul G., "The Interaction Linkage Between Family Size, Intelligence, and Sex-Role Identity," *Journal of Marriage and the Family,* vol. XXX, pp. 301-307, 1968.

* Terman, Lewis M., *Psychological Factors in Marital Happiness.* McGraw-Hill Book Company, New York, 1938.

Thomes, Mary Margaret, "Children with Absent Fathers," *Journal of Marriage and the Family,* vol. XXX, no. 1, pp. 89-96, February 1968.

* Udry, J. Richard, "Structural Correlates of Feminine Beauty Preferences in Britain and the United States: A Comparison," *Sociology and Social Research,* vol. XLIX, pp. 331-342, 1965.

* Udry, J. Richard; Bauman, Karl E.; and Chase, Charles A., "Skin Color, Status and Mate Selection," *American Journal of Sociology,* vol. LXXVI, no. 4, pp. 722-733, January 1971.

* Vener, Arthur M., and Snyder, Clinton A., "The Preschool Child's Awareness and Anticipation of Adult Sex-Roles," *Sociometry,* vol. XXIX, pp. 159-168, 1966.

* Winch, Robert F., "Further Data and Observations on the Oedipus Hypothesis: The Consequences of an Inadequate Hypothesis," *American Sociological Review,* vol. XVI, pp. 784-795, 1951.

* Winch, Robert F., *The Modern Family,* revised edition. Holt, Rinehart and Winston, Inc., New York, 1963.

Winick, Charles, "The Beige Epoch: Depolarization of Sex Roles in America," in *Medical Aspects of Human Sexuality,* vol. III, pp. 69-80, 1969; and in *The Annals of the American Academy of Political and Social Science,* vol. CCCLXXVI, pp. 18-24, 1968.

Winick, Charles, *The New People.* Western Publishing Company, New York, 1968.

CHAPTER 5   THE ORIGINS AND DEVELOPMENT OF
             HETEROSEXUALITY

* Bayer, Alan E., "Early Dating and Early Marriage," *Journal of Marriage and the Family,* vol. XXX, pp. 628-632, 1968.
* Beach, F. A., "Characteristics of Masculine 'Sex Drive'," in M. R. Jones, editor, *Nebraska Symposium on Motivation.* University of Nebraska Press, Lincoln, Nebraska, 1956.
* Bell, Robert R., and Chaskes, Jay B., "Premarital Sexual Experience Among Coeds, 1958 and 1968," *Journal of Marriage and the Family,* vol. XXXII, pp. 81-84, 1970.
Broderick, Carlfred B., "Sexual Behavior Among Pre-Adolescents," *Journal of Social Issues,* vol. XXII, no. 2, April, 6-21, 1966.
Broderick, Carlfred B., "Social Heterosexual Development Among Urban Negroes and Whites," *Journal of Marriage and the Family,* vol. XXVII, pp. 200-203, 1965.
Broderick, Carlfred B., and Rowe, George P., "A Scale of Preadolescent Heterosexual Development," *Journal of Marriage and the Family,* vol. XXX, pp. 97-101, 1968.
* Burgess, Ernest W., and Locke, Harvey J., *The Family,* second edition. American Book Company, New York, 1953.
Burgess, Ernest W., and Wallin, Paul, *Engagement and Marriage.* J. B. Lippincott Company, Philadelphia, 1953.
Caro, Francis G., "Social Class and Attitudes of Youth Relevant for the Realization of Adult Goals," *Social Forces,* vol. XLIV, pp. 492-498, 1966.
* Coleman, James S., *The Adolescent Society.* Free Press of Glencoe, Inc., New York, 1961.
Coombs, Robert H., "Value Consensus and Partner Satisfaction Among Dating Couples," *Journal of Marriage and the Family,* vol. XXVIII, pp. 166-173, 1966.
Coombs, Robert H., and Kenkel, William F., "Sex Differences in Dating Aspirations and Satisfaction with Computer-Selected Partners," *Journal of Marriage and the Family,* vol. XXVIII, pp. 62-66, 1966.
Freeman, Harrop A., and Freeman, Ruth, "Dating Between American and Foreign College Students," *Journal of Sex Research,* vol. II, pp. 207-214, 1966.
Gagnon, John H., "Female Child Victims of Sex Offenses," *Social Problems,* vol. XIII, pp. 176-192, 1965.

Gagnon, John H., "Sexuality and Sexual Learning in the Child," *Psychiatry,* vol. XXVIII, pp. 212-228, 1965.

* Goffman, Erving, *Encounters: Two Studies in the Sociology of Interaction,* Bobbs-Merrill Company, Inc., Indianapolis, Indiana, 1961.

* Goodenough, Ruth, "Dating and Security," *Understanding the Child,* vol. XXVI, pp. 59-60, 1957.

* Hardy, Kenneth R., "An Appetitional Theory of Sexual Motivation," *Psychological Review,* vol. LXXI, pp. 1-18, January 1964.

* Heiss, Jerold S., "Degree of Intimacy and Male-Female Interaction," *Sociometry,* vol. XXV, pp. 197-208, June 1962.

* Herman, Robert D., "The 'Going Steady' Complex: A Reexamination," *Marriage and Family Living,* vol. XVII, pp. 36-40, 1955.

* Hollingshead, August B., *Elmtown's Youth: The Impact of Social Classes on Adolescents.* John Wiley & Sons, Inc., New York, 1949.

Jackson, Jeffrey, "The Underdeveloped Sex," *New Society,* vol. CXXXI, April 24, 1965.

Jakobvits, Leon A., "Evaluational Reactions to Erotic Literature," *Psychological Reports,* vol. XVI, pp. 985-994, 1965.

* Kallman, Franz J., "Comparative Twin Study on the Genetic Aspects of Male Homosexuality," *The Journal of Nervous and Mental Disease,* vol. CXV, no. 4, serial no. 844, pp. 283-298, April 1952.

Kolodny, Robert C.; Masters, William H.; Hendryx, Julie; and Toro, Gelson, "Plasma Testosterone and Semen Analysis in Male Homosexuals," *New England Journal of Medicine,* vol. CCLXXXV, pp. 1, 170-1, 174, 1971.

* Landis, Judson T., "Dating Maturation of Children from Happy and Unhappy Marriages," *Marriage and Family Living,* vol. XXV, pp. 351-353, August 1963.

Landis, Judson T., and Landis, Mary G., *Building a Successful Marriage,* fourth edition. Prentice-Hall, Inc., Englewood Cliffs, New Jersey, 1963.

Leiman, Alan H., and Epstein, Seymour, "Thematic Sexual Responses as Related to Sexual Drive and Guilt," *Journal of Abnormal and Social Psychology,* vol. LXIII, pp. 169-175, 1961.

* Leuba, Clarence J., *The Sexual Nature of Man.* Doubleday, Garden City, New York, 1954.

Levine, Edward M., "The Twist: A Symptom of Identity Problems as Social Pathology," *Israel Annals of Psychiatry and Related Disciplines,* vol. IV, pp. 1-16, 1966.

Liebow, Elliot, *Tally's Corner,* pp. 138-139. Little, Brown and Company, 1967.

* Lowrie, Samuel Harman, "Early and Late Dating: Some Conditions Associated with Them," *Marriage and Family Living,* vol. XXIII, no. 3, pp. 284-291, August 1961.

Maier, Henry W., "Adolescenthood," *Social Casework,* vol. XLVI, pp. 3-9, 1965.

Maranell, Gary M., "An Examination of the Self and Group Attitudes of Adolescent Clique Members," *Kansas Journal of Sociology,* vol. I, pp. 123-130, 1965.

* Margolese, M. Sydney, "Homosexuality: A New Endocrine Correlate," *Hormones and Behavior,* vol. I, pp. 151-155, 1970.

Marth, Selden B., "Guilt Feelings and Disapproval Projections as Related to Parents, Church, God, and Fate, in Adolescent Sexual Development," *Dissertation Abstracts,* vol. XXIV, pp. 1,246–1,247, 1963.

Martin, Barclay, "Expression and Inhibition of Sex Motive Arousal in College Males," *Journal of Abnormal and Social Psychology,* vol. LXVIII, pp. 307–312, 1964.

Nichols, William C., Jr., and Rutledge, Aaron L., "Psychotherapy with Teen-agers," *Journal of Marriage and the Family,* vol. XXVII, pp. 166–170, 1965.

Pomeroy, Wardell B., "An Analysis of Questions of Sex," *The Psychological Record,* vol. X, pp. 191–201, 1960.

Reese, Hayne W., "Attitudes Toward the Opposite Sex in Late Childhood," *Merrill-Palmer Quarterly,* vol. XII, pp. 157–163, 1966.

* Rogers, Everett M., and Havens, Eugene, "Prestige Rating and Male Selection on a College Campus," *Marriage and Family Living,* vol. XXII, pp. 55–59, February 1960.

Rowe, George P., "Patterns of Heterosexual Development Among Preadolescents," presented at the 1966 annual meetings of the National Council on Family Relations.

Sagarin, Edward, "Typologies of Sexual Behavior," *Journal of Sex Research,* vol. VII, pp. 282–288, 1971.

Salmon, Udall J., and Geist, Samuel H., "Effect of Androgens Upon Libido in Women," *Journal of Clinical Endocrinology,* vol. III, pp. 235–238, 1943.

* Scott, John F., "The Role of the College Sorority in Endogamy," *American Sociological Review,* vol. XXX, pp. 514–527, 1965.

* Skipper, James K., Jr., and Nass, Gilbert, "Dating Behavior: A Framework for Analysis and an Illustration," *Journal of Marriage and the Family,* vol. XXVIII, pp. 412–420, 1966.

Stokes, Walter R., "Intelligent Preparation of Children for Adolescence," *Journal of Marriage and the Family,* vol. XXVII, pp. 163–165, 1965.

Strong, Emily, and Wilson, Warner, "Three-Filter Date Selection by Computer—Phase II," *The Family Coordinator,* vol. XVIII, pp. 256–259, 1969.

Tamm, Jurgen, editor, *Testosterone: Proceedings of the Workshop Conference at Tremsbuttel.* Georg Thieme Verlag, Stuttgart, 1967.

* Thomas, John L., "Early Teen-age Dancing and Dating Betrays Our Youth and Our Country," *Social Order,* vol. XIII, no. 1, pp. 18–24, January 1963.

* Thomas, John L., "Parents, Teen-agers and Dating Patterns," *Social Order,* vol. IX, no. 2, pp. 51–59, February 1959.

* Walster, Elaine; Aronson, Vera; Abrahams, Darcy; and Rottman, Leon, "Importance of Physical Attractiveness in Dating Behavior," *Journal of Personality and Social Psychology,* vol. IV, pp. 508–516, 1966.

Wass, Betty M., and Eicher, Joanne B., "Clothing as Related to Role Behavior of Teen-Age Girls," *MSU Quarterly Bulletin,* vol. XLVII, pp. 206–213, 1964.

* Wieland, Ralph G.; Chen, Jeffrey C.; Zorn, Elinor M.; and Hallberg, Marvin C., "Correlation of Growth, Pubertal Staging, Growth Hormone, Gonadotropins, and Testosterone Levels During the Pubertal Growth Spurt in Males," *Journal of Pediatrics,* vol. LXXIX, pp. 999–1,002, 1971.

CHAPTER 6   PREMARITAL SEXUAL BEHAVIOR

Auken, Kirsten, "Time of Marriage, Mate Selection and Task Accomplishment in Newly Formed Copenhagen Families," *Acta Sociologica,* vol. VIII, pp. 128–141, 1964.

Bair, Lowell, *Patterns of Sex and Love: A Study of the French Woman and Her Morals.* Crown Publishers, New York, 1960.

* Barnes, Kenneth, et al., "A Group of Friends," in Alastair Heron, editor, *Toward a Quaker View of Sex.* Friends Home Service Committee, London, 1963.

* Bauman, Karl E., and Wilson, Robert R., "Premarital Sexual Attitudes of Unmarried University Students in 1968 and 1972," unpublished manuscript, 1973.

* Bell, Robert R., and Buerkle, Jack V., "Mother and Daughter Attitudes to Premarital Sexual Behavior," *Marriage and Family Living,* vol. XXIII, no. 4, pp. 390–392, November 1961.

* Bell, Robert R., and Chaskes, Jay B., "Premarital Sexual Experience Among Coeds, 1958 and 1968," *Journal of Marriage and the Family,* vol. XXXII, pp. 81–84, 1970.

* Blood, Robert O., Jr., "Romance and Premarital Intercourse — Incompatibles?" *Marriage and Family Living,* vol. XIV, pp. 105–108, 1952.

Brown, Helen Gurley, *Sex and the Single Girl.* Random House, New York, 1962.

* Burchinal, Lee G., and Bock, Elmer W., "Religious Behavior, Premarital Pregnancy, and Early Maturity," *Alpha Kappa Deltan,* vol. XXIX, no. 2, pp. 39–44, spring 1959.

Burgess, Ernest W.; Locke, Harvey J.; and Thomes, Mary M., *The Family,* third edition. American Book Company, New York, 1963.

* Burgess, Ernest W., and Wallin, Paul, *Engagement and Marriage.* J. B. Lippincott Company, Philadelphia, 1953.

* Carey, Judith, and Rogers, E. Lance, "Health Status and Health Knowledge of the Student in the Changing Community College," *American Journal of Public Health,* vol. LXIII, pp. 126–133, 1973.

* Christensen, Harold T., "Child Spacing Analysis via Record Linkage: New Data Plus Summing Up from Earlier Reports," *Marriage and Family Living,* vol. XXV, pp. 272–280, August 1963.

* Christensen, Harold T., "Cultural Relativism and Premarital Sex Norms," *American Sociological Review,* vol. XXV, no. 1, pp. 31–39, February 1960.

* Christensen, Harold T., "The Method of Record Linkage Applied to Family Data," *Marriage and Family Living,* vol. XX, pp. 38–42, 1958.

Christensen, Harold T., "Normative Theory Derived from Cross-Cultural Family Research," *Journal of Marriage and the Family,* vol. XXXI, no. 2, pp. 209–222, May 1969.

* Christensen, Harold T., and Carpenter, George R., "Timing Patterns in Premarital Sexual Intimacy: An Attitudinal Report on Three Modern Western Societies," *Marriage and Family Living,* vol. XXIV, no. 1, pp. 30–35, February 1962.

* Christensen, Harold T., and Gregg, Christina F., "Changing Sex Norms in America and Scandinavia," *Journal of Marriage and the Family,* vol. XXXII, pp. 616–627, 1970.

* Christensen, Harold T., and Meissner, Hanna H., "Studies in Child Spacing: III—Premarital Pregnancy as a Factor in Divorce," *American Sociological Review,* vol. XVIII, no. 6, pp. 641-644, December 1953.
* Christensen, Harold T., and Rubinstein, Bette B., "Premarital Pregnancy and Divorce: A Follow-Up Study by the Interview Method," *Marriage and Family Living,* vol. XVIII, no. 2, pp. 114-123, May 1956.
* Clayton, Richard R., "Premarital Sexual Intercourse: A Substantive Test of the Contingent Consistency Model," *Journal of Marriage and the Family,* vol. XXXIV, pp. 273-281, 1972.
* Cutright, Phillips, "The Teenage Sexual Revolution and the Myth of an Abstinent Past," *Family Planning Perspectives,* vol. IV, pp. 24-31, 1972.
* Davis, Kingsley, "Prostitution," in Robert K. Merton and Robert A. Nisbet, editors, *Contemporary Social Problems.* Harcourt, Brace and World, Inc., New York, 1961.
* Driscoll, Richard H., and Davis, Keith E., "Sexual Restraints: A Comparison of Perceived and Self-Reported Reasons for College Students," *Journal of Sex Research,* vol. VII, pp. 253-262, 1971.
* Ehrmann, Winston W., "Non-conformance of Male and Female Reports on Premarital Coitus," *Social Problems,* vol. II, pp. 155-159, April 1954.
* Ehrmann, Winston W., *Premarital Dating Behavior.* Henry Holt and Company, New York, 1959.
* Ellis, Albert, *The American Sexual Tragedy,* second edition. Lyle Stuart, Inc., New York, 1962.
 Gallup, George, " 'Generation Gap' Apparent in Public's Views on Premarital Sexual Relations." American Institute of Public Opinion News Release, September 13, 1969.
* Gebhard, Paul H.; Pomeroy, Wardell B.; Martin, Clyde E.; and Christenson, Cornelia V., *Pregnancy, Birth, and Abortion.* Harper-Hoeber, New York, 1958.
 Goode, William J., "Illegitimacy, Anomie, and Cultural Penetration," *American Sociological Review,* vol. XXVI, no. 6, pp. 910-925, December 1961.
* Green, Arnold W., "The 'Cult of Personality' and Sexual Relations," *Psychiatry,* vol. IV, pp. 343-348, 1941.
* Hamblin, Robert L., and Blood, Robert O., Jr., "Premarital Experience and the Wife's Sexual Adjustment," *Social Problems,* vol. III, pp. 122-130, 1956.
 Harrison, Danny E.; Bennett, Walter H.; and Globetti, Gerald, "Attitudes of Rural Youth Toward Premarital Sexual Permissiveness," *Journal of Marriage and the Family,* vol. XXXI, no. 4, November 1969.
 Hartley, Shirley, "The Amazing Rise of Illegitimacy in Great Britain," vol. XLIV, pp. 533-545, 1966.
 Hollingshead, August B., *Elmtown's Youth.* John Wiley & Sons, Inc., New York, 1949.
* Hunt, Morton M., *The Natural History of Love.* Alfred A. Knopf, Inc., New York, 1959.
* Israel, Joachim, and Eliasson, Rosmari, "Consumption Society, Sex Roles and Sexual Behavior," *Acta Sociologica,* vol. XIV, pp. 1-2, 68-82, 1971.

* Kaats, Gilbert R., and Davis, Keith E., "The Dynamics of Sexual Behavior of College Students," *Journal of Marriage and the Family,* vol. XXXII, pp. 390–399, 1970.

* Kinsey, Alfred C.; Pomeroy, Wardell B.; and Martin, Clyde E., *Sexual Behavior in the Human Male.* W. B. Saunders Company, Philadelphia, 1948.

* Kinsey, Alfred C.; Pomeroy, Wardell B.; Martin, Clyde E.; and Gebhard, Paul H., *Sexual Behavior in the Human Female.* W. B. Saunders Company, Philadelphia, 1953.

* Kirkendall, Lester A., *Premarital Intercourse and Interpersonal Relationships.* Gramercy Publishing Co., New York, 1968.

* Kirkendall, Lester A., "Sex Education of Adolescents: An Exchange," *Marriage and Family Living,* vol. XXII, no. 4, pp. 317–322, November 4, 1960.

Kirkendall, Lester A., "Values and Premarital Intercourse—Implications for Parent Education," *Marriage and Family Living,* vol. XXII, no. 4, pp. 317–322, November 1960.

* Landis, Judson T., "The Women Kinsey Studied," *Social Problems,* vol. I, no. 4, pp. 139–142, April 1954.

* Leach, Edmund R., "Adolescence: II. Sins or Rules?" *New Society,* vol. I, pp. 13–15, 1963.

Linner, Birgitta, "The Sexual Revolution in Sweden," *Impact of Science on Society,* vol. XVIII, pp. 229–247, 1968.

* Locke, Harvey J., "Are Volunteer Interviewees Representative?" *Social Problems,* vol. I, no. 4, pp. 143–146, April 1954.

* Locke, Harvey J., *Predicting Adjustment in Marriage: A Comparison of a Divorced and Happily Married Group.* Henry Holt and Company, New York, 1951.

* Luckey, Eleanor B., and Nass, Gilbert D., "A Comparison of Sexual Attitudes and Behavior in an International Sample," *Journal of Marriage and the Family,* vol. XXXI, no. 2, pp. 364–379, May 1969.

Lyness, Judith L.; Lipetz, Milton E.; and Davis, Keith E., "Living Together: An Alternative to Marriage," *Journal of Marriage and the Family,* vol. XXXIV, pp. 305–311, 1972.

Macklin, Eleanor D., "Heterosexual Cohabitation Among Unmarried College Students," *The Family Coordinator,* vol. XXI, pp. 463–472, 1972.

Maranell, Gary M.; Dodder, Richard A.; and Mitchell, David F., "Social Class and Premarital Sexual Permissiveness: A Subsequent Test," *Journal of Marriage and the Family,* vol. XXXII, pp. 85–88, 1970.

* Martinez de Toledo, Alfonso, *Little Sermons on Sin.* University of California Press, Berkeley, California, 1959.

* Maslow, Abraham H., and Sakoda, James M., "Volunteer Error in the Kinsey Study," in Jerome Himelhoch and Sylvia Fleis Fava, editors, *Sexual Behavior in American Society.* W. W. Norton and Company, New York, 1955.

* Murdock, George P., *Social Structure.* The Macmillan Company, New York, 1949.

Needham, Merrill A., and Schur, Edwin M., "Student Punitiveness Toward Sexual Deviation," *Marriage and Family Living,* vol. XXV, no. 2, pp. 227–228, May 1963.

* Packard, Vance, *The Sexual Wilderness: The Contemporary Upheaval in Male-Female Relationships.* David McKay Company, Inc., New York, 1968.

Peterson, James A., *Education for Marriage.* Charles Scribner's Sons, New York, 1964.

* Pineo, Peter C., "Disenchantment in the Later Years of Marriage," *Marriage and Family Living,* vol. XXIII, pp. 3–11, 1961.

* Poffenberger, Thomas, "Individual Choice in Adolescent Premarital Sex Behavior," *Marriage and Family Living,* vol. XXII, no. 4, pp. 324–330, November 1960.

Price, Richard, "Trial Marriage in the Andes," *Ethnology,* vol. IV, pp. 310–322, 1965.

* Prince, Alfred J., and Shipman, Gordon, "Attitudes of College Students Toward Premarital Sex Experience," *The Coordinator,* vol. VI, no. 4, pp. 57–60, June 1958.

* Rainwater, Lee, *And the Poor Get Children.* Quadrangle Books, Chicago, 1960.

* Reiss, Ira, "How and Why America's Sex Standards Are Changing," *Transaction,* vol. XXV, March 1968.

* Reiss, Ira L., *Premarital Sexual Standards in America.* The Free Press of Glencoe, Inc., New York, 1960.

* Reiss, Ira L., "The Scaling of Premarital Sexual Permissiveness," *Journal of Marriage and the Family,* vol. XXVI, pp. 188–198, May 1964.

Reiss, Ira L., "Sexual Codes in Teen-Age Culture," *Annals of the American Academy of Political and Social Science,* vol. CCCXXXVIII, pp. 53–62, November 1961.

* Reiss, Ira L., *The Social Context of Premarital Sexual Permissiveness.* Holt, Rinehart and Winston, Inc., New York, 1967.

* Rettig, Salomon, and Pasamanick, Benjamin, "Changes in Moral Values Among College Students: A Factorial Study," *American Sociological Review,* vol. XXIV, pp. 856–863, December 1959.

* Robinson, Ira E.; King, Karl; and Balswick, Jack O., "The Premarital Sexual Revolution Among College Females," *The Family Coordinator,* vol. XXI, pp. 189–194, 1972.

Robinson, Ira E.; King, Karl; Dudley, Charles J.; and Clune, Francis J., "Change in Sexual Behavior and Attitudes of College Students," *The Family Coordinator,* vol. XVII, pp. 119–123, 1968.

* Rubin, Arline M., and Adams, James R., "Sex Attitudes of Sex Educators," *The Family Coordinator,* vol. XXI, pp. 177–182, 1972.

Schwartz, Martin S., "A Report on Sex Information Knowledge of 87 Lower Class Ninth Grade Boys," *The Family Coordinator,* vol. XVIII, pp. 361–367, 1969.

* Sorensen, Robert C., *Adolescent Sexuality in Contemporary America.* World Publishing Company, New York, 1973.

* Spark, Muriel, *The Ballad of Peckham-Rye.* J. B. Lippincott Company, Philadelphia, 1960.

* Stephens, William N., *The Family in Cross Cultural Perspective.* Holt, Rinehart and Winston, Inc., New York, 1963.

* Taylor, G. Rattray, *Sex in History.* Vanguard Press, New York, 1954.

Tebor, Irving B., "Male Virgins: Conflicts and Group Support in American Culture," *Family Life Coordinator,* vol. IX, nos. 3–4, pp. 40–42, March-June 1961.

* Teevan, James J., Jr., "Reference Groups and Premarital Sexual Behavior," *Journal of Marriage and the Family,* vol. XXXIII, pp. 283-291, 1972.

* Terman, Lewis M., *Psychological Factors in Marital Happiness.* McGraw-Hill Book Company, New York, 1938.

* Vener, Arthur M.; Stewart, Cyrus S.; and Hager, David L., "The Sexual Behavior of Adolescents in Middle America: Generational and American-British Comparisons," *Journal of Marriage and the Family,* vol. XXXIV, pp. 696-704, 1972.

* Vincent, Clark E., *Unmarried Mothers.* Free Press of Glencoe, Inc., New York, 1962.

* Whyte, William F., "A Slum Sex Code," *American Journal of Sociology,* vol. XLIX, pp. 23-31, July 1943.

* Winch, Robert F., "Permanence and Change in the History of the American Family and Some Speculations as to Its Future," *Journal of Marriage and the Family,* vol. XXXII, pp. 6-15, 1970.

* Zelnick, Melvin, and Kantner, John F., "The Probability of Premarital Intercourse," *Social Science Research,* vol. I, pp. 335-341, 1972.

CHAPTER 7   LOVE

Bardis, Panos D., "Erotometer: A Technique for the Measurement of Heterosexual Love," *International Review of Sociology,* vol. I, pp. 71-77, 1971.

* Baum, Martha, "Love, Marriage, and the Division of Labor," *Sociological Inquiry,* vol. XLI, no. 1, pp. 107-117, winter 1971.

* Beigel, Hugo G., "Romantic Love," *American Sociological Review,* vol. XVI, pp. 326-334, 1951.

* Bernard, Jessie; Buchanan, Helen C.; and Smith, William M., Jr., *Dating, Mating, and Marriage Today.* Arco Publishing Company, Inc., New York, 1959.

* Blood, Robert O., Jr., "Romance and Premarital Intercourse—Incompatibles?" *Marriage and Family Living,* vol. XIV, pp. 105-108, 1952.

Blood, Robert O., Jr., and Wolfe, Donald M., *Husbands and Wives.* Free Press of Glencoe, Inc., New York, 1960.

Bolton, Charles D., "Mate Selection as the Development of a Relationship," *Marriage and Family Living,* vol. XXIII, pp. 234-240, 1961.

* Burgess, Ernest W., and Locke, Harvey J., *The Family,* second edition. American Book Company, New York, 1953.

* Burgess, Ernest W.; Locke, Harvey J.; and Thomes, Mary M., *The Family,* third edition. American Book Company, New York, 1963.

Burgess, Ernest W., and Wallin, Paul, *Engagement and Marriage.* J. B. Lippincott Company, Philadelphia, 1953.

Chard, Chester S., editor, "Sternberg's Materials on the Sexual Life of the Gilyak," *Anthropological Papers of the University of Alaska,* vol. X, pp. 13-23, 1961.

Dean, Dwight G., "Romanticism and Emotional Maturity: A Preliminary Study," *Marriage and Family Living,* vol. XXIII, no. 1, pp. 44-45, February 1961.

de Rougemont, Denis, "The Crisis of the Modern Couple," in R. N. Anshen, editor, *The Family: Its Function and Destiny.* Harper and Brothers, New York, pp. 449-462, 1959.

* Driscoll, Richard; Davis, Keith E.; and Lipetz, Milton E., "Parental Interference and Romantic Love: The Romeo and Juliet Effect," *Journal of Personality and Social Psychology,* vol. XXIV, pp. 1–10, 1972.

Duvall, Evelyn Millis, "Where Do They Get Their Ideas of Love and Marriage?" *The PTA Magazine,* vol. LVI, no. 8, pp. 10–14, April 1962.

Ellis, Albert, *The American Sexual Tragedy.* Twayne Publishers, Inc., New York, 1954.

* Ellis, Albert, "A Study of Human Love Relationships," *Journal of Genetic Psychology,* vol. LXXV, pp. 61–71, 1949.

Feiffer, Jules, *Harry, The Rat with Women.* McGraw-Hill Book Company, New York, 1963.

* Freud, Sigmund, *Group Psychology and the Analysis of the Ego.* Hogarth, London, 1922.

Fromm, Erich, *The Art of Loving.* Harper & Brothers, New York, 1956.

* Goode, William J., "The Theoretical Importance of Love," *American Sociological Review,* vol. XXIV, pp. 38–47, February 1959.

* Gough, E. Kathleen, "Changing Kinship Usages in the Setting of Political and Economic Change Among the Nayars of Malabar," *Journal of the Royal Anthropological Institute,* vol. LXXXII, part 1, 1952.

* Green, Arnold W., "The 'Cult of Personality' and Sexual Relations," *Psychiatry,* vol. IV, pp. 343–348, 1941.

* Greenberg, Herbert M., and Corwin, Jeanne, "A Theoretical Discussion on Canalization as it Applies to Love in Our Culture," *Journal of Social Psychology,* vol. LVI, pp. 171–178, 1962.

Hart, C. W., and Pilling, A. R., *The Tiwi of Northern Australia.* Holt, Rinehart and Winston, Inc., New York, 1966.

* Horton, Donald, "The Dialogue of Courtship in Popular Songs," *American Journal of Sociology,* vol. LXII, no. 6, pp. 569–578, May 1957.

* Hunt, Morton M., *The Natural History of Love.* Alfred A. Knopf, Inc., New York, 1959.

* Kanin, Eugene J.; Davidson, Karen R.; and Scheck, Sonia R., "A Research Note on Male-Female Differentials in the Experience of Heterosexual Love," *Journal of Sex Research,* vol. VI, no. 1, pp. 64–72, February 1970.

* Kephart, William M., "The Dysfunctional Theory of Romantic Love: A Research Report," presented at the American Sociological Association, San Francisco, August 1969.

Kephart, William M., "Some Correlates of Romantic Love," *Journal of Marriage and the Family,* vol. XXIX, pp. 470–474, August 1967.

* Kirkendall, Lester A., *Premarital Intercourse and Interpersonal Relationships.* Gramercy Publishing Co., New York, 1968.

* Kirkpatrick, Clifford, and Caplow, Theodore, "Emotional Trends in the Courtship Experience of College Students as Expressed by Graphs, with Some Observations on Methodological Implications," *American Sociological Review,* vol. V, pp. 619–626, October 1945.

* Knox, David, Jr., "Conceptions of Love at Three Developmental Levels," *The Family Coordinator,* vol. XIX, pp. 151–157, 1970.

* Knox, David, Jr., and Sporakowski, Michael J., "Attitudes of College Students Toward Love," *Journal of Marriage and the Family,* vol. XXX, pp. 638-672, November 1968.

* Kolb, William L., "Sociologically Established Norms and Democratic Values," *Social Forces,* vol. XXVI, pp. 451-456, May 1948.

Kunz, Phillip R., "Romantic Love and Reciprocity," *The Family Coordinator,* vol. XVIII, pp. 111-116, 1969.

Landers, Ann, *Since You Ask Me.* Prentice-Hall, Inc., Englewood Cliffs, New Jersey, 1961.

Landis, Paul, *Making the Most of Marriage.* Appleton-Century Crofts, Inc., New York, 1960.

* Lantz, Herman R., and Snyder, Eloise C., *Marriage: An Examination of the Man-Woman Relationship.* John Wiley and Sons, Inc., New York, 1962.

Lewis, Robert A., "A Developmental Framework for the Analysis of Premarital Dyadic Formation," *Family Process,* vol. XI, pp. 17-47, 1972.

* Lewis, Robert A., "The Premarital Dyadic Formation Inventory: An Instrument for Measuring Heterosexual Pair Development," presented at the Annual Meetings of the National Council on Family Relations, 1972.

* Linton, Ralph, *The Study of Man.* Appleton-Century Crofts, Inc., New York, 1936.

Locke, Harvey J., *Predicting Adjustment in Marriage: A Comparison of a Divorced and a Happily Married Group.* Henry Holt and Company, New York, 1951.

Lundberg, Craig, and Moravec, Milan, "Alternatives to the Love Game," *Journal of Humanistic Psychology,* vol. XII, pp. 93-102, 1972.

* Malinowski, Bronislaw, *The Sexual Life of Savages in Northwest Melanesia.* Liveright Publishing Corporation, New York, 1929.

* Martinson, Floyd M., "Ego Deficiency as a Factor in Marriage," *American Sociological Review,* vol. XX, pp. 161-164, 1955.

* Martinson, Floyd M., "Ego Deficiency as a Factor in Marriage—A Male Sample," *Marriage and Family Living,* vol. XXI, no. 1, pp. 48-52, February 1959.

* Mead, Margaret, *Coming of Age in Samoa.* William Morrow and Company, New York, 1928.

* Miller, Walter B., "Lower-class Culture as a Generating Milieu of Gang Delinquency," *Journal of Social Issues,* vol. XIV, pp. 5-19, 1958.

Nimkoff, Meyer F., *Marriage and the Family.* Houghton Mifflin Company, New York, 1947.

* Ohmann, O., "The Psychology of Attraction," in H. M. Jordan, editor, *You and Marriage.* John Wiley and Sons, Inc., New York, 1942.

* Pineo, Peter C., "Disenchantment in the Later Years of Marriage," *Marriage and Family Living,* vol. XXIII, pp. 3-11, 1961.

* Popenoe, Paul, and Disney, Dorothy C., *Can This Marriage Be Saved?* The Macmillan Company, New York, 1960.

* Reik, Theodor, *Of Love and Lust.* Straus and Cudahy, New York, 1957.

* Reik, Theodor, *Psychology of Sex Relations.* Farrar and Rinehart, Inc., Toronto, 1945.

* Reiss, Ira L., "Toward a Sociology of the Heterosexual Love Relationship," *Marriage and Family Living,* vol. XXII, pp. 139-145, May 1960.

* Rubin, Zick, "Measurement of Romantic Love," *Journal of Personality and Social Psychology,* vol. XVI, pp. 265–273, 1970.
* Spanier, Graham B., "Romanticism and Marital Adjustment," *Journal of Marriage and the Family,* vol. XXXIV, pp. 481–487, 1972.
* Stephens, William N., *The Family in Cross-Cultural Perspective.* Holt, Rinehart and Winston, Inc., New York, 1963.
* Sussman, Marvin B., *Sourcebook in Marriage and the Family,* second edition. Houghton Mifflin Company, Boston, 1963.
  Swensen, Clifford H., Jr., "Love: A Self-report Analysis with College Students," *Journal of Individual Psychology,* vol. I, pp. 167–171, November 1961.
  Theodorson, George A., "Romanticism and Motivation to Marry in the United States, Singapore, Burma, and India," *Social Forces,* vol. XLIV, no. 1, pp. 17–28, 1965.
* Waller, Willard, *The Family: A Dynamic Interpretation.* Cordon Press, New York, 1938.
* Winch, Robert F., *Mate Selection.* Harper and Brothers, New York, 1958.
* Winch, Robert F., *The Modern Family,* revised edition. Holt, Rinehart and Winston, Inc., New York, 1963.
* Yang, Martin C., *A Chinese Village: Taitou, Shantung Province.* Columbia University Press, New York, 1945.

CHAPTER 8   SOCIAL FACTORS IN MATE SELECTION

Aberle, David F., et al., "The Incest Taboo and the Mating Patterns of Animals," *American Anthropologist,* vol. LXV, no. 2, pp. 253–265, 1963.
* Akers, Donald S., "On Measuring the Marriage Squeeze," *Demography,* vol. IV, pp. 907–924, 1967.
  Anand, K., "An Analysis of Matrimonial Advertisements," *Sociological Bulletin,* vol. XIV, pp. 59–71, 1965.
  Arkoff, Abe; Meredith, Gerald; and Iwahara, Shinkuro, "Male-Dominant and Equalitarian Attitudes in Japanese, Japanese-American, and Caucasian-American Students," *Journal of Social Psychology,* vol. LXIV, pp. 225–229, 1964.
* Babchuck, Nicholas; Crockett, Harry; and Ballweg, John A., "Changes in Religious Affiliation and Marital Stability," *Social Forces,* vol. XLV, pp. 551–555, 1967.
* Barnett, Larry D., "Interracial Marriage in California," *Marriage and Family Living,* vol. XXV, no. 4, pp. 424–427, November 1963(a).
  Barnett, Larry D., "Research on International and Interracial Marriages," *Marriage and Family Living,* vol. XXV, pp. 105–107, 1963(b).
  Bartz, Karen Winch, and Nye, F. Ivan, "Early Marriage: A Propositional Formulation," *Journal of Marriage and the Family,* vol. XXXII, pp. 259–268, 1970.
* Besanceney, Paul H., "Interfaith Marriages of Catholics in the Detroit Area," *Sociological Analysis,* vol. XXVI, pp. 38–44, 1965.
* Besanceney, Paul H., *Interfaith Marriages: Who and Why.* College and University Press, New Haven, Connecticut, 1971.

* Blood, Robert O., Jr., *Marriage,* second edition. Free Press of Glencoe, Inc., New York, 1962.

Bock, Elmer W., and Burchinal, Lee G., "Social Status, Heterosexual Relations and Expected Ages of Marriage," *Journal of Genetic Psychology,* vol. CI, pp. 43-51, 1962.

* Bumpass, Larry, "The Trend of Interfaith Marriage in the United States," *Social Biology,* vol. XVII, no. 3, pp. 253-259, December 1970.

Burchinal, Lee G., "Trends and Prospects for Young Marriages in the United States," *Journal of Marriage and the Family,* vol. XXVII, pp. 243-254, 1965.

* Burchinal, Lee G., and Chancellor, Loren E., "Ages at Marriage, Occupations of Grooms and Interreligious Marriage Rates," *Social Forces,* vol. XL, no. 4, pp. 348-354, May 1962(a).

* Burchinal, Lee G., and Chancellor, Loren E., "Proportions of Catholics, Urbanism, and Mixed-Catholic Marriage Rates Among Iowa Counties," *Social Problems,* vol. IX, no. 4, pp. 359-365, spring 1962(b).

* Burchinal, Lee G., and Kenkel, William F., "Religious Identification and Occupational Status of Iowa Grooms, 1953-1957," *American Sociological Review,* vol. XXVII, no. 4, pp. 526-532, August 1962.

* Burgess, Ernest W., and Cottrell, Leonard S., Jr., *Predicting Success or Failure in Marriage.* Prentice-Hall, Inc., Englewood Cliffs, New Jersey, 1939.

* Burgess, Ernest W., and Wallin, Paul, *Engagement and Marriage.* J. B. Lippincott Company, Philadelphia, 1953.

* Burma, John C., "Interethnic Marriage in Los Angeles, 1948-1959," *Social Forces,* vol. XLII, pp. 156-165, December 1963.

* Catton, William R., Jr., and Smircich, R. J., "A Comparison of Mathematical Models for the Effect of Residential Propinquity on Mate Selection," *American Sociological Review,* vol. XXIX, pp. 522-529, August 1964.

* Centers, Richard, "Marital Selection and Occupational Strata," *American Journal of Sociology,* vol. LIV, pp. 530-535, 1949.

* Cheng, C. K., and Yamamura, Douglas S., "Interracial Marriage and Divorce in Hawaii," *Social Forces,* vol. XXXVI, no. 1, pp. 77-84, October 1957.

* Chilman, Catherine S., "Dating, Courtship, and Engagement of Married, Compared to Single Undergraduates, with an Analysis of Early-Marrying and Late-Marrying Students," *Family Life Coordinator,* vol. XV, pp. 112-118, 1966.

* Clarke, Alfred C., "An Examination of the Operation of Residential Propinquity as a Factor in Mate Selection," *American Sociological Review,* vol. XVII, pp. 17-22, 1952.

* Cutright, Phillips, "Income and Family Events: Getting Married," *Journal of Marriage and the Family,* vol. XXXII, no. 4, pp. 628-637, November 1970.

Darlington, D. C., "Cousin Marriages," *Eugenics Review,* vol. LI, no. 4, pp. 221-223, 1960.

* Dinitz, Simon; Banks, Franklin; and Pasamanick, Benjamin, "Mate Selection and Social Class Changes During the Past Quarter Century," *Marriage and Family Living,* vol. XXII, no. 4, pp. 348-351, November 1960.

Eckland, Bruce K., "Theories of Mate Selection," *Eugenics Quarterly,* vol. XV, pp. 71-84, 1968.

*Elder, Glen H., Jr., "Role Orientations, Marital Age, and Life Patterns in Adulthood," *Merrill-Palmer Quarterly,* vol. XVIII, pp. 3-24, 1972.

*Epstein, Cynthia Fuchs, "Positive Effects of the Double Negative: Sex, Race and Professional Elites," presented at the annual meeting of the American Sociological Association, August 1971.

Fitzpatrick, Joseph P., "Intermarriage of Puerto Ricans in New York City," *American Journal of Sociology,* vol. LXXI, pp. 395-406, 1966.

*Freeman, Linton, "Homogamy in Interethnic Mate Selection," *Sociology and Social Research,* vol. XXXIX, pp. 369-377, 1955.

Gallagher, Orvell R., "Endogamous Marriage in Central India," *Ethnology,* vol. IV, pp. 72-76, 1965.

Gladden, James W., "Trends in High School Marriages and Public School Policy in the United States," *The Family Coordinator,* vol. XVII, pp. 279-287, 1968.

Glenn, Norval D., "Negro Prestige Criteria: A Case Study in the Bases of Prestige," *American Journal of Sociology,* vol. LXVIII, pp. 645-657, 1963.

*Glick, Paul C., *American Families.* John Wiley and Sons, Inc., New York, 1957.

*Glick, Paul C., "Intermarriage and Fertility Patterns Among Persons in Major Religious Groups," *Eugenics Quarterly,* vol. VII, no. 1, pp. 31-38, March 1960.

*Golden, Joseph, "Facilitating Factors in Negro-White Intermarriage," *Phylon,* vol. XX, no. 3, pp. 273-284, fall 1959.

*Goldscheider, Calvin, and Goldstein, Sidney, "Generation Changes in Jewish Family Structure," *Journal of Marriage and the Family,* vol. XXIX, no. 2, pp. 267-276, 1967.

*Gordon, Albert I., *Marriage: Interfaith, Interracial, Interethnic.* Beacon Press, Boston, 1964.

*Greenwood, David, *Essays in Human Relations,* Washington, D. C.: Public Affairs Press, 1956, pp. 48-63.

*Hart, C. W., and Pilling, A. R., *The Tiwi of Northern Australia.* Holt, Rinehart & Winston, Inc., New York, 1966.

*Heer, David M., "Negro-White Marriage in the United States," *Journal of Marriage and the Family,* vol. XXVIII, pp. 262-273, 1966.

*Heiss, Jerold S., "Premarital Characteristics of the Religiously Intermarried in an Urban Area," *American Sociological Review,* vol. XXV, no. 1, pp. 47-55, February 1960.

*Hollingshead, August B., "Cultural Factors in the Selection of Marriage Mates," *American Sociological Review,* vol. XV, pp. 619-627, 1950.

*Jacobson, Paul Harold, *American Marriage and Divorce.* Rinehart and Company, Inc., New York, 1959.

*Katz, Alvin M., and Hill, Reuben, "Residential Propinquity and Marital Selection: A Review of Theory, Method, and Fact," *Marriage and Family Living,* vol. XX, no. 1, pp. 27-34, February 1958.

Kenkel, William F.; Himler, Joyce; and Cole, Leonard, "Religious Socialization, Present Devoutness, and Willingness to Enter a Mixed Religious Marriage," *Sociological Analysis,* vol. XXVI, pp. 30-37, 1965.

*Kennedy, Ruby Joe Reeves, "Single or Triple Melting Pot? Intermarriage Trends in New Haven 1870-1940," *American Journal of Sociology,* vol. XXXIX, pp. 331-339, January 1944.

* Kephart, William N., *The Family, Society and the Individual.* Houghton Mifflin Company, Boston, 1961.

Kharchev, A. G., "Marriage in the USSR," *The Soviet Review,* vol. VIII, pp. 3–25, 1967.

Kimber, J. A. Morris, "Intersectional and Intrasectional Marriages in a Southern Bible College—16 Years Later," *Journal of Marriage and the Family,* vol. XXX, pp. 402–403, 1968.

* Kimura, Yukiko, "War Brides in Hawaii and Their In-laws," *American Journal of Sociology,* vol. LXIII, pp. 70–76, July 1957.

Kiser, Clyde V., "Assortative Mating by Educational Attainment in Relation to Fertility," *Eugenics Quarterly,* vol. XV, pp. 98–112, 1968.

Korson, J. Henry, "Residential Propinquity as a Factor in Mate Selection in an Urban Muslim Society," *Journal of Marriage and the Family,* vol. XXX, pp. 518–536, 1968.

* Landis, Judson T., and Landis, Mary G., *Building a Successful Marriage,* fourth edition. Prentice-Hall, Inc., Englewood Cliffs, New Jersey, 1963.

* Lenski, Gerhard, *The Religious Factor.* Doubleday & Company, Inc., Garden City, New York, 1961.

* Lieberman, E. James, "American Families and the Vietnam War," *Journal of Marriage and the Family,* vol. XXXIII, pp. 709–721, 1971.

* Locke, Harvey J.; Sabagh, Georges; and Thomes, Mary M., "Interfaith Marriages," *Social Problems,* vol. IV, no. 4, pp. 329–333, April 1957.

Loeb, Ruth, "A Study of Age at Remarriage: The District of Columbia, 1960–61," *Demography,* vol. V, pp. 311–317, 1968.

* Metropolitan Life Insurance Company, "Where Are the Unmarried Men?" *Statistical Bulletin,* vol. XLIV, p. 2, June 1963.

* Middleton, Russell, "Brother-Sister and Father-Daughter Marriage in Ancient Egypt," *American Sociological Review,* vol. XXVII, pp. 603–612, October 1962.

Mittelbach, Frank G.; Moore, Joan W.; and McDaniel, Ronald, *Intermarriage of Mexican-Americans,* pp. vii–83. Mexican-American Study Project, Division of Research, Graduate School of Business Administration, Los Angeles, University of California, November 1966.

* Monahan, Thomas P., "The Extent of Interdenominational Marriage in the United States," *Journal for the Scientific Study of Religion,* vol. X, pp. 85–92, 1971.

Monahan, Thomas P., "Interracial Marriage and Divorce in the State of Hawaii," *Eugenics Quarterly,* vol. XIII, pp. 40–47, 1966.

Moss, J. Joel, "Teenage Marriage: Crossnational Trends and Sociological Factors in the Decision of When to Marry," *Acta Sociologica,* vol. VIII, pp. 98–117, 1964.

* Myrdal, Gunnar, *An American Dilemma.* Harper and Brothers, New York, 1944.

Neubeck, Gerhard, "The Decision to Marry While in College," *Acta Sociologica,* vol. VIII, pp. 56–57, 1964.

Neubeck, Gerhard, and Hewer, Vivian, "Time of Marriage and College Attendance," *Journal of Marriage and the Family,* vol. XXVII, pp. 522–524, 1965.

Ortmeyer, Carl E., "Educational Attainment as a Selective Factor in Marital Status Transitions in the United States," *Demography,* vol. IV, pp. 108–125, 1967.

Podell, Lawrence, "Sex and Role Conflict," *Journal of Marriage and the Family,* vol. XXVIII, pp. 163–165, 1966.

Ramsøy, Natalie Rogoff, "Assortative Mating and the Structure of Cities," *American Sociological Review,* vol. XXXI, pp. 773–786, 1966.

Rapoport, Robert N., "The Male's Occupation in Relation to his Decision to Marry," *Acta Sociologica,* vol. VIII, pp. 68–82, 1964.

Rele, J. R., "Trends and Differentials in the American Age at Marriage," *Milbank Memorial Fund Quarterly,* vol. XLIII, pp. 219–234, 1965.

* Rettig, Salomon, and Pasamanick, Benjamin, "Changes in Moral Values Among College Students: A Factorial Study," *American Sociological Review,* vol. XXIV, pp. 856–863, December 1959.

* Risdon, Randall, "A Study of Interracial Marriages Based on Data for Los Angeles County," *Sociology and Social Research,* vol. XXXIX, pp. 92–95, November–December 1954.

Rodman, Hyman, "Technical Note on Two Rates of Mixed Marriage," *American Sociological Review,* vol. XXX, pp. 776–778, 1965.

Rosen, Lawrence, and Bell, Robert R., "Mate Selection in the Upper Class," *Sociological Quarterly,* vol. VII, pp. 157–166, 1966.

* Rosenthal, Erich, "Divorce and Religious Intermarriage: The Effect of Previous Marital Status upon Subsequent Marital Behavior," *Journal of Marriage and the Family,* vol. XXXII, pp. 435–440, 1970.

Rosenwaike, Ira, "Parental Consent Ages as a Factor in State Variation in Bride's Age at Marriage," *Journal of Marriage and the Family,* vol. XXIX, pp. 452–455, 1967.

* Rubin, Zick, "Do American Women Marry Up?" *American Sociological Review,* vol. XXXIII, pp. 750–760, October, 1968.

Rubin, Zick, "Reply to Scott," *American Sociological Review,* vol. XXXIV, pp. 727–728, 1969.

* Schmitt, Robert C., "Recent Trends in Hawaiian Interracial Marriage Rates by Occupation," *Journal of Marriage and the Family,* vol. XXXIII, pp. 373–374, 1971.

Scott, John Finley, "A Comment on 'Do American Women Marry Up?'," *American Sociological Review,* vol. XXXIV, pp. 725–727, 1969.

* Sklare, Marshall, "Intermarriage and the Jewish Future," *Commentary,* vol. XXXVII, pp. 46–52, 1964.

Smith, Carl E., "Negro-White Intermarriage—Forbidden Sexual Union," *Journal of Sex Research,* vol. II, pp. 169–173, 1966.

Snyder, Eloise C., "Marital Selectivity in Self-Adjustment, Social Adjustment, and I. Q.," *Journal of Marriage and the Family,* vol. XXVIII, pp. 188–189, 1966.

Spuhler, J. N., "Assortative Mating with Respect to Physical Characteristics," *Eugenics Quarterly,* vol. XV, pp. 128–140, 1968.

* Strauss, Anselm, "The Ideal and the Chosen Mate," *American Journal of Sociology,* vol. LI, pp. 204–208, 1946.

* Talmon, Yonina, "Mate Selection in Collective Settlements," *American Sociological Review,* vol. XXIX, pp. 491–508, 1964.

* Thomas, John L., "The Factor of Religion in the Selection of Marriage Mates," *American Sociological Review,* vol. XVI, pp. 487–491, 1951.

Trost, Jan, "Some Data on Mate-Selection: Homogamy and Perceived Homogamy," *Journal of Marriage and the Family,* vol. XXIX, pp. 739-755, 1967.

U. S. Department of Commerce, Bureau of the Census, *Historical Statistics of the United States, Colonial Times to 1957.* U. S. Government Printing Office, Washington, D. C., 1960.

* U. S. Department of Commerce, Bureau of the Census, "Marital Status and Living Arrangements: March 1971," *Current Population Reports,* series P-20, no. 225, U. S. Government Printing Office, Washington, D. C., 1971.

* U. S. Department of Health, Education and Welfare, "Marriages: Trends and Characteristics, United States," *Vital and Health Statistics,* series 21, no. 21. U. S. Government Printing Office, Washington, D. C., 1971.

U. S. Public Health Service, "Table 10," *Vital Statistics — Special Reports, 1956-1957,* vol. XLV, p. 322.

Warren, Bruce L., "A Multiple Variable Approach to the Assortative Mating Phenomenon," *Eugenics Quarterly,* vol. XIII, pp. 285-290, 1966.

Weinberger, Andrew D., "Interracial Marriage — Its Statutory Prohibition, Genetic Import, and Incidence," *Journal of Sex Research,* vol. II, no. 3, pp. 157-168, November 1966.

* Westermarck, E. A., *The History of Human Marriage.* Macmillan and Company, Inc., London, 1921.

Winch, Robert F., *The Modern Family,* revised edition. Holt, Rinehart & Winston, Inc., New York, 1963.

Winch, Robert F., and Greer, Scott A., "The Uncertain Relation Between Early Marriage and Marital Stability: A Quest for Relevant Data," *Acta Sociologica,* vol. VIII, pp. 83-97, 1964.

* Wirth, Louis, and Goldhamer, Herbert, "Negro-White Marriage in Recent Times," in Otto Klineberg, editor, *Characteristics of the American Negro.* Harper & Brothers, New York, 1944.

CHAPTER 9   INTERPERSONAL FACTORS IN MATE SELECTION

Abu-Lughod, Janet, and Amin, Lucy, "Egyptian Marriage Advertisements: Microcosm of a Changing Society," *Marriage and Family Living,* vol. XXIII, pp. 127-136, May 1961.

Baker, Luther G., Jr., "The Personal and Social Adjustment of the Never-Married Woman," *Journal of Marriage and the Family,* vol. XXX, pp. 473-479, 1968.

* Bates, Alan P., "Parental Rolls in Courtship," *Social Forces,* vol. XX, pp. 483-486, 1942.

Baxter, James C., "Parental Complementarity and Parental Conflict," *Journal of Individual Psychology,* vol. XXI, pp. 149-153, 1965.

Bayer, Alan E., "Early Dating and Early Marriage," *Journal of Marriage and the Family,* vol. XXX, pp. 628-632, 1968.

* Beigel, Hugo, "Sex and Human Beauty," *Journal of Aesthetics,* vol. XII, pp. 83-92, 1953.

* Benedek, Therese, *Insight and Personality Adjustment.* The Ronald Press Company, New York, 1946.

* Bernard, Jessie; Buchanan, Helen E.; and Smith, William M., Jr., *Dating, Mating, and Marriage Today.* Arco Publishing Company, New York, 1959.
* Bolton, Charles D., "Mate Selection as the Development of a Relationship," *Marriage and Family Living,* vol. XXIII, no. 3, pp. 234–240, August 1961.
* Bowerman, Charles E., and Day, Barbara R., "A Test of the Theory of Complementary Needs as Applied to Couples During Courtship," *American Sociological Review,* vol. XXI, pp. 602–605, 1956.
  Burchinal, Lee G., and Chancellor, Loren, "Survival Rates Among Religiously Homogamous and Heterogamous Marriages," *Research Bulletin 512.* Agricultural and Home Economics Experiment Station, Iowa State University, Ames, Iowa, December 1962.
* Burgess, Ernest W., and Cottrell, Leonard S., Jr., *Predicting Success or Failure in Marriage.* Prentice-Hall, Inc., Englewood Cliffs, New Jersey, 1939.
* Burgess, Ernest W.; Locke, Harvey J.; and Thomes, Mary Margaret, *The Family,* third edition. American Book Company, New York, 1963.
* Burgess, Ernest W., and Wallin, Paul, *Engagement and Marriage.* J. B. Lippincott Company, Philadelphia, 1953.
  Chilman, Catherine S., and Meyer, Donald L., "Single and Married Undergraduates' Measured Personality Needs and Self-Rated Happiness," *Journal of Marriage and the Family,* vol. XXVIII, pp. 67–76, 1966.
* Coombs, Robert H., "Reinforcement of Values in the Parental Home as a Factor in Mate Selection," *Marriage and Family Living,* vol. XXIV, no. 2, pp. 155–157, May 1962.
  Coombs, Robert H., "Value Consensus and Partner Satisfaction Among Dating Couples," *Journal of Marriage and the Family,* vol. XXVIII, pp. 166–173, 1966.
  Coombs, Robert H., and Kenkel, William F., "Sex Differences in Dating Aspirations and Satisfaction with Computer-Selected Partners," *Journal of Marriage and the Family,* vol. XXVIII, pp. 62–66, 1966.
* Curran, James P., "Differential Effects of Stated Preferences and Questionnaire Role Performance on Interpersonal Attraction in the Dating Situation," *The Journal of Psychology,* vol. LXXXII, pp. 313–327, 1972.
* Day, Barbara R., "A Comparison of Personality Needs of Courtship Couples and Same Sex Friendships," *Sociology and Social Research,* vol. XLV, no. 4, pp. 435–440, 1961.
  Dean, Dwight G., "Emotional Maturity and Marital Adjustment," *Journal of Marriage and the Family,* vol. XXVIII, pp. 454–457, 1966.
* Driscoll, Richard; Davis, Keith E.; and Lipetz, Milton E., "Parental Interference and Romantic Love: The Romeo and Juliet Effect," *Journal of Personality and Social Psychology,* vol. XXIV, pp. 1–10, 1972.
* Elder, Glen H., Jr., "Appearance and Education in Marriage Mobility," *American Sociological Review,* vol. XXXIV, pp. 519–533, 1969.
  Elder, Glen H., Jr., "Structural Variations in the Child-rearing Relationships," *Sociometry,* vol. XXV, pp. 241–262, September 1962.
* Green, Arnold W., "The 'Cult of Personality' and Sexual Relations," *Psychiatry,* vol. IV, pp. 343–348, 1941.

Hall, Everette, "Ordinal Position and Success in Engagement and Marriage," *Journal of Individual Psychology,* vol. XXI, pp. 154–158, 1965.

* Heiss, J. S., and Gordon, M., "Need Patterns and the Mutual Satisfaction of Dating and Engaged Couples," *Journal of Marriage and the Family,* vol. XXVI, pp. 337–339, 1964.

Hepworth, Dean H., "The Clinical Implications of Perceptual Distortions in Forced Marriages," *Social Casework,* vol. XLV, pp. 579–585, 1964.

* Hewitt, Lester E., "Student Perceptions of Traits Desired in Themselves as Dating and Marriage Partners," *Marriage and Family Living,* vol. XX, no. 4, pp. 344–349, November 1958.

* Holmes, S. J., and Hatch, C. E., "Personal Appearance as Related to Scholastic Records and Marriage Selection in College Women," *Human Biology,* vol. X, pp. 65–76, 1938.

* Holz, Robert I., "Homogamy and Heterogamy in the Marital Dyad: The Effects of Role on Need Dispositions," presented at the American Sociological Association, San Francisco, August 1969.

* Hudson, John W., and Henze, Lura F., "Campus Values in Mate Selection: A Replication," *Journal of Marriage and the Family,* vol. XXXI, no. 4, pp. 772–775, 1969.

Huntington, Robert M., "The Personality-Interaction Approach to Study of the Marital Relationship," *Marriage and Family Living,* vol. XX, pp. 43–46, 1958.

* Kerckhoff, A. C., and Davis, K. E., "Value Consensus and Need Complementarity in Mate Selection," *American Sociological Review,* vol. XXVII, no. 3, pp. 295–303, June 1962.

* Kernodle, W., "Some Implications of the Homogamy—Complementary Needs Theories of Mate Selection for Sociological Research," *Social Forces,* vol. XXXVII, pp. 145–152, December 1959.

* Kirkpatrick, Clifford, and Cotton, John, "Physical Attractiveness, Age, and Marital Adjustment," *American Sociological Review,* vol. XVI, pp. 85–86, 1951.

* Kirkpatrick, Clifford, and Hobart, Charles, "Disagreement, Disagreement Estimate, and Non-Empathetic Imputations for Intimacy Groups Varying from Favorite Date to Married," *American Sociological Review,* vol. XIX, pp. 10–20, February 1954.

Levinger, George, "Note on Need Complementarity in Marriage," *Psychological Bulletin,* vol. LXI, pp. 153–157, 1964.

* Levinger, George; Senn, David J.; and Jorgensen, Bruce W., "Progress Toward Permanence in Courtship: A Test of the Kerckhoff-Davis Hypotheses," *Sociometry,* vol. XXXIII, pp. 427–443, 1970.

* Locke, Harvey J., *Predicting Adjustment in Marriage: A Comparison of a Divorced and a Happily Married Group.* Henry Holt and Company, New York, 1951.

Lowrie, Samuel H., "Early Marriage: Premarital Pregnancy and Associated Factors," *Journal of Marriage and the Family,* vol. XXVII, pp. 48–56, 1965.

* Luckey, Eleanore B., "Perceptual Congruence of Self and Family Concepts as Related to Marital Interaction," *Sociometry,* vol. XXIV, pp. 234–250, 1961.

* Lundy, Richard M., "Self-perceptions Regarding Masculinity-femininity and Description of Same and Opposite Sex Sociometric Choices," *Sociometry,* vol. XXI, pp. 231–246, September 1958.

* Lyness, Judith L.; Lipetz, Milton E.; and Davis, Keith E., "Living Together: An Alternative to Marriage," *Journal of Marriage and the Family,* vol. XXXIV, pp. 305-311, 1972.

MacDonald, A. P., Jr., "Birth-Order Effects in Marriage and Parenthood: Affiliation and Socialization," *Journal of Marriage and the Family,* vol. XXIX, pp. 656-661, 1967.

* McGinnis, Robert, "Campus Values in Mate Selection: A Repeat Study," *Social Forces,* vol. XXXVI, no. 4, pp. 368-373, May 1958.

* Murstein, Bernard I., "The Complementary Need Hypothesis in Newlyweds and Middle-Aged Married Couples," *Journal of Abnormal and Social Psychology,* vol. LXIII, no. 1, pp. 194-197, July 1961.

Murstein, Bernard I., "Empirical Tests of Role, Complementary Needs, and Homogamy Theories of Marital Choice," *Journal of Marriage and the Family,* vol. XXIX, pp. 689-696, 1967.

* Murstein, Bernard I., "Interview Behavior, Projective Techniques, and Questionnaires in the Clinical Assessment of Marital Choice," *Journal of Personality Assessment,* vol. XXXVI, pp. 462-467, 1972(a).

* Murstein, Bernard I., "Person Perception and Courtship Progress Among Premarital Couples," *Journal of Marriage and the Family,* vol. XXXIV, pp. 621-626, 1972(b).

* Murstein, Bernard I., "Physical Attractiveness and Marital Choice," *Journal of Personality and Social Psychology,* vol. XXII, pp. 8-12, 1972(c).

Murstein, Bernard I., "The Relationship of Mental Health to Marital Choice and Courtship Progress," *Journal of Marriage and the Family,* vol. XXIX, pp. 447-451, 1967.

* Newcomb, Theodore M., *The Acquaintance Process,* New York: Holt Rinehart and Winston, Inc., 1961.

* Newcomb, Theodore M., "The Prediction of Interpersonal Attraction," *American Psychologist,* vol. XI, pp. 575-586, 1956.

Nimkoff, Meyer F., *Marriage and the Family.* Houghton Mifflin Company, Boston, 1947.

Paris, Bethel Logan, and Luckey, Eleanore Braun, "A Longitudinal Study in Marital Satisfaction," *Sociology and Social Research,* vol. L, pp. 212-222, 1966.

Pickford, John H.; Signori, Edro I.; and Rempel, Henry, "The Intensity of Personality Traits in Relation to Marital Happiness," *Journal of Marriage and the Family,* vol. XXVIII, pp. 458-459, 1966.

Pickford, John H.; Signori, Edro I.; and Rempel, Henry, "Similar or Related Personality Traits as a Factor in Marital Happiness," *Journal of Marriage and the Family,* vol. XXVIII, pp. 190-192, 1966.

* Queen, Stuart A.; Habenstein, Robert W.; and Adams, John B., *The Family in Various Cultures.* J. B. Lippincott Company, Philadelphia, 1961.

* Reik, Theodore, *A Psychologist Looks at Love.* Henry Holt and Company, New York, 1944.

* Richardson, Helen M., "Studies of Mental Resemblance Between Husbands and Wives and Between Friends," *Psychological Bulletin,* vol. XXXVI, pp. 104-120, 1939.

* Schellenberg, J. A., and Bee, L. S., "A Re-examination of the Theory of Complementary Needs in Mate Selection," *Marriage and Family Living,* vol. XXII, pp. 227–232, August 1960.

* Schopenhauer, Arthur, *The Philosophy of Schopenhauer,* Irwin Edman, editor. The Modern Library, Inc., New York, 1928.

* Secord, P. F., and Jourard, S. M., "Mother Concepts and Judgments of Young Women's Faces," *Journal of Abnormal and Social Psychology,* vol. LII, pp. 246–250, 1956.

* Smith, Eleanor, and Greenberg-Monane, J. M., "Courtship Values in a Youth Sample," *American Sociological Review,* vol. XVIII, no. 6, pp. 635–640, December 1953.

* Spuhler, J. N., "Assortative Mating with Respect to Physical Characteristics," *Eugenics Quarterly,* vol. XV, pp. 128–140, 1968.

* Stephens, William N., *The Family in Cross-Cultural Perspective.* Holt, Rinehart & Winston, Inc., New York, 1963.

Stinnett, Nick, and Montgomery, James E., "Youths' Perceptions of Marriages of Older Persons," *Journal of Marriage and the Family,* vol. XXX, pp. 392–396, 1968.

* Strauss, Anselm, "The Ideal and the Chosen Mate," *American Journal of Sociology,* vol. LI, pp. 204–208, 1946.

* Strauss, Anselm, "Personality Needs and Marital Choice," *Social Forces,* vol. XXIV, pp. 332–335, 1947.

* Stroebe, Wolfgang; Insko, Chester A.; Thompson, Vaida D.; and Layton, Bruce D., "Effects of Physical Attractiveness, Attitude Similarity, and Sex on Various Aspects of Interpersonal Attraction," *Journal of Personality and Social Psychology,* vol. XVIII, no. 1, pp. 79–91, 1971.

Strømnes, Frode J., "Development and Differentiation of Acquaintance in Engaged and Married Couples," *Scandinavian Journal of Psychology,* vol. VII, pp. 34–42, 1966.

Strong, Emily, and Wilson, Warner, "Three-Filter Date Selection by Computer — Phase II," *The Family Coordinator,* vol. XVIII, no. 3, pp. 256–259, July 1969.

* Terman, Lewis M., *Psychological Factors in Marital Happiness.* McGraw-Hill Book Company, New York, 1936.

* Terman, Lewis M., and Miles, Catherine Cox, *Sex and Personality.* McGraw-Hill Book Company, New York, 1936.

Theodorson, George, "Romanticism and Motivation to Marry in the United States, Singapore, Burma, and India," *Social Forces,* vol. XLIV, pp. 17–28, 1965.

Trost, Jan, "Mate-Selection, Marital Adjustment, and Symbolic Environment," *Acta Sociologica,* vol. VIII, pp. 27–35, 1964.

Trost, Jan, "Some Data on Mate-Selection: Complementarity," *Journal of Marriage and the Family,* vol. XXIX, pp. 730–738, 1967.

* Udry, J. Richard, "Complementarity in Mate Selection: A Perceptual Approach," *Marriage and Family Living,* vol. XXV, pp. 281–289, August 1963.

* Udry, J. Richard, "Ideal Mates, Real Mates, and Autistic Perception," presented at the annual meetings of the American Sociological Association, Los Angeles, August 1963.

* Udry, J. Richard, "The Influence of the Ideal Mate Image on Mate Perception and Mate Selection," *Journal of Marriage and the Family,* vol. XXVII, 1965.

* Udry, J. Richard, "Personality Match and Interpersonal Perception as Predictors of Marriage," *Journal of Marriage and the Family,* vol. XXIX, pp. 722-725, 1967.

Udry, J. Richard; Bauman, Karl E.; and Chase, Charles A., "Skin Color, Status and Mate Selection," *American Journal of Sociology,* vol. LXXVI, no. 4, pp. 722-733, January 1971.

* Udry, J. Richard; Nelson, Harold A.; and Nelson, Ruth O., "An Empirical Investigation of Some Widely Held Beliefs About Marital Interaction," *Marriage and Family Living,* vol. XXIII, pp. 388-390, 1961.

* Waller, Willard, "The Rating and Dating Complex," *American Sociological Review,* vol. II, pp. 727-734, 1937.

Walster, Elaine; Aronson, Vera; Abrahams, Darcy; and Rottman, Leon, "Importance of Physical Attractiveness in Dating Behavior," *Journal of Personality and Social Psychology,* vol. IV, no. 5, pp. 508-516, 1969.

Warren, Bruce L., "A Multiple Variable Approach to the Assortative Mating Phenomenon," *Eugenics Quarterly,* vol. XIII, pp. 285-290, 1966.

Williamson, Robert C., "Dating, Courtship and the 'Ideal Mate'," *Family Life Coordinator,* vol. XIV, pp. 137-143, 1965.

* Winch, Robert F., "Another Look at the Theory of Complementary Needs in Mate Selection," *Journal of Marriage and the Family,* vol. XXIX, pp. 756-762, 1967.

* Winch, Robert F., "Courtship in College Women," *American Journal of Sociology,* vol. LV, pp. 269-278, 1949.

* Winch, Robert F., *Mate-Selection: A Study of Complementary Needs.* Harper and Brothers, New York, 1958.

* Winch, Robert F., *The Modern Family.* Henry Holt and Company, New York, 1952.

* Winch, Robert F., *The Modern Family,* revised edition. Holt, Rinehart and Winston, Inc., New York, 1963.

* Winch, Robert F., "The Theory of Complementary Needs in Mate Selection: Final Results on the Test of the General Hypothesis," *American Sociological Review,* vol. XX, pp. 552-555, 1955.

Winch, Robert F., and Anderson, R. Bruce, "Two Problems Involved in the Use of Peer-Rating Scales and Some Observations on Kendall's Coefficient of Concordance," *Sociometry,* vol. XXX, pp. 316-322, 1967.

* Winch, Robert F.; Ktsanes, Thomas; and Ktsanes, Virginia, "The Theory of Complementary Needs in Mate Selection: An Analytic and Descriptive Study," *American Sociological Review,* vol. XIX, no. 3, pp. 241-249, June 1954.

Zimmerman, Carle C., and Cervantes, Lucius F., *Successful American Families.* Pageant Press, Inc., New York, 1960.

CHAPTER 10   ENGAGEMENT

Bayer, Alan E., "Marriage Plans and Educational Aspirations," *American Journal of Sociology,* vol. LXXV, pp. 239-244, 1969-1970.

* Blood, Robert O., Jr., *Marriage.* Free Press of Glencoe, Inc., New York, 1962.

Boxer, Louis, "Mate Selection and Emotional Disorder," *The Family Coordinator,* vol. XIX, pp. 173–179, 1970.

* Burgess, Ernest W., and Wallin, Paul, *Engagement and Marriage.* J. B. Lippincott Company, Philadelphia, 1953.

Cavan, Ruth Shonle, "Concepts and Terminology in Interreligious Marriage," *Journal for the Scientific Study of Religion,* vol. IX, pp. 311–320, 1970.

Cavan, Ruth Shonle, "A Dating-Marriage Scale of Religious Social Distance," *Journal for the Scientific Study of Religion,* vol. X, pp. 93–100, 1971.

Cavan, Ruth Shonle, "Jewish Student Attitudes Toward Interreligious and Intra-Jewish Marriage," *American Journal of Sociology,* vol. LXXVI, pp. 1,064–1,071, 1971.

* Farber, Bernard, *Family Organization and Interaction.* Chandler Publishing Company, San Francisco, 1964.

Hall, Everett, "Ordinal Position and Success in Engagement and Marriage," *Journal of Individual Psychology,* vol. XXI, no. 2, pp. 154–158, 1965.

Hicks, Mary W., "An Empirical Evaluation of Textbook Assumptions About Engagement," *The Family Coordinator,* vol. XIX, pp. 57–63, 1970.

Kelsall, R. Keith; Poole, Anne; and Kuhn, Annette, "Marriage and Family-Building Patterns of University Graduates," *Journal of Biosocial Science,* vol. III, pp. 281–287, 1971.

* Kirkendall, Lester A., *Premarital Intercourse and Interpersonal Relationships.* Gramercy Publishing Co., New York, 1968.

Knox, David, and Patrick, Junior A., "You Are What You Do: A New Approach in Preparation for Marriage," *The Family Coordinator,* vol. XX, pp. 109–114, 1971.

* Koller, Marvin R., "Some Changes in Courtship Behavior in Three Generations of Ohio Women," *American Sociological Review,* vol. XVI, pp. 366–370, June 1951.

Lieberson, Stanley, "The Price-Aubrzycki Measure of Ethnic Intermarriage," *Eugenics Quarterly,* vol. XIII, no. 2, pp. 92–100, 1966.

Meyer, John W., "High School Effects on College Intentions," *American Journal of Sociology,* vol. LXXVI, pp. 59–70, 1971.

Moerk, Ernst and Becker, Penelope, "Attitudes of High School Students Toward Future Marriage and College Education," *The Family Coordinator,* vol. XX, pp. 67–73, 1971.

Otto, Herbert A., and Andersen, Robert B., "The Hope Chest and Dowry: American Custom?" *Family Life Coordinator,* vol. XVI, pp. 15–19, 1967.

Rapoport, Rhona, "The Transition from Engagement to Marriage," *Acta Sociologica,* vol. VIII, pp. 36–55, 1964.

Rappaport, Alan F.; Payne, David; and Steinmann, Anne, "Perceptual Differences Between Married and Single College Women for the Concepts of Self, Ideal Woman, and Man's Ideal Woman," *Journal of Marriage and the Family,* vol. XXXII, pp. 441–442, 1970.

* Slater, Philip, "Social Limitations on Libidinal Withdrawal," in Rose L. Coser, editor, *The Family: Its Structure and Functions.* St. Martin's Press, New York, 1964.

Strong, Emily; Wallace, William; and Wilson, Warner, "Three-Filter Date Selection by Computer," *The Family Coordinator,* vol. XVIII, pp. 166-171, 1969.

* Udry, J. Richard, "Personality Match and Mate Perception as Predictors of Marriage," *Journal of Marriage and the Family,* vol. XXIX, pp. 722-725, 1967.

Wiggins, Jerry S.; Wiggins, Nancy; and Conger, Judith Cohen, "Correlates of Heterosexual Somatic Preference," *Journal of Personality and Social Psychology,* vol. X, pp. 82-90, 1968.

Yaukey, David; Thorsen, Timm; and Onaka, Alvin T., "Marriage at an Earlier Age in Six Latin American Capital Cities," *Population Studies,* vol. XXVI, pp. 263-272, 1972.

CHAPTER 11   MARITAL INTERACTION PROCESSES

* Barton, K., and Cattell, R. B., "Marriage Dimensions and Personality," *Journal of Personality and Social Psychology,* vol. XXI, pp. 369-375, 1972.

* Barton, K.; Kawash, G.; and Cattell, R. B., "Personality, Motivation, and Marital Role Factors as Predictors of Life Data in Married Couples," *Journal of Marriage and the Family,* vol. XXXIV, pp. 474-480, 1972.

* Bean, Frank D., and Kerckhoff, Alan C., "Personality and Perception in Husband-Wife Conflicts," *Journal of Marriage and the Family,* vol. XXXIII, pp. 351-359, 1971.

Bernard, Jessie, "The Adjustment of Married Mates," in Harold T. Christensen, editor, *Handbook of Marriage and the Family.* Rand McNally & Company, Chicago, 1964.

* Bienvenu, Millard A., Sr., "Measurement of Marital Communication," *The Family Coordinator,* vol. XIX, pp. 26-31, 1970.

* Bieri, J., "Changes in Interpersonal Perception Following Social Interaction," *Journal of Abnormal and Social Psychology,* vol. XLVIII, pp. 61-66, 1953.

Blanck, Rubin, "Marriage as a Phase of Personality Development," *Social Casework,* vol. XLVIII, pp. 154-160, 1967.

* Blazer, John A., "Complementary Needs and Marital Happiness," *Marriage and Family Living,* vol. XXV, pp. 89-95, February 1963.

* Blood, Robert O., and Wolfe, Donald M., *Husbands and Wives.* Free Press of Glencoe, Inc., New York, 1960.

Borke, Helene, "A Family over Three Generations: The Transmission of Interacting and Relating Problems," *Journal of Marriage and the Family,* vol. XXIX, no. 4, pp. 638-655, 1967.

* Bossard, James H. S., and Boll, Eleanor S., "Marital Unhappiness in the Life Cycle," *Marriage and Family Living,* vol. XVII, no. 1, pp. 10-14, February 1955.

Breed, George, "The Effect of Intimacy: Reciprocity or Retreat?" *British Journal of Social and Clinical Psychology,* vol. XI, pp. 135-142, 1972.

* Brim, Orville G., Jr.; Fairchild, Roy W.; and Borgatta, Edgar F., "Relations Between Family Problems," *Marriage and Family Living,* vol. XXIII, no. 3, pp. 219-226, August 1961.

* Budd, William G., "Prediction of Interests Between Husband and Wife," *Journal of Educational Sociology,* vol. XXXIII, pp. 37-39, 1959.

Buerkle, Jack V.; Anderson, Theodore R.; and Badgley, Robin F., "Altruism, Role Conflict, and Marital Adjustment: A Factor Analysis of Marital Interaction," *Marriage and Family Living,* vol. XXIII, pp. 20-26, February 1961.

* Burgess, Ernest W.; Locke, Harvey J.; and Thomes, Mary Margaret, *The Family.* American Book Company, New York, 1963.

* Burgess, Ernest W., and Wallin, Paul, *Engagement and Marriage.* J. B. Lippincott Company, Philadelphia, 1953.

* Burr, Wesley R., "An Expansion and Test of a Role Theory of Marital Satisfaction," *Journal of Marriage and the Family,* vol. XXXII, pp. 368-372, 1971.

* Burr, Wesley R., "Satisfaction with Various Aspects of Marriage Over the Life Cycle: A Random Middle Class Sample," *Journal of Marriage and the Family,* vol. XXXII, pp. 29-37, February 1970.

Cancian, Francesca M., "Interaction Patterns in Zinacanteco Families," *American Sociological Review,* vol. XXIX, pp. 540-550, 1964.

* Cattell, Raymond B., and Nesselroade, John R., "Likeness and Completeness Theories Examined by Sixteen Personality Factor Measures on Stably and Unstably Married Couples," *Journal of Personality and Social Psychology,* vol. VII, no. 4, pp. 351-361, 1967.

Clarke, Carl, "Group Procedures for Increasing Positive Feedback Between Married Partners," *The Family Coordinator,* vol. XIX, pp. 324-328, 1970.

* Clements, William H., "Marital Interaction and Marital Stability: A Point of View and a Descriptive Comparison of Stable and Unstable Marriages," *Journal of Marriage and the Family,* vol. XXIX, pp. 697-702, 1967.

Constantine, Larry L., "Personal Growth in Multiperson Marriages," *Radical Therapist,* vol. II, pp. 18-20, 1971.

Constantine, Larry L., and Constantine, Joan M., "Group and Multilateral Marriage: Definitional Notes, Glossary, and Annotated Bibliography," *Family Process,* vol. X, pp. 157-176, 1971.

Constantine, Larry L., and Constantine, Joan M., "Sexual Aspects of Multilateral Relations," *Journal of Sex Research,* vol. VII, pp. 204-225, 1971.

* Corsini, Raymond J., "Multiple Predictors of Marital Happiness," *Marriage and Family Living,* vol. XVIII, no. 3, pp. 240-242, August 1956.

* Cuber, John F., and Harroff, Peggy B., "The More Total View: Relationships Among Men and Women of the Upper Middle Class," *Marriage and Family Living,* vol. XXV, pp. 140-145, May 1963.

* Cutler, Beverly R., and Dyer, William G., "Initial Adjustment Processes in Young Married Couples," *Social Forces,* vol. XLIV, pp. 195-201, 1965.

Dame, Nenabelle G.; Finck, George H.; Reiner, Beatrice S.; and Smith, Brady O., "The Effect on the Marital Relationship of the Wife's Search for Identity," *Family Life Coordinator,* vol. XIV, pp. 133-136, 1965.

* Dizard, Jan, *Social Change in the Family,* Community and Family Study Center, University of Chicago, 1968.

* Dunn, Marie S., "Marriage Role Expectations of Adolescents," *Marriage and Family Living,* vol. XXII, pp. 99-111, 1960.

* Dymond, Rosalind, "Interpersonal Perception and Marital Happiness," *Canadian Journal of Psychology,* vol. VIII, pp. 164-171, September 1954.

Edmonds, Vernon H., "Marital Conventionalization: Definition and Measurement," *Journal of Marriage and the Family,* vol. XXIX, pp. 681-688, 1967.

* Edmonds, Vernon H.; Withers, Glenne; and Dibattista, Beverly, "Adjustment, Conservatism, and Conventionalism," *Journal of Marriage and the Family,* vol. XXXIV, pp. 96-103, February 1972.

* Ellis, Albert, "The Value of Marriage Prediction Tests," *American Sociological Review,* vol. XIII, pp. 710-718, 1948.

Ellis, Barbara Gray, "Unconscious Collusion in Marital Interaction," *Social Casework,* vol. XLV, pp. 79-85, 1964.

Eshleman, J. Ross, "Mental Health and Marital Integration in Young Marriages," *Journal of Marriage and the Family,* vol. XXVII, pp. 255-262, 1965.

* Farber, Bernard, "Elements of Competence in Interpersonal Relations: A Factor Analysis," *Sociometry,* vol. XXV, no. 1, pp. 30-47, March 1962.

Farber, Bernard, *Family Organization and Interaction.* Chandler Publishing Company, San Francisco, 1964.

Farina, Amerigo; Garmezy, Norman; and Barry, Herbert, III, "Relationship of Marital Status to Incidence and Prognosis of Schizophrenia," *Journal of Abnormal and Social Psychology,* vol. LXVII, no. 6, pp. 624-630, 1963.

Feldman, Harold, and Rand, Martin E., "Egocentrism-Altercentrism in the Husband-Wife Relationship," *Journal of Marriage and the Family,* vol. XXVII, pp. 386-391, 1967.

Ferreira, Antonio J.; Winter, William D.; and Poindexter, Edward J., "Some Interactional Variables in Normal and Abnormal Families," *Family Process,* vol. V, pp. 60-75, 1966.

Fink, Stephen L.; Skipper, James K., Jr.; and Hallenbeck, Phyllis N., "Physical Disability and Problems in Marriage," *Journal of Marriage and the Family,* vol. XXX, pp. 64-73, 1968.

* Foote, Nelson, "Matching of Husband and Wife in Phases of Development," in Marvin B. Sussman, editor, *Sourcebook in Marriage and the Family,* pp. 15-21. Houghton Mifflin Company, Boston, 1963.

Gersuny, Carl, "The Honeymoon Industry: Rhetoric and Bureaucratization of Status Passage," *The Family Coordinator,* vol. XIX, pp. 260-266, 1970.

* Glenn, Norval D., and Keir, Margaret Sue, "Divorce Among Sociologists Married to Sociologists," *Social Problems,* vol. XIX, pp. 57-67, 1971.

* Goodrich, Wells; Ryder, Robert G.; and Raush, Harold L., "Patterns of Newlywed Marriage," *Journal of Marriage and the Family,* vol. XXX, pp. 383-391, 1968.

* Gove, Walter R., "The Relationship Between Sex Roles, Marital Status, and Mental Illness," *Social Forces,* vol. LI, pp. 34-44, 1972.

Gove, Walter R., "Sex, Marital Status and Suicide," *Journal of Health and Social Behavior,* vol. III, pp. 204-213, 1972.

Handel, Gerald, "The Psychosocial Interior of Family Life," presented at the annual meeting of the American Sociological Association, San Francisco, California, August 28, 1967.

Hawkins, James L., "Associations Between Companionship, Hostility, and Marital Satisfaction," *Journal of Marriage and the Family,* vol. XXX, pp. 647-650, 1968.

* Hawkins, James L., and Johnsen, Kathryn, "Perception of Behavioral Conformity, Imputation of Consensus, and Marital Satisfaction," *Journal of Marriage and the Family,* vol. XXXI, pp. 507-511, 1969.

Hilsdale, Paul, "Marriage as a Personal Existential Commitment," *Marriage and Family Living,* vol. XXIV, pp. 137-143, 1962.

* Hobart, Charles W., and Klausner, William J., "Some Social Interaction Correlates of Marital Role Disagreements, and Marital Adjustment," *Marriage and Family Living,* vol. XXI, pp. 256-263, 1959.

Holland, David, "Familization, Socialization, and the Universe of Meaning: An Extension of the Interactional Approach to the Study of the Family," *Journal of Marriage and the Family,* vol. XXXII, pp. 415-427, 1970.

Hooper, Douglas, and Sheldon, Alan, "Evaluating Newly-Married Couples," *British Journal of Social and Clinical Psychology,* vol. VIII, pp. 169-182, 1969.

Hurvitz, Nathan, "Control Roles, Marital Strain, Role Deviation, and Marital Adjustment," *Journal of Marriage and the Family,* vol. XXVII, no. 1, pp. 29-31, February 1965.

* Hurvitz, Nathan, "The Marital Roles Inventory and the Measurement of Marital Adjustment," *Journal of Clinical Psychology,* vol. XVI, pp. 377-380, 1960.

Hurvitz, Nathan, "Marital Roles Strain as a Sociological Variable," *Family Life Coordinator,* vol. XIV, no. 2, pp. 39-42, April 1965.

* Ingersol, Hazel L., "Transmission of Authority Patterns in the Family," *Marriage and Family Living,* vol. X, p. 36, 1948.

Inselberg, Rachel M., "The Sentence Completion Technique in the Measurement of Marital Satisfaction," *Journal of Marriage and the Family,* vol. XXVI, no. 3, pp. 339-341, August 1964.

* Jacobson, Alver H., "Conflict of Attitudes Toward the Roles of Husband and Wife in Marriage," *American Sociological Review,* vol. XVII, pp. 146-150, April 1952.

* Jacobson, Paul H., *American Marriage and Divorce.* Rinehart and Company, Inc., New York, 1959.

* Kahn, Malcolm, "Non-Verbal Communication and Marital Satisfaction," *Family Process,* vol. IX, pp. 449-456, 1970.

* Karlson, Georg, *Adaptability and Communication in Marriage.* The Bedminster Press, Totowa, New Jersey, 1963.

* Kelley, E. Lowell, "Consistency of the Adult Personality," *American Psychologist,* vol. X, pp. 659-681, 1955.

* Kelley, E. Lowell, "The Reassessment of Specific Attitudes After Twenty Years," *Journal of Social Issues,* vol. XVII, no. 1, pp. 29-37, 1961.

Kerckhoff, Alan C., "Status-Related Value Patterns Among Married Couples," *Journal of Marriage and the Family,* vol. XXXIV, pp. 105-110, 1972.

Kerckhoff, Alan C., "Two Dimensions of Husband-Wife Interaction," *The Sociological Quarterly,* vol. XIII, pp. 49-60, 1972.

* Kerckhoff, Alan, and Davis, Keith E., "Value Consensus and Need Complementarity in Mate Selection," *American Sociological Review,* vol. XXVII, pp. 395-403, June 1962.

* Kieren, Dianne, and Tallman, Irving, "Spousal Adaptability: An Assessment of Marital Competence," *Journal of Marriage and the Family,* vol. XXXIV, pp. 247-256, 1972.

* Kimmel, Paul R., and Havens, John W., "Game Theory versus Mutual Identification: Two Criteria for Assessing Marital Relationships," *Journal of Marriage and the Family,* vol. XXVIII, pp. 460–465, 1966.

* Kirkpatrick, Clifford, *The Family as Process and Institution,* second edition. The Ronald Press Company, New York, 1963.

* Kirkpatrick, Clifford, and Hobart, Charles, "Disagreement, Disagreement Estimate, and Non-empathetic Imputation for Intimacy Groups Varying from Favorite Date to Married," *American Sociological Review,* vol. XIX, no. 1, pp. 10–19, February 1954.

Kogan, Kate L., and Jackson, Joan K., "Patterns of Atypical Perceptions of Self and Spouse in Wives of Alcoholics," *Quarterly Journal of Studies on Alcohol,* vol. XXV, no. 3, pp. 555–557, September 1964.

Kosa, John; Alpert, Joel J.; Pickering, M. Ruth; and Haggerty, Robert J., "Crisis and Stress in Family Life: A Re-examination of Concepts," *The Wisconsin Sociologist,* vol. IV, pp. 11–19, 1965.

Landis, Judson T., and Landis, Mary G., *The Marriage Handbook.* Prentice-Hall, Inc., New York, 1953.

* Lang, R. O., "The Rating of Happiness in Marriage," unpublished M. A. thesis, University of Chicago, 1932.

* Laws, Judith Long, "A Feminist Review of Marital Adjustment," *Journal of Marriage and the Family,* vol. XXXIII, pp. 483–516, 1971.

Levin, Gilbert, "Communicator-Communicant Approach to Family Interaction Research," *Family Process,* vol. V, no. 1, pp. 105–116, March 1966.

Levinger, George, "Marital Cohesiveness and Dissolution: An Integrative Review," *Journal of Marriage and the Family,* vol. XXVII, no. 1, pp. 19–28, February 1965.

Levinger, George, and Breedlove, James, "Interpersonal Attraction and Agreement: A Study of Marriage Partners," *Journal of Personality and Social Psychology,* vol. III, pp. 367–372, 1966.

* Levinger, George, and Sonnheim, Maurice, "Complementarity in Marital Adjustment: Reconsidering Toman's Family Constellation Hypothesis," *Journal of Individual Psychology,* vol. XXI, pp. 131–135, November 1965.

Locke, Harvey J., *Predicting Adjustment in Marriage: A Comparison of a Divorced and a Happily Married Group.* Henry Holt and Company, New York, 1951.

* Locke, Harvey J.; Sabagh, Georges; and Thomes, Mary Margaret, "Correlates of Primary Communication and Empathy," *Research Studies of the State College of Washington,* vol. XXIV, pp. 116–124, 1956.

* Locke, Harvey J., and Williamson, Robert C., "Marital Adjustment: A Factor Analysis Study," *American Sociological Review,* vol. XXIII, pp. 562–569, 1958.

* Lovejoy, Debi, "College Student Conceptions of the Roles of Husband and Wife in Decision-Making," *Family Life Coordinator,* vol. IX, pp. 43–46, 1961.

Lowenthal, Marjorie Fiske and Haven, Clayton, "Interaction and Adaptation: Intimacy as a Critical Variable," *American Sociological Review,* vol. XXXIII, pp. 20–30, 1968.

* Luckey, Eleanore B., "Marital Satisfaction and Its Association with Congruence of Perception," *Marriage and Family Living,* vol. XXII, pp. 49-54, 1960.

* Luckey, Eleanore B., "Number of Years Married as Related to Personality Perception and Marital Satisfaction," *Journal of Marriage and the Family,* vol. XXVIII, pp. 44-48, 1966.

* Luckey, Eleanore B., "Perceptional Congruence of Self and Family Concepts as Related to Marital Interaction," *Sociometry,* vol. XXIV, pp. 234-250, September 1961.

* Lynn, David B., "Sex Differences in Identification Development," *Sociometry,* vol. XXIV, pp. 372-383, 1961.

* Merrill, Frances E., *Courtship and Marriage.* Henry Holt and Company, New York, 1959.

Mitchell, Howard E.; Bullard, James W.; and Mudd, Emily H., "Areas of Marital Conflict in Successfully and Unsuccessfully Functioning Families," *Journal of Health and Human Behavior,* vol. III, no. 2, pp. 88-93, 1962.

Montgomery, James E., "The Housing Patterns of Older Families," *The Family Coordinator,* vol. XXI, pp. 37-46, 1972.

Most, Elizabeth, "Measuring Change in Marital Satisfaction," *Social Work,* vol. IX, no. 3, pp. 64-69, July 1964.

* Motz, Annabelle B., "Conceptions of Marital Roles by Status Groups," *Marriage and Family Living,* vol. XII, pp. 136-162, 1950.

Murstein, Bernard I., and Glaudin, Vincent, "The Relationship of Marital Adjustment to Personality: A Factor Analysis of the Interpersonal Check List," *Journal of Marriage and the Family,* vol. XXVIII, no. 1, pp. 37-43, February 1966.

Navran, Leslie, "Communication and Adjustment in Marriage," *Family Process,* vol. VI, no. 2, September 1967.

Nelson, Joel, "Marital Norms and Individualistic Values: A Study of Social Conditions Affecting Consistency," *Journal of Marriage and the Family,* vol. XXIX, pp. 475-482, 1967.

" 'Normal' Married Couples Lead 'Dull, Mundane' Lives," Medical News, *Journal of the American Medical Association,* vol. CLXXXIV, no. 9, p. 23, June 1, 1963.

Oates, Wayne E., "Paranoid Interaction in Marriage," *Journal of Family Law,* vol. IX, pp. 200-208, 1964.

* O'Brien, John E., "Interrelationship of Conflict and Satisfaction in Unstable Marriages: A Methodological Analysis," presented at the annual meetings of the American Sociological Association, 1972.

* Orden, Susan R., and Bradburn, Norman M., "Dimensions of Marriage Happiness," *American Journal of Sociology,* vol. LXXIII, pp. 715-731, May 1968.

* Ort, Robert S., "A Study of Role-conflicts as Related to Happiness in Marriage," *Journal of Abnormal and Social Psychology,* vol. XLV, pp. 691-699, 1950.

Osman, Shelomo, "My Stepfather Is a She," *Family Process,* vol. XI, pp. 209-218, 1972.

* Petersen, David M., "Husband-Wife Communication and Family Problems," *Sociology and Social Research: An International Journal,* vol. LIII, pp. 375-384, 1969.

Pfeil, Elisabeth, "Role Expectations When Entering into Marriage," *Journal of Marriage and the Family,* vol. XXX, pp. 161-166, 1968.

* Pineo, Peter C., "Development Patterns in Marriage," *The Family Coordinator,* vol. XVIII, pp. 135-140, 1969.

* Pineo, Peter C., "Disenchantment in the Later Years of Marriage," *Marriage and Family Living,* vol. XXIII, no. 1, pp. 3-11, February 1961.

* Pollak, Otto, "Entrance of the Caseworker into Family Interaction," *Social Casework,* vol. XLV, no. 4, pp. 216-220, 1964.

Poulson, Jenniev; Warren, Richard; and Kenkel, William F., "The Measurement of Goal Agreement Between Husbands and Wives," *Sociological Quarterly,* vol. VII, pp. 480-488, 1966.

* Preston, Malcolm; Peltz, William; Mudd, Emily; and Froscher, Hazel, "Impressions of Personality as a Function of Marital Conflict," *Journal of Abnormal and Social Psychology,* vol. XLVII, pp. 326-336, 1952.

Rappaport, Alan F.; Payne, David; and Steinmann, Anne, "Marriage as a Factor in the Dyadic Perception of the Female Sex Role," *Psychological Reports,* vol. XXVII, pp. 283-284, 1970.

Raush, Harold L.; Goodrich, Wells; and Campbell, John D., "Adaptation to the First Years of Marriage," *Psychiatry,* vol. XXVI, no. 4, pp. 368-80, November 1963.

Renne, Karen S., "Correlates of Dissatisfaction in Marriage," *Journal of Marriage and the Family,* vol. XXXII, pp. 54-67, 1970.

Rollins, Boyd C., "Consensus of Husband and Wife on Companionship Values and Marital Satisfaction: Some Theoretical Implications," presented at the National Council of Family Relations, Minneapolis, Minnesota, October 29, 1966.

* Rollins, Boyd C., and Feldman, Harold, "Marital Satisfaction Over the Family Life Cycle," *Journal of Marriage and the Family,* vol. XXXII, pp. 20-28, 1970.

Ryder, Robert F., and Flint, A. A., "Vicissitudes of Marital Disputes: the Object Test," presented at the meeting of the American Orthopsychiatric Association, St. Louis, Missouri, 1966.

Ryder, Robert G., "Dimensions of Early Marriage," *Family Process,* vol. IX, no. 1, pp. 51-68, March 1970.

Ryder, Robert G., and Goodrich, D. Wells, "Married Couples' Responses to Disagreement," *Family Process,* vol. V, pp. 30-42, 1966.

Sager, Clifford J.; Kaplan, Helen S.; Gundlach, Ralph H.; Kremmer, Malvina; Lenz, Rosa; and Royce, Jack R., "The Marriage Contract," *Family Process,* vol. X, no. 3, pp. 311-326, September 1971.

Scanzoni, John, "A Note on the Sufficiency of Wife Responses in Family Research," *Pacific Sociological Review,* pp. 109-115, fall 1965.

Scanzoni, John, "A Social System Analysis of Dissolved and Existing Marriages," *Journal of Marriage and the Family,* vol. XXX, pp. 452-461, 1968.

Steinmann, Anne, and Fox, David J., "Specific Areas of Agreement and Conflict in Women's Self-Perception and Their Perception of Men's Ideal Woman in Two South American Urban Communities and an Urban Community in the United States," *Journal of Marriage and the Family,* vol. XXXI, pp. 281-289, 1969.

Stinnett, Nick; Collins, Janet; and Montgomery, James E., "Marital Need Satisfaction of Older Husbands and Wives," *Journal of Marriage and the Family,* vol. XXXIV, pp. 428-434, 1972.

Streib, Gordon F., "Older Families and Their Troubles: Familial and Social Responses," *The Family Coordinator,* vol. XXI, pp. 5-19, 1972.

* Stuckert, Robert P., "Role Perception and Marital Satisfaction — A Configurational Approach," *Marriage and Family Living,* vol. XXV, no. 4, pp. 415-419, November 1963.

Symonds, Alexandra, "Phobias After Marriage," *The American Journal of Psychoanalysis,* vol. XXXI, pp. 144-152, 1972.

* Terman, Lewis M., *Psychological Factors in Marital Happiness.* McGraw-Hill Book Company, New York, 1938.

* Toman, W., *Family Constellation.* Springer Publishing Company, Inc., New York, 1961.

Tomeh, Aida K., "Birth Order and Dependence Patterns of College Students in Lebanon," *Journal of Marriage and the Family,* vol. XXXIV, pp. 361-374, 1972.

* Udry, J. Richard; Nelson, Harold A.; and Nelson, Ruth O., "An Empirical Investigation of Some Widely Held Beliefs about Marital Interaction," *Marriage and Family Living,* vol. XXIII, pp. 388-390, 1961.

* Uhr, Leonard Merrick, *Personality Changes in Marriage,* unpublished Ph.D. dissertation, University of Michigan, 1957.

* Wallen, John L., *Mutual Value Predictions of Husbands and Wives,* unpublished Ph.D. dissertation, University of Oregon, 1957.

Waller, Willard, and Hill, Reuben, *The Family: A Dynamic Interpretation.* Dryden Press, New York, 1951.

* Winch, Robert F., *Mate Selection.* Harper and Brothers, New York, 1958.

CHAPTER 12   SOCIAL FACTORS IN MARITAL SUCCESS

Adams, Robert Lynn, and Mogey, John, "Marriage, Membership and Mobility in Church and Sect," *Sociological Analysis,* vol. XXVIII, pp. 205-214, 1967.

* Barnett, Larry D., Research on International and Interracial Marriages, *Marriage and Family Living,* vol. XXV, pp. 105-107, February, 1963.

Bauman, Karl E., "The Relationship Between Age at First Marriage, School Dropout, and Marital Instability: An Analysis of the Glick Effect," *Journal of Marriage and the Family,* vol. XXIX, pp. 672-680, 1967.

Besanceney, Paul H., "Interfaith Marriages of Catholics in the Detroit Area," *Sociological Analysis,* vol. XXVI, pp. 38-44, 1965.

Besanceney, Paul H., "On Reporting Rates of Intermarriage," *American Journal of Sociology,* vol. LXX, pp. 717-721, 1965.

* Blood, Robert O., Jr., *Marriage.* Free Press of Glencoe, Inc., New York, 1962.

* Blood, Robert O., Jr., and Wolfe, Donald M., *Husbands and Wives.* Free Press of Glencoe, Inc., New York, 1960.

* Bossard, James H. S., and Letts, H. C., "Mixed Marriages Involving Lutherans," *Marriage and Family Living,* vol. XVIII, pp. 308-310, 1956.

* Bumpass, Larry L., and Sweet, James A., "Differentials in Marital Instability: 1970," *American Sociological Review,* vol. XXXVII, pp. 754-766, 1972.

* Burchinal, Lee G., and Chancellor, Loren E., "Survival Rates Among Religiously Homogamous and Interreligious Marriages," *Research Bulletin 512.* Ames, Iowa: Agricultural and Home Economics Experiment Station, Iowa State University, 1962.

* Burchinal, Lee G., and Chancellor, Loren E., "Survival Rates Among Religiously Homogamous and Interreligious Marriages," *Social Forces,* vol. XLI, no. 4, pp. 353–362, May 1963.

* Burgess, Ernest W., and Cottrell, Leonard S., Jr., *Predicting Success or Failure in Marriage.* Prentice-Hall, Inc., Englewood Cliffs, New Jersey, 1939.

* Burgess, Ernest W.; Locke, Harvey J.; and Thomes, Mary Margaret, *The Family,* third edition. American Book Company, New York, 1963.

* Burgess, Ernest W., and Wallin, Paul, *Engagement and Marriage.* J. B. Lippincott Company, Philadelphia, 1953.

* Cheng, C. K., and Yamamura, Douglas S., "Interracial Marriage and Divorce in Hawaii," *Social Forces,* vol. XXXVI, pp. 77–84, 1957.

* Chester, Robert, "The Duration of Marriage to Divorce," *British Journal of Sociology,* vol. XXII, pp. 172–182, 1971.

* Christensen, Harold, and Barber, Kenneth E., "Interfaith Versus Intrafaith Marriage in Indiana," *Journal of Marriage and the Family,* vol. XXIX, no. 3, pp. 461–469, August 1967.

Cole, William Graham, "Early Marriage," *The Nation,* pp. 111–114, February 1958.

* Cutright, Phillips, "Income and Family Events: Marital Stability," *Journal of Marriage and the Family,* vol. XXXIII, no. 2, 291–306, May 1971.

de Lissovoy, Vladimir, and Hitchcock, Mary Ellen, "High School Marriages in Pennsylvania Problems and School Board Policies," *The Bulletin,* official publication of the Pennsylvania School Boards Association, vol. XXVIII, June, 1964.

Eshleman, J. Ross, "Mental Health and Marital Integration in Young Marriages," *Journal of Marriage and the Family,* vol. XXVII, pp. 255–262, 1965.

Eshleman, J. Ross, and Hunt, Chester L., "Social Class Influences on Family Adjustment Patterns of Married College Students," *Journal of Marriage and the Family,* vol. XXIX, pp. 485–491, 1967.

Geismar, Ludwig L., and Gerhart, Ursula C., "Social Class, Ethnicity, and Family Functioning: Exploring Some Issues Raised by the Moynihan Report," *Journal of Marriage and the Family,* vol. XXX, pp. 480–487, 1968.

Glick, Paul C., "Health, Wealth, and Marriage," presented at the annual meeting of the American Sociological Association, San Francisco, 1967.

Glick, Paul C., "Marital Stability as a Social Indicator," presented at the annual meeting of the Population Association of America, 1968.

* Golden, Joseph, "Patterns of Negro-White Inter-marriage," *American Social Review,* vol. XIX, no. 2, pp. 144–147, 1954.

Goldstein, Sidney, and Goldscheider, Calvin, "Social and Demographic Aspects of Jewish Intermarriages," *Social Problems,* vol. XIII. pp. 386–399, 1966.

Hall, Everett, "Ordinal Position and Success in Engagement and Marriage," *Journal of Individual Psychology,* vol. XXI, pp. 154–158, 1965.

* Heiss, Jerold S., "Interfaith Marriage and Marital Outcomes," *Marriage and Family Living,* vol. XXIII, pp. 228–233, 1961.

Herrmann, Robert O., "Expectations and Attitudes as a Source of Financial Problems in Teen-age Marriages," *Journal of Marriage and the Family,* vol. XXVII, pp. 89–91, 1965.

* Jacobson, Paul H., *American Marriage and Divorce.* Rinehart and Company, New York, 1959.

* Kephart, William M., *The Family, Society, and the Individual.* Houghton Mifflin Company, Boston, 1961.

* Kimura, Yukiko, "War Brides in Hawaii and Their In-laws," *American Journal of Sociology,* vol. LXXIII, no. 1, pp. 70–76, July 1957.

* King, Charles E., The Burgess-Cottrell Method of Measuring Marital Adjustment Applied to a Non-white Southern Urban Population, *Marriage and Family Living,* vol. XIV, pp. 280–285, 1952.

Kinkade, Kathleen, *The Walden Two Experiment: The First Five Years of Twin Oaks Community.* William Morrow and Company, Inc., New York, 1973.

* Kinsey, Alfred C.; Pomeroy, Wardell B.; Martin, Clyde E.; and Gebhard, Paul H., *Sexual Behavior in the Human Female.* W. B. Saunders Company, Philadelphia, 1953.

* Landis, Judson T., "Marriages of Mixed and Non-mixed Religious Faith," *American Sociological Review,* vol. XIV, pp. 401–407, 1949.

* Landis, Judson T., "Social Correlates of Divorce or Nondivorce Among the Unhappily Married," *Marriage and Family Living,* vol. XXV, pp. 178–180, 1963.

* Landis, Judson T. and Landis, Mary G., *Building a Successful Marriage,* fourth edition. Prentice-Hall, Inc., Englewood Cliffs, New Jersey, 1963.

* Landis, Paul H., *Making the Most of Marriage.* Appleton-Century Crofts, Inc., New York, 1960.

* Lind, Andrew W., "Interracial Marriage as Affecting Divorce in Hawaii," *Sociology and Social Research,* vol. XLIX, pp. 17–26, 1964.

* Locke, Harvey J., *Predicting Adjustment in Marriage: A Comparison of a Divorced and a Happily Married Group.* Henry Holt and Company, New York, 1951.

* Martinson, Floyd M., "Ego Deficiency as a Factor in Marriage," *American Sociological Review,* vol. XX, pp. 161–164, 1955.

Mercer, Charles V., "Interrelations Among Family Stability, Family Composition, Residence, and Race," *Journal of Marriage and the Family,* vol. XXIX, pp. 456–460, 1967.

* Monahan, Thomas P., "Are Interracial Marriages Really Less Stable?" *Social Forces,* vol. XLVIII, pp. 461–473, 1970.

* Monahan, Thomas P., "Interracial Marriage and Divorce in the State of Hawaii," *Eugenics Quarterly,* vol. XIII, pp. 40–47, 1966.

Moss, J. Joel, "Teen-age Marriage: Cross-National Trends and Sociological Factors in the Decision of When to Marry," *Journal of Marriage and the Family,* vol. XXVII, pp. 230–242, 1967.

* Moss, J. Joel, and Gingles, Ruby, "The Relationship of Personality to the Incidence of Early Marriage," *Marriage and Family Living,* vol. XXI, pp. 373–377, 1959.

* Mulhearn, John, "Interfaith Marriage and Adult Religious Practice," *Sociological Analysis,* vol. XXX, pp. 23-31, 1969.

Parker, Seymour, and Kleiner, Robert J., "Social and Psychological Dimensions of the Family Role Performance of the Negro Male," *Journal of Marriage and the Family,* vol. XXXI, pp. 500-506, 1969.

* Pavela, Todd H., "An Exploratory Study of Negro-White Intermarriage in Indiana," *Journal of Marriage and the Family,* vol. XXVI, pp. 209-211, 1964.

Rodman, Hyman, "Technical Note on Two Rates of Mixed Marriage," *American Sociological Review,* vol. XXX, pp. 776-778, 1965.

* Roth, Julius, and Peck, Robert F., "Social Class and Social Mobility Factors Related to Marital Adjustment," *American Sociological Review,* vol. XVI, pp. 478-487, 1951.

Saveland, Walt, "Changing Age Patterns at First Marriage: Canada and the United States," presented at the annual meetings of the Population Association of America, April 1970.

* Scanzoni, John, "A Social System Analysis of Dissolved and Existing Marriages," *Journal of Marriage and the Family,* vol. XXX, pp. 452-461, 1968.

Schmitt, David R., "An Attitudinal Correlate of the Status Congruency of Married Women," *Social Forces,* vol. XLIV, pp. 190-195, 1965.

Schmitt, Robert C., "Age Differences in Marriage in Hawaii," *Journal of Marriage and the Family,* vol. XXVIII, pp. 57-61, 1966.

* Schmitt, Robert C., "Age and Race Differences in Divorce in Hawaii," *Journal of Marriage and the Family,* vol. XXXI, pp. 48-50, 1969.

Shipman, Gordon, and Tien, H. Yuan, "Nonmarriage and the Waiting Period," *Journal of Marriage and the Family,* vol. XXVII, pp. 277-280, 1965.

* Skinner, B. F., *Walden Two.* The Macmillan Company, New York, 1948.

* Smith, Carl E., "Negro-White Intermarriage — Forbidden Sexual Union," *Journal of Sex Research,* vol. II, pp. 169-173, 1966.

Snyder, Eloise C., "Attitudes: A Study of Homogamy and Marital Selectivity," *Journal of Marriage and the Family,* vol. XXVI, pp. 332-336, 1964.

Swain, Clark, "Responses of Family Life Professionals and Students to Family Success Indices — A Comparative Study," *Journal of Marriage and the Family,* vol. XXIX, pp. 726-729, 1967.

* Terman, Lewis M., *Psychological Factors in Marital Happiness.* McGraw-Hill Book Company, New York, 1938.

* Terman, Lewis M., and Oden, Melita H., *The Gifted Child Grows Up: Twenty-five Years' Follow-up of a Superior Group.* Stanford University Press, Stanford, California, 1947.

* Thomas, John L., "The Factor of Religion in the Selection of Marriage Mates," *American Sociological Review,* vol. XVI, pp. 487-491, 1951.

* Udry, J. Richard; Nelson, Harold A.; and Nelson, Ruth, "An Empirical Investigation of Some Widely Held Beliefs about Marital Interaction," *Marriage and Family Living,* vol. XXIII, pp. 388-390, 1961.

Uhlenberg, Peter, "Marital Instability Among Mexican Americans: Following the Patterns of Blacks," *Social Problems,* vol. XX, pp. 49-56, 1972.

* U. S. Department of Commerce, Bureau of the Census, *Current Population Reports,* series P-20, no. 26, Washington, D. C., 1956.

* Vernon, Glenn M., "Interfaith Marriages," *Religious Education,* vol. LV, pp. 261–264, 1960.
* Vincent, Clark E., "Socialization Data in Research on Young Marrieds," *Acta Sociologica,* FASC 1-2 pp. 118-127, August 1964.
* Weeks, H. Ashley, "Differential Divorce Rates by Occupation," *Social Forces,* vol. XXI, p. 336, March 1943.
* Winch, Robert F., and Greer, Scott A., "The Uncertain Relation Between Early Marriage and Marital Stability: A Quest for Relevant Data," *Acta Sociologica,* vol. VIII, pp. 83-97, 1964.
  Zimmerman, Carle C., and Cervantes, Lucius F., *Successful American Families.* Pageant Press, New York, 1960.

CHAPTER 13   SEX ROLE DIFFERENTIATION IN MARRIAGE

Ater, E. Carolyn, and Deacon, Ruth E., "Interaction of Family Relationship Qualities and Managerial Components," *Journal of Marriage and the Family,* vol. XXXIV, pp. 257-263, 1972.
* Bahr, Stephen J., and Rollins, Boyd C., "Crisis and Conjugal Power," *Journal of Marriage and the Family,* vol. XXX, pp. 360-367, 1971.
  Bauman, Gerald, and Roman, Melvin, "Interaction Testing in the Study of Marital Dominance," *Family Process,* vol. V, pp. 230-242, 1966.
  Belcher, John C., "The One-Person Household: A Consequence of the Isolated Nuclear Family?" *Journal of Marriage and the Family,* vol. XXIX, pp. 534-540, 1967.
* Blood, Robert O., Jr., *Marriage.* Free press of Glencoe, Inc., New York, 1962.
  Blood, Robert O., Jr., "The Measurement and Bases of Family Power: A Rejoinder," *Marriage and Family Living,* vol. XXV, no. 4, pp. 475-478, November 1963.
* Blood, Robert O., Jr., and Hamblin, Robert L., "The Effect of the Wife's Employment on the Family Power Structure," *Social Forces,* vol. XXXVI, no. 4, pp. 347-352, May 1958.
* Blood, Robert O., Jr., and Wolfe, Donald M., *Husbands and Wives.* The Free Press of Glencoe, Inc., Glencoe, Illinois, 1960.
  Blood, Robert O., Jr., and Wolfe, Donald M., "Negro-White Differences in Blue-Collar Marriages in a Northern Metropolis," *Social Forces,* vol. XLVIII, no. 1, pp. 59-64, 1969.
* Bossard, H. S. James, *The Large Family System.* University of Pennsylvania Press, Philadelphia, 1956.
* Bott, Elizabeth, *Family and Social Network.* Tavistock Institute, London, 1957.
  Burchinal, Lee G., and Bauder, Ward W., "Decision-Making and Role Patterns Among Iowa Farm and Nonfarm Families," *Journal of Marriage and the Family,* vol. XXVII, pp. 243-254, 1965.
* Burgess, Ernest W., and Wallin, Paul, *Engagement and Marriage.* J. B. Lippincott Company, Philadelphia, 1953
  Buric, Olivera, and Zecevic, Andjelka, "Family Authority, Marital Satisfaction, and the Social Network in Yugoslavia," *Journal of Marriage and the Family,* vol. XXIX, pp. 325-336, 1967.

Collver, O. Andrew, "Women's Work Participation and Fertility in Metropolitan Areas," *Demography,* vol. V, pp. 55-60, 1968.

Coughenour, C. Milton, "Functional Aspects of Food Consumption Activity and Family Life Cycle Stages," *Journal of Marriage and the Family,* vol. XXXIV, pp. 656-664, 1972.

* Dunn, Marie S., "Marriage Role Expectations of Adolescents," *Marriage and Family Living,* vol. XXII, pp. 99-111, 1960.

* Dyer, William G., and Urban, Dick, "The Institutionalization of Equalitarian Family Norms," *Marriage and Family Living,* vol. XX, pp. 53-58, 1958.

Elder, Glen H., Jr., "Role Relations, Sociocultural Environments, and Autocratic Family Ideology," *Sociometry,* vol. XXVIII, pp. 173-196, 1965.

* Epstein, Nathan B., and Westley, William A., "Parental Interaction as Related to the Emotional Health of Children," *Social Problems,* vol. VIII, no. 1, pp. 87-92, summer 1960.

Feofanov, Yu, "Granddaughters and Grandmothers," *Izvestia,* Moscow, 1968, *The Current Digest of the Soviet Press,* December 4, 1968.

Gibson, Geoffrey, and Ludwig, Edward G., "Family Structure in a Disabled Population," *Journal of Marriage and the Family,* vol. XXX, pp. 54-63, 1968.

Gillespie, Dair L., "Who Has the Power? The Marital Struggle," *Journal of Marriage and the Family,* vol. XXXIII, pp. 445-458, 1971.

Goode, William J., "Force and Violence in the Family," *Journal of Marriage and the Family,* vol. XXXIII, pp. 624-636, 1971.

Goode, William J., "Note on Problems in Theory and Method: The New World," *American Anthropologist,* vol. LXVIII, pp. 486-492, 1966.

Hallenbeck, Phyllis N., "An Analysis of Power Dynamics in Marriage," *Journal of Marriage and the Family,* vol. XXVIII, pp. 200-203, 1966.

* Herbst, P. G., "Task Differentiation of Husband and Wife in Family Activities," in Norman W. Bell and Ezra F. Vogel, editors, *A Modern Introduction to the Family.* Free Press of Glencoe, Inc., Glencoe, Illinois, 1960.

* Heer, David M., "Dominance and the Working Wife," *Social Forces,* vol. XXXVI, pp. 341-347, May 1958.

* Heer, David M., "Husband and Wife Perceptions of Family Power Structure," *Marriage and Family Living,* vol. XXIV, pp. 65-67, February 1962.

* Heer, David M., "The Measurement and Bases of Family Power: An Overview," *Marriage and Family Living,* vol. XXV, no. 2, pp. 133-139, May 1963.

* Heiss, Jerold S., "Degree of Intimacy and Male-Female Interaction," *Sociometry,* vol. XXV, pp. 197-208, June 1962.

* Hoffman, Lewis W., "Parental Power Relations and the Division of Household Tasks," *Marriage and Family Living,* vol. XXII, pp. 27-35, February 1960.

* Hyman, Herbert H., and Reed, John Shelton, "Black Matriarchy Reconsidered: Evidence from Secondary Analysis of Sample Surveys," *Public Opinion Quarterly,* vol. XXXIII, pp. 346-354, 1969.

* Jackson, Jacquelyne Johnson, "Marital Life Among Aging Blacks," *The Family Coordinator,* vol. XXI, pp. 21-27, 1972.

* Jacobson, Alver H., "Conflict of Attitudes Toward the Roles of Husband and Wife in Marriage," *American Sociological Review,* vol. XVII, pp. 146-150, 1952.

Kammeyer, Kenneth, "Birth Order and the Feminine Sex Role Among College Women," *American Sociological Review,* vol. XXXI, no. 4, pp. 508–515, August 1966.

* Kandel, Denise B., "Race, Maternal Authority, and Adolescent Aspiration," *American Journal of Sociology,* vol. LXXVI, pp. 999–1,020, 1971.

* Kandel, Denise B., and Lesser, Gerald S., "Marital Decision-Making in American and Danish Urban Families: A Research Note," *Journal of Marriage and the Family,* vol. XXXIII, pp. 134–138, February 1972.

* Kenkel, William F., "Influence Differentiation in Family Decision-Making," *Sociology and Social Research,* vol. XLII, pp. 18–25, 1957.

* Kenkel, William F., "Observation Studies of Husband-Wife Interaction in Family Decision-Making," in Marvin B. Sussman, editor, *Sourcebook in Marriage and the Family,* pp. 144–156. Houghton Mifflin Company, Boston, 1963.

* Kenkel, William F., "Sex of Observer and Spousal Roles in Decision Making," *Marriage and Family Living,* vol. XXIII, pp. 185–186, May 1961.

* Komarovsky, Mirra, *Blue Collar Marriage.* Random House, Inc., New York, 1964.

* Komarovsky, Mirra, "Class Differences in Family Decision-Making on Expenditures," in Marvin B. Sussman, editor, *Sourcebook in Marriage and the Family,* pp. 261–266. Houghton Mifflin Company, Boston, 1963.

* Kotlar, Sally L., "Instrumental and Expressive Marital Roles," *Sociology and Social Research,* vol. XLVI, pp. 186–194, January 1962.

* Leik, Robert K., "Instrumentality and Emotionality in Family Interaction," *Sociometry,* vol. XXVI, pp. 131–145, June 1963.

* Levinger, George, "Note on Need Complementarity in Marriage," *Psychological Bulletin,* vol. LXI, pp. 153–157, 1964.

Levinger, George, "Task and Social Behavior in Marriage," *Sociometry,* vol. XXVII, pp. 433–448, 1964.

* Lewis, Robert A., "Satisfaction with Conjugal Power Over the Family Life Cycle," presented at the annual meeting of the National Council on Family Relations, 1972.

Lopata, Helena Z., "The Life Cycle of the Social Role of Housewife," *Sociology and Social Research,* vol. LI, pp. 5–22, 1966.

Lopata, Helena Z., "The Secondary Features of a Primary Relationship," *Human Organization,* vol. XXIV, no. 2, pp. 116–123, summer 1965.

* Lovejoy, Debi, "College Student Conceptions of the Roles of Husband and Wife in Decision-Making," *Family Life Coordinator,* vol. IX, pp. 43–46, 1961.

* Lu, Yi-Chuang, "Marital Roles and Marriage Adjustment," *Sociology and Social Research,* vol. XXXVI, pp. 364–368, 1952.

Metz, Annabelle B., "The Roles of the Married Woman in Science," *Marriage and Family Living,* vol. XXIII, no. 4, pp. 374–376, November 1961.

Michel, Andree, "Comparative Data Concerning the Interaction in French and American Families," *Journal of Marriage and the Family,* vol. XXIX, no. 2, pp. 337–344, 1967.

* Middleton, Russell, and Putney, Snell, "Dominance in Decisions in the Family: Race and Class Differences," *American Journal of Sociology,* vol. LXV, pp. 605–609, 1960.

* Mitchell, Howard E.; Bullard, James W.; and Mudd, Emily H., "Areas of Marital Conflict in Successfully and Unsuccessfully Functioning Families," *Journal of Health and Human Behavior,* vol. III, pp. 88–93, 1962.

* Motz, Annabelle B., "Conceptions of Marital Roles by Status Groups," *Marriage and Family Living,* vol. XII, pp. 136–162, 1950.

Moynihan, Daniel Patrick, "Employment, Income, and the Ordeal of the Negro Family," *Daedalus,* vol. XCIV, pp. 745–770, 1965.

* Olson, David H., and Rabunsky, Carolyn, "Validity of Four Measures of Family Power," *Journal of Marriage and the Family,* vol. XXX, pp. 224–234, 1972.

Otterbein, Keith F., "Carribbean Family Organization: A Comparative Analysis," *American Anthropologist,* vol. LXVII, pp. 66–79, 1965.

Otterbein, Keith F., "Reply to Goode," *American Anthropologist,* vol. LXVIII, pp. 493–497, 1966.

Paolucci, Beatrice, "Contributions of a Framework of Home Management to the Teaching of Family Relationships," *Journal of Marriage and the Family,* vol. XXVIII, pp. 338–342, 1966.

* Parsons, Ralcott, and Bales, Robert F., *Family, Socialization and Interaction Process.* Free Press of Glencoe, Inc., Glencoe, Illinois, 1955.

Podell, Lawrence, "Occupational and Familial Role-Expectations," *Journal of Marriage and the Family,* vol. XXIX, pp. 492–493, 1967.

Pratt, Lois, "Conjugal Organization and Health," *Journal of Marriage and the Family,* vol. XXXIV, pp. 85–95, 1972.

Price, Dorothy Z., "A Technique for Analyzing the Economic Value System," *Journal of Marriage and the Family,* vol. XXX, pp. 467–472, 1968.

* Rainwater, Lee, and Handel, Gerald, "Changing Social Roles in the Working Class Family," presented at the annual meeting of the American Sociological Association, Los Angeles, California, August 1963.

* Rodman, Hyman, "Marital Power in France, Greece, Yugoslavia, and the United States: A Cross-National Discussion," *Journal of Marriage and the Family,* vol. XXIX, pp. 320–324, 1967.

Rose, Charles L., "Multigenerational Families, Intergenerational Solidarity and Social Change," presented at the annual meeting of the American Sociological Association, September 1969.

Safilios-Rothschild, Constantina, "A Comparison of Power Structure and Marital Satisfaction in Urban Greek and French Families," *Journal of Marriage and the Family,* vol. XXIX, pp. 345–352, 1967.

Safilios-Rothschild, Constantina, "Family Sociology or Wives' Family Sociology? A Cross-Cultural Examination of Decision-Making," *Journal of Marriage and the Family,* vol. XXXI, pp. 290–301, 1969.

* Safilios-Rothschild, Constantina, "The Influence of the Wife's Degree of Work Commitment Upon Some Aspects of Family Organization and Dynamics," *Journal of Marriage and the Family,* vol. XXXII, pp. 681–691, 1970.

Schmitt, David R., "An Attitudinal Correlate of the Status Congruency of Married Women," *Social Forces,* vol. XLIV, pp. 190–195, 1965.

* Silverman, William, and Hill, Reuben, "Task Allocation in Marriage in the United States and Belgium," *Journal of Marriage and the Family,* vol. XXIX, no. 2, pp. 353–359, 1967.

* Slater, Philip E., "Toward a Dualistic Theory of Identification," *Merrill-Palmer Quarterly,* vol. VII, pp. 113-126, 1961.

Sprey, Jetse, "On the Management of Conflict in Families," *Journal of Marriage and the Family,* vol. XXXIII, pp. 722-731, 1971.

Steinmann, Anne, and Fox, David J., "Attitudes Toward Women's Family Role Among Black and White Undergraduates," *The Family Coordinator,* vol. XIX, pp. 363-368, 1970.

Stone, Robert C., and Schlamp, Frederic T., "Characteristics Associated with Receipt or Nonreceipt of Financial Aid from Welfare Agencies," *Welfare in Review,* vol. III, pp. 1-11, 1963.

Straus, Murray A., "Conjugal Power Structure and Adolescent Personality," *Marriage and Family Living,* vol. XXIV, pp. 17-25, 1962.

Straus, Murray A., "Family Role Differentiation and Technological Change in Farming," *Rural Sociology,* vol. XXV, pp. 219-228, 1960.

Straus, Murray A., "Methodology of a Laboratory Experimental Study of Families in Three Societies," *Yearbook of the International Sociological Association,* 1968.

Straus, Murray A., and Cytrynbaum, Solomon, "Support and Power Structure in Sinhalese, Tamil, and Burgher Student Families," *International Journal of Comparative Sociology,* vol. III, pp. 138-153, 1962.

* Strodtbeck, Fred L., "The Family as a Three-Person Group," *American Sociological Review,* vol. XIX, pp. 23-29, 1954.

* Strodtbeck, Fred L., "Husband-Wife Interaction Over Revealed Differences," American Sociological Review, vol. XVI, pp. 468-473, 1951.

Tallman, Irving, "Spousal Role Differentiation and the Socialization of Severely Retarded Children," *Journal of Marriage and the Family,* vol. XXVII, pp. 37-42, 1965.

* Tallman, Irving, and Miller, Gary, "Class Differences in Family Problem Solving: The Effects of Language Style, Hierarchical Structure, and Role Expectations," unpublished manuscript.

* TenHouten, Warren D., "The Black Family: Myth and Reality," *Psychiatry,* vol. XXXIII, pp. 145-173, 1970.

* Terman, Lewis M., *Psychological Factors in Marital Happiness.* McGraw-Hill Book Company, New York, 1938.

Tharp, Roland G.; Meadow, Arnold; Lennhoff, Susan G.; and Satterfield, Donna, "Changes in Marriage Roles Accompanying the Acculturation of the Mexican-American Wife," *Journal of Marriage and the Family,* vol. XXX, pp. 404-412, 1968.

* Turk, James L., and Bell, Norman W., "Measuring Power in Families," *Journal of Marriage and the Family,* vol. XXXIII, pp. 215-222, 1972.

Udry, J. Richard, Review of *Blue-Collar Marriage* by Mirra Komarovsky, *Social Forces,* vol. XLV, p. 600, 1967.

* Udry, J. Richard, and Hall, Mary, "Role Segregation and Social Network in Middle-Class, Middle-Aged Couples," *Journal of Marriage and Family,* vol. XXVII, pp. 392-395, 1965.

* Udry, J. Richard; Nelson, Harold A.; and Nelson, Ruth, "An Empirical Investigation of Some Widely Held Beliefs About Marital Interaction," *Marriage and Family Living,* vol. XXIII, no. 4, pp. 388-390, November 1961.

Vandenberg, Gerald H., and Stachowiak, James G., "Patterns of Conflict and Dominance in Family Interaction," presented at the meeting of the Midwestern Psychological Association, Chicago, May 1966.

* Walters, James, "A Review of Family Research in 1962," *Marriage and Family Living,* vol. XXV, pp. 336-348, 1963.

Westley, William A., and Epstein, Nathan B., "Family Structure and Emotional Health: A Case Study Approach," *Marriage and Family Living,* vol. XXII, pp. 25-27.

Whitehurst, Robert N., "Premarital Reference-Group Orientations and Marriage Adjustment," *Journal of Marriage and the Family,* vol. XXX, pp. 397-401, 1968.

Wilkening, E. A., and Bharadwaj, Lakshmi K., "Dimensions of Aspirations, Work Roles, and Decision-Making of Farm Husbands and Wives in Wisconsin," *Journal of Marriage and the Family,* vol. XXIX, pp. 703-711, 1967.

* Wilkening, E. A., and Morrison, Denton E., "A Comparison of Husband and Wife Responses Concerning Who Makes Farm and Home Decisions," *Marriage and Family Living,* vol. XXV, no. 3, pp. 349-351, August 1963.

Winch, Robert F., and Greer, Scott A., "Urbanism, Ethnicity, and Extended Familism," *Journal of Marriage and the Family,* vol. XXX, pp. 40-45, 1968.

Wise, Genevieve M., and Carter, Don C., "A Definition of the Role of Homemaker by Two Generations of Women," *Journal of Marriage and the Family,* vol. XXVII, pp. 531-532, 1965.

* Wolfe, Donald M., "Power and Authority in the Family," in Dorwin Cartwright, editor, *Studies in Social Power,* pp. 99-117. Institute for Social Research, University of Michigan, Ann Arbor, Michigan, 1959.

* Yancey, William L., "Going Down Home: Family Structure and the Urban Trap," *Social Science Quarterly,* vol. LIII, pp. 893-906, 1972.

CHAPTER 14   EXTERNAL ROLES AND MARITAL INTERACTION

* Adams, Bert N., "Social Networks in a Middle-Sized City," unpublished manuscript, University of Wisconsin, 1965.

* Adams, Bert N., and Butler, James E., "Occupational Status and Husband-Wife Social Participation," *Social Forces,* vol. XLV, no. 4, pp. 501-507, 1967.

Aldous, Joan, "The Consequences of Intergenerational Continuity," *Journal of Marriage and the Family,* vol. XXVII, pp. 462-468, 1965.

* Aldous, Joan, "Wives' Employment Status and Lower-Class Men as Husband-Fathers: Support for the Moynihan Thesis," *Journal of Marriage and the Family,* vol. XXXI, no. 3, pp. 469-476, August 1969.

Aldous, Joan, and Hill, Reuben, "Social Cohesion, Lineage Type, and Intergenerational Transmission," *Social Forces,* vol. XLIII, pp. 471-482, 1965.

* Aldous, Joan, and Straus, Murray A., "Social Networks and Conjugal Roles: A Test of Bott's Hypothesis," *Social Forces,* vol. XLIV, pp. 576-580, 1966.

Almquist, Elizabeth M., and Angrist, Shirley S., "Career Salience and Atypicality of Occupational Choice Among College Women," *Journal of Marriage and the Family,* vol. XXXII, pp. 242-249, 1970.

Anspach, Donald, and Rosenberg, George S., "Working-Class Matricentricity," *Journal of Marriage and the Family,* vol. XXXIV, pp. 437-442, 1972.

Axelson, Leland J., "Some Differences in Perception of the Working Wife Between Husbands and Wives," presented at the annual meeting of the Southern Sociological Society, April 1970.

* Axelson, Leland J., "The Working Wife: Differences in Perception Among Negro and White Males," *Journal of Marriage and the Family,* vol. XXXII, pp. 457–464, 1970.

* Bailyn, Lotte, "Career and Family Orientations of Husbands and Wives in Relation to Marital Happiness," *Human Relations,* vol. XXIII, pp. 97–113, 1970.

Ballweg, John, "Resolution of Conjugal Role Adjustment After Retirement," *Journal of Marriage and the Family,* vol. XXIX, no. 2, pp. 277–281, 1967.

Bell, Colin, "Mobility and the Middle Class Extended Family," *Sociology,* vol. II, no. 2, pp. 173–184, May 1968.

* Bellin, Seymour S., "Relations Among Kindred in Later Years of Life: Parents, Their Siblings and Adult Children," presented at the annual meeting of the American Sociological Association, St. Louis, Missouri, August 1961.

Berardo, Felix M., "Kinship Interaction and Communications Among Space-Age Migrants," *Journal of Marriage and the Family,* vol. XXIX, pp. 541–554, 1967.

Berardo, Felix M., "Survivorship and Social Isolation: The Case of the Aged Widower," *The Family Coordinator,* vol. XIX, pp. 11–25, 1970.

Bernard, Jessie, "The Status of Women in Modern Patterns of Culture," *Annals of the American Academy of Political and Social Science,* vol. CCCLXXV, pp. 3–14, 1968.

Blood, Robert O., Jr., "Long-Range Causes and Consequences of the Employment of Married Women," *Journal of Marriage and the Family,* vol. XXVII, pp. 43–47, 1965.

* Blood, Robert O., Jr., *Marriage.* Free Press of Glencoe, Inc., New York, 1962.

* Blood, Robert O., "The Husband-Wife Relationship," in F. Ivan Nye and Lois W. Hoffman, *The Employed Mother in America.* Rand McNally & Co., Chicago, 1963.

* Blood, Robert O., Jr., and Wolfe, Donald M., *Husbands and Wives.* Free Press of Glencoe, Inc., New York, 1960.

* Blumberg, Leonard, and Bell, Robert R., "Urban Migration and Kinship Ties," *Social Problems,* vol. VI, no. 4, pp. 328–333, spring 1959.

Bock, E. Wilbur, "Aging and Suicide: The Significance of Marital, Kinship, and Alternative Relations," *The Family Coordinator,* vol. XXI, pp. 71–79, 1972.

Bock, E. Wilbur, and Webber, Irving L., "Social Status and Relational System of Elderly Suicides," *Life-Threatening Behavior,* vol. II, pp. 145–159, 1972.

Bock, E. Wilbur, and Webber, Irving L., "Suicide Among the Elderly: Isolating Widowhood and Mitigating Alternatives," *Journal of Marriage and the Family,* vol. XXXIV, pp. 24–31, 1972.

* Bott, Elizabeth, *Family and Social Network.* Tavistock Institute, London, 1957.

* Burchinal, Lee G., "Personality Characteristics of Children," in F. Ivan Nye and Lois W. Hoffman, *The Employed Mother in America.* Rand McNally & Co., Chicago, 1963.

* Burgess, Ernest W., "Family Living in the Later Decades," *Annals of the American Academy of Political and Social Science,* vol. CCLXXIX, pp. 106–114, January 1952.

Cosneck, Bernard J., "Family Patterns of Older Widowed Jewish People," *The Family Coordinator,* vol. XIX, pp. 368-373, 1970.

* Croog, Sydney H.; Lipson, Alberta; and Levine, Sol; "Help Patterns in Severe Illness: The Roles of Kin Network, Non-Family Resources, and Institutions," *Journal of Marriage and the Family,* vol. XXXIV, pp. 32-41, 1972.

Davidson, Maria, "Factors Related to Work Participation of Married Women," presented at the annual meeting of the Population Association of America, 1968.

* Dizard, Jan, *Social Change in the Family.* Community and Family Study Center, University of Chicago, 1968.

* Dotson, Floyd, "Patterns of Voluntary Association Among Urban Working-Class Families," *American Sociological Review,* vol. XVI, pp. 687-693, 1951.

* Douvan, Elizabeth, "Employment and the Adolescent," in F. Ivan Nye and Lois W. Hoffman, *The Employed Mother in America.* Rand McNally & Co., Chicago, 1963.

Dow, Thomas E., Jr., "Family Reaction to Crisis," *Journal of Marriage and the Family,* vol. XXVII, pp. 363-366, 1965.

Drabek, Thomas E., and Boggs, Keith S., "Families in Disaster: Reactions and Relatives," *Journal of Marriage and the Family,* vol. XXX, pp. 443-451, 1968.

* Duvall, Evelyn; *In-Laws: Pro and Con.* Association Press, New York, 1954.

* Epstein, Cynthia Fuchs, "Positive Effects of the Multiple Negative: Explaining the Success of Black Professional Women," *American Journal of Sociology,* vol. LXXVIII, pp. 912-935, 1973.

Farber, Bernard, "Kinship Laterality and the Emotionally Disturbed Child," *Kinship and Family Organization.* John Wiley & Sons, Inc., New York, 1966.

* Feld, Sheila, "Feelings of Adjustment," in F. Ivan Nye and Lois W. Hoffman, *The Employed Mother in America.* Rand McNally & Co., Chicago, 1963.

Fischer, Ann; Beasley, Joseph D.; and Harter, Carl L., "The Occurrence of the Extended Family at the Origin of the Family of Procreation: A Developmental Approach to Negro Family Structure," *Journal of Marriage and the Family,* vol. XXX, pp. 290-300, 1968.

* Garland, T. Neal, "The Better Half? The Male in the Dual Profession Family," presented at the annual meeting of the American Sociological Association, 1970.

Garza, Joseph M., and Rao, Nandini, "Attitudes Toward Employment and Employment Status of Mothers in Hyderabad, India," *Journal of Marriage and the Family,* vol. XXXIV, pp. 153-155, 1972.

* Gianopulos, Artie, and Mitchell, Howard E., "Marital Disagreement in Working Wife Marriages as a Function of Husband's Attitude Toward Wife's Employment," *Marriage and Family Living,* vol. XIX, no. 4, pp. 373-378, November 1957.

Gibson, Geoffrey, "Kin Family Network: Overheralded Structure in Past Conceptualizations of Family Functioning," *Journal of Marriage and the Family,* vol. XXXIV, pp. 13-23, 1972.

* Gold, M., *A Social Psychology of Delinquent Boys.* Institute for Social Research, University of Michigan, Ann Arbor, Michigan, 1961.

* Gough, E. Kathleen, "Is the Family Universal?—The Nayar Case," in Norman W. Bell and Ezra F. Vogel, editors, Free Press of Glencoe, Inc., New York, 1960.

Haavio-Mannila, Elina, "The Position of Finnish Women: Regional and Cross-National Comparisons," *Journal of Marriage and the Family,* vol. XXXI, pp. 339-347, 1969.

Hafstrom, Jeanne L., and Dunsing, Marilyn M., "A Comparison of Economic Choices of One-Earner and Two-Earner Families," *Journal of Marriage and the Family,* vol. XXVII, pp. 403-409, 1965.

Hafstrom, Jeanne L., and Dunsing, Marilyn M., "Employment of the Wife-Mother: Effect on Four Types of Family Expenditures," *Illinois Research,* pp. 4-5, 1965.

Hand, Horace B., "Working Mothers and Maladjusted Children," *Journal of Educational Sociology,* vol. XXX, no. 5, pp. 245-246, January 1957.

* Hays, William C., and Mindel, Charles H., "Extended Kinship Relations in Black and White Families," presented at the annual meetings of the American Sociological Association, 1972.

Hedges, Janice Neipert, and Barnett, Jeanne K., "Working Women and the Division of Household Tasks," *U.S. Bureau of Labor Statistics Monthly Labor Review,* vol. XCV, no. 4, pp. 9-14, April 1972.

* Heer, David M., "Dominance and the Working Wife," in F. Ivan Nye and Lois W. Hoffman, *The Employed Mother in America.* Rand McNally & Co., Chicago, 1963.

Hewer, Vivian H., and Neubeck, Gerhard H., "Attitudes of College Students Toward Employment Among Married Women," *Personnel and Guidance Journal,* pp. 587-592, 1964.

Hewer, Vivian H., and Neubeck, Gerhard H., "College Freshmen's Attitudes Toward Working Wives," *Research Bulletin of the Office of the Dean of Students, University of Minnesota,* vol. VI, pp. 1-23, 1964.

* Hill, Reuben; Foote, Nelson; Aldous, Joan; Carlson, Robert; and MacDonald, Robert, *Family Development in Three Generations.* Schenkman Publishing Company, Inc., Cambridge, Massachusetts, 1970.

Hoffman, Lois W., "Effects on Children: Summary and Discussion," in F. Ivan Nye and Lois W. Hoffman, *The Employed Mother in America.* Rand McNally & Co., Chicago, 1963.

* Hoffman, Lois W., "Mother's Enjoyment of Work and Effects on the Child," *Child Development,* vol. XXXII, pp. 187-197, March 1961.

* Hoffman, Lois W., "Parental Power Relations and the Division of Household Tasks," *Marriage and Family Living,* vol. XXII, pp. 27-35, February 1960.

Jackson, Jacquelyne Johnson, "Comparative Life Styles and Family and Friend Relationships Among Older Black Women," *The Family Coordinator,* vol. XXI, pp. 477-485, 1972.

Jacobs, Ruth Harriet, "Mobility Pains: A Family in Transition," *The Family Coordinator,* vol. XVIII, pp. 129-134, 1969.

* Johnson, Miriam M., Sex Role Learning in the Nuclear Family, *Child Development,* vol. XXXIV, pp. 319-334, 1963.

Kalish, Richard A., "Sex and Marital Role Differences in Anticipation of Age-Produced Dependency," *Journal of Genetic Psychology,* vol. CXIX, pp. 53-62, 1971.

* Kassees, Assad S., "Cross-Cultural Comparative Familism of a Christian Arab People," *Journal of Marriage and the Family,* vol. XXXIV, pp. 538-544, 1972.

Katelman, Doris K., and Barnett, Larry D., "Work Orientations of Urban, Middle Class, Married Women," *Journal of Marriage and the Family,* vol. XXX, pp. 80-88, 1968.

Keidel, Keith C., "Maternal Employment and Ninth Grade Achievement in Bismarck, North Dakota," *The Family Coordinator,* vol. XIX, pp. 95-97, 1970.

Kerckhoff, Alan C., and Bean, Frank D., "Exploration of a Circumplex Model of Interpersonal Relations," presented at the annual meeting of the American Sociological Association, 1969.

* Komarovsky, Mirra, "Functional Analysis of Sex Roles," *American Sociological Review,* vol. XV, pp. 508-516, 1950.

* Lajewsky, Henry C., "Working Mothers and their Arrangements for Care of their Children," *Social Security Bulletin,* 1959.

* Lang, R. O., *The Rating of Happiness in Marriage,* M. A. thesis, University of Chicago, 1932.

Linn, Erwin L., "Women Dentists: Career and Family," *Social Problems,* vol. XVIII, pp. 393-404, 1971.

* Locke, Harvey J., *Predicting Adjustment in Marriage: A Comparison of a Divorced and a Happily Married Group.* Henry Holt and Company, New York, 1951.

* Marcus, Peggy, "Inlaw Relationship Adjustment of Couples Married Between Two and Eleven Years," *Journal of Home Economics,* vol. XLIII, pp. 35-37, 1951.

Mayer, John E., *The Disclosure of Marital Problems: An Exploratory Study of Lower and Middle Class Wives.* Institute of Welfare Research, Community Service Society of New York, 1966.

Mayer, John E., *Other People's Marital Problems: The 'Knowledgeability' of Lower and Middle Class Wives.* Institute of Welfare Research, Community Service Society of New York, July 1966.

McGinn, Noel F.; Harburg, Ernest; and Ginsburg, Gerald P., "Dependency Relations with Parents and Affiliative Responses in Michigan and Guadalajara," *Sociometry,* vol. XXVIII, pp. 305-321, 1965.

Millman, Marcia, "Observations on Sex Role Research," *Journal of Marriage and the Family,* vol. XXXIII, pp. 772-776, 1971.

* Mussen, Paul, and Rutherford, Eldred, "Parent-Child Relations and Parental Personality in Relation to Young Children's Sex-Role Preferences," *Child Development,* vol. XXXIV, pp. 589-608, 1963.

* Nelson, Jel I., "Clique Contacts and Family Orientations," *American Sociological Review,* vol. XXXI, pp. 663-672, 1966.

* Noordhoek, J. A., and Smith, Yrsa, *Married Women, Family, and Work, vol. II: Effects on the Family.* Teknisk Forlag, Copenhagen, 1972.

* Nye, F. Ivan, "The Adjustment of Adolescent Children," in F. Ivan Nye and Lois W. Hoffman, *The Employed Mother in America.* Rand McNally & Co., Chicago, 1963.

* Nye, F. Ivan, "Employment Status of Mother and Marital Conflict, Permanence, and Happiness," *Social Problems,* vol. VI, no. 3, pp. 260–267, 1958/1959.

* Nye, F. Ivan, *Family Relationships and Delinquent Behavior.* John Wiley and Sons, Inc., New York, 1958.

* Nye, F. Ivan, "Maternal Employment and Marital Interaction: Some Contingent Conditions," *Social Forces,* vol. XL, no. 2, pp. 113–119, December, 1961.

* Nye, F. Ivan, and Hoffman, Lois W., *The Employed Mother in America.* Rand McNally & Co., Chicago, 1963.

* Nye, F. Ivan; Perry, Joseph B., Jr., and Ogles, Richard H., "Anxiety and Anti-Social Behavior in Pre-School Children," in F. Ivan Nye and Lois W. Hoffman, *The Employed Mother in America.* Rand McNally & Co., Chicago, 1963.

O'Donnell, Edward J., "The Community Welfare Family: Analogy and Analysis," *The Family Coordinator,* vol. XVIII, pp. 141–148, 1969.

* Orden, Susan R., and Bradburn, Norman M., "Working Wives and Marriage Happiness," *American Journal of Sociology,* vol. LXXIV, pp. 392–407, 1969.

* Overholser, Charles, Jr., "Marriage 1973 Style," *Family Circle,* vol. LXXXII, pp. 32 ff., 1973.

Palisi, Bartolomeo J., "Ethnic Generation and Family Structure," *Journal of Marriage and the Family,* vol. XXVIII, pp. 49–50, 1966.

* Parson, Talcott, "Age and Sex in the Social Structure of the United States," *American Sociological Review,* vol. VII, pp. 604–616, 1942.

* Peterson, Evan T., "The Impact of Maternal Employment on the Mother-Daughter Relationship," *Marriage and Family Living,* vol. XXIII, no. 4, pp. 355–361, November 1961.

* Poloma, Margaret M., and Garland, T. Neal, "On the Social Construction of Reality: Reported Husband-Wife Differences," *Sociological Focus on Sex Roles,* vol. V, pp. 40–54 (winter 1971/1972).

* Poloma, Margaret M., and Garland, T. Neal, "The Married Professional Woman: A Study in the Tolerance of Domestication," *Journal of Marriage and the Family,* vol. XXXIII, pp. 531–540, 1971.

* Popenoe, Paul, and Disney, Dorothy Cameron, *Can This Marriage Be Saved?* The Macmillan Company, New York, 1960.

Rapoport, Rhona, and Rapoport, Robert N., "The Dual Career Family," *Human Relations,* vol. XXII, pp. 3–30, 1969.

Rapoport, Robert, and Rapoport, Rhona, "Work and Family in Contemporary Society," *American Sociological Review,* vol. XXX, pp. 381–394, 1965.

Ridley, Jeanne Clare, "Demographic Change and the Roles and Status of Women," *Annals of the American Academy of Political and Social Sciences,* vol. CCCLXXV, pp. 15–25, 1968.

* Rossi, Alice S., "Family Development in a Changing World," *American Journal of Psychiatry,* vol. CXXVIII, no. 9, pp. 1,057–1,066, March 1972.

Salvo, Vincent J., "Conflict Between Familial and Occupational Orientations Among Professionals," presented at the annual meeting of the National Council on Family Relations, 1968.

Scanzoni, John, "A Model for the Analysis of Role Conflict Within the Clergy Marriage," *Family Life Coordinator,* vol. XIV, pp. 3–6, 1965.

Scanzoni, John, "A Reinquiry into Marital Disorganization," *Journal of Marriage and the Family,* vol. XXVII, pp. 483–489, 1965.

* Scanzoni, John, "Resolution of Occupational Conjugal Role Conflict in Clergy Marriages," *Journal of Marriage and the Family,* vol. XXVII, pp. 396-402, 1965.

Schlater, Jean D., and Ferrar, Barbara M., "Monetary Gain from the Working Wife's Employment," *Quarterly Bulletin of the Michigan Agricultural Experiment Station,* vol. XLVI, pp. 103-118, 1963.

* Schooler, Carmi, "Childhood Family Structure and Adult Characteristics," *Sociometry,* vol. XXXV, pp. 255-269, 1972.

* Schorr, Alvin L., "Current Practice of Filial Responsibility," in Robert F. Winch, Robert McGinnis and Herbert R. Barringer, editors, *Selected Studies in Marriage and the Family.* Holt, Rinehart, and Winston, Inc., New York, 1962.

Schorr, Alvin L., "The Family Cycle and Income Development," *Social Security Bulletin,* vol. XXIX, pp. 14-25 and 47, 1966.

Schwarzweller, Harry K., "Parental Family Ties and Social Integration of Rural to Urban Migrants," *Journal of Marriage and the Family,* vol. XXVI, pp. 410-416, 1964.

Schwarzweller, Harry K., and Seggar, John F., "Kinship Involvement: A Factor in the Adjustment of Rural Migrants," *Journal of Marriage and the Family,* vol. XXIX, pp. 662-671, 1967.

Shanas, Ethel, "Family Help Patterns and Social Class in Three Countries," *Journal of Marriage and the Family,* vol. XXIX, no. 2, pp. 257-266, 1967.

Siegel, Alberta Engvall; Stolz, Lois Meek; Hitchcock, Ethel Alice; and Adamson, Jean, "Dependence and Independence in Children," in F. Ivan Nye and Lois W. Hoffman, *The Employed Mother in America.* Rand McNally & Co., Chicago, 1963.

* Siegel, Alberta Engvall; Stolz, Lois Meek; Hitchcock, Ethel Alice; and Adamson, Jean, "Dependence and Independence in the Children of Working Mothers," *Child Development,* vol. XXX, pp. 533-546, 1959.

Somerville, Rose M., "The Future of Family Relationships in the Middle and Older Years: Clues in Fiction," *The Family Coordinator,* vol. XXI, pp. 487-498, 1972.

Spark, Geraldine M., and Brody, Elaine M., "The Aged Are Family Members," *Family Process,* vol. IX, pp. 195-210, 1970.

* Stephens, William N., *The Family in Cross-cultural Perspective.* Holt, Rinehart and Winston, Inc., New York, 1963.

* Straus, Murray A., "Social Class and Farm-City Differences in Interaction with Kin in Relation to Societal Modernization," *Rural Sociology,* vol. XXXIV, pp. 476-495, December 1969.

Streib, Gordon F., "Intergenerational Relations: Perspectives of the Two Generations on the Older Parent," *Journal of Marriage and the Family,* vol. XXVII, pp. 469-476, 1965.

Stromberg, Jerome S., "The Family and Its Kinship and Friendship Network," prepared for the annual meeting of the American Sociological Society, 1967.

* Stryker, Sheldon, "The Adjustment of Married Offspring to Their Parents," *American Sociological Review,* vol. XX, pp. 149-154, 1955.

* Sussman, Marvin B., "Family Continuity: Selective Factors which Affect Relationships Between Families at Generational Levels," *Marriage and Family Living,* vol. XVI, pp. 112-120, 1954.

* Sussman, Marvin B., "Intergenerational Family Relationships and Role Changes in Middle-Age," *Journal of Gerontology,* vol. XV, pp. 71-75, 1960.

* Sussman, Marvin B., "The Help Pattern in the Middle Class Family," *American Sociological Review,* vol. XVIII, pp. 22-28, 1953.

* Sussman, Marvin B., "The Isolated Nuclear Family: Fact or Fiction?" *Social Problems,* vol. VI, pp. 333-340, 1959.

* Sussman, Marvin B., and Slater, Sherwood B., "Re-appraisal of Urban Kin Networks: Empirical Evidence," presented at the annual meeting of the American Sociological Association, Los Angeles, California, August 1963.

* Sweet, James A., "Labor Force Reentry by Mothers of Young Children," *Social Science Research,* vol. I, pp. 189-210, 1972.

* Sweetser, Dorian A., "Asymmetry in Intergenerational Family Relationships," *Social Forces,* vol. XLI, pp. 346-352, 1963.

Sweetser, Dorian A., "The Effect of Industrialization on Intergenerational Solidarity," *Rural Sociology,* vol. XXXI, pp. 156-170, 1966.

Sweetser, Dorian A., "The Structure of Sibling Relationships," *American Journal of Sociology,* vol. LXXVI, pp. 47-58, 1971.

* Tropman, John E., "Social Mobility and Marital Stability," *Applied Social Studies,* vol. III, pp. 165-173, 1971.

* Udry, J. Richard, and Hall, Mary, "Role Segregation and Social Network in Middle-class, Middle-aged Couples," *Journal of Marriage and the Family,* vol. XXVIII, pp. 392-395, 1965.

U. S. Department of Commerce, Bureau of the Census, *Current Population Reports Series,* P-60, no. 12, June 1953.

* U. S. Department of Commerce, Bureau of the Census, *U. S. Census of Population 1960: U. S. Summary.* PC (1)—1C.

Van Den Ban, A. W., "Family Structure and Modernization," *Journal of Marriage and the Family,* vol. XXIX, pp. 771-773, 1967.

* Wake, Sandra Byford, and Sporakowski, Michael J., "An Intergenerational Comparison of Attitudes Towards Supporting Aged Parents," *Journal of Marriage and the Family,* vol. XXXIV, pp. 42-48, 1972.

* Wallin, Paul, "Sex Differences in Attitudes to 'In-laws,' A Test of a Theory," *American Journal of Sociology,* vol. LIX, no. 5, pp. 466-469, March 1954.

* Weil, Mildred W., "An Analysis of the Factors Influencing Married Women's Actual or Planned Work Participation," *American Sociological Review,* vol. XXVI, no. 1, pp. 91-95, February 1961.

Weller, Robert H., "The Employment of Wives, Dominance, and Fertility," *Journal of Marriage and the Family,* vol. XXX, pp. 437-442, 1968.

* Wilmott, Peter, and Young, Michael, *Family and Class in a London Suburb.* Routledge and Kegan Paul, Ltd., London, 1960.

* Winch, Robert F., "Further Data and Observations on the Oedipus Hypothesis: the Consequences of an Inadequate Hypothesis," *American Sociological Review,* vol. XVI, pp. 784-795, 1951.

* Winch, Robert F., *The Modern Family,* revised edition. Holt, Rinehart and Winston, Inc., New York, 1963.

Winch, Robert F., and Greer, Scott A., "Kinship, Urbanism, Ethnicity and Community Participation," presented at the annual meeting of the American Sociological Society, 1966.

Winch, Robert F., and Greer, Scott A., "Urbanism, Ethnicity, and Extended Familism," *Journal of Marriage and the Family,* vol. XXX, pp. 40-45, 1968.

Winch, Robert F.; Greer, Scott A.; and Blumberg, Rae Lesser, "Ethnicity Extended Familism in an Upper-Middle-Class Suburb," *American Sociological Review,* vol. XXXII, pp. 265-272, 1967.

* Young, Michael, and Geertz, Mildred, "Old Age in London and San Francisco: Some Families Compared," *British Journal of Sociology,* vol. XII, no 2, pp. 124-141, June 1961.

* Zimmerman, Carle C., and Cervantes, Lucius F., *Successful American Families.* Pagaent Press, Inc., New York, 1960.

CHAPTER 15   SEXUAL INTERACTION IN MARRIAGE

Bartell, Gilbert D., "Group Sex Among the Mid-Americans," *Journal of Sex Research,* vol. VI, pp. 113-130, 1970.

Beauvoir, Simone de, *The Second Sex,* edited and translated by H. M. Parshley. Alfred A. Knopf, Inc., New York, 1957.

* Bell, Robert R., *Marriage and Family Interaction.* Dorsey Press, Homewood, Illinois, 1963.

Bell, Robert R., "Some Factors Related to the Sexual Satisfaction of the College Educated Wife," *Family Life Coordinator,* vol. XIII, pp. 43-47, 1964.

* Bernard, Jessie, "Developmental Tasks of the NCFR—1963-1988," *Journal of Marriage and the Family,* vol. XXVI, pp. 29-38, February 1964.

Boyers, Robert, "Attitudes Towards Sex in American 'High Culture,'" *Annals of the American Academy of Political and Social Science,* vol. CCCLXXVI, pp. 36-52, 1968.

Brien, Alan, "Spare My Hot Flushes," *New Statesman,* p. 188, 1969.

* Brissett, Dennis, and Lewis, Lionel S., "Guidelines for Marital Sex: An Analysis of Fifteen Popular Marriage Manuals," *The Family Coordinator;* vol. XIX, pp. 41-48, 1970.

Brown, Helen Gurley, *Sex and the Single Girl.* Random House, Inc., New York, 1962.

Burgess, Ernest W., Locke, Harvey J., and Thomes, Mary Margaret, *The Family,* third edition. American Book Company, New York, 1963.

* Burgess, Ernest W., and Wallin, Paul, *Engagement and Marriage.* J. B. Lippincott Company, Philadelphia, 1953.

Cavanagh, John R., "Rhythm of Sexual Desire in Women," *Medical Aspects of Human Sexuality,* vol. III, pp. 29-39, 1969.

* Chard, Chester S., editor, "Sternberg's Materials on the Sexual Life of the Gilyak," *Anthropological Papers of the University of Alaska,* vol. X, no. 1, pp. 13-23, 1961.

* Christenson, Cornelia V., and Gagnon, John H., "Sexual Behavior in a Group of Older Women," *Journal of Gerontology,* vol. XX, pp. 351-355, 1965.

Christenson, Harold T., "A Cross-cultural Comparison of Attitudes Towards Marital Infidelity," *International Journal of Comparative Sociology,* vol. III, pp. 124-137, September 1962.

Clark, Alexander L., and Wallin, Paul, "The Accuracy of Husbands' and Wives' Reports of the Frequency of Marital Coitus," *Population Studies,* vol. XVIII, pp. 165-173, 1964.

* Clark, Alexander, and Wallin, Paul, "Women's Sexual Responsiveness and the Duration and Quality of Their Marriages," *American Journal of Sociology,* vol. LXXI, pp. 187-196, 1965.

* Constantine, Larry L., "Personal Growth in Multiperson Marriages," *Radical Therapist,* vol. II, pp. 18-20, 1971.

* Constantine, Larry L., and Constantine, Joan M., "Pragmatics of Group Marriage," *The Modern Utopian,* vol. IV, pp. 33-37, 1970.

* Constantine, Larry L., and Constantine, Joan M., "Sexual Aspects of Multilateral Relations," *Journal of Sex Research,* vol. VII, pp. 204-225, 1971.

* Constantine, Larry L., and Constantine, Joan M., "Where is Marriage Going?" *The Futurist,* vol. IV, pp. 44-46, 1970.

* Constantine, Larry L.; Constantine, Joan M.; and Edelman, Sheldon K., "Counseling Implications of Comarital and Multilateral Relations," *The Family Coordinator,* vol. XXI, pp. 267-273, 1972.

Cuber, John, with Harroff, Peggy B., *The Significant Americans: A Study of Sexual Behavior Among the Affluent.* Appleton-Century Crofts, Inc., New York, 1965.

* Cumming, Gordon, "A Study of Marital Conflicts Involving an Affair by One of the Partners," unpublished M. A. thesis, University of Southern California, 1960.

Dentler, Robert A., and Pineo, Peter, "Sexual Adjustment and Personal Growth of Husbands: A Panel Analysis," *Marriage and Family Living,* vol. XXII, pp. 45-48, February, 1960.

* Fisher, Seymour, *The Female Orgasm: Psychology, Physiology, Fantasy.* Basic Books, Inc., New York, 1973.

* Foote, Nelson, "Sex as Play," *Social Problems,* vol. I, pp. 159-163, 1954.

Ford, C. S., and Beach, F. A., Patterns of Sexual Behavior. Hoeber Medical Division, Harper and Brothers, New York, 1951.

* Friedan, Betty, *The Feminine Mystique.* W. W. Norton and Company, Inc., New York, 1963.

Gebhard, Paul H., "Factors in Marital Orgasm," *Journal of Social Issues,* vol. XXII, pp. 88-95, 1966.

Gelfman, Morris, "A Post-Freudian Comment on Sexuality," *American Journal of Psychiatry,* vol. CXXVI, pp. 651-657, 1969.

Gershman, Harry, "The Changing Image of Sex," *The American Journal of Psychoanalysis,* vol. XXVII, pp. 24-33, 1967.

Gochros, Harvey L., "The Sexually Oppressed," *Social Work,* vol. XVII, no. 2, pp. 16-23, March 1972.

* Gordon, Michael, and Shankweiler, Penelope J., "Different Equals Less: Female Sexuality in Recent Marriage Manuals," *Journal of Marriage and the Family,* vol. XXXIII, pp. 459-466, 1971.

Goshen-Gottstein, Esther R., "Courtship, Marriage and Pregnancy in 'Geula.'" *Israel Annals of Psychiatry and Related Disciplines,* vol. IV, pp. 43-66, 1966.

* Hamblin, Robert L., and Blood, Robert O., "Premarital Experience and the Wife's Sexual Adjustment," *Social Problems,* vol. IV, no. 2, pp. 122–130, October 1956.

* Hardy, Kenneth R., "An Appetitional Theory of Sexual Motivation," *Psychological Review,* vol. LXX, no. 1, pp. 1–18, January 1964.

Hastings, Donald W., *Impotence and Frigidity.* Little, Brown and Company, Boston, 1963.

Hunt, Morton, *The Affair.* The World Publishing Company, New York, 1969.

Hunt, Morton M., *The Natural History of Love.* Alfred A. Knopf, Inc., New York, 1959.

* Jakobvits, Leon A., "Evaluation Reactions to Erotic Literature," *Psychological Reports,* vol. XVI, pp. 985–994, 1965.

Johnson, Ralph E., "Extramarital Sexual Intercourse: A Methodological Note," *Journal of Marriage and the Family,* vol. XXXII, pp. 279–283, 1970.

Kaufman, Sherwin, "Impact of Infertility on the Marital and Sexual Relationships," *Fertility and Sterility,* vol. XX, no. 3, pp. 380–383, May–June 1969.

* Kenkel, William, *The Family in Perspective.* Appleton-Century Crofts, New York, 1960.

* Kephart, William M., *The Family, Society, and the Individual.* Houghton Mifflin Company, Boston, 1961.

* Kinsey, Alfred; Pomeroy, Wardell B.; and Martin, Clyde E., *Sexual Behavior in the Human Male.* W. B. Saunders Company, Philadelphia, 1948.

* Kinsey, Alfred; Pomeroy, Wardell B.; Martin, Clyde E.; and Gebhard, Paul H., *Sexual Behavior in the Human Female.* W. B. Saunders Company, Philadelphia, 1953.

Kirkendall, Lester A., and Libby, Roger W., "Interpersonal Relationships — Crux of the Sexual Renaissance," *Journal of Social Issues,* vol. XXII, no. 2, pp. 45–59, April 1966.

Kuvlesky, William P., and Obordo, Angelita S., "A Racial Comparison of Teen-Age Girls' Projections for Marriage and Procreation," *Journal of Marriage and the Family,* vol. XXXIV, pp. 75–84, 1972.

* Levinger, George, "Systematic Distortion in Spouses' Reports of Preferred and Actual Sexual Behavior," *Sociometry,* vol. XXIX, pp. 291–299, 1966.

* Lewis, Lionel S., and Brissett, Dennis, "Sex as Work: A Study of Avocational Counseling," *Social Problems,* vol. XV, pp. 8–18, summer 1967.

* Locke, Harvey J., *Predicting Adjustment in Marriage: a Comparison of a Divorced and Happily Married Group.* Henry Holt and Company, New York, 1951.

Malewska, Hanna E., and Malewska, Andrzei, "The Motivational Conflict Among Teen-agers and Its Importance for Later Satisfaction from Sexual Life," *Polish Sociological Bulletin,* vol. I, pp. 60–70, 1965.

Masters, William H., and Johnson, Virginia E., *Human Sexual Inadequacy.* Little, Brown and Company, Boston, 1970.

* Masters, William H., and Johnson, Virginia E., *Human Sexual Response.* Little, Brown and Company, Boston, 1966.

* Merrill, Francis E., *Courtship and Marriage,* revised edition. Henry Holt & Co., New York, 1959.

* Mitchell, Howard E.; Bullard, James W.; and Mudd, Emily H., "Areas of Marital Conflict in Successfully and Unsuccessfully Functioning Families," *Journal of Health and Human Behavior,* vol. III, pp. 88-93, 1962.

* Mowrer, Harriet R., "Sex and Marital Adjustment: A Critique of Kinsey's Approach," *Social Problems,* vol. I, no. 4, pp. 147-152, 1954.

* Neubeck, Gerhard, and Schletzer, Vera M., "A Study of Extra-Marital Relationships," *Marriage and Family Living,* vol. XXIV, no. 3, pp. 279-281, August 1962.

* Newman, Gustave, and Nichols, Claude R., "Sexual Activities and Attitudes in Older Persons," *Journal of the American Medical Association,* vol. CLXXVII, pp. 33-35, May 1960.

O'Neill, George C., and O'Neill, Nena, "Patterns in Group Sexual Activity," *Journal of Sex Research,* vol. VI, pp. 101-112, 1970.

* Pfeiffer, Eric, and Davis, Glenn C., "Determinants of Sexual Behavior in Middle and Old Age," *Journal of the American Geriatrics Society,* vol. XX, no. 4, pp. 151-158, 1972.

* Pfeiffer, Eric; Verwoerdt, Adriaan; and Davis, Glenn C., "Sexual Behavior in Middle Life," *American Journal of Psychiatry,* vol. CXXVIII, pp. 82-87, 1972.

* Rainwater, Lee, "Crucible of Identity: The Negro Lower-Class Family," *Daedalus,* vol. XCV, pp. 172-216, 1966.

* Rainwater, Lee, "Marital Sexuality in Four Cultures of Poverty," *Journal of Marriage and the Family,* vol. XXVI, pp. 457-466, 1964.

Rainwater, Lee, "Some Aspects of Lower Class Sexual Behavior," *Journal of Social Issues,* vol. XXII, pp. 96-108, 1966.

* Rettig, Salomon, and Pasamanick, Benjamin, "Changes in Moral Values Among College Students: a Factorial Study," *American Sociological Review,* vol. XXIV, pp. 856-863, 1959.

Roebuck, Julian, and Spray, S. Lee, "The Cocktail Lounge: A Study of Heterosexual Relations in a Public Organization," *American Journal of Sociology,* vol. LXXII, pp. 388-395, 1967.

Rubin, Isadore, "Sex over 65" *Sexology,* vol. XXVIII, pp. 622-625, 1962.

Sagarin, Edward, "Taking Stock of Studies of Sex," *Annals of the American Academy of Political and Social Science,* vol. CCCLXXVI, pp. 1-5, 1968.

Shainess, Natalie, "The Problem of Sex Today," *American Journal of Psychiatry,* vol. CXXIV, no. 8, pp. 1,076-1,084, February 1968.

Shainess, Natalie, "Psychiatric Evaluation of Premenstrual Tension," *New York State Journal of Medicine,* vol. LXII, pp. 3,573-3,579, 1962.

* Sigusch, Volkmar; Schmidt, Gunter; Reinfeld, Anje; and Wiedemann-Sutor, Ingeborg, "Psychosexual Stimulation: Sex Differences," *Journal of Sex Research,* vol. VI, pp. 10-24, 1970.

Simpson, George, *People in Families.* Thomas Y. Crowell Company, New York, 1960.

Singer, Josephine, and Singer, Irving, "Types of Female Orgasm," *Journal of Sex Research,* vol. VIII, pp. 255-267, 1972.

Smith, James R., and Smith, Lynn G., "Co-Marital Sex and the Sexual Freedom Movement," *Journal of Sex Research,* vol. VI, pp. 131-142, 1970.

* Spanier, Graham B., and Cole, Charles L., "Mate Swapping: Participation, Knowledge, and Values in a Midwestern Community," presented at the annual meeting of the Midwest Sociological Society, 1972.

Sprey, Jetse, "On the Institutionalization of Sexuality," *Journal of Marriage and the Family,* vol. XXXI, no. 3, pp. 432-440, August 1969.

* Terman, Lewis M., *Psychological Factors in Marital Happiness.* McGraw-Hill Book Company, New York, 1938.

* Thomason, Bruce, "Marital Sexual Behavior and Total Marital Adjustment: A Research Report," in J. Himelhoch, and S. L. Fava, editors, *Sexual Behavior in American Society.* W. W. Norton and Company, New York, 1955.

Thorne, Frederic, C., "A Factorial Study of Sexuality in Adult Males," *Journal of Clinical Psychology,* vol. XXII, no. 4, pp. 378-386, October 1966.

U. S. Department of Health, Education, and Welfare, "National Natality Survey Statistics," *Monthly Vital Statistics Report.* National Center for Health Statistics, March 1970.

* Wallin, Paul, and Clark, Alexander, "Cultural Norms and Husbands' and Wives' Reports of their Marital Partners' Preferred Frequency of Coitus Relative to their Own," *Sociometry,* vol. XXI, pp. 247-254, 1958.

* Wallin, Paul, and Clark, Alexander, "Religiosity, Sexual Gratification, and Marital Satisfaction in the Middle Years of Marriage," *Social Forces,* vol. XLII, pp. 303-309, 1964.

Weinberg, Jack, "Sexual Expression in Late Life," *American Journal of Psychiatry,* vol. CXXVI, no. 5, pp. 713-716, November 1969.

* Wheeler, J. I., "Psychological Effect of the Male Sex Hormone on Women," *American Psychologist,* vol. X, p. 348, 1955.

Whitehurst, Robert N., "Violence Potential in Extramarital Sexual Responses," *Journal of Marriage and the Family,* XXXII, pp. 683-691, 1971.

CHAPTER 16   FERTILITY CONTROL

* Acland, J. C., and O'Callaghan, D., "Fertility Control by Hormonal Medication," *Irish Theological Quarterly,* vol. XXVII, pp. 332-339, 1960.

* Ahearn, Nan, "Regulation of Offspring and the Roman Catholic Church," *Eugenics Quarterly,* vol. VI, no. 1, pp. 23-25, March 1959.

* Amatera, Mary, "An Investigation of Certain Economic Factors in Large Families," *Journal of Social Psychology,* vol. II, pp. 207-214, May 1959.

* Anastasi, Anne, "Differentiating Effect of Intelligence and Social Status," *Eugenics Quarterly,* vol. VI, no. 2, pp. 84-93, June 1959.

* Bauman, Karl E., "Selected Aspects of the Contraceptive Practices of Unmarried University Students," *American Journal of Obstetrics and Gynecology,* vol. CVIII, pp. 203-209, 1970.

Behrman, S. J., and Ackerman, D. R., "Freeze Preservation of Human Sperm," *American Journal of Obstetrics and Gynecology,* vol. CIII, pp. 654-664, 1969.

Blake, Judith, "Are Babies Consumer Durables?" *Population Studies,* vol. XXII, pp. 5-25, 1965.

Blake, Judith, "Family Size in the 1960's—A Baffling Fad?" *Eugenics Quarterly*, vol. XIV, pp. 60–74, 1967.

Blake, Judith, "Income and Reproductive Motivation," *Population Studies*, vol. XXI, pp. 185–206, 1967.

Blake, Judith, "Reproductive Ideals and Educational Attainment Among White Americans, 1943–1960," *Population Studies*, vol. XXI, pp. 159–174, 1967.

Bossard, James H. S., and Boll, Eleanore S., *The Sociology of Child Development.* Harper and Brothers, New York, 1960.

* Brooks, Hugh E., and Henry, Franklin J., "An Empirical Study of the Relationships of Catholic Practice and Occupational Mobility to Fertility," *Milbank Memorial Fund Quarterly*, vol. XXXVI, no. 3, pp. 222–281, July 1958.

Bumpass, Larry, "Age at Marriage as a Variable in Socio-Economic Differentials in Fertility," *Demography*, vol. VI, pp. 45–54, 1969.

Bumpass, Larry, "Stability and Change in Family Size Expectations Over the First Two Years of Marriage," *Journal of Social Issues*, vol. XXIII, pp. 83–98, 1967.

Chilman, Catherine S., "Fertility and Poverty in the United States: Some Implications for Family-Planning Programs, Evaluation, and Research," *Journal of Marriage and the Family*, vol. XXX, pp. 207–227, 1968.

Christensen, Harold T., "Child Spacing Analysis Via Record Linkage: New Data Plus a Summing Up from Earlier Reports," *Marriage and Family Living*, vol. XXV, no. 3, pp. 272–280, August 1963.

* Christensen, Harold T., and Bowden, Olive P., "Studies in Child Spacing. II. The Time-interval Between Marriage of Parents and Birth of their First Child, Tippecanoe County, Indiana," *Social Forces*, vol. XXXI, no. 4, pp. 346–351, May 1953.

Clark, Philip J., and Spuhler, James N., "Differential Fertility in Relation to Body Dimensions," *Human Biology*, vol. XXXI, no. 2, pp. 121–137, May 1959.

Clausen, John A., "Family Structure, Socialization, Personality," in Lois W. Hoffman and Martin L. Hoffman, editors, *Review of Child Development Research.* Russell Sage Foundation, New York, 1966.

* Davidson, Maria, "Predictions in Fertility," *Eugenics Quarterly*, vol. VIII, pp. 92–96, 1961.

Dobbelaere, Karel, "Ideal Number of Children in Marriage in Belgium and the U. S. A.," *Journal of Marriage and the Family*, vol. XXIX, no. 2, pp. 360–367, 1967.

Droegemueller, William; Taylor, E. Steward; and Drose, Vera E., "The First Year of Experience in Colorado with the New Abortion Law," *American Journal of Obstetrics and Gynecology*, vol. CIII, pp. 694–702, 1969.

"Drug Side Effect Stimulates Remarkable Sexual Activity," *The News and Observer*, January 15, 1970.

* Dykstra, John W., "Prenatal Influences in American Culture," *Sociology and Social Research*, vol. XLIV, no. 2, pp. 79–85, November–December 1959.

Elder, Glen, H., Jr., and Bowerman, Charles, "Family Structure and Child-Rearing Patterns: The Effect of Family Size and Sex Composition," *American Sociological Review*, vol. XXVIII, pp. 891–905, 1963.

Etzioni, Amitai, "Sex Control, Science, and Society," *Science,* vol. CLXI, pp. 1,107-1,112, 1968.

Flapan, Mark, "A Paradigm for the Analysis of Childbearing Motivations of Married Women Prior to Birth of the First Child," *American Journal of Orthopsychiatry,* vol. XXXIX, pp. 402-417, 1969.

Flemister, Carl, "Population Control and the Black Revolution," presented at Chapel Hill, North Carolina, Planned Parenthood of New York City, March 23, 1970.

* Freedman, Deborah S.; Freedman, Ronald; and Whelpton, Pascal K., "Size of Family and Preference for Children of Each Sex," *American Journal of Sociology,* vol. LXVI, no. 2, pp. 141-146, September 1960.

Freedman, Ronald, and Coombs, Lolagene, "Economic Considerations in Family Growth Decisions," *Population Studies,* vol. XV, pp. 197-222, 1966.

* Freedman, Ronald; Whelpton, Pascal K.; and Campbell, Arthur A., *Family Planning, Sterility, and Population Growth.* McGraw-Hill Book Company, New York, 1959.

* Freedman, Ronald; Whelpton, Pascal K.; and Smit, John W., "Socioeconomic Factors in Religious Differentials in Fertility," *American Sociological Review,* vol. XXVI, no. 4, pp. 608-614, August 1961.

Frejka, Thomas, "Reflection on the Demographic Conditions Needed to Establish a U. S. Stationary Population Growth," *Population Studies,* vol. XXII, no. 3, 1968.

Freund, Matthew, and Davis, Joseph E., "Disappearance Rate of Spermatozoa from the Ejaculate Following Vasectomy," *Fertility and Sterility,* vol. XX, pp. 163-170, 1969.

* Gebhard, Paul H.; Pomeroy, Wardell B.; Martin, Clyde E.; and Christenson, Cornelia V., *Pregnancy, Birth and Abortion,* Hoeber Medical Division, Harper and Brothers, New York, 1958.

Goldberg, David, "Some Observations on Recent Changes in American Fertility Based on Sample Survey Data," *Eugenics Quarterly,* vol. XIV, pp. 255-264, 1967.

Grabill, Wilson H., and Davidson, Maria, "Recent Trends in Childspacing by American Women," presented at the annual meeting of the Population Association of America, 1967.

* Grabill, Wilson H.; Kiser, Clyde; and Whelpton, Pascal K., *The Fertility of American Women.* John Wiley and Sons, Inc., New York, 1958.

Green, Ronald M., "Abortion and Promise-Keeping," *Christianity and Crisis,* pp. 109-113, 1967.

Hall, Robert E., "Abortion in American Hospitals," *American Journal of Public Health,* vol. LVII, pp. 1,933-1,936, 1967.

Hardin, Garrett, "Abortion—or Compulsory Pregnancy?" *Journal of Marriage and the Family,* vol. XXX, pp. 246-251, 1968.

Hawkins, Charles H., "The Erotic Significance of Contraceptive Methods," *Journal of Sex Research,* vol. VI, pp. 143-157, 1970.

Hzuka, Rihachi; Yoshiaki, Sawada; Nobuhiro, Nishina; and Ohi, Michie, "The Physical and Mental Development of Children Born Following Artificial Insemination," *International Journal of Fertility,* vol. XIII, pp. 24-32, 1968.

"Intrauterine Devices," *ACOG Technical Bulletin,* vol. X, 1968.

Jaffe, Frederick S., and Polgar, Steven, "Family Planning and Public Policy: Is the 'Culture of Poverty' the New Cop-Out?" *Journal of Marriage and the Family,* vol. XXX, pp. 228–235, 1968.

Kass, Roy, and Donaldson, Peter J., "Catholic Reaction to *Humanae Vitae:* Family Planning Attitudes and Practices Before and After the *Encyclical,*" presented at the annual meeting of the Population Association of America, 1970.

Kinsey, Alfred C.; Pomeroy, Wardell B.; Martin, Clyde E.; and Gebhard, Paul H., *Sexual Behavior in the Human Female.* W. B. Saunders Company, Philadelphia, 1953.

* Kirkendall, Lester A., *Premarital Intercourse and Interpersonal Relationships.* Gramercy Publishing Co., New York, 1968.

Kiser, Clyde V., "Assortative Mating By Educational Attainment in Relation to Fertility," *Eugenics Quarterly,* vol. XV, pp. 98–112, 1968.

* Kiser, Clyde V., and Whelpton, Pascal K., "Social and Psychological Factors Affecting Fertility. XXXIII. Summary of Chief Findings and Implications for Future Studies," *Milbank Memorial Fund Quarterly,* vol. XXXVI, no. 3, pp. 282–329, July 1958.

Kunz, Phillip R., "The Relation of Income and Fertility," *Journal of Marriage and the Family,* vol. XXVII, pp. 509–513, 1965.

Landis, Judson T., and Poffenberger, Thomas, "The Marital and Sexual Adjustment of 330 Couples Who Chose Vasectomy as a Form of Birth Control," *Journal of Marriage and the Family,* vol. XXVII, pp. 57–58, 1965.

Lauriat, Patience, "The Effect of Marital Dissolution on Fertility," presented at the annual meeting of the Population Association of America, 1968.

* Lauriat, Patience, "Marriage and Fertility Patterns of College Graduates," *Eugenics Quarterly,* vol. VI, pp. 171–179, September 1959.

Lucas, Roy, "Federal Constitutional Limitations on the Enforcement and Administration of State Abortion Statutes," *The North Carolina Law Review,* vol. XLVI, pp. 730–778, 1968.

* Maller, J. B., "Size of Family and Personality of Offspring," *Journal of Social Psychology,* vol. II, pp. 3–27, 1931.

Marshall, John, "A Field Trial of the Basal-Body-Temperature Method of Regulating Births," *The Lancet,* vol. II, pp. 8–10, 1968.

* Middleton, Russell, "Fertility Values in American Magazine Fiction, 1916–1956," *Public Opinion Quarterly,* vol. XXIV, no. 1, pp. 139–143, spring 1960.

Mitra, S., "Income, Socioeconomic Status, and Fertility in the United States," *Eugenics Quarterly,* vol. XIII, pp. 223–230, 1966.

Molinski, M. H., "Oral Contraceptives: Emotional Forces Affecting the Attitudes of Men and Women," *Advances in Fertility Control,* vol. IV, pp. 17–21, 1969.

Monroe, Keith, "How California's Abortion Law Isn't Working," *The New York Times Magazine,* pp. 10–20, December 29, 1968.

Morris, Miriam, and Weinstock, Edward, "Differential Effects of Education on Family Planning," *The Family Coordinator,* vol. XVIII, pp. 161–165, 1969.

* Muramatsu, Minoru, "Effect of Induced Abortion on the Reduction of Births in Japan," *Milbank Memorial Fund Quarterly,* vol. XXXVIII, no. 2, pp. 153–170, April 1960.

Namboodiri, N. Krishnan, "The Wife's Work Experience and Child Spacing," *Milbank Memorial Fund Quarterly,* vol. XLII, pp. 65–77, 1964.

Perrucci, Carolyn Cummings, "Mobility, Marriage and Child-Spacing Among College Graduates," *Journal of Marriage and the Family,* vol. XXX, pp. 273–282, 1968.

Pohlman, Edward W., "Burgess and Cottrell Data on 'Desire for Children': An Example of Distortion in Marriage and Family Textbooks?" *Journal of Marriage and the Family,* vol. XXX, pp. 433–436, 1968.

Pohlman, Edward, "Mobilizing Social Pressures Toward Small Families," *Eugenics Quarterly,* vol. XIII, pp. 122–127, 1966.

Pohlman, Edward, "Results of Unwanted Conceptions: Some Hypotheses Up for Adoption," *Eugenics Quarterly,* vol. XII, pp. 11–18, 1965.

Pohlman, Edward, "Society's Right to Force Family Size Limits: Implications for Incentives Research," presented at the annual meeting of the Population Association of America, 1970.

Pohlman, Edward, " 'Wanted' and 'Unwanted': Toward Less Ambiguous Definition," *Eugenics Quarterly,* vol. XII, pp. 19–27, 1965.

* Potter, R. G., Jr., "Some Comments on the Evidence Pertaining to Family Limitation in the United States," *Population Studies,* vol. XIV, no. 1, pp. 40–54, 1960.

Potts, D. M., and Swyer, G. I. M., "Effectiveness and Risks of Birth Control Methods," *British Medical Bulletin,* vol. XXVI, pp. 26–32, 1970.

Potvin, Raymond H., and Burch, Thomas K., "Fertility, Ideal Family-Size, and Religious Orientation Among U. S. Catholics," *Sociological Analysis,* vol. XXIX, no. 1, pp. 28–34, spring 1968.

Potvin, Raymond H.; Westoff, Charles F.; and Ryder, Norman B., "Factors Affecting Catholic Wives' Conformity to Their Church Magisterium's Position on Birth Control," *Journal of Marriage and the Family,* vol. XXX, pp. 263–272, 1968.

Presser, Harriet B., "The Timing of the First Birth, Female Roles, and Black Fertility," presented at the annual meeting of the Population Association of America, 1970.

"Profile of the American Wife," *Statistical Bulletin,* vol. LI. Metropolitan Life Insurance Company, January 1970.

Rabin, A. I., and Greene, Robert J., "Assessing Motivation for Parenthood," *The Journal of Psychology,* vol. LXIX, pp. 39–46, 1968.

Rainwater, Lee, *And the Poor Get Children.* Quadrangle Books, Inc., Chicago, 1960.

Ring, Abraham E., "Psychosocial Aspects of Contraception," *Bulletin of the American College of Nurse Midwifery,* vol. XIII, pp. 74–81, 1968.

Roach, Jack L.; Lewis, Lionel S.; and Beaucham, Murray A.; "The Effects of Race and Socio-Economic Status on Family Planning," *Journal of Health and Social Behavior,* vol. VIII, pp. 40–45, 1967.

Rodgers, David A.; Ziegler, Frederick J.; Altrocchi, John; and Levy, Nissim, "A Longitudinal Study of the Psycho-Social Effects of Vasectomy," *Journal of Marriage and the Family,* vol. XXVII, pp. 59–64, 1965.

Rosen, Bernard C., "Family Structure and Value Transmissions," *Merrill-Palmer Quarterly,* vol. X, pp. 59–76, 1964.

* Ryder, Norman B., and Westoff, Charles F., "Fertility Planning Status: United States, 1965," *Demography,* vol. VI, pp. 435–444, 1969.

* Ryder, Norman B., and Westoff, Charles F., "Relationships Among Intended, Expected, Desired, and Ideal Family Size: United States, 1965," *Population Research.* Center for Population Research, National Institute of Child Health and Human Development, U. S. Department of Health, Education, and Welfare, 1969.

Ryder, Norman, and Westoff, Charles, "The Trend of Expected Fertility in the United States: 1955, 1960, 1965," *Population Index,* vol. XXXIII, pp. 153–168, 1967.

Ryder, Norman B., and Westoff, Charles F., "The United States: The Pill and the Birth Rate, 1960–1965," *Studies in Family Planning,* vol. XX, pp. 1–3. The Population Council, June 1967.

* Sagi, P. C.; Potter, R. G., Jr.; and Westoff, C. F., "Contraceptive Effectiveness as a Function of Desired Family Size," *Population Studies,* vol. XV, no. 3, pp. 291–296, 1962.

* Samenfink, J. Anthony, "A Study of Some Aspects of Marital Behavior as Related to Religious Control," *Marriage and Family Living,* vol. XX, pp. 163–169, 1958.

Segal, Sheldon J., and Tietze, Christopher, "Contraceptive Technology: Current and Prospective Methods," *Reports on Population/Family Planning,* pp. 1–20, 1969.

* Thomson, A. M., "Maternal Stature and Reproductive Efficiency," *Eugenics Review,* vol. LI, no. 3, pp. 157–162, 1959.

Tietze, Christopher, "Induced Abortion and Sterilization as Methods of Fertility Control," *Journal of Chronic Diseases,* vol. XVIII, pp. 1,161–1,171, 1965.

* Tietze, Christopher, and Lehfeld, Hans, "Legal Abortion in Eastern Europe," *Journal of the American Medical Association,* vol. CLXXV, pp. 1,149–1,154, April 1961.

Tietze, Christopher and Lewis, Sarah, "Abortion," *Scientific American,* vol. CCXX, pp. 21–27, January 1969.

Tomasson, Richard F., "Social Mobility and Family Size in Two High-Status Populations," *Eugenics Quarterly,* vol. XIII, pp. 113–131, 1966.

"United States: The Papal Encyclical and Catholic Practice and Attitudes, 1969," *Studies in Family Planning.* The Population Council, February 1970.

"United States: Therapeutic Abortions in New York City," *Studies in Family Planning.* The Population Council, March 1970.

U. S. Department of Health, Education, and Welfare, "Advance Report Final Natality Statistics, 1968," *Monthly Vital Statistics Report,* vol. XVIII. National Center for Health Statistics, 1970.

Wattenberg, Ben J., *The Demography of the 1970's: The Birth Dearth and What It Means.* The Family Circle, Inc., New York, 1971.

Westoff, Charles F., "The Extent of Unwanted Fertility in the U. S.," presented at the annual meeting of Planned Parenthood-World Population, October 1969.

Westoff, Charles F., and Bumpass, Larry, "The Revolution in Birth Control Practices of U. S. Roman Catholics," *Science,* vol. CLXXIX, pp. 41–44, January 1973.

Westoff, Charles F.; Moore, Emily C.; and Ryder, Norman B., "The Structure of Attitudes Toward Abortion," *Milbank Memorial Fund Quarterly,* vol. XLVII, pp. 11-37, 1969.

* Westoff, Charles; Potter, Robert; Sagi, Philip; and Mishler, Elliot, *Family Growth in Metropolitan America.* Princeton University Press, Princeton, New Jersey, 1961.

Westoff, Charles, and Potvin, Raymond H., "Higher Education, Religion and Women's Family Size Orientations," *American Sociological Review,* vol. XXXI, pp. 489-496, 1966.

Westoff, Charles F., and Ryder, Norman B., "Duration of Use of Oral Contraception in the United States, 1960-65," *Public Health Reports,* vol. LXXXIII, pp. 277-287, 1968.

Westoff, Charles, and Ryder, Norman B., "Family Limitation in the United States," presented at the General Conference of the International Union for the Scientific Study of Population, September 1969.

* Westoff, Charles, and Ryder, Norman, "Recent Trends in Attitudes Toward Fertility Control and in the Practice of Contraception in the United States," presented at the University of Michigan Sesquicentennial Celebration, 1967.

* Westoff, Charles F., and Ryder, Norman B., "United States: Methods of Fertility Control, 1955, 1960, 1965," *Studies in Family Planning,* vol. XVII, pp. 1-5, 1967.

Ziegler, Frederick J., and Rodgers, David A., "Vasectomy, Ovulation Suppressors, and Sexual Behavior," *Journal of Sex Research,* vol. IV, pp. 169-193, 1968.

Ziff, Harvey L., "Recent Abortion Law Reforms (Or Much Ado About Nothing), *The Journal of Criminal Law, Criminology and Police Science,* vol. LX, pp. 3-23, 1969.

CHAPTER 17   MARRIAGE AND PARENTHOOD

Adams, Bert N., "Birth Order: A Critical Review," *Sociometry,* vol. XXXV, pp. 411-439, 1972.

Bayley, Nancy, "Research in Child Development: A Longitudinal Perspective," *Merrill-Palmer Quarterly,* vol. XI, pp. 183-208, 1965.

Becker, Selwyn W.; Lerner, Melvin J.; and Carroll, Jean, "Conformity as a Function of Birth Order, Payoff, and Type of Group Pressure," *Journal of Abnormal and Social Psychology,* vol. LXIX, pp. 318-323, 1964.

* Bernard, Jessie, "Factors in the Distribution of Success in Marriage," *American Journal of Sociology,* vol. XL, p. 51, 1934.

Bigner, Jerry J., "Fathering: Research and Practice Implications," *The Family Coordinator,* vol. XIX, pp. 357-362, 1970.

* Blake, Judith, "Coercive Pronatalism and American Population Policy," *Preliminary Paper No. 2,* (December 1972). International Population and Urban Research, University of California, Berkeley. 54p. Also published in the proceedings of the Commission on Population Growth and the American Future.

Blau, Zena Smith, "Class Structure, Mobility and Change in Child Rearing," *Sociometry,* vol. XXVIII, pp. 210-219, 1965.

* Blood, Robert O., Jr., and Wolfe, Donald M., *Husbands and Wives.* Free Press of Glencoe, Inc., New York, 1960.

* Bossard, James H. S., *The Large Family System.* University of Pennsylvania Press, Philadelphia, 1956.

* Bossard, James H. S., and Boll, Eleanore S., *The Sociology of Child Development.* Harper and Brothers, New York, 1960.

* Brimm, Orville G., Jr.; Fairchild, Roy W.; and Borgatta, Edgar F., "Relations Between Family Problems," *Marriage and Family Living,* vol. XXIII, pp. 219-226, 1961.

* Burchinal, Lee G.; Hawkes, Glenn R.; and Gardner, Bruce, "Marriage Adjustment Personality Characteristics of Parents and the Personality Adjustment of Their Children," *Marriage and Family Living,* vol. XIX, no. 4, pp. 366-372, November 1957.

* Burgess, Ernest W., and Cottrell, Leonard S., Jr., *Predicting Success or Failure in Marriage.* Prentice-Hall, Inc., Englewood Cliffs, New Jersey, 1939.

Burgess, Ernest W.; Locke, Harvey J.; and Thomes, Mary Margaret, *The Family,* third edition. American Book Company, New York, 1963.

Burgess, Jane K., "The Single-Parent Family: A Social and Sociological Problem," *The Family Coordinator,* vol. XIX, pp. 137-144, 1970.

Caldwell, Bettye M., and Richmond, Julius B., "Programmed Day Care for the Very Young Child—A Preliminary Report," *Journal of Marriage and the Family,* vol. XXVI, pp. 481-488, 1964.

Calisher, Hortense, *Textures of Life,* Little-Brown and Company, Boston, 1963.

Campbell, Frederick L., "Family Growth and Variation in Family Role Structure," *Journal of Marriage and the Family,* vol. XXXII, pp. 45-53, 1970.

Capobianco, R. J., and Knox, Stanley, "IQ Estimates and the Index of Marital Integration," *American Journal of Mental Deficiency,* vol. LXVIII, pp. 718-721, 1964.

* Chester, Robert, "Is There a Relationship Between Childlessness and Marriage Breakdown?" *Journal of Biosocial Science,* vol. IV, pp. 443-454, 1972.

* Christensen, Harold T., "Children in the Family: Relationship of Number and Spacing to Marital Success," *Journal of Marriage and the Family,* vol. XXX, pp. 283-289, 1968.

* Christensen, Harold T., and Philbrick, Robert E., "Family Size as a Factor in the Marital Adjustments of College Couples," *American Sociological Review,* vol. XVII, pp. 306-312, 1952.

Clausen, John R., "Family Structure, Socialization and Personality," in Lois D. Hoffman and Martin L. Hoffman, editors, *Review of Child Development Research.* Russell Sage Foundation, New York, 1966.

Coombs, Robert H., "Reinforcement of Values in the Parental Home as a Factor in Mate Selection," *Marriage and Family Living,* vol. XXIV, no. 2, pp. 155-157, 1962.

Crain, Alan J., and Stamm, Caroline S., "Intermittent Absence of Fathers and Children's Perceptions of Fathers," *Journal of Marriage and the Family,* vol. XXVII, pp. 344-347, 1965.

Crain, Alan J.; Sussman, Marvin B.; and Weil, William B., Jr., "Effects of a Diabetic Child on Marital Integration and Related Measures of Family Functioning," *Journal of Health and Human Behavior,* vol. VII, pp. 122-127, 1966.

* Cutts, Norma E., and Moseley, Nicholas, *The Only Child.* G. P. Putnam's Sons, New York, 1954.

Davis, Katherine B., *Factors in the Sex Life of Twenty-two Hundred Women.* Harper and Brothers, New York, 1929.

Devor, Geraldine M., "Children as Agents in Socializing Parents," *The Family Coordinator,* vol. XIX, pp. 208-212, 1970.

* Dielman, T. E.; Cattell, R. B.; and Rhoades, Patrick, "Childrearing Antecedents of Early School Child Personality Factors," *Journal of Marriage and the Family,* vol. XXXIV, pp. 431-436, August 1972.

Duncan, Beverly, and Duncan, Otis Dudley, "Family Stability and Occupational Success," *Social Problems,* vol. XVI, pp. 273-285, 1969.

* Dyer, Everett D., "Parenthood as Crisis: A Re-Study," *Marriage and Family Living,* vol. XXV, no. 2, pp. 196-201, May 1963.

Edwards, Ozzie, "Family Composition as a Variable in Residential Succession," *American Journal of Sociology,* vol. LXXVII, pp. 731-741, 1972.

Farber, Bernard, "Marital Integration as a Factor in Parent-Child Relations," *Child Development,* vol. XXXIII, pp. 1-14, March 1962.

* Feldman, H., "The Effects of Children on the Family," in Andree Michel, editor, *Family Issues of Employed Women in Europe and America.* E. J. Brill, Leiden, The Netherlands, 1971.

* Fendrich, James M., and Axelson, Leland J., "Marital Status and Alienation Among Black Veterans," unpublished manuscript.

* Fisher, Seymour, and Mendell, David, "The Communication of Neurotic Patterns Over Two and Three Generations," *Psychiatry,* vol. XIX, pp. 41-46, 1956.

Francis, Roy G., "Family Strategy in Middle Class Suburbia," *Sociological Inquiry,* vol. XXXIII, pp. 157-164, 1963.

* Freedman, Ronald, and Coombs, Lolagene, "Childspacing and Family Economic Position," *American Sociological Review,* vol. XXXI, pp. 631-648, August 1966.

* Freedman, Ronald; Whelpton, Pascal K.; and Campbell, Arthur A., *Family Planning, Sterility, and Population Growth.* McGraw-Hill Book Company, New York, 1959.

Gil, David G., "Violence Against Children," *Journal of Marriage and the Family,* vol. XXXIII, pp. 637-648, 1971.

* Greene, Gael, "A Vote Against Motherhood," *The Saturday Evening Post,* vol. CCXXXVI, pp. 10-11, January 26, 1963.

* Gustavus, Susan O., and Henley, James R., Jr., "Correlates of Voluntary Childlessness in a Select Population," *Social Biology,* vol. XVIII, pp. 277-284, 1971.

Haberman, Paul W., "Childhood Symptoms in Children of Alcoholics and Comparison Groups Patients," *Journal of Marriage and the Family,* vol. XXVIII, pp. 152-154, 1966.

Hader, Marvin, "The Importance of Grandparents in Family Life," *Family Process,* vol. IX, pp. 228-240, 1965.

Hamilton, G. V., *A Research in Marriage.* Albert and Charles Boni, New York, 1929.

Handel, Gerald, editor, *The Psychosocial Interior of the Family. A Sourcebook for the Study of Whole Families.* Aldine Publishing Company, Chicago, 1967.

* Hare, A. P., "A Study of Interaction: A Consensus in Different Sized Groups," *American Sociological Review,* vol. XVII, pp. 261–267, 1952.

* Hawkes, Glenn R.; Burchinal, Lee G.; and Gardner, Bruce, "Size of Family and Adjustment of Children," *Marriage and Family Living,* vol. XX, no. 1, pp. 65–68, 1958.

Hess, Robert D., and Shipman, Virginia C., "Early Experience and the Socialization of Cognitive Modes in Children," *Child Development,* vol. XXXVI, pp. 869–886, 1965.

* Hobbs, Daniel F., Jr., "Transition to Parenthood: A Replication and an Extension," *Journal of Marriage and the Family,* vol. XXX, pp. 413–417, 1968.

Hurley, John R., and Palonen, Donna P., "Marital Satisfaction and Child Density Among University Student Parents," *Journal of Marriage and the Family,* vol. XXIX, pp. 483–484, 1967.

* Jacobson, Paul H., *American Marriage and Divorce.* Rinehart and Company, New York, 1959.

* James, Joan, "A Preliminary Study of the Size Determinant in Small Group Interaction." *American Sociological Review,* vol. XVI, pp. 474–477, 1961.

Kopf, Kathryn E., "Family Variables and School Adjustment of Eighth Grade Father-Absent Boys," *The Family Coordinator,* vol. XIX, pp. 145–150, 1970.

Kunz, Phillip R., "Religious Influences on Parental Discipline and Achievement Demands," *Marriage and Family Living,* vol. XXV, pp. 224–225, 1963.

Landis, Judson T., and Landis, Mary G., *Building a Successful Marriage.* Prentice-Hall, Inc., Englewood Cliffs, New Jersey, 1963.

* LeMasters, E. E., "Parenthood as Crisis," *Marriage and Family Living,* vol. XIX, no. 4, pp. 352–355, November 1957.

Levy, David M., "Psychosomatic Studies of Some Aspects of Maternal Behavior," in Clyde Kluckholn and Henry Murray, editors, *Personality in Nature, Society, and Culture.* Alfred A. Knopf, Inc., New York, 1948.

Lewis, Lionel S., "Kinship Terminology for the American Parent," *American Anthropologist,* vol. LXV, pp. 649–652, 1963.

Lewis, Lionel S., "Terms of Address for Parents and Some Clues About Social Relationships in the American Family," *Family Life Coordinator,* vol. XIV, pp. 43–46, 1965.

Lewis, Robert A., "Socialization into National Violence: Familial Correlates of Hawkish Attitudes Toward War," *Journal of Marriage and the Family,* vol. XXXIII, pp. 699–708, 1971.

* Locke, Harvey J., *Predicting Adjustment in Marriage: a Comparison of a Divorced and a Happily-Married Group.* Henry Holt and Company, New York, 1951.

Long, Larry L., "The Influence of Number and Ages of Children on Residential Mobility," *Demography,* vol. IX, pp. 371–382, 1972.

* Lopata, Helena Znaniecki, "Self-Identity in Marriage and Widowhood," unpublished manuscript, Loyola University of Chicago, n. d.

Luckey, Eleanore Braun, and Bain, Joyce Koym, "Children: A Factor in Marital Satisfaction," *Journal of Marriage and the Family,* vol. XXXII, pp. 43–44, 1970.

Martin, Cora A., and Benson, Leonard, "Parental Perceptions of the Role of Television in Parent-Child Interaction," *Journal of Marriage and the Family,* vol. XXXI, pp. 410–414, 1970.

* Maxwell, Joseph W., and Montgomery, James E., "Societal Pressure Toward Early Parenthood," *The Family Coordinator,* vol. XVIII, pp. 340-344, 1969.

Mayer, John E., "People's Imagery of Other Families," *Family Process,* vol. VI, pp. 27-36, 1967.

* McIntire, Walter G., and Payne, David C., "The Relationship of Family Functioning to School Achievement," *The Family Coordinator,* vol. XX, pp. 265-268, 1971.

Meyerowitz, Joseph H., "Satisfaction During Pregnancy," *Journal of Marriage and the Family,* vol. XXXII, pp. 38-42, 1970.

Moles, Oliver C., Jr., "Child Training Practices Among Low Income Families: An Empirical Study," *Welfare in Review,* pp. 1-19, December 1965.

Morris, Gary O., and Wynne, Lyman C., "Schizophrenic Offspring and Parental Styles of Communication," *Psychiatry,* vol. XXVIII, pp. 19-44, 1965.

* Novak, Arthur L., and van der Veen, Ferdinand, "Family Concepts and Emotional Disturbance in the Families of Disturbed Adolescents with Normal Siblings," *Family Process,* vol. IX, pp. 157-172, (1970).

* Nye, F. Ivan, "Adolescent-Parent Adjustment: Age, Sex, Sibling Number, Broken Homes, and Employed Mothers as Variables," *Marriage and Family Living,* vol. XIV, pp. 327-332, November 1952.

* Nye, F. Ivan, "Child Adjustment in Broken and in Unhappy Unbroken Homes," *Marriage and Family Living,* vol. XIX, pp. 356-361, 1957.

Nye, F. Ivan; Carlson, John; and Garrett, Gerald, "Family Size, Interaction, Affect and Stress, *Journal of Marriage and the Family,* vol. XXXII, pp. 216-226, 1970.

* Overholser, Charles, Jr., "Marriage 1973 Style," *Family Circle,* vol. LXXXII, p. 32ff., 1973.

Parsons, Talcott, and Bales, Robert F., *Family, Socialization and Interaction Process.* Free Press of Glencoe, Inc., New York, 1955.

* Peterson, Evan T., and Kunz, Phillip R., "Family Size and Parental Control," unpublished manuscript, Brigham Young University, n. d.

Pollin, William; Stabenau, James R.; and Tupin, Joe, "Family Studies with Identical Twins Discordant for Schizophrenia," *Psychiatry,* vol. XXVIII, pp. 60-78, 1965.

Popenoe, Paul, and Disney, Dorothy Cameron, *Can This Marriage Be Saved?* The Macmillan Company, New York, 1960.

* Porter, Blaine M., "The Relationship Between Marital Adjustment and Parental Acceptance of Children," *Journal of Home Economics,* vol. XLVII, pp. 157-164, 1955.

Rehberg, Richard A.; Sinclair, Judie; and Schafer, Walter E., "Adolescent Achievement Behavior, Family Authority Structure, and Parental Socialization Practices," *American Journal of Sociology,* vol. LXXV, pp. 1,012-1,034, 1969/70.

Richer, Stephen, "The Economics of Child Rearing," *Journal of Marriage and the Family,* vol. XXX, pp. 462-466, 1968.

Rossi, Alice, "Transition to Parenthood," *Journal of Marriage and the Family,* vol. XXX, no. 2, pp. 26-37, 1968.

Schooler, Carmi, "Birth Order Effects: Not Here, Not Now!" *Psychological Bulletin,* vol. LXXVIII, pp. 161-175, 1972.

* Schulz, David A., *The Changing Family.* Prentice-Hall, Inc., Englewood Cliffs, New Jersey, 1972.

Schvaneveldt, Jay D.; Fryer, Marguerite; and Ostler, Renee, "Concepts of 'Badness' and 'Goodness' of Parents as Perceived by Nursery School Children," *The Family Coordinator,* vol. XIX, pp. 98–103, 1970.

Shainess, Natalie, "The Psychologic Experience of Labor," *New York State Journal of Medicine,* vol. LXIII, pp. 2,923–2,932, 1963.

* Shainess, Natalie, "The Structure of the Mothering Encounter," *Journal of Nervous and Mental Disease,* vol. CXXXVI, pp. 146–161, 1963.

Skard, Aase Gruda, "Maternal Deprivation: The Research and Its Implications," *Journal of Marriage and the Family,* vol. XXVII, pp. 333–343, 1965.

Stachowiak, James G., "Psychological Disturbances in Children as Related to Disturbances in Family Interaction," *Journal of Marriage and the Family,* vol. XXX, pp. 123–129, 1968.

Straus, Murray A., "Conjugal Power Structure and Adolescent Personality," *Marriage and Family Living,* vol. XXIV, pp. 17–25, 1962.

Straus, Murray A., "The Influence of Sex of Child and Social Class on Instrumental and Expressive Family Roles in a Laboratory Setting," *Sociology and Social Research,* vol. LII, pp. 7–21, 1967.

Straus, Murray A., and Houghton, Lawrence J., "Achievement, Affiliation, and Co-operation Values as Clues to Trends in American Rural Society, 1924–1958," *Rural Sociology,* vol. XXV, pp. 394–403, 1960.

Straus, Murray A., and Libby, Diane J., "Sibling Group Size and Adolescent Personality," *Population Review,* vol. IX, pp. 55–64, 1965.

* Stroup, Atlee L., "Marital Adjustment of the Mother and the Personality of the Child," *Marriage and Family Living,* vol. XVIII, p. 109, May 1956.

Stroup, Atlee L., and Hunter, Katherine Jamison, "Sibling Position in the Family and Personality of Offspring," *Journal of Marriage and the Family,* vol. XXVII, pp. 65–68, 1965.

Swanson, Blair R.; Massey, Randy H.; and Payne, I. Reed, "Ordinal Position, Family Size, and Personal Adjustment," *The Journal of Psychology,* vol. LXXXI, pp. 53–58, 1972.

Tallman, Irving, "The Family as a Small Problem Solving Group," presented at the annual meeting of the National Council of Family Relations, 1968.

Thomes, Mary Margaret, "Children with Absent Fathers," *Journal of Marriage and the Family,* vol. XXX, pp. 89–96, 1968.

Tomeh, Aida K., "The Impact of Reference Groups on the Educational and Occupational Aspirations of Women College Students," *Journal of Marriage and the Family,* vol. XXX, pp. 102–110, 1968.

Troll, Lillian E., "Is Parent-Child Conflict What We Mean by the Generation Gap?" *The Family Coordinator,* vol. XXI, pp. 347–349, 1972.

Tuckman, Jacob, and Regan, Richard A., "Ordinal Position and Behavior Problems in Children," *Journal of Health and Social Behavior,* vol. VIII, pp. 32–39, 1967.

* Veevers, J. E., "Differential Childlessness by Color: A Further Examination," *Social Biology,* vol. XVIII, pp. 285–291, 1971.

* Veevers, J. E., "The Child-Free Alternative: Rejection of the Motherhood Mystique," in Marylee Stephenson, editor, *Women in Canada.* New Press, Toronto, 1973.
* Veevers, J. E., "The Violation of Fertility Mores: Voluntary Childlessness as Deviant Behaviour," in C. Bydell, C. Grindstaff and P. Whitehead, editors, *Deviant Behaviour and Societal Reaction.* Holt, Rinehart and Winston, Inc., Toronto, 1972.
* Wallin, Paul, "Marital Happiness of Parents and Their Children's Attitude to Marriage," *American Sociological Review,* vol. XIX, pp. 20-23, 1954.
* Wallin, Paul, and Vollmer, Howard M., "Marital Happiness of Parents and Their Children's Attitudes to Them," *American Sociological Review,* vol. XVIII, pp. 424-431, 1953.
  Winter, William D., and Ferreira, Antonio J., "Interaction Process Analysis of Family Decision-Making," *Family Process,* vol. VI, pp. 155-172, 1967.

CHAPTER 18   DIVORCE AND REMARRIAGE

Andreyev, Yu, "Law Goes Into Force," *Isvestia, Current Digest of the Soviet Press,* October 1968.
Barnes, J. A., "The Frequency of Divorce," in A. L. Epstein, editor, *The Craft of Social Anthropology.* Tavistock Publications, Ltd., London, 1967.
Berardo, Felix M., "Widowhood Status in the United States: Perspective on a Neglected Aspect of the Family Life-Cycle," *The Family Coordinator,* vol. XVII, pp. 191-203, 1968.
Bergler, Edmund, *Divorce Won't Help.* Harper & Brothers, New York, 1948.
* Berkman, Paul L., "Spouseless Motherhood, Psychological Stress, and Physical Morbidity," *Journal of Health and Social Behavior,* vol. X, pp. 323-334, 1969.
* Bernard, Jessie, "The Adjustment of Married Mates" in Harold T. Christensen, editor, *Handbook of Marriage and the Family.* Rand McNally and Company, Chicago, 1964.
* Bernard, Jessie, *Remarriage.* The Dryden Press, New York, 1956.
* Blake, Nelson Manfred, *The Road to Reno.* The Macmillan Company, New York, 1962.
* Bowerman, Charles E., and Irish, Donald P., "Some Relationships of Stepchildren to their Parents," *Marriage and Family Living,* vol. XXIV, no. 2, pp. 113-128, May 1962.
Bronstein, Eli H., "Mexican Divorces in Light of Recent Decisions," *Bar Bulletin,* vol. XXIII, pp. 101-108, 1966.
* Burchinal, Lee G., "Characteristics of Adolescents from Unbroken, Broken, and Reconstituted Families," *Journal of Marriage and the Family,* vol. XXVI, pp. 44-51, February 1964.
* Burchinal, Lee G., and Chancellor, Loren E., "Survival Rates Among Types of Religiously Homogamous and Interreligious Marriages, Iowa, 1953-1959," *Research Bulletin,* Iowa Agricultural and Home Economics Experiment Station, Iowa State University, 1962.

* *Children of Divorced Couples: U. S., Selected Years.* Vital and Health Statistics, Public Health Service Publication #1000, Series 21, no. 18, p. 16, February 1970.

* *Civil Code of California, 1969. Statutes,* Sections 4500-4521, 1969.

* Coombs, Lolagene C., and Zumeta, Zena, "Correlates of Marital Dissolution in a Prospective Fertility Study: A Research Note," *Social Problems,* vol. XVIII, pp. 92-101, 1970.

Cuber, John F., and Harroff, Peggy B., "The More Total View: Relationships Among Men and Women of the Upper-Middle Class, *Marriage and Family Living,* vol. XXV, pp. 140-145, 1963.

Dubey, Bhagwant Rao, "Widow Remarriage in Madhya Pradesh," *Man in India,* vol. LXV, pp. 50-56, 1965.

* Duncan, Beverly, and Duncan, Otis Dudley, "Family Stability and Occupational Success," *Social Problems,* vol. XVI, pp. 273-285, winter 1969.

Foster, Henry H., Jr., "Current Trends in Divorce Law," *Family Law Quarterly,* vol. I, pp. 21-40, 1967.

Glasser, Paul, and Navarre, Elizabeth, "Structural Problems of the One-Parent Family," *Journal of Social Issues,* vol. XXI, pp. 98-109, 1965.

Glick, Paul C., "Marriage Instability: Variations by Size of Place and Region," *Milbank Memorial Fund Quarterly,* vol. XLI, pp. 43-55, 1963.

Glick, Paul C., "Permanence of Marriage," *Population Index,* vol. XXXIII, pp. 517-526, 1967.

* Glick, Paul C., and Norton, Arthur J., "Frequency, Duration, and Probability of Marriage and Divorce," *Journal of Marriage and the Family,* vol. XXXIII, pp. 307-317, 1971.

* Glick, Paul C., and Norton, Arthur J., "Perspectives on the Recent Upturn in Divorce and Remarriage," *Demography,* vol. X, pp. 301-314, 1973.

* Goode, William J., *After Divorce.* Free Press of Glencoe, Inc., Glencoe, Illinois, 1956.

Goode, William J., "Family Disorganization," in Robert K. Merton and Robert A. Nisbet, editors, *Contemporary Social Problems.* Harcourt, Brace and World, New York, 1961.

Goode, William J., "Pressures to Remarry: Institutionalized Patterns Affecting the Divorced, in Norman W. Bell and Ezra F. Vogel, editors, *A Modern Introduction to the Family.* Free Press of Glencoe, Inc., New York, 1960.

* Goode, William J., *World Revolution and Family Patterns.* Free Press of Glencoe, Inc., New York, 1963.

"Grounds for Divorce: 1968," *The New York Times Encyclopedic Almanac,* 1970.

Hansen, Donald A., "Personal and Positional Influence in Formal Groups: Propositions and Theory for Research on Family Vulnerability to Stress," *Social Forces,* vol. XLIV, pp. 202-210, 1965.

* Harmsworth, Harry C., and Minnis, Mhyra S., "Non-statutory Causes of Divorce: The Lawyer's Point of View," *Marriage and Family Living,* vol. XVII, no. 4, pp. 316-321, November 1955.

Harvey, L. V., "Marriage Failure and Mental Health," *Mental Health in Australia,* vol. I, pp. 23-30, 1965.

* Hetherington, E. Mavis, "Effects of Father Absence on Personality Development in Adolescent Daughters," *Developmental Psychology,* vol. VII, pp. 313-326, 1972.

Hillman, Karen G., "Marital Instability and its Relation to Education, Income, and Occupation: An Analysis Based on Census Data," in Robert F. Winch, Robert McGinnis and Herbert R. Barringer, editors, *Selected Studies in Marriage and the Family,* revised edition. Holt, Rinehart and Winston, New York, 1962.

* Hilsdale, Paul, "Marriage as a Personal Existential Commitment," *Marriage and Family Living,* vol. XXIV, no. 2, pp. 137-143, May 1962.

Hughes, Randall, "Divorce Reform: The New York Solution," *New York State Bar Journal,* vol. XLI, pp. 327-335, 1969.

* Jacobson, Paul H., *American Marriage and Divorce.* Rinehart and Company, Inc., New York, 1959.

* Kephart, William M., and Strohm, Rolf B., "The Stability of Gretna Green Marriages," *Sociology and Social Research,* vol. XXXVI, pp. 291-296, 1952.

Kleinfeld, Andrew J., and Moss, Guy B., "Divorce Reform Act," *Harvard Journal on Legislation,* vol. V, pp. 563-585, 1968.

* Koch, Margaret Body. "Anxiety in Preschool Children," *Merrill-Palmer Quarterly,* vol. VII, no. 4, pp. 225-231, 1961.

* Kriesberg, Louis, "Rearing Children for Educational Achievement in Fatherless Families," *Journal of Marriage and the Family,* vol. XXIX, no. 2, pp. 288-301, 1967.

Kunz, Phillip R., "Mormon and Non-Mormon Divorce Patterns," *Journal of Marriage and the Family,* vol. XXVI, pp. 211-212, 1964.

* Landis, Judson T., "The Pattern of Divorce in Three Generations," *Social Forces,* vol. XXXIV, no. 3, pp. 201-207, March 1956.

* Landis, Judson T., "Social Correlates of Divorce or Nondivorce Among the Unhappy Married," *Marriage and Family Living,* vol. XXV, no. 2, pp. 178-180, May 1963.

Lasch, Christopher, "Divorce and the Family in America," *Atlantic Monthly,* vol. CCXVIII, pp. 57-71, 1966.

* Levinger, George, "Marital Cohesiveness and Dissolution: An Integrative Review," *Journal of Marriage and the Family,* vol. XXVII, pp. 19-28, 1965.

* Levinger, George, "Sources of Marital Dissatisfaction Among Applicants for Divorce," *American Journal of Orthopsychiatry,* vol. XXXVI, no. 5, pp. 803-807, October 1966.

Levinger, George, "Systematic Distortion in Spouses' Reports of Preferred and Actual Sexual Behavior," *Sociometry,* vol. XXIX, pp. 291-299, 1966.

* Locke, Harvey J., *Predicting Adjustment in Marriage: A Comparison of a Divorced and a Happily Married Group.* Henry Holt and Company, New York, 1951.

Loeb, Ruth, "A Study of Age at Remarriage: The District of Columbia, 1960-61," *Demography,* vol. V, pp. 311-317, 1968.

McKinney's Consolidated Laws of New York Annotated, Book 14, Domestic Relations Law, Sections 1-199, 1969.

Monahan, Thomas P., "How Stable are Re-marriages?" *American Journal of Sociology,* vol. LVIII, pp. 280-288, 1952.

* Monahan, Thomas P., and Kephart, William M., "Divorce and Desertion by Religious and Mixed-religious Groups," *American Journal of Sociology,* vol. LIX, no. 5, pp. 454–465, March 1954.

Moynihan, Daniel Patrick, *The Negro Family—The Case for National Action.* U. S. Department of Labor, Office of Policy Planning and Research, Washington, D. C., 1965. (Commonly known as "The Moynihan Report.")

* Murdock, George P., "Family Stability in Non-European Cultures," *Annals,* vol. CCLXXII, pp. 195–201, November 1950.

* Nimkoff, M. F., "Contributions to a Therapeutic Solution to the Divorce Problem: Sociology," in Marvin B. Sussman, editor, *Sourcebook in Marriage and the Family.* Houghton Mifflin Company, Boston, 1963.

* Nye, F. Ivan, "Child Adjustment in Broken and in Unhappy Unbroken Homes," *Marriage and Family Living,* vol. XIX, no. 4, pp. 356–361, November 1957.

* Nye, F. Ivan; White, Lynn; and Frideres, James, "A Preliminary Theory of Marital Dissolution," read before the National Council on Family Relations, Minneapolis, 1966.

Oates, Wayne E., "The Church, Divorce, and Remarriage," *The Review and Expositor,* vol. LXI, pp. 45–60, 1964.

* Ogburn, William F., "Education, Income, and Family Unity," *American Journal of Sociology,* vol. LIII, pp. 474–476, 1948.

Ogg, Elizabeth, *Divorce.* Public Affairs Pamphlets, New York, 1968.

Parsons, Talcott, and Bales, Robert F., *Family, Socialization and Interaction Process.* Free Press of Glencoe, Inc., New York, 1955.

Paulsen, Monrad G., "Divorce: Canterbury Style," *Valparaiso University Law Review,"* vol. I, pp. 93–100, 1966.

* Perry, Joseph B., Jr., and Pfuhl, Erdwin H., Jr., "Adjustment of Children in 'Solo' and 'Remarriage' Homes," *Marriage and Family Living,* vol. XXV, no. 2, pp. 221–223, May 1963.

Plateris, Alexander A., *Divorces: Analysis of Changes, U. S. 1969.* U. S. Department of Health, Education, and Welfare, Publication No. (HSM) 73-1900, Rockville, Maryland, 1973.

* Plateris, Alexander A., *Divorce Statistics Analysis.* National Center for Health Statistics, Series 21, no. 17, Washington, D. C., October 1969.

* Ploscowe, Morris, *The Truth About Divorce.* Hawthorne Books, New York, 1955.

"Recommended Changes in New Divorce Law," Report of Special Committee on Matrimonial Law, *Bar Bulletin,* vol. XXIV, pp. 62–76, 1967.

* Renne, Karen S., "Health and Marital Experience in an Urban Population," *Journal of Marriage and the Family,* vol. XXXIII, pp. 338–350, 1971.

* Rettig, Salomon, and Pasamanick, Benjamin, "Changes in Moral Values Among College Students: A Factorial Study," *American Sociological Review,* vol. XXIV, pp. 856–863, 1959.

Rowntree, Griselda, "Some Aspects of Marriage Breakdown in Britain During the Last Thirty Years," *Population Studies,* vol. XVIII, pp. 147–163, 1964.

* Russell, Ivan L., "Behavior Problems of Children From Broken and Intact Homes," *Journal of Educational Sociology,* vol. XXXI, pp. 124–129, 1957.

Scanzoni, John, "A Reinquiry into Marital Disorganization," *Journal of Marriage and the Family,* vol. XXVII, pp. 483–491, 1965.

Schlesinger, Benjamin, "Remarriage—An Inventory of Findings," *The Family Coordinator,* vol. XVII, pp. 248-250, 1968.

Shipman, Gordon, "A Proposal for Revising Marriage License Procedure," *Journal of Marriage and the Family,* vol. XXVII, pp. 281-284, 1965.

Solovyev, N., "Why Divorces?" *Literaturnaya gazeta, Current Abstracts of the Soviet Press,* November 1968.

* Stephens, William N., *The Family in Cross-Cultural Perspective.* Holt, Rinehart and Winston, New York, 1963.

* Stroup, Atlee L., "Marital Adjustment of the Mother and the Personality of the Child," *Marriage and Family Living,* vol. XVIII, p. 109, May 1956.

* Terman, L. M., *Psychological Factors in Marital Happiness.* McGraw Hill Book Company, New York, 1938.

The Annotated Code of the Public General Laws of Maryland, 1969, Cumulative Supplement, Article 16.

"The U. S. Family: A Thriving Institution," *Population Profile.* Population Reference Bureau, Inc., July 28, 1969.

Thomas, John L. "Marital Failure and Duration," *Social Order,* vol. III, pp. 24-29, 1953.

* Udry, J. Richard, "Marital Instability by Race and Income Based on 1960 Census Data," *American Journal of Sociology,* vol. LXXII, pp. 673-674, May 1967.

* Udry, J. Richard, "Marital Instability by Race, Sex, Education, and Occupation Using 1960 Census Data," *American Journal of Sociology,* vol. LXXII, pp. 203-209, September 1966.

U. S. Department of Health, Education, and Welfare, *Converging Social Trends—Emerging Social Problems,* Welfare Administration Publication No. 6, Washington, D. C., 1963.

* Vallot, Francoise, "Les Remariages à Paris," *Population,* vol. XXVI, pp. 955-958, 1971.

* Wallin, Paul. "Marital Happiness of Parents and Their Children's Attitude to Marriage," *American Sociological Review,* XIX, pp. 20-23, 1954.

* Wallin, Paul, and Vollmer, Howard M., "Marital Happiness of Parents and Their Children's Attitudes to Them," *American Sociological Review,* vol. XVIII, pp. 424-431, 1953.

Whitaker, Carl A., and Miller, Milton H., "A Reevaluation of 'Psychiatric Help' When Divorce Impends," *American Journal of Psychiatry,* vol. CXXVI, no. 5, pp. 611-618, November 1969.

Zimmerman, Carle C., and Cervantes, Lucius F., *Successful American Families,* Pageant Press, New York, 1960.

CHAPTER 19   MARRIAGE COUNSELING AND MARRIAGE
               EDUCATION

* Allen, James E., "Training for Family Planning Counseling: The Seminary's Role," *The Family Coordinator,* vol. XVIII, pp. 70-75, 1969.

* Barrier, Dorothy E., " 'Discussion' of Aaron L. Rutledge, 'Should the Marriage Counselor Ever Recommend Divorce?' " *Marriage and Family Living,* vol. XXV, pp. 325-326, August 1963.

Beasley, Christine, "Measuring Student Achievement in a Functional Marriage Course," *Journal of Marriage and the Family,* vol. XXIX, no. 2, pp. 311–319, 1967.

Berger, Miriam E., "The Continuous Parent Education Group," *The Family Co-ordinator,* vol. XVII, pp. 105–109, 1968.

Berger, Miriam E., "Trial Marriage: Harnessing the Trend Constructively," *The Family Coordinator,* vol. XX, pp. 38–43, 1971.

Bigner, Jerry J., "Parent Education in Popular Literature: 1950–1970," *The Family Coordinator,* vol. XXI, pp. 313–319, 1972.

Blanck, Rubin, and Blanck, Gertrude, *Marriage and Personal Development.* Columbia University Press, New York, 1968.

Bloch, Doris, and Mayhew, Derryberry, "Effect of Political Controversy on Sex Education Research: A Case Study," *The Family Coordinator,* vol. XX, pp. 259–264, 1971.

* Bowman, Henry; Kerckhoff, Richard K.; Davis, Forest K.; and Sussman, Marvin B., "Teaching Ethical Values Through the Marriage Course: A Debate," *Marriage and Family Living,* vol. XIX, no. 4, pp. 325–330, November 1957.

Brashear, Diane B., "Meeting the Opposition: Sex Education and Community Support," *The Family Coordinator,* vol. XX, pp. 44–48, 1971.

* Brim, Orville, J., "Evidence Concerning the Effects of Education for Child Rearing," in Robert F. Winch, Robert McGinnis and Herbert R. Barringer, editors, *Selected Studies in Marriage and the Family,* revised edition. Holt, Rinehart and Winston, New York, 1962.

Burton, Genevieve, and Kaplan, Howard M., "Group Counseling in Conflicted Marriages Where Alcoholism is Present: Clients' Evaluation of Effectiveness," *Journal of Marriage and the Family,* vol. XXX, pp. 74–79, 1968.

Calderwood, Deryck David, "Adolescents' Views on Sex Education," *Journal of Marriage and the Family,* vol. XXVII, pp. 291–298, 1965.

Channels, Vera, "Family Life Education Through Use of Novels," *The Family Coordinator,* vol. XX, pp. 225–230, 1971.

Crosby, John F., "The Effect of Family Life Education on the Values and Attitudes of Adolescents," *The Family Coordinator,* vol. XX, pp. 137–140, 1971.

Dame, Nenabelle G.; Finck, George H.; Reiner, Beatrice S.; and Smith, Brady O., "The Effect on the Marital Relationship of the Wife's Search for Identity," *Family Life Coordinator,* vol. XIV, pp. 133–136, 1965.

Davids, Leo, "Foster Fatherhood: The Untapped Resource," *The Family Co-ordinator,* vol. XX, pp. 49–54, 1971.

Deburgerger, James E., "Marital Problems, Help-Seeking, and Emotional Orientation as Revealed in Help-Request Letters," *Journal of Marriage and the Family,* vol. XXIX, pp. 712–721, 1967.

Denfeld, Duane, and Gordon, Michael, "The Sociology of Mate Swapping," *Journal of Sex Research,* vol. VI, pp. 85–100, 1970.

De Rosis, Helen A., "Parent Group Discussion: A Preventive Mental Health Technique," *The Family Coordinator,* vol. XIX, pp. 329–334, 1970.

* Dyer, Dorothy, "A Comparative Study Relating Marital Happiness to University Courses Helpful in Marital Adjustment," *Marriage and Family Living,* vol. XXI, pp. 230–232, 1959.

* Ellzey, W. Clark, "Marriage Questionnaire Report," *Marriage and Family Living,* vol. XI, pp. 133-135, 1949.

Endres, Mary P., "The Impact of Parent Education Through Study-Discussion Groups in a Poverty Area," *Journal of Marriage and the Family,* vol. XXX, pp. 119-122, 1968.

Eysenck, H. J., "The Effects of Psychotherapy," in H. J. Eysenck, editor, *Handbook of Abnormal Psychology,* Basic Books, Inc., New York, 1961.

* Finck, George H., "A Comparative Analysis of the Marriages and Families of Participants and Non-participants in Marriage Education," *Marriage and Family Living,* vol. XVIII, pp. 61-64, 1956.

Fohlin, Mary Bercovitz, "Selection and Training of Teachers for Life Education Programs," *The Family Coordinator,* vol. XX. pp. 231-242, 1971.

* Freeman, S. J. J.; Leavens, Edith J.; and McCulloch, D. J., "Factors Associated with Success or Failure in Marital Counseling," *The Family Coordinator,* vol. XVIII, pp. 125-128, 1969.

Gadpaille, Warren J., "Parent-School Cooperation in Sex Education—How Can the Professional Help?" *The Family Coordinator,* vol. XIX, pp. 301-307, 1970.

Gehrke, Shirley, and Kirschenbaum, Martin, "Survival Patterns in Family Conjoint Therapy," *Family Process,* vol. VI, pp. 67-80, 1967.

* Golden, Joshua S., and Liston, Edward H., "Medical Sex Education: The World of Illusion and the Practical Realities," *Journal of Medical Education,* vol. 47, pp. 761-771, 1972.

Gottlieb, Anthony, and Pattison, E. Mansell, "Married Couples' Group Psychotherapy," *Archives of General Psychiatry,* vol. XIV, pp. 143-152, 1966.

Guerney, Bernard G., Jr.; Guerney, Louise F.; and Stover, Lillian, "Facilitative Therapist Attitudes in Training Parents as Psychotherapeutic Agents," *The Family Coordinator,* vol. XXI, pp. 275-286, 1972.

* Gurin, Gerald; Veroff, Joseph; and Feld, Shiela, *Americans View Their Mental Health.* Basic Books, Inc., New York, 1960.

Hardcastle, Dexter R., "Measuring Effectiveness in Group Marital Counseling," *The Family Coordinator,* vol. XXI, pp. 213-218, 1972.

Harter, Carl L., and Parrish, Vestal W., Jr., "Maternal Preference of Socialization Agent for Sex Education," *Journal of Marriage and the Family,* vol. XXX, pp. 418-426, 1968.

Hitchcock, Mary Ellen, and de Lissovoy, Vladimir, "Family Life Education in Pennsylvania High Schools," *Journal of Home Economics,* vol. LVIII, pp. 477-479, 1966.

* Hollingshead, August B., and Redlich, Frederick C., *Social Class and Mental Illness,* John Wiley and Sons, Inc., New York, 1958.

Humphrey, Frederick G.; Libby, Roger W.; and Nass, Gilbert D., "Attitude Change Among Professionals Toward Sex Education for Adolescents," *The Family Coordinator,* vol. XVIII, pp. 332-339, 1969.

Hurvitz, Nathan, "Interaction Hypotheses in Marriage Counseling," *The Family Coordinator,* vol. XIX, pp. 64-75, 1970.

Hurvitz, Nathan, "Marital Problems Following Psychotherapy with One Spouse," *Journal of Consulting Psychology,* vol. XXXI, pp. 38-47, 1967.

Hurvitz, Nathan, "The Marital Roles Inventory as a Counseling Instrument," *Journal of Marriage and the Family,* vol. XXVII, pp. 492-501, 1965.

"Is Psychiatry Becoming Oversexed?" *Medical World News,* November 12, 1965.

Israel, S. Leon, and Nemser, Sondra, "Family-Counseling Role of the Physician," *Journal of Marriage and the Family,* vol. XXX, pp. 311-316, 1968.

Juhlin, Lennart, "Factors Influencing the Spread of Gonorrhea. I. Educational and Social Behavior," *Obstetrics and Gynecology Survey,* vol. XXIII, pp. 984-988, 1968.

Kammeyer, Kenneth C. W., and Bolton, Charles D., "Community and Family Factors Related to the Use of a Family Service Agency," *Journal of Marriage and the Family,* vol. XXX, pp. 488-498, 1968.

Kerckhoff, Richard K., "Community Experiences with the 1969 Attack on Sex Education," *The Family Coordinator,* vol. XIX, pp. 104-110, 1970.

Kirby, Michael W., and Davis, Keith E., "Who Volunteers for Research on Marital Counseling?" *Journal of Marriage and the Family,* vol. XXXIV, pp. 469-473, 1972.

Kirkendall, Lester A., and Cox, Helen M., "Starting a Sex Education Program," *Children,* vol. XIV, pp. 136-140, 1967.

Krupinski, J.; Polke, P.; and Stoller, Alan, "An Analysis of Activity of an Australian Marriage Guidance Council," *Journal of Marriage and the Family,* vol. XXVII, pp. 502-508, 1965.

Kushner, Sylvia, "The Divorced, Noncustodial Parent and Family Treatment," *Social Work,* vol. X, pp. 52-58, 1965.

Landes, Judah, and Winter, William, "A New Strategy for Treating Disintegrating Families," *Family Process,* vol. V, pp. 1-20, 1966.

Landis, Judson T., "High School Student Marriages, School Policy and Family Life Education in California," *Journal of Marriage and the Family,* vol. XXVII, pp. 271-276, 1965.

* Lantz, Herman R., and Snyder, Eloise C., *Marriage: An Examination of the Man-Woman Relationship.* John Wiley and Sons, Inc., New York, 1962.

Leik, Robert K., and Northwood, L. K., "The Classification of Family Interaction Problems for Treatment Purposes," *Journal of Marriage and the Family,* vol. XXVI, pp. 288-294, 1964.

Libby, Roger W., "Parental Attitudes Toward Content in High School Sex Education Programs: Liberalism-Traditionalism and Demographic Correlates," *The Family Coordinator,* vol. XX, pp. 127-136, 1971.

Libby, Roger W., "Parental Attitudes Toward High School Sex Education Programs," *The Family Coordinator,* vol. XIX, pp. 234-247, 1970.

Lieberman, E. James, "Family Planning Counsel," *Journal of Marriage and the Family,* vol. XXX, pp. 308-310, 1968.

Luckey, Eleanore Braun, "Helping Children Grow Up Sexually," *Children,* vol. XIV, pp. 131-135, 1967.

Mace, David R., and Mace, Vera C., "Training Family Life Leaders in Developing Countries: A Seminar Approach," *The Family Coordinator,* vol. XX, pp. 23-29, 1971.

* Malfetti, James L., and Rubin, Arline M., "Sex Education: Who Is Teaching the Teachers," *The Family Coordinator,* vol. XVII, pp. 110-117, 1968.

McArthur, Arthur, "Missouri Specialists Take to the Air," *The Family Coordinator,* vol. XVII, pp. 95-96, 125-126, 1968.

* Merrill, Frances E., *Courtship and Marriage,* revised edition. Henry Holt and Company, New York, 1959.

Middleton, John T., "The Role of Values in Marriage Counseling," *The Family Coordinator,* vol. XIX, pp. 335-341, 1970.

Olson, David H., and Straus, Murray A. "A Diagnostic Tool for Marital and Family Therapy: The SIMFAM Technique," *The Family Coordinator,* vol. XXI, pp. 251-258, 1972.

Rappaport, Alan F., and Harrell, Jan, "A Behavioral Exchange Model for Marital Counseling," *The Family Coordinator,* vol. XXI, pp. 203-212, 1972.

Rice, Robert R., "The Effects of Project Head Start and Differential Housing Environments Upon Child Development," *The Family Coordinator,* vol. XVIII, pp. 32-38, 1969.

* Rubin, Arline M., and Adams, James R., "Sex Attitudes of Sex Educators," *The Family Coordinator,* vol. XXI, pp. 177-182, 1972.

Rubin, Isadore, "Transition in Sex Values—Implications for the Education of Adolescents," *Journal of Marriage and the Family,* vol. XXVII, pp. 185-189, 1965.

* Rutledge, Aaron L., "Marriage Counseling: An Overview," *Michigan State Bar Journal,* vol. XLII, pp. 27-32, May 1963.

* Rutledge, Aaron L., "Marriage Counseling Today and Tomorrow," *Marriage and Family Living,* vol. XIX, no. 4, pp. 386-390, November 1957.

Sacks, Sylvia R., "Sex Education with Teenagers: Approach and Experiences of a Family Life Educator in a Marriage Council," *Journal of Marriage and the Family,* vol. XXVII, pp. 193-199, 1965.

Schreiber, Leona E., "Evaluation of Family Group Testament in a Family Agency," *Family Process,* vol. V, pp. 21-29, 1966.

Schwartzberg, Bernard, and Hammer, Edna, "Joint Interview Sessions with Adolescent Girls and Their Mothers as a Family Treatment Tool," *The Family Coordinator,* vol. XVII, pp. 75-77, 1968.

Sholtis, Helen S., "The Management of Marital Counseling Cases," *Social Casework,* vol. XLV, pp. 71-78, 1964.

Smith, William M., Jr., "Family Relationships: Communicating a Concept," *Journal of Marriage and the Family,* vol. XXX, pp. 12-25, 1968.

Spark, Geraldine M., "Parental Involvement in Family Therapy," *Journal of Marriage and the Family,* vol. XXX, pp. 111-118, 1968.

Staples, Robert E., "Educating the Black Male at Various Class Levels for Marital Roles," *The Family Coordinator,* vol. XIX, pp. 164-167, 1970.

Steiner, George J., "Parent-Teen Education—An Exercise in Communication," *The Family Coordinator,* vol. XIX, pp. 213-218, 1970.

"The Field of Marriage Counseling," special issue of *The Family Coordinator,* vol. XXII, pp. 3-160, 1973.

* Tyndall, N. J., "Marriage in Difficulty: The Work of Marriage Counseling," *Community Health,* vol. IV, pp. 28-33, 1972.

Ulman, Neil, "The Facts of Life: More Schools Introduce Sex Education Courses," *The Wall Street Journal,* September 19, 1967.

Vincent, Clark E., "Mental Health and the Family," *Journal of Marriage and the Family,* vol. XXIX, pp. 18-39, 1967.

Wadsworth, H. G., and Wadsworth, Joanna B., "A Problem of Involvement with Parents of Mildly Retarded Children," *The Family Coordinator,* vol. XX, pp. 141-147, 1971.

Weinberger, Andrew D., "Interracial Marriage, Its Statutory Prohibition, Genetic Import, and Incidence," *Journal of Sex Research,* vol. II, pp. 157-168, 1966.

Wiechmann, Gerald H., and Ellis, Altis L., "A Study of the Effects of 'Sex Education' on Premarital Petting and Coital Behavior," *The Family Coordinator,* vol. XVIII, pp. 231-234, 1969.

Womble, Dale L., "Functional Marriage Course for the Already Married," *Marriage and Family Living,* vol. XXIII, pp. 278-283, 1961.

Won, George, and Yamamura, Douglas, "Expectations of Youth in Relating to the World of Adults," *The Family Coordinator,* vol. XIX, pp. 219-224, 1970.

Yule, Valerie, "Group Differences in Problems Presented by Marriage Counselling Clients," *Australian Journal of Special Issues,* vol. II, pp. 38-58, 1965.

Index of Subjects

Career orientation, marital success and, 298, 304

Catholicism, divorce and, 394, 408; fertility control and, 344–347; intermarriage and, 162, 164, 251–253, 257, official attitudes on, 166; marriage values and, 12, 265

Cattell, 16; Personality Factor Test, 24

Celibacy, Christian tradition and, 13

Childrearing, (see also *children*), problems in, marital interaction and, 376; wife's employment status and, 306–308

Children, desire for, marriage and, (see also *parenthood*), 1, 364; divorce and 369, 397, 398–401; effects of on parents' marriage, 365–381, 382; effects of parents' marriage on, 384–389; in remarriages, 403; influence of in family decision-making, 274; marital adjustment and, 365, 368; marriage of, parents' marital adjustment and, 387; number of (see also *birth rates*), 344–347, family decision-making process and, 271, of working mothers, 306–308; only, 367; sex-role learning by, 53; socialization of for love, 138

Chimpanzee, development of sexuality in, 82

China, family system in, 20, 285; importance of marriage in, 3

Christianity, marriage traditions and, 12; sexual values in, 103

Clergy, as marriage counselors, 417

College education, sex differences in, 29, 30

College students, contraception methods among, 355; dating customs among, 90; definitions of love among, 132; sexual involvement among, 115, 116, 118

Communication, in marital interaction, 218–220

Companionship, in marriage, 205, 211

Competitiveness, sex differences of, 25

Complementarity, mate selection and, 172; objective, 172; perceptual, 175; theory of, 175

Computer dating, 99; physical attractiveness and, 92

Condom, 353

Conflict-habituated relationships, 230

Consensus, marital interaction and, 220–223, evaluation of, 211; mate selection and, 177

Contraception, 339–363; among unmarried, 125, 355; availability of, premarital pregnancy and, 124; cross-cultural perspective on, 342–343; extramarital sex and, 128; methods of, 348–355, hormonal, 348–352, in United States, 348

Conventionality, parenthood and, 370, 382

Counseling, marriage, 416–423

Courtship (see also *dating, engagement,* and *mate selection*), duration of, 192; trends in, 190

Crow Indians, divorce among, 391

Culture (see also *social classes* and *society*), divorce and, 390–393; fertility control and, 342–343; sex-role socialization and, 51; sexuality differences and, 316

D and C, 356

Dating, as status game, 87; definition and role of, 84; motivation for, 86; partner selection in, 95; personal autonomy and, 100; physical attractiveness and, 92; social functions of, 89; steady, 96; trends in, 97, 99

Decision-making (see also *individual decision-making*), during engagement, 199; in family, 265–275, children and, 271, 274, working wife and, 304; marital adjustment and, 273–274, social factors in, 258; marital interaction process studies and, 236–239

Democratic equalitarianism, American marriage and, 13, 265, 305; ideals of mutual reciprocity in, 311–313

Denmark, working women in, 304

Dependence, interpersonal, as basis of love, 145

"Devitalized" relationships, 230

Diaphragm, contraceptive, 354

Dilation and curettage, 356

Disease, venereal, premarital intercourse and, 127

Division of labor, in family, 275–280; social class and, 276; wife's employment status and, 302, 303

Divorce, 390–415; causes of, 404, 407; children and, 369, 397–401; cross-cultural perspective on, 390–393; early marital adjustment and, 201; grounds for, 391, 411–413; legal complexities of, 410–413; United States rates of, 393–396

Double standard, American values and, 106, 107; definition and roots of, 105

Economy, family unit and, 17

Education, for marriage, 423–426; levels of, family decision-making and, 268, marital outcome and, 250–251, 257, mate selection and, 158, 159, motherhood and, 371, sex differences of, 28, status and, 248; public-school, about sex, 426–428, sex segregation in, 77, 78

Emotional involvement, premarital sexual behavior and, 110, 119, 120

Employment status (see also *occupations*), of husband, 270, 294–301; of wife, 301–308, family decision-making and, 268

Engagement, 190–199; as preparation period, 197; as screening mechanism, 194; as shift in roles, 193; personality trait matching and, 226; societal changes in, 192

England, kinship ties in, 286, 288, 291; premarital intercourse in, 115, 116; social relationships of married couple in, 308

Equalitarianism (see *democratic equalitarianism*)

Erotic needs, aging and, 328–330; ideal mate images and, 184; in engagement relationship, 195; in marriage pairs, 229; marital ideals and, 311–313; mate selection and, 172

Estrogens, contraception and, 349; sexuality and, 82

Extended family, functional differentiation and, 16; in American society, 285

Extramarital sexual behavior (see also *premarital sexual behavior*), 330–333; contraception and, 128; organized, 332

Family, as basic institution, 17; decision-making in, 265–275; division of labor in, 275–280; extended, 16, 285; functional differentiation and, 15; in American society, 8–22, 285–288, 292, equilibrium in, 20; instrumental and expressive roles in, 262–264; kinship ties and, 283, 285; satisfaction in, 204, 205; size of, 344–347, decision-making process and, 271, marital interaction and, 365, 368, marital success and, 226, preferences in, 344; stages of, 204, 205, 271

Father, roles of (see also *parenthood*), 262, in colonial America, 11, in sex-role learning, 56, 60

Females, adolescent, 74, 79, 262, sexual behavior among, 113; courtship pattern changes and, 191, 192; educational differences of, 28; ideal mate images of, 179, 181; kinship ties and, 287, 288; marital-role expectations of, 228; marriage ages of, 154; occupational differences of, 30, 31; personality patterns of, 23, 24; premarital sex standards and, 105, 106, 107, love-involvement and, 119, 120; roles of, acceptance of, 67, changes in, 36, development in, 59, in lower classes, 43, liberation movement and, 41; sexuality of, origins of, 315–317; subculture of, in United States, 73; world-orientation of, 27

Femininity, 33, 36; child's sex-role learning and, 54; unconscious, measurement of, 57

Fertility control (see also *contraception*), 339–363

Fetus, sex differentiation in, 46

Finances, between parents and married children, 292; marital success and, 250, 295

Fraternities, on college campus, dating and, 90, 91

Freudian theory, sex-role learning in, 63

Friendship, group, marital roles and, 308, versus companionate marriage, 309; versus romantic love, 134

Functional differentiation, of family, 15, 275–280

Genetics, sex differences and, 44, 46

Gilyak tribe, 141, 330

Group theory, 25

Groups, female, subculture of, 73; kinship (see *kinship groups*), male, camaraderie in, 72, subculture in, 69; peer, 69, 73, premarital intercourse and, 121; versus pair-marriage, 309, 332

Hawaii, interracial marriages in, 255

Heterogeneity, social, marital success and, 240–260

Heterosexuality, adolescent development of, 84; biological foundations of, 81; childhood prerequisites for, 60; early dating and, 98; origins and development of, 81–101

Hindus, importance of marriage among, 3

Homogamy, social, marital success and, 240–260

Homosexuality, biological factors and, 82

Honeymoon, 201

Hormones, contraceptive, 348–352; sexual development and, 46, 81, 316

Husband, effect of parenthood on, 375; high-status, 247; ideal, cultural influences and, 179; marital adjustment in, 207, 216; marital-role expectations of, 228; occupational status of, 270; roles of, 261–282, in family tasks, 277, 278, occupation and, 294–301

Ideals, cultural influences on, 179; mate selection and, 178

Incest taboos, 153

Income, from working wife, marital adjustment and, 306; marital success and, 250, 295

India, importance of marriage in, 3

Individual decision-making, on divorce, 414–415; on family sex-role differentiation, 281; on fertility control, 363; on kinship ties, 293; on marital interaction processes, 236–239; on parenthood, 383–384, 388–389; on premarital sexual values, 129; on social factors in mate selection, 168

Individualism, American marriage and, 14

Industrialization, family unit and, 17

Infancy, sex-role differentiation in, 52

Infertility, 360

In-laws, problems with, 288, 291; sharing household with, 290–292

Instrumental-expressive behaviors, in family, 262–264; theory of, 24

Interaction, kinship, 283–294; marital (see also *marital interaction*), 200–239

Intercourse (see *extramarital sexual behavior, premarital sexual behavior,* and *sexual behavior*)

Intermarriage, in United States, 159; factors predisposing to, 165; marital outcome and, 251–257; trends in, 160–161, 166

Interpersonal dependence, 145

Interpersonal rapport, 144

Intimacy, affectional, in marriage, 212 (see also *sexual behavior*)

Intrauterine devices, 352

IUD's 352

Japan, industrialization of, family unit and, 18; interracial marriage among Hawaiians and, 255

Judaism, divorce views and, 409; intermarriage and, 163, 252, 253, official religious attitudes on, 166

Judeo-Christian tradition, monogamy and, 13; sexual values in, 103

Kinship groups, functional differentiation of, 15; mate selection restrictions and, 153; ties with, marital relationship and, 283–294

Law, divorce and, 410–413; sex equality and, 42

Leaders in group theory, 25

Love, 131–151; as interpersonal process, 144, factors predisposing to, 170; as marriage criterion, 148, societal consequences of, 150; cross-cultural perspective of, 135; integrated explanation of, 143; meaning of, 131; multiple, 147; premarital intercourse and, 119, 120, 124; psychological origins of, 142; romantic, measurement of, 133, 134–135, sex differences in, 146, 323; sex as origin of, 140; socialization for, in American society, 137

Negroes, (see *blacks*)

Nuclear family (see also *family*), functional differentiation and, 16; in American life, 8–22; kinship ties and, 283, 285

Occupations, of husbands, 270, marital roles and, 294–301; of wives, family decision-making and, 268, marital happiness and, 298; marital roles and, 301–308; sex differences in, 31; status levels and, 248

Oedipus theory, sex-role learning and, 60, 63

Only child, 367

Orgasm, marital sexual adjustment and, 322

Orientals, interracial or interethnic marriages among, 159, 255

Orientation, to world, sex differences in, 27

Parenthood (see also *parents*), adjustment to, 365–381, 382; conventionality and, 370, 382; decision for, 339; impact of, 373, 375, 378; marriage and, 364–389; pressures for, 371; rewards of, 381–382

Parents (see also *parenthood*), financial exchange with, 292; image of, mate selection and, 185; marital adjustment of, effects of children's marriage on, 387, effects of on children, 384–389; mate selection roles of, 170, 186

Passive-congenial relationships, 231

Peer groups, 69, 73, 121

Permissiveness, sexual, American values and, 107

Personality, sex differences of, 23; traits, effects of on marriage, 223–226, family decision-making and, 267, in engagement, 226, mate selection and, 172, 175

Petting, premarital, definition and roles of, 111

Physical attractiveness, cultural influences and, 179, 180; dating and, 92; femininity concepts and, 74; mate selection on, 177

Physicians, as marriage counselors, 417, 418

Physiology, sex differences and, 44, 81, 315

"Pill," 348

Population, growth of in United States, 340–342, future, 361, 362; sex ratios among, mate selection and, 167

Pornography, 321

Power, as reward of parenthood, 381; within family, bases of, 265–271, wife's occupation and, 304

Pregnancy, premarital, abortion availability and, 123; contraception availability and, 124; prevalence of, 122, 123

Premarital sexual behavior, 102–130; American attitudes toward, 105, 108, recent changes in, 114; consequences of, 122, in marital adjustment, 126; cross-cultural perspective of, 102; dating patterns and, 98; intensity scale of, 109; love-involvement and, 119, 120, 124; peer group and, 121; race differences in, 109

Prestige, dating customs and, 90, 91; husband's occupation and, 296
Professions, sex differences in, 30
Projection, as reward of parenthood, 381
Propinquity, kinship ties and, 289; marital success and, 245; mate selection and, 156; social networks and, 308
Prostitution, premarital sexual behaviors and, 114
Protestantism, divorce views and, 409; intermarriage and, 162, 251-253, 257, official religious attitudes on, 166
Puberty, dating patterns and, 97; versus adolescence, 84
Puritanism, American sexual values and, 104

Race differences, in family decision-making patterns, 272; in marital stability, 395; in premarital sexual behavior, 109, 113; marital outcome and, 254-255, 256
Rapport, interpersonal, as basis of love, 144
Receptivity, sexual, 314
Religion, dating and, 92; divorce views and, 394, 396, 406, 408; fertility control and, 344-347; marriage and, 2, 162, 251-253; premarital sexual behavior and, 112, 120
Remarriages, 401-403
Renaissance, sexual values and, 104
Research, scientific (see also *methodology*), on marital success, 210; problems concerning, 5
Response, sexual, 314; patterns of, 330
Retirement, of husband, effect of on marital role, 300
Rhythm method of contraception, 352
Roles, engagement, 193; family, functional differentiation and, 15, instrumental and expressive behaviors in, 262-264; marital interaction and, 227-229, external, 283-310; parental, 376; sexual (see *sex roles*)
Roman Catholicism (see *Catholicism*)
Romantic love (see also *love*), measurement of, 133, 134-135; sex differences in, 146, 323
"Romeo and Juliet effect," 146
Russia, marriage in, 19

Science, American values and, 4; methodology of, 5
Secularism, American marriage and, 14
Segregation, sexual, in American history, 77
Separation, in engagement period, 194; marital (see *divorce*)
Sex differences, 23-49; in sexuality, future of, 317-320, origin of, 315-317; kinship ties and, 287; physiological origins of, 44, 81; romantic experience and, 146
Sex ratios, mate selection and, 167

Sex roles, acceptance of, differences in, 65; as values, 37; changes in, 32; development of, 50–80, psychoanalytic interpretation of, 63, social-psychological interpretation of, 53; equality of, hypothetical, 40, legal changes toward, 42, sexual interaction and, 311–313; in marriage, 261–282, family division of labor and, 275; socialization for, 40–80; subcultures and, in American society, 68

Sexual behavior, extramarital, 128, 330–333; in engagement, 196; marital, 311–338, aging and, 328–330, as play, 325–327, as work, 327–328, traditional picture of, 313, with parenthood, 374; marital success and, 213; premarital, 102–130; sex education and, 426–428; terminology of, 314

Sexual drive, 314

Sexual terminology, 314

Sexuality, as basis of love, 140; biological foundations of, 81; in female subculture, 74; in male subculture, 69; sex differences in, future of, 317–320, origins of, 315–317; social development and, 83

Siblings, marital success and, 226; sex-role learning and, 56, 62

Size of family, decision-making processes and, 271; in colonial America, 11; marital interaction and, 365, 368; marital success and, 226; preferences in, 344

Social classes, dating and, 89; divorce among, 394, 406; family division of labor and, 276; kinship ties and, 286, 288; marital outcome and, 245–250, 256, 257; mate selection and, 153, 157; parenthood values among, 371; premarital sexual behavior and, 119; sex-role differentiation views among, 264; sexual satisfaction among, 333, 334; working mothers and, 307

Social heterogeneity, 240–260

Social status, 247–250; dating and, 87, 90, 92; husband's occupation and, 296

Socialization, concept of, 51; for love, in American society, 137; for sex roles, 40–80, 83, 316, cross-cultural view of, 51

Society (see also *social classes*), consequences of love-based marriage for, 150; divorce and, 390–393, 405–408, 410; fertility control and, 342–343; functional differentiation in, 15; roles of, in engagement period, 198, in marital success, 240–260; sexuality differences and, 316

Soviet Union, marriage in, 19

Stability, marital, as success criterion, 240, cross-cultural perspective on, 390–393, parenthood and, 370, patterns of interaction and, 230–232, race differences of, 395, religious or racial differences and, 251–257, youthful marriage and, 243; of personality characteristics, 223

Steady dating, significance of, 96

Sterility, 360

Sterilization, in fertility control, 358–360

Subcultures, sexual, in American society, 68; decline of, 76; female, 73; implications of differences between, 76; male, 69

Taboos, 153

Tensions, in extended family household, 291; marital, 209

Terminology, sexual, 314

Testosterone, male sexuality and, 316
"Total" relationships, 232
Tubal ligation, in fertility control, 359

Understanding, in marital interaction, 215–218
United States (see also *Americans*), concept of family in, 8–22, 285–288; dating customs in, 85; divorce rates in, 393–396; mate selection factors in, 154, 169; population trends in, 340–342, 361, 362; sexual values in, 104–107

Vacuum extraction, in induced abortion, 356
Values, American, marriage and, 1, 12, 265, 305, science and, 4, sex-love fusion in, 143; fertility control and, 339, 343; interpersonal consensus on, mate selection and, 177; sex roles as, 37, 105, 106, 107; sexual, equalitarian ideals and, 311–313, in Western tradition, 103
Vasectomy, 358
Venereal disease, premarital intercourse and, 127
Victorian Age, sexual values and, 104, 111
Virginity, female, significance and prevalence of, 103, 122, 127
Vital relationships, marital, 231

Western culture, industrialization of, family unit and, 18; romantic love in, 135; traditional sexual values of, 103
Whites, divorce rates among, 395; family decision-making processes among, 272; female, occupational differences and, 32, premarital intercourse among, 113; fertility control among, 346, 347; interracial or interethnic marriages among, 159, 254–255, 256; kinship ties among, 287; parenthood values among, 371; premarital sex attitudes among, 109
Wife, dominance of, implications of, 273; effect of parenthood on, 373; employment status of, 268; friendship groups of, 309; high-status, 247; ideal, cultural influences and, 179; marital adjustment in, 207, 216; marital-role expectations of, 228; roles of, 22, 261–282, in family tasks, 277, 278, occupational, 301–308
Women's liberation movement, 41
Work (see also *occupations*), sex roles and, 43, 45, in family life, 268, 270

Index of Names